A STRONG SONG TOWS US

A STRONG SONG TOWS US

THE LIFE OF BASIL BUNTING

Richard Burton

First published in 2013 by
Infinite Ideas Limited
36 St Giles
Oxford
OX1 3LD
United Kingdom
www.infideas.com

A CIP catalogue record for this book is available from the British Library
ISBN 978–1–908984–18–0

Published in North America by Prospecta Press
P.O. Box 3131
Westport, CT 06880
(203) 903-5176
www.prospectapress.com

ISBN 978–1–935212–50–8

Designed and typeset by GRID
Printed in Britain

CONTENTS

To Elizabeth, Jamie and Jo.
This spuggy has fledged.

INTRODUCTION

Fifty years a letter unanswered;
A visit postponed for fifty years.

She has been with me fifty years.

Briggflatts

Brigflatts, 6 March 2013. The snow filling this tiny Quaker burial ground in the far north of England is delivered horizontally. It arrives on a gale that picked up its wings somewhere north of Franz Josef Land. It is barely possible to make out the simple headstones in the blizzard. Not a soul stirs. There is no birdsong. In this weather this is one of the bleakest places in Britain.

One hundred years ago, in March 1913, a thirteen-year-old boy called Basil Bunting stood in this graveyard for the first time. How little he could have known then how the spirit of this place would give him his own wings for seventy more years of what was, by any standards, an astonishing life. Along the way he was a conscientious objector, prisoner, artists' model, journalist, editor, sailor, balloon operator, interpreter, wing commander, diplomat, spy and, above all these, a poet. It wasn't just Brigflatts' spirit of place that buoyed him up through these adventures. The clink of its stonemason's chisel shaped his art. Meditation in the Quaker Meeting House shaped his philosophy. His love for the stonemason's young daughter, Peggy Greenbank, stayed alive through fifty years of separation. It was, as we shall see, one of the great love stories of the twentieth century.

* * *

A Strong Song Tows Us began three years previously. As I read *Descant on Rawthey's Madrigal* in the Upper Reading Room of Oxford's Old Bodleian library I wondered if I really wanted to write this book. As I turned the final page I saw that it was a limited edition, signed by its authors, Jonathan Williams and Bunting himself. I found myself staring at Bunting's signature – it was as intricately patterned and layered as a Lindisfarne illumination. I tried to follow its loops and curlicues. Like the bull that bellows us into *Briggflatts* it was ridiculous and lovely.

But what was it for? Bunting, for whom the slightest superfluity was an artistic failure, was one of the great parers of twentieth-century letters, a ruthless editor of his own work. He famously urged writers to use a chisel rather than a pen so as to load each individual mark with its maximum freight of meaning and intensity.[1] I was familiar enough with his habitual signature, a flowing single B with a dot. How could Bunting of all writers represent himself with this rococo fantasy? I tried to follow the ebbs and flows of his script as extravagant Bs rippled into almost formless Ns and then lurched away in search of a crowning T and plainsong G. It must have taken him longer to sign these books so generously than to complete the interviews they contain. It was, of course, entirely unlike his 'normal' signature. My foreboding about writing a life of Bunting gathered; its subject would have despised the entire enterprise.

Descant on Rawthey's Madrigal is a transcript of interviews that Williams conducted with Bunting when the poet was in his mid-sixties. Williams wanted Bunting to recall his life but his interviewee was clearly reluctant. The book begins with a statement from Bunting: 'Jonathan, I am surprised at you. What the hell has any of this to do with the public? My autobiography is Briggflatts – there's nothing else worth speaking aloud.'[2] It ends with his florid signature as though to bracket the work with a kind of benign contempt. If you want superfluous guff, he seems to be saying, take a look at *this*.[3]

For Bunting *Briggflatts* was autobiography enough. He scorned any kind of life writing as a channel into his or anyone else's art. For Bunting you can't understand a poem just by knowing the historical events that charge it. You can't even understand a poem by reading it. The only way to uncover the mystery is to *hear* it. 'Follow the clue patiently and you will understand nothing,' he writes in *Briggflatts*. When Bunting read that line the pause he inserted before the final word is pregnant with contempt for clue followers, patient or otherwise.

My concern deepened as I read those of Bunting's letters that survive in various archives in the US and UK. Is it altogether decent to write a biography of someone who loathed the idea of one, who destroyed all the letters he received and who urged his friends to destroy his own in order to make a project like this as difficult as possible?

I was encouraged, however, by the 'benign' part of the benign contempt I had detected. After all, Bunting had participated fully in *Descant on Rawthey's Madrigal* and approved publication. It reminds me of Yeats' dismissal of Friedrich Von Hügel at the end of 'Vacillation'. It is a sympathetic kind of grumpiness. In any event Bunting himself was not above using biography in pursuit of what he saw as a good cause. His introduction to his edition of the poems of Joseph Skipsey begins with a detailed account of Skipsey's life and he confesses to having sought out surviving family members for their memories. He did this because he recognised that the way to interest people in the work of a neglected poet is to tell his story, not to harangue them.[4] In a 1974 lecture on the American poet Louis Zukofsky he conceded the necessity of introducing the man in order to encourage interest in his poetry[5] and late in life he wrote another autobiography, albeit one that consists of only five words, 'Minor poet, not conspicuously dishonest.' Jonathan Williams suggested to him that this implied the virtues of modesty and honesty and asked if there were any other 'Quaker virtues' he hoped for from himself and from his friends, drawing a classic Bunting response: 'I'm not convinced I have any virtues.'[6]

My other plea of mitigation is that I consciously use *Briggflatts*, Bunting's verse autobiography, as the spine of this life. Brigflatts sits high in the Pennine mountains, which separate the east and west of northern England and are often described as the country's backbone. (The addition of the extra 'g' in Bunting's title seems to be the poet's attempt to Norse-up his dossier.)[7] Bunting's poem acts as the Pennine Chain of this book, holding its landscape together on the one hand and, I hope, providing vistas that help us see the hinterland of Bunting's work.

Briggflatts is structured in five parts, with a short coda, and this is the pattern I have tried to follow. Four of the parts broadly describe the four seasons of the poet's life. The first chapter, 'Guilty of Spring', considers Bunting's early life, his visits to Brigflatts and his eventual desertion of Peggy, his sometimes troubled times at school and his trial and imprisonment for his absolutist conscientious objection in his late teens. His sense of loss as expressed in Part 1 of *Briggflatts* is almost overwhelming:

> Guilty of spring
> and spring's ending

amputated years ache after
the bull is beef, love a convenience.
It is easier to die than to remember.

The second chapter, 'Fells forget him', describes the summer of the poet's years and a second desertion, that of his home. He moved to London to study and then fled to Paris where he met Ezra Pound, Ernest Hemingway and Ford Madox Ford and suddenly found himself at the epicentre of modernism. He returned to London and worked as a journalist before joining the Pounds in Rapallo. He married his first wife, an American, and poverty pushed them and their first child from Italy to the Canary Islands. He wrote some of his most memorable poems during this period. The rise of General Franco and the outbreak of the Spanish Civil War pushed the family back to London. His wife left him and returned to the US with their two children, while pregnant with their third, a son Bunting was never to meet. During these two decades of poverty and poetry he spent only around six months in his beloved Northumbria. He describes the consequence in part two of *Briggflatts*:

Who sang, sea takes,
brawn brine, bone grit.
Keener the kittiwake.
Fells forget him.
Fathoms dull the dale,
gulfweed voices ...

The third chapter, 'Sweet shit! Buy!', covers the poet's middle years. Bunting spent the early part of the Second World War as a balloon operator in the Firth of Forth, helping to protect convoys in the shipping lanes to Murmansk. Later in the war his knowledge of classical Persian allowed him to find work as an interpreter in Iran, and he rose rapidly through the ranks to become Wing Commander Bunting, one of the most respected intelligence officers in the region. He developed a diplomatic career in the Middle East which brought him friendships with its most important politicians. His second marriage, to a Persian girl, required him to leave the embassy in Teheran, and he became the Middle East correspondent for *The Times* newspaper until he was expelled by Mossadeq as tension between Britain and Iran over oil boiled up in the early 1950s. His expulsion began a miserable decade back in the north east of England. The poetry dried up and he struggled to find work. He eventually found a job as the Newcastle *Evening Chronicle*'s financial correspondent. 'Sweet shit! Buy!' is his crisp reflection on journalism in general, and *The Times* in particular.

'An acknowledged land' departs from biography briefly to consider *Briggflatts*, one of the three or four truly great poems of the twentieth century. The poem was inspired by the sonatas of Domenico Scarlatti, who:

> condensed so much music into so few bars
> with never a crabbed turn or congested cadence,
> never a boast or a see-here; and stars and lakes
> echo him and the copse drums out his measure,
> snow peaks are lifted up in moonlight and twilight
> and the sun rises on an acknowledged land.

'Then is Now' takes us into Bunting's winter. The phenomenal success of *Briggflatts* turned the poet into a celebrity. He was plucked from the obscurity of the *Evening Chronicle* to give readings and lecture tours in New York and San Francisco. Film crews turned up at his door to make documentaries. He was President of the Poetry Society during the ludicrous Poetry Wars. He was celebrated as one of the twentieth century's most important poets. With professional success came reunion with the children he hadn't seen since his first wife left him in January 1937. But the most important reunion of all was with Peggy, the young girl whose presence lights up *Briggflatts*:

> Then is Now. The star you steer by is gone,
> its tremulous thread spun in the hurricane
> spider floss on my cheek; light from the zenith
> spun when the slowworm lay in her lap
> fifty years ago.

A coda takes us through Bunting's final years. They were characterised by debilitating poverty, loneliness and meditation on his own past and inevitable future, as well as the broader historical narrative. The first stanza of the 'Coda' to *Briggflatts* captures human insignificance:

> A strong song tows
> us, long earsick.
> Blind, we follow
> rain slant, spray flick
> to fields we do not know.

* * *

This is not the first life of Basil Bunting. Victoria Forde included a biographical chapter in *The Poetry of Basil Bunting*, as did Carroll F. Terrell in his much earlier *Basil Bunting: Man and Poet*. Forde's chapter is particularly useful for its insights into Bunting's relationships with his elder daughters, but it is necessarily brief. Another short life is *Basil Bunting: A Northern Life* by Richard Caddell and Anthony Flowers, the strengths and limitations of which are embedded in its subtitle. The first full-length biography, Keith Alldritt's *Basil Bunting: The Poet as Spy*, appeared in 1998. The sense that it was compiled from increasingly erratic notes taken during lengthy sessions in the pub with Bunting's old friends is enhanced by some of the wilder speculations. That said, Alldritt's biography is a good story and its subject would undoubtedly have approved of its sacrifice of accuracy to imaginative narrative.[8]

In 1979 Tom Pickard proposed a biography of his older friend. 'As to writing my life,' Bunting wrote to him, 'I can't stop you, but suggest you might preface it with the enclosed note. You can't possibly get it right – even the chap who compiled an alleged chronology, one page in *Poetry Information*, got almost every item wrong.'

The enclosed note says: 'Take Heed. My biography appears in <u>Who's Who</u>, complete except for the date of my death which will not be delayed very long. Whatever else anybody writes must be looked on as fiction. Tom Pickard has a vigorous imagination and I hope whatever he writes will amuse you. I haven't read it; and once it's in print I shall not trouble to deny it unless it seems to libel someone else.'[9]

If *A Strong Song Tows Us* is 'fiction' it is at least based squarely on Bunting's own testimony. Although he urged his friends to destroy his letters many sensibly didn't and hundreds have survived. They describe his life unflinchingly. Bunting's commitment to describing the picture as he saw it never wavered, and it caused him no end of trouble.

* * *

I know that my subject would not have supported this project but I hope that he would have approved of my objective, which is to try to raise Bunting's profile for a generation that appears to be forgetting him. As we shall see, by the late 1960s some of the finest critical minds of the century were placing Bunting at the apex of literary modernism.

Thom Gunn: '*Briggflatts* is one of the few great poems of this century. It seems to me greater each time I read it.'

Cyril Connolly: '*Briggflatts* ... is the finest long poem to have been published since T. S. Eliot's *Four Quartets*.'

Hugh MacDiarmid: '[Bunting's] poems are the most important which have appeared in any form of the English language since T. S. Eliot's *The Waste Land* and such poems as W. B. Yeats' "Sailing to Byzantium" and "'The Second Coming".'

Gunn compared *Briggflatts* favourably with *The Waste Land* and Pound's *Cantos*. Sir Herbert Read compared it in durability and weight to that Anglo-Saxon icon, 'The Seafarer'.

What are we missing? How could we have got into a situation where a giant of modernism is so unloved? Mention Bunting to a literate, educated young person these days and you will be met with polite incomprehension. It wasn't always so. In the 1960s and 1970s he was arguably the world's most celebrated living poet. Gordon D. Brown recalled the Morden Tower readings of the early 1960s and the profound effect they had on Bunting's reputation, 'if we are to celebrate the 75th birthday of Basil Bunting, we should do so realizing that 75 sees the poet in a situation very different from that of 10 years ago. Yet, there is always the danger that things will repeat themselves, and, as the first flood of recognition subsides, Bunting will again be allowed to sink into a relative obscurity. We must be his guards.'[10] One is tempted to ask where his guards have been these last forty or so years. In 1988, just three years after Bunting's death, Hugh Kenner complained about our remarkable indifference to this poet, apologising in his pessimistic collection of essays on British literature, *A Sinking Island*, for having to quote such large chunks of Bunting's poetry: 'if Bunting is quoted copiously, that's to throw light on mid-century norms that couldn't accommodate him. I'd have copied out less of "Villon" and "Briggflatts" if I could assume readers familiar with them; but the dearth of such readers is precisely my point.'[11]

Bunting often reaches the heights that Yeats and Eliot reach and he always soars above contemporaries like Auden, MacNeice and Spender. The only other serious contender for the title of 'greatest British modernist poet' is David Jones, whose case has long been championed by Thomas Dilworth, among many others. In 1979 Dilworth wrote to Bunting to ask for his opinion of Jones, prompted by Hugh MacDiarmid's claim that Jones was 'the best English poet of the twentieth century'.[12] Bunting's reply is carefully considered, generous but scrupulous: 'David Jones seems to me one of the bouquet of poets who have made this century the most fruitful in English poetry since the XVIth … Most people would agree that Yeats, Pound, Eliot, Carlos Williams and Zukofsky form an astonishing centrepiece for the century's literary history and David Jones must be placed very close to them.'

Bunting went on to praise Jones's technical skill, his successful absorption of the complexities of Welsh poetry into his verse, his knowledge and versatility; but … Jones had become stuck: 'he had said his say. After *The Anathemata* he could write only what were in effect more anathemata. Considering how widely *The Anathemata* ranges, that is not a great deficiency, but it does leave him less universally available than Pound or Yeats or Zukofsky.'

In short Jones was a one-trick pony, even though that trick was brilliant, and his disciples, over whom he had no influence, bent his message in a way that was not always entirely innocent. There's no doubt that Bunting felt a close poetic bond with Jones. A few days after Jones died in 1974 Bunting paid tribute to him: 'He was the oldest – the last remaining of the friends of my youth, and also the last except myself remaining on this side of the Atlantic of the generation of writers who between 1914 and 1930 made such very large changes in the notion of poetry in twentieth-century England.'[13]

League tables are as invidious in the arts as they are anywhere else outside sport. It doesn't matter if Jones outshines Bunting slightly or vice versa. My contention is that it simply isn't possible to understand the development of literary modernism without engaging with the poetry of Basil Bunting. His friendships with W. B. Yeats, Ezra Pound and T. S. Eliot in the 1920s and 1930s put him at the heart of the modernist revolution. 'Villon', his first great poem, was as heavily edited by Pound as *The Waste Land* had been. Written when Bunting was twenty-five it bears easy comparison with two of the greatest poems of the twentieth century, *The Waste Land* itself and Pound's 'Homage to Sextus Propertius'.

No twentieth-century poet, not even Yeats, prickles the scalp quite as Bunting does. His voice is so assured, his lexical choices so deadly accurate, his timing so impeccable. There are hardly any instances in his work where you feel that he is reaching for an effect. His mastery of his material appears to be effortless, even when he delivers passages of the most precise, hard-edged beauty:

Furthest, fairest things, stars, free of our humbug,
each his own, the longer known the more alone,
wrapt in emphatic fire roaring out to a black flue.
Each spark trills on a tone beyond chronological compass,
yet in a sextant's bubble present and firm
places a surveyor's stone or steadies a tiller.
Then is Now. The star you steer by is gone ...[14]

Why then is Bunting not celebrated as he should be? There are several barriers to his proper recognition. The first is his self-rooting in the north.

Bunting's northern credentials are impeccable but they have become an obstacle to his wider recognition as one of Britain's great national poets. Bunting was in some ways the architect of his own ghetto. He played down the influence of his paternal grandparents and drew heavily on his mother's Borders family history to localise the legends and mythology that coloured so much of his work. The 'gruff Anglo Saxon brevity which survives in local speech informed his poetic language ... and the landscape and social and political environment [of the north east] provided a backdrop never far away in any part of his work.'[15] This influence is easy to exaggerate: 'Far from limiting our understanding of Bunting's achievement, it is hard to overstate the importance of Tyneside and Northumbria as recurrent presences in his work.'[16]

Not hard enough. Critics such as Richard Caddel and Peter Quartermain[17] have emphasised Bunting's northern influences, inspired, admittedly, by Bunting himself, and this has acted as a brake on public recognition of an internationally important poet. The assertion that 'Basil Bunting is the most important poet in the North-East of England since Caedmon in the latter seventh century,'[18] is well-intentioned but damaging. It isn't that it's faint praise. In itself it is a significant achievement to be the best any*thing* any*where* for thirteen hundred years, but it doesn't do justice to Bunting's importance and influence as a world poet. Nobody claims that Ted Hughes is the best Yorkshire poet since Alcuin in the latter eighth century.

It is as though Bunting had some kind of posterity death wish. Not only did he proclaim himself a poet of the North, he went out of his way to position himself as a Quaker poet of the North when not only was he not a Quaker poet, he wasn't even a Quaker. It is not my intention to disparage Bunting's Quaker influences in any way. He was well rooted in the Quaker tradition during his teenage years (notably by Ellen Fry at Ackworth School)

9

and found much in it to value in his declining years, but Bunting had a tendency to inflate the role of Quakerism in his life. He told an interviewer that he had been 'brought up entirely in a Quaker atmosphere', which, as we shall see, isn't true. The most we can say is that he was a Quaker by (secondary) schooling. Quakerism and Northumbria were very important to Bunting and his poem, 'At Briggflatts Meetinghouse', is the most exquisite meditation on meditation of the twentieth or possibly any other century. But that doesn't make Bunting a Quaker poet of the north any more than Robert Graves was a mystic poet of the Balearics or Louis Zukofsky a Jewish poet of the Lower East Side.

A second obstacle to a sensible critical and public awareness of Bunting's genius is his voice, and this for two reasons. The reading voices of most British poets of the first half of the twentieth century are remarkably similar. It isn't that you can't tell them apart, but listening to Spender, Auden, MacNeice and Day Lewis, for instance, makes you feel as though you're in a special kind of club where poetry is intoned as if from the pulpit of a particularly self-important priest. The weight of empire suffocates these voices. Even the stridently Welsh poet, R. S. Thomas, a lover of English culture but no lover of the English, is a member of the club, as are George Barker, Robert Graves, Walter de la Mare, John Masefield and David Gascoyne. Bunting described exactly the effect of listening to these poets:

> Composers are not always the best players of their own compositions, nor poets the best readers of their own verses ... Some lack a voice, or have not learned to control it. Some are so immersed in the mechanics of their craft that they, for instance, make an exaggerated pause at the line's end and lose the swing of the metre. Some have mannerisms, such as the constant repetition of a particular cadence, producing an effect rather like the detestable noise parsons make in church.[19]

You have only to listen to Masefield's toe-curling attempt at the demotic shanty in his 1941 recording of 'Sea Fever' to see Bunting's point.

But mainly we are used to *reading* these poets. When we hear poets speaking their own poetry (all of them, arguably, the worst possible readers of their own work), the uniformity of tone, pace and rhythm homogenises the output, so listening to Bunting reading *Briggflatts* comes as something of a shock. The voice, so essential to appreciating his poetry, has at the same time been a barrier to his acceptance as the great British modernist that he is. First it marks Bunting out as a nonconformist in an age of conformity.

When you hear them read you might initially mistake Spender for Day Lewis but you would never mistake Bunting for anyone else. Second it is uncompromisingly a *northern* voice and this has doubtless contributed to his reduction to a 'poet of the North' (and therefore, by implication, of nowhere else). To Richard Caddel and Anthony Flowers Bunting's voice is not merely 'northern', it is much more regionally specific than that:

> Bill Williamson in *Class, Culture and Community* describes the language of his grandfather, a miner who lived in Throckley, as being a soft Northumbrian accent with rolling 'r's, liberally sprinkled with the archaic pronouns 'thee' and 'thou'. Bunting's much-loved grandfather Isaac Taylor Cheesman and his uncle Matthew Taylor Cheesman (both Throckley men) would have used this dialect, and Bunting would have grown up used to hearing it being spoken. Bunting's own speech – both in poetry reading and in conversation – had much of this local quality. The accent which Bunting carried with him all his life is thus evidently the highly specific, local language from the place where, and the people amongst whom, he spent his childhood.[20]

Bunting is lucky that some of his more enthusiastic disciples didn't present him as a Quaker poet of Throckley. As we shall see, Bunting's deployment of his rich voice is much more calculated and complex than this suggests.

It isn't difficult to imagine the poetry establishment regarding Bunting as an outsider who was happy to remain an outsider. Bunting's voice put him at a geographical, cultural and arguably political distance from the poetry establishment. The high priest of that establishment, T. S. Eliot, was clearly unsure of how to handle Bunting, so he didn't. It was difficult to gain acceptance as a poet in the first half of the twentieth century without Eliot's endorsement and in the early 1930s Bunting mounted a sustained attack on Eliot (or rather, on Eliot's influence) that more or less destroyed any possibility of a relationship with the literary establishment. As Peter Quartermain says, 'Basil Bunting's writing is inevitably political; he is a northern nationalist and his writing is profoundly subversive of the literary establishment.'[21] But the literary establishment didn't have much time for the North either. In 1974 the Director of Northern Arts described as 'a bit fatuous' Bunting's work on behalf of Northumbrian arts. 'I'm not from these parts,' he continued. 'I'm from the Home Counties. I regard my mission as bringing arts to the North. Northumberland is dead, and its so-called folk-culture. So are the pits.'[22] He was right about something. Margaret Thatcher arrived in Downing Street just five years later and one particular British working class way of life lasted barely another five.

Carol Johnson, reviewing Bunting's *Collected Poems*, was quick to spot 'another instance of the death-wish', seeing clearly the gulf between Bunting's sense of poetic self and the wider cultural expectations of British poets in Britain: 'There are no compromises in this book: no competitive posturing for the benefit of a literary clique, none of the defenses of self pity or paranoia against the condition of the outsider. Forty years of going his own way have not diminished this poet's receptiveness to life, vitiated his sense of humor or precipitated a sterile retreat into sensibility at the expense of intelligence.'[23]

Bunting's contempt for the literary establishment is given unqualified expression in the preface he wrote for Tom Pickard's 1967 collection of poems, *High on the Walls*: 'tradition and fashion have no power over a man who has escaped education, with fresh eyes, a fresh voice, and skill to keep the line compact and musical'. He is writing about Pickard but he could just as well be describing himself. 'He is poor, and must feel the temptation to dilute his spirit till it is acceptable to the flock of inferior poets who peck up all the gleanings society leaves for literature. He has to endure the hatred of art which persists in the north of England, the insolence of officials, and of those who pirate the money subscribed "for the arts",'[24] he thundered from Wylam in September 1966. It didn't stop him from becoming President of the Poetry Society a few years later, even though he had very publicly observed that the 'most insidious charlatans fill chairs and fellowships at universities, write for the weeklies or work for the BBC or the British Council or some other asylum for obsequious idlers. In the Eighteenth Century it was the Church. If these men had to read in public, their empty lines, without resonance, would soon give them away.'[25] This may be as true today as it was in 1966 but voicing it wasn't going to drum up much establishment support for him. As Carol Johnson observed, 'So long as the practice of literature in England by original and independent outsiders remains as embarrassing as vice, and the endorsement of mediocrity a motivating factor of cultural life, Basil Bunting may continue with every reason for tranquillity of mind to ply the poetics of disregard. England does not deserve him: the only worthy successor to Hopkins ... who also had to wait.'[26] I'm not sure that Bunting would have recognised the bridge to Hopkins but the point about the 'poetics of disregard' is well made.

Bunting's voice is particularly important, however, because his poems were designed to be read aloud, to be *heard*. We learn more about how to read Bunting's poetry from the way he read it himself than from any other recorded British poet in history:

> Poetry, like music, is to be heard. It deals in sound – long sounds and short sounds, heavy beats and light beats, the tone relations of vowels, the relations of consonants to one another which are like instrumental colour in music. Poetry lies dead on the page, until some voice brings it to life, just as music, on the stave, is no more than instructions to the player ... Reading in silence is the source of half the misconceptions that have caused the public to distrust poetry ... Poetry is seeking to make not meaning, but beauty; or if you insist on misusing words, its 'meaning' is of another kind, and lies in the relation to one another of lines and patterns of sound, perhaps harmonious, perhaps contrasting and clashing, which the hearer feels rather than understands; lines of sound drawn in the air which stir deep emotions and which have not even a name in prose.[27]

Listen to Bunting once (maybe twice) and you will never again read his poetry without that voice in your head, so inseparable is it from the work. His distinctive cadences are a kind of sub-soundtrack to *Briggflatts* on which Domenico Scarlatti's sonatas float. It provides a way of *reading* poetry in both senses. As I was writing this book I was reading Bunting's near contemporary, the Irish poet Austin Clarke. Inevitably I began to read Clarke in Bunting's voice, producing some startling effects. Read in Bunting's voice this stanza from Clarke's *Song of the Books* could place you in the Borders if you replace the cod Irish names with those of Wilson and Telfer, the shepherds in *Briggflatts*:

> Dreaming of Virgil and Blind Homer,
> Schoolmasters cuffed behind a loaning
> Or clamp, hearing the cowherds, dog-boys
>   Hurrying by.
> Lurchers at heel, cold whistling fellows,
> Giddy O'Hackett, Coxcomb O'Boland,
> Buffoon O'Malachy, Pighead Moran
>   Watched on the sly,
> Irish and English words hobnobbing
> Where dealers buy,

> In Castletown or striking the cobbles
> Of Athenry.[28]

The authentic voice of the poem fixes it geographically.

But more striking still is to read the work of another northern poet, Wordsworth, as if read aloud by Bunting. Wordsworth had a pronounced northern accent. As Hazlitt observed, he talked 'with a mixture of clear gushing accents in his voice, a deep guttural intonation, and a strong tincture of the northern *burr*, like the crust on wine'.[29] In a lecture on Wordsworth Bunting observed that

> Two hundred years ago standard English had not been invented and there was neither a BBC nor a system of education determined to make us all talk alike. Wordsworth spoke as men spoke where he was born, with broad accents and a marked R. He kept his native tongue in spite of Cambridge & London & Somerset and Leicestershire. Southerners found it hard to follow his conversation ... Wordsworth did not write dialect; but he composed aloud, very loud according to the anecdotes, in the language he spoke, and that was not the Koiné we are all taught to use now.[30]

Listening to Wordsworth read in a northern accent reveals a quite different poem from the one you thought you knew and loved. Stephen Logan's attempt to reconstruct Wordsworth's authentic reading voice shows very clearly how meaning (not that Bunting would have been interested in that) and certainly understanding of even Wordsworth's best-known poems change subtly when they are read as the poet himself would have read them. 'Remember that the word "water" was unknown to him,' Bunting pointed out to an audience in 1970. 'He rhymes it with "chatter" and "shatter" because he pronounced it "watter"; and though he spells Yarrow with OW, as the map does, he rhymes it with the word he (and we) pronounce "marra", and rhyme with "Jarra".'[31]

Wordsworth's decision to retain that voice despite his many years spent away from the north west of England, and despite the substantial barrier it intruded between the poet and most of his (southern) readership, was a proudly political one, as it was for Bunting. Because we have no recordings of poets before Tennyson and Browning, linguistic orthodoxy, received pronunciation, has effectively subsumed authors like Wordsworth. Our entire understanding of Wordsworth has been hijacked and twisted by Oxbridge. As Stephen Logan says, received pronunciation is the voice of an educated minority and 'the fact that we implicitly and without question read the poets that we read in this accent might mean that we're subjecting them to a kind of sociological transformation'.[32] Wordsworth's retention of his 'burr' is a deliberate expression of allegiance to a region and a class. It is as deliberate a rejection of the establishment as Bunting's was a hundred years later.

Poetry, even 'humorous' poetry, provides few moments of genuine comedy but undoubtedly listening to Ezra Pound reading Canto XLV ('With Usura') is one such. It isn't difficult to find online and it is very funny. Where on earth did he get that accent?[33] Certainly not from his friends and family in Wyncote, Philadelphia. Bunting claims to have changed (with Louis Zukofsky) Pound's reading voice:

> I can remember our saying something to Pound ... in the days when he used to read in the Yeatsian manner, which we didn't approve of ... whenever anybody asked Yeats to read or recite, or when it came into his head to do so, he almost visibly wrapped an imaginary cloak about him and set off on one of those expeditions to the peaks of Parnassus or something, in a voice which owed more to the least desirable habits of the Church of England than to anything else: a terrible pulpit drone.[34]

The irony in this is that if Pound sounded like anyone (apart from Yeats) it was Bunting himself. Pound's pronunciation of the word 'stone' and his elongation of his Rs is pure Northumbrian.

Bunting's voice is essential to a rich reading of his poems, and in a sense he has been separated from his own work by technology. Until the publication of the Bloodaxe edition of *Briggflatts* in 2009 recordings have not been packaged with the poems, separating the reader from the authentic voice of the read. Bunting's flame has always shone more brightly in North America than in Britain, and in North America his reading voice is all but incomprehensible. Nevertheless it is hard to disagree with the poet Gael Turnbull who wrote that, 'it is by the voice that I am held. Not sound in any way cultivated for itself, as separate; but spoken and heard with the full sense that it is only by articulate speech that we can know anything, and that no word exists until it is spoken and heard.'[35]

Many of us are 'held by the voice', but we are held also by the performance. To those who know Bunting's voice only from his readings there is something puzzling about Christabel Dennison's observation in 1925 that he talked with 'the slow studied imitation of ... the Oxford accent'.[36] What sort of an accent is that for the proud northerner who had been expressing contempt for 'southron' ways since at least 1916? His friend, the poet Denis Goacher, threw some light on this:

> His own Northumbrian accent was a manufactured one. He had, in fact, a very refined voice but had two things in mind when reading his poetry aloud. He was very careful to keep the flat A's and a bit likely to roll his R's, but he certainly did not, in normal speech, roll his R's to the prodigious extent that he did when reading his poems. I never heard any sort of Northumbrian sound like that! ... Now, that is very interesting as – what shall we say – auto-biography? He is really tracing back his past, recovering the accent he was born with, with a layer of nostalgia. But, I repeat, there is an over-emphasis on regionality, because he wished to make a point *against* Southern speech. Now, I think we could agree that we none of us make our best points by being against something. So, to my mind, he spoilt the readings of his poems by concentrating on those two things. If this poem does not stand up without being read in some sort of Northumbrian accent, then it is ridiculously limited – and it is not so.[37]

I have come round to Goacher's view on this. There are none of these flat As and rolled Rs in his interviews. In fact his 'normal' voice is exactly as Christabel Dennison described it, middle class Home Counties. Bunting the poet can rarely be accused of reaching for effect; Bunting the performer always did. This is one of the many contradictions in Bunting's life and art. On the one hand we need his voice to read a poem like *Briggflatts*; on the other reading it in his 'poetry reading' voice limits the poem.

* * *

Other factors have contributed to Bunting's current neglect. Bunting in later life reflected on the penchant that his generation of poets (and the previous generation, Pound's) had for the classics:

> The world doesn't spend all its time reading books, and we all assumed that they do. We have far too many references to things. There we tumbled below Yeats. Yeats is very careful. He produces very few references to previous literature. His references are those you can find in the life around you, and that is much easier, and much better, and more provident, especially where literary fashions change. Eliot above all, of course, is using other literature all the time. Pound, to a considerable extent; Zukofsky, to some extent; me also – and that will weigh against us as the century goes on. Which of us will be remembered at this time in the next century I can't, for the life of me, imagine.

I think it's quite probable that all those I've mentioned will be remembered, but your notion of what will be remembered is often very likely to be wrong.[38]

He was confident that he would be in that select group. As he said in a television interview in 1984, 'If you have practically no readers, but those readers were people like Yeats and Pound, and Eliot, and Carlos Williams, well, you're pretty confident some notice will be taken sooner or later.'[39]

Furthermore, his association with Ezra Pound didn't help, even though, as we shall see, he forcefully rejected Pound's politics. He was no more sympathetic to the reactionary giants of twentieth-century poetry, Yeats, Pound and Eliot, than he was to the group of poets that emerged in the 1930s to replace them – Auden, MacNeice and Spender. Additionally, his total output makes a slim volume. It could have been even slimmer; he wished in later life that he had discarded more. He wasn't a lover of Shelley's poetry but he appreciated Shelley's predicament: 'I'm sure when Shelley drowned he thought "If only I could get my hands on the works. So I could destroy them. They're no good."'[40]

Another barrier is Pound's observation that his verse is 'more thoughtful than toffee-lickers require ... much more so than the public desires',[41] which points to 'difficulty' that is more apparent than real. And, of course, Bunting's best poems are long and complex and do not lend themselves readily to anthologies.

John Seed points to more complex social, political and cultural cross-currents that combined to isolate Bunting from the literary world:

Bunting's predicament was much more than a matter of his own perversity or his isolation from the networks of the English literary establishment. It was more complex than that, involving the intersection of multiple histories – an individual biography of immense complexity, literary modernism's English demise and its continuation by the political values of the extreme right, a sense of the futility of poetry in a time of crisis, the deep elitism and savage torpor of powerful literary institutions, the disruptive impact of the Depression and the Second World War on a particular generation.[42]

All true, but if we have to point to one single obstacle to proper recognition of Bunting's importance in his lifetime, and his near-disappearance since, his auto-regionalisation is the culprit.

Ezra Pound wrote both historically and prophetically to Henry Swabey in 1946, 'What the ... hell CAN you say for a pen Empire that lets best poet of the generation Bunting (B. Bunting) disappear sans trace, and no breath of curiosity even among the ten alleged literates still on the dung heap.'[43] More recently, and temperately, Peter Quartermain summed up Bunting's problem well:

> Bunting is both outside and inside the culture/the koiné at the same time, using what he subverts, subverting what he uses … The Northumbrian writer insofar as he nourishes his difference, his distinctness, his Northumbrian-ness, like any outcast views society politically, yet at the same time – if he is to write at all, if he is to be heard or to be read – he is obliged to work within the culture too, presenting himself perhaps as apolitical. Prefiguring subversion, his work equally signifies order. Which is why there are so many apparent contradictions, conflicts, and inconsistencies in Bunting's work – between the private personal verse, individual, and the public; between the strictly local and the koiné; between the insistence on the primacy of sound and the demand that the poem have matter.[44]

His deployment of his voice, as we have seen, was not straightforward. The nature of Bunting's regionalism is even more complex. On the one hand, as Matthew Hart has noted, it is only possible because of a life lived largely elsewhere, '*Briggflatts*, in the end, can't be reduced to the poetry of the North. It is only through its protagonist's metropolitan sojourn that the poem is able, in retrospect, to measure the rhythm of city and country alike.'[45]

On the other hand it is possible to see it as a kind of platform from which the poet engaged with the rest of the world. As Donald Wesling says, Bunting is 'a provincial internationalist, because from his Northern vantage he looks over the top of London for cultural values, to Italy, Persia, America. If Southron thinking is metropolitan and represents the singleness of the State, for him Northern thinking connects whatever is marginal, local, plural, adulterated, and inconvenient, with the imaginativeness of the global modernist avant-garde.'[46] Either way it was no mere isolationism. Bunting didn't retreat to Northumbria in order to avoid everywhere else.

It is the task of the rest of this book to show how Bunting navigated around these contradictory impulses. Bunting was a committed Northumbrian and I hope this book will both leave him there and yet liberate him from it. No great surprise there. Small, disorganised raiding parties have been robbing the people of the Borders of their treasures for centuries.

ONE

GUILTY OF SPRING

Drudge at the mallet, the may is down,
fog on fells. Guilty of spring
and spring's ending
amputated years ache after
the bull is beef, love a convenience.
It is easier to die than to remember.

Briggflatts I

KHAKI FEVER, MARCH 1900

I was born amid rejoicings for the relief of Ladysmith during the Boer War.
That perhaps serves to date me.[1]

By the end of February 1900 British forces had been fighting a vicious war in
Southern Africa for over four months. The British public's thirst for revenge
for the humiliating defeat at the hands of the Boers at Majuba Hill in 1881
(egged on by a hysterical *Daily Mail*) was overwhelming, but the British were
struggling. The Boers won a series of important battles and by the end of
October 1899 a garrison of fifteen thousand British troops led by Lieutenant
General Sir George White was besieged in a place hardly anyone in the
United Kingdom had heard of, Ladysmith.

This war was unusual. The quality of photographic images sent back
from the front was unprecedented thanks to a combination of new film
technology and the sharp edges caught by Africa's fierce sunlight. Moreover
for the first time ever domestic audiences could see moving images from the
front and could appreciate the full scale and bloodiness of battles fought six
thousand miles away.[2] A wave of irrepressible jingoism overtook the nation,
borne up by an enormous flood of stories, poems and music-hall songs.

During the war's early stages 'khaki fever' raged throughout the land. Kipling's 'Absent-Minded Beggar', which Mrs Beerbohm Tree recited nightly and to which Arthur Sullivan wrote accompanying music, earned at least a quarter-of-a-million pounds for soldiers' wives and children. Sub-Kiplingesque bombast formed a staple of music-hall fare, a particular favourite being Will Dalton and F. J. Willard's 'A Hot Time in the Transvaal To-night':

> There is trouble in the Transvaal,
> And England wants to know
> Whether Mister Kruger or
> John Bull shall boss the show.[3]

Khaki fever or not, the British suffered one humiliating defeat after another and sustained massive battle casualties as well as one thousand men lost to a typhoid epidemic caused by drinking water from rivers that bobbed with the rotting corpses of soldiers and horses. The public was baffled by and angry at the continuing tactical ineptness of the generals on the ground.

Troops led by Sir Redvers Buller blundered into a disastrous defeat at Spion Kop on 24 January and another at Vaalkrantz on 5 February, but eventually broke into Ladysmith on 28 February. The following day news of the relief of Ladysmith reached the world, sparking off celebrations across the Empire. The *Manchester Guardian* described the celebrations following the relief of Ladysmith:

> To describe with any degree of adequacy the excitement in London, and indeed throughout the country, consequent upon the announcement yesterday of the relief of Ladysmith would be an almost impossible task … Those around the Mansion House were electrified, and the crowd grew by thousands every minute. Men and women went frantic with delight, hats were thrown into the air, handkerchiefs were waved, and the cheers became a mighty roar … The City was excited throughout the day, and last night there was constant cheering in the streets. Nearly every omnibus and cab driver had a red, white, and blue ribbon attached to his whip. Many pedestrians were carrying Union Jacks, and everywhere there was an air of rejoicing which could not be mistaken.[4]

The new century was still young but the relief of Ladysmith was by a long way its biggest event so far. The celebrations were by no means confined to the capital. 'The scene in [Newcastle's] Grainger Street was unusually exciting, tradespeople rushing out of their places of business to procure war editions, and people assembled in groups to talk over the news. Cheers were loud and frequent.'[5]

On 1 March 1900, a cold, dark Thursday, in Scotswood-on-Tyne in the north east of England, as a delirious Empire celebrated the relief of Ladysmith, Annie Bunting gave birth to her first child, Basil Cheesman Bunting. [6]

Bunting was born as Britain was waking up to the fact that the old order was vanishing. The longest reigning monarch in British history was close to the end of her life. Her empire was at its height, with a quarter of the world's population and twelve million square miles in its control, but it faced challenges that presaged its rapid decline. British politics was entering a period of crisis on many fronts – the constitution, Ireland, rapid militarisation and the inexorable rise of suffragetism, the labour movement and socialism. The 1890s had seen a profound agricultural depression during which wheat prices dropped to half the level of those enjoyed by the previous generation of arable farmers. In the cities overcrowding and deplorable housing conditions were creating a new kind of depravity that polite society was only just discovering, in books such as Andrew Mearns' *Bitter Cry of Outcast London*, books that were in themselves fostering a new kind of poverty tourism as the middle classes shivered deliciously at the lurid behaviour of the underclass, while at the same time complaining that the most shocking activities of the remotest corners of the Empire were beginning to be enacted on their back doorsteps. Business was just recovering from a severe recession during which Baring Brothers had to be rescued by its competitors, led by the Bank of England, because of its overexposure to Argentinian securities (bankers don't read history). Prospects for the British economy were murky as foreign competition overran domestic suppliers in both agriculture and manufacturing.[7] The muscles of the relatively new trades union movement were beginning to ripple, the great dock strike of 1889 being still hot in the memories of workers and employers alike (the dockers had won). There was a huge amount of progress in the period, of course. Wages overall had risen by about a third in the final decade of the nineteenth century. Health statistics were positive, class distinctions were being slowly eroded, crime levels were dropping, although in all these areas there were still enormous regional variations. In the first ten years of the twentieth century the average wage in Durham, where agriculture successfully cohabited with mining and manufacturing, was nearly twenty-three shillings whereas in Wiltshire, which was almost exclusively rural, it was just sixteen shillings, a huge difference; and this was just the *average* wage.[8] The arts had entered a period of revolution as modernism began to sweep away Victorian realism, much of it drawing on startling new theories of the unconscious that had recently been unveiled by Boris Sidis and Sigmund Freud. The social world was being transformed as new forms of transport (and therefore of warfare) were developed[9] and electrical power began to be deployed in the home. With hindsight, of course, it's possible to point to almost any period in the last three hundred years as one of profound change but it is clear that people in the early twentieth century themselves identified a significant transition. Two months after Bunting's birth one journalist wrote that, 'we stand upon the threshold, not so much of a new century – for that merely signifies a mechanical calculation of time – as of a new era in political and social life'.[10] For some it was the beginning of the end. For others – artists, writers, musicians, activists, scientists, academics, businessmen – it was the longed-for beginning of a new beginning, the birth of a new century. It is no accident, I think, that Basil Bunting linked his birth to an iconic moment in British imperial history. He was to become an important messenger of a new world order.

PLATEFULS OF TAPIOCA, 1900–1912

Bunting's parents, Annie Cheesman and Thomas Lowe Bunting, had been married at the parish church of St Michael and All Angels in Newburn on 1 November 1898. Annie was a striking woman. A photograph taken of her at twenty-six, a year after Bunting was born, shows her to have been dark and slim, with a strong chin. Bunting himself had a Cheesman face and photographs of him in later life show a striking resemblance to his maternal grandfather Isaac.[11]

Annie, born in 1876, was the fourth daughter of Ann Forster and Isaac Taylor Cheesman, manager of the Throckley Colliery, with strong Border family connections. Ann and Isaac were both born in 1844 in the village of Ryton, seven miles west of Newcastle, on the south bank of the River Tyne. In 1881 they were living in Bank Top Cottages, Throckley, on the opposite side of the river, with their six children and Isaac's brother Edward, who was also a mining engineer. By 1891 another daughter, Maggie, had been added to the family and Edward had moved on to the Blaydon Main Colliery. Mining ran deep in the Cheesman family. Two of Bunting's Cheesman uncles, Nicholas and Matthew, were also mine managers in the Throckley pits. Bunting's grandmother, Ann, died in October 1892 and Isaac remarried in 1894. He died in the summer of 1916.

Bunting's father, Thomas Lowe Bunting, was born on 6 April 1868, the son of Mary Elizabeth Lowe, from Burton-on-Trent in Staffordshire, and Joseph Bunting, a draper from Heanor, in Derbyshire but deep in D. H. Lawrence country.[12] In 1881, when Thomas was twelve, Joseph's business, Tag Hill Draper's Shop, employed a milliner, an apprentice and a general assistant who all lived with Joseph and Mary and their children, Thomas and Harriet, above the shop. Mary died at the age of fifty-three two years later. It appears that Joseph's business failed as a result of his heavy drinking and he died at the age of fifty-four when his son was just nineteen. Thomas had to borrow from one of his uncles in order to pursue his medical qualifications in Edinburgh.

The 1901 census shows the Bunting family to have been prosperous, with an Irish male assistant medical practitioner, Lachlan Gollan, two female servants (Margaret Cowell and Isabella Bainbridge) and a further female 'visitor', Isabella Young. By 1911 the household included an Australian assistant medical practitioner, John Gormley, and two young female servants, Bessie (cook) and Barbara Clark (housemaid). The family's relationships with these young girls was deeply traditional: 'My mother's servants came to her very young, daughters of pitmen, often from her own native village. They were paid very little – about enough to buy themselves one walking-out dress every year. The rest of their clothes were provided, and of course their food. But when they married, they were married from our house and a good part of their trousseau was provided by us.'[13]

Thomas became a celebrated doctor. He received a Gold Medal at Edinburgh University in 1904 for his MD thesis on the histology of lymphatic glands and went on to establish a general practice in the West End of Newcastle as well as being the pit doctor at Montague Colliery in Scotswood and a pioneer in the new science of radiology.

Bunting remembered his father later in life:

He was a doctor – a rather remarkable one. At that time [around 1903] he would be still busy preparing the thesis … in a tiny surgery with a desk about 2 feet by 18 inches and a microscope. He managed to compare the histology … of the lymphatic glands of very nearly all the mammals, and a good many other creatures too. There was in those days an animal shop in Newcastle and he had an arrangement: when an animal died he would be called at once and go and remove the particular glands he wanted to examine before anything else was done. So he managed to have lions, tigers, leopards, monkeys, all sorts of things on his list besides the small animals he could buy for the purpose. The house was sometimes full of lizards that had escaped from their box in the cellar.[14]

Bunting was born in the family home, 27 Denton Road in Scotswood, a couple of hundred yards from the busy River Tyne. Denton Road is now the A191, entirely unrecognisable from the photographs of the early twentieth century, and the building in which Bunting was born no longer exists. Like so many parts of Tyneside Scotswood suffered uncontrollable decline in the latter part of the twentieth century as industries disappeared and mass unemployment and antisocial behaviour rose. It is now a very long way from Geordie Ridley's nineteenth-century vision of 'lots o' lads an' lasses there, all wi' smiling faces/Gawn along the Scotswood Road, to see the Blaydon Races'.[15] In 1900, however, Scotswood was a separate colliery village for the Montague coal works and, colliery aside, it was a predominantly rural environment. Bunting remembered salmon being unloaded onto carts from the nearby river[16] and that in order to get to Newcastle itself he needed to take a fairly long walk (about eight kilometres) across farmland. The house itself was not large. One of Thomas' former patients recalled the dark entrance of the Denton Road house and a contemporary photograph of the junction where the Bunting house stood suggests a rather gloomy atmosphere.[17] With Thomas' menagerie inside and the pall cast by the heavy industry outside it would have been a surreal environment in which to start life.

The Northumberland Bunting was born into was large but relatively sparsely populated. Though it was at the time the fifth largest county in England its population was relatively low; in 1891 it was just over half a million, but that population was concentrated almost entirely along the north bank of the Tyne, from Newburn to the coast, and from the mouth of the Tyne along the coast to the mouth of the River Wansbeck. It was, overwhelmingly, a coal county. Nearly nine million tons of coal were raised in 1895 and, with the expansion of the coalfield, its rapidly growing labour requirements caused increasing rural depopulation as young men and families streamed into mining towns such as Ashington and Blyth.[18] Bunting felt connected to the mining communities of the north east for his entire life: 'I knew several miner's leaders at one time and another,' he told Ezra Pound in 1934, from checkweighmen to old William Straker (the chap who had found out in the course of fifty years or so of mining politics that billiards was worse than booze). I even talked once or twice to old Charley Fenwick, before he died, a man who had been a Northumberland miner's official since the middle of last century and went down the pit to work at the age of nine. Damn it, I was brought up in all that, Joseph Skipsey is said to have dandled me when I was a baby, and he'd been down the pit before the first factory acts touched them. I was on the spot when the View Pit was flooded and forty-five men drowned, I heard what the men had to say about it and the whole cursed system when there wasn't any question of politics, mining or otherwise, but just sheer human commonsense. My grandfather, whom I knew pretty well when I was a kid, was a miner, son of a miner. I know the solidity of those people, and I watched it break up in '26, when I was all the time in a mining village, took the chair at one of Cook's meetings, stuck a knife in the tyres of a government strikebreaking lorry and tried unsuccessfully nearly every paper in the country to get the scandalous faked benches of magistrates who condemned the strikers to long terms of hard labour shown up. Not even the independent labour party's rag would publish the facts.[19]

Thomas had picked his location well. It is likely that he moved to the North East at the encouragement of his university friend, Andrew Messer. Messer was another highly successful doctor with a deep commitment to public health, but the real driver of social welfare improvements in the region was Dr J. W. Hembrough. Hembrough had been appointed Northumberland's first County Medical Officer in 1894, a position he retained until his death in 1919, and started a small health care revolution in the region. Hembrough was convinced that improved public health was dependent on better housing, cleaner water supplies and proper sewage facilities. His own careful investigations repeatedly showed that the spread of then common infectious diseases such as smallpox, diphtheria, scarlet fever, typhoid and the county's biggest and most expensive health problem, tuberculosis, were fundamentally connected to poor living conditions, and particularly to unpaved yards, inadequate and insufficient water and ventilation, uncovered drains, festering piles of refuse and overcrowded accommodation. However damning Hembrough's reports, the lack of political will to spend ratepayers' money on the problems he revealed was a persistent problem and his heroic and ceaseless battles with the local district councils on behalf of the poor must have been inspirational to the young left-leaning doctor Thomas Bunting. Although it was a time of increasing overcrowding, as the coal and arms industries blossomed, until 1904 just one man held combined responsibility for the offices of Road Surveyor, Manager of Waterworks and Sanitary Inspector. The sanitary component of this omni-job alone required him to inspect slaughter houses, cowsheds, common lodging houses and workshops while simultaneously being responsible for clearing sewers and rubbish, unblocking drains and all the other impediments to healthy urban dwelling. Thomas would have appreciated Hembrough's campaign to pave footpaths. In mining communities children would go to school with wet feet that would stay that way for the entire day. Gradually Hembrough's tireless lobbying began to bear fruit and conditions for the urban poor improved, although preventable outbreaks of typhoid and diphtheria continued to claim lives.[20] Bunting never forgot the poverty of the community in which he grew up.

Tyneside was industrialising rapidly during Bunting's early years. The Newcastle engineer George Armstrong had opened his Elswick works (a mile or so from Scotswood) in 1847 and when he moved into the arms business his workforce grew from one hundred men to over twenty thousand by 1900. Elswick shipyards opened in 1883 and eighty-four ships were launched there in the following thirty years. According to local historian Jimmy Forsyth, in the ten years leading up to the First World War eight major navies spent £670 million on warships, a significant proportion of which was built in Elswick, which could build 'an entire battleship from raw materials on site, with steel plants, engineering works, ordnance factories and plenty of cheap labour all under virtually the same roof'.[21] During Bunting's childhood the Scotswood Road was the Silicon Valley of the early twentieth century arms race, as Armstrong opened a second factory in Scotswood itself and the banks of the Tyne were turned into a heavily polluted industrial wasteland. The salmon that Bunting apparently remembered being unloaded from the Tyne disappeared very quickly and during the war a workforce of twenty-five thousand produced one-third of Britain's guns in Elswick and Scotswood. It was a gritty place in which to grow up.

Bunting described his early schooling to Jonathan Williams: 'I suppose about 1906 I did start school. I used to be taken by the housemaid. It was a long walk, about a mile and a half to the tram terminus, and then a considerable ride in the tram, and away up the hill to a part of Newcastle that is now all slums, which was then slightly shabby middle-class. There was an old lady who kept a school, a very old-fashioned kind.' The school, at 24 West Parade in Rye Hill, was owned by Miss A. M. Bell. She called it a kindergarten but Bunting doubted that she had 'the faintest notion what the word implied in the history of education. It was just a fashionable word. It was what you would call a day-nursery school in the old style.'[22] His favourite books at the time were *Grimm's Fairy Tales*, 'and there were a whole series of books by E. Nesbit; and a few things like 'Two Bad Mice' by the lady from Near Sawrey [Beatrix Potter]'.[23] Bunting also mentions the fact that he and his sister, Joyce (born in January 1902), had a governess called Miss Wraith, who was kind and loving but unsparing in the application of her cane.[24] As usual with Bunting's recollections one needs to be wary of exaggeration. Northumberland's Education Committee ruled in 1909 that there should be no corporal punishment in local infant schools and that it should be used in other schools only as a measure of last resort. All head teachers were required to keep records of any cases of corporal punishment so it is likely that cane-happy sadists, even among privately employed governesses, were on the wane by the time Bunting was twelve.

His memories of nursery school days were chiefly of a girl who was a couple of years older than him (and who helped him cheat at spelling tests) and tapioca. He wasn't a fan:

> You learned your ABC and got thoroughly rapped on the knuckles if you made mistakes. You learned by copying pot hooks into exercise books. You were supposed to learn good manners by eating up everything that was put in front of you, but I couldn't do that because she included a great deal of tapioca pudding in her menu – and tapioca is something I could never endure. I spent an awful lot of time sitting and looking at platefuls of tapioca. It would be there in front of me from the beginning of dinner time until the middle of the afternoon. If I hadn't eaten it by then I got spanked.[25]

Other than these scant details we have little material on Bunting's early years. He was characteristically unhelpful in providing more. His claim that he attended Newcastle's Royal Grammar School between 1909 and 1911 is not confirmed in the school's records but it isn't implausible.[26] The son of middle-class professional parents is unlikely to have reached the age of twelve, when he started at Ackworth School, on a combination of nursery school and a governess, although it isn't impossible.

THE SONG OF THE ACKWORTH CLOCK, 1912–1916

Ackworth School was (and still is) a co-educational Quaker school. It was founded near Pontefract in Yorkshire in 1779 by the distinguished physician and botanist John Fothergill. Bunting considered it extremely old-fashioned and decided that it hadn't changed any of its rules since Fothergill's time though it had, at least, finally introduced holidays: 'Twenty years or so before I went there, you didn't get home on holidays at all. You went to school at the age of twelve and came home permanently at the age of sixteen – meanwhile you never saw home …'[27]

Ackworth welcomed seventy-nine new scholars on 12 September 1912. Nearly half that year's intake was female.[28] Bunting's application had been approved at the School Committee meeting of 5 March and the minutes record that the annual fee was £54 (as it was for the other four 'Non Members [of the Society of Friends]' whose applications were approved at that meeting).[29] Among the seventy-nine scholars were Bunting's new friends Ernest Cooper Apperley Stephenson and John Allen Greenbank. All three left, according to the school's Admissions Book, on 25 July 1916. His friendship with Greenbank changed Bunting's life.

It is widely thought that Bunting came from a Quaker family but neither Thomas nor Annie was a Quaker and we can only guess at their reasons for sending their son to Quaker schools. His sister Joyce went to Central Newcastle High School, where she was a contemporary of the playwright and actress, Esther McCracken, and then to St Leonard's School in St Andrews. Neither is a Quaker establishment. Joyce went on to study at Edinburgh University, graduating in 1924 with a degree in medicine and surgery.[30]

We will return to Bunting's complex relationship with Quakerism but there is no denying that his secondary education was in Quaker schools. Ackworth School developed progressively during the first twenty or so years of the century. Writing in 1929 the General Committee of the School congratulated itself on the fact that 'freedom and elasticity' had been the guiding principles of the management of the curriculum; that world history and geography had supplanted 'narrower national studies'; that modern foreign languages claimed a full share of pupils' attention; that more academic and professional training was demanded of teachers and that 'more is demanded from the pupil in individual thought, reasoning and criticism'; and on the 'striking advance' that activities formerly reserved for the rich and privileged (music, singing, gymnastics, drawing) had been made available to all. As we shall see music was a very powerful force in Bunting's life and work and it can only have been encouraged by the prevailing Ackworth philosophy: 'The music offered to all pupils to-day in aural culture, instrumental lessons, and class singing and sight reading shows more advance in educational outlook and method than in any other subject that could be mentioned.'[31]

Ackworth naturally instilled 'the general Quaker attitude' and it was here that Bunting discovered the powerful rhythms of the King James Bible and particularly the second book of Kings, although he had been introduced to the Bible at nursery school: 'Every morning you had to get a large lump of the Bible by heart before breakfast At breakfast the Bible was read to you. At dinner the Bible was read to you. At tea time, after tea, the Bible was read to you again. And on Sunday there were *very* large lumps of the Bible, besides Scripture lessons in between.'[32] Although it is difficult to see how he found the time to write poetry with all this Bible he was clearly moved by the rhythms and narrative skills of Job, the Song of Songs, and 1 and 2 Kings in the Authorised Version.

The fact that the Bible played such a central role in Ackworth life can partly be explained by the encyclopaedic knowledge of it possessed by the then headmaster, Frederick Andrews. There is a story of two boys attributing their obvious lack of attention to Andrews to the fact that they had been comparing their thigh muscles. Andrews

> smiled and rubbed his long nose with his finger, then told them to look up the tenth verse of the hundred and forty-seventh psalm and write it down. That was the end of the matter. When the boys found the text, it read:

> > He delighteth not in the strength of a horse:
> > He taketh not pleasure in the legs of a man.[33]

This story says a lot about the culture of Bunting's early teenage schooling. It is characteristic of that culture that one of the biggest celebrations planned during Bunting's time at Ackworth was that to commemorate one hundred years of peace between Great Britain and the United States.[34] It isn't surprising that Bunting was happy at Ackworth. One hundred years ago the general culture of British education was still more Wackford Squeers than Frederick Andrews. In a memoir of Bunting's next school, Leighton Park School, written in 1940 the writer reflects on the style of education in the previous generation, 'The old tradition of the classical grind, the mental gymnastic of distasteful tasks, corporal punishment, fagging, excessive compulsory games, the whole of a boy's life directed on the principle that he should "work, play or sleep", no moments of leisure – this view of education was almost universal at the time.'[35] At both Ackworth School and his next Bunting escaped the worst of this.

My delight from the first time I set eyes on her

A few miles west of Sedbergh, on the north-west frontier of the Yorkshire Dales National Park, a narrow lane leads south from what is now the A683 that starts in Heysham, on the Lancashire coast, and ends near Kirkby Stephen in the Upper Eden Valley. The lane leads to the peaceful Quaker hamlet of Brigflatts, high in the Pennines. At the end of the lane the River Rawthey snakes past on its journey from Baugh Fell to the River Lune at Stangerthwaite. On the right-hand side of the lane is the stable which was built for the horses of visiting Quakers, with, as Mary Dawson described it,

> stone steps leading to an upper room where in the 18th century there was a school for the village children, run by Friends ... Near the schoolroom is the farmhouse built in 1745 by a Quaker farmer. This house was called Middle Briggflatts. Its rooms have the graceful proportions of buildings of the period. Here lived Mr. Greenbank, the stonemason, who had managed the quarry at Stonehouses in Dentdale, making black-marble mantelpieces for Victorian drawing rooms, until these dropped out of fashion and the Greenbank family moved to Briggflatts ... At the bottom of the lane was the oldest building Low Briggflatts farm, where George Fox found hospitality in 1652.[36]

Set in the middle of nine imposing yews, now as then, one wonders if it was designed in 1743 to be a place of the spirit. Brigflatts is within a couple of miles of the birthplace of the Quaker movement, Firbank Knott near Sedbergh, where George Fox delivered his great sermon in 1652. In 1652 Fox was 'moved of the Lord to go atop' Pendle Hill in Lancashire, where he had a visionary experience of 'people in white raiment'.[37] Elfrida Vipont Foulds takes up the story:

> Travelling through the Dales, George Fox came to Brigflatts, where he spent the night with Richard Robinson. Next day he attended a meeting of the [Westmorland] Seekers at Borrat, near Sedbergh, the home of Gervase Benson. When the great Whitsuntide fair at Sedbergh was in full swing, he stood under a yew tree in the churchyard and preached to the crowds which gathered round him ...[Fox] attended a great gathering of Seekers on Firbank Fell. Francis Howgill and John Audland were preaching in the little chapel near the summit, but he did not feel free to enter. Instead, he waited

outside until the congregation had dispersed for their midday meal. Later he spoke to them from a great rock close to the chapel ... A thousand Seekers listened to him eagerly, amongst them many of the Valiant Sixty who later carried his message all over the known world.[38]

At the meeting at Borrat on Sunday, 6 June 1652, the day after he spent the night at Brigflatts, Fox saw in the Westmorland Seekers the people in white raiment of his Pendle Hill vision. Thus began the Society of Friends, and Brigflatts, a tiny community of flax weavers on the River Rawthey, was at its heart. The Valiant Sixty was the name given to the first Quaker missionaries by John Handley of Brigflatts, the same John Handley who haunts the attic of the house.[39] Built in 1675, the Meeting House at Brigflatts is one of the oldest in the world.[40] It was built by the community: 'Those Friends who had good oak growing on their land gave it, and those who had none, carted it or gave the labour. At first it consisted of nothing but the bare walls and roof. There was no ceiling and each winter two Friends were appointed to stick moss under the slates to keep out the rain and snow. What warmth there was would be from a hearth fire at the west end.'[41] Today Brigflatts Meeting House is as unadorned as it was when it was built in 1675.

Bunting paid his first visit to the Greenbank family home in Brigflatts in 1913. He would spend at least a week of each of the shorter holidays and at least three weeks of the summer holiday there each year for the next four or five years.[42] Brigflatts was to become a pivotal influence on his life and work and, one hundred years later, it is virtually unchanged. John Allen Greenbank's father, also John, was a monumental mason and it is his chisel that clinks out the flinty rhythm of the opening of *Briggflatts*. John Greenbank's workshop had been situated at the end of the garden, separated from the house by an orchard, and the sound of his daily etching into stone the names of the newly dead would have rung throughout the hamlet. John Greenbank was Brigflatts' *genius loci*. The stonemason's daughter, Peggy, was eight years old at the time of Bunting's first visit. Greenbank's young sister was Bunting's 'delight from the first time I set eyes on her'.[43]

In 1913 the Greenbank household consisted of Peggy's 65-year-old widower grandfather (also a monumental mason), his son John, who was forty and married to Isabel, who was three years younger than her husband, and John and Isabel's four children. These were Bunting's close friend John Allen Greenbank, his younger brother George, and their sisters, Annie and Margaret. The 1911 census reveals that a further child had died. Margaret

(Peggy) was four years younger than Bunting. Bunting and she quickly became very close friends and it is the memory of this young love and its loss that inspired, fifty years later, some of the greatest lines of twentieth-century poetry:

Brag, sweet tenor bull,
descant on Rawthey's madrigal,
each pebble its part
for the fells' late spring.
Dance tiptoe, bull,
black against may.
Ridiculous and lovely
chase hurdling shadows
morning into noon.
May on the bull's hide
and through the dale
furrows fill with may,
paving the slowworm's way.

A mason times his mallet
to a lark's twitter,
listening while the marble rests,
lays his rule
at a letter's edge,
fingertips checking,
till the stone spells a name
naming none,
a man abolished.
Painful lark, labouring to rise!
The solemn mallet says:
In the grave's slot
he lies. We rot.

Decay thrusts the blade,
wheat stands in excrement
trembling. Rawthey trembles.
Tongue stumbles, ears err
for fear of spring.
Rub the stone with sand,
wet sandstone rending
roughness away. Fingers
ache on the rubbing stone.

The mason says: Rocks
happen by chance.
No one here bolts the door,
love is so sore.[44]

These are the opening three stanzas of Bunting's masterpiece, *Briggflatts*, written in the early 1960s, fifty years or so after the events on which they draw. The beautiful lyricism of the opening of the poem sings a song of innocence. The young love it celebrates, and the simple, peaceful environment in which it grew, were the formative influences on the poet's life. It was a life that brimmed over with drama, adventure, passion and, at times, overwhelming drudgery, but underneath it all the spring-swollen Rawthey flowed, the stonemason clinked out the names of the recently dead and the great passion of his life, Peggy Greenbank, never faded. Their parting, which was probably very early in 1918, was not intended to be final but Bunting failed to answer a letter and postponed a visit for fifty years. It was, he felt, the greatest betrayal of his life, but Peggy stayed in his thoughts throughout. It is a great twentieth-century love story and it is commemorated in one of the century's most influential and moving poems. Indeed it is a love story that is contained almost entirely *within* the poem.

A tale of blood and death

Bunting's first surviving work of fiction is a story written in autumn 1914 and submitted to Ackworth's Essay Society. '*T*' versus '*N*' is a fantasy of chivalry and adventure set in the late summer of 1812 as Napoleon begins his disastrous retreat from Moscow. Bunting helpfully explains at the outset that 'N' was 'Napolean's [*sic*] monogram. 'T' was the symbol of the Tagendbund [*sic*], a German political society, opposed to the French.' The narrator is in Paris in the autumn of 1854, 'reporting the departure of troops to the Crimea & interviewing sundry august personages for Lampton's Review, a third-rate periodical, long since defunct'. The hero of the story is one Baptiste Rénaud, a veteran of the 1812 campaign who regales his friends with a 'tale of blood & death' in a café in Senlis. Part Arthurian Romance, part Gothic horror tale, '*T*' versus '*N*' is a remarkably imaginative and confident debut. Describing the retreat from Moscow Rénaud laments that his 'brave Hussars, the Hussars of Chalons ... fell by the score. The infantry fell by the hundred. Before that awful retreat was ended, indeed, my beautiful

33

Hussars were themselves turned entirely into a regiment of light infantry. They carried their horses – inside them.' Marshal Ney has given Rénaud a vitally important communication to take to Napoleon but Rénaud is easily sidetracked by a vulnerable maiden in a bosky forest and various adventures involving a hand-to-hand fight with a German spy and chastening a ruffian for beating another vulnerable maiden with the stock of a long whip. The delay incurs the wrath of Napoleon who accuses Rénaud of spoiling his 'last chance of conquering Russia'. Rénaud is not intimidated by the legendary general: "'Sire" I replied "I have done my duty, & what you have lost by those dispatches you may well gain by these" & I flung the captured [from the German member of the Tugenbund] papers on the table; I stalked out into the sunrise, thinking bitter thoughts.' All ends well though as within weeks Napoleon has changed his position and Rénaud ends his tale with the great man thanking him for saving his army from the Tugenbund and pinning the Légion d'honneur on his chest

'*T*' versus '*N*' is a good story, told with imaginative flair and a rich vocabulary. A direct comparison with a story submitted at the same time by Bunting's friend, Ernest Stephenson, shows just how far Bunting was ahead of the field. Stephenson's story, 'A Summer Dream', is a conventional tale of murderous druids whose sacrificial blood lust is only avoided by the hackneyed device of waking up.[45]

Newcastle Lit & Phil

Bunting didn't derive all his intellectual nourishment from school, and Quakerism wasn't the only early influence on his development. Another was the Newcastle Literary and Philosophical Society. Thomas had joined the Lit & Phil in 1898 when the Buntings were living at 95 Jesmond Road, Newcastle, and was a member until he was 'resigned' after his death in 1925.[46] Founded in 1793 as a 'conversation club' the Society had long been a powerhouse of liberal enquiry (admitting women as members as early as 1804 and becoming a host for the anti-slavery movement in 1820). George Stephenson's miners' safety lamp was first demonstrated there in 1815 and in October 1880 the society's lecture theatre was the first public room in the world to be lit by electric light. There were two elements of the Lit & Phil's mission that are important to our understanding of the way Bunting was developing, a bold and eclectic lecture programme that was able to attract the most brilliant minds of the day and a deep investment in music.

By the time Bunting was thirteen the Lit & Phil was flourishing, with more than three thousand members and an average lecture attendance of nearly six hundred.[47] One of its musical advisers was the Bach scholar, choral conductor and composer William Gillies Whittaker. In 1915 Whittaker founded the Newcastle Bach Choir which gave the first complete modern performance, which Bunting attended and in which his aunt Jennie Cheesman performed, of Byrd's *Great Service* in Newcastle Cathedral in May 1924.[48] Whittaker, who was also an expert on Northumbrian folk songs, was a friend and neighbour of the Bunting family in Jesmond and Bunting frequently attended rehearsals of Whittaker's choir.[49] Many years later he told an interviewer that

> I never played anything, and it is with great astonishment that anybody ever found out that I sang. But I had an aunt who was a very good pianist. I was able to listen to good music continually from a very early age. And Dr. Whittaker, who ran the Newcastle Bach Choir in those days, was not only learned but showed great sense of music and art in general and I learned a lot from him. And Dr. Fellows [*sic*] just then discovered the manuscript of Byrd's Great Service, which had been lost for more than 300 years, and I was present at many of the services.[50]

It is interesting that Edmund Horace Fellowes isn't credited in *The New Grove Dictionary of Music and Musicians* as having discovered Byrd's *Great Service*, although his considerable editorial work on Byrd is damned with faint praise.[51] This doubtless cropped up as a topic of debate, as we shall see, in Kleinfeldt's, a public house near London's Tottenham Court Road that Bunting frequented in his twenties.

During Bunting's teenage years alone seven hundred scores were added to the Lit & Phil collection; the Purcell Society's publications were bought as well as sets of the Breitkopf and Härtel editions of Bach, Mozart and Schubert and a selection of modern British, French and Russian music. The society had a flourishing University Extension Centre (affiliated to Cambridge University) which conducted well-attended courses (average attendance was 155 at lectures) on a wide range of topics. On top of the university extension courses in 1916 alone nearly twenty 'miscellaneous' lectures were delivered on subjects as diverse as Virgil's picture of the after-life and the geology of the Dogger Bank.[52] Ezra Pound delivered a 'miscellaneous' on the troubadours in 1919.

Tick tock, tick tock, tick tock, slow

Bunting published one poem at Ackworth School, *The Song of the Ackworth Clock*, which was printed in the Headmaster's Annual Report of 1916. The clock tower surveys the life of the school through the different seasons, a stanza for each, with an extra stanza of more general reflection. *The Song of the Ackworth Clock* is therefore schematically an uncanny foreshadowing of *Briggflatts*. We can't claim too much for it, it is the work of a schoolboy, but in a limited way it looks forward fifty years to Bunting's masterpiece. *Briggflatts* also surveys a life through four seasons in four parts, with a fifth general unaligned one. To give it its due *The Song of the Ackworth Clock* has its slight charms. We tend to read into the juvenilia of writers who become celebrated rather more that it deserves. If *The Song of the Ackworth Clock* had been written by Bunting's friend John Greenbank we wouldn't be hearing notes of future masterpieces. Richard Caddel asks, 'Is it just possible to hear cadences which foreshadow the later, more subtle, concern for sound and quantity?' Maybe; just:

> When the asphalt bubbles tar,
> And lazy lads from near and far
>   Wander to and fro,
> Or seek the Elms' welcome shade
> Where record cricket scores are made,
> And Simpson's do a roaring trade.
>   Is this what you know?
> Tick tock, tick tock, tick tock, slow.[53]

I can't hear it myself and I think Caddel is on surer ground in finding 'perceptible rhythmic echoes of the Buntings' old family friend, the Newcastle pitman poet, Joseph Skipsey',[54] although the most obvious influence is Kipling.

Skipsey's presence can be felt at both ends of Bunting's life. It is harder to detect in-between. It's difficult to read Skipsey with much pleasure today. His literary world was irrecoverably swept away by the modernist revolution, and his rhythms seem artless and archaic in a way that, say, A. E. Housman's don't. He is guilty of the ultimate sin of sentimentality and yet his voice is undoubtedly authentic and surely this is what drew Bunting to him. Skipsey's poetry was part of the local song culture that Bunting drew on throughout his life. He also helped to shape Bunting's unshakeable, lifelong belief that 'meaning' in the conventional sense is unimportant in poetry. Skipsey wrote of Blake's *Thel* that it is:

> full of tenderness, sweetness, and delicacy throughout. Indeed, this is a real and genuine poem, and I say this without presuming to be able to decipher in clear terms the author's drift, for I do not regard that particular ability altogether essential before such a verdict is given, so long as the product possesses to me a meaning – an undefinable one though it may be – or constitutes spells by which visions of beauty and delight may be conjured up in my imagination, and visions of which the poet himself may never have dreamed; – for it is in the nature of things that the seer may see further than he thinks; that the singer may sing more than he knows; that, in short, the poet's words may awaken and arouse the mind of the reader to the perception of a star-like galaxy of ideas, before whose dazzling splendour the light of his own particular drift may seem in comparison but the insignificant piece of yellow flame of a farthing candle.[55]

Bunting was a great poet, and Skipsey wasn't, but nowhere does Bunting articulate their shared manifesto of the role of 'meaning' in poetry more simply, directly and beautifully than Skipsey does here. Skipsey's assessment of Blake was also soon to surface in Bunting's adolescent development.

Fabian founders

Bunting's father was also a member of the Fabian Society, the left-wing research organisation that was founded in January 1884 for the purpose of 'reconstructing society'.[56] He joined in September 1892 and remained a member until his death in 1925.

George Bernard Shaw, with his social ideal of a birthright life interest in national wealth, began contributing his formidable intellectual energy in May 1884, although he was not elected as a member until September.[57] Shaw was the driving force behind the Fabian Society from his election to the Executive Committee in January 1885, but Sidney Webb (Thomas's friend), the political scientist Graham Wallas, and W. B. Yeats's friend Annie Besant also joined the society within a couple of years of its formation. Bunting joined the Fabian Society in November 1916. His father doubtless helped out with the £1 1s 0d subscription that was paid on 23 October. He remained a member until he resigned in September 1921.[58]

By the time Bunting was born socialism, broadly defined admittedly, already had a twenty-year history in Britain but it was not a cohesive force for improving the condition of working people, with trade unionism and the early socialist societies, such as Henry Hyndman's Marxist Social Democratic Foundation, being at loggerheads. Socialists such as William Morris, leader of the Socialist League and an artist and poet, the Eton-educated Hyndman and the openly homosexual Edward Carpenter were, quite literally in some cases, not speaking the same language as the trade unions with their monomaniacal wage and conditions reformist agenda. [59] The Fabian Society had a utopian communitarian agenda from the outset but the middle-class intellectuals it attracted weren't natural bedfellows of the action-oriented unions and the Fabians quickly became a kind of proto-think tank, a 'metropolitan social research bureau, placing "facts" at the disposal of any political group which cared to study them, part of its famous strategy of "permeation"'.[60]

The Buntings' friend, Graham Wallas, was an intellectual pioneer. Shaw paid generous tribute to Wallas in his appendix on the history of Fabian economics that appeared in Edward Pease's *The History of the Fabian Society*, published in 1925. Shaw considered Wallas' *Life of Francis Place* a pivotal intervention in the intellectual development of socialism, showing Wallas' 'power of reconstructing a popular agitation with a realism which leaves the conventional imaginary version of it punctured and flaccid; and it was by doing the same for the Chartist movement that he left his mark on us'.[61] Wallas' was a powerful intellect and his contribution to the intellectual development of the Labour movement was immense.

As a Bunting family friend Wallas was to play a significant role in the intellectual environment in which Basil Bunting grew up. Bunting remembered him as a charismatic, 'inspired' and popular lecturer and he clearly put his experience as a teacher to work when he addressed the Newcastle Lit & Phil and, later in his career, at the London School of Economics: 'He could make any subject interesting. The result was that if they had to get across something which nobody on earth could be expected to take any interest in, they gave it to Graham Wallas to teach. And he would begin with a class of five and by the end of the first term he would have a hundred fighting to get in the room. I remember a series of lectures on the history of the internal organization of the War Office which began and ended that way!'[62] The distinguished economist, Lionel Robbins, later a friend of Bunting at the London School of Economics, remembered Wallas as a teacher, in which capacity 'he surpassed anyone I have ever known'.[63]

Wallas was a close friend of the Webbs. Beatrice described him as 'six foot with a slouching figure, good features and genial open smile, utterly unselfconscious and lacking in vanity or personal ambition. Without convictions he would have lounged through life – with convictions he *grinds* ... To his disciples he appears a brilliant man, first-rate lecturer, a very genius for teaching, a suggestive thinker and a conscientious writer ... A lovable man.'[64] Her observation that Wallas 'imparts the morality and scrupulousness ... [that] appeals to those of the upper and educated class who have good intentions' accurately described the Bunting milieu.[65] The academic, journalist and editor of the *New Statesman*, Kingsley Martin, remembered Wallas as, 'the most kindly of human beings, immensely stimulating and encouraging to the young. He was an eager rationalist, who resigned from the school where he taught in Highgate because he disapproved of religious instruction. He resigned from the Fabian Society in 1902 because, as he said, "the Webbs had an inadequate conception of liberty".' [66]

By the time Bunting would have become conscious of the presence of such an articulate and well-connected friend Wallas had become a considerable public figure, pacing impressively on the international stage. Beatrice Webb looked back in 1916 with a degree of pleasant surprise: 'The oddly slovenly young man of a quarter of a century ago ... is now a leader of thought, with a settled and sufficient livelihood and a body of devoted disciples ... His books are widely read in the U.S.A., his lectures are well attended, he sits on royal commissions, and is often referred to and consulted.'[67]

A loud raspberry of farewell

In 1915 Bunting discovered a copy of Walt Whitman's *Leaves of Grass* that a librarian at the school had hidden so no young people could be debauched by it (at least as he told the story over sixty years later).[68] He was captivated by its music and that same year he delivered a paper on Whitman, which he said 'won a more or less national prize – a national prize for Quaker schools, or something of the sort ... – to the great annoyance of my schoolteachers. And this caught the eye of an old gentleman living in Sheffield who got on his pushbike and rode thirty or forty miles in order to call on the fifteen year old critic of Whitman. That was no less a person than Edward Carpenter.'[69] Bunting later came to disparage Carpenter's championing of Whitman: 'Whitman's imitators were mere catchers at ideas & vague words – Edward Carpenter – with no understanding of what made him as a poet.'[70] Ackworth's headmaster, Frederick Andrews commented on Bunting's essay at the end of term gathering on 30 June 1915 that, 'Basil Bunting in an essay, with youthful ardour and perhaps more than youthful erudition, championed the poetry of Walt Whitman.' [71] Andrews went on to reflect on the standard of scholarship in the school and it is clear that Bunting was at an extreme end of the intellectual spectrum:

> An essay on a subject such as 'Walt Whitman,' always raises a certain doubt as to how much is the boy's own thought and how much he has got from books. I think the immaturity of that particular essay proves that it was strictly original, but as a further proof, since hearing the essay, I have remembered that I had a short reply to a history question by the same boy, which was answered without books or any material at hand. The question came in the ordinary course of history and was taken from an examination paper. The question was:– ' "The Spacious times of Great Elizabeth." What does this mean? Illustrate the saying from the history you have learnt.' This was the answer:– ' "The Spacious times of Great Elizabeth" Under the last of the Tudors, Elizabeth, all the knowledge, all the experience, all the discoveries, gleaned during the troublous years past were put to use, a good use, the development of England. Religion settled into an easy course of moderate toleration. The new world was explored, exploited, colonised. The new learning manifested itself in the writings of Spenser, Shakespeare, Jonson and others. The new national spirit, roused to wrath against the Spaniards, defeated them in the Channel when the Armada came up from Cadiz to conquer England. New charity made the poor law; new trade the East India Company. The whole horizon was enlarged, and England took a new place in the state system of Europe. For the first time we tasted real power, and it so intoxicated us, that we have been unable to forget it since, and always think of Elizabeth as England's Greatest Monarch.' [72]

This is not a bad spontaneous answer for a boy who, if he had turned fifteen, had only just done so. In July 1915 Bunting, along with Greenbank, Stephenson and fifteen other students passed the Northern Universities' School Certificate,[73] and in the summer of 1916 Bunting together with Stephenson obtained the Senior School Certificate (Matriculation), with Distinction in English.[74]

As if to illustrate the Quaker ambivalence to the Great War (see p.58–64) or perhaps, more accurately, to expose it, Bunting submitted an essay, 'Roncevaux', to the Ackworth School Essay Society in December 1915.

In July the following year he still considered it good enough to enter for the school's prestigious Broadhead Competition, and to help him win it 'for skill in debating ability in speaking'.[75] 'Roncevaux' can be read as a contemporary morality tale dressed up as a conventional chivalric romance, those stories of legendary heroes who 'are tragic in the highest sense of the word, for they are weighted with a burden of sorrow too heavy for any tale of lesser things'.[76] The sound of William Morris stamping around heavily behind Bunting as he wrote this essay is sometimes a little distracting.

'Roncevaux' tells the story of Charlemagne's campaign against the Saracens in Spain in 777. Hearing that the Saxons have crossed the Rhine to attack his northern border the Emperor holds a war council during which the 'faint-hearted knight' Ganelon urges appeasement of the German hordes and 'open & honest' Roland advocates speedy reprisal. The way Bunting describes the hero of the peace faction wouldn't have endeared him to the pacifists around him: '[Roland] detested [Ganelon's] cruel yet weak smile; the narrow, shifty eyes; the effeminate mode of dress & of speech; the craven heart; in fine, all the outstanding characteristics of the man who had spoken for peace.' In the battle that follows Ganelon's betrayal of the Emperor it is Roland's Frankish warriors who are glorified: 'picked veterans, dark-complexioned, rough, weather-beaten soldiers, hardened by a score of campaigns & battles against Saracens, Saxons & Lombards. There was not a novice, not a faint heart amongst all that company; nor had one man of them ever known defeat.' In Bunting's version Roland's army is wiped out in a Boy's Own bloodbath, with towers of corpses dominating the landscape, but not before Tennyson is invoked, in case anyone is still not getting the point.[77] What is provocative about 'Roncevaux' isn't its pro-war stance but its glorification of heroic battle in a submission for a Quaker school's most prestigious prize. It may be possible to argue that 'Roncevaux' demonstrates that the price of warmongering is complete destruction, but I don't think that was what Bunting was getting at. Like the final blast of Roland's horn that was heard 'from Seville in the south to Aix in the north, from the seashore in the west to Rome in the east' 'Roncevaux' seems to blow a loud raspberry of farewell to the values espoused by Ackworth School.

LEIGHTON PARK SCHOOL, 1916–1918

Despite his parting shot Bunting seems to have regarded Ackworth School with great affection. Ackworth archivist, Frederick A. Davies, recalled a former housemaster telling him that 'one dark rainy evening a man came through the front door of the school, thrust a package into his hand with a muttered "I thought my old school might like this" and disappeared. It was an autographed edition of his work.'[78] Affection then, but typically no sentiment. His start at his next school was charged with sentiment but no affection.

Bunting was becoming increasingly unsettled in this period. A letter dated 30 May 1916 to Leighton Park's Headmaster Charles Evans from Frederick Andrews at Ackworth hints at previous problems while, typically, accentuating the positives:

> I think Bunting does show real talent in literature & in grasp of history. I think his failure in Latin arises from a disinclinal [?] for its study – In fast time he has worked at the subjects he likes & given the go-bye to others – & now he finds it hard to recover lost ground. He is now much more amenable to advice & discipline – & will I think fall in comfortably with your school life ... If you have the 1918 A.O.S. report you will find on pp. 81–2 a short history answer wh. I think is good for a boy of 15 yrs of age as he was when he wrote it.[79]

His parents were aware of Bunting's educational shortcomings and possible mental instability. As Tim Newell Price, until his recent retirement Leighton Park School's archivist, says, 'the matter of "mental balance" requires some close attention. How far was it dramatic delusion – part of a front to protect his real self from the outside world? Much evidence from October 1916 suggests that he had been on the verge of insanity at times for at least a few years.'[80] Thomas Bunting sent an application form and medical report to the school on 6 June 1916 and the covering letter to Evans acknowledged that Andrews' assessment had been correct: 'the boy has not worked at subjects which did not attract him, but, from some talk I had with him recently, I fancy he is beginning to realise the folly of this'.

Thomas' application form[81] confirms that 'the boy' is not a member of the Society of Friends, that he has shown aptitude for history and English, that his favourite pursuit is reading and that he is destined for a career in 'journalism, or other writing'. It specifies that he is to learn Greek rather than German and, surprisingly perhaps, that he is not to learn a musical instrument. Thomas believed that his son would proceed to Oxford or Cambridge 'if he take a scholarship'. The form has two simple notes in Evans' hand, 'accepted' and 'Grove House'. There is something deeply poignant about this document. It compresses sixteen years of Bunting's life into terse answers to thirteen questions and, in that subdued Edwardian way, it expresses hopes and fears for a troubled boy in a deeply troubled world. As Thomas completed this form the reverberations of Dublin's bloody Easter Rising were still thudding across the Irish Sea. It had been over for barely a month and Patrick Pearse, Thomas MacDonagh and Tom Clarke had been executed by the British at Kilmainham Jail at dawn on 3 May. Another twelve rebel leaders were executed in the following days causing political uproar throughout the nation.[82] The defining naval battle of the war, Jutland, had raged during the previous week and, although it had been a British victory, it launched a deep and thick cloud across the country. The *Daily Express* headline took a pessimistic line, 'Heavy and Unaccountable British Losses'. As Thomas wrote his letter to Evans news of another naval disaster, the sinking of HMS *Hampshire*, was emerging. The loss of the *Hampshire* to a mine off the Orkneys was bad enough. The fact that it took Field Marshall Horatio Herbert Kitchener, hero of Omdurman and Secretary of State for War, down with it was a national disaster. Matters were, if anything, even worse on land. As Thomas completed his form, urging Evans to teach his son Greek rather than German, the Battle of Mount Sorrel had been bloodying the fields around Ypres for four days. Nearly fifteen thousand allied and German soldiers died around Mount Sorrel between 2 and 14 June 1916. The start of the truly terrible Somme campaign, the biggest military disaster in British history, was only three weeks away. In the context of this carnage there is something quietly moving about the ordinariness of Evans' note, 'accepted', in the top left corner of Thomas Bunting's application for a place for his son at Leighton Park School.

Less moving, but perhaps more revealing, is the medical report that accompanies the application, detailing Bunting's medical history. We learn that he had suffered with endocarditis (inflammation of the lining of the heart) at the age of six (but Thomas thought it had not left a permanent lesion), that he had already had measles, chickenpox, whooping cough, influenza and mumps, and that he had been vaccinated once in infancy. Thomas was, however, doubtful of the diagnosis of 'scarlatina' (scarlet fever). More importantly, Thomas refers to his son's 'billious headaches'. He is uncertain if they are 'gastric in origin, or true migraine'. These headaches surely explain some of what Newell Price describes as Bunting's 'wild moods' at Leighton Park.[83]

Law and liberty

The sixth form at Leighton Park was a new challenge. There were no girls for a start, and it was culturally different, 'one of the expensive public schools for the rich – the kind of place in which Cadburys and Frys get their education'.[84] He was there for just four terms, starting in September 1916, but he packed a lot in. There is a great deal of archival material relating to his time at Leighton Park and we can, for the first time, get a clear picture of Bunting as a young adult. According to Tim Newell Price, the teenage Bunting was, 'unusually precocious, forthright and determined. He was also a great poseur and rather emotionally unstable with it … he suffered the strain of containing the convictions of an unusually dedicated and outspoken adult within a youth's body.'[85]

Bunting seems to have been accepted quickly by the school community and soon involved himself in the school's cultural societies. He launched his public career at Leighton Park on 13 September 1916 when he read a paper to the 140th meeting of the Essay Society. The minute for that meeting records that

> B. C. Bunting read an essay on 'Law and Liberty'. He said that the spirit of British law was just; but the letter unjust. He laid down as the guiding principles of state affairs collectivism, liberty of conscience, equality and mercy, and looked towards a communism like that of the early Christians for the fulfilment of these ideals. The style of the essay was considered very successful in that it conveyed the desired ideas without distracting the attention. The only adverse criticism offered was upon the use of the personal pronoun: no definite decision was arrived at upon the subject by the Society, feeling being strong in both directions. The discussion which followed upon the matter of the essay was poor, owing to lack of free expression of opinion.

This rather puzzling final sentence is clarified in the report of the debate in *The Leightonian* of December 1916: 'Not a very good discussion followed, since there was unfortunately not time to consider the whole question of Socialism, and it was difficult to discuss the essay without taking up the larger issues.'[86]

Bunting's paper, 'The Relation of the State and the Individual Liberty and Law', exists in Leighton Park's archive. It is a remarkably sure-footed and mature interpretation of the law's continuing failure to live up to the principles of Magna Carta. It starts with a confident flourish:

We English are accustomed to look on our own country as the home of liberty. No-where else, say we, has man so great a measure of freedom; no-where else is equal justice so carefully maintained; no other land can boast a Magna Carta, a Habeas Corpus Act. In our arrogance we sing that Britons never shall be slaves, & far & wide we proclaim that the Union Jack means liberty, happiness & freedom from oppression. We rarely stoop to argue with those who question our superiority; and yet it behoves us as a nation either to cease from this bombast, or to bring forward proofs of the truth of our professions.

Bunting's argument in this essay rings with the preoccupations of his later life: 'Greed, that greed which is so common that economists call man a "covetous machine", has brought about the downfall of Christendom … The greed of manufacturers created modern poverty.' He defines the spirit of British law:

All men are equal, & have equal rights in all things: everyman, while bowing in matters of state to the will of the majority, is free to hold & to express any beliefs whatever: & the precedents of Pym and Hampden show that conscience has an absolute veto on any law: & the trial of prisoners shall be conducted with every mercy of safeguard for the liberty of the prisoners. Or, in fewer words, Equality; Freedom of conscience; Collectivism in state affairs; & Mercy. These are the watchwords of the Social Revolution.

I have utterly failed to be happy here

Minutes of a meeting of the (Senior) Essay Society on 9 October 1916 report that he was elected as a member of the society and, furthermore, that he and one N. L. White 'were elected representatives of the Society on the Union Committee for the coming year'. Bunting was also 'appointed to serve on the Committee to arrange for next meeting'. It had been a busy meeting for him. Newell Price provides a useful gloss on this. Leighton Park had been established:

to provide a very broadly based 'polish'. Learning to manage a community was part of it, especially for those who were (in due course) expected to play a leading role in public life. The Union Committee was a mixture of senior boys and masters in a school which turned out to be more like an enlarged country house family served by a small team of private tutors. The Committee decided about everything from expenditure on newspapers, a wide range of hobbies and societies and the running of games. They even appointed the cricket professional. Leighton Park was still essentially like that when Basil Bunting arrived.[87]

It's unlikely that Bunting's views on cricket were valued too highly[88] but the fact that he was elected to this important committee within a month of joining the school indicates that he was not entirely unclubbable. Nor was he averse to the society scene. He was elected a member of the Debating Society on 17 November 1916 and to the committee on 29 January 1917, and he was also elected a member of the influential Literary, Historical and Archaeological Society (LHA) in his first term.

All this committee work notwithstanding Bunting had a terrible start at Leighton Park, being 'defiantly homesick' according to Newell Price. Within a month of arriving he wrote an extraordinary memorandum to the head teacher, Charles Evans. It is extraordinary enough to quote in full:

I am not good at expressing myself in speech, so I beg you to read this instead.

I think I ought to leave this school at once for several reasons.

1. I have utterly failed to be happy here, I do not quite know why. But I think there must be some great underlying difference between North & South which makes people with Northern manners comfortable & easy to deal with, but people with the Southern manners are, for me, utterly impossible & hateful. Yet the rules of this, as of all schools, compel me to associate with them.

2. They seem to have no conception of any but physical pain, & put me thro' hourly mental torture without probably knowing it. Also (tho' this hasn't happened to me) there is some bullying. At supper without a prefect last night, the whole school turned on one helpless & harmless little new [chap]. And, of course, when the master came in, the new chap got an equal punishment with the rest And I had to sit by, impotent to stop it.

3. Last night in your speech you said "LPS has public school fees so as to get the public school class of men". That means, so as to exclude all boys who are unable to pay public school fees. I consider this as typical of the school. They have borrowed from the public schools all that there is bad & vile in that system; whether they have borrowed the good or not I cannot say, but I have only seen the bad. There is a system of making new boys sing in the dormitories. There is no real harm done, & it would be reasonable in a school with long traditions of it. But L.P.S. is too young to have traditions, & the pain and torture to the new boys should have been sufficient to prevent this feeble imitation of the public school.

4. They have no respect whatever for property. Every Sunday hats are jumped on. Every day coats & mackintoshes are torn. And I am sorry to say that things have disappeared from my locker. I do not know whether wilful destruction is ever pardonable, but if someday they should turn on my coat it is a fact that I cannot afford to have it maltreated. I could scarcely have come here at all but for the hope of a scholarship from Ackworth.

For all these reasons (and there are many included under number one), I think it is your duty to give me my fare to Newcastle with whatever shreds of character you can give me.[89]

It is hard to imagine a private school student delivering a rant like this is 2013, let alone 1916. Some fascinating 'boy-is-father-to-the-man' themes emerge from it – the uncompromising distaste for the South and bad 'southern manners', the non-intervention (in the bullying episode), the acute sense of fairness, the revulsion against capital, the lack of respect for 'tradition', the studied poverty (one of the most celebrated medics in the North of England could probably have been leaned on for a coat repair), the need for truth ('tho' this hasn't happened to me') and, above all, the sheer bloody-minded *nonconformity* of it. I'm a northerner, get me out of here.

Evans annotated Bunting's memorandum. It appears that it was Evans who underscored 'the whole school', adding in the margin '25 boys present'. About the bullying he asked 'Why so? Why not stop the bullying?' and about the 'equal punishment given' he notes 'no punishment given'. His only remark on Bunting's assessment of the previous night's speech is 'mis statement' and on Bunting's fourth point he notes 'public position of coats' regarding the lack of respect for property and 'eatables?' regarding the alleged theft. 'Prefects to enquire' is his last note. It all points to a bout of hysterical paranoia on Bunting's part.

Bunting had delivered his memo to Evans early on the morning of Monday 23 October. Shortly afterwards Evans wrote a file note to himself about Bunting's outburst and about another recent 'episode' (an unauthorised trip into Reading the previous Saturday). The note starts:

Glad he is safe – there satisfaction ends
    16½   juvenile escapade?

Consideration for others $\begin{cases} \text{Home} \\ \text{LPS} \\ \text{Ackworth} \end{cases}$

Want of manliness – of backbone cowardice. Reason given for
    going down town.
A stupid thing to do.
He needs grind & pluck ...
Had he any real grievance? I am quite open to think he had but
    evidence at present is against it

Ackworth success
    F. A's letter
    Miss Hartley's letter
    Bernard Shaw touch.

This last is a perceptive observation.

The following day Evans wrote to Thomas Bunting and Thomas wrote to
Evans, their letters crossing in the mail. This is Evans' account of Bunting's
busy weekend:

> I wonder what sort of letters Basil writes to you. My impression is that he gets
> along satisfactorily for the most part with periodic outbursts or nerve storms,
> which make him very miserable. I have known of two such definitely since
> you were here. One of them came to a head this last week-end, and sent him
> to me with the enclosed document in his hand (please return this). This was
> early on the Monday morning, and the boy was evidently suffering very great
> excitement. (The extraordinary thing, however, is that I found he had come
> straight from an interview with another master, in which he had not appeared
> at all outwardly overwrought, and at which he had made arrangements to
> read an essay here next month). I gave him a general word, and told him to
> come to see me last evening. I then went through the document, first of all
> from the point of view of the things he said about the School and showed
> him how time and again he magnified small things into great. I think it took
> him a little by surprise to find that I know quite well to what he was referring
> in saying that some bullying took place, and could tell him just who was
> responsible for the small things that have occurred. It was also a new point of
> view to him that he and another big boy had any responsibility with regard
> to stopping "ragging" at supper when many other boys happened to be away.
>
> I then adopted quite another tone in addressing myself to the seriousness
> of the position he was taking up; I told him plainly that if he allowed these

outbursts to continue, and to master him, he would find in time that he could not live with any of his fellows, North country or South country, and that he would become a recluse, separated from others almost altogether. I showed him into how many things he was already fitting in the School, and begged him to face life and not to be so absolutely self-centred as he is. I put before him several ways in which he could reasonably let himself go and give himself to others, and said that in this is his great hope in preventing these disturbances wrecking his life.

The net result is that for the time Basil was quite re-conciled and saw the commonsense of what I was saying. We shall make continued and increased efforts to help him in right ways, and to see that he has companionship that he can enjoy. A great difficulty is that he is so conceited about the value of some of his work, and therefore notice of it and interest in it (for it is good) will do him harm if we are not careful. I am glad to say that he is showing considerable concern for all his work, including the less interesting subjects such as Latin.

Meanwhile Thomas expressed similar concerns:

Mrs Bunting is considering the advisability of spending a week end in Reading about Nov 10th. But we feel uncertain of the effect on Basil. It might help him to settle down, on the other hand it might disturb him just as he is beginning to settle. You will probably be better able to judge than we, will you kindly give us your opinion?

Judging from his letters Basil is still unhappy, though not so violently as at first; & it seems to depend more on his state of mind than on anything external. In fact he seems hysterical.

"I don't know" he says "exactly why I am unhappy. If I did know I might get it put right, but it's something indefinite that is in everything about Leighton & Reading, something poisonous in the atmosphere, something foreign & unfriendly in even the nicest of the people" – "I'm never happy – except when I get away alone into the country" – "I can't get my work done for thinking. I've tried every way to stop thinking. I've tried whistling at my work, reading back numbers of Punch; I've tried working a double rate, & working at Fabian essays, or economics, but I can't stop thinking."

These extracts will perhaps illustrate his present way of thinking – or at least show his interpretation of himself, which is possibly a very different thing. I should not like him to know that I have sent you extracts, but they may aid you in deciding whether Mrs Bunting should come to Reading.

If you think she should come would you mind mentioning what you think the most suitable hotel for her to stay at, or would it be better to stay in London, & come up to Reading in the day time?

Thomas answered Evans' letter on 26 October, reporting that Bunting had written them two 'quite reasonable, and not unhappy letters' when he returned to school, but that on 3 October he had sent one in a different tone:

very unhappy, & unreasonable. "I think I'm going mad here I can't work, nor anything – just dream of home." "I'm sure I shall die slowly here, first my sense, then my body". His mother replied to this, and immediately there came a Telegram telling us to disregard his last letter. The next day there came a very curious letter from him. He said that he vastly preferred to stand alone to fight the devil Despair, "who has been at me ever since I can remember", in privacy. That for a time, at Ackworth, he had tried to tell us what he really felt; but as it did no good, and was called whining, he left off telling us, that he had now tried again to tell us how he felt, but that as we didn't want to know how he felt, and how he ought to feel, he would try once more to stand alone. He ended by saying that we were not to worry, he would beat everyone to everything yet, & he quoted 'Peer Gynt' "to myself enough, & Emperor of myself". It was a theatrical letter, after this came one or two quite reasonable, & ordinary letters, perhaps rather high strung; and lastly Sunday's letter which began by saying that he must whine, though he had promised not to do so. I gave you the essence of the 'whine', it was followed by two or three pages of reasonable, though perhaps hypercritical, matter. Even the 'whine' was less unreasonable than some previous letters. I certainly agree with most that you say of him. There is brain storm, or hysteria; with intervals of what is probably nearly normal thought, though he may perhaps regard the intervals as having been periods of self suppression. I think too there is some semi-conscious posing. I can't help feeling that in the midst of it he stands outside of himself, and admires his own attitudes, which may nevertheless be quite sincere.

I was very sorry to observe the tone of his note to you, particularly of its last paragraph. One phrase I disliked for another reason. Basil knows that his going to Cambridge or Oxford depends on his getting a Scholarship. But no such condition applied to his going to Leighton Park. That was definitely decided before we were aware that there was any prospect of a Scholarship from Ackworth, & I thought that Basil knew this.

On the whole I am inclined to be encouraged by your report, & the improved tone of Basil's letters home; I am extremely pleased to hear that he seems to be working even at the less interesting subjects. It does look as though his nerves were quietening, and that he may yet settle well in his new surroundings.

Thomas' letter ends by expressing genuine regret and surprise at the trouble Bunting was causing Evans and gratitude for the 'care and insight' which Evans was applying to the case. The record of the correspondence on the subject ends with a letter of 30 October from Evans urging Annie to visit her son as she had planned and reassuring Thomas that Bunting had 'made no demur to the fact that there are many exaggerations in what he wrote'.

I have dwelt on this episode because it throws so much light on Bunting's state of mind as he faced the challenge of adulthood in a world at war. Bunting's parents had clearly feared for their son's sanity for some years. Evans, no doubt familiar with homesick boys, took a pragmatic line but applied it with sensitivity. There is more than homesickness in Bunting's *cri de cœur* though. Hysteria, histrionics, self-absorption, exaggerated showmanship and depression all jostle to the front of Bunting's 'explosion'. We need to keep this episode in mind when we come to his exploits in the 1920s and 1930s.

Matters clearly improved though and Evans (the son of a previous Ackworth headmaster and himself a former teacher at the Yorkshire school as it happens) clearly treated the episode with the firm-but-fairness characteristic of the time. Indeed, Bunting went on to become a prefect.[90]

Towards the end of term Evans filed a note on Bunting for the forthcoming reports:

> 1916 Decr. G. There is no doubt ['in our mind' erased] that he is making a
>   place for himself in the school
> A. Might devote himself more keenly
> B. Essays (needs a hobby) – but not much to show

It could have been a lot worse. The end of Bunting's first term at Leighton Park was considerably better than its beginning.

Essays and debates

On 5 February 1917 the sixty-ninth meeting of the school's Literary, Historical and Archaeological Society was devoted to 'a discussion on what should be the terms of a just and permanent peace', with eighteen members and three visitors present. Bunting's contribution was held to be 'easily the best in point of literary style, it was also quite witty'. Bunting argued that

i. The guilty must be punished as
ii. Justice includes punishment.
iii. There must be no more war waged for money.
iv. All men must work for their own living.
v. The Moslem empire should centre at Baghdad.
vi. China must reform.
vii. Manchuria (?), Egypt, and India must be independent.
viii. Racial leagues to be formed (e.g. Jewish (?) League, Latin League, Slav League)

More witty than logical by the sound of it. Unfortunately this paper has not survived; it would be interesting to know how Bunting worked his Fabian point three into his proposed peace treaty.

The Leightonian of April 1917 reports that at the Senior Essay Society of 26 February 'B. C. Bunting read an essay on "Blake", whom he admired as a prophet rather than as a poet, and whom he considered to be a genius of the type that creates, as opposed to that which perfects. The essayist showed a great command of language.'[91] Blake was clearly considered exotic enough to warrant his own blanket of inverted commas. We can detect Skipsey's influence again in Bunting's essay on Blake. In the introduction to his edition of Blake's poems Skipsey had also pointed out that, at least in the *Book of Thel*, Blake was a better prophet than he was poet: 'for though he poured forth a multitude of writings – his so-called prophecies – many passages of which are written with absolute sincerity … yet as there is in these, according to those most competent to judge, a lack of organic, not to say a lack of harmonic organic unity, and cannot in any just sense be termed poems …'[92]

In fact the conclusion that Bunting used Skipsey's edition of Blake in preparing his own essay is inescapable. By the end of Bunting's life Blake had fallen from grace almost entirely. Blake's mysticism was 'spurious', he wrote to Tom Pickard in 1974, and about as 'authentic as the current gurus in the USA. Or Madame Blavatsky … he was too lazy to write poetry properly once he'd learned that he could get away with the sort of stuff Macpherson put into Ossian.'[93]

At Meeting 141 of the Debating Society (date unrecorded but probably in the final week of February) Bunting seconded the opposition to the proposition that, 'In the opinion of this house the savage man is happier than the civilised man', seemingly with an element of belligerence: 'he said that his opponents had misrepresented the savage that he really was lean, hungry, cold and afraid and in short miserable. He also accused his opponents of insincerity.'[94] Bunting had probably seen more lean, hungry, cold, afraid and miserable people than most of the boys at Leighton Park, though he wouldn't have described them as savages.

Bunting proposed the motion that democracy is a better form of government than aristocracy at the Debating Society meeting on 12 March 1917 and generally Bunting's second term seems to have gone well for him. Evans's file note written on 17 April reports that Bunting's 'appointment as a prefect shows that we recognise ['a' erased] great development in character: he knows that we regard the appointment as something of an exp/t. & we trust he will respond thoroughly to the confidence we are reposing in him'.[95] He had come a long way in four or five months.

In July 1917 the school suspended the normal timetable for a week, as it had done for several years in the summer term, while the boys pursued a communal project, in this case a social survey of the local village, Shinfield. Bunting joined the 'Social Section', doubtless looking for ammunition for his budding Fabianism, and was also appointed the group's reporter. His report, 'The Present Social Condition of Shinfield', again evinces a remarkably assured prose style for such an apparently troubled young man. He bristles at one local capitalist in particular:

> It would be well if the Village Hall were under village control. But Mr Curtis rules it for the adult school, & refuses to allow dancing & whist drives. His terms are, £5 until 10 o'clock at night, exclusive of chair hire, & after 10, 10/- hourly. This is in effect a prohibition against its use for parties of any sort. Even 'refined concerts' cost £3 per night. The Parish Council cannot buy it, & is unwilling to build a new one, while there is a hall in existence. The Fire Station is under the same control, and is without either firemen or horses.[96]

Bunting casts a cold eye on local politics, health care, schooling and housing and there is an observation that the local church is, 'sufficiently ritualistic to drive a few parishioners into dissent', that is an early manifestation of the authentic Bunting voice. Wages in the village were low because agricultural trade unionism had 'barely touched Berkshire yet'. Towards the end there appears a passage which could have been lifted directly from Robert Tressell's *The Ragged Trousered Philanthropists*, which had been published three years previously: 'The land is owned by various farmers, by Mr. Cobham, & by a mysterious company for whom Mr Curtis has done building. The chief employers of labour are Mr. Cobham, Mr. Ravenscroft, and Mr. Penington, of farmhands, & Mr. Lucas of farmhands & mechanics, who look after the agricultural implements which he hires out.' It's hard not to see Sweater, Rushton, Grinder and Didlum of Mugsborough Council lurking in the background, preparing a bid to take over Shinfield's entire assets for £1 and sell them back for thousands.

In the same month Evans' file note reports that Bunting had been awarded a Royal Life Saving Society bronze medal and that in general, 'In work want of balance in character has played ['less' erased] a smaller part than before: grind at uninteresting work must be faced and carried through. He has justified his appt. as a prefect.'[97] Bunting continued to make good progress.

The minutes of the seventy-third meeting of the LHA on 5 November 1917 record the results of a debate about the merits of the politicians of the moment; British Prime Minister, David Lloyd George, US President Woodrow Wilson, and the Russian Prime Minister, Alexander Kerensky.[98] Bunting presented Kerensky as 'an impassioned idealist, with a commanding personality, and a practical statesmanlike grasp of present problems'. Bunting (or Kerensky) won the ensuing debate by one vote over Wilson, Lloyd George coming in 'a very poor third' according to *The Leightonian* of December 1917, not altogether surprisingly given the way the war was going.

Later that month Bunting read an essay to the (Senior) Essay Society entitled 'A Revival of a Forgotten Art: A Romantic Allegory'. He must have been reading Edgar Allen Poe:[99]

> There lies in the island of Britain a vale more beautiful than man has ever dreamed. Tall mountains guard it, & the flanks they give the world are so bleak & so uninteresting, that for many years no man has essayed them. But, beyond the summit of the greatest, lies ravine [*sic*], & beyond the ravine, the vale. Few trees cheer the way; the pass to the great canyon is difficult & dangerous; & the black stream that has carved for itself this channel swirls & bubbles with a sound of all foreboding.

The story concerns a young witch and wizard who are sent by the master wizard to collect a rare weed for some unspecified act of magic. The enchanter has warned them on no account to enter the vale where 'a fearful fate' would await them. They fail to find the weed despite diligent searching but then spot a specimen in the forbidden land of the vale; 'small wonder they disobeyed'. In a kind of reverse Fall they find themselves suddenly alive: 'an intense wonder seized their souls, & they felt, for the first time, things, & that they were alive'. The Edenic reference is well trailed: 'He glanced towards the ravine & shuddered; for the home that had harboured him lay like the abode of Satan on Eden's bounds, &, like the snake's slimy track, the watercourse retired in sinuous curves to the depths of the abyss.' The young couple are befriended by a 'gaunt hermit' who shelters them in his cell for the night. At midnight they are visited by the enchanter, an outlandish figure with 'fangs polluted by unholy orgies', who offers to make the hermit, in return for his two 'children', 'abbot of the richest foundation in Britain'. The hermit's somewhat dismissive reply ('Fudge') sets off a debate about liberty and God that ends in another reversed myth, this time Faustian. The wizard agrees to let the hermit keep the children and teach them the true ways of liberty and nature but only for six months. In November he will return to destroy them and the whole vale if they refuse to renounce 'this madness'. The day of reckoning is marked by a colossal storm: 'A rusted suit of armour stood in a corner; the busy maid had polished it to a semblance of its old glory, but it was treacherous and weak. An old sword, dented & battered leant against the wall. As in a dream the boy suffered himself to be armed & girded: as in a dream he saw the hermit unbar the door: dreaming still, he stood a moment on the threshold. Then, raising the cross of his sword hilt to his lips, with a valiant cry he rushed into the storm.'

This is important as Bunting's second surviving work of fiction. There wasn't much more to come. It is a carefully constructed and elegantly written allegory of good and evil but any ballooning temptation to read into it more than it deserves is rapidly punctured by the surviving minute of the meeting that was filed on 12 November 1917: 'B. C. Bunting read an essay entitled "The Revival of a Forgotten Art". This was an allegory, medieval in plot and style, very modern in its moral. The essayist has a great power of description ...'

To this point all is true. Bunting does indeed describe the vale and the holy lake with real Gothic verve, and the moral, with its Fabian triumph of liberty over capitalism, could hardly be more 'modern'. But, the minute writer continues, 'his paper was felt to be somewhat spoilt for the listeners by his amusement at the more lurid patches of it. It was discussed whether an essay of this sort was of any real value to the society.' The ensuing debate went in Bunting's favour but the presenter's sniggering clearly robbed the allegory of some of its power.[100]

Bunting resubmitted his allegory for another prize but wasn't given a place because it contained 'too little substance and too much flamboyant description'. That was a rather unfair judgement. The flamboyant description is powerful for such a young writer; the judge doesn't seem to have appreciated that whiff of Poe. The account of the discussion of Bunting's verse submission is even more damning: 'One judge thought that it would fit well into a poem on "Freedom & Nature", while the other thought that as a fragment it contained little to make it part of the whole promised by the title or at least that a whole with such a part had better remain unwritten.'[101] The poem didn't survive Bunting's ruthless self-editing; probably a good thing.

Bunting also entered the 1917 Elocution Competition, which contained four elements – a prepared speech, an unprepared speech, a reading and a recitation. The judges' reports for three of these survive. For the set speech Bunting took as his text, 'A School should be judged by the boys it turns out' and the judges reported that he was 'a fluent speaker, & attempted to make a slashing attack on our Public School System, arguing that our Civil & Diplomatic Services, & our Ruling Classes, recruited from our Public Schools, are a failure, & that Athletics are the very foundation of our Public School System. This took most of the time at his disposal. An introduction of this immoderate length was quite out of proportion, & upset the balance.'

He had chosen Coleridge's 'Kubla Khan' for his recitation and the judges' report on this is perhaps the first example of the way Bunting's voice could unsettle the establishment: 'This is a difficult piece, but proved an excellent choice, as Bunting, in a sound effort, did some justice to it. In three or four places, however, his emphasis was at fault; and further there were several verbal inaccuracies. It is a pity that Bunting failed to adapt his strident voice to the room, which re-echoed his twang in a painful way.' Bunting's twang was to re-echo through rooms in Europe and America with immense power and drama for another sixty years. The report on 'prepared readings' praised Bunting's careful preparation of his extract from 'The Golden Age', being 'easy to follow, without hesitation & freer than usual from mannerisms'. Bunting was awarded second place in the 1917 Elocution Competition.

Two years before Bunting's arrival at Leighton Park the outgoing (and first) Chairman of Governors, Jonathan Backhouse Hodgkin, had inaugurated the 'JBH', an annual public speaking competition. Bunting could have written JBH's six golden rules himself as instructions to young poets in how to address their readers:

1. Conciseness: It is a painful thing to listen to diffuse addresses. Many people, when they have said what they meant to say, start afresh and say most of it again in different words ...

2. Clear Enunciation: Much of the effectiveness of speech is lost if parts of it are not distinctly heard ...

3. Earnestness: I should therefore like each competitor to choose his own subject, so that he may be able to forget himself in his desire to convince his hearers.

4. Simplicity and Lucidity of Literary Style: ... I should like all tricks of oratory or evidence of self-centredness to be discouraged.

5. Sympathy with Audience: A speaker who can convince his audience that he is in sympathy with them ... will do much to secure their sympathy with him, even when their general attitude is hostile.

6. Presence of Mind: ... I should like a decided preference given to those competitors who speak without notes.[102]

These principles chime with those Bunting later articulated for poetry. It is impossible to believe that they were not on his mind as he embarked on his career as a poet. Perhaps it is not surprising then to discover that a winner of the J. B. Hodgkin Speech Competition of 1917, with a speech on Conscientious Objectors, was one Basil C. Bunting.[103]

Bunting's final recorded contribution at Leighton Park was to the Hobbies Competition in December 1917 and he was commended for the originality of his researches into the 'employment of men and women in the British Isles'. He'd had another busy term. Evans' file note on Bunting at the end of that term was positive:

Dec. 1917 A boy of considerable power – with evident difficulties of wh. he has been made well aware!

The restraint shown in public appearances in the last week is very encouraging – it has allowed his good points [emended from 'his good parts'] to show themselves & is of good promise for the stand on the question of military service wh. he believes he is called to make. Much interest in his schol. exerc. work in January & shall follow his career with ['great' erased] interest.

His 'schol. exerc.' was going well enough for his application to Peterhouse, Cambridge to proceed but it was not successful. A letter from H. J. Edwards to Evans, dated 16 February 1918, explains why:

> The examiners reported that his work in Ancient History and Medieval European History was very promising, as regards both style and matter. In the paper of General Questions there were signs of immaturity and of a certain recklessness; and his English essay made a very unfavourable impression for its lack of taste and even of sense. His French was fair: in Latin he only just qualified.

> It was felt that there was a possibility of brilliance in him, but that his work was as yet too uneven and unbalanced to merit the award of a scholarship.

Quaking leadership

Bunting attended Leighton Park school at a time of rapid expansion, materially if not financially. New buildings were springing up. After a generously supported appeal for funds, Peckover Hall appeared, 'a fine example of a modern building' according to governors writing in 1940.[104] The number of boys however stuck obstinately at around one hundred, and the school was in constant financial peril. An old boy and former Governor, Kenneth Wright, wrote that 'Charles Evans had many virtues as a headmaster … but the ability to administer and to exercise financial control was not among them.'[105] The school didn't even employ a bursar until Evans retired in 1928. Evans' stewardship has been divided into a period of success (while Bunting was there) and failure during the 1920s when continuing financial problems and lack of discipline destabilised the school,[106] but even the successful period was clearly marred by a static headcount and crumbling finances. Evans was an engaging and charismatic leader with his constant motion and 'intellectual twinkle'.[107] With so few boys in the school he would have been a direct influence on most of them, with his deep love of the natural world and his fervent but undogmatic brand of Quakerism. S. W. Brown drew a fine picture of the man:

> He tried to know everyone and he practised the arts of developing intimate and self-revealing contacts. His casual remarks, made while walking round the farm buildings or some other part of the park, would suddenly lift his companions – small boys or prefects, or O.L.s [Old Leightonians] visiting because they liked him and liked his ways – from mental apathy into a

consciousness of their own importance. There was something psychic about the way he did this, its suddenness, its aptness, with his quiet hesitating voice, unmusical but sympathetic, his slightly bent figure, pausing as he spoke to point out some object that took his fancy. Those delicate and scholarly hands that were never in his pockets would gesticulate as he spoke, gently but expressively. He was gentlemanly always, with fine instincts and perceptions, never thrusting himself into company where he was not welcome, or into conversations that were foreign to his nature.[108]

It is easy to imagine Evans defusing Bunting's hostility to his new environment with his combination of gentle humour and resolute belief in people.

From histories of Leighton Park one gains a distinct impression that Evans' stewardship was generally liberal, sophisticated and cultured. One near-contemporary of Bunting's, Eric Southall, however, remembered music teaching at the school as 'very poor': 'The small orchestra had few players and, as was general in those days, no wind or brass ... I don't recall Mr Ballard [music and geography teacher from 1895 to 1918] ever playing to us at a school concert or at any other times. Nor were the visual arts cultivated.'[109] (Rather remarkably the school seems to have had no dedicated teacher of English between 1896 and 1919.[110]) There may be a touch of pique in this (Southall was clearly a talented musician) as Brown recalls that music flourished at Leighton Park at precisely this period: 'in place of the miscellaneous items of songs, recitations and pieces by the band, whole evenings were spent on the works of single composers – on Mozart, Purcell, Bach, Coleridge-Taylor and in 1916 on Glinka, Moussorgsky and Tchaikowski.'[111] So, *pace* Southall, it's likely that Bunting's musical interests developed at Leighton Park. Certainly the school's Literary, Historical and Archaeological Society was taking modern literature seriously, with readings of poetry by Newbolt, Masefield, Kipling, Brooke, Tagore and the plays of Arnold Bennett and John Galsworthy. Bunting's first two published poems certainly show the strong influence of two of these poets.

Evans was anxious to build the sixth form but only about fifteen boys were admitted to it each year at that time. Although his parents sent Bunting to Leighton Park with a view to him progressing to Oxford or Cambridge, to some extent that went against the Quaker grain. Many Quaker parents (not that the Buntings were Quakers) were hostile to Oxbridge because those universities had denied admission to members of the Society of Friends until 1854. Quakers had not been able to take an MA (and therefore were barred from teaching) at Oxford and Cambridge until 1871. Thomas was an unusual parent, perhaps precisely *because* he was not a Quaker, in valuing university education in its own right. Many Quaker parents, while in no way undervaluing the acquisition of knowledge, felt that Oxford and Cambridge provided education that was inferior to that which might be got in the 'real' world.[112]

Quakerism in any event was at odds in principle with the entire private school ethos. The Society of Friends were dissenters who had a long history of exclusion from privileged English society and yet, in a school such as Leighton Park (and Ackworth), it had in a sense created an institution that could be socially divisive and with rules that could seem derived from the necessary discipline of a military environment. On the other hand it was, of course, an opportunity to inculcate and preserve traditional Quaker values of self-reliance and the ability to think for oneself, as well as to protect the school's charges from a society that encouraged ambition above principle.

But the Society of Friends' ambivalence towards Oxbridge was as nothing compared to its leadership's moral desertion regarding the war. Bunting was considering his future, and Cambridge was a possibility, but he was clearly a very confused young man. Bunting's second publication of 1916 appeared in *The Leightonian* in December. 'Keep Troth' is straight out of the 'Vitaï Lampada' school of jingoism, but as Richard Caddel says it is 'in no way militaristic',[113] and to be fair the young poet catches Newbolt's tone and rhythms well:

> And while we're still at school, boys,
>   The principle's the same;
> Stick to the golden rule, boys,
>   Play up, and play the game.
>   What do you do for England,
>   Who does so much for you?
>   Keep troth, speak true for England,
>   Be straight, keep troth, speak true.

No doubt the Quaker sentiment of the final line of this stanza caught the eye of *The Leightonian*'s editor. As Caddel observes, the remarkable feature of 'Keep Troth' is the fact that it reveals nothing of his current enthusiasms, Whitman, Blake, Kerensky. One might have expected at least some of the fiery mysticism or blazing revolutionary activism he was absorbing to bubble to the surface, but if they did the waves of Newboltian convention submerged them entirely. As a vanishingly small moment in twentieth-century poetry 'Keep Troth' clearly points in the wrong direction. Compared with another poem written in 1916, H. D.'s 'Amaranth', its plodding metre thumps out a death march for Georgian poetry where H. D. asserts the new all-questioning, self-confident modernist note:

> I was not asleep.
> I did not lie asleep on those hot rocks
> while you waited.
> I was not unaware when I glanced
> out toward sea,
> watching the purple ships.[114]

Taken broadly as a 'war poem' though 'Keep Troth' is surprisingly mainstream. We now think of the poetry of the First World War as overwhelmingly critical of political and military leaders' strategy and tactics, articulating a sense of hopeless valour in the teeth of insuperable horror, but this is largely because the poetry that has survived (because it is the best) was written by poets – Wilfred Owen, Isaac Rosenberg, Siegfried Sassoon and Robert Graves – who subscribed to the view that it was the futility and horror that needed to be in a perverse sense celebrated. In fact, of the 2,225 poets who published during the years of the war hardly any expressed the views that have for generations of students defined its poetry. Read in this context 'Keep Troth' is absolutely of its moment.[115]

'Roncevaux' and 'Keep Troth' essentially reject mainstream Quaker attitudes to war, but during the course of Bunting's four terms at Leighton Park something momentous happened to change his position. We have to see this shift in the context of Quaker leadership on the issue.

The war naturally had a significant impact on school life during Bunting's entire time at Leighton Park. There were material changes, needless to say – the school clock wasn't permitted to strike the hours and possible damage from air attack needed to be insured against – but the effect of the war on Quaker institutions' sense of self was much more dramatic. In some quarters there was a lack of confidence in the relevance of traditional Quaker beliefs and practices to the circumstances of a long and bloody war. For example, in 1914 Leighton Park's Debating Society carried a motion in favour of rounding up and imprisoning all German nationals but voted strongly against conscription. Two years later it reversed that decision. *The Leightonian*'s report of that debate on conscientious objection of 23 October 1916 shows how important this subject was to the boys. Nearly all members of the school attended and the minute book of the Debating Society confirms that the meeting was 'open to the school and to visitors. It was well attended, only a few members of the school being absent.'[116] I think it is inconceivable that Bunting was not at that meeting, but with one hesitation. It took place the night before Bunting's extraordinary explosion at Evans about the 'pain and torture' culture of the school. Perhaps he was busy polishing his script.

On the one hand generations of Quakers had deplored any kind of violence and witness against war had become part of the fabric of the Society. On the other hand this was a very different kind of war and many Quakers were uncomfortable about not making the sacrifices that were expected of the rest of society. This ambivalence was etched into Quaker school life. Bunting, a non-Quaker, became a conscientious objector in the First World War; his close Ackworth friend, Ernest Cooper Apperley Stephenson, a committed Quaker, fought and died in it.[117] Britain's public schools had started to become militarised during the Boer War and by 1914 there were twenty thousand schoolboys in the Officer Training Corps.[118] At Leighton Park, however, Evans refused any kind of military training although the boys did make large quantities of splints for wounded soldiers. They supported a local hostel for Belgian refugees and visited German prisoners of war at a camp on Newbury race course. By the time Bunting arrived, every boy was expected to devote one hour of his spare time each day to working in the school's gardens and in 1917 much of the school's energy was devoted to growing crops. Brown reports that, 'crops of potatoes were grown, and squads went as far afield as the allotments on Manor Farm to help. The boys bought spades and forks to the value of £6. The spirit in the school at this time appears to have been splendid.'[119] By the time twenty boys and three masters attended the school's first agricultural camp at Lincombe Farm near Stourport-on-Severn in spring 1918 Bunting was in prison.

For the organ of a Quaker school *The Leightonian* seems to have been fairly even-handed in its treatment of serving soldiers and conscientious objectors. The December 1918 issue is apparently proud of both and announces the consequences of Bunting's adherence to his belief that 'the principle's the same' without condemnation or praise. Bunting would have been aware of Quaker ambivalence since 1914 when Ackworth's Frederick Andrews had refused to criticise 'Old Scholars' who chose to fight in spite of the fact that he doubted the possibility of ending war by means of war: 'If a man has no conscientious convictions against war, I honour him for enlisting.'[120] Such compromise was bound to attract criticism, and it did. And at

Leighton Park Charles Evans adopted a pacifist position while at the same time ensuring that old boys' military deeds were fully appreciated in *The Leightonian*. Some Quaker families were divided by this issue of conscience, just as the Society of Friends as a whole was divided, many taking a strongly pacific line, others providing outspoken support to the prosecution of the war. By June 1915, for instance, nearly two hundred Ackworth Old Scholars had joined up and Andrews had received many letters from them: 'I don't wonder at these boys … feeling the call of their country, because we have tried to instil into them those very principles of liberty and fair-play which are being outraged. They have heard at School of the contributions that small nations have rendered to civil and religious freedom, such as Athens at Marathon and the Netherlanders in their heroic resistance to Philip and the Duke of Alva.'[121] It just doesn't work. Invoking the spirit of Marathon to promote world peace wasn't even papering over the widening Quaker crack. 'The position of ours that Friends take with regard to National Service is liable to be misunderstood', Andrews complained.[122] It was misunderstood because it was completely incoherent. Just after the war the Secretary of the Ackworth Old Scholars Association (AOSA) reflected ruefully on the divisions, sometimes bitter, that the war had thrust upon the entire Quaker community and on him in particular, having been the 'target fired upon from all sides'. His conclusion is bizarrely neutral: 'We are neither pacifists nor militarists, Quakers nor Jingoes. To us it matters not in what direction the service of any Old Scholar has lain during the war.' How could an explicitly Quaker institution take such a position? The answer, in a stroke of dazzling Jesuitry, is by splitting the moral responsibilities of the AOSA from those of the school, the only common denominator for those the association served. Having made this daring moral leap he goes on to celebrate the values that underpin it: 'The fact which does interest us is that, according to the light within them, Old Scholars have done their duty in so many varied ways. Inasmuch as Old Scholars have endeavoured to live up to their convictions, we see in it the result of their Ackworth training, and the practical expression of their School motto. It is of this that we are proud, and for this reason we gladly record their service in "battlefield, prison cell, or scene of unaccustomed labour".'[123]

This bewildering statement suggests that such all-encompassing neutrality is the only sane response to what had become perhaps the bloodiest war ever. With this kind of ethical leadership it's not surprising that so many Quakers found themselves in such a deep moral bind. This failure of leadership was not lost on the Ackworth community. In his biography of Frederick Andrews, Isaac Henry Wallis quoted one of these deeply confused young men: 'Many of us were in great distress of mind and in grave doubt as to what we ought to do. We had learned our peace principles at the feet of F. A. and we naturally looked to him for a clear lead. Alas he never gave one. I never understood why.'[124]

One consequence of the Quaker leadership's failure to articulate a coherent response to the war was the enlistment by 1917 of, remarkably, nearly a third of all eligible Quakers,[125] the desire to make a contribution outweighing the certainty that participating in war was wrong. To be fair to the Quakers the rest of British society was just as divided. A recent study by Adam Hochschild has shown how families, friendships and communities were split, sometimes irrevocably, by the war. Along with the boy who became Britain's greatest modernist poet, some remarkable people found themselves in jail for their beliefs during the First World War, including a future Nobel Prize-winner, Bertrand Russell, a future Cabinet minister, several future MPs and a distinguished investigative journalist who became the Labour Party's chief spokesman on foreign affairs in the House of Commons. Ramsay MacDonald, who narrowly escaped jail for his anti-war position and was under heavy police surveillance, was Britain's Prime Minister by 1924.[126]

Bunting's J. B. Hodgkin Speech Prize paper was, according to Leighton Park's archivist, 'remarkable, as courageous and fearlessly demonstrative as it was inflated with his usual posturing. This was to be his ultimate show-down, determined and uncompromising. His witness was carefully prepared, starting with the selection of his JBH topic and possibly (was it part of his plan?) leaving school two terms earlier than he expected in order to face a Tribunal at the earliest opportunity.'[127]

In this vacuum of moral leadership Bunting had to make his own decision about his conscience. Ellen Fry or Charlemagne? In the event it was a mixture of both, Fry's pacifism prosecuted with steely Carolingian ruthlessness. Bunting waged his peace.

NEWCASTLE 'CONCHY', 1918

Peterhouse's identification of 'recklessness' and 'brilliance' is a fair characterisation of Bunting at eighteen. Just two months later, on 17 April 1918, Bunting was in front of the Newcastle Military Tribunal in an uncompromising mood. (He had attended a 'Preliminary Examination' by the National Service Representative at 26 Northumberland Street on 16 March 1918.) The report in the following day's *North Mail* is a fascinating display of just how far Bunting could get under the skin of the establishment, even at eighteen:

> In a long statement the lad, who carried himself with great self-possession, objected to war, to non-combatant service because it released a man for combatancy, to national service because it helped the prosecution of war, and to leaving his present occupation of 'desultory reading' because he thought he was doing his duty as a 'citizen of the world' in remaining as he was. He had been educated in Quaker schools.
>
> In reply to Mr George Renwick, the applicant was quite prepared to let the German hordes overrun England.
>
> 'Are you taught those principles in these Quaker schools?' asked Mr Renwick.
>
> 'The whole atmosphere is one of pacifism,' came the reply.
>
> Further replies of an equally uncompromising character led Mr Renwick sarcastically to observe: 'You would rather stay here and let other men die for you in France?'
>
> 'Yes,' interposed the objector.
>
> 'You are a beauty, you are!' said Mr Renwick.
>
> On hearing that the tribunal would grant him non-combatant service, the applicant inquired about appealing, whereat Mr Renwick indignantly broke in: 'I want it to be clearly understood that I absolutely object to that – a boy of 18 coming here with such views'.

It is easy to laugh at blimpish Mr Renwick, who was probably still spluttering when he got home, but we need to put this exchange in context. For a start Renwick, a local politician and businessman who would become Conservative MP for the newly created constituency of Newcastle upon Tyne Central in the December 1918 general election, had five sons away at war in various capacities so Bunting's arrogant dismissal of their sacrifice must have touched him at a deeply personal level. (All five of the Renwick boys survived the war prompting their father to fund the Grade II listed Renwick Memorial at Barras Bridge in the heart of Newcastle's university area.) More importantly though, in April 1918 it was not at all obvious that the war was reaching its final stages and that an armistice would be signed by November. If anything the German position had been hugely bolstered by the previous year's Bolshevik revolution in Russia and the Treaty of Brest-Litovsk which was ratified in March 1918 and in which Russia ceded to Germany part of Ukraine and all of Poland, Finland, the Baltic states and the Caucasus. This sudden gain of territory three times the size of Germany was a significant threat to the Allies, and particularly to Britain. With their Turkish allies Germany now had a real opportunity to expand into Asia Minor and threaten Britain's position in India. The British War Cabinet believed that the decisive battle to end the war could not take place until 1919, possibly 1920. Moreover the British army was seriously under strength, having suffered nearly 800,000 casualties in 1917, and just a few weeks before Bunting's tribunal, on 21 March, Ludendorff's storm troopers had broken through British lines at the second battle of the Somme. Operation Michael began with a shock and awe barrage that put Gough's 5th Army into complete disarray. The German artillery began at 4.40 a.m. and fired, on the first day alone, 3.2 million rounds, one-third of them chemical.[128] It was followed by a release of tear gas and then the far deadlier mustard gas over the British trenches, after which seventy-six elite German divisions arrived out of the mist in a devastating assault that saw seven thousand British infantrymen killed by the end of the day. A further ten thousand men were wounded and twenty-one thousand were taken prisoner on a single day that saw German troops capturing over ninety-eight square miles of territory and bringing them within twelve miles of Amiens. By 5 April the Germans were in Amiens' suburbs and the hole punched in Gough's line had separated him from the 3rd Army on the one hand and the French army on the other. The scale of the German victory can be measured by the fact that the Kaiser awarded a 'victory' holiday to German children.[129]

Just the week before Bunting's tribunal the British public had received news that Operation Michael had been replaced by Operation George as Ludendorff switched his attack to Flanders, driving Horne's 1st Army and Plumer's 2nd Army back over the strategically important Messines Ridge. A British victory was not in the air as the young Basil Bunting tormented George Renwick at Newcastle Tribunal on 17 April 1918. The British Empire had lost over 900,000 military personnel, over 720,000 of them from the British Isles, and patriotic feeling was running high.[130] In the context of such colossal sacrifice Bunting's principled pacifism was courageous or selfish, depending on how you look at it. In 1918 there wasn't much doubt about the way to look at it. The 900,000 deaths were dwarfed by the numbers of wounded and diseased men returning from the front and it is doubtful that many of the 160,000 premature British widows and their 300,000 fatherless children had much that was positive to say about conscientious objectors.[131] As Adam Hochschild shows, hysteria against pacifists was encouraged by the authorities:

> A pamphlet by 'A Little Mother' typically declared that 'we women ... will tolerate no such cry as "Peace! Peace!"'... There is only one temperature for the women of the British race, and that is white heat ... We women pass on the human ammunition of "only sons" to fill up the gaps.' It sold 75,000 copies in a few days. 'The conscientious objector is a fungus growth – a human toadstool – which should be uprooted without further delay,' screamed the tabloid *John Bull*. The *Daily Express* declared that COs were financed by German money. [132]

On 4 May 1918 *John Bull* published a cartoon showing a CO sitting comfortably at home with the caption 'This little pig stayed at home'.[133] and a postcard reproduced by Hochschild depicts the conscientious objector at the front. A caricature brutal German soldier is bayoneting the campest possible (and long-haired of course) British CO in the buttocks while the CO, betraying no sign of not enjoying the experience, flirts:

> Oh, you naughty unkind German –
> Really, if you don't desist
> I'll forget I've got a conscience,
> And I'll smack you on the wrist![134]

For the vast majority of British people Bunting was fungus, a pig, a homosexual. The self-appointed scourge of obscenity, James Douglas of the *Sunday Express* reacted predictably to the publication in 1918 of A. T. Fitzroy's novel about homosexual conscientious objectors, *Despised and Rejected*. His rant in *London Opinion* of 24 August remarkably brings together three of these elements (money, fungus and homosexuality) in one hysterical paragraph:

> A thoroughly poisonous book, every copy of which ought to be put on the fire forthwith, is *Despised and Rejected* ... Of its hideous immoralities the less said the better; but concerning its sympathetic presentation, in the mouths of its 'hero' and other characters of pacifism and conscientious objection,

and of sneering at the English as compared with the Hun, this needs to be asked: What is the use of our spending hundreds of thousands of pounds on propaganda, and tens of thousands more on Censorship, while pestiferous filth like this remains unsuppressed? ... I imagine that it will not be long, after the authorities have examined this literary fungus, before [the author] is a Daniel brought to judgment.[135]

With this kind of cheerleading the voices of reaction were overwhelming. If nothing else one has to admire the physical bravery of young COs in 1918. The title of the reviled novel tells the whole story. Mr Renwick was furiously spluttering on behalf of the many.

Bunting's confident appearance before the Newcastle Military Tribunal was reported in predictably sneering tones in the local press, the *Illustrated Chronicle* and the *Newcastle Weekly Chronicle*, presumably delighted to be prejudicing the outcome of Bunting's appeal. The *Illustrated Chronicle* ran the story under a rabble-rousing headline: 'NEWCASTLE "CONCHY" Would sooner see Huns Over-running Country Than Kill a Man':

An 18-year-old youth applied at Newcastle Local Tribunal yesterday for exemption on conscientious grounds. He stated that he was a student of History, and had because of his views, sacrificed a scholarship at Peterhead [*sic*]. He had been educated at a Quaker school, where the whole atmosphere was one of pacifism. He had a conscientious objection to killing a man; it was manifestly wicked to do so after months of preparation. He could not take up non-combatant service because that meant releasing a man to do what he himself objected to do. By continuing his studies he considered he was doing what was best in the interest of the country. He would sooner see Germans over-running this country than kill a man.

On 20 June 1918 a local historian, F. W. Dendy, heard the appeal for the Northumberland Appeal Tribunal and Bunting was given one month to take up agricultural work or to sign up for combat.[136]

The young Bunting must have felt intensely isolated in his defiance. At least 1.6 million British servicemen were wounded or fell seriously ill during the war. Bunting was one of just 16,500 men who had declared their refusal to serve on grounds of conscience.[137] Of these the vast majority were granted some form of exemption or accepted national service in a non-military capacity, that is they accepted the authority of the tribunal, leaving just 1,298, including the young poet, who didn't and who were sent to prison, less than 1 per cent of the 1 per cent. These prisoners, as Alyson Brown has shown,[138] provided the British authorities with a significant administrative and moral problem. Absolutists like Bunting became victims of a cycle of arrest, conscription, court martial and then imprisonment, a cycle that merely repeated once the sentence had been served.

Prison was not kind to COs and several died as a result of the harsh conditions they faced. According to Gilbert Murray, in his preface to Stephen Hobhouse's *An English Prison from Within*: 'Of the 54 men [COs] who have died since arrest, 8 died actually in prison, 1 in an asylum, and 11 in Home Office camps, and 6 committed suicide. Thirty-seven men have become mentally affected, while 189 have been released from prison because of their shattered health …'[139] Whatever it was that compelled these young men to avoid conflict it certainly wasn't cowardice.

It seems ludicrous now that a principled young man should have been sent to prison straight out of school six months before the capitulation of the German army. But, as we have seen, there was no way of foreseeing that collapse and in any event Britain took some of the moral high ground by being one of only two nations in the First World War to even recognise the existence of conscientious objection.[140]

The Leightonian of December 1918 reported on the whereabouts of recent leavers. E. P. Southall, who we last met complaining about the music, was in prison and Bunting was serving 'a sentence of 112 days in Wormwood Scrubbs, after refusing agricultural work on the ground that in effect that was sending another man to fight for him'.[141]

Ordeal by chicken

We tend to think of boys leaving school and going straight to prison as a relatively recent phenomenon. During the war years, however, many Quaker boys refused service, although not all of them ended up in Wormwood Scrubs. After his arrest Bunting was transferred to Fenham Barracks, where he enjoyed the doubtless generous hospitality of the Northumberland Fusiliers for a month,[142] after which he spent the next six months or so in Wormwood Scrubs, various military hospitals and Winchester Prison (where the COs circulated an underground newspaper called *The Whisperer*). Bunting did talk about his early prison experience many years later to his friend Peter Quartermain. Fenham Barracks was a large, crowded, underheated eighteenth-century-style room … Many of his companions there were pickpockets and thieves. Most of the prisoners were grown men and rough, not middle class boys of eighteen. There were a few blankets for which the prisoners fought. One prisoner, a large angry man, managed to get hold of two blankets and gave one of them to Basil. It turned out that his benefactor, the only person in the room to treat Basil with kindness, had committed a double murder. He had poisoned two women.[143]

Even if Bunting's imagination plays the lead role in this story there's no doubt that conditions were harsh. According to Adam Hochschild, 'those refusing conscription were sentenced to hard labour. For the first two weeks, a prisoner was given no mattress to sleep on in his seven-by-twelve-foot cell. Prison labour usually consisted of sewing a daily quota of thick canvas mailbags with a big skewer-like needle.' Towards the end of 1917 imprisoned COs had their daily bread allowance halved to just 11 ounces; that's a piece of bread roughly four inches square.[144]

Bunting gave a fuller account to *The Leightonian* in a letter that was published in the July 1919 edition:

'I am able to answer your letter myself, because it arrived here just two or three days after I was released under the Cat and Mouse Act. I spent all last winter and autumn in Wormwood Scrubs Prison, making mailbags and twisting ships' fenders. I forfeited my remission, because, for some while before the armistice I refused to do prison work, so I was not released till the end of January. Then I had divers adventures, into which I need not now enter, and after a long sojourn in a military hospital, whither I was sent to get rid of a septic ulcer, I found myself on Salisbury Plain. There, after I had visited Stonehenge, and satisfied my curiosity as to the internal appearance of Y.M.C.A. huts, I repeated the farce of refusing to obey an order, for which I was court-martialled a second time, and sent to do a year's hard labour in Winchester Civil Prison. There were only half a dozen C.O.'s left there, all the rest having been released under the twenty months order, and since I did not see why the rest of us should be left behind, I went on hunger strike. They were very merciful with me. I have come to the conclusion that they only wanted an excuse to let me out, because three days proved sufficient to do the trick, and they gave me six weeks (till June 15th) to do as I like in.'

On June 24th, however, B.C.B. visited the school in person, and informed us cheerfully that he was now living in London and avoiding the police.[145]

Bunting also talked about his prison experience to his friend, the poet and actor, Denis Goacher. Goacher was well aware of Bunting's self-mythologising tendencies ('it was sometimes quite difficult to disentangle the real truth from his Ford Madox Ford-ing of it') but he was sure he had the essence of Bunting's first imprisonment:

> What they did was to put you in a totally darkened cell, without a window, without any heating, and no furniture whatever, no clothes whatever. (It was up North, remember, Newcastle.) You just had to lie, when you could sleep, on the floor, naked; and you were allowed, once a day, a bowl of water and a crust of bread. This lasted for three days and you were then examined by a doctor, to see what condition you were in. If he considered that your condition was sufficiently sound, you went back on that regime for two days. If, at the end of say five or six days, your condition had deteriorated, you were then given a minimum of clothing and a little bit more food and water. At the end of that three days, in a slightly improved condition, you were put back on the no heating, no clothes and no light whatever. The idea, of course, was to break your spirit. Well Basil, who was a tough man, survived this for six weeks, and at the end of the six weeks he was still unbroken. So they let him out, and he was set to work making jute bags, which they had to do for twelve hours a day. Very bad food, of course. He discovered, I don't know how, that these bags were being used for the Services, so he refused to make them. He was slapped back in a cell and it started all over again ... Basil told me that this experience embittered him for life. He didn't make any bones about it. He said it coloured all he thought about England, about the Establishment, the 'Southrons' as he called us.[146]

Bunting may have been characteristically reluctant to talk about his time in prison, but others weren't. Another imprisoned Quaker CO, Stephen Hobhouse, described long rows of cells, four or five storeys of them, facing each other across an open area: 'Across the central space at first-floor level is stretched a wire netting to catch an unhappy man trying to commit suicide from above.' All the cell doors had peepholes, 'through which at times could be seen the sinister eye of the warder spying on the inmate from without'. Warders sometimes padded silently along the corridors in felt slippers, to catch the prisoners unawares. Two of the day's meals consisted only of porridge, dry bread, and salt; the third was mostly potatoes. Prisoners were allowed to send and receive one letter a month – but none at all for the first two months.[147]

In 1982 Bunting recalled the prison regime in 1918 in a letter to Tom Pickard: 'In 1918 all the writing even the most privileged were allowed was confined to a slate. When you had filled the slate you wiped it off and started again. Most of us didn't even have a slate. You were allowed to receive one letter and write one, as much as you could get onto one very small sheet of notepaper, every month after the first three, which were blank, provided you broke no rules meanwhile. You were allowed to talk, an hour a day, after the first two years, which were silent.'[148]

Bunting later put his prison experience to very good use. While 'Villon', written in 1925 but not published until 1930, may be Bunting's starkest expression of prison life his review of Conrad's novel, *The Rover*, in the *transatlantic review* of August 1924 gives a better flavour of his time in prison:

> I read *Romance* for the first time in the solitude of an English prison. The Book of Kings, Isaiah's harsh splendour and the voluptuous majesty of the Song of Solomon had tempered my weariness for several months, but somehow – a reminiscence of schooldays, perhaps – I always looked upon the Bible as prison reading. *Romance* was a real book, a book written by man and not by the heavy finger of God. In that emptiness, where no new thing ever enters, it took possession of my eyes and ears. My cell grew full of aromatic bales, fading into the shadows of Don Ramon's warehouse; Thomas Castro walked with me around the patch of rotting cabbage-stalks that was our daily exercise ground; even Seraphina visited me occasionally, keeping modestly to the dark places, an indistinct but sympathetic form. It was all amazingly concrete. I *saw* that warehouse; I saw the bay and its town, the hovels, the cathedral, the palace; I watched the hanging of the pirates at Kingston; and when I came to the long trial at the end of the book I heard the rustle of the public and the muttering of the turnkeys to one another.[149]

This lengthy aside on Conrad's collaboration with Ford Madox Ford, the novel *Romance*, in a review of Conrad's *The Rover* is typical of Bunting's cavalier approach to book reviewing. It extols Conrad's qualities as a writer, but rather shirks the responsibility of a reviewer to say something interesting about the book under review: 'It would be useless … as well as impertinent for me to expatiate on Mr. Conrad's themes or to discuss his stories. Those who do not already know them can only truly satisfy their curiosity by reading them. I would like to write about *how he does it*. I wish I knew.'

Bunting didn't like talking about his time in prison. He slid off the subject rapidly in *Descant on Rawthey's Madrigal* by invoking Graham Wallas and setting off a useless research trail for would-be biographers. His long spell in jail wasn't 'a matter of much interest nowadays. The jails have been altered. Anybody who wants to know what they were like can get from a library Graham Wallas's book on the subject which has some footnotes by me and which was the main evidence before the Royal Commission that reformed the prisons.'[150] Nobody has been able to find this book. That is because it doesn't exist. Bunting's contribution to prison reform is elsewhere.

The Quaker conscientious objector Stephen Hobhouse spent two terms in prison, one in Wormwood Scrubs and the other in Exeter. The experience had shattered his health but on release he quickly plunged into a huge task. Hobhouse was Beatrice Webb's nephew and the Webbs were at that time working hard on the state of British prisons as part of their monumental work on English local government. They set up the Prison System Enquiry Committee (a sort of unofficial counterpart to the hugely influential Gladstone Committee that had been set up in 1894), which included Bernard Shaw and Lawrence Housman, under the chairmanship of Sir Sydney Olivier (a socialist ex-Governor of Jamaica), and Hobhouse was appointed as the committee's Secretary with sole responsibility for collating information and writing a report. When it was published in 1922 that report immediately became an 'acknowledged landmark in prison reform'.[151] *English Prisons Today: Being the Report of the Prison System Enquiry Committee* is an exhaustive account of the nature and roles of British prisons at that time and buried within its 749 pages I believe we can find Bunting's contribution. Graham Wallas isn't mentioned anywhere in those pages, and neither is the non-existent Royal Commission, but this volume surely contains whatever contemporary views of prison Bunting expressed. The chapter on political offenders draws in a sympathetic and deeply affecting way on the anonymous personal statements of some two hundred COs, of whom it is inconceivable that Bunting was not one, especially given that the Chairman, Sydney Olivier, was a close Oxford friend of Graham Wallas. Hobhouse's uncle, Leonard Trelawny Hobhouse, one of the great liberal intellectuals of the day, was also connected to Wallas as he was Britain's first Professor of Sociology at LSE from 1907 until his death in 1929.[152] It is also possible, of course, that Bunting contributed actual footnotes as well as personal testimony to this progressive report, including the moving 'Specimen of Evidence' supplied by one CO as an appendix. I think Bunting was genuinely misremembering rather than trying to lay a false trail because he disliked expressing his opinion about his prison experience. After all, he needn't have mentioned it to Jonathan Williams at all. Hobhouse and Brockway did have enormous impact. Margery Fry called it the 'Bible for the reformers',[153] and the newly appointed Chairman of the Prison Commission, Sir Maurice Walker, immediately did everything possible to put the report's recommendations in place and, according to Hobhouse's biographer, *English Prisons Today* 'had perhaps greater practical success than any single volume on prison reform that has ever been published. If it had achieved nothing but the abolition of the iniquitous silence rule it would have been worthwhile, and one finds a certain satisfaction in the fact that a Quaker did so much to remove an enormity first introduced into prison by well-intentioned but wrong-headed Quakers two centuries earlier in Pennsylvania.'[154] Graham Wallas, social pioneer though he was, didn't reform British prisons; Stephen Hobhouse did.

Bunting was emphatically correct about one thing though. After reading the stories about life in prison as a CO in Hobhouse and Brockway's report no one would require any further gloss from Bunting. His prison experiences and those of the other COs surveyed by the Prison System Enquiry Committee, as we shall see, underpin Bunting's first great poem, 'Villon'.[155]

By the end of the war imprisoned conscientious objectors were certainly flexing their muscles. In May 1918 conscientious objectors jailed in Liverpool announced that they would 'break all prison rules they considered "inhuman and immoral," including the rule of silence. For ten days the prison resounded with talk, laughter and singing. Then the warders cracked down, moving the men they thought to be ringleaders to other prisons. Some COs went on hunger strikes, only to find themselves force-fed like the suffragettes.'[156] Bunting's story, as told late in life, was different. He told Carroll F. Terrell that he went on hunger strike and vowed to die there if he wasn't released.

> After he'd been on the strike for a week, the warden played, said Basil, a dirty trick. Each day, a beautiful, plump, enticing roasted stuffed chicken was placed without comment in his cell. The very odor was enough to drive a hungry man to distraction. He was sorely tempted, but he never touched the chicken. The warden concluded that if this ploy didn't work, nothing would. Probably also that a man of such sterling character ought not to die in prison. So, on the eleventh day of the strike four or five days after the chicken torture, he was discharged a free man.[157]

There are a number of factors that might lead us to doubt this tale. It is true that English prison authorities were sensitive to the hunger strike tactic. The suffragette movement had been using it since the beginning of the century to great effect. Suffragettes were usually released after six days as the last thing the authorities wanted to do was create martyrs of the women. But conscientious objectors were not likely martyrs. Their constituency was, as we have seen, tiny, and outside it they were despised. It is doubtful that the prison governor would waste something as valuable as a chicken three days running on a CO. He would have been an unusual prison governor indeed if he had recognised 'a man of sterling character' lurking inside a notorious coward, for that is what COs were regarded as. Furthermore the war was over; why go to the trouble of roasting chickens when a door could be left open accidentally one dark morning? Most compelling of all though is the fact that this story comes at the very end of Terrell's long account of his visit to Bunting in Northumbria. As we shall see the poet teased and misled his guest mercilessly during his entire stay. I suspect the chicken story was his parting shot.

The story, true or not, was immortalised by Pound in Canto 74:

> Bunting
>   doing six months after that war was over
>   as pacifist tempted by chicken but declined to approve
> of war "Redimiculum Metellorum"
>   privately printed
>   to the shame of various critics[158]

My business was to be a poet

From the age of five Bunting, 'never had any reason to change the conviction then borne in me that my business was to be a poet … my father used to read poetry to us from the earliest years and included amongst the poems for the children a number of the less recondite bits of Wordsworth. It made a great impression on me early in life.'[159]

Poetry was certainly an important component of Bunting family culture. He was given Rossetti's poetry at the age of fourteen, and 'got an enormous lot of them by heart'.[160] In an interview in 1981 he recalled that, 'by the end of my childhood I was familiar with most of Wordsworth, except for a good deal of "The Prelude". When I was about the beginning of my teens I read Rossetti's translations of the early Italian poets. And when I was about 15 I came across Walt Whitman … At a later date I would have to add Horace, in Latin.'[161]

Bunting's sister, Joyce, told Victoria Forde that it amused her to think that 'up to the age of 8 or 9 if asked what I would be when I grew up, I always said, "a poetess"'. For Joyce this soon faded, but Bunting remained faithful to his nursery school ambition: 'when Basil was 12 years old, our parents encouraged us and a cousin to write poems about a holiday we had had in the Lake District by offering a small prize and Basil won it'.[162]

By the time Bunting left Leighton Park he had published three poems, the two school poems we know about and a third that apparently won a prize and was published in the *Leeds Mercury*.[163] Bunting claimed in *Descant on Rawthey's Madrigal* that he 'wrote always' but had had the 'good sense' to destroy all his early work:

> I could see that they were no good. I didn't always have that much sense immediately, but I remember sending one [poem] to a London paper when I was about 17, and the editor, a kind-hearted fellow though an extremely bad poet himself, sent for me and said, well, we can't print this, it's not good enough. But it's getting on for it, you know. You must just try a little harder and you'll have it ... But mostly I had the sense to destroy them before I got to showing them to anybody. And I think the earliest poem that I preserved is only a fragment of one that I wrote in 1923.[164]

At the age of nineteen Bunting was introduced to the poetry of Ezra Pound and T. S. Eliot. According to Bunting he 'had arrived via a somewhat strange route at the conclusion that poetry should try to take over some of the techniques that I only knew in music. So that when I discovered Eliot writing poems and calling them "Preludes", even though the resemblance to, say, Chopin's Preludes was slight and superficial, I was extremely interested. He was obviously thinking on lines not dissimilar from my own.'[165] He was a poet throughout his life (although he gave up in his early fifties until he was rescued by the young Newcastle poet, Tom Pickard), but alongside the poetry for the next twenty to thirty years there was an awful lot of rough and tumble life to be lived. To some extent this was self-willed. He looked back in the mid-1970s on a life lived consciously: 'It was always my idea, when I was a youngster, that there were a certain number of things which every man ought to do, to experience, without which he would hardly be whole, and my notion was that somebody like Sir Walter Raleigh was such a person one ought to be; he did a mass[ive] variety of things, did them all well, some of them supremely well.'[166]

76

How does the first part of Bunting's verse autobiography represent his tumultuous youth? Barely at all in terms of coverage of events. It starts and ends in Brigflatts and appears to go nowhere else in-between. In twelve beautiful thirteen-line stanzas the poet celebrates love and mourns its loss, blaming himself, guilty of spring. We will come to *Briggflatts* later. Here it is enough to say that the sexual relationship with Peggy that he remembers is qualified by a note: '*An autobiography*, but not a record of fact. The first movement is no more a chronicle than the third. The truth of the poem is of another kind.'[167]

Throughout this chapter I have tried to trace the events of Bunting's early life while examining the many political, intellectual and cultural influences that he encountered. The rapidly industrialising Tyne, Montgomery Colliery and the poor miners who visited his father's surgery in Scotswood and provided a platform for his lifelong dislike of capitalism; the family friend Joseph Skipsey who brought that world into poetry; the Cheesman family, which provided a strong sense of the northern-ness that he never lost; his father's restless, enquiring mind and progressive views, his love of poetry, particularly Wordsworth, and the hills of the Lake District where he had taught Bunting to climb; the extensive collection at the Newcastle Lit & Phil, where Bunting absorbed so much north country history and folklore, and the lively lectures on all aspects of the arts and sciences; the music of Scarlatti, J. C. Bach and Monteverdi that he absorbed at school and the Lit & Phil; his parents' early involvement in the Fabian Society with its progressive democratising principles, and the presence of the foremost British social scientist of the time, Graham Wallas, as a family friend; the gentle Quaker Greenbank family, the timeless mysterious serenity of their hamlet and Meeting House at Brigflatts and the time spent there with the great love of his life, Peggy Greenbank; his pacific Quaker education, under inspiring leaders like Frederick Andrews and Charles Evans, that led to his imprisonment for refusing to fight in the First World War, refusing even to accept work that made another man available to fight.

Within three years he was in prison again, this time in Paris, and for persistent drunken violence.

TWO

FELLS FORGET HIM

Who sang, sea takes,
brawn brine, bone grit.
Keener the kittiwake.
Fells forget him.
Fathoms dull the dale,
gulfweed voices …

Briggflatts II

LONDON, 1919–1923

The Leightonian of July 1920 reported that Bunting was 'still at the London School of Economics. He is hoping to go to Russia shortly via Copenhagen, but the Danish authorities say that the "desire to study Danish literature" is not a good enough lie and refuse to *viser* his passport. Meanwhile he has been appointed to write articles on English art, music, and literature, for a Roumanian newspaper. He is also growing a beard.'[1]

Having been rejected by Cambridge the London School of Economics (LSE) was the obvious university for Bunting to go. New, progressive, social sciences oriented and founded by the Fabian movement, it had rapidly become a powerhouse of liberal intellectualism since its foundation in 1895. Bunting didn't exactly seize his opportunity.

He enrolled in October 1919 and left (formally at least) in April 1923 without taking a degree, but having 'got enough of all that [economics] to last me a lifetime'.[2] This was quite literally true. He had absorbed enough to earn a living as a financial commentator until the very end of his career as a journalist, and Eric Mottram noted in his diary of 2 August 1966 that during a lunch in Buffalo, New York, Bunting had 'talked very good economics indeed'.[3] As late as 1979 he gave a 'long and informed disquisition on money,

79

banking, and economics' to Carroll F. Terrell during an extended discussion of Pound's Douglasite economic theories (which Bunting came to deride).[4]

Graham Wallas would have been a strong influence on his decision to enroll at LSE and there was doubtless some fatherly arm-twisting behind it. Wallas had turned down the role of founding Director of LSE in 1895 but had joined as a teacher of politics when the school opened and was still there when he retired in 1923, continuing to teach occasionally until his death in 1932.

The school was formally founded in 1895 and quickly became an important institution, the kind of establishment that was then common in the rest of Europe, a polytechnic for training the next generation of the business and administrative elite. This was at some variance from its benefactor's desire that LSE encourage socialism.[5] In that same year LSE had been at the vanguard of the new discipline of economics, offering the first BSc degree in the subject, and following this in 1909 with the creation of a Department of Sociology. The London School of Economics combined academic rigour in the new social sciences with a proudly utilitarian streak, offering vocational courses in management and administration for instance.

We know something of the scope of Bunting's intended learning at the London School of Economics from his contemporary, the distinguished economist Lionel (later Lord) Robbins:

> The first year course for the B.Sc. (Econ.), then even more than now, was widely spread: Elements of Economics (Dr [Hugh] Dalton), with applications in Money, Banking and International Trade (Dr [T. E.] Gregory), Economic History (Professor [Lilian] Knowles), British Constitution (Mr [Hastings] Lees Smith), Logic and Scientific Method (Dr [Abraham] Wolf), Geography (Dr [Hilda] Ormsby) – this, together with a translation paper, was what we were expected to cover in the short space of nine months ... The majority survived it satisfactorily and were in a position to proceed to more intensive studies in the final with a very satisfactory grounding and with a wide range of interests suitably kindled.[6]

This is a stellar line up of tutors. Hugh Dalton was later to become Chancellor of the Exchequer in the Labour government that came to power under Clement Attlee in 1945. Hastings Lees Smith became a Cabinet Minister in 1931. Lilian Knowles was the first of only two Professors of Economics appointed at London University before the Second World War and she was Dean of the Faculty of Economics from 1920 to 1924, the first female Dean of Faculty at London University. She was widely recognised as a superb teacher. Hilda Ormsby was to be the only female founding member of the Institute of British Geographers. Indeed Bunting may have owed more to Ormsby than a fleeting interest in geography as she worked as a cartographer for the naval intelligence division of the Admiralty during the Second World War.[7]

Unhappily, even with a faculty as distinguished as this, Bunting did not find himself in Robbins' 'majority':

> The lectures ... were extremely good and well delivered; although we did not know it, it would have been relatively easy to have passed the intermediate examination ... on the strength of lecture notes alone. Indeed, this was done by a fellow student, Basil Bunting the poet, who having been distracted by other matters during the greater part of the session, borrowed my notes at the end and, having read them intensively for three or four days, lying on the grass in the Green Park opposite Buckingham Palace, emerged from the ordeal triumphant.[8]

It is possible that Bunting was acquainted at LSE with a man who was later to become an influential socialist economist, Piero Sraffa. Sraffa was a friend of Antonio Gramsci, perhaps the most important Italian Marxist of the period, and Filippo Turati, Italy's foremost socialist. Two years older than Bunting, Sraffa attended the London School of Economics in 1921 and 1922, becoming one of the most important economists of his generation and a major influence on Wittgenstein's *Philosophical Investigations*. Sraffa was a frequent visitor to Rapallo, Bunting's home for part of his twenties and thirties. His father, the lawyer and academic Angelo Sraffa, had a villa, San Michele, in Rapallo[9] and he was one of the patrons of the concerts Bunting helped Ezra Pound to organise there in 1933.[10]

It is possible, as Lionel Robbins' biographer, Susan Howson, says that Bunting and Robbins met at the Fabian Research Department,[11] but they lived in the same house in St John's Wood for a period. Robbins was certainly an important early influence on Bunting. Bunting wrote to Pound later that Robbins was,

> a bloke abt a year or two older than me, good war record, son of the chap who used to be president or secretary or something of the National Farmers Union – anyway a man of some importance. I met him just before I went to the L.S.E. and did him the bad turn of persuading him to go there too ... He was one of the first people I met to show any interest in [Clifford Hugh] Douglas.

81

Subsequent hostility is at least not result of ignorance, as in many cases. Tastes more or less better class Bloomsbury – i.e., aware of a lot of things you might not expect a prof of economics to have heard of. First person, I think, to show me any of Eliot's work, certainly first to show me bit of Ulysses in The Egoist (or was it Portrait of J.J.?) ... He used to like yr works and probably still does.[12]

Bunting used the Fabian common room above its shop in Westminster when he was a student at the London School of Economics. He recalled that, 'when I was in London in 1919 I usually got my food, apart from my supper at night and breakfast in the morning, by having tea and toast in the Fabian common room which was above its shop in Westminster and there I must have met all of that famous gang sooner or later, and some of them frequently. Some of them I was on such terms with as a young man can be with those who are very much his seniors.'[13]

The other meeting place he used in this period was, 'the Mecca café, in Gentry Lane closer to the street where the offices of the *New Age* were. And there I used to go and sit with [Alfred Richard] Orage [editor of the *New Age*] and [Clifford Hugh] Douglas, and occasionally Marmaduke Pickthall, the great translator of the Koran.'[14] This highlights one of the problems of transcribing from old taped interviews. There is no 'Gentry Lane' in London's West End. The offices of the intellectual weekly, the *New Age*, were in Cursitor Street and the newspaper was printed in Rolls Passage off Chancery Lane (easily confused with 'Gentry'), about 50 yards from the London School of Economics. Bunting started to show up at the fringe of a group that collected around Orage, including Douglas and Wyndham Lewis, in 1919 and the early part of 1920.[15] It couldn't have been later than that because the celebrated orientalist Marmaduke Pickthall, who had converted to Islam in 1917 at the age of forty-two, left Britain for India in 1920 and didn't return until 1935. Douglas was an engineer turned economist whose theory of social credit had a profound influence on Ezra Pound. As a young economics student Bunting would have valued his brief acquaintance with Douglas. At that time Douglas was looking for a publisher for his first book, *Economic Democracy*. Orage serialised it in the *New Age* in 1919 and Douglas took Orage on as a collaborator on his second, *Credit-Power and Democracy*, which was published in 1920. Douglas had become concerned with the nature of the money supply in capitalist economies and developed a theory to rectify its anomalies. Pound clearly didn't understand Douglasite theory even in 1920, when it had become the driving force of the *New Age*, as his review of *Economic Democracy* in the *Little Review* in April 1920 shows.[16] Pound may have been attracted by the part of Douglas' theory that calls for the destruction of the power of 'money-lenders'. Social credit quickly became seen as anti-Semitic and Pound's own anti-Semitism was gathering force at this time. The *New Age* of March 1920 carried a piece by Pound that praised Douglas' 'profound attack on usury'.[17] Douglas was not anti-Semitic[18] and he regarded fascism as evil, but once Oswald Mosley's British Union of Fascists took to social credit it became linked inextricably with anti-Semitism.[19]

Orage himself was widely credited with bringing the British modernist movement together by providing it with an intellectually credible forum. Pound had been writing for him since 1911 and he published rare (at that time) essays on Freud, Wyndham Lewis, Herbert Read and T. E. Hulme. He promoted Fabian socialism and the works of Nietzsche, as well as Douglas.

Bunting liked Orage 'very much'.[20] Towards the end of his life he told Carroll F. Terrell how Orage 'by paying Pound regularly for contributions in his own name as well as several pseudonyms, literally kept him from starving ... According to Basil, Orage began to show signs of fear, mental stress, and symptoms of paranoia by 1922 ... [but he] could not provide any certain evidence that Orage's mental state in any way contributed to Pound's mental state.'[21]

Bunting did not meet Pound in 1919, but Pound was certainly an important part of Orage's circle at the time. His contributions to the *New Age* had started in 1917 with a series of articles, 'Studies of Contemporary Mentality' on the stupidity of British journals and magazines. Towards the end of that year he began to write art criticism for the *New Age* as B. H. Dias and in December he began a series of astonishing music reviews as William Atheling. Pound was tone deaf, knew nothing about music and got away with, for example, a description of part of Beethoven's Kreutzer Sonata where 'the piano jabs in, and jerks on the violin, tum, tum, ti, ump, tum, tump, ti ump'.[22] Pound earned four guineas a month from the *New Age* and later described it as 'the SINEWS of his income in the period',[23] but Bunting's claim that Orage had 'literally' kept Pound from starving is an exaggeration. By that time Pound had married Dorothy Shakespear, the daughter of Yeats' former lover Olivia Shakespear, whose parents had settled on her an annuity of £150 per annum, more than enough to keep the couple from starving, and Pound did generate other income from his tireless output.[24] Possibly Bunting didn't run into Pound in 1919 because Pound and Dorothy spent quite a large part of that year in France.[25]

A reluctant student

Bunting's student dossier is a delight. It shows that the relationship between the benign, but necessarily slightly formal, broadly sympathetic and supportive, but nonetheless a little bewildered academic and the feckless student who is supposedly in his charge hasn't changed much in a hundred years.

Bunting applied for admission to the London School of Economics on 21 August 1919 and paid the £15 15s fee. At this time he was living at 44 Hamilton Gardens in St John's Wood, as was Lionel Robbins.[26] The views around his 'garret' in St John's Wood inspired the earliest poem he preserved, 'Weeping oaks grieve, chestnuts raise'.

By the autumn of 1919 he had moved, according to a postcard to an unnamed London School of Economics authority, to the much more convenient address of 20 Great James Street near Holborn. He started solidly but after just two terms of his first year he was restless and agitating for a move. An extract from a letter to the Academic Registrar, dated 14 March 1921, requests that Bunting be excused for having been absent without leave for two terms of the previous year, 'in order to journey to Russia to study Communistic conditions there'.[27]

A letter from the Secretary to the Academic Registrar on 26 May 1921 shows that Bunting's application had been successful, and the interruption of his course of study during the third term of the session 1919–20 and the first term of the session 1920–21 was excused.

Bunting spent the second half of 1920 travelling in Northern Europe, returning to the London School of Economics in January 1921. He wrote to Lionel Robbins from Copenhagen with a full account of Danish particularity:

> The Danes are a curious race. They ride their bicycles on the wrong side of the road.

> Now every Dane has a bicycle, or, if he is too old, a tricycle, and every morning every Dane pedals to his work, every evening he pedals home again, and after dinner he pedals to the Tivoli to ride on the roundabouts, bet on the mechanical horses, and see the famous clown who performs nightly in the

open air theatre there what he calls 'Balleto pantomimes'. There is no trace of dancing about it, and the fun is extremely crude, but let that pass.

On his bicycle the Dane is a beautiful creature, but off it he does not feel at home, and looks as awkward as an automaton. Luckily he speaks either English or German or both, for his own language is a hideous affair of snorts and grunts, and Swedes and Norwegians say they can learn English more easily than Danish.

He eats twelve or thirteen meals a day, to the amazement of foreigners. He has Morgenkaffee twice, and then breakfast: more coffee meals, tea at 4, dinner at five, more coffee and beer and punch, and then a grand extra big coffee meal to finish up with, and a bottle of Pilsner to wash it down. All this is very expensive. But what he eats! Not bread and butter, but butter, beautiful butter, with a little slice of Ruybread hidden away behind it somewhere. And wonderful coffee.

Also he smokes. His pipe is about a yard long, and the bowl holds a good pound of tobacco. He smokes it after every meal, and at pauses between whiles as well. Luckily baccy is cheap – about ½ lb for about 9d. ...

... The Dane drinks Swedish Punch. Now this is a marvellous drink, and I can recommend it to you ... It is sweet and very pleasant, and while still you sit at table you can drink bottle after bottle with no visible effect. But rise once, and drunkenness is upon you. The after effects are not so good. But it is a drink worth trying, if you don't know it already. It should be drunk iced like champagne. A Norwegian skipper, his chief engineer, two American-Swedish sailors (skippers, both) and a Swedish economist, with me sat and drank four bottles of it, in a café in the Radhusplads [Rådhuspladsen] on top of the usual supply of excellent Pilsner. Then we topped it with Madeira, and Rum, and felt sufficiently bad. It was an excellent drink.

Bunting goes on to praise Copenhagen's architecture, girls and Tivoli. The girls were beautiful, the whores less so: 'They are fat, not good-looking, even less attractive than the English variety ... I'm off to see Litvinov on Monday. May go to Stockholm next.'[28]

Maxim Litvinov was a Russian diplomat who had been based in London as a representative of the Bolshevik People's Commissariat of Foreign Affairs from early in 1918. In 1919 he went to Copenhagen as head of the Soviet delegation negotiating the exchange of prisoners of war. It is unclear what Bunting was looking for from a meeting with Litvinov, but at the very least he would have wanted endorsement for a smooth transition to Russia.

Bunting gave the fullest account of his Scandinavian adventure to Lionel Robbins in October 1920:

I never reached Russia: the police were too efficient for me. First of all in Copenhagen Litvinov wouldn't see me, or more accurately, his secretary wouldn't let me see him. So I went to Stockholm, to see Frederick Ström [by then the head of the Stockholm Comintern group that negotiated with Western Europe]. He was pleased and helpful, but when he finally made up his mind to let me thro by Reval [Tallinn], he got instructions from Copenhagen not too [*sic*]. He advised me to try and get to Archangelsk or Alexandrovsk via the Arctic, and I set off by the Lapland train, after infinite passport difficulties with the Norwegian Authorities. It's a wonderful country, and all that, and the Finmark coast is even better: but that's beside the point. I reached Hammerfest, two short days from Russia, and then two detectives came on board, arrested me, and locked me up, with a gaoler who was afraid of me and six or seven selected criminals, mostly drunken Laps. I was deported to Newcastle, no reason assigned. Every port we came to the police had a fresh idea. One lot arrested me, another set me loose, another wanted me put in irons; anon there came more detectives, disguised as Consulate officials, and at N/C were more detectives, dressed up as customs officers. Before I started I was warned by someone that there was an International dossier out against me, but I wouldn't believe it!

This letter reveals that Bunting had made a 'bargain' with his father. Thomas funded the Russian escapade but his son forfeited his right to further education, forcing this pioneer of the gap year to start looking for a job, not very successfully, on Tyneside as his father refused to allow him to go to London to look for work:

An uncompromisingly truthful advertisement in the Athanaeum and the Statesman, brought me two copies of a tract on the Resurrection of the Dead, and a leaflet printed in two colours on The Evils of Drink. There are no jobs to be had in the northern Trades Union world. At present I have two prospects, both very unlikely, one a bi-weekly column on Trades Union Affairs in the local liberal paper, the other a job that Cadbury has been advertising, on their [added by hand: 'Oh! Grammar! How a Typewriter undoes thee!'] private paper to keep their workpeople from striking.[29]

His recent reading material, by his own account 'some queer stuff', is not what we might expect from an emerging poet:

My Arctic jailer produced two German books for me, a romance about the coming war, written in 1906, and differing from [Erskine Childers'] Riddle of the Sands only in being rather more capable, rather more knowledgeable, rather more frank, and rather duller; and the commanders account of the first voyage of the Deutschland, which, in spite of its technicalities and its very colloquial style, was extremely fascinating. It took my breath like a novel by Defoe, and I read it all at a sitting. Hairrrbrreadth escapes! Daring! Triumph of the legitimate hero, and <u>no women in it</u>! [added by hand: 'Lieber Gott! What a beast of a typewriter!']

At least his German was coming on, although his Russian was 'progressing slowly'. More surprisingly he reveals, after a more conventional appreciation of Swift's poetry, a remarkable admiration for the work of Anatole France:

at last I have read La Revolte des Anges ... What a book! I do not think it is equal to Penguin Island, but it is more coherent, and the incidents are delicious. Who else would have materialised the Angel when the hero was in bed with another man's wife, just ... Gibbon says these things are best left in the decent obscurity of a learned language, so I leave you to find the French. Who else would make another Angel earn its living as a 'Russian lady'? And who but Anatole France would finish the novel with the triumph of Satan, and his assumption of the exact state just vacated by Ialdabaoth?

Gentle things like Chapmans Homer, Complete Angler, Lambs Letters, Gibbon and Boswell, fulfill my list. The last two have been a standby for years.

Bunting's 'bargain' with his father didn't last long. On 6 December 1920 Bunting wrote to Miss MacTaggart at LSE from his parents' house in Portland Terrace, Jesmond, excusing his absence and telling her that he was, 'anxious to resume my course. Could I return to the School in January and take Intermediate in June? Or could I return in April and take Intermediate in June, using the interval to relearn Latin, Greek, German, etc.?'

The school's Secretary, E. V. Evans, replied to reassure him that it would probably be acceptable for him to return in the summer term and sit his examination in July, and to ask his reason for his travels in Europe so that he could account for the absence to the university. Bunting replied on 4 January 1921, with more details of his trip, saying that he'd decided to resume his studies that term.[30]

The Lent term began on 10 January 1921 and Bunting was relatively diligent, attending 64 of the 99 lectures at which he was expected. If we exclude Economic Theory, which he attended just once out of the ten lectures, his record is surprisingly good at over 70 per cent. He was certainly active politically. The London School of Economics student magazine, *Clare Market Review*, reported that Bunting had organised a London University social credit study circle. Of one Socialist Society meeting Lionel [Robbins] wrote cryptically in his diary, 'A meeting. Bunting and "Absolute Dictatorship".'[31]

By the autumn of 1921, however, he was troubling the authorities again. A letter to Dr Edwin Deller, the recently appointed Academic Registrar of London University, from Sir William Beveridge, then Director of the London School of Economics, dated 10 November 1921, formally requests a further interruption in Bunting's studies stating that, 'Mr. Bunting finds that residence in London has a deleterious effect upon his health, and his doctor has advised him to spend the next six or nine months abroad.' Having passed the exams the previous July he was entitiled to study for a year at an approved foreign university. Bunting, characteristically, had requested the as then unapproved University of Freiburg. There was some doubt about whether Bunting could study there and still sit his finals in 1923, but the application was granted on 15 December. The idea that the University of London, then barely eighty years old, and LSE at twenty-five or so, between them might *not* approve a course of study at one of the oldest universities in Europe may seem odd, especially when one considers Freiburg's outstanding reputation in the social sciences. No doubt the fact that Freiburg is in Baden-Württemberg had an effect on a still war-conscious establishment.

In June 1922 Bunting requested leave of absence again: 'My doctor has advised me not to use my eyes for reading and writing for about a week, and to spend all my time in the open air. I wish, therefore, to be excused from attending at the school during the present week, I enclose the doctors certificate.' The doctor's certificate, from M. M. Richards of 30 Guildford Street, London WC, is dated 12 June 1922: 'Mr Bunting is suffering from eye strain and should do no work for a few days.'

Evans' response is sympathetic, but puzzled: 'Thank you for your letter and medical certificate. I have given instructions for your absence from lectures to be excused. An application was, by the way, made at your request to the University last Autumn for leave of absence to be given to you to attend the University of Freiburg. This application was granted, but as you do not appear to have availed yourself of the Senate's permission I am wondering what the position is.'

So having been granted it, Bunting turned down the opportunity to study at Freiburg. He had attended just 137 out of 268 lectures in 1921–22 and he managed only one more term, Michaelmas 1922, at the London School of Economics before disappearing again.[32]

Bunting's student career reached a glorious climax in April 1923. On 17 April Evans politely enquired, 'I am informed that you did not attend any lectures at the School last term, and I am wondering what are your plans with regard to your Final Examination.'

By now Bunting's father was involved once again.[33] Thomas wrote from Jesmond, in that slightly hesitant, anxious voice ('almost essential') we may remember from Leighton Park days, on 26 April, that his son had,

> written asking my consent to his spending the next six months in France & Germany instead of in London. Would you be kind enough to advise me on the subject?
>
> My son's final examination is in October this year, & it is almost essential that he should get his degree then. I am anxious he should do nothing to militate against this. If, under these circumstances, you think the residence in France & Germany is the wisest (or even a wise) course I shall agree to it. But I am anxious first to have your views, & shall be indebted to you if you will let me have them.

Too late. Bunting struck first. He wrote to Evans' secretary, Mrs Mair, on 23 April 1923 from the Grand Hôtel de l'Univers in Rue Grégoire de Tours, Paris 6e:

> I have abandoned my intention of getting the B.Sc. Econ: I am now attempting to earn my living in Paris. If any part of my fees is returnable, please send it to me here.
>
> My reasons for abandoning the course are:
> (I) It interfered with my pursuit of literature.
> (II) It did not seem to lead to any secure employment.
> (III) It ceased to interest me for its own sake.
> (IV) It appeared (to me) to have turned several intelligent men into dullards, & I did not desire a similar fate.
>
> I am now seeking employment as a bargee.

Mrs Mair replied with a straight face on 26 April: 'Thank you for your letter of April 23rd. I am afraid that one of the regulations of the School is that fees are non-returnable and I cannot therefore return any part of the sessional fee paid by you in October.'

Bunting's course leader, Dr T. E. Gregory, replied to Thomas with characteristic early twentieth-century British restraint, informing him of Bunting's decision, summarising the whole tale and noting: 'as your son has not been here since Christmas I am not really in a position to say to what extent he is fit to go in for the examination, and in any case he seems himself un-anxious to sit'.

In October 1923 Lionel Robbins had dinner with a postgraduate student, Rajaram Narayan Vaidya, and Elizabeth Allen, the vice-president of the Students' Union. Vaidya told Robbins that Bunting had left London for Paris suddenly on 20 April, but Robbins already knew. Bunting had written to Robbins on 22 April to tell him where he was and that he had left unpaid debts to Jacques Kahane and Vaidya. He asked Robbins to take over the debt and pay the £2 to each of their friends as they were both 'very hard up'. Bunting expected to be able to repay Robbins by the middle of May. In fact the debt wasn't repaid until Bunting returned to London three years later.[34]

The final item in Bunting's student dossier is a reply from Evans to 'The Rt. Hon. Sidney Webb, M. P.' of 26 April 1926. Webb appears to have asked him for a reference for Bunting:

> I have your card regarding Mr. Basil Bunting. I have not seen or heard anything of this young man for three years, and he never sat for his degree examination. He came to the School in October 1919, but interrupted his course during that session in order to go to Russia to study conditions there. (He did not reach Russia, however, being intercepted and deported by the Norwegian Police Authorities for some passport troubles.) He settled down more or less steadily to work in January 1921, and passed his Intermediate. He then started to work for the Final Examination, but attended irregularly, appearing to lose interest in economic studies, and finally I received a letter from him in April 1923, which I have copied out as I think it will amuse you.
>
> It is a case in which I should find it very difficult myself to give a testimonial. Mr. Bunting had ability, I believe, but he did not attack his work at the School with real interest, and did not keep closely in touch with any member of the staff. His honours lecturer, Dr. Gregory, saw very little indeed of him.

Attached to this letter, in a handwritten note dated 26 April 1926 to Evans' secretary, is Bunting's London School of Economics epitaph: 'Mrs Mair. I don't know if you remember Basil Bunting – bearded & rather an oddity.'

Six hundred black-hearted villains

Although he didn't refer to it explicitly in *Descant on Rawthey's Madrigal*, in 1922 Bunting became Secretary to Major Harry Barnes MP. Barnes, a Coalition Liberal, had been elected at the age of forty-eight to the newly created constituency of Newcastle upon Tyne East in the so-called 'Coupon Election' of 14 December 1918.[35] Barnes had won with an impressive 23.4 per cent majority over the Labour Party candidate and he remained the constituency's MP until the 1922 election when he was ousted by Labour's Joseph Bell in an election that saw the Liberal parties heavily punished by the electorate for their internal divisions.[36]

There must have been a strong local reason for the former Commanding Officer of the 2nd Volunteer Battalion Northumberland Fusiliers, Major Harry Barnes, to take on as his assistant so locally notorious a conscientious objector as Basil Bunting. Either Bunting had made an outstanding impression on the military authorities at Fenham Barracks during his incarceration there, or there was a friends-and-family connection to Barnes. I think the former is unlikely.

During nearly four years as MP for Newcastle East Barnes made just four interventions in the House of Commons. Hansard gives a strong impression of the character and values of Bunting's first employer. His first contribution was during the debate on the King's Speech on 13 February 1919. William Brace, the Labour MP for another constituency that had been created for the 1918 election, Abertillery, had moved an amendment to add the following words to the end of the King's Speech: 'But regrets the absence of any mention of definite proposals for dealing with the present causes of industrial unrest and for securing, as regards wages and working hours, conditions of labour that will establish a higher standard of life and social well-being for the people.'[37] A serious industrial crisis had developed with strikes on the Clyde as well as in London and Belfast and Barnes' lengthy speech opposing the amendment shows him to be above all a Liberal loyalist.[38] He clearly understood working-class grievances but argued strongly for a solution to them that benefited British society as a whole by devolving the responsibility for finding it to the place where the grievance was being aired.[39] Barnes' later contributions show him to be a pragmatic Centrist. He argued against nationalising the railways in the same speech and five days later he supported a bill that temporarily gave the government emergency powers that would protect his 'rights as a private Member [as well as] the rights of the electors'.[40] His interventions on housing in March 1919 and the old age pension in June, as well as his publications on tax and housing show him to be particularly concerned with social issues as the country eased out of a devastating war. Devolution, the role of the state, the politics of a Conservative–Liberal coalition government, the publication of Graham Wallas' *The Great Society* in 1914 – it seems that Barnes and his colleagues were tackling issues that the British electorate has been led to believe are peculiarly modern.

Bunting clearly could have made no contribution to Barnes' Commons speeches and we know nothing of his work with the MP, but we can assume that the bulk of his activity supported the MP's social welfare preoccupations. Barnes was an architect by training and a property and tax expert. From 1910 to 1918 he had worked in the Valuation Department of the Inland Revenue and it is likely that the financially literate Bunting would have appealed to him. In his final year in parliament Barnes published his *Valuation & Revaluation for Poor Rate and Income Tax (Post War)* and *Housing: The Facts & The Future*. These almost criminally tedious volumes would have stretched Bunting's patience. If Bunting worked on these books, and he almost certainly did, it isn't surprising that he didn't see fit to mention it in *Descant on Rawthey's Madrigal*.[41] Bunting recalled the period without much warmth in 1969: 'I was young then and I imagined that members of Parliament were serious people. That must have been one of the worst parliaments of all time. Six hundred black-hearted villains. Not that I think that things have improved much.'[42] We have seen just how 'serious' Harry Barnes was. Bunting makes a political rather than autobiographical point here.

IN PARIS THERE IS NO ONE DULL, 1923–1924

Since Bunting was attending the London School of Economics, albeit sporadically, in the autumn of 1922 we must assume that he worked for Barnes while still technically a student. We don't know exactly when Bunting left Barnes' employment but Barnes lost his job at the election of 15 November 1922 and we can reasonably speculate that it was very shortly after that. In any event, as we have seen, Bunting left London for Paris on 20 April 1923 with no money and began 'the usual sort of adventures that young men have until Pound found me a job as one of [Ford Madox] Ford's young men for the time being'.[43] It seems that he quickly found some (badly) paid life-modelling work as he wrote to Lionel Robbins on 1 May:

> Unfortunately, Robbins, there is no trades union in this business. Individual bargains & don't they put it across the poor foreigners! This week I am doing 7 hours a day at one of the most respectable academies, for which I shall touch 80 francs at the end of the week, plus a subscription from the students. In England I could get 15/- a day for the same work. In America, a dollar an hour. Well, anyway, I've got nearly two months of this work, & I hope to learn in that time enough French to get a job on the barges. Paris – Lyons – Marseilles – & then I'll take a summer tramp somewhere or other.

This long letter continues with his early observations of life in Paris, including some rather unpleasant reflections on the local women. He was much more positive about café life, the food and wine, the language and, particularly, the waiters, 'Waiters are the glory of Paris. I set no limit to the admiration that may be legitimately paid to them.' The architecture of public buildings is 'hideous beyond anything I have ever seen', Notre Dame in particular needing 'breeches or some such wear to hide its external genitals'. Good French art was difficult to find; sanitation was inadequate; French morals were better than British in matters of money but hypocritical in matters of sex. Bunting found it particularly irritating, in view of the generally casual attitude to sex, that he was required to wear, when modelling before young girls, 'a pair of striped bathing drawers that stretch from knees to navel'. His chief delight in Paris was a Rabelaisian sign outside a café which showed a naked waiter 'walking between the tables, balancing three trays, one in each hand, & one on the end of his erect penis'.[44] He had been in Paris for just ten days but he had formed a view.

The modelling work was precarious. He told Robbins that he was 'out of work till October. Models are as thick as dust in the Montparnasse cafés now because all the artists have gone away for the summer & the schools are closed.' He was hoping to find work 'stevedoring or portering at the markets', and he had developed some new complaints. The views (excepting that from the Pont du Carrousel at sunrise) were ordinary; the revues 'much over-rated'; the women (again) even worse than American women; the people 'mostly dull'. 'Still,' he told Robbins, 'I like Paris, & don't intend to leave it. It is deuced comfortable.' It could have been more comfortable if he had accepted a 'fine offer – new suits, 2000 francs and a voyage in central Europe to become bugger to an entertaining old gentleman, but I turned him down. That was financial folly. Still, I value my liberty, and buggery is a profession in which one works twenty-four hours per day.' He had already met Pound at this point: 'Pound entertains me. So does Nina Hamnett.'[45]

He found some work charring and tutoring 'to a lovely girl of fourteen – I wish it had been a permanent job – a ravishing Juliette!'[46] But it wasn't. In the summer of 1923 Bunting decamped to Bourron-Marlotte, about two miles from the artists' colony at Grèz-sur-Loing, to stay with a 'pleasant but dull old boy, who gives me very little time to write or think'. The dull old boy was the English artist and art collector Arthur Heseltine, uncle of the musician Peter Warlock (Philip Heseltine) with whom Bunting was to have a fine time in London's Fitzrovia a few years later. He wrote to J. J. Adams that before he left Paris he had discovered that 'most of the "artistic" bunch of Montparnasse are bores'.[47] 'France,' he observes, 'is traditionally the home of wit. I suppose the government, true to the motto "Egalité", serves out the available wit all round, & the separate portions are not enough to go very far.' He is moved to a sudden burst of apparently impromptu satire:

> In Paris there is no one dull,
> No one a block-head or a fool.
> Wit is the birth-right of the masses.
> Wit sparkles from the dotard's glasses;
> Wit in the maiden's tongue resides
> And – hidden somewhere else besides;
> Wit is the basis of their laws;
> Wit opens every Frenchman's doors,
> And every woman's legs (the whores!)
> And all the visitors are witty
> In the gay intellectual city.
>
> Perhaps you wouldn't notice it.
> They do not always show their wit –
> Their conversations are often boring –
> Their faces, too, are reassuring,
> Placid & flat, debauched & bleary.
> Their deeds & thoughts & looks are dreary.
> Their learning is not evident.
> Their work is heavy, tho' well-meant,

Both flatulent and constipated,
Pompous & pious & inflated;
Or else loose-bowelled and ecstatic;
Or too-much-laboured-empty-Attic,
Yet themselves aver they've wit
And that's strong evidence of it.

It's their reserve that makes them seem
Like other folks. Their leader's dream
It wise to exercise their wit
In private places where they – sit
And make a canvas for their art
On walls of places where they – .
Their privy walls are covered over
With witty words that stink to Dover.

But still they are not witty born
Nor yet by learning. They would scorn
To get wit in that prosy way.
They buy it with their carte d'indentité.

This rather enjoyable neo-Augustan squib didn't make it into Bunting's *Collected Poems*; indeed this may be its first publication in full.

A flabby lemon and pink giant

Ford Madox Ford arrived in Paris with Stella Bowen in September 1923, and that autumn the *transatlantic review* was born in slightly bizarre circumstances. Ford recalled that:

> my brother stood beside me on a refuge half-way across the Boulevard St Michel and told me that some Paris friends of his wanted me to edit a review for them. The startling nature of that coincidence with the actual train of my thoughts at the moment made me accept the idea even whilst we stood in the middle of the street. He mentioned names which were dazzling in the Paris of that day and sums the disposal of which would have made the durability of any journal absolutely certain. So we parted with the matter more than half settled, he going to the eastern pavement, I to the west.

Ten minutes after, I emerged from the rue de la Grande Chaumière on to the Boulevard Montparnasse. Ezra, with his balancing step, approached me as if he had been awaiting my approach. – He can't have been. – He said:

'I've got a wonderful contribution for your new review,' and he led me to M. Fernand Léger, who, wearing an old-fashioned cricketer's cap like that of Maître Montagnier [the *avocet*] of Tarascon, was sitting on a bench ten yards away. M. Léger produced an immense manuscript, left it in my hands and walked away … Without a word.[48]

Pound had by this time known Ford for fourteen years. The novelist May Sinclair had introduced them in 1909 when Pound was struggling to establish himself in literary London and Ford, then Ford Madox Hueffer, was editing the newly established *English Review* from a flat above a fishmonger in Holland Park. Ford was the grandson, on his mother's side, of the Pre-Raphaelite painter Ford Madox Brown. His mother had married a German music critic and Ford was happy to emphasise his German-ness until war broke out in 1914, at which point he rapidly changed his surname. Bunting was, as we shall see, struck by Ford's grotesque appearance, but he was by no means the first. Wyndham Lewis described Ford memorably as, 'a flabby lemon and pink giant, who hung his mouth open as though he were an animal at the Zoo inviting buns – especially when ladies were present. Over the gaping mouth damply depended the ragged ends of a pale lemon moustache … a typical figure out of a Conrad book – a caterer, or corn-factor, coming on board – blowing like a porpoise with the exertion – at some Eastern port.'[49] Ford was a notorious, and brilliant, fabricator of stories. The poet Richard Aldington described him as 'a sort of literary Falstaff' whose ability to exaggerate could spin out of control even with the most gullible audience. Aldington described a conversation at his parents' home:

The food and wine were good, and Ford, ever susceptible to the genial influences of the table and good fellowship, opened the flood-gates of his discourse and babbled o' the green fields – I should say, of celebrities – in his most imaginative strain. A scholarly recluse like my father … was an ideal subject for Ford's experiments. He sensed the virgin sucker at once. So we had the stories about Ruskin, and my uncle Gabriel and my aunt Christina [Ford never shied away from his Pre-Raphaelite connections]; the Conrad and James stories; the story of the abbé Liszt's concert and how Queen Alexandra took the beautiful infant Ford on her knees and kissed him; the 'old Browning' stories, and the Swinburne stories; gradually working back through the 19th century. My father was swimming in bliss, although once or twice he looked a little puzzled. And then Ford began telling how he met Byron. I saw my father stiffen ... [50]

Pound and Ford became firm friends. Ford published Pound's sestina, 'Sestina: Alteforte', in the *English Review* as May Sinclair had suggested, giving him his first break in literary London.

Pound repaid the favour in Paris by providing Ford and the *transatlantic review* with a deranged White Russian sub-editor, one E. Séménoff,[51] who was immediately convinced that Ford was a Russian agent, and, as his private secretary, Basil Bunting, 'an English Conscientious Objector, an apparently mild, bespectacled student. He too was starving.' By that evening Ford possessed 'all the machinery of a magazine – sub-editor, secretary, contributions, printers, subscribers [...] It was as if I had been in one of those immense deserts inhabited by savages who have unknown methods of communication over untold distances.'[52] The *transatlantic review*, a pivotal instrument of literary modernism, was launched just three months later in December 1924 (though dated January 1925). The contents list of the two volumes reads like a roll call of modernism, with poems by H. D., F. S. Flint, William Carlos Williams, E. E. Cummings (in upper case guise) and two of Pound's Cantos; a serialised novel by Conrad (with Ford) and stories by John Dos Passos and Jean Rhys; letters from H. G. Wells, Pound and T. S. Eliot; the score of a sonata by George Antheil and a song by Erik Satie; reproductions of paintings and drawings by Braque, Gwen John, Man Ray, Picasso, Nina Hamnett and Brancusi; essays by Gertrude Stein, Paul Valéry, Havelock Ellis and Djuna Barnes; work in progress from Joyce, Conrad, Jean Cocteau and Hemingway. Ford memorably described the milieu in Paris as the *transatlantic review* was born:

> Paris gyrated, seethed, clamoured, roared with the Arts. Painters, novelists, poets, composers, sculptors, batik-designers, decorators, even advanced photographers, so crowded the boulevards that you could not see the tree-trunks. They came from Tokio, they came from Petrograd; they poured in from Berlin, from Constantinople, from Rio de Janeiro; they flew in locust hordes from Spokane, from Seattle, from Santa Fé, from all the states and Oklahoma. If you had held up and dropped a sheet of paper on any one of the boulevards and had said: 'I want a contribution,' a thousand hands would have torn you to pieces before it had hit the ground ... [53]

All this, of course, was happening at the same time as that distinct strain of Parisian Dada was tearing itself apart. In 1923 Paris Dada was effectively dead and was replaced in 1924 with its more portentous younger sibling, André Breton's Surrealism.[54] Bunting knew many of the Surrealists, without ever having been particularly influenced by them, 'I just enjoyed the liveliness about the place and tried to take my part in it.'[55] Although he acknowledged that in his 'earliest poems … you'll find many places I think where the sound is underlined by purely Surrealistic words'. The closing couplet of his 1925 poem 'Villon' is surely one such:

> How can I sing with my love in my bosom?
> Unclean, immature and unseasonable salmon.[56]

Harriet Monroe, the editor of *Poetry*, was one of many who were confused by these lines. In November 1930 Bunting wrote from Brooklyn to praise her stewardship of *Poetry* and to express hope that he would be able to meet her in New York City before he had to leave at the end of the following February.

> On a postcard which followed me here from Italy you ask me 'Why salmon?' It would be easy to answer why not? But though I am shy of giving partial explanations which often seem to mislead people, which is probably worse than leaving them in the dark, I will say that by line 180 odd I have been angling a long time for a very big fish and only landed something for which the Board of Fisheries formula seems an exact and fitting description.[57]

At twenty-three Bunting found himself, albeit briefly, at the epicentre of an intellectual earthquake that changed the artistic landscape for ever:

> It was the strangest type of set-up you can imagine. One young man after another performed the same functions, oh, for many years … You did all sorts of things. I acted as assistant-editor, and sub-editor, and various other things for the *transatlantic review*, which he was starting. I also bathed the baby, and answered the telephone. I corrected the proofs and made various alterations of my own – some of them with and some of them without his knowledge. I changed a few words in a Ford–Conrad novel which I was reading the proofs of at that time too. Nobody troubled … What else did I do? Chiefly I kept him company.[58]

It has only recently emerged that Bunting played an important part in the shaping of Ford's *Parade's End*. He told Gael Turnbull that he 'helped correct the proofs of the first book of the *Parade's End* sequence. Ford had some sort of verbal tic, ending sentences with the same word. B. had crossed this out through the whole ms. At first FMF seemed upset. Then sat counting them, up to 40 or more. Then let B. finish.'[59]

Bunting stayed with Ford and Stella Bowen for a short time. Bowen recalled that Bunting, a 'nice young man ... slept in a damp, little store-room beyond our kitchen and was kept on the run by Ford for eighteen hours a day. He endured much in the cause of Literature.'[60] When Ford, Bowen and daughter Julie moved Bunting moved with them into, if anything, even more unlovely accommodation, 'The studio was immense. It had neither gas nor electricity, and its kitchen was a black underground dungeon, reached by a perilous flight of narrow, slippery stone steps. There was a gallery at one end, filled with stacked canvases, and here the unfortunate Bunting had his shakedown.'[61]

Ford described Bunting to the British short story writer and poet, A. E. Coppard, in preparation for Coppard's visit to Paris, as 'a dark youth with round spectacles, in a large Trilby hat and a blue trench coat with belt who shall hold up a copy of the TRANSATLANTIC REVIEW towards passengers arriving at the barrier and smile'.[62]

Ford was by no means immediately impressed by Bunting. The day after the momentous meeting with his brother in the middle of the Boulevard St Michel Ford asked Pound where his 'Conscientious Objector was. He ought to have brought those MSS. round to me that morning. Ezra said: "Oh, he ... That'll be all right ... You mustn't keep his nose too close to the grindstone ... He's not used to discipline. But he'll be invaluable ... That's what he'll be ... Only your excremental *Review* will be in the gutter tomorrow ... "'[63]

Ford had taken on at the same time Ernest Hemingway as a second sub-editor (alongside the Russian lunatic who was able to find communists breeding in every drawer), having been persuaded by Pound that the young man shadow boxing in Ford's office was, in fact, the 'finest prose stylist in the world'.[64] Bunting quickly found himself in jail, having converted into alcohol the entire advance that Ford had given him against his salary as, according to Ford, he 'embarked on a career of martial adventure'.[65] Ford's account of Bunting's adventure is a minor comic masterpiece. As we shall see, its surreal prison scene sits underneath Bunting's first great poem, 'Villon'. Never referred to by name in Ford's memoir, *It Was the Nightingale*,

Bunting is only ever the 'Conscientious Objector' or the 'bespectacled student'. Bunting clearly threw himself fully into the spirit of the times:

> The ten shillings or so that I had given that studious and bespectacled young man as earnest money had proved his undoing. He had been really near starvation, having been earning what living he did earn as an artist's model. So, instead of spending the money on a square meal he laid it out on the normal products of the Dôme. That is not a good thing to do.
>
> When he got home he found that his concierge's lodge had been moved to the other side of the passage: its furniture was quite different and the concierge was a new man. In his own room an aged gentleman was sitting on the bed. The aged gentleman threw him down the stairs. The kindly *agent* to whom he told this unusual story patted him on the back and recommended him to go home, as a good, spectacled student should.
>
> The young man walked round the block and tried again. Things were worse. The strange concierge blocked the way. The young man knocked him down ... The aged gentleman was still on the bed. This time he held a gun. Outraged by their offences against the laws of hospitality the young man smashed some windows, defiled the staircase, yelled at the top of his voice, and got into bed with the concierge's wife.
>
> When the *agents* arrived in great numbers the young man made a spirited attempt to bite off the nose of the sergeant in charge of them. He was carried, spread-eagled, to the Santé. Next morning a kindly magistrate told him he had acted very wrongly. Poets have a certain licence, but his deeds were not covered by that indulgence. The concierge pleaded for him; the old gentleman pleaded for him; the sergeant, who was a poet too, if a Corsican, asserted his conviction that the prisoner was an excellent young man. He had indulged too freely in the juice of the grape – but to indulge freely in wine was in France an act of patriotism.
>
> He was ordered to pay frs. 15 for injuries to the aged gentleman; frs. 12 for the broken window; frs. 5 for the cleaning of the staircase and frs. 9 to the wife of the concierge, all these with *sursis* – the benefit of the First Offenders Act. He expected to go free and unmulcted.
>
> Alas, a much more dire offence was alleged against him. He had been found to be in possession of a prohibited arm! The weapon was a penknife, three inches long. But the blade could be fixed. It was one of the Scandinavian, barrel-shaped affairs that some gentlemen use for cleaning their finger-nails. The unfortunate young man was remanded in custody.

The kindly sergeant did his best to lighten the irksomeness of the young man's captivity. He visited him in his cell, declaimed to him his own *vocéros* and other poems to the glory of the vendetta. He listened with attention to the poems of the young man and to the music of Mr Pound, who had brought his bassoon and rendered on it the airs to which the poems of Arnaut Daniel had been sung. That sergeant even brought half-bottles of thin wine and slices of the sausage called *mortadella*. With this he fed the captive. It is good to be a poet in France.

The Higher Court before whom the case was tried was less placable. The poor young man had just, when Ezra visited me, been sentenced to a fine of frs. 4, with frs. 66 for costs and, it having been discovered that as a conscientious objector he had been in prison in England; he was sentenced to expulsion from France: − Ezra's proposition now was that I should pay the fine and approach the authorities with assurance of the excellence of the young man's poetry and of my conviction that he would not further offend ... I had never read the young man's poetry and I had only seen him for ten minutes at the Dôme, so I knew little about his character. But I perjured myself all right. I did it rather reluctantly, for I dislike the militant sides of the characters of conscientious objectors and, having once seen a man's ear bitten off by an American trooper, I felt some distaste at the idea that my own nose might leave my face between the teeth of an English poet ... Eventually, on the assurance that the young man was in my service, the authorities decided that as long as he kept that job he might stay in Paris.[66]

Pound recalled an interchange of his own with the 'kindly sergeant', 'the officer learning that I was a man of letters, and concerned with the welfare of another man of letters, produced from his pocket a poem of his own, with the lady's name running in acrostic down the initial letters, and when I had read it said in a tone of apology, "Ça plait beaucoup aux dames."'[67]

We should register the 'definitive' version of this story that Bunting gave to Carroll F. Terrell at Orono in 1980, although Terrell freely admits that even this account is 'at best impressionistic' as he didn't write it until several hours after he heard it:

A friend of mine had received a hundred pounds which in those days was quite a lot of money so he invited me along with another friend on a party to celebrate. We went out on the town. Around midnight the other friend gave up and left, but we kept on drinking and celebrating until quite late in the morning until he gave up. After that, I had nothing to do but to go home. The

Paris streets laid out in the time of the Empire often had four corners which looked exactly alike, so that my hotel on one corner looked like the one on the next corner. My taxi driver drove up in front of one which I took to be mine. I got in and found my room but the damn key wouldn't work! That got me quite frustrated and furious. Finally, I had to relieve myself on the wall of the stairs, but I went back and tried to knock the door down. Eventually the noise aroused the concierge whose husband appeared. He'd never seen me before so concluded I was a burglar who had broken in. I'd never seen him before, and couldn't imagine what he was protesting about or why he should be trying to kick me out of my own hotel. Finally, he threatened to call the cops if I wouldn't leave quietly. I invited him to do so and while he was gone jumped into bed with his wife. She was fairly old but made up for a lack of youth by a whole lot of enthusiasm. Imagine my chagrin and surprise, right at the height of my own enthusiasm, to be dragged out of bed by the police, who for some mysterious reason wanted to take me to jail. Well, now, as an innocent man, it was my duty to refuse to go. I was outnumbered, but while they were trying to restrain me, I managed to give one of them a good swift kick in the pants. In the end, they overpowered me. By this time I could be charged with a number of crimes: minor ones such as disturbing the peace, but also serious ones such as resisting arrest and what the French call 'rebellion'.

The next day I was herded into the *grande salle* along with a flock of petty thieves, pickpockets, prostitutes, pimps, and other assorted characters. I happened to have a copy of Villon in my pocket, so while waiting my turn, I sat on a bench reading him, quite aware of the ironies. For Villon himself, centuries before, had sat in the same salon and waited his turn before the magistrate. Here it was that Ezra found me. He was always interested in helping young writers in trouble; but I think it was seeing me reading Villon that really got him. After he heard my story, he rushed away to get lawyers and money or whatever to get me off and see justice done.

The case came to trial. But since a key witness in the prosecution's case was the wife of the hotel keeper, I was saved. She refused to say anything against me or support any of the story the police were telling. She told them that I was a very nice, polite, young man and she hadn't seen me doing any horrible things they were accusing me of. Thus, I was only sentenced to two weeks in jail. But it was probably lucky things happened the way they did. If the hotel keeper hadn't come and got me away from the door I was hell-bent to break down, I'd have doubtless been killed. I found out afterwards that sitting in the middle of the room facing the door was an old man with a loaded pistol. If I had come through it, he had every intention of shooting to kill.[68]

The 23-year-old Bunting was probably feeling pretty sorry for himself. As he said at a reading in London over fifty years later: 'I suppose young men are attracted to people like Villon. Villon was very sorry for himself and young men are all sorry for themselves, and I suppose I must have been too about 1925.'[69]

Ford's account of the offence differs from Bunting's only in minor detail, but their description of the trial and sentence could hardly be more different. In any event Bunting's tenure at the *transatlantic review* was short-lived. He worked on the first issue only and was replaced in early January 1924 by Ivan Beede, who 'wore large, myopic spectacles in front of immense dark eyes, wrote very good short stories about farming in the Middle West and boasted of his Indian blood'.[70] Ford's account of Bunting's departure beautifully captures the essence of both men:

> The conscientious objector had had to go. He had worked quite well till Christmas. I sent him to England to do some private work for me and to get a rest. Whilst there he discovered inside himself that I regarded him as an object of charity, and resigned his post in a letter of great expletive violence. I had never regarded him as an object of charity, but as one who was by turns quite useful and a great nuisance. As he had had nowhere to go to after he left the Santé, I had taken him to live with me. His salary was rather small, so he was really under no obligation to me … He was eventually arrested and conducted to the frontier. I regretted it, because he appeared to be a young man of real talent. He has since pursued the career of a poet and savant in a country bordering on France … [71]

Certainly Ford was already looking to replace Bunting by the end of December.[72]

Although it is difficult to reconcile the 'nice young man' of Bowen's memory with the psychotic nose biter of Ford's there is something about Ford's style that suggests he relished embellishing this story. JC described this feeling well in the *Times Literary Supplement*:

> Ford is a loquacious writer, and there is often an air of untrustworthiness when he's about. In a yellowing article from *The Times* pasted into [a second-hand copy of Ford's *Joseph Conrad: A personal remembrance*] … we found this: 'Almost everything Ford wrote about Conrad has a false ring, even when it may be asserted to be the literal truth'. Having devoured the book that very evening, our impression was the opposite: 'almost everything' had the ring of truth, even when implausible.[73]

I too take 'almost everything' in Ford's account of Bunting's Parisian escapade to be essentially true. In his (possible) embellishments reside the essential Bunting.

Bunting liked Ford, although he wasn't sure that the feeling was mutual. In 1930 William Carlos Williams invited Bunting to a function that Ford was to attend in New York but Bunting was 'not so sure that Ford would be at all pleased to see me again'.[74] He complained in a letter to Bernard Poli that all Ford's biographers had 'missed the point':

> what's it matter if he told lies? He was a writer of fiction. What does matter is his kindness to young men and men in distress, his readiness to talk to them at length, without being patronising or pedantic, his willingness to consider everything, the tolerance in his frivolity, the care for living English, the generosity, the fun. Ford did a great deal of good one way or another, and has never been given full credit for it. He was a good poet and a good novelist too. To dwell on what was comical or exasperating in him is to mislead a generation that cannot meet him.[75]

In *Descant on Rawthey's Madrigal* he remembered his time as Ford's companion:

> He liked eating and drinking expensively and well and he wanted somebody to talk to meanwhile. Now Ford may have been the biggest liar you like. No doubt he was quite a considerable one, but he was always exceedingly entertaining and the untruths were there not for the sake of untruth but for the sake of turning a mediocre story into a very good one. To feed in his company while he talked was always a pleasure. I'd say he was a kind-hearted man, and I'm fairly sure that the root reason behind a large party he gave that year was not so much that he was anxious to entertain his literary friends as that he thought it a good opportunity for me to dance with the daughter of one of his American colleagues whom I suddenly had a fancy for. Unfortunately he didn't ask me beforehand whether I could dance! It was rather a failure.[76]

Nearly fifty years later Bunting edited a selection of Ford's poems and without claiming too much for them pointed carefully at some of their attractions. He noted Ford's muscular approach to writing: 'Ford sweated up his halliards like a sailor. He took a fresh purchase and another swig again and again till the sail's last wrinkle was smoothed out.'[77] In another way, though, Bunting used Ford's ambiguities to reinforce his own tirelessly offered message about the importance of imperfection of meaning in poetry: 'Some vagueness is inherent in his subjects; words – and ears – flinch from some precisions. There are explorations that can never end in discovery, only in willingness to rest content with an unsure glimpse through the mists, an uncertain sound of becks we shall never taste: approximations.' [78] At this point Bunting's introduction changes direction abruptly and, unusually, to illustrate the character of the man rather than the work of the artist. As he had in his letter to Bernard Poli he praised Ford's kindness, and having established Ford's human credentials Bunting turns on Hemingway, who had caricatured Ford ruthlessly in *Fiesta, Or the Sun Also Rises* and particularly in *A Moveable Feast*, with a burst of sustained, cold fury:

> Among the young men who owed Ford thanks, few owed more than Ernest Hemingway ... But his sketch of Ford in *A Moveable Feast* ... [is a] deliberately assembled [lie] to damage the reputation of a dead man who had left no skilled close friend to take vengeance; a lie cunningly adjusted to seem plausible to simple people who had never known either Ford or Hemingway and to load his memory with qualities disgusting to all men and despicable to most.[79]

How Ford would have relished the fact that half a century later his bespectacled student had taken revenge on his behalf against the shadow-boxing bully whose literary career had benefited so greatly from Ford's generous patronage.

As we have seen Ford recalled that Bunting left the *transatlantic review* because while he was in England he decided that Ford regarded him as an 'object of charity'. In a radio interview in 1974 Bunting remembered events differently. On the one hand Ford was:

> the most friendly and tolerant boss you could possibly have. I occupied a room on one side of the studio, Ford and his wife were in rooms the other side. But if I turned up at breakfast in the morning with an unannounced and unintroduced young lady Ford would never turn a hair, merely shout that we wanted four eggs or something like that. Altogether life could have been very comfortable. I left for a reason which it is a little difficult to explain. The great drawback to working with Ford at all times was that he was overcome so easily by little worries. Small things would go wrong, they would pile up and then instead of doing a little general cursing and getting on with it as most folk do, Ford would weep on your shoulder. It's very uncomfortable for a young man of twenty-two to have someone a generation older than himself and very heavy weeping on his shoulder and in the end I couldn't put up with it and moved on.[80]

One of the reasons for Bunting's abrupt departure from Paris was probably embarrassment. Bunting expanded on the dance at the American Embassy in a letter to Carolyn Burke, biographer of the poet and artist, Mina Loy, written in July 1980. Loy frequently visited Ford for tea and Bunting fell 'at least half in love' with her. He was struck by her 'dark, melancholy beauty that didn't seem to sentimentalise itself', a beauty ('Oval face, thin eyebrows wide of the eyes') that he celebrated in his Ode 17, 'Now that sea's over that island'. Loy was nearly twenty years older than Bunting but 'not only did they share an affinity … but Mina let him imagine that she enjoyed his attentions'.[81] Ford, as we have seen, frequently sent Bunting to the Gare de Lyon to greet his friends and visitors and on one occasion he was sent there to meet Loy's sixteen-year-old daughter Joella with a bouquet of flowers on her return from holiday:

> From then on, the young man found himself 'split, as it were, between mother and daughter.' Bunting took every opportunity to call, until it occurred to him that Ford had concocted the plan as a way of ridding Mina 'of my altogether too young attentions. I felt as much attached to her as ever,' he went on, 'but it was Joella I now wanted to make up to.' Next Ford threw a party intended, Bunting thought, to give him the occasion to woo Joella. But the young man, who could not dance, spent the evening glowering at her partner, Tristan Tzara. Mina tried to make up for the evening by inviting him to a gala at the American Embassy. 'I had had enough drink already to set free my taste for mischief,' Bunting recalled in a letter that must be quoted at length: 'When I came in some American lady, goodness knows who, introduced me to a very august looking female sitting with another like her in full evening regalia with a very cutaway bodice. She was said to be the wife of the missionary bishop of somewhere or other. As she held out her hand for it to be kissed in the French fashion I reached beyond it and scooped her exuberant bosom out of its corsage. Scandal. She, however, seemed to like it, set about drinking a great deal, and was presently doing cartwheels on the dancing floor. The scandal of the bishopess (or whatever you call her) was at its worst just as Mina Loy and Joella arrived.' Joella told him to leave, and he slunk off 'in disgrace'. When sober, he was so worried that Mina and Joella were angry that he left Paris without saying goodbye.[82]

This incident is recalled in the closing couplet of Bunting's ode to Mina Loy:

> Very likely I shall never meet her again
> or if I do, fear the latch as before.

In an uncharacteristic departure from his usual line Bunting threw a little light on his 'adventures', particularly the troubles with the Parisian authorities, in a letter to Eric Mottram, written more than fifty years after the events:

> When I got drunk with Boris de Kruschev and locked up in the Conciergerie to be tried for a long list of miscellaneous offences I was alleged to have committed, but chiefly for kicking a cop, Ezra, looking for a chess opponent, missed me from the café and looked around, most generously getting me a (damn bad) lawyer and so forth. That was just before I joined Ford Madox Ford on the *transatlantic review* (no capitals, which upset the critics). The dungeon of the Conciergerie was, probably still is, the same in which Villon landed for burglary, and they stuff everybody in there who is waiting to be tried, whores, thugs, tax-dodgers, pickpockets, all higgledy piggledy. Ezra never stopped marvelling that I was there, with a tattered copy of the Grant Testament in my pocket. I knew a great deal of it by heart then, and I think that's what first drew EPs attention to my merits, if any. Amusing, afterwards, to have been in there with Grosse Margot and the rest of them.[83]

Bunting is misremembering or romaticising a little here. He wouldn't have needed a lawyer before he joined Ford. An account in a 1982 interview is probably closer: 'I was in Paris with no money, and I used to play chess in a café with a lot of Poles and other oddments about the place, and Ezra wanting a game of chess, came in. Having tried a couple of Poles, he also tried me, and we became quite friendly.'[84]

Closer still, perhaps, is an account written in a letter to James Leippert nine years after the event:

> I met him [Pound] in Paris about ten years ago playing a swashbuckling kind of chess. I believed then, as now, that his 'Propertius' was the finest of modern poems. Indeed, it was the one that gave me the notion that poetry wasn't altogether impossible in the XX century. So I made friends. I was then digging the roads outside Paris for a living. I got locked up for a colossal drunk. It was Ezra who discovered me, still half blank with something approaching D.T.s, and perjured himself in the courts to try to get me off. When I came out of quod, and was working as a barman at the Jockey, he introduced me to Ford Madox Ford and I became sub. and sec. to the Transatlantic Review.[85]

In his last letter to Mottram Bunting followed his tale of his encounter with the Parisian authorities with an extraordinary meditation:

Jails and the sea, Quaker mysticism and socialist politics, a lasting unlucky passion, the slums of Lambeth and Hoxton – these have had some effect, I think; but all the reviewers are likely to notice is that my verse has a rather superficial resemblance to Ezra's. One man, one only, in the quarter century the stuff has been in print, one only, has noticed my manipulations and adaptations of Greek metres. No one, until I proclaimed it myself, perceived Horace somewhere in my background. Condensation must be due to Ezra because he made use of my pun: not, of course, to Dante. And the word Wordsworth has only come into their writings since I practically put it there for them. I don't want to minimise my debt to Ezra nor my admiration for his work, which should have 'influenced' everybody, but my ideas were shaped before I met him and my technique I had to concoct for myself. And, back to condensation: I could never get Ezra to do what I thought enough of it. I've usually more to the page than he has. And the silly bugger despised Wordsworth. Oh well! More shreds for your waste paper basket.[86]

As we have seen, Bunting requested that the people he wrote to destroyed his letters. We should be deeply grateful that Mottram had the good taste not to shred this lyrical, passionate, monumental statement.

RAPALLO, 1924–1925

Bunting returned to Newcastle to find his father desperately ill with what Bunting described as 'a particularly persistent & violent form of angina'. He described to Adams a harrowing encounter with Thomas during the previous week:

He was brought home in a taxi by his partner, after a very bad attack. He had another attack on the way home & then he lay on the sofa and had another. His face went a dirty grey colour, almost heliotrope, & it looked as though all the flesh had fallen off it & left just the skull & the skin. His eyes sank back into his head behind perpendicular black cliffs. There were huge deep lines where a normal man of sixty has wrinkles. He stared & stared at the back of the sofa & held tight to it. You know the Greco 'Agony in the Garden'? Greco knew how agony manifests itself but he was afraid of exaggerating & so he's very much understated it. My father was like that Christ, only far worse, far more intensely hurt. He couldn't speak – not for weakness, he was no weaker than usual, but for sheer agony. All of him concentrated on that burning pain, & the most dreadful fear in his expression ... I was also once locked up in a cell with a homocidal [*sic*] maniac who got a terrible fear at times that shone out of him like a flaming light, but it was not so terrible as the fear I saw in my father.[87]

There is horror in this account but little genuine affection, and yet when his father died Bunting 'read the whole of Hardy in three weeks to quiet my soul'.[88]

The problem was compounded by the fact that Bunting's mother was also ill with angina and that his sister was very busy at her own practice. Thomas' health improved sufficiently for Bunting to get away again after a couple of months in England. After another spell in jail in Genoa[89] he went to Rapallo to find Pound, who wasn't there. Bunting stayed on though and earned a living sailing boats carrying sand for construction from Sardinia to the Ligurian coast. This was his first experience of sailing, an activity that became a significant part of his life until the Second World War, after which he never went to sea again.[90] Bunting was one of those celebrated by Pound in Canto 23:

> And in the morning, in the Phrygian head-sack,
> Barefooted, dumping sand from their boat
> 'Yperionides! [91]

He learned how to handle 'the big lateen sails' of the sand boats before sailing 'a fair amount at Amalfi in a little lateen rig. Then I bought a boat on the beach near Rapallo – quite a large boat, 26 or 28 feet long I think, undecked, a heavily built fishing boat. Perfectly good once I'd repainted her. She'd looked pretty bad on the beach. I bought her for four pounds and sailed that for some years.'[92] He had bought the boat on the beach at Chiavari, ten kilometres or so down the coast from Rapallo, according to an interview in 1981, by which time it had grown a little: 'It was a great, heavy fishing boat, 32 feet long, half decked. It was fully rigged, good sails, good rope, wanting nothing but a lick of paint. It cost me £4. I suppose a similar boat today would cost me six or seven thousand at least now.'[93]

Pound and Bunting had been reunited in Rapallo by 12 March when Bunting 'just stopped by for tea' at Pound's apartment.[94] Bunting described his reunion with Pound in a letter to James Leippert: 'I climbed a mountain, and on top of the mountain, to my astonishment, Ezra appeared. So I saw more of him. He was busy writing his first opera, and I was busy with poems.'[95] Thirty-six years later this scene had collected some incidental detail:

One day I walked up the mountain. I had to walk in those days, there were no cable railways and no roads. I walked up the mule track and there was a little inn at the top. As I passed the inn someone rushed out of the doorway and began shouting, 'Bunting! Bunting!' And I looked around and there to my astonishment was Ezra Pound, followed almost immediately by Dorothy, running after me up the mountain.[96]

His father had encouraged in Bunting a love of walking and climbing, particularly in the Lake District. 'My father used to take me up to Capheaton sometimes and he knew some of the Swinburnes,' he told an interviewer in 1978.

We walked about the park and looked at the lake and so forth and it's just chance that when I was a small boy Swinburne never had met me. He'd do what he would always have done, what he did to all the children on Putney Heath: he'd pat me on the head and present me with half a crown. And that would have been very interesting to me because when he was a little boy of eight or nine, as I, he was taken to Grasmere where he met an old gentleman who patted him on the head, but did not offer him half a crown – he was too frugal – and that was William Wordsworth![97]

According to Victoria Forde Thomas Bunting was:

an experienced climber ... and saw to it that Basil at ten began climbing big boulders. Walking and climbing were sometimes serious undertakings, and at twelve a friend was giving climbing lessons to Basil who remembers him as 'occasionally a little impatient, what the hell'. With a shake of his head, Bunting described to me the simple preparations for climbing in those years, relishing the story about the time that his father and a group of climbers struggled to the top of a mountain in Switzerland only to find a shepherd there, calmly eating his lunch and enjoying the view. However, as late as 1982 he still shuddered to remember the time he was alone, climbing in the fog, when he slipped to a chalk ledge between two steep sides about a thousand feet from his starting point at the base.[98]

Bunting was prone to exaggeration, if not outright invention, but in a sense even those of his stories that we might not take entirely at face value are important in building a picture of the man and the poet. Even if some of the detail is embellished all his tales *could* have described events as they happened, and the fact that he tells them says something about the way he wanted the world to see him. That anyone would climb a mountain in fog, alone and in a place where it is possible to fall down a steep ledge is beyond the understanding of this writer at least, but that doesn't make it impossible.

Forde continues with another Bunting walking story, this one perfectly plausible:

> Though he had difficulty walking without a cane during the last few years of his life, Basil spoke to me proudly of the vigour which until those final years had kept him walking about twenty miles every afternoon. Even in 100° heat he walked daily in Persia, and once in 129° without a hat. In this connection he told me about Ezra Pound in Italy inviting him to take 'a long walk'. He laughed at himself, remembering that after his extensive preparations, Ezra was satisfied with only one or two turns around the promenade, about two and a half miles.[99]

There is, of course, a long history of writers composing on long, solitary walks. Apart from Wordsworth one thinks of Rousseau, Mary Wollstonecraft, Virginia Woolf and, more recently, the German writer W. G. Sebald. Bunting, however, seems to have been a more gregarious walker. We know that he enjoyed walking holidays in the 1930s. Matthew Kahane offers a story that has some quintessential Bunting in it:

> I have heard my father [Jacques Kahane] say that he was a friend of Basil Bunting, I take it in the 1930s, and that they went on at least one walking holiday together, I believe in Wiltshire and the area of Salisbury Plain, during which they quarrelled bitterly over which of them was to carry the bar of soap they shared in his rucksack ... The point of this particular story, in my father's retelling of it, was that even good friends, of open and straightforward character, could quarrel about some trivial matter when it was taken past some point – and that we (my sister and I) should never allow some trivial point to spoil a friendship.[100]

Jacques Kahane, 'universally loved and never to be sufficiently lamented', was a significant influence on Lionel Robbins' life. The two had been introduced by Bunting during their first year at the LSE and became great friends, travelling together to Salzburg where 'the vagaries of the exchange in hyper-inflation permitted us, poor students, to buy front-row stalls and sit just behind Richard Strauss conducting the Mozart cycle at the first festival'.[101]

The 'mountain' on which Bunting re-encountered the Pounds was almost certainly Mount Rosa which rears up nearly 700 metres behind Rapallo. It is difficult to believe that after so steep a climb Bunting passed up the opportunity for refreshment as he reached the Hotel Ristorante Montallegro on the right-hand side of the shady ilex-lined path that approaches the Sanctuary of Montallegro, but we must take his story at face value. He described the terrain himself as 'steep and rugged ... a mountain with no path at all and the devil to climb'.[102] It was one of the Pounds' favourite hikes and when the funicular to which Bunting refers opened in August 1934 Pound refused to use it.[103]

Weeping oaks and sequent graces

Two short poems survive from this period. 'Weeping oaks grieve, chestnuts raise' and 'Farewell ye sequent graces' were written in 1924 and became the first two odes in 'The First Book of Odes' in Bunting's *Collected Poems*. The first appears to take the opening of Eliot's *The Waste Land* as its point of departure:

> Weeping oaks grieve, chestnuts raise
> mournful candles. Sad is spring
> to perpetuate, sad to trace
> immortalities never changing.[104]

Bunting linked music and poetry from the outset of his career. He described his longer poems, with the exception of 'Chomei at Toyama', as sonatas. The odes, however, reach back to choral elements in classical Greek drama. In his first collection, *Redimiculum Matellarum*, which appeared in 1930, and where 'Weeping oaks grieve, chestnuts raise' was called 'Sad Spring', he referred to them as 'carmina' so it is clear that he intended them to be seen (and read) as songs. 'Weeping oaks grieve, chestnuts raise' is a world-weary song. Victoria Forde observes that it is difficult 'to believe this youthful ennui, especially for readers who know that at this time he is 24, poor but hale and hearty, and enjoying life with Pound and Yeats in Rapallo. Even if he is looking back at the chestnut trees of Paris, it still seems a pose ... preserved for the melody of some of its lines.'[105] There is indeed a laconic pose struck in some of these lines:

Weary on the sea
for sight of land
gazing past the coming wave we
see the same wave

'Farewell ye sequent graces' reached back to nineteenth-century wistfulness:

Farewell ye sequent graces
voided faces still evasive!
Silent leavetaking and mournful
as nightwanderings
in unlit rooms ...

but 'Weeping oaks grieve, chestnuts raise' is more powerful, closing with a celebration that is far from melancholy, reminiscent in tone of Siegfried Sassoon's beautiful 'Everyone Sang' written five years previously:

drift on merciless reiteration of years;
descry no death; but spring
is everlasting
resurrection.

A sense of release similar to Sassoon's emerges from this studied lament about a world that is fated to recreate itself perpetually. In fact the poem is not about Paris, it is about London's Regent's Park. At a reading in London in 1980 Bunting said of 'Weeping oaks grieve, chestnuts raise' that:

This is the oldest fraction that I've preserved. It's only a little bit of what was a poem; the rest of it was too dreadful to preserve at all. And really it concerns Regent's Park. You know, I used to live just round the corner from Regent's Park, in a little garret, and I was often there, and that avenue of horse chestnut trees is in the spring so magnificent. I was in love with Regent's Park and once wrote a poem to say quite falsely that it was the finest park in all Europe and all the rest of it. It had to be abolished, that poem, it wasn't good enough, but I did feel very strongly about Regent's Park.[106]

LONDON, 1925–1928

Bunting returned to England around the time of his father's death in February 1925. He told Pound that he would never have left Rapallo if his father hadn't 'begun to die'.[107] Thomas' obituary in the *British Medical Journal* begins conventionally enough:

> The announcement of the sudden death of Dr. Bunting, on February 18th, has been received with deep regret by the medical profession of Newcastle and Tyneside. It was known to his intimate friends that his health had recently given cause for anxiety, owing to attacks of precordial pain, which were believed to be anginal. Some months ago he had taken a rest from his professional duties, but he had returned to work and was quietly carrying on when the blow fell.

Thomas' obituarist goes on, however, to offer some personal observations of a man who was clearly an exceptional person as well as an outstanding medic:

> The writer of this note had the opportunity of reading the thesis which won this distinction [the Gold Medal at Edinburgh] for Dr. Bunting ... and was much impressed by the originality of the views therein expressed, many of which have since been accepted ... Eventually he took up the study of radiology and visited various important centres where x-ray work was being carried on, and he had already achieved considerable success in the practice of it when the war broke out; this gave him the opportunity he required. He was appointed radiologist to the Northumberland War Hospital at Gosforth. Those of us who were his colleagues have cause to remember his patience, his urbanity, and the great assistance he rendered to the visiting staff. Nothing seemed to be a trouble to him if he could be of service in clearing up a doubtful point in diagnosis.

Having established Thomas' sensitive professional side the obituary goes on to describe a man who generally quietly carried the day in spite of his progressive tendencies:

> Dr. Bunting was keenly interested in the politico-social movements of the times. A man of rather advanced views, he did not hesitate to express his opinions, but he never unpleasantly enforced these, nor did he disagreeably differ from an opponent. It was this circumstance which made him so beloved by all, and caused him to be chosen as the mouthpiece of the medical profession when disputable matters had to be considered by a joint body of the profession and insurance, health, or education authorities. At committee meetings on national insurance matters there was no one, quite independently of the subject under discussion and the divergent views expressed, who was

more carefully listened to than the subject of this memoir. He had a wonderful grasp of the intricacies of the Act, what it could and what it could not do, and as he invariably spoke from conviction the opinions he expressed carried great weight and were received with respect.[108]

We learn from Thomas' obituary in the *Lancet* that he had started his career with a short spell as asylum medical officer near Buxton, and that his work on the histology of lymph glands had won for him a Fellowship of the Royal Society of Edinburgh. In 1911 he had passed the degree of Bachelor of Hygiene and the Diploma of Public Health both with honours, at the University of Durham. The *Lancet*'s obituary also traces the source of Thomas' 'advanced' social views:

> Dr. Bunting was also interested in social questions, an interest which dated from his student days when he was associated with Prof. Patrick Geddes's work in founding the Town and Gown Association, for promoting students' sympathies in the welfare of the poor of Edinburgh.[109]

Popular and successful, Thomas was laid to rest in Old Jesmond Cemetery on 21 February 1925, just a few weeks before the Montague Colliery disaster of 30 March 1925, when water from a nearby pit flooded the mine, killing thirty-eight people. The medical profession attended Thomas' funeral in numbers and the various organisations with which he was connected were all represented: 'The British Medical Association was represented by Dr. R. A. Bolam. Dr. Bunting passed away at the comparatively early age of 57 years, before he had time to enjoy the fruits of the greater success which we all believed was in store for him. He left a widow, one son, and a daughter, who is in the medical profession.'[110] We learn a good deal more about Thomas from these notes than from anything the 'one son' wrote or said.

Bunting worked for a while as the British correspondent for *Rivista di Roma*, until he discovered 'that enterprising review hadn't the remotest intention of ever paying for its contributions'.[111] He didn't see Pound again for roughly another five years, but they exchanged letters every six months or so, and he never lost touch with Pound again, although their friendship was seriously tested by Pound's anti-Semitism in the 1930s.

He spent a week in May 1925 with the eccentric poet J. J. Adams and his lover, the artist Christabel Dennison, at their unhappy home in Primrose Hill in north London. Christabel's first impression was not positive. 'He has a horrible face,' she wrote in her diary on Sunday 11 May 1925. 'Heavy features, smooth & white with a farouche moustache, perpetual nervous smile. Speaks with a slow studied imitation of what they call the Oxford accent … I try to be a good hostess & not to show that I don't like his face … ' By the following day she was beginning to change her mind about her visitor: 'B is a good guest. He makes his own bed & only wants a few raw tomatoes for breakfast.' Christabel's version of events doesn't make Bunting's holiday sound idyllic but by the end of the week she had warmed to him considerably:

> Bunting's visit had worked out better than I expected. He hadn't been here a day before John was infinitely bored & looked silent & sullen in B's presence, so that I had to keep on talking with bland cheerfulness about nothing to keep it from being noticed. But B. did notice. He stayed in bed in the morning till J. had gone & then absented himself till last thing at night. Then it would always be me who called out. 'Hallo Bunting, had a good day?' To-night he came home early & said to me so humbly, 'Do tell me if I'm in the way & I'll go out to the pictures?' Which I told John & John was touched & turned nice to him. Have spent much tact & energy telling J. things I learnt talking to B. about his shyness & fear of people not liking him, & this together with most bombastic accounts of his exploits & adventures with women – which I did not recount to John.

A degree of domestic harmony appears to have prevailed by the end of Bunting's visit. The following Sunday Christabel records a 'pleasant day. Bunting getting on with John. John happy. We eat raw cabbage with evening meal. Bunting said, "What pleasant meals you have here."'[112] Bunting liked Christabel, who died just a few months after his visit. He wrote to Adams in February 1926 that: 'Christabel was very kind and gentle – too gentle and sympathetic for her own comfort in a world based mostly on callousness.'[113]

Thomas' death altered the Bunting family's situation significantly. His will shows that he left £600 to his sister Sarah, £300 to his other sister, Harriet, and the rest to Annie but Annie, used to the prosperous life of marriage to a successful doctor, apparently swiftly found herself short of money. Thomas' estate, however, was valued at £12,547 15s 10d, the equivalent of £600,000 (nearly $1m) today, and even though it was resworn as £10,924 10s 2d, that is still a significant legacy. Annie sold the family home in Jesmond and moved to a substantial, semi-detached, redbrick house with a spectacular view west up the Tyne valley. Here at 242 Newburn Road in the village of Throckley, seven miles west of Newcastle, she was closer to other members of the

Cheesman family. Bunting described his attempt to support his mother in his 19 February letter to Adams:

> I became one of the ignoble army of lecturers who pretends to educate adults. I lecture on economics to working men, confuse their minds with the technicalities of the money market, and get two pounds a week for it. The institution that employs me thus wanted to make me its boss, so I took on a lot of extra, unpaid work – coaching a 'Little Theatre', boiling down Frazer and Freud and so on – and then they announced they couldn't raise money enough to pay my salary.

The school he taught in was the Adult School in Montague Street, Lemington, a few hundred yards from the house he had been born in. Once again it was a family connection that took him there. The school had been founded in 1913, with funding from the Joseph Rowntree Trust, by Bunting's uncle, Andrew Messer. Bunting told Lionel Robbins in October 1926 that 'lecturing to working men was the only thing I could get in the North – quite amusing, but not enough of it to keep me. It is pleasant to listen to unsophisticated views on the foreign exchanges, the origins of religion or the literary merits of various Victorians and the lectures are quite easily prepared, But thirty bob a week is less than my expenses.'[114] He was less generous about it to Adams, describing the classes as comprising elementary schoolteachers ('the stupidest people in the world'), trades union officials ('far from bright') and a 'hotchpotch of detestable people who have obtrusive souls and want something for nothing'.[115] He consoled himself by reading Dante, Wittgenstein, Eliot, Dryden and Pope's *Dunciad*.

Bunting returned to London and lived at 5 Osnaburgh Terrace near Regent's Park in a 'small but decent' room overlooking 'a good church'. He repaid the debt to Robbins that he had incurred when he fled to Paris in 1923 ('I've owed you this money for a Hell of a time, but I've never forgotten it for a moment') and explained his plan: 'After messes and muddles inherited from my father; after two years of job-hunting without an atom of success in the North, I'm settling here again to try the cheaper kinds of journalism – not that I want it to be cheap, but that seems to be the kind there is a demand for.'[116]

He told Pound that he was 'becoming industrious' and 'laying the foundations of three books simultaneously ... a book on Dickens as a stylist and a master of form, which badly needs doing. A book on music halls, not gossipy but treating the thing seriously as it deserves. A book on the comparative anatomy of Prisons.'[117]

He began to meet some of the leading literary figures of the day, including T. S. Eliot, D. H. Lawrence and members of the Bloomsbury Group, various of whom he described to Victoria Forde with characteristic brevity:

Q. Roger Fry?
A. Fidgety.
Q. Clive Bell?
A. (Dismissed with a 'hmph').
Q. Forster?
A. Nice enough chap, but the whole Bloomsbury Group didn't really like anyone not wealthy, with an inheritance, and educated.[118]

He elaborated on this many years later. Asked what it was that he disliked so much about Bloomsbury he was able to reply quite specifically:

What I resented about the Bloomsbury group in particular might be said to be two things: one, a certain cocksureness which in particular made me distrust Maynard Keynes. The other was that they were all of that well-to-do middle class, bordering on country gentry who felt that if you couldn't afford to live in Bloomsbury or Regent's Park or some similar, desirable, but very expensive part of the world, well, poor devil, there wasn't much to be expected from you.[119]

He also remembered his first meeting with T. S. Eliot in 1926 with little affection: 'he spent a long time urging upon me the necessity to read Dante. And being a modest young man and not wanting to put him off his stride, I never once mentioned that I had already read Dante and knew a good deal of the *Inferno* by heart. So that, perhaps, I wasted that first interview.'[120] Bunting sent some poems to Eliot in 1926 but heard nothing from him. By the following spring he was beginning to understand that Eliot wasn't the most reliable of correspondents. He told Pound that he had intended to send him a (now lost) story called 'The Salad Basket', but Eliot had his only copy and, 'letters to him are invariably met with the assertion that he had gone into the country and would be back in a fortnight'.[121] He prodded Eliot on 4 April 1927:

You will remember that I called on you in the autumn, introducing myself with Pound's name, and that subsequently, by your request, I sent you samples of the kind of journalism I was then doing, together with two or three of my poems, the bad as well as those I think good. I have not heard from you since.

Could you let me have my roll of typescript back? Pound has asked me to send him something for Exile, and I think I sent you my only copy of a story which might serve his purpose, called 'The Salad Basket'.

I suppose I may take it, from your silence, that there is no prospect of my being allowed to do a few reviews for the Criterion?

Eliot replied almost immediately to apologise for the delay and to return the material Bunting had requested, adding that he had seen enough to assure him that he would like Bunting to review for the *Criterion* and that he would send him something in a couple of months or so. 'I should very much like to see more of your original work, such as "The Salad Basket."'[122]

Bunting and Eliot were by no means close but they kept in touch. Bunting recalled meeting him again, in a vignette from 1940s London:

More astonishing [than Schmidt's, also in Charlotte Street], a restaurant, I forget its name, further up the street on the other side, where I used to go for a modest meal which was quite adequate Parisienne cookery, cheap. I went back there one day about 1947 and found the same little room, but instead of the tables with the checkered cloths on them, there were tables with the most wonderful damask, these little shaded lights, and all the rest of the deluxe styling. I looked at the menu – I got a terrible shock! The prices were prodigious. I did eat my meal there and paid for it – it nearly broke me. That night I was having dinner with T. S. Eliot in the Cafe Royal. I told him of my astonishment. He said, let me guess which one it is. He named it at once, adding, 'I believe that is now the most expensive restaurant in Europe.'[123]

The depth of their relationship is measured by the fact that Eliot is an incidental bystander in a story about restaurant prices.[124]

Villon

The fifteenth-century French poet François Villon was much in vogue in the 1920s. Pound had completed his own operatic treatment of Villon's *Le Testament de Villon* in Paris before Bunting arrived there,[125] but was still ostensibly working on it with George Antheil in February 1924 in Rapallo. The concert version was premiered on 29 June 1926 in Paris[126] and the

BBC broadcast a version of the scores in 1931. Justin McCarthy's play, *If I Were King*, an imaginative reconstruction of Villon's swashbuckling life, was released as a film in 1920. Rudolf Friml's hugely popular operetta, *The Vagabond King*, which appeared in 1925 was based on McCarthy's play and Villon was also a major character in the 1927 film *The Beloved Rogue*. Bertolt Brecht based the poet in his *Baal*, written in 1918, on Villon. A poet who was unknown as such in his own time had won global recognition across a broad cultural spectrum by the time Bunting started his own 'Villon'.

Villon was born as François Montcorbier (or François des Loges) into poverty in 1431 but entered the University of Paris and took Bachelor's and Master's degrees there. We know little of Villon's life but some events were recorded by the Parisian authorities, the first being a knife fight involving Villon, two priests, a Breton scholar and a girl named Isabeau. Villon spent much of his life in various prisons, and what we know of these experiences is contained in his *Testament*. He disappeared from history at the age of thirty-two.

Because Bunting published little and destroyed most of what he wrote we have little sense of his early development as a poet. He emerges with a fully developed, mature voice in 'Villon'. As Philip Norman said in a feature on Bunting in the *Sunday Times* over forty years later, in 'Villon', 'he seemed to conquer poetry all at once'.[127] 'Villon' is a poem that is worth looking at more closely for a number of reasons. First, it is an exceptionally good and greatly overlooked poem, certainly one worth being distracted by. Second, it is Bunting's first substantial poem to survive into his *Collected Poems* in 1968, so it is developmentally important. It is also a poem that draws on his own experience of prisons in England, France, Italy and Norway in the previous six years. Before we look at the poem, however, we need to clear away a pile of undergrowth that has collected around one word. That word is 'sonata'. All Bunting's longer poems, with the exception of 'Chomei at Toyama', are 'sonatas'. But what does that mean?

Bunting was asked in April 1976 what he meant by his assertion that *Briggflatts* was 'organised on musical analogy'. His reply is an important statement:

> You could quite easily borrow the formal organisation which developed in the 18th century and early 19th century that is used in musical sonatas and symphonies and so forth. It's a matter of making the rhythms develop and shift around themselves chiefly, partly having something to adapt in the way

of matter to that. The thing seems to have happened, whether consciously or not, first with Walt Whitman, and was later developed by Pound. Whitman's best pieces are very much like what Lizst was writing at the time – as far as form goes. Pound takes over that general idea in 'Homage to Sextus Propertius'. And I carried the analogy further. Eliot did something not quite the same, at the same time. I pointed out to him – he hadn't noticed it himself – in 1922 or 1923, that the form 'The Waste Land' took, if you omitted the short fourth movement, is exactly that of a classical sonata. This seems to have stuck in his mind, so that when he wrote the 'Four Quartets', each of them an exact copy of the shape of 'The Waste Land', he calls them quartets – quartets being normally a sonata form. He takes it a rather different way than I would have done, but it is making use of what you can derive from the musical form, and doing it with great skill.[128]

Bunting's frequently articulated belief in the inextricability of music and poetry was, as we have seen, a guiding principle of his own work since the very beginning of his career. The two forms are 'twin sisters born of the primitive dance'.[129] His notes for a lecture at Newcastle University show that he presented nineteenth-century poetry as providing, Whitman excepted, no more than minor variations on 'the general Spenserian model of English poetry'. He traces a tradition of 'cadence' in English prose from Miles Coverdale's English translation of the Psalms to Swift's *Tale of a Tub* via two of Queen Mary's three Oxford martyrs, Thomas Cranmer (who wrote the 1549 Book of Common Prayer) and the preacher Hugh Latimer, Robert Burton's *The Anatomy of Melancholy*, Sir Thomas Browne's *Religio Medici* and *Hydriotaphia* and James Macpherson's *Ossian*.[130] Bunting believed that Whitman was the only nineteenth century poet who moved this particular tradition forward:

> What Whitman adds to this is to make *all* the words part of the machinery which causes them to cohere into a poem. The echoes & repeats are not confined to cadences. But he usually avoids immediate repeats or repeats that are too exact & obvious. Yet the taking up of a sound or rhythm again & again in a poem has just the same effect as taking up a theme, more or less transformed, has in music.[131]

Bunting isn't saying that Whitman is the nineteenth-century's greatest poet. Wordsworth was. Wordsworth was, for Bunting, the greatest narrative poet since Chaucer, but what Whitman did for prosody paved the way for Pound's

Homage to Sextus Propertius and the modernist revolution in poetry. (Bunting also saw Hardy as an honorable proto-modernist.)[132] As Peter Makin says,

> it is fundamental to Bunting's idea that the word-sound it concerns is a shaping not of the prettier glitterings of aural surface (consonant patterns and the like) but of what is much more basic in the English language: rhythm. Thus Pound's *Propertius* was a springboard for real development because its aural shaping was essentially rhythmic ... The return to earlier-stated melodic themes, 'more or less transformed', is one of the builders of major structure in post-Renaissance Western music. Thus the concluding event in classical sonata form is the return of a melodic motif or motifs in a changed key. If a rhythm motif in poetry can do what a melodic theme does in music, rhythm ceases to be mere texture and becomes structure maker.[133]

This was quite different from the lesson T. S. Eliot tried to teach Bunting. Asked in 1981 how he started a new poem Bunting said that his poems 'would usually begin by catching a rhythm which is not overdone', a trick learned from Eliot: 'Eliot once told me when I was very young and I said I had some difficulties about what to say because I hadn't the experience, and he said, "You don't bother about what you have to say. Try like me, write rhymes, quatrains, and the rhymes will tell you what to say." That I suppose must be how he wrote "Burbank with a Baedecker" and so on.'[134] A few years later he illustrated Eliot's point about rhyme by referring to, 'the poems of the hippopotamus cycle, the Sweeney ones for instance, you will soon observe that Eliot is doing just that. Those poems are based on words that rhyme and not on any philosophical basis.'[135]

Bunting believed that what Whitman and Pound took from music 'was chiefly the notion of modifying a theme, a rhythmic theme, especially, and – bit by bit – until it could be merged in a counter-theme or in some other way combined with it. Pound was fascinated by the idea of fugue, but he found it necessary to change that notion fundamentally, and use images rather than rhythms to carry on a counterpoint in the reader's mind.'[136] Bunting was aware that the connection between music and poetry could be exaggerated ('they're twins, but they're not identical twins')[137] but he believed that 'music and poetry are very very closely intertwined, and ... as soon as you begin to part them things begin to go wrong'.[138] Bunting was keen to draw a distinction between the way he and Eliot had used a 'form'. 'I've never wanted to be precise in his sense of precision', he explained to Victoria Forde in 1972:

Now to follow anything very closely, as the young Eliot followed certain verse forms – Jacobean blank verse for instance – is to some extent to be controlled by the model instead of controlling it. Music has suggested certain forms and certain details to me, but I have not tried to be consistent about it. Rather, I've felt the spirit of a form, or of a procedure, without trying to reproduce it in any way that could be demonstrated on a blackboard. (There's no 'one-one' relationship between my movements and any of Scarlatti's.) You could say the same of the detail of sound. Eliot – and Kipling – show prodigious skill in fitting words to a prearranged pattern, very admirable: yet they don't do it without losing some suppleness … I never have, on the one hand, something I want to say, and on the other, a form I want to say it in. My matter is born of the form – or the form of the matter, if you care to think that I just conceive things musically.[139]

But in what sense can a poem be said to be a 'sonata'? We have seen that Bunting was dismissive of Eliot's 'Preludes', although not entirely so. In an interview in 1981 he observed that they 'didn't have much relation to preludes of early pianists but nonetheless the aim was a similar one, and the effect was often very similar – some of them, not only like Chopin, but rather like preludes from Bach's to his fugues. Something of that must have been in Mr Eliot's mind I thought. Perhaps it wasn't. Perhaps the title was just a catch. I don't think so though.'[140] It's true that there doesn't seem to be much structural correlation between Eliot's poem and, say, Chopin's music. There is also the metaphysical problem of a prelude existing in the absence of the thing to which it is a prelude. Can a prelude exist if its reason for existing doesn't? Bunting's relationship with the sonata form was much more developed. Although he doesn't seem to have acknowledged it Pound's influence may have been critical here. According to David Gordon, Bunting learned from Pound in 1922 that Joyce had planned *Ulysses* as a sonata and Pound would have introduced Bunting to the work on the eighteenth-century sonata of the Paris Conservatory's professor of harmony, Albert Lavignac, whose 'consummate manual', as Pound called it, *La Musique et les Musiciens*, had been published in 1895.[141] Lavignac described the sonata carefully:

Every Sonata regularly constructed contains a first movement called the *Allegro*; a slow movement, the *Andante* or *Adagio*; and an animated *Finale*.

Between the first and second movements, or between the second and third may be introduced a short piece – a *Minuet*, *Scherzo*, or *Intermezzo*.[142]

Lavignac describes the five-part structure of the eighteenth-century sonata as first theme and second theme in the Allegro; development of the themes with variations in the Andante; and return to the two themes in the third Finale (which is followed by a coda). So, as Gordon says, 'the sonata form develops *two tonally contrasting themes* through *three basic stages*'.[143] So how does this relate to 'Villon'? Two themes are certainly announced in the first section. In the first, Villon reflects on the difference between the world promised by art, religion and power ('the Emperor with the Golden Hands, the Virgin in blue') and the reality of life in prison. The second theme, a series of relaxed quatrains with a folksy ABAB rhyme scheme, shows art triumphing over death:

> Remember, imbeciles and wits,
> sots and ascetics, fair and foul,
> young girls with little tender tits,
> that DEATH is written over all.
>
> Worn hides that scarcely clothe the soul
> they are so rotten, old and thin,
> or firm and soft and warm and full –
> fellmonger Death gets every skin.[144]

The sonata analogy leads us to expect development of these themes in the second section, but with a perceptible change of pace, tone and rhythm, and the change of key in 'Villon' is immediately obvious:

> Let his days be few and let
> his bishoprick pass to another,
> for he fed me on carrion and on a dry crust,
> mouldy bread that his dogs had vomited,
> I lying on my back in the dark place, in the grave,
> fettered to a post in the damp cellerage.

The second section develops the art versus death theme by showing how artists, Villon (and by implication Bunting), are imprisoned by powerful, violent forces. A central section of heavy iambic tetrametre and a dominating AABB rhyme scheme gives this section an authority that Villon's bitter voice in the first lacks:

> They took away the prison clothes
> and on the frosty nights I froze.

I had a bible where I read –
that Jesus came to raise the dead
I kept myself from going mad
by singing an old bawdy ballad
and birds sang on my windowsill
and tortured me till I was ill.

One senses Bunting's own prison experience showing through here. The tone has changed from the theatricality of the first section to one of thoughtful honesty, a listing of the facts of the case. Its close is a bleak analysis. Homer and Dante live, but Villon?

Blacked by the sun, washed by the rain,
hither and thither scurrying as the wind varies.

Villon's fate is random, attested by Bunting's abandonment of recognisable metre.

The two themes of the first section return in the lyrical third section of 'Villon'. In the first section the poet (either of them) had been unable to trace a link between beauty ('A blazing parchment,/Matthew Paris his kings in blue and gold') and the reality of life, in or outside prison:

It was not so,
scratched on black by God knows who,
by God, by God knows who.

In the third section the poet sees how the two are reconciled. Man's eternal suffering is a direct consequence of his thirst for beauty:

below me the ports
with naked breasts
shipless spoiled sacked
because of the beauty of Helen.

And the second theme, art triumphing over death, returns in its developed guise. Art supplies form to life:

precision clarifying vagueness;
boundary to a wilderness
of detail; chisel voice
smoothing the flanks of noise;

125

catalytic making whisper and whisper
run together like two drops of quicksilver.

So Bunting's description of 'Villon' as a sonata is not fanciful. The poem
follows the developmental theme and changes of pace and tone followed in
sonatas composed by Johann Christian Bach and Domenico Scarlatti. That
in itself, of course, doesn't make it a good poem.

I want to look briefly at the opening of 'Villon' to show how Bunting
handles the contradictions that fuel the poem. Bunting sets the scene by
introducing the imprisoned poet:

> He whom we anatomized
> 'whose words we gathered as pleasant flowers
> and thought on his wit and how neatly he described things'
> speaks
> to us, hatching marrow,
> broody all night over the bones of a deadman.
>
> My tongue is a curve in the ear. Vision is lies.
> We saw it so and it was not so,
> the Emperor with the Golden Hands, the Virgin in blue.
> (– A blazing parchment,
> Matthew Paris his kings in blue and gold.)
>
> It was not so,
> scratched on black by God knows who,
> by God, by God knows who.
>
> In the dark in fetters
> on bended elbows I supported my weak back
> hulloing to muffled walls blank again
> unresonant. It was gone, is silent, is always silent.

We 'anatomized' Villon. He is dead and we have dissected what is left of him,
his corpse in the metaphor, his poetry in reality. But 'anatomized' carries the
strong counter-suggestion of *giving* Villon an anatomy, shape, structure, life.
The process of anatomising juxtaposes life and death carefully. Bunting also
clearly has in mind the common sixteenth-century sense of 'anatomize' as
a comprehensive and systematic exposure of a person's moral faults, the
sense in which Oliver seeks to 'anatomize' his brother Orlando to Charles
the Wrestler in the first scene of *As You Like It*. The poet is dead, the poetry

alive. The dead poet 'speaks'. That word's occupation of its own line brings the reader up short because of the prosaic quotation that precedes it. The quotation is from Clément Marot's preface to his 1533 edition of Villon's poems. Marot (who returns in a different guise a few lines later), a member of the royal household of François I, also spent much of his career in prison as a consequence of his Protestant activism. Marot was an acclaimed wit who prized wit highly and who fully acknowledged Villon's own. As a courtier, however, and the son of a courtier (his father had been poet to the court of Anne of Brittany), he seems to have found Villon's low birth and vulgarity inexcusable. So his supercilious comment, in Bunting's translation at least, damns with the faintest possible praise – 'how neatly he described things'. We have been lulled into the mood of polite sixteenth-century manners by Marot's lines and we are surprised when the dead poet suddenly 'speaks/ to us'.

As he speaks the poet works: 'hatching marrow,/broody all night over the bones of a deadman.' The dominant theme in these lines is the process of nurturing something to life. The eggs that the poet is 'hatching' as he broods are marrow/Marot and bones. He makes life out of death. He is, in a sense, bringing Marot to life, creating his own *Collected Poems* in his dungeon, as well as giving himself immortality in verse. But marrow is not just the animal life force; it is also the best part of anything, its inner meaning or purpose. Villon/Bunting in expressing themselves in poetry are doing that which defines them as beings. And hatching does not relate only to birth. It is also the process of marking a drawing or painting with fine, close diagonal lines to evoke shades, textures and colour, a technique that developed in the Middle Ages and which Villon's near contemporary, Albrecht Dürer, made his own. Hatching is particularly useful in black and white representations of full colour images. Bunting artfully prefigures the glorious luxury of the following stanza with the hatching image, as well as the immediate return to bitter monochrome. Marrow (pronounced marra) has another submerged meaning that may be unfamiliar to those who don't know Bunting's northern English. In the north of England marra is a friend or companion, a peer or one of a pair, a match in a contest. The poet is incubating other poets, strengthening the link between Bunting and Villon as poets and as prisoners. Kenneth Cox thought the line 'broody all night over the bones of a deadman' mere decoration, that it 'only adds atmospheric effect'.[145] It clearly does a great deal more than that. Even the condensation of 'dead man' into one word works hard. He is not a dead man; being dead he has lost his humanity and metamorphosed into something else, something quite different, a 'deadman'. There is very little in Bunting's poetry that is merely decorative. He was too good an editor, and he had Pound constantly looking over his shoulder.

The phrase 'hatching marrow' is the pivot of these lines, signposting a number of routes into the next stage of the poem. Monochrome and colour, life and death, friends and enemies, Villon's poetry and Marot's dead prose, art and criticism, prison and freedom, a dead man speaking; in just six lines Bunting keeps so many meanings and contradictions in play that they threaten to spin out of control, but they never do. Indeed, the second stanza develops new pairings and contradictions. 'My tongue is a curve in the ear' suggests that we are doomed to incomprehension, reaching forward into the fourth stanza where the poet in his dungeon speaks to 'muffled walls blank again/unresonant. It was gone, is silent, is always silent./My soundbox lacks sonority.' What the poet says is not what the listener hears and what the seer sees simply deceives him: 'Vision is lies./We saw it so and it was not so.'

At this point we are launched abruptly into another world:

> the Emperor with the Golden Hands, the Virgin in blue.
> (– A blazing parchment,
> Matthew Paris his kings in blue and gold.)

But it is an illusion, 'it was not so.' More pairings: art and life, vision and reality, speech and sight, lies and truth, secular and religious, state and church. Victoria Forde notes that, throughout 'Villon', 'the constant grouping and regrouping of subjects has the kind of intricacy and precarious stability of a steadily shifting kaleidoscope design'.[146] The reader needs to give way to these mutiple 'meanings' and hold them as equal possibilities. As Bunting wrote to Donald Davie fifty years later, 'critics sometimes forget that other poets besides Dante can bundle two or three different meanings into a sentence on occasion'.[147]

The emperor with the golden hands is lifted from Villon's:

> Voire, ou soit de Constantinobles
> L'emperieres au poing dorez.[148]

The reference may be to Byzantine iconography. The complex of buildings at the Byzantine court housed an extraordinary quantity of Christian relics, more than 3,600 representing 476 different saints. These treasures conferred enormous political and religious power on Constantinople during the early

Middle Ages. Of these buildings two in particular were outstanding not just because of the prestige of the relics they contained but because they were vitally important parts of the court's ceremonial life. One of these was the Church of the Virgin of the Pharos which housed Christianity's most important relics, those of Christ's Passion – the crown of thorns, the cross, the nails, the sponge, fragments of Longinus' spear – as well as an imprint of Christ's face, one of his sandals and the right arm of John the Baptist. The other important building was Hagios Stephanos, the Church of St Stephen of Daphne, the first martyr of the Christian church, which was built specifically to house St Stephen's right arm. Within the Church of St Stephen was a portico called 'the Golden Hand'. According to Ioli Kalavrezou this was an extremely important location, being the place where 'the emperor and the empress would show themselves to the courtiers and dignitaries after the coronation, and where the adoration and acclamations would take place … a pivotal point in the processional entries and exits of the emperor from and to the palace, and also the place where he would be awaited and acclaimed on the major feast days.' Villon, and by extension Bunting, consciously evoke the holiest of holies and the most politically loaded location in the entire early medieval world.[149] The glory of the emperor is conferred by God directly through the presentation of the royal crown by the holy, golden hand. Bunting silently amends Villon by shifting the plural to 'hands' and away from 'l'emperieres'. It is the emperors of the golden hand that Villon conjures rather than the emperor of the golden hands.

Matthew Paris, the thirteenth-century English monk and historian, illustrated his manuscripts with exquisite, brightly coloured miniatures. Bunting's deliberate archaism, replacing the required apostrophe with 'his' ('Matthew Paris his kings'), subtly roots the image in the early modern period and suggests a religious dimension. This grammatical aberration was popular from the fourteenth to the eighteenth centuries and lingers in perhaps its most famous incarnation in the Book of Common Prayer, first published in 1549, 'And this we beg for Jesus Christ his sake'.

The glory of all this art, holiness and supreme imperial power, however, is illusory and we return with this insight to a world of bleak monochrome:

> It was not so,
> scratched on black by God knows who,
> by God, by God knows who.

The artist uses his primitive tools to reverse out his message from a black surface, emphasising the theme of inversion that permeates the poem. Who is the artist? All three possibilities leave us in the dark. Either God knows who the artist is but we don't, or God is the artist, or nobody, including God, knows who the artist is. These three lines are despairing. The four heavy beats, 'It was not so', allow no room for ambiguity. This vision of artistic anonymity and futility sets up the brutish inarticulacy that follows.

The glorious world of colour is, of course, set against the monochrome of the coal mine. Anonymous miners, 'God knows who', would leave messages 'scratched on black' for their marrows. The contorted prisoner/miner writhes against his fate:

> In the dark in fetters
> on bended elbows I supported my weak back
> hulloing to muffled walls blank again
> unresonant. It was gone, is silent, is always silent.

Is this Villon or Bunting? In fact it is both, plus another prisoner-poet. Bunting explicitly invokes Sir Walter Raleigh, imprisoned in the Tower of London by Elizabeth I after his secret marriage to one of her maids of honour. Raleigh expressed his frustration at imprisonment in 'The Ocean to Cynthia':

> But now, close kept, as captives wonted are,
> That food, that heat, that light, I find no more.
> Despair bolts up my doors; and I alone
> Speak to dead walls; but those hear not my moan.

Bunting invoked Raleigh to balance the books. Villon had been imprisoned in Paris for drunken violence, as had Bunting. But Bunting had been a prisoner of conscience, a political prisoner like Raleigh, towards the end of the First World War and soon after in Norway, if we are to take at face value his claim to have been on a mission to Quakerise the revolution fomented by Lenin and Trotsky in Russia.

We have looked at just eighteen lines of a poem that consists of more than 160. The purpose of this has been to attempt to show just how complex and exciting 'Villon' is. It is a forgotten gem of modernist poetry. With its rich structure, swooping rhythms and intense condensation it deserves to be considered alongside Eliot's *The Waste Land* and Pound's 'Homage to Sextus Propertius' as a third pillar of the modernist revolution in poetry. Pound performed the same kind of surgery on 'Villon' as he had on *The Waste Land* and when one considers his legacy it is impossible not to be rocked by Ezra Pound's genius.[150] Bunting was to write more great poems (notably 'The Well of Lycopolis' and his poem of the Second World War, 'The Spoils') but he didn't hit the form of 'Villon' for another forty years, and then he surpassed it.

Too complicated for me!

After 'Villon' Bunting's poetry became increasingly authoritative. Two poems written in 1926, 'I am agog for foam' and 'After the grimaces of capitulation' survived his ferocious self-culling. He was beginning to feel more confident. At the end of 1928 he sent 'Aubade' ('After the grimaces of capitulation') to Pound and asked, 'Is this a poem? Have I found my voice? Everybody says it is exceedingly disagreeable of me to be unpleasant about sunrise and the loud chorus of complaints encourages me to think that I must have done something of my own at last.'[151]

'I am agog for foam', which Bunting told Louis Zukofsky that Yeats particularly liked,[152] is an exquisite love poem dedicated to Peggy Mullet (who is not, as is often suggested, Peggy Greenbank from Brigflatts):

> I am agog for foam. Tumultuous come
> with teeming sweetness to the bitter shore
> tidelong unrinsed and midday parched and numb
> with expectation. If the bright sky bore
> with endless utterance of a single blue
> unphrased, its restless immobility
> infects the soul, which must decline into
> an anguished and exact sterility
> and waste away: then how much more the sea
> trembling with alteration must perfect
> our loneliness by its hostility.
> The dear companionship of its elect
> deepens our envy. Its indifference
> haunts us to suicide. Strong memories
> of sprayblown days exasperate impatience
> to brief rebellion and emphasise
> the casual impotence we sicken of.
> But when mad waves spring, braceletted with foam,

towards us in the angriness of love
crying a strange name, tossing as they come
repeated invitations in the gay
exuberance of unexplained desire,
we can forget the sad splendour and play
at wilfulness until the gods require
renewed inevitable hopeless calm
and the foam dies and we again subside
into our catalepsy, dreaming foam,
while the dry shore awaits another tide.[153]

The poem starts at low tide with the poet at one with nature in a kind of dynamic inertia. Underneath the 'midday parched and numb' is 'expectation', the immobility is 'restless', the sterility 'anguished', 'indifference' threatens annihilation. With full tide comes intense erotic fulfilment as 'mad waves spring, braceletted with foam', intense but brief before the 'inevitable' subsidence of tide and desire. 'I am agog for foam' draws heavily on Mallarmé's 'Les Fenêtres' and Bunting had doubts about its lasting value but retained it in his various collections out of deference to Yeats.[154]

Bunting's first translation to survive into *Collected Poems*, 'Darling of Gods and Men', also dates from 1927. Pound had been encouraging young poets to translate the classics for many years, apparently unconcerned that his own translations had aroused the derision of readers who had even a scant knowledge of the original. 'If Mr Pound were a professor of Latin,' snorted Professor William Gardner Hale of the University of Chicago, when he read the parts of Pound's 'Homage to Sextus Propertius' that Harriet Monroe dared to print in *Poetry*, 'there would be nothing left for him but suicide.'[155] 'Translation is ... good training', Pound wrote in 'A Retrospect' in 1918[156] and in 'Notes on Elizabethan Classicists', published in *The Egoist* the previous year he justified his cavalier approach to the technicalities of translation as an artistic *obligation*:

A great age of literature is perhaps always a great age of translations; or follows it. The Victorians in lesser degree had FitzGerald, and Swinburne's Villon, and Rossetti ... we have long since fallen under the blight of the Miltonic or noise tradition, to a stilted dialect in translating the classics, a dialect which imitates the idiom of the ancients rather than seeking their meaning, a state of mind which aims at 'teaching the boy his Latin' or Greek or whatever it may be, but has long since ceased to care for the beauty of the original; or which perhaps thinks 'appreciation' obligatory, and the meaning and content mere accessories.[157]

Bunting, as we shall see, strongly endorsed Pound's position in a review of E. Stuart Bates' *Modern Translation* in the *Criterion* in July 1936. The job of the translator is to 'make an English poem, not to explain a foreign one'.[158] In his *Collected Poems* Bunting collected many of his translations in a section he called 'Overdrafts', a subject about which he sadly came to know quite a lot. His only comment on these translations is an oblique statement of his modus operandi, 'It would be gratuitous to assume that a mistranslation is unintentional.'[159]

'Darling of Gods and Men' renders Lucretius' invocation to Venus directly in clear, confident modern English, entirely free of the archaisms from which many previous translations suffer:

> Therefore, since you alone control the sum of things
> and nothing without you comes forth into the light
> and nothing beautiful or glorious can be
> without you, Alma Venus! trim my poetry
> with your grace; and give peace to write and read and think.[160]

Finding publishers for his poetry was, however, a challenge. He submitted some to *Poetry* in 1926 and asked for them to be returned if Harriet Monroe was 'unable to use them'. Monroe's handwritten note on the letter is deadly, 'Ret'd too complicated for me!'[161]

Humanity, information, throb

The Leightonian of October 1927 reported that 'Basil Bunting is understood either to have shaved or to have grown a beard (we forget the phase) and to spend his evenings as Musical critic of *The Outlook*.'[162] Apart from the slightly dippy review of Conrad's novel *The Rover* in the *transatlantic review* of July 1924 the bulk of Bunting's journalistic output during the 1920s appeared in *The Outlook*, a Conservative London weekly to which his old friend Lionel Robbins contributed regularly in 1926 and 1927. It is likely, as Susan Howson says, that Robbins had a hand in finding Bunting work there.[163]

Bunting wrote reviews and articles from February to October 1927, when he became the paper's official music critic until it closed in 1928. Otto Theis, the literary editor of *The Outlook*, was looking for a music critic and had called Bunting at Kleinfeldt's, a pub in Charlotte Street in London's West End, where he was a regular. 'I used to go to Kleinfeldt's to meet Nina Hamnett, and then people came to meet both of us there, and, gradually, from being a quiet place where a small number of people met from time to time, it became more and more crowded.' Bunting claimed to have told Theis that he didn't know 'a damn thing' about music,[164] but he got the job anyway.

The pub Bunting (and many others) referred to as 'Kleinfeldt's' was never so-called. The licence to run the Fitzroy, described by Augustus John as 'the Clapham Junction of the world',[165] was bought in 1919 by Judah Morris Kleinfeldt, an immigrant from Polish Russia, who had arrived in London with fourpence in his pocket and who quickly became an influential figure in the Jewish community of London's West End. Previously called the Hundred Marks (because it was the favourite pub of the West End's German community that had grown rapidly until war became inevitable), the Fitzroy, situated on the corner of Charlotte Street and Windmill Street, acquired its current name as soon as Kleinfeldt bought the licence.[166] It quickly became the epicentre of London's Bohemia. The undisputed queen of Bohemia was Bunting's friend, Nina Hamnett, who had rejected her Welsh background for study at the London School of Art before spending time in Montparnasse with her lover, Roger Fry ('fidgety'), where she was influenced by Modigliani and Sickert. It was Hamnett who decided to settle her court at the Fitzroy where 'sitting erect on her bar stool, she ruled supreme'.[167] Hamnett bought the pub an autograph book which, as Sally Fiber says, 'vividly reflected the artistic and literary clientele of the tavern from 1927 to 1930', the time of Bunting's apparent near-residence there.

> The customers not only signed their names but composed music, did sketches and wrote poetry. E. J. Moeran, the volatile Irish composer, scribbled eight bars of his *First Rhapsody*, while Peter Warlock (Philip Heseltine), Constant Lambert, Michael Birkbeck and Dennis Arnold all contributed some music. Artistically Nina set an example by sketching people drinking at the bar, and Geoffrey Nelson drew the 'snob windows'. But the most famous artist was undoubtedly Augustus John.[168]

Bunting professed to detest London, and he probably did, but his relationship with the city was complex. Later in life he was astonished by the deterioration he perceived in London, and cast an enrosed eye on the Bohemia of the 1920s. 'How can a city which once was more than half civilised,' he asked Roger Guedalla in his 70s, have become so barbarous within my lifetime? There used to be teashops in no hurry, restaurants where half a bottle of tolerable claret cost less then a shilling, a Café Royale where you were sure to meet someone worth talking to, and reasonably efficient cheap public transport. There was a madam – what was her name? – in Jermyn Street whom any personable young man could count on when his pockets were empty for a guinea, tea and toast, and chatter; and Harold Monro feeding poor poets while he listened; and the shop in Red Lion Street where pork and pease pudding cost one penny, take it away, or a halfpenny more for the use of a plate.[169]

Bunting was in love with one of Nina Hamnett's friends, Helen Rowe, during this period. According to Susan Howson he may have lived with her for a short time.

But, as Lionel [Robbins] recorded in his diary, by 1921 she had a child by Dr Hans Egli, who was also at the London School of Economics in 1919–21 and whom she married. Lionel did not identify her husband, but Bunting did when he wrote to Ezra Pound in December 1926. She was a fine writer, Bunting told Pound, 'who was about to do good work, when she got married, produced three infants and became so taken up with domestic duties that I doubt whether she will ever make time to do anything'.[170]

There's no doubt that Bunting had a close relationship with Helen Rowe. Two days after he fled London for Paris in 1923 he wrote to Robbins:

I ran away from London on Friday. I have quarrelled with Helen (my fault) & London has become unbearable to me.[171]

Helen was much on his mind at that time. He was still in touch with her in May 1925. Christabel Dennison recorded in her diary for 18 May that Bunting, during his week-long holiday with her and Adams, 'left to go into the country for a day or two. I devine to look up his old love Helen Egli whose husband is away on military service in Switzerland.' [172]

He dedicated a poem he wrote in 1927, 'Empty vast days ...' to Helen:

Empty vast days built in the waste memory seem a jail for
thoughts grown stale in the mind, tardy of birth, rank and inflexible:
love and slow selfpraise, even grief's cogency, all emotions
timetamed whimper and shame changes the past brought to no utterance.

Ten or ten thousand, does it much signify, Helen, how we
date fantasmal events, London or Troy. Let Polyhymnia

strong with cadence multiply song, voices enmeshed by music
respond bringing the savour of our sadness or delight again.[173]

The notion that 'shame changes the past brought to no utterance' eerily
reaches forward nearly forty years to *Briggflatts*. As a statement about his
relationship with Helen Rowe it seems to me that Bunting here regrets an
opportunity unfulfilled, an affair acknowledged but unconsummated. The
replacement of Helen of Troy by Polyhymnia suggests that an erotic interest
has been transferred to an artistic obligation, a greater, almost sacred
good.[174] Another poem that survives from 1927, 'Personal Column', suggests
that the relationship with Helen Rowe, however it was configured, had left
him emotionally disarrayed:

> ... As to my heart, that may as well be forgotten
> or labelled: Owner will dispose of same
> to a good home, refs. exchgd., h.&c.,
> previous experience desired but not essential
> or let on a short lease to suit convenience.[175]

It isn't a good poem and we must assume that it survived the poet's self-
editing because it had such charged autobiographical significance.

Bunting's inaugural contribution to *The Outlook* was 'Throb: An Inquiry',
a satire on contemporary British journalism that appeared on 19 February
1927. The 'greatest journalist in England' advises Bunting's imaginary
friend that to 'succeed in journalism ... you must make your stuff Human,
Throbbing, and Informative. Informative you are; Human you may become;
but you will never manage the Throb.' Bunting and his wannabe journalist
friend set off to discover Throb, encountering a fourth dimension, Snap, on
the way. Having found some of the great prose stylists of the previous three
centuries (Browne, Gibbon, Johnson, Swift and Burke) disastrously lacking
in Throb, the pair turn to modern journalists to see if they can do better,
and of course they can:

> After a very short study we discovered that there are two distinct schools of
> reporting, the one in use in twopenny papers, the other in penny ones. The
> 'Times' of January 26th, 1927, describes an incident thus: –

> Two horses attached to a van bolted from Lumley-street into Oxford-street
> yesterday and then turning into Duke-street ran on the pavement and crashed
> into the window of S. and M., Limited, costumiers and furriers.

"Attached" means "harnessed," not "glued" or "nailed".

The 'Evening News,' January 25th, 1927, has it: –

Many pedestrians in Oxford-street to-day ran wildly for safety when a pair of horses, attached to one of Selfridge's vans, took fright, bolted, and careered madly along the busy street, etc., etc.

Commas, used by the 'Times' for formality, are used here for speed.

The 'Times' account is Informative, The 'Evening News' account is Human, Throbbing and Informative. The most obvious difference between them is that while the 'Times' begins by relating the matter in hand the 'Evening News' practises a kind of inversion and puts one of the minor consequences first.

The purpose of the inversion is to make the article Human. That conventionally depraved half-wit, the Office-boy, for whom journalists delight to toil, is sure to be tickled by a vision of pedestrians (staid persons) running wildly, whereas he might be bored by mere runaway horses.[176]

This gentle satire is designed to amuse but it makes a serious point about persuasive prose, suggesting that Bunting had been studying his craft. It foreshadows an essay written eight years later when Bunting was living in Tenerife. In 'Observations on Left-Wing Papers', unpublished until 1995, he advised newspapers and journalists on the use of propaganda:

Propaganda can only have a durable effect when it is based on full and exact information, without exaggeration or false implication. If you write 'Negroes are lynched' the public will understand you to mean 'all (or at least a great proportion of) negroes are lynched'. But when it has had time to reflect, it perceives that this is not true, and you not only fail to produce the effect you intended but actually create distrust and hostility in your readers ... The argument against lynching is that it is wrong for a fragment of the public to take the law into its own hands, and that it is wrong to discriminate against a man on racial grounds. Effective propaganda against it can only be made on those lines, backed up with accurate information.[177]

In other words effective journalism needs to rouse and persuade, while being believable, just and informative: Humanity, Information, Throb.

'Alas! The Coster's End' which appeared on 26 March 1927 is a remarkable display of retail prescience that anticipates today's battle for the hearts and minds of consumers. It effectively predicts the death of the High Street eighty years before it started to happen, although Bunting does stretch this one observation out to a half page; more signs of craft. The article laments the enforced disappearance of costermongers from London's streets. Costermongers were the mobile street traders who distributed vegetables, fish and meat to the suburbs from central markets such as Covent Garden (fruit and vegetables), Smithfield (meat) and Billingsgate (fish). The following sentence could, modernised a little, be seen in any lament for the demise of small retailers in 2013:

> To-day the poor shopkeeper, like the coster, is browbeaten as an economic anachronism by the apologists of the big multiple shops; the coster has been tamed by the Board of Education and lives as decent and orderly a life as his means permit; but the old rivalry is still there and it looks as though the shop may triumph awhile over the barrow before it too gives way before the ten thousand branches of Stunter's Stupendous Stores.

Bunting was learning to disguise his own views and prejudices to appeal to his readership. It is amusing to see him celebrating a disappearing London that in reality he had come to detest:

> Needy ghosts who write books of Oriental travels for illustrious authors must henceforth journey to Constantinople to see a Bazaar instead of strolling observantly down Berwick Street of a Saturday evening between stalls canopied with lace and draped in real silk stockings at three-and-six the pair. The prodigal strewings of vegetable matter in the gutters will be missed by Borough scavengers, themselves vegetating on the Dole. What will bank holiday be like without a Pearly King or Epsom without a 'moke'?[178]

The extent of the development of Bunting's craft is demonstrated by this willingness to write what his audience wanted to read rather than what he necessarily believed. There is another small example of this in his next article in *The Outlook*, which was a review on 7 May 1927 of *London's Squares and How to Save Them*: 'The sentimental Cockney middle-classes will certainly resist such a deprivation [of "fresh air, sunlight, greenness and good-temper"] with all their usual posthaste fervour as soon as it is too late to prevent it. The hoardings are up around Mornington Crescent, Endsleigh Gardens have become a Friends' House.' The conversion of a public space into a Quaker Meeting House is hardly something one would expect Bunting to have objected to very strongly, but *The Outlook* was a conservative weekly and, with the memory of the sacrifice of the First World War still fresh in the public memory, pacifists were a legitimate target. 'Endsleigh Gardens have become a Friends' House' was Throb. But he wasn't yet a master of disguise and he couldn't keep it up. A few lines later he lets his true Fabian colours show:

> while all other important cities have such gardens [as those in Bloomsbury], publicly owned and open to the public, we in London have allowed them to be private property, shut up, hidden behind forbidding iron railings and generally deserted. It is nothing to be proud of that it was possible for so long to prevent patients from the adjacent hospitals from walking in Queen's Square or that the gardens of Russell Square should be reserved for the use of a handful of residents who are careful to lock the gate after entering.

So he still had a bit to learn and though he was on form in this review his closing observation might have jarred with a few of his readers: 'It is possible but unlikely that these fickle forces will combine to give the squares to the people, but is more probable that London will continue to edify us with an exhibition of that imbecile corporate timidity known approvingly to England as "muddling through".'[179] This had, perhaps, Humanity, but no Throb. Interestingly, three weeks later his review of Edgar Thomas' *The Economics of Small Holdings* gave him a platform for a similar assault on 'the system', but he gave the opportunity a wide berth so perhaps he had been warned to throw a blanket over the Fabian fire, at least as far as readers of *The Outlook* were concerned.[180]

His next assignment, a review of three recent titles on crime and punishment, was a gift for so experienced a convict. 'Crime and Punishment' appeared in the issue of 4 June 1927. It is a thoughtful and insightful consideration of Andreas Bjerre's *The Psychology of Murder* and E. Ray Calvert's *Capital Punishment in the Twentieth Century*. A third title, Sydney A. Moseley's *The Convict of To-day*, is put away in a dismissive final paragraph that smokes with contempt: '"The Convict of To-day" is a poor journalistic write-up of English prisons, full of irrelevancies and inaccuracies. It is difficult to believe that the author is really as ignorant, prejudiced, and sensational as he appears in his work.'[181]

Calvert's abolitionism gets a solid B+, Bunting noting that 'the argument is bad though the conclusion is true'. Calvert's book is still occasionally cited[182] but Bunting believed Calvert should have waited to read the translation from the Swedish of the late Andrej Bjerre's masterpiece of 'field-naturalist' criminology, the clear pick of the three titles under review.

It is astonishing how contemporary many of the subjects on which Bunting ventures opinions now seem. His next target, on 16 July 1927, was the UK's public library system which seems today to be in some kind of nuclear winter. Lack of insight into popular culture and popular taste was the problem for Bunting as it is for today's vote mining front bencher:

> It is no use blaming the public for its garish taste. We are democratic and State-educated. We know what we want, and we are entitled to get it, whether we choose to pay for it privately at the bookseller's, by voluntary co-operation at the circulating library, or by the compulsory co-operation of a rate in support of the Borough or County Library. Unfortunately, many librarians take our insistence ill. They regard themselves as missionaries of Culture and plenipotentiaries of Education, and it gives them the hump to have to circulate a hundred copies of 'Did She Fall?' and only one of 'Science and the Modern World.' They regret, lecture, protest, conduct propaganda, mutinously continue to buy and stock works of acknowledged intelligence that leave their shelves so seldom that it would be cheaper and as satisfactory to borrow them from the Central Library for Students.[183]

Bunting was becoming as skilled at manipulating his constituency as any politician, although he couldn't resist the opportunity for a spot of light class warfare, setting the 'high-brow middle class of to-day' against working class readers: 'Some of the most illuminating comments on Richardson I have heard were uttered by a cook, and one of the best critics of poetry in the second half of last century was Joseph Skipsey, a working miner.' Needless to say the library system, its funding, philosophy and organising principles, were decidedly tilted against the latter.

Bunting's articles for *The Outlook* offer a fascinating example of the tightrope many of us walk between principle and profession. It must have been a relief for Bunting to get onto relatively neutral ground by contributing to *The Outlook*'s regular 'Some of Our Conquerors' column. He used his first, on the dancer Lydia Sokolova, to showcase her interpretation of Stravinky's 'The Rite of Spring', choreographed by Léonide Massine in 1920, and the second, on Nina Hamnett, to attack contemporary art and art criticism.[184] The article on Hamnett that appeared in the issue of 24 September is provocative, an early example of his lifelong need to undermine the establishment:

Most of the pictures, the good as well as the bad, that are exhibited in London are so monotonously alike in subject matter and technique that the painters have to invent mannerisms to distinguish their own work from the general level of dull competence. The bewildered critic, surrounded by bowls of geraniums, dishes of apples, landscapes, roofscapes, and nudes, or portraits which might all have been painted from a group of half-a-dozen assorted models rigged up in miscellaneous suits and surroundings, tries in vain to appraise them by the minute criteria of craftsmanship … with the aid of a labyrinthine technical vocabulary scarcely surpassed by that of medicine. But it would take more hard words than even Mr. Bell has learned to persuade us that many of these masterpieces are anything but careful imitations of what was being done in Paris when the painter passed his pupil-year there. A few well-defined designs that can be learned by heart in half a year, two or three tricks of colour conscientiously repeated, laborious drawing painfully dissimulated as careless ease – that is the London Group as well as the Academy.

The dismissal of the Academy is to be expected but the casual sideswipe at the Bloomsbury art critic, Clive Bell, and the Bloomsbury Group generally, effectively widens the notion of the 'establishment' that is under attack. Who does Bunting advance as the alternative to this tide of conformism? Wyndham Lewis, Isaac Rosenberg's friend David Bomberg and, naturally enough, his own drinking buddy, Nina Hamnett, artists who have 'perilously kept their independence in a wilderness where the pleasant fruits of patronage don't grow'. Bunting emphasises the humour in Hamnett's work, seeing her as the 'contemporary representative of the long line of English Comic draughtsmen that extends from Hogarth', and he uses his own experience of her life in the Fitzroy Tavern to describe her art: 'She seems to view the world as an agreeably ridiculous place, a huge bar-room, full of Rabelaisian tipplers, sometimes sad, always hard up, but never without a joke. She has something of the spirit that animated the immortal partnership of Boz and Phiz.'

In-between the two 'Some of Our Conquerors' pieces there were reviews of John Macy's *The Story of the World's Literature* (on 23 July), Harold Montgomery Belgion's translation of Ramon Fernandez's *Messages* (6 August) and René Fülöp-Miller's *The Mind and Face of Bolshevism* (27 August). Macy's survey suffers a real drubbing, chiefly, one suspects, because he had published those horrible sham translations from Hugo and de Musset and pulled your leg by turning Villon at his most straightforward into – well, let us be polite and call it Wardour Street English? Do you imagine *that* to be a translation that renders

> Plus becquetez d'oyseaulx que dez à couldre

as

> Our cheeks, ah me,
> Like thimble-tops are full of hollows small?

What cheeks? What hollows small? 'Translation,' you write elsewhere, 'should be one of two things, strictly literal, or recreated art in the language of the translator.' Which is this?'[185]

The notable feature of Bunting's positive review of Fernandez's *Messages* is its criticism of Belgion's translation. This may be because it is a pedantic and precious translation, or it may be because Montgomery Belgion was, as we shall see, one of Pound's 'bloomsbuggers'.[186] Bunting rejected the opportunity that Fülöp-Miller's apologia for Bolshevism gave him to express his own Fabian brand of socialism. Instead he turned his review into an attack on the cult of the 'new': 'it never occurs to Herr Fülöp-Miller to trace his list of 'amazing' *isms* not to Bolshevik theories but to the painters and poets of Montparnasse, who are more likely to be Camelots than Communists'.[187]

Bunting contributed two more book reviews in October 1927 before becoming the newspaper's full time music critic towards the end of the month. His review of Jack Lindsay's *William Blake: Creative will and the poetic image* appeared on 1 October and gave him an opportunity to rehearse his (or at least Skipsey's) view that Blake was a better metaphysician than poet, while lambasting Lindsay for his execrable prose. Lindsay, like the subject of his book, 'was always running for shelter under hard words borrowed from the more illiterate philosophers'. Bunting seems to have taken a real dislike to Lindsay. Born in Australia in 1900, he moved permanently to the United Kingdom in 1926 and as a prolific author and publisher (he wrote 170 books in a long life that ended in 1990) he and Bunting would have been moving in similar circles. We can't assume that Bunting's hostility was excited by any personal animus but 'Mr. Lindsay and Mr. Blake' is more *ad hominem* than was Bunting's usual style, although he was always forthright. Indeed Bunting's style in this particular review is adversely affected by the very problem he identifies in Lindsay's: 'Are we so dull as to be unable to accompany Mr. Lindsay in his critical excursions? It is to be hoped that, having by now read some of the other Centenary books, he is ashamed of this sneering superiority, which he assumes on almost every page.' Bunting's own sneering superiority mars this, his penultimate review in *The Outlook*.[188]

His final outing before becoming the paper's music critic was a review of *Hymen, or the Future of Marriage*, written by another Australian, the sexologist Norman Haire. By now Bunting was seriously off form and the patronising tone he adopts suggests that his reviews were becoming more about him than about the book supposedly under consideration. Norman Haire wasn't exactly a lightweight. Not only was he controversial, but already at the age of thirty-five, when *Hymen, or the Future of Marriage* was published, he was also a globally recognised pioneer in sexual studies, including the Steinach vasectomy to increase male potency, which he performed on W. B. Yeats in 1934. After a little headmasterly fun with Haire's name ('The cautious Mr. Haire runs a little way behind the hounds') he coyly introduces his own love life to protest at what is, after all, a serious sociological study of the role of sex in society. Haire, a friend of Havelock Ellis and the first sexologist to have a Harley Street consultancy, deserved better than this response to his contention that marriage was *not* instituted for the procreation of children:

> Heaven forbid! Man is a jealous animal, and the clash of desire and jealousy that the Restoration wits could not contrive to soften will never be avoided by mere benignity. The question (which Mr. Haire avoids asking) is whether it is better in the mind to suffer the pangs and buffets of outrageous jealousy or for us all to consent, as now, to nurse a certain proportion of unacted desires in consideration of being allowed to have our wives and husbands more or less to ourselves. The reviewer is not to answer the question he asks, thank goodness! He is neither philosopher nor prophet, and finds his own very simple love affairs embarrassment enough without undertaking to regulate those of the world at large.[189]

So, one might ask, why are you reviewing this book? It is an abdication of journalistic responsibility similar to that of his review of Conrad's *The Rover*. I doubt that Norman Haire had ever heard of Restoration wits. If anything Bunting's review becomes even more pompous, patronising, self-serving and embarrassing, but we probably have enough evidence that it was time he moved on to a subject about which he knew something. Bunting was writing for his audience, of course, but it is easy to see what he meant when he told Victoria Forde that he wouldn't have liked himself much in his *Outlook* days (see p.145). Two observations stand out from 'What are we coming to?'. The first is that Haire's book quotes 'from learned scientific books long passages in praise of incest', passages that doubtless informed the conversation with the recently Steinached W. B. Yeats a few years later (see p.173–4). The second is Bunting's uncanny ability to showcase ideas that seem particularly relevant in 2013, in this case not to his credit. 'How glad we are to learn, on page 92,' he sneers airily, 'that long before Mr. Haire's earthly paradise is established, "Society will have recognised and legalised the citizen's right to suicide!"' Game, set and match to Haire.

For all his talents Bunting of *The Outlook* is sometimes difficult to like. To be fair to him he was doing a job that he detested. In 1927 he wrote to his twelve-year-old cousin, Billy Swann, back in Throckley:

> I sometimes see people playing [tennis] on the hard courts in Lincoln's Inn Fields when I am on my way to the dusty offices of dreary editors in Fleet Street, who say 'Nothing today, thankyou' as though I were a peddlar selling bootlaces instead of the Celebrated Mr Bunting trying to sell articles, but sometimes they print things and then the chief troubles are:-
>
> (a) that they don't pay enough.
>
> (b) that they don't pay at all unless you go round and bother them.
>
> (c) they always choose the bad articles instead of the good ones, and the worse an article is the surer they are to stick your name at the bottom of it in big letters so that you get a bad reputation instead of a good one.[190]

Young Billy might well have asked himself what he'd done to deserve this tale of woe from the glamorous capital.

Mostly I wrote drunk

Bunting told Jonathan Williams in a televised interview that his music criticism was 'not art in any sense. I was merely a journalist who knew nothing whatever about music pretending to be a music critic. That went well enough. England was full of highbrow papers in those days ... I even wrote High Tory leaders [for *The Outlook*] though I was a socialist.'[191] None of his identifiable contributions to *The Outlook* was a leader although, as we have seen, he was indeed usually able to disguise his socialism.

Bunting wasn't proud of his music criticism. He told Victoria Forde that a young man earning his weekly guineas is not particular what he writes. Indeed, *The Outlook* told me that when I wrote sober I was too highbrow for them, so mostly I wrote drunk, and goodness knows what foolish things I may have written. Besides, I hardly recognise the author: I am not the same person I was fifty, forty, thirty years ago, and I don't think I would like my early self very much if I met him – too conceited by far, and even more ignorant than I am today.[192]

This casual self-deprecation belies a considerable sensitivity to music. In *Descant on Rawthey's Madrigal* Jonathan Williams took the poet back to the link between Chopin's and T. S. Eliot's *Preludes* and nudged him on to the next stage of his thinking:

I had thought all along that the sonata was the more likely one to be of use. But I got off on the wrong foot trying to imitate Beethoven's sonatas, using extremely violent contrasts in tone and speed which don't actually carry well onto the page, and had to puzzle about that for awhile before I discovered it was better to go back to a simpler way of dealing with the two themes and to take the early or mid-eighteenth-century composers of sonatas – John Christian Bach and Scarlatti – as models to imitate.[193]

We have seen Bunting's advanced use of the sonata at work in 'Villon', but he admitted that in his early twenties he couldn't make much of a Bach sonata. In any event his period at the *Outlook* was clearly one of musical self-development:

Before my twenties ended, after I had that spell as music critic on the *Outlook* and was able to spend some money on scores and to listen with the scores before me, I could for a number of years – I've lost the art now – read a score and hear in my mind pretty roughly, but accurately enough for my general purposes, how the thing goes. So I read quite a lot of music of that period. Not precisely the same as is now fashionable – Vivaldi was not above the horizon at that time.[194]

Bunting wanted to get 'the public to take notice of composers despised at that time',[195] and he singled out Monteverdi, Schoenberg and the Elizabethan composers. He clearly felt himself to be part of the musical public education revolution that Edward Clark had started at the BBC in 1924, deliberately giving 'the public what it didn't want until it changed its mind and did'.[196] In 1970 he recalled the squalid state music was in in England before that [Clark]. As late as the middle twenties I remember a respected critic excusing Beethoven's late quartets on the ground that the poor chap was deaf and couldn't hear the ghastly noise they made. Caruso sang 'The Yanks are Coming' and Dame Clara Butt never gave a concert without 'Home Sweet Home' and 'Love's Old Sweet Song'. Even the cultured few limited their pleasures to Beethoven's successors or to Wagner and Verdi. Only the real intellectuals could put up with Debussy. Stravinsky was to be endured, but Schoenberg was merely a mad pedant. Mozart was not often heard, Handel only in edited versions: and musical history began with Bach, who was to be put up with in spite of his dryness and terrible difficulty.[197]

Seen against this philistinism Bunting's crusading was brave and principled.

The Outlook, however, supplied more than intellectual stimulation. It provided Bunting with an element of stability in what had become a fairly chaotic life:

> I suppose I made, between what the *Outlook* paid me and what other jobs I was able to get on the strength of that one – writing music for a monthly magazine, an occasional review for the *Musical Times*, sometimes standing in for one of the daily newspaper critics, and so on – I made something like 250 pounds a year. You multiply that by five and you've got the present equivalent. It's not bad for a youngster of 27.[198]

This recollection, forty years after the event, of a new-found and unfamiliar financial security is seriously compromised by a letter he wrote to Lionel Robbins at its apparent height. In September 1927 he asked Robbins for a loan of £20 with no great hope that his request would be granted. He had pawned all his possessions except his typewriter and had 'only a very few pounds in prospect'. He was expecting an advance from Duckworth for a book on pubs that never materialised, and he was trying to sell a 'wardrobe-trunk, a kind of portable pantechnicon of a brute of a box ... I hate the monstrous thing, but it will hold all one's clothes and half one's household effects into the bargain.'[199]

On 29 October 1927 Bunting began (with a review of four recent piano concerts)[200] an almost unbroken run of weekly music articles and reviews that lasted until 19 May 1928. With the responsibility he seems to have discovered a sudden desire to serve the reader thoughtfully:

A seat on the fence may afford a wide view of the contemporary scene, but it gives no one a lead. The critical journalist, writing for a mainly non-technical public, is called upon to give a very decided opinion; if he falters modestly or seeks refuge in discussions of technique he is abdicating his function.[201]

His judgements certainly weren't infallible. Arnold Bax's reputation has survived this mauling in the same article:

> Bax is an excellent specimen of the composer whose work has been instructive and valuable to contemporary musicians, but does not seem likely to interest another generation … That he should ever have written this dull work [*Fantasy Sonata*] betrays his crucial fault – a strained, mechanical, and often trite invention used to cover an embarrassing lack of imagination.

In a review of the same concert *The Times* described it as 'full of characteristic poetic feeling … beautiful in sound'. [202]

Bunting's tone in his music articles for *The Outlook* is frequently condescending and scornful but he was capable of unalloyed praise as well. He applauded Segovia's sublime guitar artistry on 12 November 1927: 'Segovia does not play his guitar with his mind and fingers only but with something much deeper and more fundamental – his soul, his whole life. One feels that Segovia without his guitar would be like a dumb man; he is like a poet, with it.'[203] He was enthusiastic about Peter Warlock's 'Capriol', which may have encouraged their first meeting a few months later. He championed the out-of-fashion Liszt, the Italian composer, Ferruccio Busoni, the 'pagan mystic' Stravinsky and the (then at least) bewildering Arnold Schoenberg. He attacked the musical establishment fearlessly, for demanding subsidies for opera, for failing to plan the London season to avoid musical feast and famine, for preventing the British public from hearing Schoenberg's 'Gurrelieder' for eighteen years. He described the London music scene as 'a wilderness of dull days when nothing is to be heard but mediocrities playing to a meagre audience of deadheads, pupils and relatives'. He warily celebrated William Walton's early work and was willing to handle roughly popular favourites such as Schubert and Beethoven, Elgar and Franck. And almost anything, it seems, was better than 'the purely descriptive talent of Dr. Vaughan Williams, whose Lark ascends apparently interminably'.[204]

In March 1928 he was scornful of the undiscriminating (mainly Italian) audience at the Aeolian Hall and the Poltronieri Quartet they were applauding, an ensemble which seemed to prefer noise to music; enchanted by the harpsichordists Mme Wanda Landowska at the Wigmore Hall and Mrs Gordon Woodhouse at the Aeolian, although unfortunately 'Madame Landowska also composes. Alas!'; impressed by the folk singing of Ursula Greville at the Purcell Rooms and Elisabeth Schumann's lieder; and disgusted by Sir Thomas Beecham's butchery of Handel's 'Solomon'.[205]

The Outlook was nearing the end of its life and Bunting had only three more music pieces and two book reviews to come. On 19 May he signed off for ever with a review of *Human values and verities* by Henry Osborn Taylor. After months of deriding composers, performers, ensembles and audiences one cheers silently that he was able to leave on a positive note, mainly. All Mr Taylor writes 'has pondered breadth and is worth serious consideration. His writing is clear and, in the best sense, popular. A little too much unction here and there is easily forgiven.'[206]

His piece on Elizabethan composers encouraged Philip Heseltine and the Scottish composer and music critic, Cecil Gray, to seek him out in Kleinfeldt's, ostensibly to discuss sixteenth-century music but as likely is the fact that Heseltine recognised a kindred spirit in Bunting. In that period Heseltine and fellow composer Jack Moeran were leading a life of drunken chaos in rural Kent, behaviour that frequently attracted police attention, as when he was arrested for riding his motorbike naked. Hesletine moved to Eynsford in Kent with his lover, Barbara Peache, Moeran, 'his Maori factotum Hal Collins, and a number of cats'[207] in January 1925. Better known as Peter Warlock, Heseltine was a talented composer. By the time he met Bunting he was well known for *The Curlew*, which linked four poems by Yeats as a song cycle, but he was perhaps even better known as the inspiration for the characters of Julius Halliday in D. H. Lawrence's 1920 novel *Women in Love* and the irrepressible drunk, Coleman, in Aldous Huxley's 1923 satire of the post-war cultural elite, *Antic Hay* (a novel that also caricatures Wyndham Lewis and Nancy Cunard). There's no doubt that Elizabethan music was discussed by Gray, Bunting and Warlock in Kleinfeldt's in the 1920s, just as Shakespeare was, perhaps, fifty years later by Oliver Reed, Peter O'Toole and Richard Burton in the Duke of Hamilton a couple of miles up the hill. By 1928 when Warlock met Bunting his fortunes were waning. He had little money and less work and his musical self-confidence had deserted him. We can get some sense of his lifestyle from a letter written to his friend the bon viveur Bruce Blunt on 20 July 1928: 'Please excuse this tardy reply – I have been in soak for several days and even now (10 a.m.) can, as you see, barely hold a pen.'[208]

Towards the end of the year Warlock was living in London and spending considerable time in the British Library (at that time housed in the British Museum in Bloomsbury) researching an anthology of drinking songs. Kleinfeldt's is a few hundred metres from the rear entrance of the museum and since Warlock was spending at least as much time in pubs as in the library it seems reasonable to date Bunting's acquaintance with him to late 1928 and early 1929. His letters of the time show him to be considerably more preoccupied with contemporary than with Elizabethan music, lending weight perhaps to the possibility that his relationship with Bunting was as social as it was professional. To be fair, Warlock was a genuine expert on Elizabethan music, and he had attempted to correct what he saw as Fellowes' hijacking of the Byrd *Great Service* discovery.[209] Bunting, too, retained his devotion to Elizabethan music for the rest of his life. Asked, at the age of eighty, which five recordings he would save from a flood he had no hesitation: 'The Monteverdi bit out of Ariosto ... Some Dowland played by Julian Bream ... A concerto grossi from Corelli ... Any of D. Scarlatti's five hundred or so harpsichord sonatas played by Ralph Kirkpatrick ... And maybe Stravinsky's *Petrouchka*.'[210]

It is also possible that the artist Nina Hamnett was the main attraction as she and Heseltine had been friends since 1920 when Hamnett was installed in Modigliani's studio near the Café Mère Charlotte in Paris. According to Bunting Heseltine and Gray 'used often to come to Kleinfeldt's to drink with me and talk about music. And that was useful because both of them knew more about 16th century music than I did, and in those days hardly anyone knew anything about it. All the present knowledge was simply non-existent in 1926 and 1927.'[211]

SIMONSIDE INTERLUDE, 1928

The Outlook died in 1928 of 'a libel action that it didn't want to face'[212] leaving Bunting once again penniless, but a meeting with Margaret de Silver, the wealthy widow of prominent American civil liberties activist, Albert de Silver, who had died under an express train in 1924, gave Bunting the opportunity to escape a London he detested. At that time Margaret was lonely and depressed, dispensing largesse until she met the Italian revolutionary Carlo Tresca in 1931 and found a new investment focus. It is possible that she was attracted by Bunting's Quaker credentials – she was herself from a wealthy, elite family of Philadelphia Quakers – but her artistic philanthropy was well known and she welcomed many writers as friends to her sophisticated Greenwich Village home.[213] It is easy to mock de Silver's perhaps undiscriminating generosity, as her good friend, the novelist Dawn Powell did: 'October 6 [1933]: 24 days to raise $500 to save rent, piano and all establishment my cocksureness of future got us into. Decided to do play on Margaret and her house – the fortunate rich woman surrounded by artists, radicals, schools, dancers, etc., all telling her she's a bourgeois. Her constant expiation of sin of wealth.'[214]

On the record Bunting himself remembered Margaret de Silver more generously and, naturally enough, certainly not as undiscriminating:

> She had been left a great deal of money by her husband ... and she spent [it] in the course of her lifetime very largely on subsidizing artists, poets, politicians, lawyers, civil liberties, etc. Before she died, I believe she got rid of practically all of it, just giving it away in this very wonderful and rather discriminating generosity. I met her and found when she had left London that she had left word with Otto Theis that I was to have a subsidy of 200 pounds a year for two years to give me a chance to get going writing. I could hardly refuse! It was the greatest possible help.[215]

Off the record he was less generous, although sufficiently oblique to remain loyal. During a conversation with Carroll F. Terrell in 1979 he remembered Margaret as his salvation as an artist:

> These memories led to the story of John J. Adams, who was sort of an Eliot on one side and a nature lover and vegetarian on the other. He was also the ugliest man in London with a head and face which suggested nothing so much as a bedraggled horse. His chances of getting married seemed to be nil until someone introduced him to the ugliest woman in London, who also happened to be one of the wealthiest women in England. They married and lived quite happily until she died. But before dying, she exacted a promise from him to marry her best friend, who was the second ugliest woman in London. He did with happy consequences. He had inherited all his first wife's wealth. The happiest consequence of all was that, with John J. Adams's encouragement, his new wife became a great patron of struggling artists.
>
> The context of the story suggested he was talking about ... Margaret de Silva [*sic*], but he wouldn't say so directly. I had the impression he didn't want to be so ungallant as to nominate any candidate for unqualified ugliness.[216]

Bunting was tired of London and his first instinct was to get as far away from urban life as he possibly could.[217] Armed with Margaret's bursary he immediately fled back to the north of England. He lived for about six months in the Simonside Hills in Northumberland, sharing a small cottage with Ned Wilson, a local shepherd. He remembered that the cottage, Coldside, was seven miles to the nearest cigarette shop and four miles from the local pub.[218] This is a bit of Bunting hyperbole, although to be fair to him he was recalling distances from fifty years previously. Coldside Farm is five miles from Rothbury (for cigarettes) and a few hundred yards from the Crown and Thistle public house (which almost certainly sold cigarettes). Nevertheless it was as remote a location as one could find in England, and still is. Only fifteen thousand years ago this part of the world was buried under a kilometre of ice and it feels, more than other parts of northern England, as though that is its natural state, as though the windswept wilderness of the Simonside Hills is showing itself briefly and reluctantly before it welcomes back the ice. It is a cold, unforgiving and beautiful landscape, perfect for a lover of Wordsworth seeking to chisel out his own poetic epitaph. According to Caddel and Flowers, Wilson had moved to Coldside as he was unwell and he and his wife let a room to guests to supplement their reduced income. Wilson's daughter 'who was six at the time, remembers Bunting with his moustache and pipe – not surprisingly she found him intimidating! He was writing during the time he was staying with them, and she was under strict instructions not to disturb him.'[219]

The Crown and Thistle in Forestburn Gate now calls itself The Gate, but it is still really the Crown and Thistle. The pub sign that swings alarmingly in the gusts that roar down from Simonside, just two miles to the north west, depicts a gate sure enough, but a small red velvet crown is perched surreally on the left-hand post and two blowsy thistles bloom underneath the other. In 1928 the building was shared by a blacksmith, Robert Carmichael, and a publican, the pub being the tiny back room. Astonishingly the one photograph that was hanging on the wall of the Crown and Thistle when I visited in 2012 is of Forest Burn AFC, winners of the Coquetdale League 1928–29.

In later life Bunting was not above spinning tall tales about the folly of the inhabitants of the rural north for credulous American friends. He told Carroll F. Terrell a story about a Simonside shepherd who in his whole life never got further than a small market town nearby, and that only a couple of times. But when he was quite old, he was called upon to be a judge of sheep in some national contest near London. The managers of the contest provided him with a first class train ticket, expenses, and a fancy hotel room. Basil got much fun out of the man's trying to get out of train windows, not finding the door, and his general disorientation in the modern world. After it was all over, they put him onto the underground for King's Cross Station, so that all he saw of London was through the window of the train. When they asked him later at home what he thought of London, he said all he could remember about it was that it was very dark.[220]

Bunting's audience doesn't appear to have asked itself how many sheep trials took place within a tube ride of King's Cross, even in 1928.

By his own admission[221] he didn't achieve much in England but two poems from 1928 survived into *Collected Poems*, 'The day being Whitsun' and 'Loud intolerant bells'. 'The day being Whitsun' evokes a wet and dreary quotidian London:

> The day being Whitsun we had pigeon for dinner;
> but Richmond in the pitted river saw
> mudmirrored mackintosh, a wet southwest
> wiped and smeared dampness over Twickenham.
>
> Pools on the bustop's buttoned tarpaulin.
> Wimbledon, Wandsworth, Clapham, the Oval. 'Lo,
> Westminster Palace where the asses jaw!'[222]

So far, so dismal. Bunting is in south London, and far from happy. (Peter Quartermain has pointed out that Whit Sunday in 1928 fell on 27 May, shortly after *The Outlook* folded.[223]) We imagine his wet bus journey from Richmond in south west London to Westminster via the suburbs of Twickenham, Wimbledon and Wandsworth and up through Clapham, past the Surrey County Cricket Club ground at the Oval, over Vauxhall or Lambeth Bridge to the Houses of Parliament where politicians debate ('asses jaw'). 'Asses jaw' also invokes a biblical scene of course. In Judges Samson takes bloody revenge on the Philistines for the loss of his wife: 'And he found a new jawbone of an ass, and put forth his hand, and took it, and slew a thousand men therewith. And Sampson said, With the jawbone of an ass have I slain a thousand men.'[224] The suggestion is that although politicians are asses their talk can be lethal. We might think that he has in mind the First World War, a conflict he considered an unnecessary and unjustified construct of the European business and political elite, but the final stanza of the poem suggests that his gloom is deepened not by the political classes but by their victims:

> Endless disappointed buckshee-hunt!
> Suburb and city giftless garden and street,
> and the sky alight of an evening stubborn
> and mute by day and never *rei novae*
> *inter rudes artium homines.*
>   never a spark of sedition
> amongst the uneducated workingmen.[225]

The quotation from Livy is a little ugly, but it doesn't spoil the surprising turn the poem takes. Perhaps his time teaching at the Adult School in Lemington had convinced him that a proletarian revolution was impossible in a society that accepted the insults and injuries the ruling classes inflicted upon it with cheerful stoicism.

'Loud intolerant bells', by constrast, attacks the Church as the chief agent of betrayal, a target that was highlighted by the title under which it appeared in 1930 in Burling's first collection, *Redimiculum Matellarum*, 'While shepherds watched'. Its first stanza contains hints of the Georgian style from which Bunting was desperate to distance himself:

> *Each fettered ghost slips to his several grave*

> Loud intolerant bells (the shrinking nightflower closes
> tenderly round its stars to baulk their hectoring)
> orate to deaf hills where the olive stirs and dozes
> in easeless age, dim to farce of man's fashioning.

To my ears there is something a little too Rupert Brooke about these tender closings and dozing olives, but the second stanza is a less bucolic call to action:

> Shepherds away! They toll throngs to your solitude
> and their inquisitive harangue will disembody
> shames and delights, all private features of your mood,
> flay out your latencies, sieve your hopes, fray your shoddy.

The Church then will rob you of your humanity, and the deft reference to the Inquisition suggests that it will do so by force. To retain our simple virtues and pleasures we must get away from the Church and the final stanza makes it clear that there is no point in trying to reach beyond the Church to get direct access to the mysteries it has politicised for itself and its blood brother, the ruling elite:

> The distant gods enorbed in bright indifference
> whom we confess creatures or abstracts of our spirit,
> unadored, absorbed into the incoherence,
> leave dessicated names: rabbits sucked by ferrets.[226]

Even if they cared the pagan deities would be unable to help. They have been sucked dry by priests.

These short poems provide a useful opportunity to assess the development of the 28-year-old poet's technique, for there is a great deal going on under their surfaces. They also help us to understand what Bunting meant by his insistence that sound in a poem carries 'meaning'. In 'Loud intolerant bells' Bunting weaves a web of sound which gives the stanzas a unique musical quality, and the music of the language both expresses and creates some of the complex tensions in the poem. The bells evoke musicality immediately and the repetition and echoes of particular sounds help to structure the poem. Of course, good poetry always uses music and metre to deliver and create meaning, but here Bunting focuses very deliberately on sound as an *object*, as well as a mechanism, and in particular 'tolling', a word that also intimates rhythm. Specifically 'tolling' suggests monotony and regular, restricted ('fettered') measure. The sound doesn't ring out a melody but 'tolls' ominously.

The sound 'toll' appears four times in the first two stanzas: 'intolerant', 'olive', 'toll … solitude'. But even these few cases have an audible impact. In both stanzas the first 'toll' echoes disturbingly in the word that follows ('intolerant … olive'; 'toll … solitude'). The sound invades the peace of the language, occupying the phonetic space of the words 'olive' and 'solitude'. This is emphasised at a semantic level in the second stanza where the 'inquisitive harangue' of the tolling threatens to 'disembody' and 'fray' the shepherds' privacy and 'solitude'. The effect is condensed in the phrase 'toll throngs to your solitude', whereas in the first stanza the echo of 'intolerant' in 'olive' is protracted over three lines. This compression amplifies and intensifies the effect, and amplification (noise) could be read as a negative and disruptive force in the poem. The very first word, 'loud', threatens the other images in the first stanza: the 'shrinking nightflower closes/

154

tenderly round its stars to baulk [the loud bells'] hectoring'. The parenthesis emphasises discomfort in these two lines, the whole threatened image trying to defend itself within a protective shield, the parenthesis closing around the lines reflecting the nightflower closing around its stars. And at a denotative level the image is comparatively 'tender' and vulnerable, in contrast to the loud, obnoxious bells.

In the third and fourth lines the noise seems to lose some of its potency: the hills and olive are 'deaf' to the bells' 'oratory', and 'dim to farce of man's fashioning', the artificial, regulated, *fettered* tolling of the bells. As the landscape changes space is opened up. The antiquity of nature ('stars', 'hills', 'easeless age') is contrasted with the modern 'farce' of man. However, the latent threat, which initially provokes the actively defensive image of 'the shrinking nightflower', hasn't disappeared in this landscape, as the 'toll' from the word 'intolerant' echoes in the word 'olive'. This epitomises the subtle and powerful tensions Bunting conjures within the poem's soundscape. The olive, a symbol of peace, is disturbed in its 'easeless age'; it 'stirs and dozes' rather than sleeping peacefully. Without the word 'easeless' we might be tempted to read the two verbs in a tranquil isolation. The words 'deaf', 'stirs', 'dozes', and 'dim', however, are separated by 'easeless' – an uncomfortable, *uneasy* presence in the stanza. I read 'easeless' as a word which interrupts and at the same time captures the entire movement of the stanza, positioned in the final line to remind us of the unsettling presence of the bells which dominates the first three lines. All the natural images seem vulnerable and threatened.

The poem has an extraordinary sonorous density. An ABAB rhyme sequence reflects the regularity of tolling, amplifying the pervasive bells. It is another structural restraint which contains the natural images that struggle for freedom: shepherds, stars, 'abstracts … absorbed into the incoherence'. The regularity of a rhyme scheme like this might suggest the inflexible and restrictive conventions of pre-modernist poetry. In the first stanza the end rhyme traces the now familiar conflict between indifference and restriction. 'Closes' rhymes with 'dozes' to suggest a quiet resilience to the impotent bells, unable to wake or startle the 'deaf hills' and 'olive', and unable to permeate the nightflowers' 'tender' protection of its 'stars', closed off to the noise. But the images are also *closed* within the rhyme pattern. 'Hectoring' and 'fashioning' couple to evoke a sense of harassment and artificiality, antagonising the dozing and closing. There is a similar antagonistic effect in the second stanza where 'solitude' rhymes with 'private features of your mood', and 'disembody' with 'fray your shoddy'. This alternating rhyme pattern both emphasises and *enacts* the tensions and conflicts.

The poem's epigraph: '*Each fettered ghost slips to his several grave*' reaches into the final lines. This world we have 'desiccated' and subordinated with a Christian totalitarianism is a world that is dying *within us*, closing a silent grave around itself like the nightflower closing itself around its stars in the first lines. Christian symbolism has even appropriated the most natural spiritual images, such as the stars which primitive man used to navigate through the incoherence and beautiful enormity of the world, and shepherds, nomadic men who live freely within it in a close relationship with nature. The sound of Christianity ('Loud intolerant bells') saturates the poem. The epigraph comes from Milton's 'On the Morning of Christ's Nativity' so the presence of Christ is with us from the very beginning. The 'fettered ghosts' are those of a 'damnèd crew' that 'Our Babe to show his Godhead true,/ Can in his swaddling bands control ... ' The conflicts Bunting approaches in this poem reflect the conflict between monotheism and paganism that is integral to the narrative Milton weaves in his. Milton's poem is utterly engrossed in the music and sounds of God, his voice, man's voice, nature's voice, and the resonant and spiritual relationships and clashes between them.

Bunting absolutely loathed this kind of analysis. His frequent quarrels with academia were, as Peter Lewis says, motivated by a desire to 'protect poetry from ... a type of analytical criticism that promised to offer up its "meaning" or "message" or "significance"'.[227] Bunting may have scorned it but this analysis of 'Loud intolerant bells' is an attempt to show how much craft underpins this poem. Every word works hard to pull together complementary and contradictory 'meanings', but every word too is a note in the overall music of the poem. The poet was mastering his craft during his twenties and if 'Villon' is the most impressive expression of that craft his early lyrics are evidence of very precise technique.

RAPALLO, 1928–1930

These years in England, 'earning a very meagre living and growing stupid', had been largely wasted but,

> then I kicked, decided that I'd rather not earn a living than write any more reviews for weeklies, and have been the better for it ever since. I tried my own North Country for a while, and it wasn't so bad but I got very little done that

I wanted to keep, so I took advice and went to Berlin and it was the worst thing I ever did. In the end to save my sanity I went suddenly to the station and bought a ticket for Italy to look up Pound again. And here I've been ever since, with the exception of eight months in the States to get married.[228]

After six months in the Simonside Hills Bunting first 'cleared off to Germany – but for a very short time, for I found I didn't like the Germans at all. And then into Italy again. I went to Rapallo and settled down there close to Pound.'[229] Pound wrote to his mother in October 1928 from Rapallo: 'Bunting is exmusic critic of the no longer extant London 'Outlook', wanted or rejected by the police in several countries.'[230] Buried in all this is a casually announced, anonymous tragedy. Bunting wrote to Pound at the end of 1928, 'I am off for the continent, and I hope to be in Italy sometime in the spring and I hope to visit Rapallo and I hope to see you there. My girl died.'[231]

Bunting was back in Rapallo when Pound wrote to his mother from there on 3 March 1929[232] and by the summer he was in love. Marian Gray Culver, from Eau Claire, Wisconsin, was in Venice as part of the European tour her father had presented her with on her graduation from Columbia University. Marian recalled their meeting on Corpus Domini day some forty years later: 'We were both staying in a pension in the Clock Tower in Venice. We watched Mussolini's Black Shirts give an exhibition to the music of "Giovinezza" and watched a solemn procession march around the Piazza and into St. Marks. There was even a Cardinal from Rome present to mark the occasion.'[233]

Marian was immediately impressed by his erudition. 'B's standards were very high & I can remember his going over my library (I carried Van Doren's anthology of World Poetry around Europe with me). Basil got hold of it while we were in Venice ... & he went thru it page by page saying "Shit, Shit, Shit, Shit; he's left out the best poems in most cases! (and quoted them) He doesn't know a God-damn thing about Poetry etc. etc."'[234]

When Bunting met Marian he was trying valiantly to interest the newly established publishing company, Wishart & Company, in a translation of Paterne Berrichon's 1912 biography of his brother-in-law, Jean-Arthur Rimbaud. He wrote in April 1929 to C. H. Rickword at Wishart to offer it as a 'companion book to your brother's' for 30/- per thousand words, noting along the way that the originating French publisher, Mercure de France, would require £24 for the rights. At that price he could guarantee to finish in two months 'well done, an improvement on the original etc. etc.'[235]

Rickword wasn't especially impressed by this idea. Berrichon was out of date, Mercure wanted far too much money 'and so, if I may say so, do you. Even the great Scott Moncrieff only gets about a pound per thousand!'[236] Charles Kenneth Scott Moncrieff was the period's most celebrated translator from French and was just completing his masterly translation of Proust's *A la Recherche du Temps Perdu*. Bunting was never short of chutzpah.

In this letter Rickword also told Bunting that Higgins had mentioned to him the fact that Bunting had 'unearthed an Austrian' whom he considered worth translating. 'Bertie has got the details wrong again,' Bunting replied. 'It is not an Austrian but a Hungarian and I haven't unearthed him, he is confoundedly famous already. Name of Jokay, novelist. Probably some little bits of his big output are translated already.'[237] Most of Mór Jókai's output had been available in English for over twenty years. Rickword wasn't very interested in this idea either. [238]

Bunting was restless as soon as he arrived in Rapallo. He told Louise Morgan as early as April 1929 that he was by no means sure that he would stay: 'I am fond of the place, but after Ezra & Yeats & Antheil are gone it might be as well for me to make a change of scene & avoid being bored in a place where I've never yet made any but good memories. So I don't know where I'll be in June. I don't want to live in London again yet not before 1930. And France is still forbidden. Perhaps the south of Italy – or Greece.'[239]

The tiny resort, however, and its celebrated artists stirred Bunting's creativity. Five of the poems he wrote in 1929 went the distance to *Collected Poems*. 'Dear be still!', a poem 'which is quantitative', as he told an audience in February 1982,[240] is a riposte to Andrew Marvell's 'To his coy mistress', celebrating delayed gratification:

> Dear be still! Time's start of us lengthens slowly.
> Bright round plentiful nights ripen and fall for us.
> Those impatient thighs will be bruised soon enough.[241]

He was still experimenting with metre. As Victoria Forde points out, the music of 'Dear be still!' revolves around the skilful use of spondees[242] but there is still a languorous *fin de siécle* tone about this poem.

Generally the 1929 odes show the poet in an uncompromising mood. Ode 11, 'To a Poet who advised me to preserve my fragments and false starts', is a harsh riposte to what was probably well-meant advice:

Narciss, my numerous cancellations prefer
slow limpness in the damp dustbins amongst the peel
tobacco-ash and ends spittoon lickings litter
of labels dry corks breakages and a great deal

of miscellaneous garbage picked over by
covetous dustmen and Salvation Army sneaks
to one review-rid month's printed ignominy,
the public detection of your decay, that reeks.[243]

Ode 12, 'An arles, an arles', takes a slightly more light-hearted view of the role of the poet but it is hardly free from bitterness:

An arles, an arles for my hiring,
O master of singers, an arlespenny!

–Well sung singer, said Apollo,
but in this trade we pay no wages.

I too was once a millionaire
(in Germany during the inflation:
when the train steamed into Holland
I had not enough for a bun.)

The Lady asked the Poet:
Why do you wear your raincoat in the drawing-room?
He answered: Not to show
my arse sticking out of my trousers.

His muse left him for a steady man.
Quaeret in trivio vocationem.

(he is cadging for drinks at the streetcorners.)[244]

Victoria Forde detects 'ironic humour' in this poem[245] which, I think, underplays the poet's resentment that his work should be so little valued. The poem draws on a real experience. Bunting told a creative writing class many years later that he had once had to leave his overcoat on at a party so as 'not to show my arse sticking out of my trousers'.[246]

An arles is an advance payment on a signed contract and the salon scene in the poem is bracketed by his plea for cash at the opening and his destitution at the end, 'arles' playing off 'arse'. In between, in a beau monde vignette, the poet's honesty causes him to blow his opportunity to raise funds from a benefactress. The implication is that by holding up a mirror to the world the poet automatically excludes himself from it.

Bunting wrote to Otto Theis' wife, Louise Morgan, in April 1929. He had been entertaining Margaret de Silver's son for the previous ten days or so and, Pound being away in Venice, his chief source of conversation was W. B. Yeats. He gave an intriguing glimpse of the ageing poet: 'He walks about – absent: sees nothing, apparently. But his huge curiosity is busy all the time, & in the evenings there comes upon him an urgent need of conversation and he lets loose metaphysics, mysticism, anecdotes, literary criticism and the history of Ireland all stirred up well together. References to Sligo have the power of making him look almost young again.'[247]

At some point in 1929 Bunting went south. He wrote to Otto Theis on 28 Setember 1929 from Santa Caterina, Amalfi, telling him that 'Counting syllables is the only way to write!', and adding a poem that has not been published previously:

> Do not think I am contented here
> Although I am idle, wellfed and brown.
> >There's nothing to see but the sun
> >And nothing but the wind to hear.
> The sea is always flashing messages
> But I can't decode his conversation
> >Mountains give no occupation
> >To the mind: damn'd sterile ridges
> As to the natives, they are gay but dull,
> And that imbecile who tries to teach me
> >Is the blockhead of Italy:
> >Teacher! Pah! Qu'il me lèche le cul!
> Besides this, to say nothing of the flies
> Or of the other visitors, the wine
> >Is Spanish toothwash (that's wine) –
> >And the long and short of it is
> I may turn up in London any day
> And put up with the noise, to get blotto
> >In some good pub with you Otto,
> >And listen to what you've to say![248]

He wrote to Louise Morgan, by now Theis' wife and working for *Everyman* magazine, from Amalfi on 18 October. He was at that time probably briefly juggling two romances, one with Marian and one with Antonietta, with whom he shared, as we shall learn, 'submarine Amalfitan kisses'. Morgan had asked Bunting to help her source a photograph of Ford Madox Ford but he couldn't be of much help. Ford, he told her, had 'quarrelled with everybody, even Ezra' and no one seemed to know where he was. In any event there weren't many pictures of Ford in existence because he was 'too watery-bovine … to want his photo broadcast'. Although he couldn't help much with the photograph he was keen for commissions from *Everyman*. Perhaps his anecdote about Yeats looking 'almost young again' had interested her enough to ask for an article on Yeats because Bunting told Morgan that he didn't know Yeats' poetry well enough to write one until he returned to Rapallo the following month, but that he could write articles on Pound and Eliot straight away as he knew their work 'almost by heart'.[249]

Bunting, disguised as 'the late Mr Surtees', sent an article on Yeats to Morgan from Rapallo early in the new year. He had been busy:

> I was in bed with the liver, and then my mother came here and then I went to Switzerland on a job for W.B.Y. and then it was Xmas, so I had a hell of a time getting back to work at all. This is done straight onto the machine at midnight with a very bad cold, in the hope that in those conditions all highbrow inclinations, (as well as all sense of the English language I fear), will be in abeyance. Hence the resurrection of the late Mr Surtees, who contributed once or twice to the Outlook. I can say nothing in favour of this timeserving and unscrupulous journalist except that he gives all his earnings to me – and that he is not known to Yeats![250]

Bunting wrote again to Morgan on 6 May 1930, two days before he left Rapallo for Frankfurt (to hear an Antheil opera), London and then New York, in a beleagured but cheerful mood. He enclosed an article which he hoped might get an airing in *Everyman* and, unusually, he wasn't too worried about money: 'My clothes are appalling, my prospects nil, I am quite cheerful and not bothering at all.'[251] He was cheerful sometimes but he was occasionally sleeping rough in London and he wrote to Pound in June that he had

> got through one of the worst five weeks I have ever spent (including night on the embankment and Primrose Hill) and having apparently landed (but it is not quite sure yet) a commission to translate Lionardo da Vinci [*sic*] for the Mandrake people, two drafts have turned up that have been wandering

uselessly about the world for over two months and I am able to go to the blooming U.S.A.

He asked Pound for introductions in the US. His earnings in five 'fairly strenuous weeks' had been 31 shillings and 6 pence (around 30p a week at a time when the average weekly salary in the UK was £3.75).[252]

A NEW YORK INTERLUDE, 1930

Marian Culver, twenty-nine, of Wading River, New York, and Basil Bunting, thirty, of Rapallo were married on 9 July 1930 (not 1929 as in some accounts, including, surprisingly, Marian's own)[253] at Riverhead, Long Island. They lived in Wading River for a while and then moved to an apartment at 62 Montague Street in Brooklyn Heights. Marian taught English in state schools and Bunting tried to find paid writing work. Bunting claimed to be almost allergic to artistic society, as we have seen, but in New York the Buntings' friends included the poets, William Carlos Williams and Louis Zukofsky, as well as the French critic René Taupin, the American artist Adolf Dehn, recently returned from Europe, and the Hungarian musician Tibor Serly.[254]

On 11 July 1930 Bunting sent a postcard to Zukofsky which started a lifelong friendship:

Dear Mr Zukofsky – Ezra Pound says I ought to look you up. May I?'[255]

Nearly four years Bunting's junior, Zukofsky had grown up as a Yiddish speaker in New York's Jewish community. He became a Marxist early in life and his youthful poetry impressed Pound. Zukofsky is another relatively uncelebrated genius. His 'A Foin Lass Bodders' of 1940 is proto-rap:

> You may go now assuredly, my ballad,
> Where you please, you are indeed so embellished
> That those who've relished you more than their salad
> Days'll hold you hallowed and away from shoddy –
> You can't stand making friends with everybody.[256]

I think that Zukofsky is the closest poet to Bunting in spirit. For Zukofsky, as for Bunting, the sound of a poem was its most important quality: 'The melody! the rest is accessory: ... /My one voice.'[257] Elsewhere in *"A-12"* Zukofsky is more explicit:

I'll tell you.
About my *poetics* –

$$\int_{\text{speech}}^{\text{music}}$$

An integral
Lower limit speech
Upper limit music

No?[258]

As Charles Bernstein says, 'The music of poetry, in Zukofsky's sense, refers to the intricate patterning of sound that everywhere pervades his work. This poetry leads with sound and you can never go wrong following the sound sense, for it is only after you hear the words that you are able to locate their meanings.'[259] It is true that close attention to sound patterns delivers Zukofsky's message just as close attention to syntax usually delivers Yeats'. The clue is here:

> *The vowels*
>   *abide*
> *in consonants*
>   *like*
>
> *Souls*
>   *in*
> *bodies* –[260]

In 'Peri Poietikes', in a sideswipe at Sir Philip Sidney, Zukofsky ridiculed poets who were obsessed by metre, much as Pound had complained of English translators of Homer who were 'deaved with syntax.'[261]

> What about measure, I learnt:
> *Look in your own ear and read ...*
> Mind, don't run to mind
> boys' Greeks' metres gnome,
> rummage in tee tomes, tee-tums,
>   tum-tees.[262]

Zukofsky also shared Bunting's preference for controlled simplicity:

Everything should be as simple as it can be,
Says Einstein,
But not simpler.[263]

Zukofsky is more playful than Bunting, but rarely as sonorous: 'For Zukofsky, it's all about toggling: between I and I, it and we, eye and you, seen and unseen, present and absent, here and there; a re-doubling-as-re-doubting of the senses. "See sun, and think shadow".'[264] Bunting was himself well aware of the ludic quality of Zukofsky's poetry in contrast with his own, or indeed with most poetry written in Britain, seeing immigration as the key factor, and noting that homonyms and puns are:

> a constant feature of his poetry, connecting things together; not only as jokes, [but as] a serious means of knitting together the poetry; as would be done, by an English poet, rather with the ancient cousinships of words which you hardly even notice. Puns are much more prominent. That is more natural to an American than to an Englishman because of the difference that has grown up between the two dialects because of the immigration.[265]

The image of Zukofsky pirouetting with cap and bells around an unsmiling Bunting as the English poet chisels his great monument is a caricature of course. Bunting's poetry has its light-hearted moments and Zukofsky wouldn't exactly fill out an anthology of twentieth-century comic verse. But caricatures can be useful shorthand and certainly reading Zukofsky alongside Bunting is fascinating. They have distinct voices but they wind around each other and you can often hear phrases in both poets that could have been written by the other. Bunting wouldn't have written:

> Ye nó we see hay
> io we hay we see
> hay io we sée no ... etc

but a few stanzas earlier there is a short passage of Buntingesque lyricism:

> Neither can bent hobnails flung
> chance's play equated aleatorical notes
> hurt public oblivion, no more
> than skiddaw rock emitting tones:
> the sea is our road

the land for our use,
damp cannot warm the houses —[266]

It's hard to keep Bunting's voice out of these lines. It is not my intention to denigrate the earlier lines from Zukofsky as nonsense. It is a carefully wrought adaptation of an Arapaho song, but one cannot hear Bunting in it. These quotations from Zukofsky are taken from the middle of *"A"*, an enormous poem in twenty-four parts that he wrote between 1928 and 1974, but Bunting's influence can be felt throughout Zukofsky's work, and vice versa. The stonemason in *Briggflatts* appears as a prototype in Zukofsky's *4 Other Countries*:

Sculptures
    in the shadow
of round
    wall —

Primitive
    monumental
nameless
    as the carver

Who hewed —
    constraining
his shapes
    to rocks [267]

Zukofsky's poem 'The' contains only five words, including the title:

The

The
desire
of
towing

Zukofsky explained to Ian Hamilton Finlay that 'he'd been thinking of tugboats, "which *tow* very seriously"'.[268] 'The' is a masterpiece of condensation and so close to the spirit of the opening lines of the 'Coda' to *Briggflatts* that the two poets seem to be operating in tandem. The only overlapping feature is the reference to towing, but both are infused by the spirit of a relentless sea-borne force that drives our destinies. 'The' had a profound effect on Bunting. He wrote to Pound in 1935 that he had been 'looking at [Zukofsky's] "The" again the other day I thought it much more accomplished than anything I'm ever likely to do.'[269]

Bunting reflected towards the end of his life that 'you could go a long way before you found two poets who are so close in their general ideas who remain so completely different.[270] A few months before his death he returned to the theme:

> The curious thing is that he and I, from the moment we met, which would be in 1930 I think, until within a couple of years of his death, were very, very close in writing. Everything I wrote I sent to Zukofsky and paid great attention to whatever he said about it. And about three quarters of what he wrote he sent to me with the same object and for the same thing, close, detailed criticism which he usually attended to – not always, but usually. Our output certainly must look very different. His is very different indeed from mine, mine very different from his. And though somebody looking at our verse might think we came from quite different points of view, he would be wrong ultimately. The conception of what a poem is, and what it should be, and what it should be about, and so on, would be pretty much the same.[271]

In spite of the opportunity to spend time with Zukofsky and William Carlos Williams Bunting was dismissive of his time spent in the US, although he recognised that in 1930, at the depth of the Depression, his timing wasn't perfect:

> I soon found out that I wasn't going to earn anything in America. American papers didn't at all like my way of things. It was better to go back and see how long we could live on nothing in Italy – rather than the very short time you can live on nothing in the United States ... I was ready to write music criticism for anybody who would employ me. I think I did some for one of the Philadelphia papers. There were some for the *New York Times* and some in *The Nation*, but you didn't get much for them and there weren't many of them in the first place. There certainly was no living in it.[272]

Bunting wrote to Harriet Monroe, somewhat tactlessly misspelling her name, on 2 August 1930: 'I am now in the United States, and seeing what prices you Americans charge for eats I could very well do with the price of my "Villon". If I were likely to be in Chicago before the end of September I would collect it in person. But I am never likely to reach Chicago at all, nor to get farther than the Brooklyn cemetery unless I can collect it before that. Besides, I have got married and my wife eats too.'[273]

Bunting's heart was never in journalism but the American media seems to have been more inhospitable even than the Fleet Street he detested. He complained to Pound: 'Journalism, nix. The atmosphere of Irita Van Dorens office at Herald Tribune nearly finished me off – the rows of books for review, the general tiredness of books in everybody, the hatred of the authors who inflict them on them.'[274]

Marian's recollections of Bunting's attempts to secure paid writing work in 1930 pull no punches, although she admits that 'it is almost impossible for me to give … any account of Basil Bunting that is not highly emotional'. She told Roger Guedalla that Bunting wrote nothing for any paper while in New York.

> He had lunch with Malcom Cowley but they did not hit it off & no writing of Basil's appeared in the Nation. Much to my disappointment since this was the kind of writing I had hoped he would do. During his stay in N.Y. Basil made no attempt to work, to obtain commissions, and did not even (except for the luncheon w[ith] Cowley) present the letters of introduction to possibly productive contacts with which Pound had supplied him in quantity.[275]

By his own account he had been 'disgustingly lethargic. It seems as though Italy were the only climate in which I can get up any energy',[276] but the problem was clearly more deep-rooted than that. It had been building up since his troubled adolescence. He wrote to Pound: 'I fell into worse than doldrums a while ago and still cant get up anything like distant relative of energy. Why I cant say. It's a recurrent disease with me. Environment has something to do with it, but I don't think suffices to explain it.'[277]

But it wasn't completely miserable. Bunting and Marian had an active social life. William Carlos Williams wrote to Zukofsky in January 1931: 'The Buntings … and I had supper in Brookly [sic] last week.' Bunting was part of a team that 'flayed' Carlos Williams for his naive reverence for classical Greek beauty.[278]

These were Prohibition years in the US. Alcohol hadn't been freely available since 1920 and many years later Bunting recalled the comedy of Prohibition in conversation with Victoria Forde: 'He told me that once in Rhode Island when Margaret de Silver said she would have to go to New

York because she was out of whiskey, Bunting forestalled her by going out and asking the first policeman he saw where he could find a bootlegger. "You came to the right person," the officer replied. "I'm the only bootlegger in town!"'[279] He told *Contempo* magazine in 1932 that prohibition 'is the most effective red-herring yet invented. It beats even religion for keeping people from thinking about more fundamental structural defects in their society. It beats even baseball.'[280]

Towards the end of 1930 Bunting's six month visa was due to expire. According to Marian this in itself was no excuse to return to Italy. She wrote in 1968 that

> he could have renewed it by going to Canada but did not choose to do this. Instead acting on a suggestion from Pound, Basil decided to give up trying to make a go of it in N.Y. & decided we should go to live near Pound in Rapallo. The idea thrilled me, but I was reluctant to leave a good job and proceed with these plans when we had no means of support ... From this time on our life was one nightmare, for me, at least, of financial insecurity.[281]

REDIMICULUM MATELLARUM

During his tumultuous time in Rapallo, Paris and London Bunting had been writing the poems that would form his first collection, *Redimiculum Matellarum* ('necklace of chamberpots'), which was published privately in Milan in 1930 and priced at 'Half a Crown or Twelve Lire'. Everything about this slim volume is interesting, from the copyright line: 'This volume is copyright in all civilised countries but not (yet) in the United States. March 1930' to the epigraph: 'La même justesse d'esprit qui nous fait écrire de bonnes choses nous fait appréhender qu'elles ne le soient pas assez pour mériter d'être lues'[282] to the preface: 'These poems are byproducts of an interrupted and harassed apprenticeship. I thank Margaret De Silver for bailing me out of Fleet Street: after two years convalescence from an attack of journalism I am beginning to recover my honesty. Rapallo, 1930'; and then triumphantly to the poems, nearly all of which survived Bunting's editorial scythe in his first *Collected Poems*. *Redimiculum Matellarum* starts with 'Villon'. A section head 'Carmina' is followed by a rather Yeatsian epigraph on the title page:

> Coryphée gravefooted precise, dance to the gracious music
> Thoughts make moving about, dance to the mind's delicate
>   [symphony.

These lines are from a subsequently discarded poem. (A coryphée is a leading ballet dancer just beneath the soloists in importance.) The poems in 'Carmina' are 'Weeping oaks grieve', 'I am agog for foam', 'Against the tricks of time' (which was omitted from *Collected Poems* although the five central stanzas appear as 'Farewell ye sequent graces'), 'After the grimaces of capitulation', 'Narciss, my numerous cancellations prefer' and 'Empty vast days'.

A second section, 'Etcetera', consists of six short poems: 'An arles, an arles for my hiring', 'Loud intolerant bells', 'Dear be still!', 'Chorus of Furies (overheard)', 'Darling of Gods and Men' and 'As to my heart'.[283]

The final page of *Redimiculum Matellarum* has a quotation from the epilogue of book six of Jean de La Fontaine's *Fables*:

> Bornons ici cette carrière,
> Les longs ouvrages me font peur.[284]

The only review that *Redimiculum Matellarum* attracted was by Louis Zukofsky in the June 1931 issue of *Poetry*, and that review was observant rather than evaluative,[285] although Pound immortalised it Canto LXXIV:

> hast killed the urochs and the bison sd/ Bunting
>   doing six months after that war was over
> as pacifist tempted with chicken but declined to approve
> of war 'Redimiculum Matellorum'
>   privately printed
>   to the shame of various critics
> nevertheless the state can lend money
>   and the fleet that went out to Salamis
>   was built by state loan to the builders
>   hence the attack on classical studies
> and in this war were John Gould, Bunting and cummings
> as against thickness and fatness[286]

By May 1930 Bunting reported to Louise Morgan that *Redimiculum Matellarum* was 'actually selling and now nearly out of print – without ads or reviews I think that is pretty good.'[287]

RAPALLO, 1931–1933

On their return to Rapallo from New York the Buntings settled down

> half-way up the mountain, and on the whole it was a very pleasant time. I
> got a good deal of poetry written, I enjoyed conversation, enjoyed sailing my
> boat, enjoyed the sunshine. And enjoyed having a baby. My first daughter.
> Pound was there then and various other people. Yeats was there. I saw a
> good deal of Yeats. But of few others. I don't enjoy literary society or literary
> conversation.[288]

Annie Bunting had joined her son in Rapallo in the spring of 1930. This
was more than a vacation since, according to Victoria Forde, her furniture
followed from Newcastle upon Tyne later in the year: 'If she had left Italy
when Basil went to the United States, she had returned and moved into her
own apartment before Basil and his wife arrived in Rapallo in February
1931 since Marian remembered her already there and well liked by Dorothy
Pound.[289]

Marian was pregnant with their first child for most of 1931 and in
November she went to Genoa to give birth to Bourtai, named after the nine-
year-old bride of Genghis Khan, a procedure that was at least partly funded
by the $50 1931 Lyric Prize Bunting had just received for 'Villon' from *Poetry*,
as Pound had predicted – 'I spose Basil B's 50 will be absorbed in maternity
fees.'[290] Marian had a difficult time giving birth to Bourtai and she remained
in hospital for several weeks. She recalled in 1968 that

> when Bourtai was born we did not have one cent, but on that day Basil got
> a poetry prize for $50.00 which paid the hospital expenses. Pounds gave us
> $300 & when I had to stay in the hospital (no pre-natal care) from Nov 8 to
> Jan 13th my family & everybody pitched in so we were inundated with cash –
> We stayed w. Mrs. Bunting after I came home from hospital – it was fantastic.
> I was so nervous I cried if the baby slept & if she was awake I was sure that
> 10 lb. hunk would die if we didn't fight for her life every minute. [Annie] was
> a meticulous housekeeper – she had a beautiful kitchen but wouldn't let me
> cook a chicken in it for fear of getting it messy. When we left she had the
> whole apartment re-decorated and the furniture re-covered.[291]

Bourtai clearly recovered quickly from her difficult birth. Within months
Bunting wrote to Dorothy Pound that she 'has demonstrated reactionary

instincts by tearing up the portrait of Lenin. Ezra thinks that qualifies her for the Balilla.'[292] Marian claimed that the $50 prize from *Poetry* comprised Bunting's entire earnings during their seven year marriage and yet that, with her allowance, they lived in 'comparative luxury'.[293]

A beautiful lyric embedded in the second part of *Briggflatts* describes Bunting's life in Italy. In Bunting's recordings of the poem you can almost feel him relaxing into it. Although loaded with self-recrimination it captures a sense of ease and fulfilment that appears nowhere else in *Briggflatts*:

> It tastes good, garlic and salt in it,
> with the half-sweet white wine of Orvieto
> on scanty grass under great trees
> where the ramparts cuddle Lucca.
>
> It sounds right, spoken on the ridge
> between marine olives and hillside
> blue figs, under the breeze fresh
> with pollen of Appenine sage.
>
> It feels soft, weed thick in the cave
> and the smooth wet riddance of Antonietta's
> bathing suit, mouth ajar for
> submarine Amalfitan kisses.
>
> It looks well on the page, but never
> well enough. Something is lost
> when wind, sun, sea upbraid
> justly an unconvinced deserter. [294]

Rapallo was indeed a kind of paradise. Yeats loved it:

> 'Sligo in heaven' murmured uncle William
> When the mist finally settled down on Tigullio.[295]

Yeats described Rapallo's irresistible charm in 'A Packet for Ezra Pound':

> Mountains that shelter the bay from all but the south wind, bare brown branches of low vines and of tall trees blurring their outline as though with a soft mist; houses mirrored in an almost motionless sea; a verandahed gable a couple of miles away bringing to mind some Chinese painting. Rapallo's thin line of broken mother-of-pearl along the water's edge ... On the broad pavement by the sea pass Italian peasants or working people, people out of the little shops, a famous German dramatist, the barber's brother looking

like an Oxford don, a British retired skipper, an Italian prince descended from Charlemagne and no richer than the rest of us, a few tourists seeking tranquillity.[296]

The famous German dramatist was Gerhart Hauptmann whose appearance in Rapallo Bunting gently satirised in 'Aus Dem Zweiten Reich':

> The renowned author of
> more plays than Shakespeare
> stopped and did his hair
> with a pocket glass
> before entering the village,
> afraid they wouldnt recognize
> caricature and picturepostcard,
> that windswept chevelure.
>
> Who talked about poetry,
> and he said nothing at all;
> plays,
> and he said nothing at all;
> politics,
> and he stirred as if a flea
> bit him
> but wouldnt let on in company.[297]

By 1931, when Bunting wrote 'Aus Dem Zweiten Reich', the 69-year-old Hauptmann was a Nobel laureate with thirteen novels and thirty-two plays under his belt.

Rapallo's other resident Nobel laureate, W. B. Yeats, described Pound's apartment:

> I shall not lack conversation. Ezra Pound, whose art is the opposite of mine, whose criticism commends what I most condemn, a man with whom I should quarrel more than with anyone else if we were not united by affection, has for years lived in rooms opening onto a flat roof by the sea. For the last hour we have sat upon the roof which is also a garden, discussing that immense poem of which but seven and twenty cantos are already published.[298]

Bunting thought Pound's apartment 'queer ... like a couple of parallel corridors cut into sections. Unfinished wall decorations. Drawings by Lewis, scupltures by Brzeska, etc. His wife's excellent watercolours everywhere ...

Small magazines lying about. Not very many books. There is no alternative to the homemade chairs.'[299]

Ezra Pound had moved to Rapallo with his wife, the painter Dorothy Shakespear, in 1924, after sixteen years in London and Paris, and he stayed there until he was arrested for treason in May 1945. He wrote most of *The Cantos* in Rapallo and ran his 'Ezuversity' from their attic apartment in Palazzo Baratti, a huge and impressive building on the seafront, just behind the Lungomare. (If you look up at Palazzo Baratti from the sea the Pounds' apartment occupied the right half of the top floor.)

The Buntings lived at Villa Castruccio, 'a peasant's cottage',[300] on a path going uphill from the Funivia in Rapallo (the house is still there but it is no longer called Castruccio) until late 1932, when they moved to an apartment at Corso Cristoforo Colombo 30/7 nearer the seafront. W. B. Yeats and his wife George had taken an apartment in what was then and is still one of the largest and most impressive buildings on the west side of the River Borte, Palazzo Cardile on Corso Cristoforo Colombo, from 1928 to 1930. Homer and Isabel Pound, Pound's parents, took it when the Yeatses departed.

Bunting saw plenty of Pound: 'I didn't on the whole work with Pound. I did some odd jobs for him. Proof-reading, things of that sort. Otherwise we met very frequently, I dare say, four times a week, and we'd spend several hours together in the afternoon or evening. That was always instructive and useful. Pound was very willing to impart whatever help he could.'[301]

Ezra's savage disciple

Bunting continued to write and to mix with the artistic community that was gathering around Pound in Rapallo, earning him Yeats' description as 'one of Ezra's more savage disciples': 'He got into jail as a pacifist and then for assaulting the police and carrying concealed weapons and he is now writing up Antille's [*sic*] music. George and I keep him at a distance and yet I have no doubt that just such as he surrounded Shakespeare's theatre, when it was denounced by the first Puritans.'[302] Many years later Bunting told the Yeats Summer School in Sligo that Yeats was 'disturbed by my conversation, though he is also kind enough to say that he had admired my verse. The conversation was about God and the church, and young men are apt to be very summary in their judgements of such matters, and crude in expressing them.'[303] This impression was confirmed by Bunting's chance remark about Shelley:

We were sitting inside the café on a wet afternoon, eating cakes, George Antheil and I, when Yeats joined us. He must have said something about Shelley, when I, intending to wave a red flag at the bull to liven up the afternoon, announced that there was no good in Shelley whatsoever, except perhaps that he had recommended incest, which I said, must be the best foundation for domestic tranquility. Yeats did not bother to come to Shelley's rescue, but began considering my proposition about incest in detail. I forget what he had to say about it, but presently he said: "Ssshh! If the general public could overhear the conversation of poets, they would hhhang the lot of us."[304]

Bunting recalled their meeting in Rapallo: 'I dined or lunched or supped or underwent some similar formal presentation in the flat he had taken at the top of a big modern block overlooking the bay. I remember nothing about it, but a little later at some similar meeting he astonished me by reciting to his guests the whole twenty-eight lines of one of my poems, word-perfect, though to me, at first, almost unrecognisable in his hieratic chant.'[305]

The poem Yeats recited was 'I am agog for foam'. Shortly after meeting Bunting Yeats asked him to dinner, Bunting recalled at a reading in London in 1980,

and meanwhile he had taken the trouble to look at what little work I had available then and do you know, the old man had (it's mere decency of course to learn two or three lines out of the poet you're entertaining and quote them – it shows you've read the thing) but he read all the twenty odd lines of this poem, he spouted them off by heart and much later again he referred to it and obviously Yeats liked it; so though it's early stuff and not the stuff I've devoted myself to trying to make it has his sanction.[306]

Ezra's savage disciple was sufficiently close to Yeats to witness (with Pound) Yeats' emergency will on 21 December 1929 (although, as he freely admitted, 'the next passerby would have done as well for that')[307] and to collect his children, Michael and Anne, from their Swiss school in May 1930.[308]

Bunting enjoyed the great man's company: 'Yeats liked gossip. He was ready to talk about anything at anytime. He was always entertaining, often very intelligent on whatever you chose to talk about.'[309] There was a dark side to Yeats' gossip however. After a confusing anecdote about an encounter in Cefalu between the occultist Aleister Crowley, his student, the British Modernist novelist Mary Butts, and a goat, Bunting noted that sometimes 'his pleasure in scandals which must have been terrible to the people concerned rather disgusted me'.[310] Bunting certainly was no more overawed by Yeats than he had been by Eliot:

> If conversation were in any danger of flagging, you could always revive it by a reference, in any context, to George Moore. Yeats's invective about Moore was always as fresh as though their difference had happened only yesterday … Fortunately, one of the first pieces of literary work I ever did had been done for George Moore, so that the bait was always at hand and the big fish always rose to it.[311]

Victoria Forde offers some details about the relationship between the Bunting and Yeats families, gleaned many years later from Bunting's 'American' family: 'Yeats's father, the painter Jack Butler Yeats, gave the first Bunting child a playhouse, and W. B. Yeats himself became a friend of Basil's mother, a great reader of astrology books. For the rest of her life she remembered with pride that she had read Yeats' horoscope.'[312] Forde does not record the source for this and it neatly encapsulates the problem of writing an authoritative life of Bunting. For a start, Yeats' father, John Butler Yeats, had died in February 1922, nearly ten years before Bourtai was born. WBY's brother, who *was* Jack,[313] may have supplied the playhouse but who is remembering? Bunting? Bourtai? Marian? It is understandable that someone who was four years old at the time doesn't know the difference between W. B. Yeats' brother and his father but it throws some doubt on the anecdotal evidence that has been used to build a picture of Bunting's life. In fact Bunting was quite explicit about the source of the playhouse; Yeats himself was the donor: 'Yeats was kind and thoughtful of other people. His children possessed a very splendid Wendy-house, but had grown out of it. He handed it over to my little daughter and she and the dog wore it out in a year or two. It must have been troublesome to arrange its transport to Italy. We could never have afforded such an expensive toy.'[314]

My guess is that Bunting himself originated the confusing wrinkle to the playhouse story. There is also something very Bunting about the idea of his mother being a 'great reader of astrology books'. Bunting had an interesting take on Yeats' magic.

> Yeats was ill a good deal of the time. He had the disease which was called, in those days, Malta fever, because Maltese were said to catch it from the goats whose milk they drank; but it had been called relapsing fever, a better name, since patients are continually getting better and then suddenly showing

175

all the symptoms again as badly as ever or even worse. At one time Yeats certainly thought that he was dying, and that is why Ezra Pound and I were suddenly called to witness his will. However, he got better again and again and relapsed again and again. At one time he would be strolling about the town – a little town still in those days – and at another he would be what the hospitals now call 'serious'. This went on so long that he began to think he had been bewitched, so that the doctors were helpless: what he needed was a powerful and well-disposed wizard. But for magic he had only himself to rely on in that time and place, and he was often too ill even to think fruitfully about magic. However he did at last convince himself – perhaps I ought to rephrase that – he did at last manage to humbug himself into believing that his illness was caused by a certain ring he wore, and the next time he was strong enough to venture out, he and Mrs Yeats made their way to the end of the mole and cast the ring into the sea, with the appropriate formula; and it seemed to work, for that time he did not relapse, which confirmed him in his half-belief in magic.[315]

In his Sligo lecture Bunting padded out his recollections of Yeats in Rapallo with a tedious story involving himself, Ezra and Homer Pound, the Italian poet Sem Benelli, Yeats and a suicidal Persian cat. He was aware that he was padding it out. He described the lecture to the editor of *Agenda*, William Cookson, as 'a lot of desultory blah but leading gently to some suggestions that I think are not without relevance. At any rate it isn't disguised in the jabber of literary criticism.'[316] He was also well aware that his audience knew a great deal more about Yeats than he did but these personal anecdotes, however tangential to his subject, gave him a slight edge. When he returned to his subject, leaving the deranged cat 'sitting in the sun with that kindest of old men [Homer Pound]', it was to the subject of magic:

> Sometimes he tried to convince me that magic, theosophy, and the rest of his paraphernalia were not just a subjective source of symbols for him, but were real, objective happenings. He gave me some notion of Madame Blavatsky, and her mixture of obvious charlatanry with feats which he thought she really believed, and which he was, provisionally, willing to believe. I had met Annie Besant and had been impressed by the force of her personality, but Yeats said she was not to be mentioned in the same breath with Blavatsky.[317]

Bunting regarded Yeats' 'half belief' in magic as a kind of poetic pragmatism. Rosicrucianism, theosophy and freemasonry equipped Yeats with a set of symbols that had not been worked to death by previous poets (as legendary Ireland had been so worked), and it was too precious a resource to allow scepticism to get in the way of its exploitation, even if the scepticism was there underneath. Yeats belonged with the mass of semi-religious people: his 'faith' was no less real than it was for a 'great many people who have what they call religious beliefs' but he was no mystic: 'Their faith is not that of the mystics who have seen God nor the philosophers who have invented him. In most cases I think it is merely self-indulgence, and in others, as with Yeats, a utility, a means to perfectly human ends.'[318]

Bunting also rightly detected a political dimension to Yeats' magic. Yeats' commitment to the occult and to reactionary politics are inextricably linked[319] and Bunting's observation that magic is 'primarily a means of exercising power or persuading yourself that you can' is acute:

> love of power underlines a great deal of what is not even superficially mystical in his poetry. He thought of himself as one of a governing class, with obligations, but with privileges too. Disdain of shopkeepers, readiness to snub stone-breakers with political opinions, contempt for the mob, even when the mob was an abstraction, show clearly enough that Yeats felt he had a right to power that he did not share with the greater part of mankind. If you have none of the real power of armies and police and huge fortunes, magic is an unsatisfactory, but often irresistible way of pretending to yourself that you have an equivalent.[320]

Bunting was also correct to point out that we tend to view Yeats' 'Fascism' (and that of Eliot, 'the more insidious for being disguised as an English gentleman', and Pound) through a false prism. Fascism is a technical term that requires careful handling. Partly we are so horrified by the brutal excesses of inter-war Fascist machines that there is a feeling that to treat the subject as suitable for serious debate is to invite its reappearance. Partly, too, by the time Bunting was addressing the Yeats Society in Sligo in 1973 the prevalence of Marxist critiques of twentieth-century political history had debased the term. The problem of assimilating into a Marxist system a proletarian-based revolution that, ideologically at least, is the antithesis of that system had reduced Fascism to little more than paramilitary capitalism. We retain the term because its disturbing associations are useful, but its all-inclusiveness has rendered it virtually meaningless.[321]

Ideologically Fascism is committed to continual renewal and to continual preservation, fusing past and future. Another way of putting it is that it is, as Stanislav Andreski demonstrated, both the 'extremism of the centre' and the 'centrism of the extremists'.[322] But in the 1930s those forces were already clearly classifiable. Fascism was founded on a strong sense of racial and national identity, an urgent militarism that expands that racism and nationalism into foreign affairs, a violent antipathy to socialism (although not to a number of significant socialist principles), and a clearly defined ruling elite, supporting a charismatic leader whose presidency over a totalitarian state is uninterrupted. Yeats, Eliot and thousands of other intellectuals were 'Fascists' in this sense. Fascism was intellectually, morally, socially and philosophically defensible, even attractive, in the first half of the 1930s. As Gertrude Himmelfarb observed, 'passive, social anti-Semitism was "the prerogative of English gentlemen"'.[323] The evil that Fascism spawned was unimaginable to the fashionable intellectual elite in 1932 and we should not allow anachronistic judgements to prevail. Eliot's casual anti-Semitism is disgusting: but it doesn't make Eliot a Nazi sympathiser. Yeats' flirtation with Eoin O'Duffy's Blueshirts was borne of a desire for national resurgence, not racism. Pound was a different matter. Pound couldn't accept that *any* intellectual could be honest in opposing Fascism. In *British Union Quarterly*, an unashamedly Fascist review, he 'chided Eliot for declaring that there was no "intellectual interest" in British Fascism, and when he claimed that "Mr Bunting considers himself anti-fascist, nevertheless he and Mr Jorian Jenks [a regular contributor to the paper] are ineluctably OF the same party, when you get down to any real bedrock, to any real honesty."'[324]

Marian Bunting's recollection of Pound's politics, although clearly based on considerable personal contact with him, seems wide of the mark. 'I can say with certainty,' she wrote in 1968,

> that Pound was hostile to Mussolini & scornful of him at the time when we left Italy for Tenerife in September, 1933. Mussolini had refused to allow Hemingway to come into Italy & this was one count against him. We felt we were likely to be spied upon there & while conversing in public places we never mentioned Mussolini's name – used a substitute. The only praise I heard of him was that he had forbidden Italians to shoot small birds. His law against profanity was considered absurd since both Basil & Ezra enjoyed the lusty fertility of the Italian's swearing.[325]

In fact Pound had written approvingly about Mussolini's regime to Harriet Monroe as early as 1926[326] and on 30 January 1933, eight months before the Buntings left Italy, Pound had an audience with Mussolini in the Palazzo Venezia in Rome during which he presented Douglas' Social Credit theory as a natural economic policy for a Fascist state, and after which he 'swiftly developed a world view in which the Fascist leader played a central part, and was portrayed as the ideal ruler, but where Social Credit rather than Italian Fascism was the political dogma.'[327] Perhaps Marian was trying to protect her ex-husband from the toxic effect of association with Pound in post-war America, although she didn't try to protect him from much else.

Bunting for his part found Pound's Fascism incredible even in the mid-1930s. He told Pound in September 1936 that 'Angold accuses you of connections with the British Union of Fascists: which I refuse to believe ... I am not a Left sucker, I don't go mad at the idea of a blasphemy against democracy, don't think I'm talking blindly. But they spell Finance with three letters, J E W, and that's all you'll get out of them.'[328]

If we must judge Yeats, Eliot and many others, we should be scrupulous about doing so by the standards of the poets' own times, not ours. Bunting recognised this:

> What these poets and many other writers really had in common was a love of order. With order in society it matters little whether you are rich or poor, you will not be harassed by perpetual changes of fortune, you can plan your life's work within known limits ... Yeats's love of order is something he shared with Dante and Shakespeare and probably far more than half of the world's great poets, as well as with nearly all the philosophers and historians.[329]

Pound does not survive scrutiny by any standards.

Piera's book

Bunting may not have enjoyed 'literary society or literary conversation' but he certainly involved himself in the high-octane artistic community that gathered around Pound in Rapallo. A contemporary article, 'Prominent Literati Arriving at Rapallo to Pass Winter Season', catalogues the poet's illustrious neighbours:

> Gerhardt Hauptmann, venerable figure of the literary constellation, is shortly due from Switzerland ...

> Ezra Pound is here busily working upon his new opera, which should shortly be completed. He is living with his parents at the beautiful home of William B. Yeats, who is in Dublin arranging for the presentation of one of his dramas.

Nancy Wilcox McCormick, Chicago sculptor, recently stayed with Mr and
Mrs Homer Pound, parents of the poet, after coming from London where she
completed a bust of Gandhi ...

The poet, Basil Bunting, whose wife is from Wisconsin, is rejoicing in the
arrival of a baby daughter born in the Protestant Hospital at Genoa. The
daughter was christened Bourtai Bunting in honor of Genghis Khan. Since
this happened Mr Bunting has given birth to two lines of inspired verse each
month.

... Edmond Dodsworth, Italian translator of William Blake and W. H.
Hudson, recently moved here

... Max Beerbohm, with his wife Florence Khan, former actress from
Tennessee, is busy in his white villa on the Ambrogian Hill.[330]

The *transatlantic review* in Paris, Kleinfeldt's in London's Fitzrovia, Rapallo
with the cream of Europe's artists; for someone who didn't enjoy literary
company Bunting certainly knew how to find it. Massimo Bacigalupo
describes 'Il libro di Piera', a unique record of cultural Rapallo:

Here [Caffè Aurum, on the ground floor of the Pounds' apartment block]
Ezra and Dorothy took their meals, entertained guests, and EP met his
associates to launch ventures like the *Supplemento Letterario del Mare* (1932–1933)
and the concert seasons of the Amici del Tigullio (1933–1939). EP was friendly
with the hotel proprietors, the Majerna family, and gave their young daughter
Piera a leather-bound autograph book on the first page of which he wrote 'Il
libro di Piera'.[331]

'Piera's book' contains a stave from Pound's opera, *Villon*, signed in April
1929 by Pound and George Antheil. Yeats, too, contributed a stanza to
Piera's book:

Much did I rage when young,
Being by the world oppressed,
But now with flattering tongue
It speeds the parting guest.
W B Yeats, April 17, 1929

As Bacigalupo says, Piera's book is a 'document of the lively and creative
Rappalo milieu during the EP era'. After Yeats' poem: 'we find the
signatures of Gerhart Hauptmann, Filippo Tommaso Marinetti, and many

others, among them the co-editor of the Literary Supplement of *Il Mare*, Gino Saviotti, and three younger contributors: the Northumbrian poet Basil Bunting, the German Eugen Haas, and the Spaniard Juan Ramon Masoliver, who was to become an important critic and translator'.[332] Saviotti was the author of *Mezzo matto*, a novel which Pound admired and which won the 1934 Viareggio Prize. Haas was an accomplished watercolourist and Masoliver (who later became Pound's secretary) was a pioneer of Surrealism.

In the way that it records an artistic milieu Piera's book is similar to the Fitzroy tavern's guestbook. The patron and hostess, Pima Andreae, kept a Rapallo guestbook that performs a similar function. She entertained the local artistic community at her home, Villa Andreae. The villa's guestbook was signed on 28 July 1932 by Ezra, Dorothy, Homer and Isabel Pound and by Basil and Marian Bunting. It records that they listened to a concert that day by the composer and violinist, Tibor Serly, and the pianist, Geza Frid.[333]

Bunting certainly used his own music criticism to advance his credentials. In the summer of 1933 Pound organised performances of Mozart's sonatas for violin and piano in the Teatro Reale in Rapallo. Bunting confusingly previewed the concerts, which had already taken place on 26, 27 and 28 June 'under the auspices of the Fascist Institute of Culture', on the front page of *Il Mare* on 1 July.[334] The public response was sufficiently enthusiastic to encourage Rapallo's authorities to allow Pound to use, free of charge, the local town hall. The organising committee – Bunting, Pound and Eugen Haas – according to advertisements, 'had been professional music critics on journals in large European cities and offered their guarantee of the high quality of performers and programmes'.[335] According to Victoria Forde Bunting insisted that 'his connection was quite incidental. His self-effacement or perhaps his feelings about the "overpowering" Olga Rudge, Pound's mistress, who had a part in it may have kept him from associating himself with this project closely.'[336] In fact Bunting had been an 'active participant in the early concerts', according to R. Murray Schafer.[337]

Bunting later claimed a much more significant role in this than was at the time apparent, and, indeed, if the following story is broadly true (which I take it to be) his accidental discovery of some Scarlatti and Vivaldi manuscripts affected significantly the listening tastes of the twentieth century. Asked about Vivaldi in an interview primarily about Pound in 1982 he said:

> I don't suppose he [Pound] even knew the name of Vivaldi when I first met him. Now, Vivaldi came up in the most peculiar way. I was living in a house

in Rapallo, close to where the daughters of an Italian musicologist lived …
He had been in the Italian diplomatic service, and wherever he went he went
into all the libraries and copied out, and otherwise got hold of, all the ancient
music he could. His name was Chilesotti. One day the Chilesotti girls came
into my house, three of them, and we fooled about, as we often fooled about.
And they found on my desk some manuscript where I was busy transferring
to stave some music that was in the tablature for the lute. And they said,
'Why, that is just what Daddy's old chest is full of!' This electrified me, and I
begged them to fetch Daddy's old chest around to me. Which they did. And
there was I, and got Gerhard Münch and his wife in by that time, and the
three of us opened Daddy's old chest. And the very first thing on the top of
it we came on, was an opera by Alessandro Scarlatti that nobody had ever
heard of before or knew existed. And then, under that, other things and other
things. Various stuff from lute tablatures in Italian and in Spanish and in what
not. And finally, a trio sonata or two by Vivaldi. Nobody had ever heard of
these bloody things! We took them round to show Ezra, in great excitement.
Münch and his wife turned some of the stuff into piano and violin, piano and
voice. Ezra rushed off to Rome, to tell Mussolini that he had got a glorious
find of some sort, and he wanted money to start a series of concerts, which he
did. Mussolini produced the money, and the concerts were founded. And year
by year they played a good lump of Mozart and a good lump of what we put
out from the Chilesotti manuscripts. And that was where Vivaldi came from.
And Pound very rightly told Olga, who had this job in Siena on the musical
Academy there, to look up everything that she could about Vivaldi, and press
it as far as she could. So that in fact the mechanics of the great Vivaldi revival
came entirely from Olga Rudge, urged on by Ezra Pound, but Ezra was put
on the track by the sheer accident that put them my way.[338]

Bunting's exact role in the discovery of this treasure is unclear, although
here he clearly puts himself centre-stage. In his account of the discovery
published in the *Musical Times* it is interesting that he made no such claim, nor
does he mention Vivaldi.[339] In any event Pound, of course, effortlessly took
the credit for it and assumed responsibility for managing its dissemination,
culminating, as Humphrey Carpenter says, in a Vivaldi week in Siena in
September 1939 in which well-known Italian musicians performed the
'works that Olga and Ezra had discovered'.[340]

A few weeks before Bunting left Rapallo Zukofsky arrived.[341] Bunting,
resplendent in a red jacket, met him at Genoa to take him to Rapallo, which
they reached in time for lunch at the Albergo Rapallo with the Pounds.
Zukofsky stayed with Homer and Isabel Pound, in Yeats' old apartment on

the Via Americhe. He was supposed to eat his meals, for which Pound paid, with the Buntings but sometimes, according to Charles Norman, 'when he tried to slip out to have breakfast by himself, Homer Pound, towering above him, would bar the exit. "'In Idaho," he would say, "if anyone tried to refuse hospitality –." He left the sentence unfinished. But it sufficed. Zukofsky usually breakfasted with Homer and Isabel Pound.'[342]

'Tea with Ezra and Dorothy which lasted for hours every afternoon became a ritual for these two younger poets. Money had poured in after the birth of Bourtai, especially from Margaret de Silver, so that Bunting had bought a crude sailboat which Zukofsky enjoyed sharing some days.'[343] Sometimes they saw Pound out in the ocean 'rowing strenuously seaward on a *pontone*, a raft consisting of two pontoons and a board for seat. He liked to swim by himself.'[344]

Sweatin' away at Firdusi

In 1930 Bunting began his lifelong affair with the tenth-century Persian poet, Hakīm Abu'l-Qāsim Ferdowsī Tūsī Ferdowsi. He had found a copy of part of Ferdowsi's epic, the *Shahnameh*, in a stall on the quays in Genoa, a book

> tattered, incomplete – with a newspaper cover on it marked 'Oriental Tales.' I bought it, in French. It turned out to be part of the early 19th century prose translation of Firdausi, and it was absolutely fascinating. I got into the middle of the story of the education of Zal and the birth of Rustam – and the story came to an end! It was quite impossible to leave it there, I was desperate to know what happened next. I read it, as far as it went, to Pound and to Dorothy Pound and they were in the same condition. We were yearning to find out, but we could think of no way. The title page was even missing. There seemed nothing to do but learn Persian and read Firdausi, so, I undertook that. Pound bought me the three volumes of Vullers and somebody, I forget who, bought me Steingass's dictionary, and I set to work. It didn't take long. It's an easy language if it's only for reading that you want it. It's difficult to speak.[345]

The 'somebody' who bought him the Steingass was, according to Forde, his wife, who had acquired it in New York, although Dorothy Pound was also involved.[346] Bunting wrote to Dorothy from Rapallo in September 1932 while she was staying with her mother in London to ask her to visit a dealer in oriental books in Great Russell Street to price a good classical Persian dictionary and a copy of the seven volume 1880 French edition of the *Shahnameh*. Not that he had any money to pay for them.[347] By then he had acquired a grammar and was finding it 'amazingly easy' to master classical Persian, although the heavy borrowing from Arabic was causing him problems.

Pound wrote to the *Morning Post* to showcase Bunting's Persian credentials, with a little Poundian exaggeration: 'With all due respect to Mr. Drinkwater as an outstanding representative of English letters, I suggest that the English poet most qualified to represent your country at a celebration of Firdausi should be a young man who reads Persian, who writes Persian, and who is actually engaged in the almost impossible task of translating Firdausi into a suitable English metre. Perhaps Mr. Drinkwater could find a post in his suite for Basil Bunting.'[348]

In fact, however, far from being 'in the same condition' Pound was dismissive of this enthusiasm. While he immortalised Bunting's enthusiasm for Ferdowsi in 'Canto 77':

> If Basil sing of Shah Nameh, and wrote
> ... *Firdush*' on his door [349]

he dismissed it privately, writing to William Carlos Williams on 16 February 1935: 'Buntin' sweatin' away at Firdusi, which he aint yet found a way to make readable. Dirty dumb middle eastern fat heads.'[350] As far as Pound was concerned Bunting was still struggling with it three years later. He wrote to Otto Bird from Rapallo on 9 January 1938: 'Bunt'n gone off on Persian, but don't seem to do anything but Firdusi, whom he can't put into English that is of any *interest*. More fault of subject matter than of anything else in isolation.'[351]

Pound didn't have a clue about the 'subject matter' of course, and Bunting would not have agreed with him even if Pound had understood Persian. His work on Persian translation continued during his time in the Canary Isles, and proved a serious irritant to Pound. Some of it was light-hearted, such as Sa'di's:

> Powder and lipstick and lace on their drawers
> Are all very well for young women and whores,
> They look a bit more human in that sort of stuff;
> But for a man, cock and balls are enough.

> Which doesn't seem likely to get a place in my collected works but is worth at any rate oral preservation. Literal, nearly: last line word for word.[352]

Within twelve months Pound told Bunting he was 'bored' by the Persian translations. He wrote to Bunting on 17 January 1935:

> You bloody bullheaded ape ...
> All this snotten and shitten belly-button gazing etc ... no fkn/USE.

> Wot I feel about yr/ persins, is tha shucks wot does it matter if some nigger knifed a few others ... You av/ a rty TELLING the fukn STORY in the simplest possbl langwidg/ and then see if you help it by fussin with the ornaments and oriental currleywigs.[353]

Bunting seems to have taken only mild offence at this nuanced critique, but the disagreement prefigured a much more serious rift a few years later.

In his preface to Omar Pound's *Arabic & Persian Poems* in 1970 Bunting explained the misunderstandings that have surrounded the classics of Persian literature, on the way making a prescient point about the symbiosis of Islamic and Western culture:

> Persian poetry has suffered badly, Arabic rather less, from neo-Platonic dons determined to find an arbitrary mysticism in everything. You would think there was nothing else in Moslem poetry than nightingales which are not birds, roses which are not flowers, and pretty boys who are God in disguise ... There are difficulties in the way of a more satisfactory account of Persian poetry. Hafez, for instance, depends almost entirely on his mastery of sound and literary allusion, neither translatable. Manuchehri's enormous vigour and variety expresses itself often in patterns as intricate as those of a Persian carpet. Even dons are put off by the vast size of Sa'di's *Divan*, and fail to find the key poems ... Sooner or later we must absorb Islam if our own culture is not to die of anaemia. It will not be done by futile attempts to trace Maulavi symbols back to Plotinus or by reproducing in bad English verse the platitudes common to poetry everywhere.[354]

The mysticism, nightingales and roses, he considered, got you as close to Persian poetry as you would be to English if you had only read Oscar Wilde and Aubrey Beardsley. Fitzgerald was the only translator who 'got the hang of even a quarter of it'.[355]

Bunting applied for a Guggenheim Fellowship in 1932 'to translate Ferdausi's Shannameh into English verse. Its eight times as long as the Illiad and will take most of my lifetime, but the Guggenheim would enable me to get a start on it. I don't know another poem as good except Homers.'[356] Bunting's application to the John Simon Guggenheim Foundation, stamped

1 December 1932, describes his project as 'ultimately, to translate the whole of the epic poem, the "Shahnamah" of Abu'l Kasim Mansur Firdausi into verse. Immediately, to make a beginning of this enormous task and to complete my preparation for the undertaking by further study of Persian literature and poetry.' He estimates that the work would take at least fifteen years but that a Guggenheim would get him started, and 'My ultimate purpose? To make a respectable contribution to civilisation as I understand it.'[357] His application, though unsuccessful, had an impressive list of sponsors – Yeats, Pound, Ford Madox Ford and Harriet Monroe.

Bunting's Persian translations, including some previously unpublished material, have recently been collected by Don Share.[358] Bunting's earliest surviving translation from Persian, 'When the sword of sixty comes nigh his head', is from Ferdowsi and was written in 1935, but he also translated from Rudaki, Manuchehri, Sa'di, Hafiz and Obaid-e Zakani. Today's classical Persian scholars and translators regard Bunting's translations with respect. Parvin Loloi suggests that Bunting's 'versions from Hâfiz are free, but perceptive and vivid accounts of their originals, and confer more of Hâfiz' poetry than many more pedantically accurate versions … one can only regret that [they] should be so few in number, since they speak eloquently of the possibilities of this kind of translation.'[359] Dick Davis is more cautious in his admiration but finds Bunting's translations 'fresh and strong … vivid in their feeling'.[360]

Now that sea's over that island

Bunting's Persian translations were outshone by a burst of intense poetic creativity in the early 1930s. Marian Bunting's claim in 1968 that 'domestic troubles, plus no money, put poetry in the background after our first child was born', is not borne out by Bunting's preserved output of the time. Marian thought that poetry did not return to Bunting until 1936, when 'in London … Basil read some poems to Helen Egli in our apartment, the old excitement and thrill came back. The trouble was he could not & would not work at his poetry, or at journalism as he called all other kinds of writing.'[361] Marian's memory, as we shall see, was not entirely reliable when it came to the decade or so she spent with Bunting.

In fact 1930 was a fertile year for the poet. He completed some of his most anthologised poems, and the ones by which he was best known until the publication of *Briggflatts*, including 'Gin the Goodwife Stint' and

(*top left*) Thomas Lowe Bunting, c.1916.
(*top right*) Annie and Basil Bunting, 1901.
(*below left*) Basil and Joyce Bunting, c.1904.
(*below right*) Basil and Thomas Lowe Bunting, 1916.

5. (*top*) Denton Road, Scotswood, c.1908. The Bunting family home is located between the two small boys standing in the street. Thomas used the building as his surgery when the family moved to Jesmond Road in Newcastle.

6. (*below*) Ackworth School leavers, 1916. Bunting stands at the far right of the back row. John Allen Greenbank is at the far left of the back row. Ernest Cooper Apperley Stephenson is seated, arms folded, in the middle row. Frederick Andrews is seated third from left in the middl row.

PASS-
PORTS

20   23   26

28   33

7. (*top*) Bunting's passport photographs, 1920–1933.

8. (*below*) Marian and Basil Bunting, Rapallo beach, 1933.

9. (*top left*) Basil and Bourtai Bunting, Ra[
c.1933.

10. (*top right*) Marian, Annie and Basil Bu
on the balcony of Annie's apartment, Ra[
1932.

11. (*below left*) Marian and friend (Berthe)
Rapallo, 1933.

12. (*below right*) Architect and designer
Giulio Minoletti, essayist and Surrealist Ju
Ramon Masoliver, Bunting and artist Eug
Haas, Rapallo, 1933.

13. (*top right*) Marian, Bourtai
and Roudaba Bunting, Las
Arenas, Canary Islands,
December 1934.

14. (*below right*) Basil and Bourtai
Bunting, Las Arenas, Canary
Islands, December 1934.

15. (*top left*) The Thistle, c.1938.

16. (*top right, below right*) Bunting in uniform, c.1942.

17. (*below left*) Bunting standing (*rear, right*) next to Violet Harris and her father, George. Seated (*left to right*) are Violet's Aunt Lizzie, her cousin, Jean, and her mother, Jessie. This photograph was taken in the garden of the Harris family home in Wellesley Road, Methil, in 1941.

ipse delineavit 1939

Bunting MS 348/2

18. Basil Bunting, self portrait, 1939.

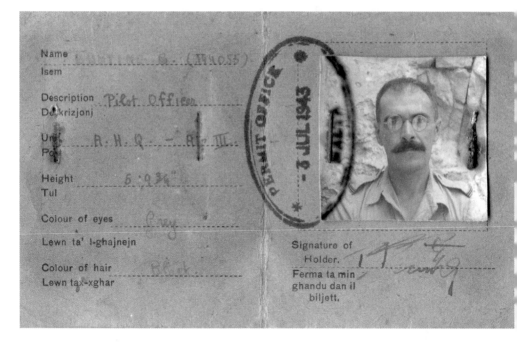

19. (*top*) Bunting's Maltese ID card, July 1943. It reveals him to have been 5' 9¾" with grey eyes.

20. (*below*) Wing Commander Bunting, c.1945.

'The Complaint of the Morpethshire Farmer'. Bunting correctly said in an interview many years later that 'the attempt to transliterate dialect is a disaster',[362] and although these poems only flirt with dialect they do so sufficiently to damage them irretrievably in my view. His justification was that they were 'attempts to make use of the ballad form for ballad purposes', an enterprise that had become entirely irrelevant in the intervening years as the ballad form effectively no longer existed in popular consciousness.[363] The ballad form has indeed become dated but in these poems it is not just the form that seems locked in a vanished age. 'Gin the Goodwife Stint' and 'The Complaint of the Morpethshire Farmer' fail to reach beyond their limited subjects to some universal truth. They don't quite work as poems and it is an unhappy irony that they should be seen as exemplars of Bunting's early poetry.

> The ploughland has gone to bent
> and the pasture to heather;
> gin the goodwife stint,
> she'll keep the house together.
>
> Gin the goodwife stint
> and the bairns hunger
> the Duke can get his rent
> one year longer.
>
> The Duke can get his rent
> and we can get our ticket
> twa pund emigrant
> on a C.P.R. packet. [364]

Emigration of poor farmers from the north of England to Canada is also the theme of the complaint:

> And thou! Thou's idled all the spring,
> I doubt thou's spoiled, my Meg!
> But a sheepdog's faith is aye something.
> We'll hire together in Winnipeg.
>
> Canada's a cold land.
> Thou and I must share
> a straw bed and a hind's wages
> and the bitter air.[365]

'Crazy Jane' it isn't. Bunting knew it was flawed. At a reading in London in 1980 he said that he hadn't read it:

for a long time, chiefly I suppose because the matters it deals with cleared up long ago. I'd no sooner written the 'The Complaint of the Morpethshire Farmer' than it was out of date, for the Forestry Commission came and took all the land and drained it, and then the farmers got rich instead of being extremely poor. But in the 1920s a large part of Northumberland, a great deal of many other counties I suppose, remained in a real mess. The landlords didn't put in land drains, which would make the ground tolerable for grass, because what they wanted was lots of heather to fill it with grouse, who live on heather, and so be able to get enormous fees from people who wanted to shoot the grouse. It was a bit hard on the farmer, and this was a protest against that.[366]

More successful were his meditations on art, 'Nothing', which was published in Zukofsky's February 1931 edition of *Poetry* as 'The Word', and 'Fruit breaking the branches'. In the *Poetry* version the poem that follows 'Nothing' in *Collected Poems*, 'Molten pool, incandescent spilth of' is an appendix, 'Appendix: Iron', to 'The Word'. But the triumph of 1930 was Bunting's poem to Mina Loy, 'Now that sea's over that island':

Now that sea's over that island
so that barely on a calm day sun sleeks
a patchwork hatching of combed weed
over stubble and fallow alike
I resent drowned blackthorn hedge, choked ditch,
gates breaking from rusty hinges,
the submerged copse,
Trespassers will be prosecuted.

Sea's over that island,
weed over furrow and dungheap:
but how I should recognise the place
under the weeds and sand
who was never in it on land I don't know:
some trick of refraction,
a film of light in the water crumpled and spread
like a luminous frock on a woman walking
alone in her garden.

Oval face, thin eyebrows wide of the eyes,
a premonition in the gait
of this subaqueous persistence
of a particular year –
for you had prepared it for preservation
not vindictively, urged
by the economy of passions.

Nobody said: She is organising
these knicknacks her dislike collects
into a pattern nature will adopt and perpetuate.

Weed over meadowgrass, sea over weed,
no step on the gravel.
Very likely I shall never meet her again
or if I do, fear the latch as before.[367]

I think that Carolyn Burke is correct in seeing this poem as essentially autobiographical: 'The intricate network of flea-market finds that filled her apartment found its way into the "knicknacks", and Cravan's fate [Loy's second husband who had drowned] echoed in the subaqueous persistance/ of a particular year.'[368] David Annwn has shown, however, that a more subtle reading is possible, one which reflects on Loy's qualities as artist and poet.[369]

Something missing

The earliest of Bunting's adaptations and translations to survive were written in 1931. The two-part poem, 'Vestiges', is a 'presumably exact version' of Genghis Khan's correspondence with Chang Chun taken from Emil Bretschneider's *Mediaeval Researches from Eastern Asiatic Sources*,[370] and 'Yes, it's slow' is the first of Bunting's translations from Horace to survive:

Yes, it's slow, docked of amours,
        docked of the doubtless efficacious
bottled makeshift, gin; but who'd risk being bored stiff
every night listening to father's silly sarcasms?[371]

Even casual readers will notice the deliberately introduced anachronisms in this poem (gin for instance). Bunting was following in the tradition established by Pound's 'Homage to Sextus Propertius'. He claimed in the appendix on translation that would have appeared in *Caveat Emptor* in 1935, had it ever found a publisher, that 'a good translator will employ anachronisms as often as seems needful to avoid the kind of obscurity that gives footnotes an excuse'.[372] Harry Gilonis has shown just how expert is another 1931 translation from Horace, 'Please stop gushing about his pink', brilliantly employing a device known as 'hypallage' that is 'usually near unachievable in English'.[373]

The major works of 1931 were, however, the longer poems. 'Attis: Or, Something Missing' and 'Aus Dem Zweiten Reich'. 'Parodies of Lucretius and Cino da Pistoia can do no damage and intend no disrespect', he said of the former.[374] While pointing at Shelley's 'Alastor: Or, The Spirit of Solitude' 'Attis' draws on a legend which seems to have emerged as early as 1200 BCE, although it is likely that Bunting picked it up from a poem by Catullus. Attis, a young Phrygian, sails from the mainland and begins a cult, worshipping the Anatolian Mother Goddess, Cybele. Attis castrates himself in a frenzy as a way of preventing his ever loving a woman other than Cybele. The myth (and Catullus' version of it) deliberately confuse male and female and Bunting's Attis seems to represent modern man as emasculated and modern society as debased. As Philip Hobsbaum says, 'Modern man may not be impotent but something is missing from his society and he is presented in anarchically free verse as dishevelled and ineffectual.'[375] Of all Bunting's work 'Attis: Or, Something Missing' seems to invoke the spirit of *The Waste Land*, and perhaps that is why some commentators have assumed that it satirises T. S. Eliot. The first part shifts the scene from Anatolia to the Cheviots in northern England:

> Out of puff
> noonhot in tweeds and gray felt,
> tired of appearance and
> disappearance;
> warm obese frame limp with satiety;
> slavishly circumspect at sixty;
> he spreads over the ottoman
> scanning the pictures and table trinkets.
>
> (That hand's dismissed shadow
> moves through fastidiously selective consciousness,
> rearranges pain.)

There are no colours, words only,
and measured shaking of strings,
and flutes and oboes
enough for dancers.
.... reluctant ebb:
     salt from all beaches:
disrupt Atlantis, days forgotten,
extinct peoples, silted harbours.
He regrets that brackish
     train of the huntress
driven into slackening fresh,
expelled when the
     estuary resumes
colourless potability;
     wreckage that drifted
in drifts out.

'Longranked larches succeed larches, spokes of a
stroll; hounds trooping around hooves; and the stolid horn's
sweet breath. *Voice*: Have you seen the
fox? Which way did he go, he go?
There was soft rain.
I recollect deep mud and leafmould somewhere: and
in the distance Cheviot's
heatherbrown flanks and white cap.

Landscape salvaged from
evinced notice of
superabundance, of
since parsimonious
soil .....

                    Mother of Gods.'

Mother of eunuchs.

Praise the green earth. Chance has appointed her
     home, workshop, larder, middenpit.
     Her lousy skin scabbed here and there by
     cities provides us with name and nation.

From her brooks sweat. Hers corn and fruit.
     Earthquakes are hers too. Ravenous animals

191

are sent by her. Praise her and call her
Mother and Mother of Gods and Eunuchs.[376]

Bunting, to me, in this complicated poem mocks the modern human condition rather than any one exemplar of it. He accepted its obliqueness and celebrated it. He wrote to Harriet Monroe that 'Ezra says *Attis* is obscure, from which he deduces that he is getting old. It certainly wouldn't be easy to write a synopsis, but I think it's really fairly plain for all that, if the reader doesn't spend time and energy looking for a nice logical syllogistic development which isnt there.'[377]

'Aus Dem Zweiten Reich' is altogether more straightforward. The poem is 'a description of the Germany just before Hitler's time ... I got in before the novelists did',[378] a rueful reference to Christopher Isherwood whose novels about Weimar Berlin had by the time of Bunting's remark been transformed into the phenomenally successful musical *Cabaret*. Bunting described 'Aus Dem Zweiten Reich', many years later, as 'very obviously a Scarlatti sonata',[379] but for me this pushes the sonata model too far. 'Aus Dem Zweiten Reich' is a light, uncomplicated mockery of a Germany he despised, whereas 'Attis: Or, Something Missing' is a rich, dark, complex mockery of the world and all it contained.

The clarity comes from the corpse

The year 1931 was productive but 1932 was a watershed in Bunting's development. He considered 'Two Photographs' to be the 'central work' in his *Collected Poems*, a 'turning point; before that, if it comes off, it's pretty much almost by accident, you could say. They hit it by chance. But in "Two Photographs", and in every subsequent poem, I knew what I was doing; the poem does what I want it to do. It's the first poem I wrote that does *exactly* what it's intended to do. And all the rest, after that, do that too.'[380]

It's true then that you still overeat, fat friend,
and swell, and never take folk's advice. They laugh,
you just giggle and pay no attention. Damn!
                    you don't care, not you!

But once – that was before time had blunted your
desire for pretty frocks – slender girl – or is

the print cunningly faked? – arm in arm with your
fiancé you stood

and glared into the lens (slightly out of focus)
while that public eye scrutinised your shape,
afraid, the attitude shows, you might somehow
excite its dislike.[381]

I don't think that Bunting meant to suggest that this was a great poem but that he had at last found his technique. Technically it is assured and from 1932 on his work is confident and independent, with fewer classical allusions and more direct, one might say more Yeatsian, engagement with the world around him. The other poems of 1932, 'Mesh cast for mackerel',[382] 'The Passport Officer' and his major work of the 1930s, 'Chomei at Toyama', have none of the world-weary, stage poet about them.[383] That is not to say that they weren't brilliantly crafted. He said of 'Chomei at Toyama' many years later that

> not all, but three quarters of it is in quantitative metres. In that case nearly all of them altered Greek metres … and nobody, for all these many, many years, nobody has ever observed that this is … organised by quantity. Perhaps because when it was done the line endings seem to come in odd places and so I changed the line endings, and they come rather where it helps the person to read it instead of where the metre comes.[384]

Certainly by 1932 Bunting had found his own unique voice and you can hear his frustration about his supposed 'influences' in a letter he wrote to Harriet Monroe in November 1932. Eliot, he said, disliked 'Chomei' partly because, 'he says it echoes Pound … But Pound supposes it to contain echoes of Eliot. I'm not aware of echoing anybody. Except Chomei: his book was in prose and four to five times as long as my poem, but I think everything, or nearly everything relevant in Chomei has been got into the poem. The curiously detailed resemblances between mediaeval Kyoto and modern New York are not my invention, and I didn't feel called on to disguise them.'[385]

On the other hand he had told James Leippert the previous month that 'so far as I know my "Chomei" has only two admirers, but they are Pound and Yeats. Eliot is said to have said that it couldn't be good because I had never been in Japan! Which, if true, is an example of what ten years at the head of a dull "heavy" can do to a man.'[386] He eventually came round to Eliot's view. Many years later Bunting told Gael Turnbull that the reason Eliot rejected 'Chomei at Toyama' for the *Criterion* was that Bunting had never lived in Japan and didn't know any Japanese, a view with which Bunting had some sympathy.[387] In fact 'Chomei at Toyama' has always had its admirers. Victoria Forde considers it Bunting's best long poem after *Briggflatts* and Lorine Niedecker adored it.[388]

Bunting was rightly proud of its technique. He told the editor of *Agenda*, William Cookson, that 'the day somebody discovers the prosodical basis of 'Chomei', if it ever comes, my bones will turn over in the grave and cheer'.[389] But he was aware of its flaws and there is something about Eliot's criticism that rings true. Thirty years or so later a reviewer of *Briggflatts* pointed out that literature 'for Bunting is a function of his experience, not a substitute for it',[390] and it is striking how much Bunting's best poems are based on the poet's own experiences – 'Villon' on prison life, 'The Spoils' on war, 'Briggflatts' on his entire life – and how comparatively weak are those, such as 'Chomei at Toyama', which aren't. He knew this. He said that Sir Walter Raleigh 'was a great poet, a pirate, a statesman, and a million other things. You can't write about anything unless you've experienced it: you're either confused in your subject matter or else you get it wrong.[391] The fact that 'Chomei at Toyama' doesn't quite equal 'Villon' and 'Briggflatts' in its conviction doesn't, of course, mean that it is not an important poem.

Bunting explained the genesis of 'Chomei at Toyama' at a reading at St Andrew's Presbyterian College in 1976:

> Long ago I came across a little volume which included an Italian prose translation of a prose book of essays written by a Japanese who died about the year 1200 and it had notes to it, learned notes. As I read it, it seemed to me that Chomei had so shaped his volume of essays that it was equivalent to an elegiac poem – but, of course, such a thing would have been quite outside any tradition he knew of, and when he wrote it he was, for those ages, an old man, well over sixty and without the energy to invent a new form. I thought 'oh well now I'll do what Chomei would have done if he could, and I'll write a poem of it.' So I made a poem and altered it a good deal here and there and transferred some of the learned notes into the poem itself.[392]

'Chomei at Toyama' takes as its source a thirteenth-century Japanese essay, *Hojoki* ('An Account of a Ten Foot Square Hut'), by Kamo no Chōmei that had been translated into Italian by Marcello Muccioli. Chōmei, having witnessed a series of natural disasters, including the great fire of 1177 in Kyoto, then the capital of Japan, and having been politically disappointed withdrew from the court and built a hut in the Hino mountains. He lived from then on in isolation as a reclusive Buddhist and reflects, in Bunting's poem, on matters universal and local, from:

> Whence comes man at his birth? or where
> does death lead him? Whom do you mourn?
> Whose steps wake your delight?
> Dewy hibiscus dries: though dew
> outlast the petals.

> I have been noting events forty years.

to:

> On the twentyseventh May eleven hundred
> and seventyseven, eight p.m., fire broke out
> at the corner of Tomi and Higuchi streets.
> In a night
> palace, ministries, university, parliament
> were destroyed. As the wind veered
> flames spread out in the shape of an open fan.
> Tongues torn by gusts stretched and leapt.
> In the sky clouds of cinders lit red with the blaze.
> Some choked, some burned, some barely escaped.
> Sixteen great officials lost houses and
> very many poor. A third of the city burned;
> several thousands died; and of beasts,
> limitless numbers.

> Men are fools to invest in real estate.

> Three years less three days later a wind
> starting near the outer boulevard
> broke a path a quarter mile across
> to Sixth Avenue.
> Not a house stood. Some were felled whole,
> some in splinters; some had left
> great beams upright in the ground
> and round about
> lay rooves scattered where the wind flung them.[393]

He told William Carlos Williams that 'it was much more difficult than you may imagine to keep Chomei clear, and couldnt have been done if I hadnt had the japs own book (italian translation) in front of me and kept as closely to it as the condensation of verse would permit. In short it's a collaboration between me and a corpse of sixty-five, and the clarity, such as it is, comes from the corpse.'[394]

'Chomei at Toyama' is an important poem, and Bunting's serious intent in it is unquestionable. Pound admired its discipline with good reason, but reading the correspondence between Bunting and Pound in the early 1930s can be a challenging exercise. For the most part the subjects are extremely abstruse, the finest possible points of, for instance, classical Japanese scholarship, banking theory and Elizabethan metre. It is easy to assume that not much fun was had at the Ezuversity at times. But it wasn't all hard theory. Among Gael Turnbull's papers are two poems that Bunting wrote in Rapallo 'to amuse Pound'. Neither has been published before. The first is titled 'Dialogue: Non-Platonic':

> THE TRAVELLER: Sir, I would like you to see
> This very fine perfume invented by me.
> It penetrates more than the smell of a bug.
> It's stronger than chloroform, attar of roses
> Or lemons in blossom. Its virtue suffuses
> Itself through the body – one drop on the skin
> Will make your intestines smell pleasant within,
> The sweat of your arm pits will be such a liquor
> As ladies delight in, and as for your feet,
> Wherever you set them a footprint of sweet
> Honeysuckle will be and inhere in the street
> For a month. It will vanquish the stifling fug
> Of the Tube or the odour of petrol and rubber
> In Great Portland Street or convert the damp slubber
> Of stale fish in Billingsgate into a chic-er
> Aroma than Coty can furnish, and quicker
> Than any explosion or Edison's brains
> It will make a Kurot of the sewers and drains –
> You can sell off your urine for Clicquot!
> If you want to deodorize belches and farts
> To a delicate flavour of Pekoe
> Or conquer the stench of your sexual parts,
> We have tried out the mixture on several tarts
> And assure you it makes the vagina distill
> An odour of oranges. Now Sir, I will
> Take your order?

THE CUSTOMER: That's a poor stunt.
Can't you make oranges smell like a cunt?

The second, 'Grandma's Complaint' is more succinct:

Yesterday morning my old man Jack
Left off his waistcoat and got a stiff back;

And the day before that the doddering wreck
Left of his collar and got a stiff neck.

I wish to the Lord that the bloody old crock
Would leave off his trousers and get a stiff cock.

Pound clearly enjoyed these diversions. Bunting sent him a truncated
limerick from Tenerife in 1935:

What a pity that Bela Bartok
Cannot give his smug public a shock
By writing in parts
For the hiccups and farts
And conducting his piece with

Yes, obviously.[395]

Poetry, the Bri'ish number

By 1930 Bunting the poet was in play, although the material world was
already leaving him behind. Pound had heard about Bunting's nights on
the streets:

I hear via Lunnon that Mr. Buntin' left them parts wearin the full regalia of
the reignin' house of Assam. He'd been sleeping on the Embankment for a
time previous.[396]

His friends were aware of the mild paranoia that he had started to display
at Leighton Park School.[397] Zukofsky's reply suggests that there was already
a cartoon element to Bunting's behaviour, 'The last I heard of Buntin' some
mysterious "they" wuz planning to send him to Colorado.'[398]

In 1927 the 23-year-old Zukofsky had sent Pound 'Poem beginning "The."'
Pound published it in *The Exile* and suggested to Harriet Monroe that she
give Zukofsky an issue of her magazine, *Poetry*, to edit. The result was the
'Objectivists' issue of February 1931. Pound had been Harriet Monroe's

197

'foreign correspondent' since she founded *Poetry* in 1912. He had effectively launched the Imagiste movement in the second (November 1912) issue. In fact the 'Imagistes', Pound's friends Richard Aldington and H.D., were unaware that they were part of a movement. H.D. was barely aware that she was a *poet* at that stage, let alone part of the vanguard of the 'American Risorgimento' that would make the Italian Renaissance 'look like a tempest in a teapot!'[399] At the outset Imagisme had no manifesto, no followers and no practitioners, but it was the birth of Pound the impresario. As Humphrey Carpenter puts it, Imagisme 'was just a clearing of the ground, a blast to announce the appearance of a new circus-act'.[400] Imagism (it became Anglicised in 1913), however meretricious, represented the first contractions of the birth of Modernist poetry.

Nearly twenty years later Objectivism was only slightly better conceived. William Carlos Williams recalled the birth of Objectivism in his autobiography: 'With Charles Reznikoff, a New York lawyer and writer of distinction, and George Oppen, in an apartment on Columbia Heights, Brooklyn, we together [with Zukofsky] inaugurated, first the Objectivist theory of the poem, and then the Objectivist Press. Three or four books were published, including my own *Collected Poems*. Then it folded.'

Objectivism was a reaction against Imagism which, according to Williams, had been 'useful in ridding the field of verbiage' but which had run its course because it lacked any structure: 'It had already dribbled off into so called "free verse" which, as we saw, was a misnomer. There is no such thing as "free verse"! Verse is measure of some sort. "Free verse" was without measure and needed none for its projected objectifications. Thus the poem had run down and became formally non extant.'

The Objectivists argued that the poem is an object, 'an object that in itself formally presents its case and its meaning by the very form it assumes. Therefore, being an object, it should be so treated and controlled – but not as in the past. For past objects have about them past necessities – like the sonnet – which have conditioned them and from which, as a form itself, they cannot be freed.' It followed that, the poem being an object ('like a symphony or a Cubist painting') the poet's job must be to create a new form for the poem, 'to invent, that is, an object consonant with his day. This was what we wished to imply by Objectivism, an antidote, in a sense, to the bare image haphazardly presented in loose verse.'[401]

Hugh Kenner, in his ground-breaking study of Modernism, *The Pound Era*, sees a direct US–Paris axis underneath Objectivism, 'The Parisian 1920s underlie the term, language as if indifferent to hearers, and an American quality underlies it too, American preference for denotation over etymology, for the cut term over association and the channelled path.'[402] In a nutshell Objectivism (vanished within a year and barely ever a movement as such) eschewed symbolism.

Although Bunting agreed with Zukofsky that poetry was a kind of craft, he wasn't greatly interested in Objectivism. He sent an open letter to Zukofsky to *Il Mare* in October 1932 specifically refuting Objectivism as a 'flight into darkness'.[403] Privately he confided to Pound that 'Oglethorpe University wants a harticle on Hobjectivists not by Zuk. I may send them something … but probably not. I don't know at all clearly what Zuk means by Objectivists.'[404] Asked much later if he felt that his poetry had enough in common with the other Objectivists to merit inclusion in *An 'Objectivists' Anthology* he was dismissive:

> Precious little. That was also Zukofsky's view. I think that he would probably have omitted me altogether but submitted to pressure from Pound, possibly also from Reznikoff. I wasn't anxious to be with them because I didn't like the manifesto he had decided on. And this in spite of the fact that so far as there is any having things in common, some general principles which were very much akin to the same general principles Ezra had laid down long before, and Wordsworth a hundred years before that again, apart from a few general principles, there wasn't much to have in common; but those I did have with Zukofsky.[405]

Although he didn't see himself as an Objectivist he thought the term perfectly adequate to describe Zukofsky:

> There is a sense in which 'Objectivist' is not too bad a term for Louis and the people who are closely connected with him. The idea was a double one: one that a poem is an object which must stand by itself, a thing, and should have ideally no connection whatever with the chap who wrote it. It's just a thing in itself … And secondly that the proper matter for poetry is objects, things about the place, which is of course derived from Wordsworth ultimately, though Wordsworth didn't put it that way in his own prose writings. And you don't bother yourself about your own inner feelings. Wordsworth did of course in 'The Prelude' and 'The Excursion', but those were written about that and he treats his own things as things instead of expanding on his heart and this, that and the other. Zukofsky wanted to look at the things about him and put them down as things, and he wanted the completed poem to

be a thing, totally independent of its author. In those two points I would be in complete agreement with him, though we differed very strongly on many other things.[406]

Pound bombarded Zukofsky with advice during the latter part of 1930 in a tyrannical campaign of micromanagement in which Bunting's name featured frequently. If Zukofsky's Objectivist issue were to be a success Pound thought Bunting could be drafted in to edit his own 'British' edition. He wrote to Zukofsky on 24 October, 'This also wd. make it a murkn [American] number; excluding the so different English; though you cd. be broadminded an mention 'em in a brief article Basil's from L'indice; or a condensation; or yr. own. If you cover yourself with glory an' honour, H. M. might even let Basil try his hand at showin what Briton can do.'[407]

Zukofsky saw Bunting's role differently, as adding 'the "Foreign critic sees us" in a later issue,'[408] but Pound wasn't easily deterred. He told Zukofsky on 25 October, 'You can in ten lines of yr, prose cover the facts re/Bunting and J. Gorrdun Macleod. whose Ecliptic is now pubd.'[409] Three days later, reflecting on Bunting's prospects, he wrote again, 'As to Basil/ I spose his six months visa will make it oblig: fer him to git out of the U.S.A. I want to insert him as Eng. Correspondent for H & H or Poetry or everywhere possible: to choke off snot from Beligions Ray Mortimers and bloomsbuggers in generl/ (confidenshul as is most of the rest).'[410] 'Beligions' was the British essayist, Montgomery Belgion, and 'Ray Mortimers' was Raymond Mortimer, a British art historian who was closely associated with the Bloomsbury group. Pound already clearly saw Bunting as the antidote to the British arts establishment.

By 6 November Zukofsky had his contributors pretty much in place. He told Pound that it included Bunting for 'a poem or so, because, I wrote him, & to introduce him previous to the subsequent English issue you plan'.[411] By 9 November he had decided that

> Basil: Will be the only Englishman I'll print. Apprenticeship or Debut for his appearance as coming Eng. corresp. If he doesn't send new stuff – I'll have to choose from Redimiculum (of which Harriet doesn't know) – possibly Sad Spring or Against the Tricks of Time or While Shepherds Watched or Chorus of Furies or To Venus. None of these as good as Villon but handling of quantity always pretty expert. Myself – liked his traduction of La Bonne Lorraine – ending possibly too uniwersul … Will hint to Harriet he should be prized when I see her in Chicago Dec 19 …[412]

In the end he selected just one poem by Bunting for the issue, 'Nothing', here given the title 'The Word' for the only time.

Zukofsky's lobbying for Bunting was successful. He wrote to Pound in February 1931 celebrating the, 'good news about Basil's British number: Harriet evidently thought I was a nice boy suggesting it and accepted Basil's proposition after I told him to write to her. He ought to criticize my number – and perhaps invite one American to contribute – preferably one who did not appear in my Feb. issue.'[413] Pound already knew. On 22 January 1931 he wrote to Zukofsky that 'Basil writes me that our sportin' frien' Miss Monroe has axd him to do a Bri'ish number.'[414] The letter that Zukofsky had urged Bunting to write to Monroe was written on 15 December 1930, the day after Zukofsky had visited Bunting in Brooklyn. He lists a number of poets he would include in a British number including J. Gordon MacLeod, W. H. Auden, J. J. Adams, Bertram Higgins, John Collier and possibly Edgell Rickword and Peter Quennell.[415] This seems a fairly undistinguished list today and the quality issue was, as we shall see, not lost on Bunting even then.

Pound wrote to Monroe on 16 February, still pressing Bunting's case:

Bunting said some question of his doing an Eng. Number or getting Brit. Mss/ had arisen. He don't see how he can solicit mss ['especially from men whom he knows very slightly' added by hand] unless he has some sort of standing, such say, as Zuk. had in doing the American number. Macleod (J. Gordon) has sent me a mss/ and with that to start on I think Bunting could find enough material.

I think that if you decide to let him do a number it wd. be advisable to submit to him whatever English stuff you have already on hand. The more material to choose from (even he don't use a line of it) the better the number will be, i.e. greater enlightenment and knowledge of the FIELD in the mind of the selector.

BB's copy of Poetry not yet here. He spent an hour on mine the other evening and did not feel he cd. raise against it the objections he had some months ago raised against Amurikun poesy in general …

… Basil is quite aware that the Yenglisch cant be lined up to as stiff standard or provide any sort of intellectual unity. ['That don't mean that there is no way of assessing values' added by hand]

By way of further endorsement of Bunting's merit Pound appended a note from William Carlos Williams to this letter: 'I liked, we liked, Bunting – also his bride, whom you have not seen. They must be in Rapallo by now. He is a piece of metal sure enough. Fine chap and his poetry the most seductively musical that I know. It has a weird effect on me. I hope to the god of fishes and swollen prostates that he gets out a book for my pleasure soon. I enjoy reading him.'[416] Williams never lost this feeling about Bunting's work. He told Zukofsky nearly twenty years later: 'My taste has developed so that ... I can't read anything but the sort of work represented in the Active Anthology, your work for instance, Basil's work and some of the other work presented there.'[417]

Bunting expressed his own concern about being properly commissioned to edit an issue before soliciting contributions in early March. Now back in Rapallo, he wrote to Monroe on 5 March that he was 'diffident about definitely asking for material unless I can say that I am really commissioned to do so. One of my possible contributors [the Australian poet Bertram Higgins] has gone to Papua in search of gold and may shortly be eaten by the cannibals who abound there, so I want to get busy pretty soon, (before the savages).'[418]

It seems that Bunting quickly changed his mind about a formal editorship as Monroe replied to him on 19 March agreeing with him 'that it is inadvisable to offer you the editorship of the number, as in Zukofsky's case; indeed, distance makes it impracticable – it was difficult enough in February, with Zukofsky only 60 miles away'. Instead Monroe wanted him to encourage the poets he had mentioned the previous December to send their submissions directly to her, while he prepared an article about the 'English situation'. She told Bunting that Michael Roberts had also offered to write an article and that it might be interesting to include both. Roberts had also recommended including Julian Bell, William Empson and Cecil Day Lewis.[419]

Bunting started work and reported to Monroe on 1 May that he had contacted the poets and enclosing his own 'Attis' and 'Fearful Symmetry' as well as submissions from Bertram Higgins (which he later agreed were 'uninteresting')[420] and J. J. Adams.[421] By July his foreboding about the quality of a British number was gathering:

> I am very sorry no one else [apart from Higgins and Adams] seems to have
> sent anything to you. I thought you would get something from Macleod at

least and probably Auden and Rickword as well. Unless you can get something from these yng men it hardly seems worthwhile to have a special English number, since the rest of the existing English poets, so far as I know anything about them, are not worth printing: this is not intended to be fearfully high praise for the abovementioned.[422]

By October the issue was put to bed and he was already regretting missing one particular young writer: 'Putnam has published a poem by a young man who ought to have been mentioned if I'd known of him – name of Becket, Irish, I believe.'[423]

The 'Bri'ish number' would be the February 1932 issue of *Poetry* for which Bunting selected the first part of a long poem, 'Buckshee', by Ford Madox Ford, two poems by Michael Roberts, Julian Huxley's 'Spitsbergen Summer', two poems by Cecil Day Lewis, three by M. G. Gower, J. J. Adams' 'The Sirens' and Gordon Macleod's 'Foray of Centaurs', along with his own short poem 'Muzzle and jowl and beastly brow'. If there is any music in this selection it is drowned by Bunting's angry barrel scraping.

What is astonishing about Bunting's British number is his 'Comment' piece, 'English poetry today'. Bunting's must be the most bad tempered garland of other men's flowers ever constructed. He begins by excoriating contemporary English poetry (that is poetry written in English by British writers): 'There is no poetry in England, none with any relation to the life of the country, or of any considerable section of it.' The establishment is to blame:

> the rulers of England for a generation or more have never been indifferent to literature, they have been actively hostile. They have even set up and encouraged the frivolous imbecilities of cat-poetry, bird-poetry, flower-poetry; country-house Jorrocks-cum-clippership poetry (as Mr. Masefield does it); country-family cleverness (the Sitwells); and innumerable other devices for obscuring any work that smells of that objectionable quality, truth.[424]

Bunting was onto something here. Masefield had been appointed poet laureate in 1930 and his style of pastoral nostalgia promoted conservative values in an uncertain world. Clipper ships and R. S. Surtees' comic working-class sportsman, John Jorrocks, evoke an early nineteenth century landscape (and seascape) of honest endeavour, imperial security and political innocence that bore no resemblance to the turbulent 1930s. You don't have to be a conspiracy theorist to imagine that the establishment was engineering a cultural shift in its own favour when, in 1933 and at Masefield's suggestion, George V established the annual gold medal for the first or second poetry collections of British citizens under the age of thirty. Such a prize was unlikely to encourage the subversive or experimental. Nor was Bunting alone in seeing the Sitwells as cheerleaders for mediocrity. In *New Bearings in English Poetry* F. R. Leavis had famously derided them as belonging more 'to the history of publicity rather than of poetry'.[425]

Bunting saw T. S. Eliot's magazine *The Criterion*, not unreasonably, as the literature department of the establishment, and he had no fear of expressing his contempt for it:

> Mr. Eliot's *Criterion* is an international disaster, since he began to love his gloom, and regretfully, resignedly, to set about perpetuating the causes of it – kings, religion and formalism … *The Criterion* has gone about the business of blunting the English intelligence as systematically as the quarterlies of a century ago, but less crudely … Mr. Eliot's intelligence, turned to the work of drugging intelligence (having first, let's charitably suppose, drugged itself), can do much more havoc in England than in America; for kings, priests and academies are not living issues in the States … I have nothing to say against his poetry, amongst the finest of the age; but against his influence on the poetry of others, the involuntary extinguisher he applies to every little light, while professing, maybe truly, to hate the dark.

Bunting realised too late that he wasn't doing himself any favours with his principled assault on Eliot. He wrote a slightly panicky letter to Harriet Monroe from Rapallo on 21 January 1932: 'Enclosed is a mitigatory letter, which please print if possible in the same number with my article, if not, in the next. I don't want to call Eliot names, as I almost appear to in the article as it stands.' The letter itself is hardly a model of retraction:

> I see from the proofs of my article on English poetry, which arrive at this remoteness too late for revision, that it might appear to a rapid reader that I was making a personal attack on Mr Eliot, whereas I want to have it quite clear that it is only his influence I want to denounce; his influence acting probably far beyond his intentions, maybe even contrary to them. So far as I am aware he has always encouraged whatever decent poetry came his way, independent of its political, religious and so forth aspects. It is the pressure of his phenomenal prestige that extinguishes the sparks, etc. It is all so much weight added to the existing inducements to retrogression in England. If the mournful cadences of The Waste Land have turned out to be as hypnotically

effective as the Eat More Fruit advts., it is, of course, Mr Eliot's fault, but in a sense in which one might as justly call it his misfortune.[426]

The damage had probably already been done. Bunting had already published 'Attis, or: Something missing' which (according to Michael Schmidt) satirised Eliot as the eunuch.[427]

Harriet Monroe may have thought that Bunting was digging himself into an even deeper hole with this passive aggressive recantation. Although the February issue provoked a lively correspondence, selections of which were printed in the April issue, Bunting's letter was never published. In any event she had had quite enough of Pound's disciples and wrote to him on 17 December 1932, 'You think a lot of Zukofsky … while I think he is no poet at all, his 'objectivist' theories seem to me absurd, and his prose style abominable. Bunting's verse and prose are better, but after all he is no great shakes. If these are the best new ones in sight, the magazine may as well quit.'[428]

Bunting didn't blame Eliot himself for the work of his followers. In his essay on Eliot in *The New English Weekly* of 8 September 1932 he announced at the outset that he was not concerned with Eliot's opinions which had had, 'an illegitimate influence, that is to say, imitators have tried to make poetry out of Eliot's emotions instead of their own, have borrowed the content of his verse instead of studying its form and applying its devices … to matter of their own'.[429] He explained his position once again over forty years later: 'when one attacked Eliot that didn't mean that one didn't value Eliot; it meant that one felt he ought to be up and doing with the same sort of vigour and uncompromisingness of Pound, Zukofsky and Carlos Williams. Perhaps it was unfair because I've never myself been as uncompromising as them either.'[430]

Given the tone of Bunting's assault on Eliot it wouldn't be surprising if Eliot had felt distinctly undervalued by the younger poet. Eliot might have been the archdeacon of modernism but Bunting had no patience with his absorption in his own role, with the fact that, as Wyndham Lewis memorably put it, he went around disguised as Westminster Abbey.[431] He explained his frustration with Eliot to Morton Zabel, Associate Editor of *Poetry*, in January 1933, 'Eliot apparently finds a need to complicate himself and erect artificial selves and stalk about on stilts. He mistrusts his own verve and so cheats the reader.'[432]

None of this mattered greatly because, as Bunting continued in his 'Comment' essay, the British poetry-reading public was equally moribund: 'the divorce between literature and the British subject is complete. The gulf is unpassable. The intelligent reader in England is the frequenter of two small public-houses in Bloomsbury, plus a few isolated idiosyncratic scholars in the provinces.'[433] The consequence of a philistine establishment encouraging mediocre poets to write for an indifferent public was, of course, disastrous, breeding middlebrow contempt on the one hand and involution on the other: 'When they see what is given out publicly as poetry, men of good but not specifically literary intelligence conceive a contempt for poetry similar to that traditional amongst the army and hunting people, and still fostered in the schools.' The result? Poetry

> withdraws into itself. It can reach but a small audience, small enough to have special learning and, as it were, passwords; too small to hope to influence even a corner of the national culture, so that, proposing no end but the exercise of its special knowledge, it delights more and more in approximations to the acrostic, less and less in true concision, which implies force and clarity as well as paucity of words. The cure? – I can see nothing for it but patience.[434]

One might think that Bunting's misery is complete, but he has barely started. Having surveyed the scorched earth of contemporary British poetry he becomes more granular. Roy Campbell ('the successor to Mr. Masefield, if not in the Laureateship at least in middle-class favor') has Masefield's 'meaningless violence' and 'coarse, primitive, but often strong beat'. Campbell's poetry is 'good enough for the *New Statesman*, but not for export or cold-storage.' So no place for Campbell in the British edition. Nor was there a place for John Collier who had 'lapsed into a novel called *His Monkey's Wife: or, Married to a Chimp*. (And there's an end of him? as formerly of Mr. Huxley?)' Bunting was correct in this. Collier pretty much abandoned poetry after the modest critical and commercial success of his first novel, *His Monkey Wife*, in 1930. He concentrated on novels and short stories and became a prolific writer of screenplays for film and television. Bunting regarded Collier as, 'something between a pimp and a buffoon in person, but his poems move me even when I have very little idea of what he is driving at'.[435]

Bunting wasn't particularly impressed by the poets he *did* include. J. J. Adams, for example: 'neither sends his manuscripts to editors nor revises them for publication, having had his exhibitionism removed by psychoanalysis, as it might be his appendix. His poetry is therefore unfinished, profuse, abounding in lax passages: often as full of dross as unsmelted ore.' But even so Adams was better than most: 'it seems to me that his satiric-ironic method, even in its crude state, is individual enough and enough of an improvement, as method, over the usual thing, to attract a great deal more attention ... A good editor would take Mr. Adams in hand and force him to revise and cut; but it is better to have him unrevised than not at all.'[436] Bunting didn't give up on Adams. Nearly forty years later in an essay on Herbert Read Bunting asked if it is 'irrelevant that I find in Read's 1923 volume [*Mutations of the Phoenix*] phrases here and there that have the very tone of that strange man, John J. Adams, who will be dug up one day by the scholars? But Adams has more emotion.'[437]

Macleod enjoyed an easier ride. *The Ecliptic* 'interested me more than any new thing since *The Waste Land*' and in 'The Foray of Centaurs', Macleod 'seems to have been preoccupied with the versification, which is consummate, even surpassing the best of *The Ecliptic*'. On the other hand 'the force of the poem' isn't clear to Bunting, it isn't well organised, and 'there is not much zeal in it; and zeal, if not indispensable to poetry, is at least at present a desideratum. But who in England can be zealous, being hopeless?'

Are there any redeeming features? Well, nearly: 'Of the group of young men who edited *The Criterion* about five years ago in opposition to Mr. Eliot's *ex cathedra* decrees, two have not yet given up the attempt to do something worth the effort.' These two are Edgell Rickword who may 'produce a sufficient body of good stuff for us to remember him by' and Bertram Higgins who is, at least 'not a case for despair'. And then there's W. H. Auden, but 'most of his poems seem fragments only. Some are rather silly. Lack of content is always detectable, even the satire becoming frivolous from lack of depth.' But at least Auden's case is 'far from hopeless', although looking back forty or so years in 1975 it had become clear that it was indeed hopeless:

> When Auden sent his first book to Rapallo I thought there was something there that ought to be encouraged. Pound didn't. Pound thought there was nothing there and there'd never come out of it anything but bunk. I tried to write and suggest to Auden the way I thought things should go. He wrote back, quite pleasantly, but stating that what he really wanted to do was go on teaching rugby football at a prep school.[438]

The other poets Bunting included, Day Lewis, Gower and Roberts, don't merit even a negative mention and, unlike Auden, didn't get to be damned with faint damnation forty years later. It is surprising that Bunting overlooked Clere Parsons, an English poet who had died in 1931 at the age of twenty-three. Parsons, like Bunting, believed that the meaning of poetry is communicated through sound and rhythm. The evidence of *Poems*, published the year after his death by Faber, suggests that he would have been a significant voice in twentieth-century poetry.

Poetry's doubtless rather bemused American subscribers might well have been asking themselves why, if British poetry is *this* bad, it is being visited on them at all. Bunting, too, may have asked himself why he had bothered. He concluded his introduction to the cream of British poetry in despair, 'There is a long and dreary list of highly advertised failures, beginning with the Sitwells; but nothing with which to prolong a catalogue, if each item is to have the interest of a possible winner. Adams, Macleod, Rickword, Higgins and Auden exhaust the category; and two of these are long shots, and one really belongs to the last generation.' Zukofsky told Pound in April 1931 that Bunting, 'shd. go to it anyway & remove some of the monthly manure by the way',[439] but it seems that Bunting thought he had merely added to it.

By this time Bunting had seen two of his poems published in *Poetry*, 'Villon' in October 1930 and 'Nothing' in February 1931.[440] Pound had, as ever, been working hard behind the scenes on Bunting's behalf. He had written to Monroe in November 1929 to urge her to consider 'Villon' for a prize: 'I don't think you will have any trouble in accepting this poem of Bunting's [Villon] ... you will probably find same ... well in the running for one of the heavier prizes.'[441] And he was happy to clear up, in that Poundian way that almost always made matters more incomprehensible, Monroe's suspicion about her new contributor's name: 'Bunting has had a fit of modesty and refuses to divulge his heroic past. He is far from a pseudonym. Old Saxon tribal ending in =ing. Northumberland."[442]

Monroe reprised part of 'Villon' in the November 1931 issue of *Poetry* to mark Bunting's award of the Lyric Prize. Bunting managed to be simultaneously generous and unappreciative in acknowledging receipt of the prize. He wrote to Monroe in January 1932: 'I don't know what I ought to say about my prize. It went some way towards paying the expenses of my daughter's birth, arriving the same day. But I am inclined to quarrel with the judges in that they preferred me to Zukofsky, who in my judgment had the better claim on any laurels that were going.'[443] Zukofsky followed up the Objectivist issue of *Poetry* with an Objectivist anthology which was published in 1932 but Bunting seems not to have involved himself in it. In October 1931 Zukofsky wondered aloud to Pound why, 'didn't I ever hear from him re- the Anthology. Too late now – but give him my best – the Trotzskiite.'[444]

For Bunting the poet 1932 was a good year. His 'Verse and Version' appeared in *Il Mare* on 1 October 1932. He contributed the first two sections of 'Villon' to Ezra Pound's *Profile*, published in May 1932 in Milan, a collection of poems, 'which have stuck in my memory and which may possibly define their epoch, or at least rectify current ideas about it in respect to at least one contour'.[445] For the first time Bunting was published in the company of some of the greatest writers of the age, Eliot, Yeats, William Carlos Williams, Joyce, Marianne Moore and Cummings among them. In the same year he also contributed four poems to Sherard Vines' *Whips & Scorpions: Specimens of Modern Satiric Verse 1914–1931*.[446] In summer 1932 Zukofsky published his long-awaited *An "Objectivists" Anthology* with poems mainly from the Objectivist issue of *Poetry* from the previous year (but also with poems from Pound, 'Gentle Jheezus sleek and wild', and Eliot, 'Marina', who had not been included in that issue of *Poetry*). Bunting's contribution to the anthology was a fragment of 'Attis: Or, Something Missing'. To Bunting's fury Yvor Winters launched a scathing attack on Zukofsky in a review of *An "Objectivists" Anthology* in *Hound and Horn*:

> Mr. Zukofsky's preface is so badly written that it is next to impossible to disentangle more than a few intelligible remarks … It is symptomatic of the intellectual bankruptcy of the middle generation that Mr. Pound will actively back such a man, that Mr. Eliot, Dr. Williams and Miss Moore have been willing to put up with him … none of the talented writers of Mr. Zukofsky's generation are included, and theories that Mr. Zukofsky struggles hopelessly to express, the methods of composition that he and his friends have debauched till they no longer deserve even ridicule, seem to be sinking rapidly to lower and lower literary levels.[447]

Bunting wrote to James Leippert, editor of the new *Lion & Crown* magazine, on 30 October 1932: 'Hound and Horn has recently published Y Winters disgusting review of Zuks Objectivist anthology … please run a fair review of that anthology as soon as you can, since that is ultimately the best answer to such disappointed spite … I have sent a letter to H & H which if it doesn't get printed will at least make them sit up.'[448]

It would indeed. The letter was printed; Bunting described Winters'
review as 'the vomit of a creature who ... found his own name omitted from
an anthology that proposed to sample everything at this moment *alive* in
poetry'. He claimed that his own poem in the first pages of the anthology
was a direct attack on Winters himself. 'No fool much likes being laughed
at,' he continued. 'He was afraid, maybe, to go for someone who seemed to
have discovered the disgrace he fondly believed secret, so he turned his spite
on the anthology's editor.'[449] Marian Bunting recalled in 1969 that 'Basil
slashed [Winters] to pieces ... He loathed him & his works.'[450] Winters'
response in the same issue rather suggests that he didn't understand the fact
that he had been insulted rather than challenged by Bunting. The 'something
missing' is genitalia. Typically Bunting worked the machismo exchange up
in an account he gave of it to Gael Turnbull many years later. Winters, he
told Turnbull, 'wrote to him in Italy, making a physical challenge of it! It so
happened that Gene Tunney was there, and wrote back for him, saying that
he (Tunney) would accept the challenge on Bunting's behalf. They didn't
hear from Winters again!'[451] Gene Tunney was at the time the heavyweight
boxing champion of the world. What actually happened was that Bunting
wrote the following letter to *Hound and Horn* containing a masterly put-down:
'Yvor Winters' offer to take me on at prose, verse or fisticuffs (180 lbs was,
I think, the weight he mentioned) shows a stout heart, but I am afraid such
an unequal spectacle would draw no good gate. Winters would be better
matched in all these respects with Gene Tunney.'[452]

Pound had conceived *Profile* as a 'critical narrative, that is I attempted to
show by excerpt what had occurred during the past quarter of a century'.
The following year he followed up with a new anthology, *Active Anthology*,
which collected an 'assortment of writers, mostly ill known in England,
in whose verse a development appears or in some case we may say "still
appears" to be taking place, in contradistinction to authors in whose work
no such activity has occurred or seems likely to proceed any further'.[453] It is
astonishing that the ringmaster of literary modernism could introduce the
most gifted writers of a generation with a sentence as horrible as that. But
there is no doubt that they were the most gifted writers: Williams, Zukofsky,
Aragon (translated by Cummings), Cummings himself, Hemingway,
Marianne Moore, Oppen, D. G. Bridson, Bunting and, of course, Pound.
This is quite a list. Not many editors have selected ten contemporary poets,
nine of whom would be literary household names eighty years later. What's
really surprising about this anthology is the amount of it given over to

Bunting, who occupies nearly a quarter of the book (51 pages out of 216 pages of poetry). The fact that Bunting takes 25 per cent of a book with so stellar a line-up indicates his gathering importance. In fact though Pound himself points out that he had confined 'my selection to poems Britain has not accepted and in the main that the British literary bureaucracy does NOT want to have printed in England'.[454] Pound introduced Bunting as a slightly special case:

> Mr Bunting probably seems reactionary to most of the other contributors. I think the apparent reaction is a definite endeavour to emphasize certain necessary elements which the less considering American experimenters tend to omit. At any rate Mr B. asserted that ambition some years ago, but was driven still further into the American ambience the moment he looked back upon British composition of, let us say, 1927–8.[455]

This is a strange observation. Pound included Bunting's most progressive poems to date, including 'Villon', 'Attis – Or, Something Missing' and 'Chomei at Toyama', poems that challenged the literary status quo as much as did those of William Carlos Williams or Zukofsky.[456]

Bunting had a special role in the creation of the *Active Anthology*, one that seems to have cast a long shadow across twentieth-century poetry. The year before he died he recalled that:

> In 1930, or thereabouts, Ezra decided to make an anthology called the *Active Anthology* and he was too … busy, so he picked out great lumps of Zukofsky and great lumps of me and said, 'that's the core of it; now you do Carlos Williams and Marianne Moore' and I forget who else, two or three others. So I had to read all the works of Carlos Williams and pick out what I thought were the best for the anthology. And I did that, and for years and years and years after, until Williams was quite an old man, every anthology that included Williams had poems selected from my selection.[457]

The only obscure inclusion in the anthology is that of the author and long-time BBC producer, Douglas Geoffrey Bridson. By the time he retired from the BBC in 1969 Bridson was widely seen as the organisation's 'cutural boss'.[458] In the 1930s Pound held Bridson in high regard, bracketing him with Bunting as the twinned hope for the future of British poetry. In a letter to the American poet T. C. Wilson in January 1934 he complained that, 'Surely Bunting and Bridson must be better than Eliot's deorlings.'[459] More than a year later he wrote to Eliot himself to encourage him to consider the two young poets, Bridson was only twenty-four at the time, as a kind of pair: 'However, gor ferbidd that I speak modest ever again about anything I find fit to recommend. If you print Brid.[son] you can print Bunting's Firdusi, which certainly is good enou(bloody)gh fer 'em.'[460]

Active Anthology was sufficiently visible to attract a satirical attack in 1934 when Samuel J. Looker mocked Pound's collection as Ephraim Pundit in *Superman: being the complete poetical works of Robert Baby Buntin-Dicebat*. Looker thought that Pound's circle showed real contempt for its readership. 'When the dead dogs of romanticism are indecently buried', he wrote in a spoof introduction,

> I shall feel much happier about the state of modern poetry and criticism. That they are dead at all is largely if not entirely due to my activity. English-speaking poetry, not to say the Italian and Bantu, owes to me an almost unpayable debt, which, with the usual snout-like quality of their skunkish kind, modern critico-poetico imbeciles will not make the slightest attempt to repay, nor do I expect even elementary gratitude from this collection of critical cowards, intellectual impotents, eunuchs, and mangy doctored cats and jackals.[461]

A very sympatico old Jap

From January 1932 Bunting tried to interest Harriet Monroe in 'Chomei at Toyama' and, from July, James Leippert, of *The Lion and Crown*. He had sent Monroe some fragments of the poem but withdrew them in February, preferring to try to find a home for the whole poem.[462] The problem with Leippert was that he wouldn't pay so *Poetry* was a far better option.[463] (Bunting mischievously suggested in 1984 that Zukofsky wrote poems with lines containing only two words because *Poetry* paid by the line.[464]) Leippert was desperate to secure contributions from Pound but Bunting, by then acting as Pound's informal secretary, continued to rebuff, though not in an unkindly way, Leippert's entreaties throughout 1932. He suggested a number of alternative contributors, including J. J. Adams:

> Have suggested to John J Adams he should send you something. What he writes isn't fashionably dressed. End-stopped blank verse. But if you look further into it you will find a skill in satire and irony that no one else has just now. He's the most unpublished man of his age I know of. Nobody likes satire that isn't utterly obvious and on obvious subjects … I suppose Adams is as old

as Pound and Eliot and he's only made a few appearances in print – partly his own fault since he makes no effort to get printed and MSS have to be dragged out of him.[465]

But if Leippert *must* have Pound the best he could offer was translations of the articles Pound had written for *Il Mare*. The value of this would be to remind parts of the literary world that Pound still mattered: 'The fact that Ezra spotted quite a number of winners – Williams, Joyce, Eliot, Lewis, H.D., Aldington, etc etc – at that period [before the war], before anybody else had so much as heard of them, if insisted on, may make some of the literary snobs take more notice of what he has to say NOW.'[466]

Another way to Pound's heart though, Bunting suggested, would be to publish Bunting. Pound was a great admirer of what the *Little Review* had achieved and saw *The Lion and Crown* as a possible successor:

> I am sorry to keep thrusting myself forward, but I really think [Pound] would consider publication of my 'Chomei' a long step in the direction of a new 'Little Review'. Maybe he would modify his opinion if he saw it in print! I too, however, think 'Chomei', in spite of defects I haven't been able to remedy, a poem which, whatever its worth or worthlessness in itself, might have a useful influence; showing, for instance, that poetry can be intelligible and still be poetry; a fact that has come to be doubted by the generation that took most of its ideas indirectly from Eliot.[467]

The following day Bunting urged 'Chomei' on Monroe once again[468] and she seems to have asked to see the whole poem.[469]

Bunting apologised to Leippert for his long silence in January 1933, the confusion of a house move and a fortnight 'on the sick list' being the reason. He wrote to congratulate Leippert, in a rather tepid way, for his first issue of *The Lion and Crown*, as 'pleasantly got up and as good as a mag need be, but not as good as it could be. There is a too goddam gentlemanly air about your contributors, including me (the thing having been written with the Criterion in view). It is true that some camouflage of that sort aids chances of survival, but it also produces premature senile decay, as in Eliot's quarterly tombstone.' A string of criticisms of individual contributors follows, trumped by a bizarre conclusion, 'On the whole, therefore, a success. Congratulations.'[470]

On the same day he wrote to Morton Dauwen Zabel, Associate Editor of *Poetry*, to explain that the reason he was resisting the suggestion of publishing parts of 'Chomei' rather than the entire work, which would have taken up about eighteen pages of the magazine, was that it depended

> in a very high degree on the general design: the balance of the calamities and consolations pivoted on the little central satire, the transmogrification of the house throughout, the earth, air, fire and water, pieces, first physical then spiritual make up an elaborate design which I've tried not to underline so that it might be felt rather than pedantically counted up. Also the old boy's superficial religion breaking down at the end needs what goes before to give it relief, and what goes before needs the breakdown to anchor it to its proper place.[471]

This abridgement problem was, as we shall see, to resurface decades later, when his international reputation was secure and he became eligible for inclusion in anthologies.

By March 1933 he had given in and reluctantly accepted Zabel's proposal to publish fragments of 'Chomei' even though 'the picking out of four somewhat "poetical" bits rather misrepresents the very sympatico old Jap'.[472] Pound had, as always, been agitating behind the scenes. He had written a typically forthright letter to Harriet Monroe early in 1933 saying: 'If you don't print Bunting's long poem I shall have to believe that you have had a really acute attack of the kind of inferiority complex that has upheld your hatred of having good stuff in the magazine, even when you have tolerated and permitted it.'[473] The September 1933 issue of *Poetry* carried seven fragments of 'Chomei at Toyama', around 150 lines, being about half of the whole poem. Bunting and Monroe had nearly fallen out over the poem during the previous summer, after Bunting's testy announcement on 2 August that Pound was to publish the poem in its entirety in his 'Active Anthology' which was due to be published in October.[474] He demanded the return of his fragments which, he felt, she had accepted the previous December but had not published. Monroe reacted quickly and a mollified Bunting thanked her on 30 August for both proofs of the poem that was about to be published and a welcome cash advance.[475]

Essays in criticism

A number of essays written in the early 1930s show how Bunting was developing intellectually. The longest of these, 'The Written Record', probably written in the late 1920s, remained unpublished until Richard

Caddel collected the essays in 1994.[476] It mounts a sustained attack on the 'modern-western vogue of the illusion of Permanence' in literary criticism, that sense that understanding a work of art is possible only with a kind of scientific rigour and the precision of expression that are commonly understood by the priesthood that administers the rites, scholars. Its chief exponent, in Bunting's view, was T. S. Eliot, 'Archdeacon in the Province of Literary Criticism', particularly as he presents himself in 'Tradition and the Individual Talent'. Eliot's contention that 'criticism is as inevitable as breathing' was anathema to Bunting.[477] Basil Bunting would not countenance for a second the notion that 'fitting in is a test of … value'. The canon, 'paper art', once established simply creates exponentially more paper – commentaries, interpretations, theories – all of no real value. Against the Sisiphean misery of professional critics in the academy of the precise Bunting celebrates ambiguity in an essay which, if it is a bit of a rant, is a learned one. He engages with logic and philosophy on their own terms and comes out of the encounter rather well. There is much in 'Tradition and the Individual Talent' with which Bunting would have agreed so one has to assume that his attack was in some way political.[478] In any event he was brave to take on Eliot so directly at this stage of his career. Either that or he was banking on modernism moving on, leaving Eliot marooned in the new establishment while he himself became a mover in the next revolution. If so he was a generation ahead of his time.

'Some limitations of English' was written by November 1930 and published in *The Lion and Crown* in October 1932. It moves the attack from the priesthood to the very medium of its communication, showing with a clear grammatical eye why 'our philosophy and our religion are bound to a stupid monism derived from the grammarbook'. 'The Lion and the Lizard' remained unpublished in Bunting's lifetime. He uses a comparison of Edward FitzGerald's translation of *Rubáiyát of Omar Khayyám* with Omar's original to launch a general attack on English poetry: 'English poets are too often on their dignity, they strive too constantly to be sublime and end by becoming monotonous and empty of life-giving detail, like hymn-tunes. They have often been the slaves rather than the masters of their metres. (The sonnet exploited Wordsworth, not he the sonnet.)'[479]

T. S. Eliot finds himself in the dock again. He is identified as the exemplar of those poets who 'have sought yet remoter abstractions even by forced adjectives, and conceits, like some of Mr. Eliot's, painful to follow. They have often thought more carefully about the impression made by their own personality than about that made by the ostensible object of their verse.' Bunting singles out Eliot's 'Ash-Wednesday' as a poem that 'might serve to demonstrate many of these errors'. [480]

These seem to me to be angry essays. As Caddel points out they are 'noteworthy for their spirit of *attack* ... As such, they reflect a radical, even subversive temperament in Bunting which has perhaps not yet been fully recognised.'[481] As Peter Nicholls noted in a review of *Three Essays*, they 'give access to some of Bunting's most deeply-felt ideas' while revealing 'that habitual movement of his thought which so impressively places the detail of poetic language at the very centre of our large concerns'.[482] In 1934 Bunting told Zukofsky that, 'half the evils in the world come from verbalism, i.e. imagining that abstract words have anything more than a grammatical meaning or function. Adjectives, numbers, symbols like the word God, eat away all sense of reality and land us in every kind of social and economic mess, when people begin to think they correspond to anything genuine.'[483]

The essays, particularly the first two, also seem to me to be closely linked, written in a tight sequence. The tone of professional disdain doesn't let up at any point. It is though a very different disdain from that shown in some of Bunting's articles in *The Outlook*. Here we sense a deeply committed mind engaging with subjects that it really cares about, very personal statements that carry none of the baggage or compromise of an identifiable readership that mattered to it.

Perhaps the most succinct description of his view of society in the 1930s, however, appears in a letter to Ezra Pound written in 1931. Once again it addresses issues that British society is struggling with as I write; how to punish bankers and media barons, the financial politics of devolution, supertax, reform of the House of Lords. It is incredible how little progress we have made:

> If Wales and the North don't rise this autumn, there's little hope of anything but extinction. The new program of the T.U.C. should be drawn up quite simply, thus:
>
> 1. Hang Rothschild and a select retinue of 'merchant bankers'.
>
> 2. Confine Rothermere in Broadmoor Criminal Lunatic Asylum with public warning to Beaverbrook and the Berries.
>
> 3. Warn Australia Canada and S Africa that if they don't both pay up their proportionate share of the cost of the fleet and loosen up a bit on the

immigration restrictions, they will be put up for public auction to any buyer who cares to undertake the job of reconquering them, such as Germany or U.S.A.

4. No import dues, and a bloody big supertax.

5. Abolish the game laws.

6. Abolish the Home Office.

7. Confiscate the Church lands and royalties.

After that elect a new House of Commons and omit to summon any of the hereditary peers to parliament.[484]

Bunting certainly had a reasonable amount of his prose published in the early 1930s, with regular appearances in the Rapallo weekly newspaper, *Il Mare*, including a Pound–Bunting double-header on Scriabin on 8 July 1933.[485] *Il Mare* published a literary supplement every second issue which, Bunting claimed improbably in a letter to James Leippert, is 'read all over Italy'.[486]

On 26 May 1932 *New English Weekly* ran Bunting's remarkable essay on 'Mr. Ezra Pound'. Remarkable because of the sure-footed way it summarises Pound's pioneering literary scholarship and remarkable too in identifying an unjustly neglected poem, 'Homage to Sextus Propertius', which Eliot had unaccountably excluded from his selection of Pound's poems in 1928 (and again in 1948):[487] 'In my considered opinion, "Propertius" was the most important poem of our times, surpassing alike "Mauberley" and "The Waste Land".' Bunting marshals the evidence in favour of Pound's genius like a barrister:

> He was [first] heard of as a scholar, explaining the 'Spirit of Romance', the poets of Provence and Tuscany, the French and Spanish epics. He translated Bertran de Born, Arnaut Daniel, Guido Cavalcanti, the Anglo-Saxon 'Seafarer'. He interested himself in every branch of the technique of verse, rhymed, rhymeless, accentual, quantitative, alliterative, as strict as the ballade and altogether free. He wrote Sapphics successfully in English, and a Sestina stronger than, and almost as musical as, Spenser's. He made himself, early in his career, one of the most consummate masters of the techniques of versification that our literature has ever seen.[488]

All this enormous achievement, Bunting reminds us, was *before* his pioneering work on modern French poetry, Catullus and Propertius, Japanese Noh theatre, Chinese classical poetry, Fenellosa, Cavalcanti; before his discovery of Joyce and Eliot, his study of music, his book on Antheil and his Villon opera; before his 'two long poems of modern life', 'Hugh Selwyn Mauberley' and 'Homage to Sextus Propertius'. Ten lines into this essay one realises afresh just how much the world of letters lost when Pound disintegrated into an anti-Semitic amateur economist and Mussolini worshipper. Pound taught a generation of poets to *condense*, to rid their work of superfluous words. Humphrey Carpenter says that Pound 'cited with delight Bunting's discovery that a German–Italian dictionary rendered *dichten* (to write poetry) as *condensare*, to condense',[489] and in Pound's *ABC of Reading*, published in 1934, there is a chapter heading 'DICHTEN = CONDENSARE', and acknowledgement of 'Mr Bunting's discovery and his prime contribution to contemporary criticism.'[490] In fact, however, Bunting had intuited the connection. He wrote from Tenerife to thank Pound for the mention but to correct him: 'Mention of me an ad gratis: however, dichten–to condense aint nobody's property unless Hitler wants it for the Reich. But I didn't get it mucking about with a dictionary, but because I have some feeling for words of Indo-European origin which has often been useful: and when it occurred to me that this word might be useful to you, I then looked it up and confirmed what was already my firm belief.'[491]

Bunting never failed to acknowledge his debt to Pound although he was always careful to contextualise it. Nearly fifty years later the editor of *Agenda*, William Cookson, asked Bunting if he could reprint the *New English Weekly* article on Pound in a special Pound issue, prompting an anguished response, 'No no no no no no. The article you have exhumed from the New English Weekly is altogether too jejune for any purpose worth considering this lifetime later. Leave it to be dug up, if it ever is dug up again, by the pedants who will gnaw any carrion when I'm dead (and out of copyright).' He went on to tell Cookson how the article had originated and his account shows why the article seems so remarkable. It was an inside job.

I've been trying to recollect how it came to be concocted in the first place. There was a time when The Listener asked for a piece on Ezra to go with something or other the BBC was doing, and what I said was, they said, far too highbrow for their readers. They wanted something in the style of 'Told to the Children'. So Ezra and I got together and made what we thought was the simplest possible statement of his career, something that might do for a publisher's blurb, only longer. We cut out anything that we thought too hard for a middling intelligent child of ten, but the Listener still found it too hard, so it went elsewhere ... I perceive in it bits that sound like me and bits that are certainly Ezra shifted over into my words; and it has none of the things that I would have said if I'd been writing for, for instance, the Criterion which might have irritated EP. In short it's a joint performance of a chore neither of us fancied ... I would never, on my own, have bothered with his 'studies of modern French poetry'. I would have left the Treatise on Harmony to slumber undisturbed. On the other hand, it is me rather than Ezra who insists on the merits of Propertius, but too circumspectly, for Pound would not have liked me *at that date* to draw attention to the relationship with Whitman. The bit of balls about 'Trois Contes' is, again, pure Ezra – bunkum to me.[492]

In 1979, at a conference on Pound in Durham, Bunting revealed another Poundian hoax, the sleight of hand that underpinned 'Hugh Selwyn Mauberley' itself, the unravelling of which served only to highlight Pound's skill. Pound had planned to collaborate with Eliot to write not a great poem but simply one that was better than any of their contemporaries could have written. 'The point about *Mauberley* is an odd one,' Bunting told James Laughlin and Lawrence Pitkethly in 1982:

> Pound and Eliot got together and decided to do a great hoax. They would produce a poet, an imaginary poet, who would have all sorts of virtues, but always all the vices they believed belonged to English poetry, and was therefore a complete failure – though he had to be good enough to be convincing, to be someone Eliot and Pound could take an interest in. And they set to work on it. But in fact Eliot was lazy and didn't, and the whole thing was done by Pound. That was *Mauberley* ... They got their notion of doing it, I'm sure, by their reading of Samuel Butler which happened about that time, just about the beginning of the First World War, or a little after the beginning of it.[493]

CANARY ISLES, 1933–1936

It appears that Bunting had been planning to leave Italy for some time. Money was the problem. He told James Leippert in January 1933 that 'an old peasant gave me a mongrel dog (and its kennel) for Xmas. Together with baby and cat, the household is now complete. If I had enough money to keep all these creatures fed and those that need it clothed and my boat painted and to buy a few books I need and pay my worst debts, I'd be perfectly comfortable.'[494] A letter sent to Morton Zabel on the same day explains that he is not prepared to finance a collection of his own since 'I have no intention of wasting my substance, which never more than barely suffices my family, on printing it myself. I should say, my wife's substance, because my own doesn't even cover the cigarettes I smoke.'[495] By March he reported to Zabel that he had not possessed trousers of his own for months and that the only pair he could borrow didn't fit.[496] Some of this constant penury was clearly self-inflicted. Marian later recalled that 'both Basil and his mother were wildly extravagant – almost penniless, he took the train from Rapallo to Genoa each morning to visit me at the hospital – travelling 1st class when there was a 3rd class coach on the train'.[497]

Pound told Zukofsky in April 1933 that Bunting was going to Spain, prompting Zukofsky to ask if he had gone 'for good? & does that mean the next war?', but Bunting recalled that he left Italy for the Canary Isles towards the end of 1933 because it was cheaper.[498]

Many years later he reflected on his time in Paris and Rapallo in a letter to the editor of *Nine*, Peter Russell: 'What went on in Paris and Rapallo … ? Mainly a comedy. Most of the dramatis personae were comically vain, and the clash of their vanities was funny. Little by little the spectacle reduced my own vanity to manageable proportions, but that didn't appear to be the usual result.'[499]

His wife remembered their life in Rapallo as a more private drama. 'He was out of this world – he didn't know up from down except in literature, music, and poetry. I had the best years of my life with him,' she recalled in 1968,

> and they were some of them pretty bad. He had chosen to make no attempt to earn a living – let ordinary men do this if they wanted to. We lived & lived well in Rapallo on $35.00 a month my parents sent me. Married him to support him while he wrote poetry, but he took me away from my job to live in Italy – the insecurity was horrible for me – didn't seem to bother him.[500]

He clearly wasn't a perfect father. Pound's daughter, Mary de Rachewiltz, said that Pound's mother, Isabel, 'raised her hands in despair at the mention of B.B. – he had parked the pram with two infants on the Rapallo Lungomare, went into a café and forgot all about them'.[501]

The move from Rapallo to the Canaries seems to have been a subject of domestic dispute. Victoria Forde claims that Marian believed that Bunting's mother would help her to prevent the move and that she 'tried to use all their money to pay bills, but on the day that Mrs Bunting was to arrive they left for the Canary Isles'.[502]

The Canary Isles (named after the wild dogs that once inhabited the islands, not after the songbird) consist of seven main and six smaller islands in the Atlantic Ocean, sixty-five miles west of Cape Yubi on the southern coast of Morocco. After three weeks on the island the Buntings were struggling to find accommodation and the poet's first impressions were of a colourless landscape: 'Just got back from a visit to the local Sahara. Seven or eight miles wide and ever so many long, sand covered with loose pieces of pumice about as big as a man's head. A sort of pale grey thorn scrub, and a few camels eating it. A sort of green shrub much rarer, and a goat or two eating that.'[503]

Although the Buntings lived an impoverished life in Tenerife, it had its colourful compensations:

Alarming bus ride with driver just lively drunk, most dangerous road I ever travelled, hairpin bends with precipices beneath every ten or fifteen metres. Took it at thirty-five miles an hour. Shot the conductor clean out of the bus at one corner, but he wasn't killed. Missed a child by about one inch, and nearly got busted by the one railway engine on the island. Total casualties (twenty minute ride), one billy-goat, fairly and squarely squashed according to all the rules of the game, after a chase of about fifty metres.[504]

He wrote to Pound a few months later that 'the people of this island so unspeakable, and the food so uneatable, they make prolonged residence impossible, in spite of great cash saving'.[505] He even refused to learn Spanish because 'the natives are so disgusting'.[506] He loathed the island and its people. As early as April 1934 he told Pound that the family was returning to Rapallo as soon as convenient, provided no war developed to prevent it.[507]

Alcohol clearly played a big part in local life. He related a tale of drunken woe to Pound that is ironic given Isabel Pound's memories of Bunting's paternal care in Rapallo:

detecting and getting rid of a dipsomaniac servant during last twentyfour hours has left me a bit bewildered. She got dangerous at the end, otherwise I dare say she would have gone on puzzling us some while longer. Its incredible the cunning of that gentry. She took Bourtai out for a walk to the lowest ginshop in the neighbourhood, kept her there three and a half hours and finally fell down on the highroad, leaving the kid in the middle of heavy motor traffic all alone.[508]

The locals were bad enough, but even they were better than the visitors: 'An aroma of tourist about the towns, not much to my liking – too strongly flavoured with German.'[509] The climate, the scenery and the prettiness of the women seem to have comprised Bunting's lasting memory of the Islands:

> There are perpetually clouds being blown up against the mountains. Rain doesn't fall. The clouds simply condense on the mountains and the water trickles from the condensed cloud into the ground and has to be mined from the galleries in the mountains. The sky is very often overcast for a long time. Still, through the clouds enough sunshine comes to sunburn you faster than the bare sun on the Mediterranean.[510]

Bourtai, was similarly struck by the climate. Her recollections of it are remarkable considering she was four years old when she left the Canary Isles. She remembered unusual weather, 'red rain once or twice when the Sahara sand coloured it, a hurricane which lifted the thatched roof of a peasant's cottage straight up in the air, and all the trees down in the garden. Frighteningly, the window before which Marian was holding her youngest daughter while she was looking out at the chaos was broken immediately afterwards.'[511]

Bunting described the vagaries of the climate in Tenerife to Pound:

> The east wind blew for over a week. It picks up fine black dust in the Sahara and carries it here, and on out into the Atlantic ... The air is so dry it cracks your lips. The moisture condenses round the particles of dust, and then it rains in torrents. I was in a taxi, crossing the island, when the rain began. It wasn't water that fell, but thin mud mingled with oil. I never saw anything so extraordinary ... and since there's no provision for rain, no drains, everything was flooded, a torrent eighteen inches deep tearing down the mainstreet of Santa Cruz, stinking of this filthy oil.[512]

This letter rather bears out Marian's claim that Bunting's grip on personal finance was at best fragile. He is crossing the island in a taxi when the storm blows up, but in the same letter he complains that, 'the impending breakdown of the attempt to live cheaply and manage that way, leaves me a bit in the air. It is clear we can never, anywhere, rely on what Marian's parents dish out, so that even here, at 40% saving on Rapallo prices, we can't live. Its also clear that I have no money earning qualifications.'[513]

Bourtai also recalled moving home a few times, 'once from Hotel La Orotava to a favourite place, a small house at Salto del Barranco among banana plantations near Puerto Cruz. Here a woman living next door invited them to help themselves from her garage full of bananas whenever they wanted.'[514]

Marian sent a postcard to Pound's parents in Rapallo telling them that: 'We have a good house which we rent completely furnished. It has a lovely tropical garden & we grow our own vegetables. The children are very well and enjoying the bathing beach here. Basil finds it hard to work in this climate but hopes to do something now we have house.'[515] The new house was comparative luxury for the Buntings. He enthused to Pound in March 1935, 'We have got a house again, furnished, for six months … nice garden, bit of land, equivalent of three hundred lire. About eight or nine rooms, plus bath etc.'[516] In fact, according to Marian housing was scarce in Tenerife and the family moved nine times before finally settling at Casa Fortuna, Las Arenas, Puerto Cruz de Tenerife, where they stayed for two years until they left for England.[517]

Perhaps the climate affected Bunting's spirits. He became 'very gloomy' in the Canaries and wrote there 'The Well of Lycopolis', 'which is about as gloomy a poem as anyone would want.'[518] He told Pound in 1934 that his 'personal depression' was 'deep and durable',[519] and he was beginning to overreact to relatively trivial matters. Pound wrote to Zukofsky in May and mentioned a letter he had received from Bunting: 'Note from pore ole Bzl/ all of a tetter cause he has taken the trouble to try to tell you sumfin or other. Evidently thinks you've a weaker head than I think you have. At any rate you had orter be glad he takes thet much interest'.[520]

Not all his income came from writing while he was in the Canaries. He did odd jobs and handouts arrived periodically from Margaret de Silver and from Marian's parents. Marian's parents were sending $50 regularly each month,[521] and Bunting justified to Pound his sponging on a father-in-law he seems to have despised: 'If my father in law has more money than he needs and does nothing for it but bleed the pore buggers who want offices and houses in a country town in Wisconsin, I don't see why I, who do something I conceive to have a certain degree of use, shouldn't get as much of it as I possibly can … The drawbacks are practical, not moral. It's a fairly difficult job bleeding flints.'[522] A few months later he wrote to Pound that 'Marian's Pa brought off another lucrative real estate deal a while ago, the news has just leaked through. To celebrate it, he deducted the cost of Xmas presents for the children from the monthly cheque.'[523]

Bunting's poetry from 1933 and 1934 is not conspicuously distinguished. A translation from Catullus, 'Once so they say', peters out in despair:

> I will talk to you often in my songs, but first I speak to you, bridegroom
> acclaimed with many pinebrands, pillar of Thessaly, fool for luck, Peleus,
> to whom Jove the godbegetter, Jove himself yielded his mistress,
> for the sea's own child clung to you

> *- and why Catullus bothered to write pages and pages of this drivel mystifies me.*[524]

'How Duke Valentine Contrived', also written in 1933, takes the theme of 'The day being Whitsun', the urge the powerful feel to destroy the people and institutions which impede their political advancement, but delivers it in casual, throwaway lines that emphasise the cruelty without being in any way convincing:

> The Duke's soldiers
> were not satisfied with plundering Liverotto's men
> and began to sack Sinigaglia, and if he hadnt
> checked their insolence by hanging a lot of them
> they would have finished the job.[525]

Bunting wisely left both these poems out of *Collected Poems*. More convincing were the odes, 'Vessels thrown awry', which reflects on the different experiences of statesmen and workers, 'An appleblossom to crocus' and 'Two hundred and seven paces', both of which take a wry view of urban life. Reading 'Two hundred and seven paces' to a London audience nearly fifty years after it was written he explained that

> there used to be a pub in the Kennington Road – it was still there two or three
> years ago but they've pulled it down at last – where when I was in my 20s it
> was possible to go in and get a pint of beer, a cut off the joint, two vegetables,
> and a plate of apple tart for 10 pence. (Yes, think of the days you've missed.)
> And in there I heard this gentleman:

> Two hundred and seven paces
>   from the tram-stop
> to the door,

> a hundred and forty-six thousand
>   four hundred
> seconds ago,

two hundred and ninety-two thousand
    eight hundred
kisses or thereabouts; what else

let him say who saw and let
    him who is able
do like it for I'm

not fit for a commonplace world
    any longer, I'm
bound for the City,

cashregister, adding-machine,
    rotary stencil.
Give me another

double whiskey and fire-extinguisher,
    George. Here's
Girls! Girls!"

I still like that you know, crude as it is, after all these years it has a certain life in it.[526]

On the Orotava Road

The birth of the Buntings' second daughter, Roudaba, on 4 February 1934 in Santa Cruz was an uplifting event. Perhaps Roudaba was so named to exorcise Marian's difficult first childbirth with Bourtai. Roudabeh was Rustam's mother in Ferdowsi's *Shahnameh*. According to Ferdowsi, Roudabeh felt intense pain while giving birth and fell unconscious. Her husband, Zaal, remembered that the legendary bird Simorgh had given him a feather to use in time of great danger. He told his mother-in-law, Sindokht, to light a fire and he conjured up Simorgh by placing the magical feather on it. Simorgh told Zaal that Roudabeh would give birth to a courageous and heroic child but advised Zaal that

> for this noble child to be born you must prepare a sharp knife and summon a wise and experienced doctor. Then have her attendants make Rudabeh drunk with wine, so that she forgets her fear and becomes insensitive to pain. Next the doctor must cut open the mother's womb and bring this lion cub forth: then he must sew up the womb. Meanwhile, you must grind certain

herbs that I shall name, together with musk and milk, and dry the mixture in
a shady place: then reduce it to powder and apply it to the scar, which you
must also stroke with one of my feathers ... Rudabeh will soon be out of pain
and danger.[527]

By following Simorgh's advice to have what later became known as a
Caesarean section Roudabeh gave birth easily to the prodigious Rustam.
This is pure speculation of course but Bunting had by now been steeped
in Ferdowsi for three or four years and it is attractive to think that Marian
and Bunting chose their second child's name as a kind of charm against a
difficult second childbirth.

Although she was too young to remember life in the Canaries, she does
remember her father as the dapper young man in photographs of this time
and recalls hearing of the lively parties in Italy of "Haas, Mas, and Baz",
Eugene Haas, Masoliver and Bunting.'[528]

With the notable exception of Diana Collecott, Bunting scholars (and his
biographers) have rather overlooked the importance of Bunting's relationship
with the German artist Karl Drerup and his Jewish wife, Gertrude. The
Drerups lived in Tenerife from 1934 to 1937, Fascism having followed them
around Europe until they emigrated to the US. The Nazis made life in their
homeland untenable; Drerup's graduate work from 1930 to 1933 in Italy at
the Accademia di Belle Arti in Florence was destroyed by Mussolini's rise
to power and when they fled to Madrid in 1933, and then to the Canary
Isles, they couldn't have known that Francisco Franco's revolution was about
to tear Spain apart. Drerup cast a wry gaze over the anti-Semitism of his
native land. Bunting wrote to Zukofsky in October 1935: 'Certain German
towns having ordained that Jewish cars may not park in their streets, Drerup
is trying to think out a process for circumcising cars.'[529]

The Drerups lived in Puerto de la Cruz (formerly Puerto Orotava) which
had an established British colony and regular German and American
visitors. The Buntings found that they were unable to pay the rent on their
hillside home overlooking the port and the Drerups moved in when Bunting
and Marian moved to a simple cabin in a banana plantation. As Diana
Collecott points out in her illuminating essay on Drerup in Tenerife the
Buntings and Drerups had much in common,

> not the least of which was their pacifism and liberal politics. They had all
> been living in Italy, where Bunting's teacher was Ezra Pound in Rapallo,

and Drerup's was Felice Carena in Florence; Gertrude and Bunting were both gifted linguists who had studied at the London School of Economics, and Gertrude and Marian were keen tennis players. The Drerups were comparatively well off, as long as Drerup could receive financial support from his family in Germany, supplemented by Gertrude's English teaching.[530]

Bunting and Drerup were fascinated by the peasant life around them. One of the best poems Bunting wrote in Tenerife, 'The Orotava Road', closely observes the simple rural scenes that Drerup illustrated:

> Four white heifers with sprawling hooves
> > trundle the wagon.
> > Its ill-roped crates heavy with fruit sway.
> The chisel point of the goad, blue and white,
> > glitters ahead,
> > a flame to follow lance-high in a man's hand
> who does not shave ...
>
> > Camelmen high on muzzled mounts
> boots rattling against the panels
> > of an empty
> > packsaddle do not answer strangers ...
>
> Milkmaids, friendly girls between
> > fourteen and twenty
> or younger, bolt upright on small
> trotting donkeys that bray (they arch their
> > tails a few inches
> > from the root, stretch neck and jaw forward
> to make the windpipe a trumpet)
> > chatter. Jolted
> cans clatter.[531]

Many years later, at a reading in London in 1980, Bunting expressed some surprise at the enduring appeal of 'The Orotava Road':

A couple of years ago I got a letter from the Canary Isles. To my great astonishment they now have a university there – it wouldn't have been imaginable in my day – and a professor wrote and said that he had made a translation, in fact a very good translation of a poem of mine, which he had read some time or other to his father, or was it his grandfather, I forget what, who was in the Canaries when I lived there and who said that it was the most perfect picture of the islands he'd ever come across.[532]

Bunting was making no money in the Canaries, but it seems that this was a consequence of his unwillingness to compromise. Pound wrote to Rabindranath Tagore seeking funding for him from the Roerich Museum: 'Bunting has done what I think a very good condensation of Cho Mei, and writes Persian very beautifully (I mean as far as the handwriting goes. I don't know any, so I can't tell whether it is correct). He has no money, and simply will not melt himself into the vile patterns of expediency.'[533] As William Carlos Williams wrote to Zukofsky in January 1934: 'Bunting is living the life, I don't know how sufficiently to praise him for it. But it can't be very comfortable to exist that way. I feel uneasy not to be sending him his year's rent and to be backing at the same time a book of my own poems. It's dog eat dog in the end I suppose anyway you look at it.'[534]

Living from odd jobs and handouts was clearly unsustainable so he used some new funds from Margaret de Silver to try his hand in the Algarve on the southern coast of Portugal. Marian was not impressed:

> He found a place in the Algarve, miles from civilization and expected me to follow him there with a 2 year old and a 6 month old baby. To get there entailed travelling 3rd class on a Spanish ship – 1st class is reputed to be filthy, and taking a bus from Cadiz through all of Portugal in mid-summer. I did not have the money to do this and refused to take the trip. I felt Basil would be forced to go to England to get a job and earn a living of some kind for us. I did not dream that he would return to go on living on hand-outs from my family.

> He returned and there was nothing left for us after that.[535]

According to Victoria Forde while Bunting was away the Drerups helped Marian move from the house which they were waiting to move into to the pension Las Arenas run by Dr Isadore Luz and Baron and Baroness von Louen. 'The Baroness was the widow of the Kaiser's youngest son, a mentally deficient boy who committed suicide when she ran away with the Baron. Since by Hitler's order the Germans could not spend their money outside of Germany, there were not many tourists. So the proprietors took in the Buntings at low rates.'[536] This slightly mangled bit of German history hardly does justice to what must have been a fascinating milieu. After an unhappy childhood during which she suffered deeply from her parents' disintegrating marriage Princess Marie Auguste married, at the age of just seventeen,

Prince Joachim of Prussia, the youngest son of Kaiser Wilhelm II. Joachim, who was five years older than his bride, was a Captain in the Fourteenth Regiment of Hussars. The families were, naturally enough, deeply embroiled in the First World War. Joachim was with the German Army on the Russian front and Marie Auguste's father, Prince Eduard, was also in the German Army, serving with the Crown Prince, Joachim's brother, in the Verdun area. According to Countess Emilie Alsenborg, who served as one of Empress Auguste Viktoria's ladies-in-waiting, Joachim was an epileptic, spoilt child who was physically, mentally and morally weak. At the time of their wedding Joachim was in love with another woman, Erna von Weberhardt, whom he robbed of an enormously valuable collection of jewellery in order to pay off his equally enormous gambling debts. Astonishingly this theft became a factor in the Kaiser's war strategy (particularly in regard to Zeppelin raids on London) as these highly politicised, aristocratic families jockeyed for position in an attempt to suppress the scandal. Joachim was forced into marriage with Marie Auguste as part of this plot, so by the time of their marriage he was already an unattractive catch. In 1919, amid rumours that Joachim was physically abusing her, she left him. Prince Joachim's mental state was already weakening when Marie Auguste filed for divorce, although the estranged couple were still married when Prince Joachim shot himself with a revolver at his home on 18 July 1920. By the time Joachim killed himself the 'mentally deficient boy' was a thirty-year-old wife beater, thief and sociopath with serious mental and physical health problems. It's no wonder that she left him.

In 1924 Princess Marie Auguste became engaged to a wealthy businessman but she broke off the engagement on the eve of the wedding and disappeared for three years before marrying, on 27 September 1926, her childhood friend, Baron Johannes Michael von Loën, who was four years her junior. By 1930 this woman, having moved in (or been a pawn of) the highest levels of European society and politics, was running a pension in Santa Cruz. Bunting appears to have overcome his intense dislike of 'the Germans' to take advantage of the need of these particular Germans for rental income.

The family moved to the new pension in July 1934. Bunting had written to Pound from Lisbon on 23 June 1934 and told him he expected to find a place there for the family. He had been badly shaken up by three fatal accidents he had witnessed in Lisbon during the week, including 'a woman cut in two by a railway train within three feet of me', but generally the Portuguese were far more tolerable than Spaniards.[537] By 18 July he was back in Tenerife and reporting that all the houses in Portugal had been taken up for the summer, but that they may try again in autumn because although outside Lisbon the country was 'amazingly primitive' it was cheap.[538] He does not tell Pound that he was away when the move occurred but he explains the circumstances: 'Check from Eauclaire failing to turn up, irate landlady seized all baggage, down to the babies napkins. We moved to another pension [and] … now inhabit with German aristos: Roudaba is actually swaddled in napkins from the august arse of an imperial highness.'

The previous pension had 'possessed bedbugs, lice, mice, fleas (more than the usual large Canary quota) and the worst cook without exception on the entire face of the globe. Sometimes one couldn't swallow his productions, other times one swallowed them and they came back. Here we get excellent food but not enough.'[539] The new pension owned by the German 'aristos' threw up challenges of its own. He wrote to Pound the following March:

> Three weeks before we left the pension the chaufeur [sic] there was found in bed with the twelve-year old housemaid. The other servants rigged up a mirror and even succeeded in taking a photograph of the rape in progress. Next day everything returned to normal, except that the chaufeur was strutting more than usual because everybody knew of his conquests. Our own twelve-year old, Bourtai's nurse, may or may not be a virgin. I wouldn't trust anybody but a surgeon to say.[540]

The fact that the other servants rigged up a mirror to set up a photoshoot rather than acting to stop the rape says something about the prevailing culture. Bunting later 'calculated the rape-rate at one woman in six on Tenerife. Have no data for the seduction rate, but imagine four of the remaining five would barely cover it.'[541]

By 1934 Hitler's tentacles had spread as far as this, the furthest outpost of Europe. 'I'm sick of all the bloody Huns, all alike,' Bunting told Pound in April. 'Here they all talk Hitler, except the tailor who told me some specific instances of people who had NOT talked Hitler, had gone back to Germany and been instantly sent from the port to the Concentrazienslager. They all evidently think all the other Germans and an appreciable number of Spaniards and English must be Hitler spies, which makes them extremely enthusiastic Nazis.'[542] By October Hitler was having a direct affect on Bunting's life: 'Our aristocratic landlord turns out to be a pal of Roehm, hence his sourness in speaking of Hitler.' Ernst Roehm, the too-powerful head of the Brownshirts, had been murdered by Hitler's SS just four months earlier. 'Hitlerian finance is forcing our local Hohenzollern back to Berlin. But the pension will carry on a few months longer I think, after which we will have to swim to Europe if we haven't raised the fare otherwise.'[543] Just a month later he reports that the 'Local Boches all now completely bankrupt. We have this pension to ourselves, Baron Loen and the Princess of Anhalt doing the cooking when the cook is drunk, which is pretty often.'[544]

The Well of Lycopolis

The Canaries did not bring out the best in Bunting the poet or, perhaps, the man. Apart from 'The Well of Lycopolis' and 'The Orotava Road' Bunting preserved only a handful of adaptations and translations. 'You leave', for instance, when first written acknowledged itself as a translation from the fourteenth-century Persian poet, Hafiz,[545] but by the time it reached *Collected Poems* Hafiz had disappeared. The reason, Bunting said, was that 'if I'd thought there was very much of Hafez left in the product, I'd have put it in with the other translations'.[546] Bunting clearly thought he had made a new poem, albeit based on a theme by Hafiz, but as Parvin Loloi and Glyn Pursglove have shown it is actually a very accurate translation.[547] 'When the sword' is a more straightforward translation from Ferdowsi. 'O Ubi Campi!' ('The soil sandy'), written in 1936, is a 'poem about the farm troubles in the United States in the middle of the '30s,' he told an audience in 1995,[548] but although thematically similar it is no return to the complaining Morpethshire farmer:

O ubi campi!

The soil sandy and the plow light, neither
virgin land nor near by the market town,
cropping one staple without forethought, steer
stedfastly ruinward year in year out,
grudging the labour and cost of manure,
drudging not for gain but fewer dollars loss
yet certain to make a bad bargain by
misjudging the run of prices. How glad
you will be when the state takes your farm for
arrears of taxes! No more cold daybreaks
saffron under the barbed wire the east wind

thrums, nor wet noons, nor starpinned nights! The choir
of gnats is near a full-close. The windward
copse stops muttering inwardly its prose
bucolics. You will find a city job
or relief – or doss-and-grub – resigned to
anything except your own numb toil, the
seasonal plod to spoil the land, alone.[549]

There is not a hint of sentimentality here. The 'flurry of the grouse' and the 'lowing of the kye' have been replaced by irony, 'ubi campi' (fruitful fields) contrasted with the American Dust Bowl.

'The Well Of Lycopolis', however gloomy, was on the other hand a major achievement. The odes are effective enough, some of them are very beautiful, but Bunting was much more powerful when he worked on a larger canvas. He was aware of this:

> I am impelled by love of a larger shape, more architectural, which has been so much neglected … The Well of Lycopolis begins and ends as I intended, but the middle movements fail to fill out the shape as they should … Chomei has the shape, but at the cost of some pretty dull brickwork. No one else but Eliot seems to care about the plan – they all get engrossed in detail – and Eliot is apt to make the plan to[o] plain – council houses where we want temples. ('Quando flautos, pitos')[550]

'The Well of Lycopolis' is a very carefully constructed poem. Bunting explained to a London audience in 1982 that it was

> the most disgruntled of all my works, the one which takes the gloomiest view of everything I suppose … I used large passages some from Villon, some from Dante, translated in my own manner, as a large part of the body of the poem. I learned of it from Edward Gibbon … He describes … the Well of Lycopolis which is visited by the Emperor Hadrian … There are four parts, they're not very long. The 1st part has the epigraph … which of course is the opening in Villon of the Lament of the Belle Heaulmiere. The Belle Heaulmiere was the wife or daughter of a helmet maker, and in Villon's day, the 1400s, next to the goldsmiths the helmet makers were the most skilful, the most highly paid, much the richest of the artisans. They were the foundation of what became the middle class. Many heaulmieres became bankers just as goldsmiths did. They were rich people. So when you read the people discoursing on Villon who treat La Belle Heaulmiere as a prostitute it is absolutely wrong. She was

nothing of the sort. She was a rich woman, and she had no doubt spent her money and become poor and all the rest of it, but the man she is regretting and worried about is not as you find in half the French editions of Villon, a pimp. Nothing of the sort. He's her boyfriend, that she no doubt is exploited by in every possible way but he's the boyfriend of a rich woman … I use her for the introduction of Venus the first part being a dialogue between the goddess Venus, and the goddess Polymnia, the muse of the more complicated kinds of song.[551]

Part I describes the meeting of the poet, Venus and Polymnia in a setting that is far from salubrious. To some extent we have been set up for this by the epigraph to the poem, 'cujus pota signa virginitatis eripiunter' (by the drinking of which [the well of the title] the signs of virginity are taken away), taken from note 112 in chapter 27 of Gibbon's *The Decline and Fall of the Roman Empire*, a 'very convenient fountain' as Gibbon says,[552] and by the epigraph to Part I, the quotation from Villon's 'Les Regrets De La Belle Heaulmière' ('Advis m'est que j'oy regretter' or 'by chance I heard the belle complain'). Here it is:

Slinking by the jug-and-bottle
swingdoor I fell in with
Mother Venus, ageing, bedraggled, a
half-quartern of gin under her shawl,
wishing she was a young girl again:
'It's cruel hard to be getting old so soon.
I wonder I don't kill myself and have done with it.

I had them all on a string at one time,
lawyers, doctors, business-men:
there wasnt a man alive but would have given
all he possessed
for what they wont take now free for nothing.
I turned them down,
I must have had no sense,
for the sake of a shifty young fellow:
whatever I may have done at other times
on the sly
I was in love then and no mistake;
and him always knocking me about
and only cared for my money.
However much he shook me or kicked me I

loved him just the same.
If he'd made me take in washing he'd
only have to say: 'Give us a kiss'
and I'd have forgotten my troubles.
The selfish pig, never up to any good!
He used to cuddle me. Fat lot of good it's done me!
What did I get out of it besides a bad conscience?
But he's been dead longer than thirty years
and I'm still here, old and skinny.
When I think about the old days,
what I was like and what I'm like now,
it fair drives me crazy to
look at myself with nothing on.
What a change!
Miserable dried up skin and bone.

But none of their Bacchic impertinence,
medicinal stout nor portwine-cum-beef.
A dram of anaesthetic, brother.
I'm a British subject if I am a colonial,
distilled liquor's clean.
It's the times have changed. I remember during the War
kids carrying the clap to school under their pinnies,
studying Belgian atrocities in the Sunday papers
or the men pissing in the backstreets; and grown women
sweating their shifts sticky at the smell of khaki
every little while.
Love's an encumbrance to them who
rinse carefully before using, better
keep yourself to yourself.
What it is to be in the movement!
'Follow the instructions on page fortyone'
unlovely labour of love,
'or work it off in a day's walk,
a cold douche and brisk rub down,
there's nothing like it.'
Aye, tether me among the maniacs,
it's nicer to rave than reason.[553]

Venus' rather improbable claim to be a British subject is validated by the
fact that she is a Cypriot, Cyprus having been declared a Crown Colony by

the British in 1925. 'Every little while' was a popular sentimental song of the
second part of the First World War, with sugary lyrics that describe a world
in which there was no place for 'sticky shifts'.

Bunting caught working-class vernacular in a way that Eliot, for instance,
never did. Giving it to the goddess of love is a stroke of genius. The poem
gathers pace as the poet takes Venus to visit Polymnia, the goddess of music,
song and dance. Polymnia is as grumpy as Venus:

> Took her round to Polymnia's, Polymnia
> glowering stedfastly at the lukewarm
> undusted grate grim with cinders
> never properly kindled, the brass head of the
> tongs creaking as she twitched them:
> 'Time is, was, has been.'
> A gassy fizzling spun from among the cinders.
> The air, an emulsion of some unnameable oil,
> greased our napes. We rhymed our breath
> to the mumble of coke distiling.
> 'What have you come for? Why have you brought the Goddess?
> You who
>
> finger the goods you cannot purchase,
> snuffle the skirt you dare not clutch.
> There was never love between us, never less
> than when you reckoned much. A tool
> not worth the negligible price. A fool
> not to be esteemed for barren honesty.
> Leave me alone. A long time ago
> there were men in the world, dances, guitars, ah!
> Tell me, Love's mother, have I wrinkles? grey hair?
> teats, or dugs? calves, or shanks?
> Do I wear unbecomning garments?'
>
> 'Blotched belly, slack buttock and breast,
> there's little to strip for now.
> A few years makes a lot of difference.
> Would you have known me?
> Poor old fools,
> gabbing about our young days,
> squatted round a bit of fire

just lit and flickering out already:
and we used to be so pretty!'[554]

The line 'Time is, was, has been' is a reference to the Faust-like medieval monk and scholar, Roger Bacon. Friar Bacon was said to have created a brazen talking head which could answer any question. In Robert Greene's play about Bacon, *The Honourable History of Friar Bacon and Friar Bungay*, written in the late sixteenth century, the Brazen Head speaks three times to Bacon's hapless servant, Miles, before falling to the floor and shattering: 'Time is ... Time was ... Time is past.'

The chief event in Part I of 'The Well of Lycopolis' is the reduction of love and music to such dereliction, but it is almost overshadowed by Polymnia's heartless rejection of the poet. In just four lines she mocks his ambition:

> There was never love between us, never less
> than when you reckoned much. A tool
> not worth the negligible price. A fool
> not to be esteemed for barren honesty.

The poet has never put music into his words, has failed, is failing, will always fail.

Part II of 'The Well of Lycopolis' starts in a very similar mode to Part II of 'Villon'. In 'Villon' it is:

> Let his days be few and let
> his bishoprick pass to another,
> for he fed me on carrion and on a dry crust ...

Part II of 'The Well of Lycopolis' also starts with a hearty curse:

> May my libation of flat beer stood overnight
> sour on your stomach, my devoutly worshipped ladies,
> may you retch cold bile.[555]

Bunting continues to contrast music hall sentimentality with the reality of the lives of the goddesses:

> 'Let's be cosy,
> sit it out hand in hand.
> Dreaming of you, that's all I do.'

'Dreaming of you, that's all I do' is the first line of Beth Slater Whitson's 1909 song, 'Meet me tonight in dreamland'. Dreamland for Polymnia was less romantic:

> Open your eyes, Polymnia,
> at the sleek, slick lads treading gingerly between the bedpots,
> stripped buff-naked all but their hats to raise,
> and nothing rises but the hats;
> smooth, with soft steps, *ambiguoque voltu*.

The Latin phrase 'ambiguous looks' is a quotation from Horace's 'Be patient' and is there to suggest the androgyny of the 'sleek, slick lads' with their lack of erections. Polymnia's world is sexless:

> Daphnis investigated
> bubless Chloe
> behind a boulder.
> Still, they say,
> in another climate
> virgin with virgin
> coupled taste
> wine without headache
> and the songs are simple.
> We have laid on Lycopolis water.

And the target of this accusation of passionless impotence? Bloomsbury:

> The nights are not fresh
> between High Holborn and the Euston Road,
> nor the days bright even in summer
> nor the grass of the squares green.

Part III piles up fresh images of decay and disappointment in a way that occasionally suggests *The Waste Land*:

> – with their snouts in the trough,
> kecking at gummy guts,
> slobbering offal, gobbling potato parings,
> yellow cabbage leaves, choking on onion skin,
> herring bones, slops of porridge.
> Way-O! Bully boys blow!
> The Gadarene swihine have got us in tow.[556]

Bunting undoubtedly has the shanty, 'The Banks of Newfoundland', in his sights,[557] but 'swihine' shows that he has more than half an eye on Eliot's

> O O O O that Shakespeherian Rag –
> It's so elegant
> So intelligent.

Part IV begins with a quotation from Canto VII of Dante's *Inferno*:

> Ed anche vo' che tu per certo credi
> che sotto l'acqua ha gente che sospira.

In Dorothy Sayers' translation this is:

> Further, I'd have thee know and hold for true
> That others lie plunged deep in this vile broth.[558]

These are the Wrathful, those who tear each other 'piecemeal with their teeth', and they announce Bunting's reflections on war which, by 1935, he was certain was inevitable:

> Surrendered in March. Or maybe
> ulcers of mustard gas, a rivet in the lung
> from scrappy shrapnel,
> frostbite, trench-fever, shell-shock,
> self-inflicted wound,
> tetanus, malaria, influenza.
> Swapped your spare boots for a packet of gaspers.
> Overstayed leave.
> Debauched the neighbour's little girl
> to save two shillings ...
> muttering inaudibly beneath the quagmire,
> irresolute, barren, dependent, this page
> ripped from Love's ledger and Poetry's:
> and besides I want you to know for certain
> there are people under the water. They are sighing.
> The surface bubbles and boils with their sighs.
> Look where you will you see it.
> The surface sparkles and dances with their sighs
> as though Styx were silvered by a wind from Heaven.[559]

'NO one will publish the W of L,' he wrote to Zukofsky in October 1935. 'Perhaps as well, not sure I want it published.'[560]

He has gnawed too much on the bridle

Bunting kept up his journalism in the mid-1930s. William Carlos Williams wrote to Zukofsky in September 1934 saying, 'Just received Bunting's criticism of my book, not bad. In fact he has done me a service that is of great value. Why not a world with a few more Bunting's in it? Damn 'f I know.'[561]

This was in response to Bunting's review in *Westminster Magazine* of Williams' recent poetry. In it Bunting praised Williams' 'extraordinary technical virtuosity' and drew a parallel between Williams and Yeats: 'Nobody else has taken America for a permanent subject. Whitman's was Democracy, an abstraction a much more competent technician would have found as difficult to keep at heel ... He is like Yeats a national and nation-making poet.' His verdict was unequivocal: 'In case the implicit intention has been missed let me state plainly that Williams is one of less than a dozen poets now writing who have a reasonable certainty of literary longevity and whose work repays study.'[562]

An informed and detailed article on the coup that started the Spanish civil war in the *Spectator* in July 1936 shows an appetite for political analysis that would resurface when Bunting worked for *The Times* in Teheran. General José Sanjurjo's botched coup on 17 and 18 July split an already deeply divided nation but Bunting denied that the coup was Fascist and with extraordinary prescience described its likely consequences: 'General Franco, who is believed to be a moderate republican, may be forced into the arms of the Monarchists, or driven to disguise a purely military dictatorship as Fascism. His manifesto commits him to nothing ... In my opinion, the Left has the better chance in the long run, for it has, in Spain, the better cause. You cannot starve a nation for ever. But the long run may be a Marathon of blood.'[563] Three years of vicious civil war followed the coup in which the Republicans (broadly the left) were defeated by Franco's Nationalists.

Bunting also reviewed E. Stuart Bates' *Modern Translation*, negatively, in *Criterion*.[564] His by now familiar haughty put-down enters as early as the close of the first paragraph: 'Closing Mr. Bates's book, one may repeat his introductory statement: the subject of modern translation "does not appear to have yet been dealt with".' Bates' error was to engage with modern translation without proposing a plausible theory of it, without properly engaging with Dryden's identification of different types of translation as metaphrase, paraphrase and imitation, and most egregiously of all, without any reference to Edward Fitzgerald or Ezra Pound. His review of Janko Lavrin's *Aspects of Modernism* in the same issue is also largely dismissive but he admires from a distance Lavrin's clinical approach: 'In a series of skilful dissections we are invited to the mortuary table to contemplate the remains of lately adulated leaders of literary fashion. We have the sensation of assisting at a slightly cynical burial-service.'[565]

In September 1936 Bunting reviewed three books on desert adventures in the *Spectator*. *The Paradise of Fools* by Michael Mason and *Adventure in Algeria* by a former French Foreign Legionnaire, Brian Stuart, pass muster, although at that time Bunting knew as much about the desert as did most of his readers. *The Scourge of the Desert* by Operator 1384, however, is handled roughly: 'Operator 1384 has "adhered strictly to facts, and related no incident which did not actually occur and in which he did not personally take part." I don't believe him. A stage American and stage Arabs uttering Hollywood dialogue amongst scenery kindly lent by the British film industry at its worst surround his incredible adventures. People who read beyond page 15 without being paid for it deserve to have to finish the book.'[566] Bunting was soon to have some 'incredible adventures' of his own in the desert.

He appeared to extend the suicide mission over the British literary establishment that he had set off in his attack on Eliot in 'The Written Record' with an uncompromisingly hostile review of Malcolm Muggeridge's *The Earnest Atheist* in *New English Weekly* in October 1936. Muggeridge's study of Samuel Butler infuriated Bunting and the impression that its author was influential in London literary circles wasn't going to prevent Bunting from fully expressing himself in what Peter Quartermain calls 'an almost text-book example of a devastating exposure of individual Grub-Streetism'.[567] It is, indeed, almost surgical in its dismemberment of Muggeridge:

> I don't know Mr. Muggeridge's circumstances, but dare swear his 'study' of Butler, from the false implication in the title to the scamped précis of 'Erewhon Revisited' in the final chapter, would not have been brought to any length if he had expected to be called upon to foot the printer's bill. I doubt whether his contentions would have been those I think I can disentangle from the bluster, if he had taken time to disentangle them a little more himself … The author who most delighted in tumbling the dull-witted into false analogies and specious inductions has found another victim posthumously, one who perhaps has never read how Wordsworth murdered Lucy because she bored

him. Or perhaps he has: no beacon can put a Muggeridge on guard against his own lack of humour.[568]

Bunting goes on to mock Muggeridge's judgement and ridicule his learning. Whatever influence the author of *The Earnest Atheist* did have in literary London it certainly wasn't going to be exercised on Bunting's behalf after this hatchet job. Marian Bunting recalled that he wrote this review in 'one of his ferocious hate-moods ... [the review] was murderous ... Both his mother and I tried to keep him from sending it in, but he was adamant.'[569]

In fact Bunting had unwittingly put his finger on the issue with his remarks about money. Muggeridge had begun his book on Butler with no great enthusiasm but he was desperately short of money, confiding to his diary that 'I badly need some money, and feel cynical enough to do nearly anything to get it.'[570] He had sent advance copies to friends who advised him to change the proofs substantially. Hugh Kingsmill warned him that he would be 'flayed alive by every single critic'.[571] He was right. Bunting was by no means the only commentator to be deeply disturbed by *The Earnest Atheist* and its debunking of Butler, the great Victorian debunker. The *Sunday Times* devoted two articles by Desmond MacCarthy to attacking the book. Stephen Spender 'singled out the harsh tone and barbed rhetoric of the book as its own worst enemy'.[572] E. M. Forster wrote that the book was 'an attack so disgruntled and so persistent that it may well be the result of a guilt complex' and the *Daily Herald* called it 'an extravagance of peevishness and spitefulness'.[573]

It is often said that Bunting's review of *The Earnest Atheist* further prejudiced the London literary elite against him[574] but there is no real evidence of that having happened. First, Muggeridge's book had been universally panned and its author would have had no reason to single out Bunting's review from all the rest. Second, Muggeridge himself later acknowledged that it was a poor book and that his own circumstances while writing it had affected his depiction of Butler.[575] Third, Muggeridge doesn't appear to have been unduly upset by the hostile reception his book received. He noted in his diary of 16 November 1936 that he'd 'had a happy day. In the morning there were newspaper cuttings about *The Earnest Atheist*, which I read twice.'[576] And fourth, Muggeridge at the time was no more a part of that London literary elite than was Bunting, although he certainly later became an influence. I think we can detect Bunting's own hand in this deft bit of mythmaking. Bunting would certainly have known Hazlitt's warning to Wordsworth: 'He did not court popularity by a conformity to established models, and he ought not to have been surprised that his originality was not understood as a matter of course. He has *gnawed too much on the bridle*, and has often thrown out crusts to the critics, in mere defiance or as a point of honour when he was challenged, which otherwise his own good sense would have withheld.'[577] He has gnawed too much on the bridle. There's a badge that Bunting would have worn with pride.

Chess with Franco

Bunting's politics were regarded as complex by his friends. Pound wrote to Zukofsky in July 1938 hoping that he and 'BZL' would accept the dedication of his forthcoming *Guide to Kulchur*. Zukofsky described Bunting's obscure position thus: 'Dear Ez: Can't guess what Kulchah is about, but if you want to dedicate yr. book to a communist (me) and a British-conservative-antifascist-imperialist (Basil), I won't sue you for libel, and I suppose you know Basil. So dedicate.'[578]

Zukofsky gently satirised Bunting in his 1961 short story, *Ferdinand*: 'An Englishman, who loved to sail with them in a catboat someone had given him, analysed international desirabilities for them, as though they depended on English common sense and England's will to rid itself of the thieves in the Merrie Isle. A decent British empire, he believed, could be the best government in the world.'[579]

In fact Bunting's politics in the 1930s were relatively straightforward. In his 'Observations on Left-Wing Papers', written in November 1935, he is explicit that he is not a communist but, it seems to me at least, only just:

> Personal. I am not a Communist, nor have much sympathy with the communist dogmas: but the revolution I desire has several things in common with the communist revolution. I am also in favour of any serious improvement on existing conditions in the world at large, and a strong communist movement in the U.S.A. would certainly improve existing conditions, provided it were a movement based on fact and action, not merely another of the ineffective emotional disturbances that have from time [to time] wasted themselves in vague aspirations and popular phrases in the United States. Such a movement must be built up from the workingman, not down from the 'intellectual'.[580]

The political situation in Europe was heating up towards the end of the Buntings' time in the Canary Isles, although Marian claimed that the American Ambassador in Spain 'didn't even see the war coming & was caught up there for 6 months'.[581] Bunting claims to have played 'indifferent' chess with Franco when he was the military governor of the islands.[582] This is certainly possible as Franco had arrived in Tenerife as military governor of the Canary Isles on 23 February 1936, four months before the Buntings fled to the UK. Bunting had a knack of being in the thick of things. The military rebellion that sparked the Spanish Civil War was announced in the Canary Isles on 17 July 1936, after months of intrigue including a (now famous) secret meeting between Franco and Emilio Mola in La Esperanza forest in Tenerife.

Not long before the Buntings left the Canary Isles he described to Pound a storm that seemed to mirror the political turbulence in Europe,

> two days of fury not seen here for a generation, they say. The houses aren't built for it and I had a worrysome night, especially after the neighbours roof rose up and flapped away like a seagull. One of our cedars came down – all I could hear above the gale was a noise like tearing calico – and every tree in the garden lost some of its bigger branches, so that the litter is inconceivable. A huge eucalyptus three yards from our front gallery, and another cedar that leans over the roof and kept banging on it, as though there were half a dozen heavy men fighting in an upper story [sic], were the chief trouble … We were in the lee of twelve thousand feet of mountain. What it must have been like on the other side I cant easily imagine, there were pretty big things floating about in the atmosphere on our side.[583]

Pound spotted the irony. He wrote to Zukofsky from Rapallo on 23 July 1936: 'That pore fool Basil has got to London, having gone to Canaries for QUIET.'[584]

ENGLAND, 1936–1938

Bunting was desperate to get out of the Canaries for the entire time he was there. In January 1936 he told Pound that they had 'taken Taupin's house at Nyack on Hudson. New York will destroy me with noise and very likely starve me, but a word now and then with somebody who has something in his head will do me good.'[585] This escape from the Canary Isles to New York was indefinitely postponed.

Finally in July 1936 he wrote to Pound that the family had, 'escaped from Tenerife (formerly Isla del Infierno)' and were staying temporarily at 2 Doughty Street in London wc1. The journey to Southampton had not been pleasant: 'Union Castle Line seeking to pay off overdraft by starving passengers: fog in channel, delay, avoided collision with big French cargo boat by eighteen inches measured. Ship six days late from Cape Town, one of which added between Tenerife and Sthampton. Roudaba celebrated embarkation by swallowing a big button, hullabaloo, messy voyage.'[586]

By the beginning of September they had moved to 6 South Hill Mansions, South Hill Park, near Hampstead Heath.[587] After the Buntings fled Franco's coup Gertrude Drerup escaped to Holland with an English family and for a while Drerup joined Bunting in London.

We have very few descriptions of the Buntings' family life at this (or any other) time but Victoria Forde's conversations with Roudaba and Bourtai provide a glimpse into it:

Life in England must have been quite difficult for the family, living for a time with Mrs Bunting in London and for a time alone. But the children were kept free from these concerns. Bourtai can vividly picture the Christmas tree her grandmother trimmed for them and the quintuplet dolls she loved to undress completely so that her mother and grandmother would have to dress them up again. Like an echo from Basil's own early education, Bourtai remembers both her parents reading to her from an early age, especially 'The Cat Who Walked by Himself' from the *Just So Stories*. The music Basil taught her to appreciate was quite different from Byrd's Service, but more in line with the bawdy songs he enjoyed all his life: 'Rollicking Bill the Sailor', for one, and an American Civil War shanty she still sings, for another. While they were living at South Hill mansion with a view of Round Pond at Hampstead Heath, she obediently kept away from the swans though she was always allowed to run excitedly to meet the hot cross bun man. She also remembers being frightened when she rode the elephant at the London Zoo where her parents had taken her.

Rou's clearest and happiest memory is riding on her father's shoulders with Bourtai walking, holding his hand, to see the Punch and Judy shows. Bourtai's memory is of her own turn on his shoulders so she could look down into the crowd to see where Punch had thrown out the baby. That he was preparing his children to love the kind of entertainment he himself enjoyed is evident from a letter he sent me fifty years later: 'Years ago I would have said take your students to the pantomime at the Elephant, but they pulled down the Elephant long since, and though there may still be theatres in the suburbs or in south London where they keep up the old Victorian pantomime, the lush ones in Central London are just what you might see anywhere – no real fun.'[588]

This domestic idyll was about to be shattered. Apparently driven to the end of her tether by their constant poverty Marian borrowed £1 from her mother-in-law and left home with their two children in early January 1937. She was five months' pregnant with their third child at the time. Having gained custody of the children she returned to her home in Eau Claire, Wisconsin, where Rustam, a boy his father never saw, was born on 15 May.[589]

'From "Faridun's Sons" by Firdusi' was published by T. S. Eliot in *Criterion* in April 1936.[590] Bunting did not include this overdraft, a translated fragment of Ferdowsi, in *Collected Poems* but its tone suggests some of the grief he felt at the separation from his children. Faridun prepares to greet his homecoming army led by his son, Iraj, but Iraj's head is returned in a box, wherupon Faridun 'fell from his horse like a dead man'.[591] The poem is a translation so the subject matter is fixed but it is not difficult to imagine that the poet is expressing his own sense of deep loss:

'Never fancy Fate favours you,
the heavens turning above us
ready to snatch whatever they smile on.
Defy them, they smile. Call them Friend,
they never return your devotion.'

Bunting wrote to the Pounds after Marian left:

The whole mess that's been gathering constantly thicker for now three years broke just at Christmas and Marian and I are separate ... I'm now able to say clearly that what has prevented me doing any intelligent work during nearly two years has been the utterly miserable situation at home. You can't, or at least I can't, manufacture literature while crisis after crisis at rapidly decreasing intervals keeps you in constant suspense and profound wretchedness ... Marian finally kidnapped the children, and I am unhappy about them. Moreover she seems to think that since she has nearly all the money, it is reasonable that I should be left with nearly all the expenses – the lease of this flat, for example ... The thing that drags most heavily on work is the impossibility of bringing Marian to any durable arrangement on any point whatsoever, so that everything is perpetually in suspense. That is still so. At the best it will be a slow, difficult business for me to make any escape from the financial quagmire I find myself shoved into: the emotional one is likely to be far more tenacious.[592]

Bunting's friends seem to have had little sympathy for him in his marital difficulties, clearly feeling that art came first. Pound complained to Zukofsky from Rapallo in March 1937 that 'Las' I heard of Bzl his wif had left and took the chillens. It wuz preyin on his cerebrum/ why? Some folks iz never satisfied'[593] Pound may have felt thoroughly vindicated by the course of the Buntings' marriage. Bunting told Zukofsky that when 'Ole Ez found me and Marian drinking German beer to celebrate two years of [marriage], he bade us cheer up, the first seven years are the worst.'[594] This may seem tactless since this letter was congratulating Zukofsky on his recent marriage, but the tone is playful. Bunting and Marian split after seven years, and they clearly hadn't been easy ones. Zukofsky replied to Pound in April 1937 saying, 'Yes Basil wrote me about the mess. Easy enough to understand *why* he feels as etc. But the worst of it is he's prob. so in the dumps, he won't even write. Maybe if he cd. be published – .'[595] Perhaps only a poet could believe that being published could compensate for being separated from one's children by three thousand miles of ocean.

By December 1936 Pound was writing to Bunting from Rapallo in an austere mood:

> The poet's job is to *define* and yet again define till the detail of surface is in accord with the root in justice. [Rot] to submit to the transient. But poetry does not consist of the cowardice which refuses to analyze the transient, which refuses to see it.

> The specialized thinking has to be done or literature dies and stinks. Choice of the *field* where that specialized analysis is made has a percentage of relevance. In no case can constipation of thought, even in the detail, make for good writing. LUCIDITY.[596]

Not many concessions to Bunting's emotional turmoil there. In any event it was around this point that Bunting the poet dried up for nearly thirty years. His 1935 collection, *Caveat Emptor*, was never published although it was regarded as a milestone of modernism by modernist poets. William Carlos

Williams wrote to Zukofsky in March 1943 suggesting some scripts ('not my own') that James Laughlin could publish in his New Directions imprint: 'Basil Bunting's Caveat Emptor of which I have the ms, J.L. refused it a long time ago – it's better than the work of any Englishman he's published.'[597]

Apart from 'To Violet', some Odes written in the late 1940s and 'The Spoils', the published poet disappears until his magnificent re-emergence with *Briggflatts* in 1965. He told Dorothy Pound in November 1946 that 'I have written nothing (except official reports, "appreciations", & such) since Marian walked out on me.'[598]

Marian Bunting's account of her marriage to the poet makes for uncomfortable reading. It needs to be heavily discounted because, as we have seen, by her own admission she found it impossible to write about her life with Bunting without becoming highly emotional. There is more than emotion at work in this account:

> He worked systematically at learning Persian while we lived in Brooklyn & I taught school, & for a period in Tenerife, but from the moment we landed in the Canary Isles he became so enmeshed in his hatred of the islands, and Spaniards, and so frustrated by the hatred the English in the islands felt for him & by (our estrangement) ['his impotence' written above 'our estrangement'] that he was almost insane. The idea of working for a living was so hateful to him that he screamed & raved if it was ever mentioned. It took me years to get the courage to open my mouth to express an opinion after I returned to America & I was amazed at the freedom with which my sisters-in-law conversed and expressed opinions before their husbands. I was told to shut up & never open my mouth. B. regretted audibly and in public that I was too old when he married me (I was younger than he) and that if he had caught me 10 or 15 years earlier he could have brought me up right. His second marriage at 50, was to a 14 year old girl, so this was really a strong feeling. He developed a crush on a 12 yr. old 'chica' we employed at Las Arenas, Puerto Cruz, Tenerife. This was so slavish & so absurd I felt ashamed, because the other Spanish servants were snickering about it & the little girl, Juana, found it distasteful. Basil was broken hearted when we moved from a pension to 'La Casa Las Arenas' because, I learned with surprise, his main interest in moving there was to have privacy to teach Juana English. Juana did not want to learn English and Basil was genuinely dejected for days. My surprise was because I thought his liking for little girls was an act he put on like his pretending to have visions that told him not to do things (a là Yeats). He only tried the vision thing once. This was useful at the time he tried it out, but he knew better than to try it twice.

Hilaire Hiler, when I told him at a party in New York that I was going to marry Basil Bunting, commented "But Bunting is insane! He's raving, totally mad!" He was. He screamed & slashed out at me because I couldn't be in 2 places at once, and often. Our children were subjected to, or were affected by his violent tantrums. The son, born after I left him, was our only normal child.[599]

The other reason to put pressure on Marian's account is its near hysteria. The implied physical and sexual abuse seems almost designed to discredit her ex-husband in a way that couldn't be seen as libellous. None of it rings quite true. How could his pretence to have visions be an act if it happened only once? Could their children really be said to be 'abnormal', especially in the light of the fact that Bunting had congratulated her on her parenting (see p. 421)? And by the time their parents split weren't they too young in any event to have been traumatised in the way Marian suggests? Even the public statements about wishing he had met Marian ten to fifteen years before he did, while tactless, would have put her in her mid to late teens; hardly the confessions of a paedophile.

In any event Bunting had a far more interesting gloss on his relationship with Juana. For Bunting it was part of a traditional Spanish way of life that had lasted for centuries. Pound had a puzzling reference to Bunting in Canto 81:

> Basil says
> they beat drums for three days
> till all the drumheads were busted
> (simple village fiesta)
> and as for his life in the Canaries ... [600]

The editors of *Paideuma*, a journal devoted to Pound studies, asked Bunting for an explanation of these lines, eliciting a fascinating story of traditional rural Spanish customs:

I was fortunate enough to be invited to spend Easter one year with an uncle or cousin of J. R. Masoliver (and therefore also a relative of Bunuel) who was the lord of a large village in Aragon ... At that time it was a perfect survival from the middle ages, with a wall around it and no house newer than four or five centuries old, and it had kept its mediaeval practices long after almost everywhere else had given them up ... The village had an hermandad, which behaved most of the year as other hermandads did – it buried people, especially the poor, or those who required special celebration, and to do this the brothers dressed in voluminous black smocks and huge black hood-masks, shaped much like the white ones of the Ku Klux Klan. That preserved their anonymity and therefore the merit of their charity. But at Easter everybody in the village, strangers too and even women, became for a day or two members of the hermandad and hid themselves in these hideous costumes. You couldn't tell who was a man and who was a girl unless you heard their voice. Then everybody took drums, huge drums, biggish brass drums or side drums, and beat them in one dull repetitive rhythm all the time Jesus was harrowing hell – that is, from noon of Good Friday (the agony on the cross) till noon of Easter Sunday (the resurrection). There was no pause for meals or sleep. The drums went on all night, only becoming slightly less noisy as one by one was destroyed by the violence with which they had to be beaten. I was hidden in the proper mask and smock and provided with a big drum and a very sturdy drum stick, more like a club or a cosh, and banged away like everybody else. As long as your drum lasted you must go on beating it, pausing only to drink wine … My hands blistered, each in turn, and the blisters burst, and it hurt like hell; so after about a day and a half I sneaked away and let the devil rejoice at my cowardice.[601]

After this splendidly evocative story Bunting turned to Pound's reference to his life in the Canaries, and explained the relationship with his criada in a way that can only be properly understood in the context of a society where such deep traditions persist:

We had a criada of our own in Tenerife, but I could never get my Wisconsin wife to understand that it wasn't just cheap labour – we had undertaken serious responsibilities. A criada is a girl who comes to live in your house and does all the jobs she can without pay, though she gets her clothes and her food. Gradually she learns house work and civilised behaviour, until she marries: whereupon you are expected to provide a dowry, and you will be judged to some extent by how well you have brought her up … But Marian thought of the criada as just a kind of slave who was so dumb that she didn't make you pay wages, and it was all I could do to get her to dress the girl decently. She could not realise that it was a relationship intended to last for life, in which money played a very small part, but in other ways you owed as much to the girl as she did to you.[602]

Perhaps Bunting was 'broken hearted' because his wife had prevented him from fulfilling his part of a centuries-old contract.

Even heavily discounted, however, Marian's account of the marriage suggests that Bunting wasn't an easy man to live with in his thirties. Their mutual acrimony had been festering for years when Marian wrote this letter. In January 1940 Bunting told Karl Drerup that he had received from Marian 'the cruellest, wickedest letter I have ever seen'. She had begun divorce proceedings during the previous September,

> as soon as the war made it practically impossible to oppose her effectively. She has invented a new lie for this purpose – she says I attacked her with an axe. She pretends to believe that I want to kill my children, and therefore I shall never see them again unless she becomes satisfied that they would be safe in my presence. She says she will have Roudaba give evidence in court about my cruelty – my dear daughter that was not even three years old when she was taken from me … She says it never mattered to her how poor I was, it was only my murderous violence that she could not stand.[603]

It is a heartbreaking letter.

COUP D'ÉTAT, 1936

Bunting arrived back in the UK during an eventful year. As soon as he arrived an attempt (on 16 July) was made on the life of the controversial King Edward VIII. In October the Battle of Cable Street took place between Oswald Mosley's British Union of Fascists, the police and anti-Fascist demonstrators, and the following day the iconic Jarrow March began, bringing protesting shipyard workers on the long walk to London from Tyneside. But all this was nothing compared to the crisis precipitated by King Edward VIII's relationship with the American socialite, Wallis Simpson. Edward had already rattled royal protocol watchers earlier in the year when he publicly oversaw the proclamation of his accession to the throne accompanied by Simpson, who was then still married to the shipbroker Ernest Simpson. By November a real constitutional crisis was brewing. The King told the British Prime Minister Stanley Baldwin of his intention to marry Simpson and Baldwin told the King that the British people would not accept her as their Queen. The King then announced that he would abdicate if the government opposed the marriage. The crisis raged through November, but it raged privately. There was a complete media blackout, even though the crisis was being widely reported overseas, particularly in the US. The British people and their representatives in parliament had no idea that there was a crisis, let alone a serious one. The issue even divided the society that *was* aware of it. A bizarre alliance of politicians including Churchill and Lloyd George, Mosley's fascists and the communists supported the King. *The Times* and most of the rest of the media opposed the King but newspapers owned by Lord Beaverbrook and Lord Rothermere, the *Daily Mail* and the *Daily Express*, supported him. The media blackout ended when the hapless Bishop of Bradford, Alfred Blunt, referred to the crisis in what he thought was a low key speech to his diocesan conference on 1 December.

This combination of Royal politics, hobbled democracy and press connivance with the rich and privileged pushed so many of Bunting's buttons that it is not at all surprising that he found himself at the thick of it. His otherwise abjectly miserable letter of January 1937 to the Pounds crackles into life when he describes his part in the 'coup d'état':

> The only time I broke free from my personal affairs for a bit since September, was during the coup d'état. I got in a round-robin to King Edward at the very start, offering to go to any length whatsoever to dish Baldwin, and succeeded in keeping my very short tail of young men together and active during the crisis. The police finally ousted me from the lobby of the House of Commons. The crowd at the Palace didn't respond. But the conspirators managed the whole show very efficiently. Lack of exact information was a huge handicap. The week-end difficulty of getting in touch with Churchill or Wedgwood, and the absence of Lloyd George, made it impossible to put my proposals before anyone of importance until it was clearly too late to carry out my plan (to occupy Printing House Square and prevent the Times appearing unless the Astors and Walters consented to change its policy). I would have had to recruit more men, and couldn't do it without help at a moment when people were actually being gaoled for singing 'God Save the King' in the street. The so-called Fascists would do nothing effective, while dishing Edward's chances with the crowd by claiming that he was one of them, the rotten liars.

> Nobody any longer has any doubt that the South Wales speech was the clue to the whole business. [The King had made a speech in Wales that suggested he was likely to seek to impose his political views on parliament.] But at the time the press was so unanimous (Beaverbook and co didn't support Edward, they merely didn't support Baldwin as heartily as the rest) that the people at large were deceived. They didn't see that there was a coup d'état at the expense of parliament and electorate, they only saw a marriage about which

they were divided, but the unco' guids who always speak first anyway had the opportunity of making themselves heard, the others hadn't: and that I suppose stampeded parliament in the end. In the North it seems crowds in the cinema were hissing Edward and shouting 'She's nowt but a bloody hoor' and so forth.

The success of the wage-parers and purity-fiends is making itself felt already. I'm not clear what it portends. The whole thing is conditioned by the danger of war, which makes everybody chary of going very far against our masters. BUT King George [who had succeeded Edward after his abdication] has been publicly hissed. That appearance at the window in Piccadilly a day too early has made people look on him as a usurper.

Now it doesn't seem to me to matter two hoots who is King, but it matters enormously whether we elect a parliament, or merely a cabinet. I don't know whether the unpopularity of the new King can be made to work against the gang, but I hope it will. What seems quite certain is that not only no great change, but not even any substantial alleviation of the lot of the poor in England is going to be possible in future without civil war.[604]

The Thistle

Separated permanently from his wife and three children by the Atlantic Bunting decided that 'the best way to face up to the difficulty of life was to get a little boat and live on that. At least you were away from the mass of apes that call themselves mankind.'[605] He bought the *Thistle*, a six tonner, in Essex and lived aboard it for a year, apparently very enjoyably. 'One can live awfully cheaply that way.' He stayed in Essex for a while before sailing up the English Channel intending to make a crossing to France but fell foul of nautical bureaucracy: '… the boat, to get its papers completed for foreign trips, has to have its whole pedigree. It has to know all its owners back to the day it was built, and I couldn't get the list completed. So I got stuck in Devonshire and spent a very pleasant winter going out with the herring fishermen and helping the seine-net men on shore.'[606]

Bunting had become a skilled sailor in Rapallo and Amalfi and the *Thistle*, which cost him £100, was an easy vessel for him to manage. He wrote to Karl Drerup in January 1938 from Dittisham in Devon, where the *Thistle* was anchored for the winter:

I have left off being anything but a sailor. I see nobody but fishermen and naval men, and do scarcely anything but look after the "Thistle". Of course, she is a very little yacht. I could not buy the sort of boat I really want. She is very shallow, so that she does not stand up well to the sea: and she has a big open cockpit which makes her dangerous in rough water: and there is very little room in the cabin – only three feet six inches high – and so on. But she is a good ship of her kind and brought me safely about four hundred miles, in conditions she was never meant for.[607]

He had been distressed by the separation from his children and the *Thistle*, his own prescription, was working slowly and he was 'less easily upset now'.[608] Indeed he seems to have thoroughly enjoyed his single-handed voyage to Devon from Kent. There had been a 'most hospitable yacht-club at Ramsgate' and in Dover he met a 'famous Dutch yachtsman who has been round the world alone in his boat'. After he left Dover he became caught in a gale and the subsequent five-day calm left him becalmed at sea without sleep or food. Near Southampton he passed a large German liner (possibly the *Pennland*) on which 'there was a big group of sailors near the stern doing some work, and when they saw my beard ("Russian") they all ran to the side and gave the clenched fist salute and began to sing the "Internationale". They didn't seem to care what the passengers thought about it.'[609] He spent almost a month in Southampton mostly talking to a whaler who had been captain of a Cunard liner and a Commander in the Navy. By that point he had become enough of a seaman to be able to enter Lulworth Cove in Dorset 'against strong, gusty winds – a tricky business – on a day when, it seems, no other boat could (or would) do it.' He sailed on to Devon and spent time, ill and depressed, in Torquay before sailing to the estuary of the River Dart, 'a very beautiful place – a wide, enclosed stretch of water surrounded by high hills covered with forest – mostly oak, beech and elm, but with a good many Mediterranean pines and a few palms and eucalyptuses. There are vines and figs and agaves in the cottage gardens, for this corner of England is nearly as warm as the Riviera, though much rainier.'[610]

He spent the winter on the Dart estuary and went to the local pub less to drink the very cheap local cider than to talk to the men of the village, 'kind and good natured'. In December 1937 there were strong rumours of war and mobilisation and Bunting expected to be conscripted 'to navigate a trawler or other small coastal vessel', but the emergency passed. He was hopeful of a job censoring films in Singapore for the British Colonial Service that he had applied for but it came to nothing.

Bunting occupied himself on the *Thistle* by rewriting Shakespeare's sonnets. Richard Caddel says that Bunting started improving Shakespeare at school, 'cutting out the inessential bits, straightening the syntax and so on to reveal the essence of the poems'. These exercises have not survived but Caddel reproduced some examples of his 'radical attack', apparently from the late 1920s in a Basil Bunting special issue of *Durham University Journal* in 1995. [611]

Bunting's arrangement of Shakespeare's 'Sonnet 22'.

Bunting told Denis Goacher that when he was living on his boat in Devon, if he'd got nothing better to do he would take a few of Shakespeare's sonnets and cut out every single word that he considered unnecessary.[612] Goacher also dates this to the 1920s and sees it as one of the ways Bunting learned his craft, but it is clearly from the period Bunting spent on the *Thistle* in the winter of 1937/8, long after he'd found his voice. Bunting had never been overawed (or even all that impressed) by Shakespeare; the fact that

Shakespeare revolutionised the sonnet by treating it with disrespect being almost the only good thing he could find to say about him. 'Everybody treats Shakespeare as the greatest writer,' he complained. 'All English must be subordinate to Shakespeare. And when I look at English literature and think what has moved you most, what does continually move you most, what is the most lively and lifelike of English literature, it's Charles Dickens. Over and over and over again it's Charles Dickens, a far greater writer than Shakespeare.'[613]

His time on the *Thistle* was good therapy. He told Pound when he was desperate for work in the US the following year that 'sailing the Thistle for a year was at least a man's life, not this louse-like writing for money ... the Thistle served her main purpose in getting me through the worst period I've had ... Harpooning congers, netting herring, is a good life. If ultimately they won't let me write what I have to write, I'd liefer be a fisherman than another thing.'[614]

Let them remember

Only one poem, the sonnet 'Let them remember', survives from Bunting's time on the *Thistle*. It is a haunting statement about his separation from his children, as his brief note in *Collected Poems* makes clear: 'In Samangan Rustam begot Sohrab.'

> Let them remember Samangan, the bridge and tower
> and rutted cobbles and the coppersmith's hammer,
> where we looked out from the walls to the marble mountains,
> ate and lay and were happy an hour and a night;
>
> so that the heart never rests from love of the city
> without lies or riches, whose old women
> straight as girls at the well are beautiful,
> its old men and its wineshops gay.
>
> Let them remember Samangan against usurers,
> cheats and cheapjacks, amongst boasters,
> hideous children of cautious marriages,
> those who drink in contempt of joy.
>
> Let them remember Samangan, remember
> they wept to remember the hour and go.[615]

Apart from 'Let them remember', written in 1937, and a poem dedicated to Margaret de Silver's daughter, Anne, 'Not to thank dogwood', written in 1938, Bunting's entire published output from these years was a review of two poetry translations, from Chinese and Greek, in the April 1938 edition of *Criterion*, in which he mounted an energetic defence of translation of the spirit rather than the word of the foundation works:

> There are those who love dead languages because they were once alive and those who like them better as dead as possible, who hate being reminded that they ever were alive and free from literary affectations and who would be distressed if they could possibly be convinced that the earliest poets did not conform to a standard of insipidity that did not yet exist, but must have shared the vocabulary and syntax of the unread mob and taken their rhythms from the play of limbs in dancing and of fingers on the lute, not from the calculations of prosodists. Every revivification of poetry has taken the same route, towards the language of the streets and the cadences of song or bodily movement: but their knowledge teaches nothing to those who fear life, the life of 'the people' above all. It is 'vulgar'. It is 'in bad taste'. It threatens to wake them up. The perverse arrangements of a University [both volumes had been published by Cambridge University Press] encourage those least fitted to feel the power of ancient poetry to undertake to translate it from living Greek into dead English.[616]

Nellist's Nautical Academy

After a happy year on the *Thistle* he ran out of money, sold his boat for nearly £200 and enrolled in 1937 at 'a very peculiar place', Nellist's Nautical Academy, 'a cramming school for people who want certificates to be mates or masters'.[617] Nellist's Nautical School had been opened in the early 1920s by John Nellist, who had been born in 1870 in Robin Hood's Bay, in South Shields. The *Edinburgh Gazette* of 19 June 1923 records 'John Nellist, residing and carrying on business under the style of Nellist's Nautical School of Navigation at 4 Charlotte Terrace, lately carrying on the same business at the Seamen's Institute, Coronation Street, both in South Shields, county of Durham, and previously at 19 Dockwray Square, North Shields, Northumberland, nautical instructor.'[618] The school was later run by his two sons, John (Jackie) and William George (Billy), who had learned their craft as assistants to their father, from a Victorian terraced house, Mercantile Marine at 10 Summerhill Terrace in Fenham, just a couple of hundred metres from Bunting's first school, Miss Bell's, in West Parade.

There is real relish in Bunting's recollection of Nellist's:

When I first saw it I couldn't believe my eyes. I walked in asking for Mr. Nellist and was shown into a room in an old house across which I couldn't see because of the thickness of the tobacco smoke – all these men smoking pipes. No window was ever opened, the smoke just accumulated and got thicker and thicker like London fog ... You learned the routine things, how to handle the nautical tables and the theory of navigation and so forth. I picked and chose. Because of my eyes I couldn't hold a certificate, so that didn't enter into the matter at all. I just wanted to know enough to handle a boat intelligently. They were very pleased, for they had not had anybody wanting to read sailing stuff as against steamship stuff for a long time. That brought me into classes where I would not otherwise have been at all, of course; and into one class where I was with a number of shipmasters reading for the extra masters certificate. And there old Mr. Nellist explained to us the various ways of correcting the error of the sextant. There was one way, now outdated, called taking the angle of the arc, about which you were required to know something. He explained this. He said: "Now, ye dinna need to knaw much aboot it, cause its outa date. And if the examiner say to ye, what aboot the angle off the arc, ye just say to that Board of Trade Examiner, bugger the angle off the arc, there's a new method!" I wonder how many of them did that?

Bunting remembered sitting next to a fellow examinee during a mock examination at Nellist's:

The man – a mate reading for master – sitting next to me was given two or three old charts of the Red Sea and the Indian Ocean and told to make a bridge-book for the ship from Suez to Karachi. The obvious thing, of course, was simply to take the ship down the Red Sea, noting the various lights you'd see on the way, any special dangers, and around the bottom of Arabia and up again to Karachi. This man next to me had not had an opportunity yet during the examination of showing off his knowledge of the way to set out a great circle route. So he set to work. He took the latitude and the longitude of both places, applied his mathematics and worked out the great circle route. And it was only when he came at last – towards the end of the time allowed for the question – to transfer it to the chart that he discovered he'd taken his ship across the middle of the Arabian Desert.[619]

UNITED STATES, 1938–1939

Equipped with Nellist's nautical education (and a new sextant) in 1938 Bunting launched his career at sea. He sailed to Montreal from Middlesbrough on 16 April 1938, a journey that would take about twelve days.[620] His plan was to take a bus to Boston to look for work and if not instantly hired there to carry on to New York. He did find work. He told Jonathan Williams that 'in America I sailed other men's boats, a big schooner and so forth.'[621] But the Second World War put paid to all that. He was 'awhile in New York and in Los Angeles. No good. Couldn't get anything to do. I had to live off my mother.'[622] He tried, perhaps audaciously for a poet so little known, to sell some manuscripts. He wrote to a collector to explain that 'Unfortunately my income is not sufficient to permit the donation of manuscripts. I have several for sale from $150 up. I have also a copy of "Redimiculum Matellarum", Milan 1930, now exceedingly rare, with which I might be induced to part for about twice that sum.'[623]

He spent time with Zukofsky and nearly became a commercial fisherman. Lorine Niedecker, Zukofsky's former lover and the only female poet to be associated with Objectivism, recalls that she nearly met him on this visit.

> Some mention at the time of his going into the fishing business (he had yeoman muscles LZ said and arrived in New York with a sextant) with my father on our lake and river but it was the depression and at that particular time my dad felt it best to 'lay low' so far as starting fresh with new equipment was concerned and a new partner – the market had dropped so low for our carp – and I believe BB merely lived a few weeks with Louie without engaging in any business. He's probably a very fine person and I've always enjoyed his poetry.[624]

You will NEVER get the hang of fascism

Zukofksy wrote to Pound in July 1938 that 'Basil wuz here for 2 months, trying to get job as navigator on yacht, or wut else, & now has gone for west coast on chance that there might be a job out there for an extra in the movies. I hope he lands one. Things probably not so hopeful there either.'[625]

Bunting was paying $25 per month for a small apartment at 427 S. Figueroa Street in Los Angeles which he had reached by Greyhound bus via Washington, Chattanooga, Memphis, Dallas, El Paso and Phoenix. In August he wrote a very long letter to Karl Drerup, who was planning a similar trip to the west coast and had asked for Bunting's advice. Bunting suggested that Drerup take a different route, via Albuquerque, Las Vegas and Santa Fe: 'These towns, which are close to big Indian Reservations, are all "artist colonies" … probably unbearably arty, but there must be money about somewhere.' He was in good spirits. He liked Los Angeles more than any other American town he had visited. He was happy in his little downtown apartment where he was delighted to find that refrigerator, gas stove, hot water, and electric light, as well as good furniture and even sheets and towels were included in his rent. 'And they go over the place once a week with a vacuum cleaner.' Wine was cheap and some of it 'not at all bad'. On the other hand work was hard to find – 'The Japs and Mexicans will work for less than you need to keep alive.' Fortunately Margaret de Silver had made it possible for him to carry on for at least another month.[626] He would have stayed in Los Angeles if the British navy hadn't intervened, 'wanting to make a sailor of me during the late perils and not even refunding my wildcat fare when they called it off'.[627] Meanwhile Pound was haranguing Bunting about his inability to appreciate the value of Fascism. In a letter to Bunting of 24 November 1938 he drew a rather implausible analogy:

> You will NEVER get the hang of fascism if you persist in E habit of regarding every ACT as a precedent.
>
> Surgeon amputates leg/NOT as precedent/ he dont mean to go on amputating the patients leg every week or year.
>
> Operations to save life/ ONLY in an emergency/What are called CONTINGENT. Things to be done ONCE and NOT erected into a system.[628]

Bunting didn't want to get the hang of Fascism and he loathed Pound's anti-Semitism, which he described as an 'obsessive redherring' in a letter to Dorothy Pound.[629] Bunting and Pound had been corresponding about economics, communism, anti-Semitism and Fascism since 1934 and the correspondence had become increasingly fractious.

Pound and Lionel Robbins had already fallen out spectacularly over Douglas' economic theories. Pound wrote a series of increasingly rude and aggressive letters to Robbins which rarely rise above invective and barely skirt theory. Robbins emerges with enormous credit from the spat. In August

1934 Robbins put Pound in his place in a way that Bunting, a London School of Economics drop out, never had the intellectual authority to do, although he knew a lot more about economics than Pound did. It was a letter that, as Robbins' biographer Susan Howson says, Robbins clearly enjoyed writing:

> I am neither over 80 and paralysed nor a God damned English mutton. I am a type you have not encountered recently – a man who can think logically and without prepossession.
>
> Put your questions by all means. There is a large sum of money for the charities of Rapallo if I am worsted.
>
> But don't think I don't know you already – a damned good poet led up the garden path by a set of second rate moth-eaten currency cranks. Don't you realize that I'm as good a specialist on money as you are on poetry? What would you say if Mr. Selfridge came and tried to tell you how to write verse?
>
> Well you see I'm more tolerant to *you*. Come and feed with me next time you're in London instead of seeing that dull dog Douglas. You shall have some good wine and a completely painless extraction of all your fallacies.
>
> *Extract from a future history of poetry* In the year 1934 the economist Robbins persuaded Pound that he was making a fool of himself about Douglas. Thank Gawd! After that he wrote good verse again.

According to Howson Robbins added a postscript which suggested to Pound that if he wanted to know more about him he should ask Bunting, which Pound did, but the correspondence became no more amiable after that. Pound acknowledged Bunting's attempt to take some of the heat out of the conversation. He wrote to Robbins in September 1934: 'even Buntin sez I got to be lenient cause you got wife and family and can't afford to lose yr/ job/ … ' But the rest of his letter is not a model of leniency: 'Read tr/ Jefferson (if as a god rotted Briton you have heard of him) … read up on Monte dei Paschi your a buggarin prof/ PAID to know a subject. even by so lousy and obscurantist a gang of counterfeiters as the London School/ but you orter know a bill from a mortgage … YOU are just plain DUMB.'[630]

Robbins' diagnosis of Pound's problem – 'a damned good poet led up the garden path by a set of second rate moth-eaten currency cranks' – is brilliant. If Pound had followed Robbins' advice the literary landscape of the mid-twentieth century could have been very different. Pound's incarceration in St Elizabeths psychiatric hospital after the Second World War effectively finished him off as a poet and, more damaging yet, as an editor. Although it is doubtful that Robbins could have cured Pound of his Mussolini worship.

In March 1935 Bunting wrote to Pound that 'you surely got a bloody big bat in the belfry about economics. It seems to me just one of a good number of matters that are all pretty equally wrong.'[631] An extraordinary tirade from Pound[632] that started: 'You really BLOODY fool/ "Go Douglas" your arse. As you never see any printed matter, you [sic] ignorance may be an alibi', and carries on in much the same vein for two pages, brought an exasperated response from Bunting. 'It makes me irritable trying to answer a letter that doesn't say anything,' he wrote, and it is true that Pound's letter says absolutely nothing about anything, but does so in an extremely intemperate way. 'Calling me a bloody fool,' Bunting continued, 'does me no good unless you attempt to show WHY.'[633] Bunting's lengthy, reasoned letters seem to have goaded Pound further. By January 1936 Bunting pointed out to Pound, quite fairly, that 'a chap who writes the letters you've been writing lately obviously isn't at his best … I desire to continue profiting by you, but don't get any profit out of mixed abuse and political intolerance. A bad bargain for you? I don't give anything in exchange? That's your affair. If I'm not worth better than what I've got lately I'd rather be dropped. I would lose a good deal, no doubt of it. I've enough confidence in my own abilities to think you'd lose something too.'[634] Tempers settled a little after this warning shot across Pound's bow, but by the end of 1938 Bunting had had enough of Pound's lunacy, the catalyst being a letter that Pound wrote to Zukofsky on 2 December 1938, preposterously blaming the Rothschilds, rather than the Nazis, for the persecution of Jews in Germany. Bunting saw the letter and wrote an angry rejection of its contents to Pound: 'No, I am sorry, and thankyou: but I cant take it. I wish I were not as much indebted to you as I am.' He goes on to berate Pound for his failure to acknowledge fascist atrocities such as Guernica and for the 'abomination' of his anti-Semitism:

> Every anti-semitism, anti-niggerism, anti-moorism, that I can recall in history was base, had its foundations in the meanest kind of envy and in greed. It makes me sick to see you covering yourself with that filth. It is not an arguable question, has not been arguable for at least nineteen centuries, Either you know men to be men, and not something less, or you make yourself an enemy of mankind at large.

> To spue [sic] out anti-semitic bile in a letter to Louis, as I yesterday accidentally discovered you to be doing, – to Louis who has shown his devotion to you over

many years, and who even now insists that you are to be forgiven because after all you are Ezra – to write such a letter is not a mere lapse of taste: it is uncommonly close to what has got to be called the behaviour of the skunk.

He broke off his relationship with Pound in a sign-off that was written more in anger than in sadness: 'I suppose if you devote yourself long enough to licking the arses of blackguards you stand a good chance of becoming a blackguard yourself. Anyway, it is hard to see how you are going to stop the rot of your mind and heart without a pretty thoroughgoing repudiation of what you have spent a lot of work on. You ought to have the courage for that: but I confess I don't expect to see it.'[635]

Zukofsky's response to Pound takes a strangely neutral poisition, but ends with precisely the same sentiment that Bunting's had: 'your letter which offended Basil because he feels I'm a very Jewish Jew, which I don't feel, was written to me. It was none of his business to take it upon himself etc, but I admire him for having done it, whatever reservations I may have as to the usefulness of his action. He thinks it may lead you to think again. Frankly, I don't.'[636] Bunting's hostility to Pound over his absurd letter to Zukofsky may have been exacerbated by the fact that he felt deeply indebted to his Jewish friends at the time. 'Do you know,' he wrote to Karl Drerup in January 1938, 'I believe at this time you are my only close friend who is not a Jew? You and I will have to get circumcised. Only the Jews have stood by me in real misfortune.'[637]

In spite of their quarrel Pound's fundamental honesty about poetry meant that he never failed to promote Bunting to anthologists and editors who asked him for contributions. He wrote to Douglas McPherson in September 1939 saying, 'There is plenty of room for a new mag ... But you must realize *first*, that the actual output of good poetry is *very* small ... Were I forced to make one I shd. have to go into retrospect as far as my own *Active Anthology* and take Bunting's "Northern Farmer" and a few other pages of him, plus a couple of Angold's satires ... Plus a few poems by Cummings ... ten lines quoted from my new *Cantos* ... If you can find *six* pages outside that lot, go to it.'[638]

Pound had sincere belief in his protégés. He told Zukofsky in 1940 that 'mebbe if you and Boozle B[unting] & me & the kumrad keep at it, we'll evolve a style of the period'.[639] In June 1955 Pound tried to enlist William Carlos Williams' support in persuading Lawrence Ferlinghetti to include

Bunting in his new Pocket Poet series: 'if yu write em yu cd/putt in a plug fer Basil the Bunter, that wd. circumvent the idol of yr. optic Mr Ellyut.'[640]

London, Paris, Rapallo, New York, Spain: Bunting accounts for his twenties and thirties with characteristic obliqueness in *Briggflatts*. Here is part of the poem that deals with London:

> Poet appointed dare not decline
> to walk among the bogus, nothing to authenticate
> the mission imposed, despised
> by toadies, confidence men, kept boys,
> shopped and jailed, cleaned out by whores,
> touching acquaintance for food and tobacco.
> Secret, solitary, a spy, he gauges
> lines of a Flemish horse
> hauling beer, the angle, obtuse,
> a slut's blouse draws on her chest,
> counts beat against beat, bus conductor
> against engine against wheels against
> the pedal, Tottenham Court Road, decodes
> thunder, scans
> porridge bubbling, pipes clanking, feels
> Buddha's basalt cheek
> but cannot name the ratio of its curves
> to the half-pint
> left breast of a girl who bared it in Kleinfeldt's.
> He lies with one to long for another,
> sick, self-maimed, self-hating,
> obstinate, mating
> beauty with squalor to beget lines still-born.[641]

It is not very self-forgiving.

* * *

Bunting was still in New York in December 1938. Zukofsky wrote to William Carlos Williams on 3 December 1938: 'I'm very sorry I was out the other night when you dropped around – if it was Thursday, I went uptown to see Basil. I'd enjoy it a lot, if you feel like it, if you'd come here next Thurs. or the Thurs. after., I could make some supper – and if you'd like to see Basil, I'll try and shanghai him.'[642] And on 12 December he was still trying to fix up the rendezvous: 'If you can possibly come here this Thursday without inconveniences, do so – because I arranged for Basil to come that night, & René [Taupin] may possibly show up, too.'[643]

However, Bunting was, as usual, struggling to make ends meet in New York. 'NOTHING,' he wrote to Pound in November 1938, 'from digging to reviewing will yield me a living. I am now lying about imbecile books for cigarette money.'[644] Fortunately global events came to his rescue.

When war was declared Bunting, according to William Carlos Williams, 'rushed across the United States from California to go to England, as fast as he could, to enlist'.[645] Caddel and Flowers say that he explained his reaction to the outbreak of the Second World War as follows: 'During the First World War it was possible to believe, I did believe, that it was a totally unnecessary war fought for purely selfish ends, to get hold of markets and things like that. You couldn't believe that, in the second one at all. It was perfectly obvious for years beforehand that nothing short of war and violence would ever stop Hitler and his appalling career.'[646]

Many participants made the same case, and no doubt it is true. But we shouldn't lose sight of the fact that Bunting at eighteen, psychologically vulnerable and having been immersed in private Quaker education (however inept its moral leadership) for six years was not the poverty scarred, worldly, forty-year-old wanderer, sea dog and convict who engaged so energetically with the second war.

No conscientious objections this time.

THREE

SWEET SHIT! BUY!

Heart slow, nerves numb and memory, he lay
On glistening moss by a spring;
as a woodman dazed by an adder's sting
barely within recall
tests the rebate tossed to him, so he
ascertained moss and bracken,
a cold squirm snaking his flank
and breath leaked to his ear:
I am neither snake nor lizard,
I am the slowworm.

Briggflatts III

THROCKLEY, 1939–1940

We know more about Bunting's war service now than we did just a few years
ago. In 2010, under the twenty-five year rule (Bunting died in 1985), the Royal
Air Force released as much information about his record as we are ever likely
to receive from that source. We now have his 'Promotions, Reclassifications,
Reversions' and 'Movements' as both aircraftman and officer. Having been
rejected by the navy and army, apparently on health grounds, Bunting was
eventually accepted by the RAF although he had to wait until September
1940 to enlist. He had been largely unoccupied since his return from the
US, apart from a series of six history lectures that he gave to working men
in Lemington in September and October 1939. By early November he was
complaining to Zukofsky that his earnings had 'dwindled to £5 – and led
to such a mass of red tape that I am determined never to have anything to
do with a body which evidently exists to put as many hindrances as possible
in the way of education.'[1] It seems, however, that he may have pitched

these lectures inaccurately. It all 'grouped very nicely around Alexander, Abu Bekr, Genghis, and Columbus: or if you prefer the thinkers to the men of action, Isocrates, Al-Ghazzali, Galileo, Andy Jackson.' He seems to have been surprised that the 'workingmen listened politely and asked no questions whatever. They were not interested in anything except Marx.'[2] Although Bunting claimed that his classes were reasonably popular he was asked at least one question which ought to have suggested to him that he wasn't taking his students on a journey to enlightenment. He reported this 'jewel of half-knowledge' to Zukofsky: '"Please, what was the connection between this Caliph Omar and Omer that wrote the Iliad?"'[3]

In May 1939 Bunting reported to Karl Drerup that Britain was on a war footing: 'tanks on all the roads, trenches in every garden, balloons anchored at sea off the Tyne, big guns on railway trucks travelling to the coast to go to Gib[raltar] or Malta'.[4] By October this activity had been scaled up. He wrote a vivid account of Britain at war to Zukofsky:

> When it began, the weather improved instantly, which of course shows that Jehovah approves. Also the lights went out. It is inconceivably dark without the moon. From my doorstep I should see a largish industrial town & a number of big industrial villages: but an hour after sunset I might as well be looking at a totally uninhabited stretch of country. Occasionally a furnace flares up for a moment, but not often. Even the tramcars which pass the house are so dark that in about a hundred yards they become invisible – though not inaudible … We all carry gasmasks – little kids making mud-pies in the gutter & Lord Mayors at public functions. Drunks take their gasmasks to gaol with them, judges have theirs on the desk before them.[5]

Bunting was waiting to know what 'they' wanted of him. Annie was concerned about him. She told Karl Drerup that, 'Basil is still here with me. He has not found any work yet, and gets very depressed about it sometimes. He has very few friends here, and does not go out much.'[6] He was already feeling a burden on his mother and he planned to borrow a tent and take a long walk along Hadrian's Wall and then across the heather and bogland to the mountains. His frustration spilled into a letter to the *Manchester Guardian* in June 1939:

> I learn from your leading article that General Valle has given a list of ships attacked or sunk in Barcelona harbour by the Italian Air Force. You do not state whether our Government has sent in any claim for compensation. Since

the responsibility is now admitted there can be no excuse for overlooking it. It would hardly be consistent with our national independence to acquiesce in acknowledged acts of war against us, particularly since the nearness of these attacks to the time of our agreement with Italy makes them conspicuous examples of treachery.

Our Government 'reserved the right' to exact damages from Franco for ships sunk by his forces. It is surely extremely important that those claims should be fully met before there is any question of loans, public or private, to Spain. But if Italy asserts responsibility for some of the sinkings, it is Italy that should be made to pay.[7]

This strikes me as the view of someone who wants to be seen to be involved at *any* level rather than that of an economist of war reparations.

By October he had a sniff of a job at the Ministry of Information. He told Zukofsky that a friend of his uncle, who was a cabinet minister, thought he should be employed to write 'articles for America', but that when he went to the ministry he found it 'four times overstaffed with the nephews, daughters, etc of the men in charge. Hardly a journalist among them.'[8] This rather improbable acquaintance was Buck de la Warr or, more properly, Herbrand Edward Dundonald Brassey Sackville, 9th Earl De La Warr, two months older than Bunting and the Labour Party's first hereditary peer in 1923. By 1939 he was Secretary of the Board of Education in Chamberlain's government and Bunting was urging him, in English and Persian, to put in a word for him to his 'bosom pal ... the Secretary of State for War', the long-forgotten Leslie Hore-Belisha.[9] One might wonder how the gritty, unemployed, seemingly unemployable Bunting might move in a circle that included an Old Etonian toff like de la Warr (pronounced 'Delaware' of course). The only point of connection, apart from Bunting's uncle, seems to be that de la Warr had been a conscientious objector at exactly the same time as Bunting, although the 9th Earl de la Warr spent no time in Wormwood Scrubs.

Bunting's first brush with espionage occurred in this period. A few years later he was to be deeply involved in the real thing. 'Imbeciles in a motorcar the other day,' he wrote to Zukofsky in November 1939, 'tried to get a village policeman to arrest me as a spy. I was out for a walk. Fortunately it was an intelligent policeman, who realised that spies don't make themselves conspicuous by growing beards. After some talk I suggested to him that he might also enquire whether the motorcar was stolen, which he proceeded to do, very thoroughly, to the enormous indignation of the four fools in it.'[10]

He had been told by the Admiralty that he would have to wait a long time for a commission but that he could join as a rating, and he had volunteered for the minesweepers as a seaman as early as January 1940 but failed the medical.[11] Even so, warned of the dangers of the job by an old captain at the Merchant Marine Office, he was so miserable about his impending divorce that he would have been 'glad to be blown up, if it were done thoroughly'.[12]

His misery deepened in March when he was 'completely laid out – entire guts red hot, appendix howling'. A doctor was called and insisted that he be operated on immediately, but Bunting could afford neither the time nor the money involved. While his illness raged he was called to an interview at Army Intelligence in London, blaming influenza for his wretched physical condition so as not to invite further medical enquiries. He was pleased with the interview but lost fourteen pounds in weight on the three-day trip. When he returned he was called for another interview at the Admiralty, this time in Newcastle, but he was sent away and told to go to hospital. By the time a third interview, with the skipper of a coasting steamer, came round he could hardly walk and one of his uncles (at his own expense) called a consultant who confirmed that he had three conditions which combined to give the impression of acute appendicitis – a kidney stone and two other unidentified problems that were causing spasms in his colon. Miraculously the following day, 'the spasms ceased'.[13]

Eventually he managed to persuade a doctor who had known his father to allow him to memorise the eye test and he was able to join the Royal Air Force. By July 1940 he was a balloon man, 'the only thing the doctors would pass me for', though as yet without a posting.[14] In August he complained to Zukofsky that he was 'idle ... no nearer a job ... The army (intelligence), air force (balloons) and children's evacuation people have all got me listed for jobs at short notice, but nothing comes of it.'[15] He was also desperate for news of his children. By then he had not heard anything from Wisconsin, apart from a few lines his lawyer managed to obtain, for the fifteen months since he left the US. He told Zukofsky that he was paralysed by the loss of his children and the 'bitter, gratuitous, vindictive wrongs' he suffered at the hands of his ex-wife.[16]

BALLOONS IN HULL, 1940

Bunting was finally accepted into No.3 Recruits Centre at Padgate in Warrington on 21 September 1940 as Aircraftman Second Class. Padgate (now a housing estate) had been opened in April 1939, so before Britain was formally at war, as a national training centre for RAF recruits. Bunting recalled that the recruits 'were all Welshmen and many of them didn't understand English. Amusing blokes.'[17] Padgate was to become an important camp and by 1943, as the RAF stepped up its bombing campaign in Germany, Padgate's intake rose to fifteen hundred recruits per week. Bunting spent just six days there before joining 653 other airmen and twenty officers at 942 Squadron, Balloon Command, at No.17 Balloon centre in Sutton-on-Hull in East Yorkshire on 27 September 1940, 'weather intermittent rain or drizzle ... 23 balloons shining, 17 balloons sleeping', according to the Operations Record. Bunting thought it a 'terrible bore'.[18] 'They' believed that he was 'too old for anything except the damned balloons' after he had been trained.

A balloon barrage had been part of the defence strategy for British cities since 1929. Balloon barrages forced enemy aircraft to fly higher and consequently to drop their bombs less accurately and they made them more vulnerable to searchlights, anti-aircraft fire and fighter aircraft. They also acted as deterrents to dive-bombing. On the other hand the balloons were as dangerous for unwitting British pilots as they were for the enemy and, of course, a collection of highly visible aerial objects drew attention to the target.

Balloon Command had been formed in November 1938 and consisted of five groups, each of which was further divided into Balloon Centres. The Hull Centre (No.17) was in No.33 Group headquartered in Sheffield. The first balloons had flown from Hull on 17 July 1939 and by the start of the Hull Barrage on 1 September 1939, just two days before Britain declared war on Germany, just six balloons were flying at war sites. By the time Bunting arrived the Hull Barrage alone was flying over seventy.

Those of us who have no experience of the Second World War tend to scoff at barrage balloons as a gimcrack response to the terrifying Luftwaffe, if, that is, we know anything about them at all. In fact they were a vital part of Britain's defence strategy and when Bunting joined it 17 Balloon Centre was one of the most important in the country. A month after Bunting arrived Hull flew more balloons (seventy-two) than any of the UK's forty-one Balloon Centres except Glasgow and London.[19]

Hull, to be fair, was a particularly dangerous place and Bunting would have been happy to move on as quickly as he did. The Luftwaffe regarded the city as a primary target before the war started.[20] The Log of 942 Squadron recorded the death of two airmen and a civilian during the month of Bunting's arrival. But an element of deep amateurism suffuses the story of No.17 Balloon Centre. The following passage from Leonard Bacon's history of the Hull station could be instructions received from Home Guard HQ by *Dad's Army*'s hapless Captain Mainwaring:

> The personnel at the No.17 Balloon Centre assisted by the crews of four nearby Balloon Sites was to form part of the defence of Sutton on Hull by taking over a road block, install a machine gun post at Noddle Hill Farm and with the defence posts at the Centre, cover Wawne Road ... The Crews from the Waterborne Barges were to assist Royal Navy personnel in the immobilisation of the Docks and when that role was completed some were to become part of defence of the City Keep, while others join crews from land Sites already in place on the railway embankment running the North edge of King George Dock, it was there *they were to resist the enemy's entry into the Docks until the last!*[21]

It is easy to poke fun at a war fought at this local micro-level but there were periods of intense activity and danger. Hull took twenty-two bombing raids between February and early May 1941. A large parachute mine fell in the city centre causing major destruction on the night of 7 May. Raids on the following two nights killed more than five hundred civilians and injured a further 325.[22] The record of an evening picked at random (5 November 1940) from Bunting's posting at Hull tells its own story:

> 17.39 hours 'D' Flight report bombs and heavy gunfire very near, 17.41 hours 'C' Flight reports heavy explosions. 17.43 hours Red warning. 17.43 hours 'D' Flight report Sites 8 & 27 machine gunned. Site S down for topping-up. Balloon will be examined for punctures before flying. (No punctures found.) 17.50 hours GY report HMD 'Student Prince' in action against enemy a/craft flying SW at 2000. 18.10 hours 'D' Flight Site 27 reports 2 enemy aircraft coming in from river. Bombs dropping near 'D' Flight HQ. 18.11 hours and 18.18 hours, 'B' and 'A' Flights respectively report heavy explosions on Lincs. side of river. 18.14 hours 'E' Flight report a 'plane S of Site 83, also one or two explosions S of site. 18.27 hours air raid message White. 18.30 hours GT

report 'HMD Student Prince' fired on a/craft because guns on Lincs. coast were already firing before a/craft was within range. Therefore 'S. Prince' presumed a/craft to be hostile and opened fire. Immediately after guns at Spurn opened fire.[23]

And so on through the night. It was a frenetic, round-the-clock defence and repair operation. Bunting was pleased to be moved on from it after ten weeks or so.

Bunting didn't talk much about his eighteen months or so inflating balloons in Scotland and the north of England and one can see why. It was considerably less glamorous than his later war career, although that didn't prevent an element of myth-making collecting around the activity. Lorine Niedecker wrote to Zukofsky on 18 May 1941: 'So – and Basil is over the North Sea with a machine gun in a balloon and he sees the end of the world.'[24]

BALLOONS IN SCOTLAND, 1940–1942

On 9 December 1940 Bunting joined 948 Squadron at Rosyth on Scotland's Firth of Forth, having been promoted to Aircraftman First Class on 28 November. The squadron's main activity on the day Bunting joined was the condemnation and evacuation of the Band Hall at Methil[25] and he immediately found his circumstances much more congenial:

> the very first day I was there [in Hull] a notice appeared asking for volunteers for what was described as difficult and dangerous work at sea. And I thought, well, that's the job for me. And went for it. The people I left behind at Hull were killed in the great raid on the docks which took place almost immediately after I left. I found that the 'dangerous and difficult work at sea' turned out to be the most comfortable you could find in the Royal Air Force. We worked on these large yachts that millionaires had built before the War. The masts had been taken out of them, of course. They were running on diesel engines. We lived in berths that had been built for the Rothschilds, and we ate very well. The crews were mixed – partly RAF, partly Navy, partly civilian fishermen. We got on very well together. On my boat, the Golden Hind, it was extremely difficult to get anybody to take the day off when they had a day in harbour. We had to make it compulsory to go ashore, otherwise they wouldn't. Oh yes, I enjoyed that year. That was 1940 and some of 1941 …[26]

According to Peter Quartermain the job of the *Golden Hind* was to escort convoys across the North Sea to the Arctic Russian port of Murmansk, although 948 Squadron's Operations Record doesn't support that.[27] Few other details of his fifteen months in Scotland survive, although many years later he related a tale to Peter Quartermain from late in 1941: 'Alloa, Fife: Bunting, B., Leading Aircraftsman, Serial number 1119305, learning how to drive an army lorry, at the front of a large convoy, spots up ahead an archway, on the left side of the road, on which, as he gets nearer, he can read "George Younger's Brewery." So he leads the whole convoy into the yard. "We all got a free drink," he said.'[28]

Although the Band Hall was a priority for the men on the day he arrived Bunting was immediately pitched into intense activity at Rosyth. During January 1941 the 'efforts of all Sections of the Squadron have been directed towards the earliest possible establishment of the Methil Barrage ... Six vessels [including the *Golden Hind*] fitted with winches have docked at Methil during the month, also the R.A.F. Pinnace. Instructions have been received from Higher Authority to fly balloons from these vessels at the earliest opportunity.'[29]

The 'D' Flight barrage was installed on 9 February and three days later the *Golden Hind* was damaged in a collision with the jetty at Methil as the ships were withdrawn from the harbour because of bad weather. Squadron 948's activity was a constant round of inflating, deflating and repairing balloons. In Methil in July 1941 alone 93 new balloons were sent up, 138 were topped up, 22 were repaired and 5 salvaged, all involving 482 tubes of hydrogen.[30] Methil was by some way the biggest of the Forth barrages. The month before Bunting left 948 Squadron it used more tubes of hydrogen (a key measure of activity) than the Aberdeen, Oban, Dundee and Aultbea barrages combined.

Bunting wrote lightly about his time in the North Sea but it could be hard and dangerous work. He gave an example to Gael Turnbull:

We had been lifted from the water by a depth charge dropped by a German plane, and the leak that caused opened dangerously during a hard easterly gale while we were lying in Leven roads. Our crew, all over age for other service except two boys (who were very frightened), had to keep the pumps going while the job was done by men up to their waist in water in the narrow bilge, without elbow room. We got free and into Methil in time, where engines did the pumping till we could take the Golden Hind (no less a name) to Burnt Island for repairs.[31]

Certainly life aboard the *Golden Hind* seems to have been better than life ashore. In a letter to Zukofsky written in September 1941, mystifyingly damaged by the censor, he wrote that '[long blank] I have been without a change of linen, without a bath, sleeping in a horrible smell in an unventilated room with [blank] men in it, shaving [long blank] out in the street from a bucket: scrubbing floors without soap, polishing brass without metal polish, washing dirty dishes in cold water, in all the time left over from "duty". It's better now I am back on board.'[32] Time spent ashore wasn't all drudgery. He spent six weeks at headquarters in Rosyth in September and October learning to drive and repair lorries, and 'having to look smart, for a change, and do all the stupid military things'.[33]

During his time in Scotland Bunting became friendly with a local girl, a fourteen-year-old secretary called Violet Harris. Violet offered to type Bunting's poems and he dedicated a farewell to art to her, 'To Violet, with prewar poems'.

> These tracings from a world that's dead
> take for my dust-smothered pyramid.
> Count the sharp study and long toil
> as pavements laid for worms to soil.
> You without knowing it might tread
> the grass where my foundation's laid,
>
> your, or another's, house be built
> where my weathered stones lie spilt,
> and this unread memento be
> the only lasting part of me.[34]

He told Zukofsky in September 1941 that he had sought a 'minor promotion, not willingly' that would increase his wages by sixpence a day. The reason he wanted this promotion was 'to save for Violet', so he clearly had a long-term relationship in mind.[35] *Poetry* had offered to publish 'To Violet, with prewar poems' in the September issue, something that pleased him mainly because Violet would see her name in print. Although he longed for a job in Persia he was desperate not to be separated from Violet.[36] Violet's family clearly saw nothing in the friendship to discourage. He told Zukofsky that but for her parents a day ashore meant a day on the streets and he visited Violet's aunt for supper, so tired that he fell asleep at it.[37] By February 1942 he was deeply attached to Violet who had by then become a clerk at the Leven Gas Company, running a small office in Methil. 'Her gentleness and gaiety are my chief assets,' he told Zukofsky. 'I fancy she is beginning to rely on me as much as I on her: and I dread a parting.'[38] Violet had made a 'tolerable life into a good one' and she had finally helped him to recover from the bitterness he felt at Marian's departure.[39]

Bunting wrote movingly of his experience in the North Sea in his war poem, 'The Spoils':

> Tide sang. Guns sang:
>> 'Vigilant,
>> pull off fluffed woollens, strip
>> to buff and beyond.'
> In watch below
> meditative heard elsewhere
> surf shout, pound shores seldom silent
> from which heart naked swam
> out to the dear unintelligible ocean.
> From Largo Law look down,
> moon and dry weather, look down
> on convoy marshalled, filing between mines.
> Cold northern clear sea-gardens
> between Lofoten and Spitzbergen,
> as good a grave as any, earth or water.
> What else do we live for and take part,
> we who would share the spoils.[40]

These lines are about 'what the tide says, rippling round the anchor chains of the ships assembling in the Firth of Forth for the Archangel convoy; the contrast of leisurely fishing with the need to prepare to face very ultimate things'.[41]

In fact Bunting enjoyed his luxurious lifestyle in Fife for the last three weeks of 1940, all of 1941 and the first three months of 1942. By then technology was automating balloon activity and Bunting's position was becoming redundant. He wrote to Karl Drerup on 1 April 1942:

> I can tell you very little of what I am doing. No enemy has ever come within range of my machine-gun, except Hess: and I was asleep when he passed, & none of the men on deck knew how to fire the gun, though a merchant ship near us did have a shot at him. The work was formerly dangerous, though not fearfully so. But now it is uneventful and boring. I was in some of the heavy bombings on the Mersey and at Hull before they sent me to be based in Scotland: but for well over a year I've seen very few bombs. I expect to be

transferred to a more risky job – still at sea – before very long, but I know nothing definite about it.[42]

The hyperbolic reference to action on the Mersey can only relate to his week at the recruitment centre at Padgate. In later life he was sanguine about his ballooning. He told Gael Turnbull that he 'went up to 7,000ft under a barrage balloon, wrapped in a blanket. Next chap not so lucky.'[43]

PERSIA, 1942–1943

Bunting's letter to Drerup was written on his last day at Methil. 'One day last April,' he told Zukofsky in October, 'a drifter came out from Port Edgar to my yacht, bringing a two-page signal from the Ministry; and waited while I packed my kit and left Scotland and the North Sea for "Overseas Posting". I got 48 hours embarkation leave – and that was cut short by telegram. When I joined my new unit in the south of England I found I was posted as interpreter.'[44]

Unimpressed by the requirement to 'go back to this damned old business of flying balloons ashore' Bunting had applied for and acquired a posting to Persia on the strength of his knowledge of classical Persian,[45] and on 2 April 1942 during a severe thunderstorm that lasted for most of the month[46] Bunting joined 929 Squadron at Queensferry, still at Forth, for a month in preparation for service overseas.[47] On 29 April he joined the newly formed 982 (Balloon) Squadron at Chessington, according to his service record 'in formation and will proceed overseas', and two days later, on 1 May 1942, he was promoted to Leading Aircraftman: 982 Squadron's destination was Persia. On 6 May the squadron embarked on a thirteen-hour overnight train journey to Glasgow, from where it set sail on 10 May on its voyage round the Cape of Good Hope. From 7 May 1942, according to a cryptic and somewhat detached note in Bunting's service record, he was serving in Iraq. Within a few days of leaving port, 'regular lessons in Persian [had] been arranged ... Our instructor [is] L.A.C. Bunting who has a sound knowledge of many languages and is quite an authority on certain literary subjects.'[48] Bunting did not enjoy the voyage on this 'appalling troopship, like a bad canto from the Inferno, so overcrowded, such foul food'.[49]

The squadron arrived at Freetown, Sierra Leone, on 22 May for four days of rest and recuperation before heading off for Durban in South Africa where they arrived on 9 June. This part of the voyage made an impression on Bunting. He wrote to Dorothy Pound after the war that the place he really wanted to see again was Africa. 'I want to know what is behind the Lion Mountains from which Sierra Leone gets its name, which are lovely – as sharp of outline as the Appenines above Rapallo, but covered in bright green forest. I liked Zululand too: to say nothing of the Zulus themselves.'[50] Bunting enjoyed wandering alone in the bush, meeting Zulu farmers and Indian settlers who had set up as market gardeners. 'Bathed from surfy beaches,' he told Zukofsky, 'pulled wild guavas, bananas, etc.'[51]

The squadron enjoyed a month at the Cape, with plenty of sporting fixtures and visits to local townships, before embarking once again for a passage across the Indian Ocean on an American troopship (less crowded and better food) on 7 July. By now Bunting had written a textbook on Persian in fairly challenging conditions and had been promoted to 'Acting Unpaid Corporal', which seems to have annoyed him. 'I get nothing for interpreting,' he told Zukofsky, 'and am annoyed to think that I'd have been a fully paid corporal long since if I'd still been at home.'[52]

On 23 July they arrived in Karachi (mistakenly – they were supposed to have gone to Bombay) and the following day set up a miserable camp eight miles from the city. Many of the men succumbed to stomach complaints, probably because 'the food is monotonous and served with flies'.[53] The men kicked their heels playing football and cricket but Bunting involved himself in the local culture:

I made one or two friends – a learned Brahmin, who talked about religion; a Gujerati poet with the same name as Mahatma, M. K. Gandhi; a Persian restaurant keeper from Most Sacred Yazd in the Eastern desert. There was a dinner party in a chemist's shop one Sunday, with chutneys that cried aloud for the Fire Brigade. Good mangoes in the bazaar, tasting strongly of turpentine. Paludè, in tall glasses. Palm toddy, and a mad old Englishman, down a backstreet. And a wild animal, cat kind, that growled outside my tent one night for quite a while. I think it was a leopard or an ocelot – as big as an Alsatian dog or bigger.[54]

On 30 August they embarked on the *City of London* for the final leg of their journey to Basra which they at last reached on 6 September after a journey that had taken four months. The following day a convoy of thirty-four vehicles took the entire squadron on an eighty-five mile desert journey to Ahwaz, near the Iranian border with Iraq, which was to be their permanent base. While they built the base they waited for their supplies.

The first supply of hydrogen didn't arrive until the last day of October and the first balloons followed on 6 November. But by then the plans of Allied Military Command had moved on and on 19 November 982 Squadron learned with 'deep regret' that it was to be split into detachments at Teheran and Bahrain.[55]

Bunting was not impeccably equipped to fulfil his translation brief. He recalled that 'I never expected to hear [Persian] spoken or to speak a word of it. In fact, I didn't hear a word of it spoken until I arrived in Persia and was called upon to interpret for a court martial. You can imagine how difficult that was. I hope they put the right man in jail. Very fortunately it wasn't one of those cases where it would require shooting or hanging.'[56]

He already had experience of trying to use a medieval language to communicate. His Italian had been learned from Dante and 'it was as if someone came along in England speaking a Chaucerian mode'.[57] In Persia he was able to communicate with the Luri and Bakhtiari tribesmen, whose dialect is similar to early medieval Persian, far better than with Teheranis. The Bakhtiari, a tribe from the south west of Iran, consider themselves to be descendants of Shah Fereydun, a legendary figure from Ferdowsi's *Shahnameh*. The Bakhtiari had played a significant role in Persia's Constitutional Revolution and continued to have enormous influence on Iranian politics in the 1940s, as we shall see, particularly in the figure of Morteza Quli Khan. Bunting was correct about the Bakhtiari dialect. No less a figure than Sir Austen Henri Layard ('Layard of Nineveh') had observed that: 'The Bakhtiari speak a Persian dialect which is generally known as the Luri, and is a corruption of the pure old Persian without the modern intermixture of Arabic and Turkish. They maintain, indeed, that it is the 'Farsi Kadim', the language of the ancient Persians. It more nearly resembles the language of the 'Shah-Nameh' than it does that of the works of the later Persian poets and of modern Persian literature.'[58] Layard, like Bunting, loved the Bakhtiari people,

> a splendid race, far surpassing in moral, as well as in physical, qualities the inhabitants of the towns and plains of Persia—the men tall, finely featured, and well built; the women of singular beauty, of graceful form, and when young almost as fair as Englishwomen. If the men have, for the most part, a savage and somewhat forbidding expression, it arises from the mode of life they have led from time immemorial. They are constantly at war, either among themselves or with the Persian Government, against which they are in chronic rebellion.[59]

Bunting wrote to Louis Zukofsky about his adventures with the tribesmen: 'My men became the envy of other units. And out of hours (and out of bounds) they entertained me every now and then as Bakhtiaris should, with pipes and drums, dancers and singers, sweetmeats and rice and strong drink, and a man to fan me all the evening – very welcome in the terrific heat of Khuzistan (139^0 in the shade – and it had been 145^0 a little earlier).'[60] Bakhtiari hospitality impressed Bunting. Asked to recall one meal that stuck in his memory above all others he had no hesitation: 'During the War I drove up to dine with some Bakhtiari in the mountains of central Persia. We began with alternations of tea and whisky and little sweet cakes for nine or ten hours. About nine o'clock in the evening we sat down to a large plate of porridge, followed by half a turkey per man, smothered in rice, followed again by a leg of mutton per man. Then we were allowed to retire to bed; a good thing, since I was half dead.'[61]

Bunting was mainly occupied managing a gang of labourers who were impressed to the point of devotion by Bunting's knowledge of their language and poetry and the fact that his children were named after national heroes and heroines. He was also busy interpreting evidence at courts martial, working from 4 a.m. until 7 p.m. in one of the world's most testing climates, regularly pushing 120^0 in the shade. He also had one of his periodic run-ins with the authorities, having become 'quite innocently' involved in what he described as a 'shindy' in the local town. His punishment, twenty-one days confinement to camp and fourteen days stopped pay, prompted him to ask to be reduced from his rank and transferred to another unit, but even Bunting didn't think that was likely.[62]

THE MEDITERRANEAN, 1943–1944

Bunting volunteered a little information about this part of his war to Jonathan Williams:

> I found myself in charge of a vast number of Luri workmen, and that was simple enough. I got on very well with them. We wandered about the country a bit, then went off in pursuit of the Eighth Army. We had to take in some shells, because it had become obvious that the Germans were not going to get down through the Caucasus while there was Stalingrad on the flank … They were simply unable to capture Stalingrad, so we could be spared. There was a hell of a great convoy of lorries full of shells waiting for anyone that would take them. Our squadron leader, without asking whether anybody

could drive or not said, oh, we'll take them. Then they found that by putting on everybody who had ever taken a milkcart a hundred yards down the street and by making all the officers drive, we could just manage. We had to take on a few Indian drivers as well to cross the desert. We set off and were a month getting from Basra to Tripoli. A month of very hard fare, yet one of those I've enjoyed most in my life. Seeing vast stretches of the desert; and from El Alamein onwards there was this vast pile in all directions of abandoned, broken arms, broken guns, broken airplanes, broken cars and lorries, lying about. One of the two or three most astonishing things I've ever seen in my life – I've described it in 'The Spoils.' As I said, we went to Tripoli, and one or two of us went as far as Wadi Aqarit, where the fighting was going on at that moment. There I was obliged to take a commission, which I'd never wanted, and I set off to Cairo.[63]

On 29 March 1943 Bunting was posted to Headquarters Middle East Command in Cairo for two months until he was discharged as an airman on 1 June and granted the commission he'd 'never wanted' the following day as Flying Officer on probation. On the day he received his promotion 982 Squadron was posted to Tripoli where Bunting and a friend apparently played an elaborate practical joke on their comrades:

> He and a friend were visiting some natives in the desert where they saw a strange looking tree which bore castor nuts, from which a certain useful oil could be pressed. They took a bag of the nuts back to the squadron and explained to the cooks that they were a delicate native spice used to flavor all kinds of food. The cooks believed the story and used the nuts wantonly. The next day, half the squadron spent most of their time running for the latrines while Basil and his friend slapped their knees with laughter. The culprits were discovered and reduced to the ranks, but Basil thought it was worth it.[64]

He remained in Tripoli for three weeks or so, long enough to witness Operation Scipio, the Battle of Wadi Akarit, before being posted with 229 Squadron to Air Headquarters Malta in Valetta on 21 June 1943. He spent fourteen months in Malta, moving to Krendi (a 'strange landing ground' according to Air Vice-Marshall Sandy Johnstone, with a runway 'constructed hard against the edge of a cliff'),[65] on 4 October 1943 and then to Hal Far on 10 April 1944, where he stayed until 16 August 1944. Along the way his promotion, to Flying Officer on probation, was confirmed on 2 December 1943. Johnstone's account of 229 Squadron's arrival in Malta shows just how ad hoc operations in the Mediterranean theatre could be:

229 Squadron had had an interesting career as it had arrived in Malta as 603 Squadron … after having flown off an aircraft carrier midway between Gibraltar and Malta. It had been their intention to make only a transit stop in the island for refuelling purposes before proceeding to the Western Desert where the ground crews of the unit, having travelled out by sea, were already waiting for their aircraft to turn up.

Intensive operations were taking place in Malta when they touched down and it was decided that the sixteen Spitfires would serve a more useful purpose on the island than in the Western Desert, so they were retained. Consequently, it was found there were two 603 Squadrons – one in Malta with aircraft, but no ground crews, and one in Egypt with ground crews, but no aircraft.[66]

229 Squadron ran Spitfire operations in Malta and Sicily, patrolling over Allied Cruisers and Destroyers and attacking enemy airfields in the region. On Christmas Day 1943,

in view of attacks on shipping it was decided to station one complete flight at Catania in Sicily. Eight pilots in 8 Spits of "B" Flight and the I.O. with 32 N.C.O.s and airmen in 2 Dakotas flew to Catania to form 229 Detachment. It is regretted the move took place over Christmas but all the airmen had an enormous Christmas dinner before climbing into the Dakotas. The ground crew welcome the change but the aircrew are not so eager, most of them already know Catania and the work of convoy escort is equally as tedious whether it is done from Malta or Sicily.[67]

The 'I. O.' was Bunting. This part of the war seems to have oscillated between intense activity and suffocating tedium for Bunting's unit. On the one hand he told Dorothy Pound that he had been responsible for arranging 'the "war-room" for Eisenhower for the Sicilian invasion, & then went over to Catania with a fighter-squadron: captured Cotrone [Crotone in Calabria] on my own initiative: in Naples during the fighting north of the City – I just missed being blown up by the delay-action bomb which destroyed the Post Office there.'[68] On the other hand the Operations Record reports many days in Sicily without a single operational flight,[69] and is occasionally reduced to reporting non-military issues in order to fashion a daily entry. On 14 January 1944, for instance, 'F.O. Bunting with two Italian sub. Lieutenants searched neighbouring peasants house for stolen blankets with no result except to make an impression. F/Sgt. Manley was requested to shoot a sick dog.

After passing through the dog the bullet ricocheted and just missed a high American Officer.'[70]

Bunting sent his own version of dealing with Catanian peasants to Dorothy Pound: 'When I wasn't busy with "warfare" in Sicily I was organising a peasant's market in Catania, tracing lost persons in Randazzo and Enna, or riding a motorbicycle up Etna. Randazzo really was bashed, by artillery, during a big battle. Some Maltese nuns got me to trace their relatives there, & so I am now being prayed for in perpetuity in two convents. I haven't noticed any good effects.'[71] He told Gael Turnbull, many years later, that he had swapped a bottle of Scotch he had got from Malta for two BSA motorbikes. His Spitfire mechanics equipped one with a pair of Rolls Royce Spitfire cylinders and he reached 110 mph on it on the airstrip.[72]

He described a life of intense attention to detail:

> De-briefing is taking a pilot's report and cross-examining him to compare what he actually did on a sortie with what he was instructed to do. In a Fighter Squadron, the Operations Officer and the Intelligence Officer are one and the same man. He receives a rather general order from H. Q and works out all the implications down to the exact minute of every detail, using not only all the official information he has on file, but also his personal knowledge of his pilots, their capacity & temperament. He then 'briefs' everybody concerned – passes on the now exact orders together with every scrap of useful information he can get – where the flak is, what the route looks like, what sort of bloke commands any enemy squadron likely to intercept them, & so on. He checks the planes as they go off, investigates crashes at take-off & reports to H. Q. When the sortie is over, he interviews each pilot separately and compiles an exact narrative of all that took place or was seen. That is the 'de-briefing', which has to be done like lightning and still remain perfectly accurate. It is good mental training: you can almost feel yourself getting shrewder in your estimate of men. I am glad I had a year of it (even though, in action, as we mostly were, you get hardly any sleep or food, being always at work), & I think it probably helped me in surpassing other political intelligence officers and minor diplomats who had not had any similarly strenuous training.[73]

One such debriefing occurred after a raid on Rapallo itself. 'It was a flight of Mitchells that first bombed Rapallo,' he wrote to Dorothy Pound after the war. 'They were sent to get the Zoagli viaduct but couldn't get into it because of weather conditions. One of them landed at Catania where I was, for the moment, in charge, and I had to de-brief the pilot. It was part of the preparation for Anzio.'[74]

The deaths of so many of these young pilots haunted the poet, and their ghosts made occasional appearances, as we shall see, in Bunting's post-war poetry. He hated having to record the details of their deaths as part of his duty.[75] A later letter to Dorothy, the main thrust of which was to refute the Pounds' 'redherring of anti-semitism', described the composition of 229 Squadron, of which he was Operations Officer, as 'extremely polyglot. You heard Czech and Polish, Belgian, Afrikaans, Yankee, Cockney, Maltese and Hebrew being spoken in the mess ... It was a Jew who was killed before he could be decorated after landing on an enemy aerodrome and carrying off one of his mates who had just been taken prisoner there after parachuting ...'[76]

Bunting's unit was clearly stretched:

> I found myself practically in charge of a unit working beyond its strength. The C.O. was in Malta, the Flight Commander always away. I had to take all responsibility. I've even signed documents as Medical Officer! ... I planned operations, interpreted orders from above, ruled everything, without official authority or backing. I even started and regulated a civilian market (not black but stripy), caught and punished thieves, traced a spy, instituted liaison with an Italian regiment. Between Xmas day and 1st April I had ten hours of liberty all told.[77]

It isn't surprising that his unit was this stretched if a story he told Gael Turnbull was true. At one point he was given half a squadron of Spitfires, half a squadron of Mosquitos and a free hand to clear the Adriatic of German reconnaissance planes. 'We did.'[78]

On 1 April 1944 229 Squadron left Catania by road 'and reached Messina, where it was accommodated in barracks'. After a day in Messina 'getting baths' the men were ferried to Reggio on 3 April in landing craft where they boarded a train to Catanzaro. The train stopped at Pellaro to enable Bunting and an adjutant, accompanied by the engine-driver, to buy a barrel of the famous local wine for the men. Unfortunately for them, according to the squadron's log, the two heroes 'having sampled the barrel too freely, sold the wine at a little over half price, to general satisfaction'. They continued by train to Naples for the next two days and then by truck to Bellavista where, on 6 April, 'by the hospitality of Professor Doctor Frollo, some of the officers made the acquaintance of certain Neapolitan young ladies who proceeded to make our stay pleasant'. On 10 April Squadron 229 left Naples on SS *Leopoldville* and anchored in the Clyde on 22 April, from where they went by train to Carlisle and Leicester on the following day. From 24 April

Squadron 229 covered the invasion of Normandy from an airfield near Hornchurch in Essex.[79]

The difference in conditions in different theatres was enormous. Bunting told Turnbull that in Sicily he had direct contact with Eisenhower during the Sicilian invasion, 'But they lost very few pilots at all. They were highly skilled. When Normandy came up, the squadron was taken back to England to do cover work and close support, because of this. "It was terrible. Even during the Battle of Britain, if a pilot did two or three sorties in a day, it was considered a lot. My pilots were going out six or seven times in a day. Working low all the time. They were just worn out completely, in no time. We lost nearly every one."'[80]

PERSIA 1944–1946

After a week at No.1 Personnel Dispatch Centre West Kirby in August 1944 Bunting was posted to Headquarters Royal Air Force Middle East Cairo on 22 August. He travelled to Persia on 8 September and joined the Combined Intelligence Centre in Baghdad, Iraq, on 29 September, though he continued to be based in Iran.

Bunting loved Persia, 'one of the most civilized countries in the world'[81] and Isfahan, the former capital of Persia, was his favourite city of all. By the time he left in 1946, after his first posting, he had trained a new generation of diplomatic Arabists: 'Got them on Shia theology, present position of darvish orders, family tree of the Qajar dynasty, detailed history of oil concessions, etc ... And the Tribal Map of Persia, the first thing of its kind ... There is no other Tribal map so detailed & careful, at least outside India.'[82]

Although the Middle East theatre was recognised as the key to victory for both the Allies and the Nazis, access to the rich oilfields being the strategic imperative, when Bunting arrived in Persia in September 1944 the British had been running a distinctly unimpressive intelligence operation in the region for five years, with four major stations, at Jerusalem, Aden, Cairo and Baghdad. In December 1939 John Shelley had been sent out to strengthen the Secret Intelligence Service's presence in the region, one of his key objectives being to establish a full SIS station in Teheran. At that point British agents in Iran, mainly British businessmen, were run from the Baghdad station, but businessmen were seen to be compromised by their desire to do nothing to offend the Iranian authorities that might affect their businesses, particularly running agents from Iran into the USSR. Shelley proposed that SIS should open permanent stations in Baghdad and in Tabriz in the north.[83] He spent a few months setting up the Teheran station which began operations in April 1940 and conspicuously failed to cover itself in glory:

> The first full-time representative, whose instructions were to concentrate on the Caucasus and South Russia, stayed barely a year, by which time little progress had been made in penetrating the Soviet Union. In April 1940 London asked Teheran to look into the possibilities of using as agents smugglers working across the Soviet-Iranian frontier. Evidently nothing resulted, for in January 1941 the Army Section at Head Office noted that the Soviet Central Asian Military District was 'a veritable "black spot" to us as 83000 [Teheran] has so far failed to obtain a single item of military information from this area'. It was hoped, however, that matters might improve as an additional officer had been sent out at the end of 1940 specifically to concentrate on Soviet military information.[84]

Persia was neutral at the outbreak of the Second World War. Ruled in authoritarian style by Reza Shah since 1925, Persia had imposed Western dress on its reluctant subjects but was not aligned to any particular Western faction. The culture, nevertheless, was pro-German and the Persian press was relentlessly anti-British.[85] Reza Shah was convinced that Iran was in some way special to Hitler as the home of the historic Aryans. As early as 1936 Hitler's cabinet had formally exempted Iranians from the Nuremberg Racial laws because they were 'pure-blooded Aryans',[86] a calculated political move that suggests that Germany foresaw the role that Iran might play in the coming conflict. After the war had begun the Germans promised Reza Shah that they would return oil rich Bahrain to Iran when they won.[87] Once the Soviet Union signed the 1939 Non-Aggression Pact with Germany the two sides worked closely to foment rebellion in Iran. In May 1941, according to Abbas Milani, the British Embassy in Teheran started to develop strategies to deal with the likelihood of a German or Russian occupation of northern Iran: 'In August 1941, the British Embassy reported that Germans had been "planning a coup" in Iran. Nazis had also found willing allies in leaders of the Qashgai tribes who not only helped hide two of Nazi Germany's spymasters – Berthold Schulze-Holthus and Franz Mayer – in their midst, but declared themselves ready to help a massive uprising in favour of Germany.'[88]

In 1941 a new head of station had been appointed in Teheran. The new man, Wilfrid Hindle, stayed in post until the end of 1942 but the ability of Teheran to ruffle feathers elsewhere in the security and military establishment was undiminished by his arrival. In August 1941 Iran was occupied by British and Soviet troops as fears of an Axis invasion of the country grew, and it appears that during this time intelligence took a back seat locally as the security situation required urgent stabilisation. By the time Bunting arrived, then, British intelligence in the region was at best patchy. Bunting told what is perhaps his longest war story in 1978:

> During the war I captured, for instance, a very famous German spy and I was asked, what should we do with him? I said, send him to Australia, he'll make a damn good immigrant, and this was accepted by the English government and the Australian government. Unfortunately our treaty with the Russians obliged us to send him back to Germany. But he escaped – we probably arranged for him to escape. That's the way we dealt with spies. Of course, when he was captured and being sent for interrogation and he asked me what was going to happen to him, I said, 'Of course we usually hang spies.' But nobody ever had the slightest intention of doing that sort of thing to him.

> But I captured an American girl once. She was a silly bloody girl. It's true that she had done extraordinary things, but always by the folly of other people, not because of her own cleverness. She came from Chicago and imagined that she could be like Mata Hari. She went off to Mexico City. She had no papers, so they chucked her straight out. She managed to get into Brazil and then into Argentina – still with no papers. Then she got to South Africa, where she managed to become the mistress of a British official. She at last got some information and she sent it to the Japanese – it wasn't very much. Then she went, with the help of the British official, to India. She couldn't do very much in India, so she arrived in Persia where she had the brazen cheek to go and make herself the mistress of an intelligence officer in the South of Persia and he sent her up to Tehran finally where she became the mistress of a man in the Embassy. I still hadn't heard of her yet, you see. Then one of my Russian colleagues in Isfahan said: 'There's a queer specimen coming down here this weekend. You'd better look into her.' I began making enquiries and we had her letters looked at and so on and here she was in constant correspondence with the Japanese to try and do down the United States. I'm sure it was purely a matter of silly girl vanity, you see, nothing more. But I caught her, as she'd obviously got to be stopped, and I sent her back to Tehran. My impression was, since we always treated all these people with extreme gentleness, that nothing much could happen to her. She'd get a spanking and go back to Chicago. But in fact we handed her over to the Americans and I was told that three days afterward they shot her. That's the way they behaved. We were absolutely frightened of them.[89]

Typically Bunting offered this insight into his war experience to illustrate the treatment of Pound by the American authorities after the war, rather than as an interesting story in itself.

Teheran was a tiny station and Bunting was in the thick of it. Iran was not a negligible theatre, however. Russian intelligence had probably exaggerated the threat of an Axis invasion but the Joint Intelligence Sub-committee believed that in the summer of 1941 the number of German nationals in Iran had reached five thousand, and that they constituted 'a very highly developed German Fifth Column' with well-advanced plans to exert pressure on the Iranian government.[90] The Iranian government continued to protest that its position was scrupulously neutral, but Italian intelligence gave a strong indication that Germany was talking to Teheran about the possibility of expanding Iranian territory in the event of a collapse of the Soviet Union and that, in any event, Teheran was strongly predisposed to Germany and would throw off the mask of neutrality as soon as German troops appeared in the Caucasus. The joint Soviet and British occupation was a way of getting the Allied retaliation in first. The primary objective was to ensure the expulsion of the German Fifth Column but protection of the oil fields and refineries and pressure on the Iranian government to adopt Allied-friendly policies weren't far behind.[91] German desperation for oil meant that an attack on Iraq and Iran was regarded as inevitable by 1941, although there was consensus that a complete Russian collapse was a prerequisite.

There can be little doubt that British security operations in the Middle East were a shambles during the war. The official history of the security services of the time points to an impossibly confusing chain of command in the region. The Security Service in London failed consistently to co-ordinate activity with the Security Intelligence Middle East (SIME) organisation, which was itself part of a separate body called Middle East Intelligence (MEIC). The problem was compounded by the fact that Iraq and Persia were handled by another organisation, Combined Intelligence Centre Iraq and Persia (CICI), which arose from the fact that for most of the war there were two commands in the Middle East, Middle East (MEF) in Cairo, and Persia and Iraq (PAIC) which was headquartered in Baghdad. There were many more layers in the swirling hierarchy of responsibility and command, but these alone are sufficient to demonstrate that Bunting was operating in impossible circumstances.[92]

You wouldn't recognise the old bum

After the war the deployment of British intelligence services overseas was directed specifically towards those countries that were deemed particularly vulnerable to the influence of Communism. In the Middle East, according to Keith Jeffery's definitive history of the service, 'beyond sizeable stations in Istanbul, Cairo and Jerusalem, SIS was pretty thinly spread, and tackling Communism in Iraq and Iran largely depended on liaison services'.[93]

Bunting, by now Vice-Consul in Isfahan, having been promoted to Acting Flight Lieutenant in November 1944, wrote to Zukofsky on 21 April 1945:

> my taste for variety has certainly been gratified in this war. I have been on almost every British front worth being on except Dunkirk, travelled through every rank from Aircraftsman First Class to Squadron-Leader (equals Major, to forestall your question), seen huge chunks of the world that I wouldn't otherwise have visited, been sailor, balloon-man, drill instructor, interpreter, truck driver in the desert, intelligence officer of several kinds, operations officer to a busy fighter squadron, recorder of the doings of nomadic tribes, labour manager, and now consul in a more or less crucial post.[94]

He was well placed. He described his situation to Karl Drerup:

> I am sure you would like Isfahan. My lawn is studded with bright flowers, just like a Persian brocade ... I have a nice Persian house built around a garden, and another garden opening from it, where there are fruit trees, and where I keep my five alarming watch-dogs. Beyond, there is a brook, and then more gardens – Isfahan is so full of gardens that from a little distance you would think the minarets rose straight out of a forest ... We go hunting – lie behind piles of stones near the snow on the mountains while the beaters surround and drive an enormous area of country, and the animals appear all of a sudden, and they may be deer or moufflon or ibex, or they may be a wolf, leopard or bear.[95]

Bunting was quickly well-connected in the region. He told Drerup that he had to know

> everybody of any influence in the whole of Central Persia – officials, rich men, tribal chiefs, soldiers – and I spend a fair amount of time travelling about the mountains and deserts in an old Ford as far as it will take me, and then on a horse or on foot. I not only see wonderful places and picturesque

people, I get a good view of mens motives, a much more varied view than is possible at home; and I step at will, as it were, from the present into the Middle Ages, from the Middle Ages into the age of the Nomads, and back again.[96]

Bunting was, once again, at the heart of the action. 'By some unlucky chance,' he told Zukofsky,

since the day I took over here, the centre of tension in Western Asia has been Isfahan, and my reports have had to be long, and I know that many were copied for the Ambassador and at least one went straight by plane to the Prime Minister. Not reports which I enjoyed writing, those. I have the impression that the situation in Persia, which has been kept dark for so far, is going to be made public soon, and though I don't suppose there will be any details given, you may be able to read between the lines of eventual newspaper reports what a strenuous time I've had.[97]

He quickly befriended General Abbas Garzan in Isfahan. Garzan, he wrote to Dorothy Pound, was a

queer and charming character: a good soldier, an honest official, with a sense of humour equal to anything that could possibly turn up, and no respect for snobbery or convention. He married a girl straight out of the local brothel, to the horror of the wives of his staff, and she was a kind and admirable woman. I helped him catch a gang of arms smugglers, and he helped me to the extent of making me almost (though not quite) free to use Persian military intelligence. And I think it must have been he who told Colonel Shivrani to lend me a cavalry horse and groom ... for the whole time I remained in Isfahan.[98]

He recognised the sudden change in his fortunes:

The missionaries and bankers treat me with respect and keep away from me. The Persian officials are good fellows ... and they and the landlords and the chiefs of the Bakhtiari tribe regale me with mounds of rice, acres of mutton steaks, and gallons of vodka at shooting parties, garden parties, receptions, dances and just plain parties without a label. Even the service, the niggardly old Air Force, provides me with a car and a house and four excellent servants, and pays for my drinks and cigarettes, and the Persian army lends me a horse and groom. I keep five large dogs and two sentries in and out of my garden, and altogether you wouldn't recognise the old bum in his present surroundings.[99]

Almost as soon as he arrived in Isfahan he tried to arrange for his daughter Bourtai, by now fourteen, to meet Omar Pound in Europe and travel with him to Persia. He wrote to Dorothy Pound in May 1947 that he was trying to persuade Marian to let Bourtai join him but she was 'proving a hard nut to crack'. His new boss was Sir John le Rougetel, who had a daughter, Bridget, about Bourtai's age. He liked le Rougetel already, although he later came to see le Rougetel as part of the problem of British engagement with the region rather than part of the solution.[100] Marian cancelled the trip at the last minute, after Bourtai's passage had been booked.[101]

Even when discounted for Bunting's proneness to exaggeration (or outright invention) his stories from Persia are still wonderful. He told Gael Turnbull, for instance, that when he was first in Persia

> one morning a man arrived at the door with a horse for him. Sent for his personal use by one of the Persian generals. Bunting had to apologise, that he could not ride. Then the message came back, 'We will teach you!' He attended the cavalry riding school, run by the acknowledged best cavalry teacher in the world. 'The first day we started off bareback, riding facing backwards. The next day we were standing up on the horse. It went on like that. By the end of the week, we were getting off and on the horse while it galloped. To finish, we all rode to the top of a steep mountain, and back again. Coming down the horses were sliding most of the way on their rumps. But I learned to ride! …'
> He saw two public hangings. One was of a doctor, who had murdered a lot of patients, for money. But he was away off at the edge of the crowd, and there really to keep an eye out for undercover agents. The other was a rebel who had been a ringleader in a conspiracy. He had helped to uncover the plot, and had to attend as the official British representative. 'They did it from one of the city gates. Just drove a lorry underneath. He choked to death. It isn't very pleasant at all.'[102]

Gael Turnbull told Michael Shayer about how Bunting

> once slept with a Persian whore at the expense of His Majesty's Government, to get information about the Russians … And Michael tells me of, at the Rutherfords, some talk of sexual morality and he tells of a visit to the head of the Shi'a sect of Islam, in Iraq, on official business. A very saintly man, who has since become so venerated since his death. 'He entertained me very well. A full set of courses, and wines, and coffees. And then he asked me, "Do you prefer girls or boys?" It was only right he should.' Apparently, too, he *did* enjoy that hospitality.[103]

Bunting's job in Isfahan was clearly dangerous, but danger was one of the few subjects that he never felt any compulsion to embellish. He played it down to Zukofsky:

> the Persian government insisted on providing me with a guard of soldiers (I was vice-consul and credited locally with the most hairraising anticommunist performances) which I found a nuisance. An English newspaper (Reynold's) without even Tass to inspire it credited me with an attempt to burn down the city of Yazd and massacre the inhabitants ... Sometimes the soldiers didn't recognize me and I had trouble getting into my own house: and there was dismay when I fetched a Russian consul home to dinner. The danger (of me being assassinated) was, I think, imaginary, though they did have a shot at one of my colleagues (Communists did). I wore a pistol after dark for a week or two, out of deference to the Chief of Police.[104]

He even played down the danger he caused to himself:

> I have just distinguished myself by smashing my car twice in one month, after never having had an accident of any sort in my life before. The first time I hit a mis-lighted lorry in the dark, the second a wheel came off when it was travelling at high speed on a very busy road, and though I failed to kill anyone, the car ultimately turned over and gave me a bang on the head which kept me dazed for three days. I fear the insurance agent has ceased to love me and will buy me no more free drinks.[105]

Bunting's appointment as Flight Lieutenant was confirmed on 16 January 1946 but by June he was on his way home with the rank of Acting Squadron Leader. He wrote to Zukofsky from a transit camp in Cairo:

> So my responsibility for telling our two governments what happens in Western Asia – between the Jordan and the Indian border, between the Hadhramaut and the Ukraine – is ended at last. So are the pleasant journeys ended, amongst mountain tribes, long trips on horseback, moufflon hunts, banquets with provincial governors and cocktail parties with diplomats ... All the tribesmen had the same question: 'Why are you taking these officers away from us? Who will be left to understand the Kurds and tell the Powers what we need?... The Bakhtiari sent a note to the British Govt asking for my return to Persia.[106]

Given what happened to the Kurds in the second half of the twentieth century this is prescient. Victoria Forde quoted this letter to Zukofsky in her short life of Bunting and when Bunting read the proofs he wrote 'modestly' to her saying, '"I'd rather have all this omitted … It sounds too presumptuous altogether." But he had written these same stories of life in Persia to others. They had sounded so amazing to his daughter Roudaba that not until much later did she realise that the lavish banquets with the tribesmen in the mountains, the princes he rode with, and the exotic animals he wrote about, the leopard which jumped onto his lap, were not just fantastic stories for her amusement.'[107]

Bunting readily acknowledged that the war had been good to him. He told Peter Quartermain that it 'did me a lot of good: it gave me confidence, assurance in myself as a man of action; it gave me power of decision under great responsibility. It gave me authority: I learned my Wing-Commander-act.'[108] Bunting's various reflections on his war show a man at ease with his contribution:

'War … an activity which has pleasures of its own, an exercise of certain faculties which need exercise: in which death is neither a bugbear nor a consummation but just happens.'[109] And, 'freedom from war, like freedom from poverty, can be pursued at the expense of things better worth preserving than peace and plenty, of which, I should say, the most important, and the most threatened, is personal autonomy'.[110]

Many years later he told an interviewer that 'I can say with complete immorality that I enjoyed the war very much. I managed throughout to keep things lively for myself.'[111] He told another interviewer about the challenge of performing with the Northern Sinfonia Orchestra, reading his poems with the music of Vivaldi, Corelli and Albinoni: 'I will be reading some of my poems, of course, at the concert. But not being a trained opera singer, I cannot throw my voice softly. That is why mechanical aid is needed [i.e. loudspeakers]. Otherwise I think I would manage all right. I used to have to bawl orders at 600 men in South Africa during the war, and I was for a time a sailor as well and used to plenty of hailing.'[112]

It is hard to reconcile this dynamic self-possession with the life he led in the twenty years that followed his expulsion from Iran in 1953.

Ezra … indomitably out of date

Bunting had disappeared from the literary world during the war years leaving barely a bubble at its surface. Pound wrote to the Japanese modernist poet Katue Kitasono from Rapallo on 29 October 1940: 'Any news of living authors would be welcome. Gornoze what's become of Possum and Duncan and Angold or the pacific Bunting.'[113] As the war ended he was making the same complaint. He asked Robert Duncan on 24 January 1946 if there was 'any news of Bunting or Nancy [Cunard] or anyone',[114] and he reported to Dorothy Pound on 31 January that there was 'still no news of Basil ...' On 2 April 1946 he told William Carlos Williams that he knew 'mostly who's alive and who's dead = but no news of Bunting or of Nancy Cunard'.[115] By this time Pound was incarcerated in a psychiatric ward in Washington DC.

The following month he told Dorothy that 'Jas [Laughlin] thinks Basil was on a trawler – Oh hell. I thought it was groundwork @ air base.'[116] He complained again to Dorothy in late March and again in early May about the lack of news of Bunting's fate.[117] He wrote to Dorothy's son Omar on 3 May 1946 that 'Navy or Air Force ought to trace Basil (best Eng. poet of his decade)',[118] but Dorothy told him later that month that 'Basil can't be traced unless we can give his date of birth & the ship he served on – Somebody will hear abt. him I suppose, in time.'[119] By 1949 even Bunting was complaining about it. He wrote to Margaret de Silver: 'I am losing track even of my more personal American friends. Only Zukofsky writes regularly, and Dorothy Pound passes on the news from Ezra's loonybin. I've lost track of Archie Roosevelt somewhere in the Levant. I've not heard from Drerup for ages. I think Carlos Williams has forgotten he ever knew me.'[120] He'd had no time to write letters but wouldn't have written even if he had the leisure because, as he wrote to Drerup, 'it is so easy to give away secrets unintentionally'.[121] Moreover all this action had driven literature from Bunting's horizon entirely. He told the poet Robert Creeley that 'I regret the time I waste on earning a living, but not the sea and the desert and the unremitting need of knowing facts, calculating character or forseeing [*sic*] the run of events. If ever I met a poet (English or American) in Persia or Arabia or Cyrenaica I never knew it: we talked about rainfall, tribal movements, the price of whisky, where the game has gone, anything except literature.'[122]

Pound had been having a bad time. He had been broadcasting pro-Axis propaganda from Rome since 1935 and had been indicted for treason in the United States in July 1943. As the war ended the US authorities were put in an awkward position. The administration was legally obliged to prosecute Pound but the situation was complicated by Pound's high profile, doubts about his sanity and the fact that, in reality, there were rather more pressing issues confronting the nation. On 24 May 1945 Pound was arrested and taken to a US prison camp near Pisa where he was treated with extraordinary brutality. He began to write the *Pisan Cantos* while housed in one of the death cells, a six-foot wide steel cage with a concrete floor and no shelter from the blistering heat, no communication with other prisoners and in the glare of powerful floodlights that kept him from sleeping at night. He was kept in inhumane conditions in this 'Disciplinary Training Center' until the middle of November, when he was transferred to a jail in Washington DC. An intricate legal battle ensued which centred on the issue of whether or not Pound was sufficiently mentally stable to stand trial. In December a psychiatric report by four doctors judged him unfit to plead and he was transferred to St Elizabeths Hospital on 21 December, and there one of the finest literary minds of his generation was incarcerated for the next twelve years, during which time a struggle for the very soul of Ezra Pound developed, conducted by his friends and lawyers but fuelled by the hatred the two women in his life, his wife Dorothy and his mistress Olga Rudge, felt for each other. At its peak St Elizabeths housed over eight thousand patients. As we shall see the British political establishment used Bunting very badly after the war but maltreatment of cultural heroes was not a uniquely British embarrassment. However un-American his activities, however disgusting his anti-Semitism, the US authorities' persecution of Ezra Pound was a shameful dereliction of cultural duty, robbing the world of one of its great geniuses, albeit a flawed genius.

Bunting was willing to help but was doubtful of the likely impact. In a letter of 19 October 1946 to William Carlos Williams Zukofsky copied part of a letter which Bunting had written to him:

From Bunting:

'Please ask Bill Williams to convey to Dorothy that I will do anything for Ezra that may be in my power: but that I don't think there is anything in my power. Let her have my address and tell her my mother often wishes to hear from her. We cannot help Ezra by asserting his literary value. In fact, the only defence likely to go down with a tribunal would be, that he was so easily tricked & outwitted by Fascists of high position who ministered to his unfortunate appetite for flattery: and I daresay that would be too humiliating for him to own to. Otherwise, so far as I can see, they must endeavour to prove him mad: an untrue defence, but it could easily be supported from his eccentricities.'[123]

Bunting wrote to Dorothy in November 1946 offering to use his contacts as best he could on Pound's behalf, but he was far from confident that any action could succeed in the prevailing climate:

> The US public has made up its mind that he is guilty, & must, if possible, be allowed to forget him, before anything effective can be done … My power to help is very limited indeed. I have very few contacts at all. The best would be Archie Roosevelt, but he is not at present in America: through him, we might ultimately be able to get Eleanor's [Roosevelt] powerful help, but I think, only after Archie returns & after a longish time for the public to lose interest. I am pretty sure Archie would trust me, & I believe the Roosevelt family think a lot of him. I don't think it would be any use for me to approach Field-Marshall Wilson: he would listen attentively to what I might say about Iraq or Persia, but probably not on any other subject. Eisenhower wouldn't remember me – I only actually met him twice.[124]

Pound, apparently annoyed, annotated this letter. He underlined the word 'guilty' and put two question marks in the margin.

'Ezra – in correspondence – seems indomitably out-of-date', Bunting wrote to Zukofsky in January 1947.[125] They seem to have tried to put their disagreements of the 1930s behind them. In March 1947 Bunting wrote to Pound's daughter, Mary, newly married to Boris Barrati, that he had received 'an ebullient note from Ezra, wishing he could have a job on my (imaginary) "staff" in Teheran. He would enjoy Persia, I believe: a country where they still make beautiful things by hand. But I am myself a hard mouthful for the Russians to swallow (an "international reactionary") and I am afraid Ezra's sudden appearance in a country they covet would be altogether too much for them!'[126] Bunting's generosity of spirit is striking, considering the abuse Pound had directed at him over the years. He berated Zukofsky for his principled refusal to visit Pound. Pound was

> an old man in distress, who seems to look to me and Eliot for a kind of help no one else can give him. Omar says his father waits eagerly for letters from me, and is quieter for days after one. Well, how could I hold back? Eliot describes him as the same, except that all the eccentricities have become exaggerated tremendously. Of his two or three letters to me, the greater part was so incoherent as to be incomprehensible. Eliot says he does not realise his situation in the least. He refused peremptorily to let me approach the Roosevelts or Lord Wilson to help in getting his conditions eased a little, at a time when I could have done so with some prospect of success.[127]

A little disingenuous this, in view of the letter he had written to Dorothy Pound six months previously.

THROCKLEY, 1946–1947

As the war ended Bunting, back in Throckley, was considering his options. These were writing for a living ('unpleasing'), settling in southern Italy (he liked Policastro and the villages near Reggio and Cotrone) or 'out of political cussedness' in Andalusia or Spanish Morocco. Sierra Leone would have been nearly perfect but too expensive and Persia best of all but 'the Russians would kick up such a row'.[128] He told Zukofsky of a plan to buy a boat and sail to Sierra Leone, Greece and Malabar.[129] He also told friends[130] that he was planning (and had apparently begun) a book about his experiences in Persia. It is a great pity that this was never written as Bunting captured the charm and eccentricity of Persia beautifully in letters. In December 1946 he wrote to Ezra Pound lifting scenes and anecdotes, seemingly at random, and weaving them into a memorably exotic narrative:

> sitting in judgment in the mountains, in support of the Ilkhan, in an embroidered tent pitched in a grove by a spring, and while the shaggy plaintiff was expounding his case there was a leopard slowly crossing the snow field on the mountain opposite: or capping quotations from the older classics with the aged Poet-laureate and an ex-Prime Minister, by moonlight, in a garden, with girls passing the wine: or Shalamzar, the palace of the Ilkhan of Bakhtiari, under a prodigious alp, remote from all roads, where the largest carpet I have ever seen is also one of the finest, & the few chairs have little mirrors set in them and the huge ceiling is of polished walnut: but everybody sits on the floor and the darvish outside, in his wolfskin with his two headed axe over his shoulder, sings a long ballad about the magical deeds that were done in – 1943! There are also Ra'is Touma's Assyrian trousers – sky blue, wide, short, with a spray of roses embroidered on each cheek of the arse, which he wore with dignity – And the Mujtahed's funeral, with the horse-tail standards, the black banners of the Abbasides, & the men scourging themselves with chains while dancing before the corpse: and the six horsemen who apologised for stopping my car: 'We were only waiting to murder a man, your Honour', and they did murder him an hour later … the Armenian archbishop of Jerusalem swapping cups with me & drinking first to demonstrate the absence of poison.[131]

This is heady stuff. We lost a great travel writer when Bunting decided that he could no longer risk the Persia book. His account of his journey from London to Teheran is a catalogue of rich incidents:

I flew to Cairo – a little less noisy without the troops – visited a friend at Ismailiya, where we got caught by a fierce sandstorm, out on the lake in a very tippy dingy – flew to Baghdad, more old friends, including the ferryman who embraced me: Abbas Hilmi, the anti-British stalwart of the Arab League, who cheerfully informed me that he was in Baghdad without papers, though he is still 'wanted' for his share in Rashid Ali's rebellion. Behauddin Pasha gave me a fine lunch & told queer Kurdish stories. And I went again to one of those indescribable music halls, where you leave your rifle at the door but pistols are allowed, and are often used either to criticize the performance or argue with a man on the other side of the balcony. Then by car to Teheran – two very long days of high passes & deep gorges. The Irani Kurds were on the move – luggage tied on to the sheep's back: the men dressed in their best – striped peg-top trousers, sash, very white shirt with very long sleeves turned back & tied over the jacket sleeve, the jacket tight, very short, in contrasting stripes, & the heavily fringed black turban over all: with rifles & cartridge belts. The women wear turbans too, and a rather shapeless frock open down the front to below the navel, so that you see their great udders going floppety flop as they jog along with a load on their head & a child on their back (but the young girls look very nice that way). The little boys wear carbines, & to me their faces always look like those of Edinburgh urchins – freckly, blue-eyed, oval. At one place we disturbed thirty or forty vultures eating a dead donkey. They lurched to the side of the road all together, too full of corpse to fly, and others who had been circling overhead swooped down to take their places, even before the car was past ... I haven't looked up my old friends here yet, but happened to meet one of the Bakhtiari Khans in the street, & got a surprisingly warm welcome. I believe he was really very glad to see me. I also, conforming to Persian custom, had my Friday picnic in a garden near Demavend village, by a stream, huge mountains all around: jug of wine (or anyway vodka) and all that, but no 'Thou' to sit beside me in the wilderness, only a ragged boy who made my tea & brought me meat and eggs.[132]

If he had had the opportunity to thread these observations and anecdotes into a narrative of mid-century Persia it would probably be the definitive account today, he understood the country and its people so intimately. Bunting knew though that the Foreign Office would do its best to prevent him publishing a book on Persia because so much of his experience there was gained on secret business in the service of the British government, although it's difficult to see what more he could have lost. As we shall see, the British government didn't cover itself in glory when he left its service. He wrote to Ezra Pound in March 1947: 'I saw Eliot the other day, & promised to keep in touch with him. I must drop the book I began on Isfahan – can't afford to be "indiscreet" now. But I may get time to do some writing nevertheless. Eliot says: poems. Perhaps: but tranquillity is hard to get – He was kind and very friendly.'[133]

If Britain lost a significant travel writer to the Official Secrets Act it lost an even more significant diplomat. Bunting wrote an extraordinary twenty-page letter to Zukofsky in November 1946 in which he described the politics of the Middle East in such intimate detail that one imagines it can only have been written for posterity. He couldn't possibly have imagined that Zukofsky, who had barely stepped out of Manhattan for the previous twenty years, would be interested in these tales of Bahrain, political intelligence work, Basra, slavery and piracy, orientalists, oil, the Kuwait–Iraq dispute, the role of the Americans in the oil dispute, the source of disputes, the facts that have been distorted by media, the Arab world's indifference to comfort and Western theorists' assumption that it was a priority, the fact that economics are irrelevant to the Arab mentality, the problem with newspapers, the lie campaign against the Poles, a thousand of whom had been in his care in Isfahan. Eighteen pages into this spectacular diatribe he pauses for breath and with deep, if unintended, irony writes: 'Dear Louis, you must be bored to tears by now. I have no news.'[134]

I am for thwarting the government

He might have had a good war but it changed him utterly. In 1946 Pound tried to incite him to edit a magazine. Bunting gave Dorothy his reasons for not doing any work of that kind in a letter on 10 December 1946 that is heavily annotated by Pound's pencil. It is a long statement of a new Bunting. Although we have been able to follow his activities during the war it hasn't been possible to follow his development in the same way as he was incommunicado for such long stretches of it. We have barely heard from him since we left him complaining to Zukofsky and Drerup about having no war work early in 1940. He emerges in this letter to Dorothy Pound with newly felt responsibilities: 'I want, if convenient, to earn a living, so as to help my children through their education. Bourtai thinks in terms of the University, Roudaba wants to breed horses ... I don't think Marian can provide all this unaided.' More fundamentally though divorce and war had altered him permanently:

> the circumstances under which Marian got first a separation and then a divorce, so that I was completely cut off from my children, reduced me to a state in which it took all my resolution and ingenuity to keep alive and sane. Unexpected success as a soldier and as a minor diplomat set me up again, but did it by bringing out things in me that could hardly have been suspected before, at least by me. In short, it is not merely that I have had more experience, but the experience has been different in kind. I no longer feel, as I did in 1938, that I have nothing to say, but I do not know, except in some details, what it is I want to say, and I don't think I shall know for some time yet to come ... our old preoccupations now seem to me very out-of-date. I cannot go back to them if I wanted to. I do not like what has happened and is happening, but to revive, for instance, Douglas, would seem to me like pretending that nothing really had happened. So that if I were to produce a paper now, I am afraid it would be one of which Ezra would not approve. (I am for thwarting the government – all the governments, especially the more powerful and effective ones: and for not reforming backward nations: and for pushing economics out of the limelight for a century or so; and limiting free compulsory education to reading, writing and 'rithmatic.)

Perhaps that final sentence contains the seeds of some of the tensions ahead. Governments didn't necessarily want operatives who secretly wished to thwart them in the great post-war rebuild. Another reason for not editing a magazine was Bunting's disillusionment with poetry:

> Leave out the various shams, and the rest all leads to Zukofsky, and nobody can read Zukofsky! Yeats, Ezra & Carlos Williams; Eliot; Marianne Moore; are all in a sense stages on the road to a degree of subjectivity so extreme that, in Zukofsky, it fails to realise that there is an outside world which will necessarily fail to understand ... [Pound's] conspicuous success must convince him that the road is the right one, even for those who go much further along it than he has done. The little magazines in general just wallow in its dusty ditches, without a trace of Ezra's metric skill or Zukofsky's logical consistency. Clearly I am not the right person to rally them.[135]

Pound annotated this letter so heavily that reading it is almost like overhearing their conversation. Bunting would have been surprised at how much Pound actually agreed with, and less surprised at the intemperate tone of his disagreement. 'It is a shame that this is all so negative,' Bunting wrote, 'for

I would have liked to oblige E.P.' 'To hell with the personal angle', Pound raves from the margin.[136]

In the end he decided to 'use the lump of money they gave me to buy a boat and to live again at sea – it's cheap there – and to write. But, before I could get anything done, the Foreign Office stepped in with the offer of a job, and it would probably be well paid and I had to take it.'[137] He told Dorothy Pound in January 1947 that he was negotiating the price of a yacht, 'just small enough for me to manage alone, & large enough to live in fair comfort with a number of the more necessary books.' He planned to take *Idonea*, a twelve-ton ketch, to the Mediterranean the following year.

The Foreign Office had written to him in 'vague terms' about returning to Isfahan but he was distrustful, believing that the government was trying to get someone with private income for the job to 'do the work for less than it costs ... Firdusi won't impress them. The old fashioned cultured diplomat survives in the "Levant Service", but not in Downing Street. Sir Reader Bullard valued my knowledge of Persian poetry, and might put in a word for me if they consult him, but his successor as Ambassador doesn't know me except as a name at the foot of uncomfortable "appreciations".'[138] There had been a prospect of a new Vice-Consulate at Behbehan which was going to be offered to Bunting so he could keep an eye on the Kuhgalu tribes but he wasn't disappointed that the scheme fell through. 'I don't love barbarians for their barbarism,' he told Dorothy, 'and there would have been little else at Behbehan.'[139]

The Foreign Office finally offered Bunting a post in Isfahan but the salary was insulting, £990 ('or £90 more than is paid to a fairly good mechanic') for a job that involved 'much entertaining & constant travelling'. Bunting had spent over £2,000 per annum during his first posting in Isfahan and claimed not to have been extravagant as his two predecessors had each spent about £3,000. Prices in Persia had risen by 1000 per cent since 1940 but the Foreign Office didn't seem to want to acknowledge that.

He turned the job down and bought the yacht, although the rationing system made provisioning it impossible as you could not buy ahead in 1947. He asked Dorothy Pound to send some 'unsolicited parcels', which he would pay for, to get round this problem.[140] He had nearly provisioned *Idonea* – the shopping list he sent to Dorothy is a post-war rationing horror story that included tinned butter and tinned bacon but, mercifully, 'Spaghetti (not tinned)' – when the government offered him a job in Teheran at a sensible salary (double the previous offer, although he claimed that 'they' cut his pay by £1 a day in April 1948),[141] and he jumped at it. He wrote excitedly to Dorothy on 20 February 1947 that he would 'live in sight of Mt. Demavand – 19,000 feet of pure snow cone'. Isfahan it wasn't but he was delighted with the appointment and planning the acquisition of a new rifle, 'something capable of stopping a bear or a wolf'.[142]

Perhaps, as Carroll Terrell observes, the letter from the Bakhtiaris had worked.

TEHERAN, 1947–1950

Tea, we drink. They don't understand coffee, they are one of the five great tea nations, and their tea is very good indeed. After putting the boiling water on the tea they keep the pot very hot in the embers of charcoal, and pour out small glasses of it, diluted if necessary, and take a piece of smashed sugar-loaf (or sometimes an acid-drop or similar boiled sweet) between their teeth and suck the tea through that … tea is protocol here. If you visit an official you drink three glasses of tea, very hot, before getting down to business: and you give him three glasses of it if he visits you. A round of visits such as you must make at the Persian New Year is a test of tea-drinking capacity. I have had fifteen glasses of it in one afternoon.[143]

Bunting's job at the British Embassy in Teheran was immense. He was 'chief of all our Political Intelligence in Persia, Iraq, Saudi Arabia, etc.'[144] in the world's most explosive theatre. The job required intense 'astuteness and tact' as he wrote to Zukofsky in May 1947.[145] Nonetheless he longed for a less abstracted life, something more tangible. He wrote to Dorothy Pound in May 1948:

I like a new landfall, certain graces of men and trees and hills, the greased leathern hides of Zulu girls, the lack of cupidity in remote places and places grown out-of-date, Portuguese sailor's shirts. I like the monkeys to be in the trees, not on chains; bougainvillea; the banyan; the snake-guarded wild bananas in bush you must cut as you go; a life more physical, less logical, less covetous, less distilled out of the past, than the chained life we lead. That's why I enjoyed the war, why I love a barbarian girl, why I hate earning a living.[146]

He was unable to afford a house in Teheran itself and moved instead to a village seven miles from town and fifteen hundred feet above it. 'It's a nice enough building,' he told Dorothy, 'with a pillared terrace in front and a big garden. The diningroom and drawing room are run into one, intended to be separated by a curtain, but by leaving it as it is I have a huge room with only a pillar in the middle to divide it.'[147]

Bunting found himself at the heart of the British establishment and he was never going to be entirely comfortable there. 'Friction with the Embassy nabobs is very severe,' he told Dorothy in the same letter. 'I wouldn't be surprised to be chucked out. There are two particularly pompous, self-complacent, hollowskulled jackasses, who are in the two places next to the Ambassador, and one or other of them is sure to be able to dish me in the end. They have made it impossible for me to work effectively and very difficult to remain courteous. And I never saw such a jumble of petty jealousies before.' He must have prevailed in his battle with the jackasses however. Six months later he wrote to Dorothy to report progress: 'I can claim a sort of victory in the work. I have really done what was never even attempted before, and done it well enough to astonish my diplomatic bosses into (probably temporary) respectful attention, so that my personal status here has improved out of all recognition in the past two months.'[148] After the British Ambassador in Iran, Sir Reader Bullard, retired in 1946 Bunting believed he was the only employee of any Western government who understood the region.[149]

His letters of this period, particularly those written to Louis Zukofsky, are full of lurid tales and chance encounters at the edge of civilisation. Describing a trip to Luristan he recounts how he ran into some highwaymen:

> Luristan is full of castles inhabited by the same old robber barons the history books dilate on. My car broke down in sight of one such castle, and three pretty ruffians came out to collect the spoils. I was alone, but I was able to bluff them. I had in my bag an American insecticide which is sold under pressure in a case very like a hand grenade, and which hisses when you open the valve. I persuaded them it was a sample atomic bomb which I was taking to the Embassy, and that, since I didn't really understand its mechanism, it was liable to go off at any minute. They swallowed enough of that to retreat to a considerable distance, where they watched till the car got under way again. The conversation took about twenty minutes, disagreeable ones, for I had a diplomatic bag with me, and to have lost that to robbers would have been a serious business … And on the top of a hill the car surprised a young girl having a bath in a puddle. She snatched up her frock to put it on, but the wind filled it and carried it away, and we last saw her chasing downhill like a gazelle stark naked after her only garment.[150]

You can't imagine that he was making this stuff up.

One of these letters to Dorothy Pound also contains the first indication of a turn in Bunting's emotional life. An old friend and colleague, Ronald Oakshott, had settled in Isfahan while Bunting was in Teheran. He had married a young Armenian wife and her two younger sisters lived with them in a household that lacked any trace of the 'conventions which we have got so used to that we have forgotten that they are merely conventions'. It was a simple lifestyle:

> Beds, for instance are places where you sleep, and when you feel like sleeping you get into the nearest one, irrespective of who else may be there already. Clothes are for warmth and for making a show in the street, and when you are at home and the room is warm, you take off as many of them as makes you comfortable, without the least regard to how much of yourself you exhibit. The vodka bottle gets into very strange places. Work is very like Nausicaa's washing-day 'What shall we do today? Let's wash the clothes.' – a kind of play that never seems to grow stale and become a burden as household chores do in Europe, and that is always mixed up with singing and often interrupted by dancing, and never has to be done on time or against the grain. These girls are peasants, of course, born in a Kurdish village, and perhaps more Kurdish than Armenian in everything except their religion, which sits on them very lightly. Their ambitions are simple and obvious – to see Teheran where there are so many cinemas, to acquire a gold bracelet, to have a ride in my car. It is restful to be among people who are happy and unhampered, who have so few wants and make so few demands on one. I wish I had the sense to marry someone of their sort.[151]

After Oakshott died in the early 1950s Bunting painted a memorable picture of his friend's lifestyle for Louis Zukofsky:

> From the other side of the compass I am asked to compose an epitaph for my old friend Oakshott, Sima's plus que père, who died drunk a couple of years ago. Banking was his trade, intoxication his calling. He distrusted cars, but would sniff out any bottle within walking distance and had sworn to reduce Persia to Islamic obedience by emptying every bottle in the land. He died with his task less than half accomplished but it has since happily been taken up by the Minister of the Interior … He drank not less than six bottles of brandy during a day's journey from Mosul to Suleimania and at the end of it received the local notables flat on his back in the middle of the vice-consular sittingroom without the slightest loss of dignity or scandal. I was there, officially superintending the move … His dog bit a piece out of the seat

of my trousers and a larger bit out of the leg of an Iraqi colonel, but even that didn't mar the occasion.[152]

Oakshott had been 'a substitute for a father to Sima [one of the sisters] as long as she could remember' and his friendship with Bunting clearly facilitated a romance, which had developed considerably by April the following year. He had taken a week's holiday in Shiraz and Persepolis with two 'Saqis', the two sisters, 'with one of whom I intend to commit matrimony if the gods permit ... I only realised how deeply I love her while we were in Shiraz and quarrelling about the amount of wine she insisted on swallowing.'[153] That week he met the national champion nose-flautist 'who kept making the most beautiful noises in the room next door. He said it was the spirit of the kisses he believed Sima and I were exchanging.'[154]

There are the alps

His reflections about the change wrought on his life by the war and its aftermath, by the 'circumstances that obliged me to abandon the reflective life for the active one, as seaman and airman and diplomat, and I have no doubt gained something by the change, but I have lost a lot ... action is a lust that is hard to abandon',[155] indicated that he expected to write nothing, or nothing of interest, until he lost his job. In fact, however, he wrote some memorable poetry in the second half of the 1940s.

'Search under every veil', written in 1947, seems to draw on his experiences in the Middle East but is applicable to any society:

Search under every veil
for the pale eyes, pale
lips of a sick child,
in each doorway glimpse
her reluctant limbs
for whom no kindness is,
to whom caress and kiss
come nightly more amiss,
whose hand no gentle hand
touches, whose eyes withstand
compassion. Say: Done, past
help, preordained waste.
Say: We know by the dead

they mourn, their bloodshed,
the maimed who are the free.
We willed it, we.
Say: Who am I to doubt?
But every vein cries out.[156]

He told Zukofsky that the change of weight in the middle of this poem
was deliberate: 'up till then I have only a stock sentimental poem which I
attempt to raise suddenly onto another level altogether. The fact that you
don't grumble at the sentimental beginning is quite possibly due to what is
thus reflected back from the end, which I think I couldn't have got in the
same light movement.'[157]

'See! Their verses are laid', written in 1948, has a deliberate muscularity
in its opening lines:

See! Their verses are laid
as mosaic gold to gold
gold to lapis lazuli
white marble to porphyry
stone shouldering stone, the dice
polished alike, there is
no cement seen and no gap
between stones as the frieze strides
to the impending apse:
the rays of many glories
forced to its focus forming
a glory neither of stone
nor metal, neither of words
nor verses, but of the light
shining upon no substance;
a glory not made
for which all else was made.[158]

Zukofsky objected to some of the vocabulary in 'See! Their verses are laid'
and Bunting agreed that 'impending' is 'weak, but I couldn't find what's
wanted', but he defended 'shouldering': 'What's the word for quarter of the
solid formed by the rotation of an elipse on its axis, and has it an adjective?
"Shouldering" probably has for you moral echoes which haven't worried
me. I meant it just physically, in which sense it is exact.'[159] Bunting clearly
felt that he had been too oblique in 'See! Their verses are laid' and felt the

need, unusually, to add an explanatory note to *Collected Poems*: 'A friend's misunderstanding obliges me to declare that the implausible optics of this poem are not intended as an argument for the existence of God, but only suggest that the result of a successful work of art is more than the sum of its meanings and differs from them in kind.'[160] Thomas Cole detected Yeats' 'Lapis Lazuli' somewhere behind 'See! Their verses are laid'.[161] There is a clear thematic link, but for all its charms 'See! Their verses are laid' is not 'Lapis Lazuli'.

He was also busy translating and adapting from Persian 'All the teeth ever I had' and 'Came to me' from Rudaki,[162] 'Shall I sulk because my love has a double heart?' from Manuchehri in 1949, and 'Last night without sight' and 'This I write' from Sa'di.[163] Twenty years later Bunting used a reading of 'Last night without sight' to illustrate his contention that Orientalists and translators had overstressed the mysticism of classical Persian poetry:

> When you hear people talking as though the Persian poets were all mystics and thought of nothing but mysticism, in fact what it means is that the selection of Persian poets dealt with by European orientalists are mostly mystics, but they are a very tiny section and a very uncommon section of Persian literature. In fact Sa'di, who is read by westerners to some extent, had a piquant mixture that you can twist and make them sound mystical, was in fact not mystical in the least.[164]

This is a translation from Sa'di but surely the spirit of Yeats' 'The Song of Wandering Aengus' is never far away from it:

> Last night without sight of you my brain was ablaze.
> My tears trickled and fell plip on the ground. That I with
> sighing might bring my life to a close they would name
> you and again and again speak your name till
> with night's coming all eyes closed save mine whose every
> hair pierced my scalp like a lancet. That was
> not wine I drank far from your sight but my heart's
> blood gushing into the cup. Wall and door wherever
> I turned my eyes scored and decorated with shapes
> of you. To dream of Laila Majnun prayed for
> sleep. My senses came and went but neither your
> face saw I nor would your fantom go from me.
> Now like aloes my heart burned, now smoked as a censer.
> Where was the morning gone that used on other nights

to breathe till the horizon paled? Sa'di!
Has then the chain of the Pleiades broken
tonight that every night is hung on the sky's neck?[165]

Zukofsky included two fragments of Bunting's translations from Sa'di

Night swallowed the sun as
the fish swallowed Jonas.

and Lucretius ('Darling of Gods and men...') in his *A Test of Poetry* in 1948.[166]

Bunting's major achievement of the 1940s, however, was not a translation but a generous tribute to the friend with whom he had fallen out so badly ten years previously. 'On the fly-leaf of Pound's Cantos', written in 1949, is a moving, if slightly Ozymandian (in the hostage-to-fortune sense), monument:

There are the Alps. What is there to say about them?
They don't make sense. Fatal glaciers, crags cranks climb,
jumbled boulder and weed, pasture and boulder, scree,
et l'on entend, maybe, *le refrain joyeux et leger*.
Who knows what the ice will have scraped on the rock it is smoothing?

There they are, you will have to go a long way round
if you want to avoid them.
It takes some getting used to. There are the Alps,
fools! Sit down and wait for them to crumble![167]

'Once,' Bunting told an audience in 1982,

in the period when you were supposed not to say a word to anybody for many years, Pound sent me a little tape which he had spoken. It had a small amount of letter on it, and then having exhausted what he had to say I suppose, it wasn't much, he started reading my poems. He read them very well, and he read them right through until he came to 'the fly-leaf of Pound's Cantos'. And then he started it, and half way he got stuck. He started it again and he got stuck half way. He started it a third time. He said 'God damn it. I can't!'... he had obviously felt this as an enormous compliment.[168]

There is no doubt that Pound thought Bunting had paid him an immense compliment. When Denis Goacher visited Pound in St Elizabeths Hospital in 1954 Pound told him that Bunting had written a small amount of extremely good poetry, 'some of which I even remember'. Then, according to Goacher,

> he brought out his copy of the collected *Cantos* up to that date, because he had been re-reading them for the purposes of *Rock Drill*. There was, in front, a letter from Basil Bunting containing his poem 'On the fly-leaf of Pound's Cantos', which begins 'There are the Alps'. Pound took out this letter, in which Basil had typed out the poem, and when he read this to me, he broke down in the middle of it. He couldn't finish it because he was so upset. It is not often that one poet gives another poet as great a compliment as that.[169]

Bunting was enjoying life, although Margaret de Silver wouldn't have guessed it. She wrote to Bunting in 1948, prompting a reply from Teheran that rekindled their correspondence for several years. The subtext of these letters seems to be an attempt by Bunting to emotionally blackmail Margaret into renewing her bursary from the late 1920s. By this time he had been on a payroll of sorts for eight years and yet, even though the salary was 'nominally good … they juggle with it so wildly that I have actually grown poorer instead of richer during my time here'.[170] It seems inconceivable that this could be the case given he was not supporting his two children and had not at that stage remarried. Indeed even the remarriage was a problem:

> I've been working, and the work has got sillier and sillier, more and more futile delays, bureaucracy gone mad. In addition I've been illish, not in bed but near it. Brrr. Grrr. Finally, Sima has changed her mind and doesn't want to marry me after all, which is depressing, even though she may yet change it back again. She was an unexpected stroke of fortune in my middle-age, and now I feel like the chap who hears that he has won the lottery, and then that they have made a mistake over the number and he hasn't after all. I believe I told you about Sima – very young, beautiful, barbarous (Kurd and Armenian), without any of the usual assumptions and inhibitions. She was bound to get tired of me in time, but I'd hoped it might last a few years.[171]

He wrote on the same day to Dorothy Pound that colleagues had been congratulating him on his 'escape' from Sima; she would have acted as a brake on a career that he neither wanted nor sought. 'Just another savage won't do,' he told her. 'It was the particular brand of barbarism.'[172] When his secretary saw his face after Sima left him, she locked up the small arms and hid the key.[173]

He told both Margaret and Dorothy that he was considering not renewing his contract when it became due in March 1949, the work was so life-sapping. 'If I had just a little more money ...' He believed that he had a few poems still to write, 'but I'll never get them out unless I stop working for the government'. It isn't very subtle. A year later he wrote again. Margaret's heart must have sunk even further at the dismal opening: 'My dear Margaret, When shall I get a little leisure again?'[174] By then he had married his 'wild girl' and had left the embassy as a consequence but the weariness of this letter is overwhelming:

> In a few months now it will be ten years since I had any rest at all except the few months of demobilisation, when I was looking for work. From 40 to 47 I had just over fourteen days leave and worked mostly at tasks far more continuous and often more strenuous than fell to most men. From 47 to today I've had a period when it was necessary to waste a certain amount of time, not to employ it sensibly or for pleasure, and a longer period now growing intolerable of work at a pressure equal to that of the war in its more strenuous phases. Since February this year I have had two days precisely in which I was free to do what I fancied – no Sunday off, no Friday off – and most days I have worked more than ten hours, often fourteen or fifteen for weeks together. It is stupefying. When I look back without actually tasking my memory I can remember only the few hours here and there when there was nothing official to be done – walks ashore in Scotland, amongst the bushes by the river at Ahvaz, through the bush at Durban, shooting in the mountains over Isfahan ... I spent sixteen hours every day under a sun dispensing 145 Fahrenheit in the shade chasing around driving Bakhtiari workmen to greater efforts ... sat for three twelve hour tours and one of seventeen hours every four days at the telephone collating the reports of the Sicilian landings ... rose at five and worked until the night raiders came home about midnight or later every day at Catania ... worked, as they told me, an average of eighteen hours a day for over six weeks at the beginning of the invasion of France, until for lack of sleep I nodded off riding my motor-bicycle down the runway of the airfield.[175]

If only, he seems to be musing, I knew some wealthy patroness of the arts who could relieve me of all this Sisyphean toil so I could buy a boat and read.

I'm getting too garrulous

On 2 December 1948 Bunting married Sima Alladadian, a Kurdo-Armenian from Isfahan, at the embassy. Bunting's profile locally was high; the Persian press went 'all gooey over my marriage and splashed baseless romances all over its columns for several weeks, and I haven't resented the silliness'.[176] There followed a six-week honeymoon in England. 'It was amusing,' he told Dorothy Pound in a letter in April 1949, 'to see how it struck someone who had never been in any city bigger than Teheran, nor ever seen the sea nor ridden in a train. We spent all our money on clothes. I think the Times printing office made the biggest impression, closely followed by Kew.'[177]

Bunting had anticipated problems with the Foreign Office eight months previously. He told Dorothy Pound in April 1948 that the FO would

> not approve and may forbid. There is a new law to discourage the bloody slaves my compatriots from marrying foreigners by refusing to give their wives citizenship, so that they become stateless and have to find Nansen passports. Above all, the difference of manners and habits makes what is a suitable and right match in Persia very shocking for the English community, so that I shall not only marry a Wop or Wog, but also a child by their standards, and be accounted a Nasty Old Man. But Sima who is actually fourteen (though we have agreed to call it sixteen to appease the English) would probably have been married to a still older man at least a year ago but for some odd circumstances which have left her the ward of an ageing, hard-drinking ex-British officer 'gone native'.[178]

Marriage forced Bunting to leave the Foreign Office and he became the Iran correspondent of *The Times*, although he suggested to Zukofsky that he had left the embassy of his own accord.[179] It could be, however, that the Foreign Office was concerned that Bunting had himself gone native, and not just by marrying a Persian wife. In May 1967 Bunting wrote a letter to Dorothy Pound that contained an early version of the poem 'Under sand clay', a poem that touched on desert politics. The poem mentions Bunting's first encounter with the Aneiza tribe without hinting at the turbulent politics underneath. 'Abdulaziz Ibn Saud was a member of it, and brought up in the desert,' he explained to Dorothy.

> I have an unbounded admiration for that last of medieval kings, who tried so hard to reconcile kingship with his conscience. When Rashid Ali escaped

to his court, Abdulaziz had a fearful problem. (a) The then all-powerful allies demanded that he should be surrendered (b) Abdulaziz abhorred Rashid as a rebel against kings, who should help each other (c) If he didn't surrender him, it might mean war against both the Hashemi kingdoms, Iraq and Jordan, both backed and equipped by the allies. (d) The Qur'an is silent about refugees. BUT (e) sanctuary is an ancient, sacred custom, and if God as author of the Qur'an says nothing about it, that's because he took it for granted that everyone respected the custom. So the king argued with himself, with his advisers, with his ambassadors here and there. His telegrams at that time were apt to begin with long prayers to almighty God. In the end he did right, pensioned Rashid at the risk of ruining his kingdom and destroying his dynasty. I don't think he ever really hesitated. He delayed announcing the decision, partly from dread of the consequences and partly till he was sure that he was getting the best terms that he could from God for doing right. There were many similar struggles, though that was the most striking and important. (It never occurred to any of these old barbarians that international law would protect the protectors of a refugee.) Don't ask how I know all this. The facts might as well be public, but the evidence is still very secret. I tried to minimize allied pressure on the old ruffian, and I don't think it was ever really severe; but he feared it.[180]

The suggestion that Bunting may have been using his influence in support of local, tribal rather than strictly British ends may have curtailed his career for these were not merely tribal squabbles. Although if you take out the word 'telegrams' this account could have come straight from Ferdowsi, in fact it describes momentous power struggles at the heart of the world's most turbulent and politically sensitive region, events that continue to reverberate to this day. The intimacy with which he recalls the main protagonists shows that Bunting was at the heart of it. 'There are other men,' he told Dorothy

> I'd like to get into verse somehow; but their qualities seem to need something more argumentative and expansive than poetry. Nuri as Saed – his wisdom needs demonstrating, an historian's task. Behauddin Nuri, who found all men funny, and so managed to be the most tolerant and gentle of Arab statesmen. The cunning of king Abdullah, like a story from the Dark Ages, original, naïve, without any conscience at all (which prevented him from having the kind of success Abdulaziz had). And Morteza Quli Khan, the aging barbarian revolutionary, who ordered his clothes from St. James's Street, but refused to wear a collar and tie with them.
>
> I'm getting too garrulous.[181]

Bunting's friendship with some of the most important politicians in the region shows that he had been operating at the highest political level throughout the Middle East, not just in Iran. A coup in Baghdad in April 1941 overthrew the pro-Allies' Regent, Abd al-Ilah, who had largely been controlled by the Prime Minister Nuri al-Said. Nuri fled to Jordan and the Iraqi nationalist, Rashid Ali, immediately forged an alliance with Nazi Germany, prompting a British counter-coup in May which reinstalled Nuri al-Said as Prime Minister in the British occupation. Rashid Ali fled to Germany while he negotiated with King Abdulaziz ibn Saud for sanctuary in Saudi Arabia. The pro-British Nuri signed the Anglo–Iraqi Treaty in 1948 sparking off angry popular demonstrations in Baghdad. The six-year British occupation of Iraq was bad enough; a treaty that gave the British even more influence over Iraqi affairs was deeply unpopular. Bunting may have thought that Nuri al-Said's wisdom needed demonstrating but to his countrymen he was little more than a traitor, albeit an enormously powerful one.[182]

King Abdullah of Jordan certainly was 'cunning'. He had been agitating since the 1930s to turn 20 per cent of Palestine into a small Jewish state while merging the remaining 80 per cent into Transjordan, as it then was. When this move failed he entered into secret negotiations with the Jewish Agency for Palestine in 1948 over the partition of Palestine, still with the aim of annexing all of Arab Palestine, a plan that was supported by the British government. When the state of Israel was established in May of that year Abdullah joined a pan-Arab military assault on it. By 1949 however he was back in secret negotiations with Israel and his compromise, the annexation of the West Bank into what was now Jordan left a disastrous political, military, cultural, religious and social legacy that continues to fester to this day.

Morteza Quli Khan whose clothes came from St James's Street belonged to the Duraki clan which had ruled the Bakhtiari tribe continuously for nearly four hundred years. From 1934 he was the supreme tribal leader of the Bakhtiaris and one of the richest and most powerful men in Iran. In 1939 Reza Shah, in an attempt to curb Bakhtiari power, launched a legal case against Morteza Quli Khan to force him to sell all his considerable property to the state but he delayed it for long enough to be rescued by the Allied invasion of Iran in 1941. When the war ended Morteza Quli Khan was still Governor General of the Bakhtiari province, still the richest tribal leader in Iran and still a personal friend of the Persian celebrities of the day.

Bunting's friends were the most important men in the region. The nature of his work is well illustrated in a letter he wrote to Dorothy Pound in September 1948:

> Talking of opium, last night I supped with a colonel of police and an ex-governor general of one of the southern provinces, who, after much vodka and endless kebabs, produced the most sumptuous opium outfit I have ever seen – the charcoal in a chased silver brazier, the pipe of the finest porcelain, and ebony, in a soft leather case embroidered with silver thread, the tongs of silver, etc. etc. A special carpet, very fine, was brought for the brazier to rest on. I smoked my two pipes as I always do when these people press me, and I am getting quite skilful in manipulating it.[183]

He might have become skilful at manipulating it but not necessarily of mastering its effects.

> Once I and a couple of friends – one of them happened to be the head of the Persian Secret Police at that time – were smoking opium round my stove in my living-room and drinking vodka, drinking tea and smoking another pipe when the stove went out. Now in Persia the usual way of lighting a stove is to pour paraffin over it and just light the paraffin. We forgot that the coals all being still hot and the thing full, when you poured paraffin in, would carburette on its way down and when you put a match to it would cause an explosion. So the thing did explode – little bits of the stove flew in all directions – very nearly cut off my friend's head – and all the curtains and carpets and hangings everywhere were on fire and we sat there without moving, laughing ourselves silly at the sight of it while the servants came in and put the fire out.

One has to wonder how funny it seemed to the servants, who hadn't spent the day drinking vodka and smoking opium. 'That's the effect of opium,' he continued with unintended irony, 'Nothing more exciting than that, it's cheerful.'[184]

The Times is bellowing

Bunting blamed institutional racism for his departure from the embassy, but Tom Pickard has speculated that the Foreign Office may have considered that Bunting could better serve British interests as a journalist and that it was the embassy itself that was behind his move to *The Times*. They would have been aware that *The Times* had no local correspondent and getting their own man into the job would have made it easier to present the British point of view as objective reportage. Bunting wrote to Charles Deakin, Foreign Editor of *The Times*, in early November 1948 to ask if he needed a correspondent in Iran, as the newspaper hadn't had a man on the spot for some time.[185] Two months later he told Deakin that he had 'reason to suppose that my appointment would not be unwelcome to our Embassy and that I could hope for their help in appropriate matters'.[186]

According to his employment file Bunting began work for *The Times* as special correspondent in Teheran on 28 January 1949 on a salary of £350 per year, with £50 towards his travel expenses. The work was harder than embassy work, he told Margaret de Silver in September, but it got him out from behind his desk: 'I spend a fortune in petrol and am as handy in the Teheran traffic with a big car as any of the taxidrivers from constant practice. So I get about three times as many interviews into a morning as I could on foot, feeding the afternoon and evening session at the typewriter.'[187]

For all his complaints, he had more free time at *The Times* than he'd had for years. In February 1949 he and Sima visited a friend who had a camp in the mountains, helping him make a bridge across the river between his camp and the road and then going hand-net fishing. This was a regular visit. The previous year he described short weekends at the camp where 'the vodka is too plentiful, but the river is cold and very fast, just melted snow from the summits. And the fish is fried in batter and tastes excellent.'[188] On another occasion they had a picnic by another river in even higher terrain, 'with a stream far too fast and cold to bathe in, under white mulberry trees, the mulberries dropping over us as we sat'. On this occasion there was a bull tethered nearby which 'snorted only for the fun of it and was friendly beneath the conventionally fierce exterior'.[189] On another occasion he drove to Isfahan and back and had a morning free to eat 'the excellent kebab at Nejafabad and bought their cotton sandals there and watched Sima and her cousin trying to catch fish in the Zayandehrud by hand and tumbling in'.[190]

Robert Payne visited Bunting in the spring of 1949 during a cultural mission to Persia sponsored by the Asia Institute of New York, and acknowledged that he owed 'a special debt to Mr. and Mrs. Basil Bunting of the London *Times*, who allowed me to keep them awake at Teheran over their own Scotch whisky on too many nights'.[191] Payne had asked a Persian poet to describe the Persian sky and was told to 'think of a waterfall of blue wine in the sunlight':

I spent days bathing in this waterfall in the garden of an English poet not far from Shamran, up the sloping road which eventually loses itself in the snows of the Elbruz mountains. It was a small garden, full of dying roses, for summer was coming on. There was a red-tiled swimming-pool, and the poet was credited with possessing the best cook and the best collection of whisky in Teheran. He possessed a passionate love of Persia, translated their poetry superbly, knew many Persian dialects and thought the world and ambition well lost as long as he could remain in his garden, with his exquisitely handsome Armenian wife, his books and his pipes ... He had quelled a German-aided revolt of the Bakhtiari tribesmen almost single-handed, and to that extent he may have altered the course of the war, for the Germans were within an ace of succeeding in creating a foothold in Persia. I had heard about him in China. Ezra Pound had said once: 'If I was a younger man, I would go to Teheran just to see him.'[192]

In the same piece Payne also relates a conversation he had with Bunting, which demonstrates his love for the Iranian people

'The people are entrancing. There is nothing in the world like them. I don't know what it is – a strange mixture of licence and dignity. They live their lives without subterfuges; they have all the dignity of the desert Arabs without the Arab hysteria. It is the only place in the world where it is impossible to be bored. Do you remember the inscription on the tomb of Hafiz:

"When thou passest by the head of this tomb, invoke a blessing,
For this is a place of pilgrimage for all the libertines of the world."

They are gay and charming and effervescent – much more than the French. They know their own minds. They have decided what is due to God, and what is due to themselves. And they cannot be completely serious: as soon as they make the effort, they realise how ridiculous they are. They give the impression of knowing all the answers, as perhaps the Chinese do, and so they play, even when they are most miserable.'

Bunting liked Payne immediately, or at least he told Dorothy Pound that he did, but he may have been being polite as she had introduced Payne to Bunting.[193]

In fact Payne's book annoyed Bunting and his position had hardened considerably by March 1953 when, desperate for work, he told Zukofsky that he wouldn't contact Payne: 'He is too fantastic a fool and too unblushing a charlatan for me to be indebted to him.'[194] He wrote in despair to Margaret de Silver in May that he wished he 'could write impudent nonsense like

Robert Payne who seems to get at least a living by it'.[195] And by 1979, 'If you can find six consecutive words in his piece,' he wrote to Tom Pickard, 'which do not contain a lie or imply one I'll be astonished ... He visited Persia for fourteen days with a party of old women, and wrote a book about it within a few weeks of getting home. He knew nothing, cared nothing, kept his eyes shut tight for fear a fact or two might put him off his stride.'[196]

As if to illustrate precisely Payne's point, however, in June 1949 Bunting told Dorothy Pound a wonderful story that again suggests that Bunting would have written a pungent book about Persia:

> A friend of mine – another Ezra [Horesh] – was returning from my house to the city in a small open car, when he was hailed by an Arab crying 'Stop'. He didn't stop, whereupon the Arab began to abuse him thoroughly in his own language. As it happens, Ezra is bi-lingual in Arabic and Persian, so he stopped the car, beckoned the Arab over, and hit him on the head with the handle of the jack. A police car which was passing took both of them to the police station and before the magistrate. The magistrate asked: 'Why did you hit this man on the head with the handle of a jack?'
>
> Ezra said: 'Because he abused me.' The magistrate asked: 'What did he say?' Ezra told him. The magistrate turned to the Arab and asked: 'If someone said this to you in Baghdad what would you do?' The Arab said: 'I would rip up his belly.'
>
> The magistrate gave sentence: 'I cannot let you off. You were seen to hit this man over the head with the handle of a jack, so I fine you the minimum, five tumans. If you care to pay twenty tumans you may hit him over the head with the jack itself.'[197]

These were good times for Bunting and he expressed an unusual degree of contentment in his correspondence. Zukofsky wrote to William Carlos Williams from Brooklyn on 3 June 1949: 'A letter from Basil after visiting Meshed with his young Persian bride and the Sanctuary there "done in mirror work", along with two poems not weaker in gusto. He seems to lead an enviable life tho he says all the American journalists descended on him more or less together after he came back to Teheran.'[198]

After intelligence work journalism seemed fatuous, little more than gossip. 'Here it is hot,' he complained to Zukofsky in June 1949 'and distinguished visitors keep me from my rest, chasing the news about them. Does anybody really care if the Regent of Iraq had dinner with the Prime Minister of Iran?'[199] It was high level, colourful gossip though:

Nasr. Khan Qashqai turned up at a party yesterday: first time I've seen him in four years, looking large as well as cunning and rather goodhumoured, with a hooky nose and incongruous brown eyes à la cow and a suit that didn't fit him at all. I forget how many hundred thousand nomads he thinks he governs, but a lot of them go their own way and he has to make the most of it. A few years ago the tribe was really run by his thirteen year old wife, a girl of fierce and indomitable passions, sharing the name of my daughter Roudaba ... And the Prime Minister, always the Prime Minister, with his arabesque of whisker, shaking hands all round and wondering each time 'Who the devil is this now? I ought surely to know' and disguising his ignorance with a clever set of politenesses designed to find out whether he ought to ask after the wife or who. I like the upright old Turk, and have more respect for the contents of his skull than I used to.[200]

By August he was beginning to despair. He told Zukofsky that without Sima

there'd be nothing for me in this life beyond the contact with Persia which helps to clarify Persian poetry here and there ... Do you know I've worked seven days every week (except one when I worked six) And twelve to sixteen hours every day since February? That's almost as strenuous as the war, and without any such motive. The prospect of even two or three days break has practically disappeared. Sima suffers by my overwork, too. I have no time to play ... The Times is bellowing for two long articles, the Abadan Daily News is waiting for its weekly column, there are a dozen shorter items to be sent to Near and Far East Agency, and I have promised a report on local opinion to the Embassy ... I have to make up the time we lost by obeying the royal command to be part of a huge crowd having a magnificent supper with King Abdullah of Jordania, which lasted hours and hours at my busiest time: but Sima was pleased because the little King ... spoke to her and to no other female, and because there was a good puppet show and some very good Armenian dances, and because she astonished some Kurds by addressing them in their own language ... I was bored, even by the whisky, but it was Sima's first taste of splendours.[201]

And by September he was finished with it. 'I am bogged down in the price of cotton piece goods and the prospects of selling steel rails and other bloody nonsense. My ancient hatred of journalism was well justified.'[202]

The good times were coming to an end. A three-day trip through the forests of Mazanderan and 'over the spectacular pass from Chalus'[203] wasn't much compensation for the fact that Teheran's charm was beginning to fade.

With only seven free days since the previous February he was beginning to feel that his time was up, especially with Sima eight months pregnant with their first child. Money was becoming short and he calculated that by March his earnings would be the equivalent of the salary he had paid his chauffeur when he had that luxury at the embassy. He tried to find work with the Anglo Iranian Oil Company but discovered that it applied strictly a policy of not recruiting anyone over the age of forty. He summed up his employment prospects in a burst of prescience:

> Roughly, from the employer's point of view, I am a man who was a writer, with a little political experience in extreme youth, very varied journalistic experience (but none in the office), a successful military career, some years of diplomacy and the prestige of the 'Times' job here. I am an 'expert' on the Middle East, on literature and on counterespionage … none of which is awfully urgently required in business. It is held that the high positions I have filled disqualify me for subordinate ones, which is unfortunate. I have 'administered' a fairly large organisation (however I hate administration). Might be a very good policeman or professor or leader-writer or reviewer (though by now bored with most books). I know by experience that my political judgment is much shrewder than most mens, that I can detect, often where others cant, that I can write very clearly about complicated matters and remain interesting, that I am capable of long periods of extremely hard work … and that I cannot sit in an office for very long without chafing.[204]

His diagnosis was accurate and his condition would blight the next fifteen years of his life.

Meanwhile, in February 1950 Sima-Maria Bunting was born, Bunting's first child with Sima. Sima had insisted on Maria so Bunting 'stuck Sima on in front to distinguish her from ten million other Marias'.[205] Finally in April 1950 he told Dorothy Pound that he would return to Britain in three days time: 'I lost (chiefly through the sin of not having joined twenty years ago) the job which provided most of my money, and the Times had none worth mentioning, though Hugh Astor swore that he would make them at least double my pay.'[206] Hugh Astor was then deputy Middle East Correspondent for *The Times* and since his father was the proprietor and Chairman of the newspaper he was in a good position to fulfil his promise. At this time Bunting hadn't fallen out with *The Times* and he wrote of Astor as 'a pleasant young chap with a brain'.[207] Given his subsequent treatment by *The Times*, and the fact that Astor was on the board by 1956, it isn't surprising that he makes, as we shall see, an unflattering appearance in *Briggflatts*. In spring 1950, however,

Bunting was looking to ingratiate himself with the Astors in order to secure future employment at *The Times*. He went so far as to 'wilily' import into the UK caviar and vodka for Hugh's father, John Jacob Astor, 1st Baron Astor of Hever, these being 'about the only things a millionaire can't buy in England – and I hear he was pleased, but that only improves prospects on the Times'.[208] A year later he told Dorothy Pound that he had received an invitation from Astor and again couldn't go.

> It's wonderful what a little caviar & vodka will do to a millionaire oppressed by an inherited conscience. I think he looks on Ezra Horesh and Abufazle Solimani-Kashami as the picturesque figurines in the corner of a bleak canvas. It was a dark tea-house at the foot of a pass, in violent snow, surrounded by huge mountains. The lorry drivers were singing over their tea after lunch. Solimani had vodka, the place supplied opium, in every lull you could hear the unhappy jackals outside. A change from Carlton House Terrace & Cliveden. And the idea that Solimani, so little lawabiding, was a colonel of police, crowned Astor's enjoyment.[209]

He broke his journey to Throckley in London where Eliot was 'invisible, wrapped in rehearsals'.[210] 'T.S.E. said to have become very frail,' he told Zukofsky. 'I've missed seeing him, unfortunately, in spite of his apparent anxiety for a meeting. It may be managed this month. I gather he has something to say or discuss that wouldn't go adequately into writing. I've not seen him for several years and have no clue to what's on his mind.'[211] Perhaps he didn't have much on his mind at all: 'Eliot went off to the USA after feeding me at the Café Royal. Conversation rather more malicious than it used to be, but good.'[212]

Poems 1950

Bunting's second collection, *Poems 1950*, was assembled by Dallam Flynn (or Dallam Simpson) and published in 1950 by Cleaners Press in Galveston, Texas. One of Pound's disciples, Flynn published Bunting at Pound's instigation. Bunting claimed that he had virtually no connection with its publication, but he told Dorothy Pound in April 1949 that he was busily typing up a 'lot of stuff that isn't in the Active Anthology to send him'.[213] He certainly didn't have much to do with it. It's inconceivable that he would have missed the misprint he complained about to Zukofksy: 'There are a number of misprints: few vexing. But the metamorphosis of fiends into friends is rather startling. Not a good omen, one would suppose. Perhaps the reverse would be worse.'[214]

Asked by an interviewer many years later how he became involved with Flynn Bunting replied: 'God only knows, I don't. I was in Persia and thinking of anything rather than literature or poetry or publishing when I got a letter from Texas offering, nay begging, to be allowed to do a volume of my work and I saw no reason why not; and that's all. I only set eyes on him once in my life, several years later.'[215]

Faber and Faber refused to publish a British edition of *Poems 1950* unless Flynn's bizarre preface was removed. It features a sustained attack on John Berryman that seems to have no place in a preface to Bunting's poetry, and is more or less unintelligible throughout. Flynn, for instance, claims that 'The Complaint of the Morpethshire Farmer' 'in an instant explains away four centuries' of decadent verse, and leaves us supporting a somewhat vapid bellows, from which, a rather pyrexial feline has just bounded'.[216] Pound's daughter (by Olga Rudge, not Dorothy), Mary de Rachewiltz, described Flynn as 'mad as a hatter and physically a hybrid of Errol the actor, Red Eric and Ezra Pound'.[217] Bunting, however, while not admiring it (he told Dorothy Pound that it completely baffled him[218] and he told Gael Turnbull that when he saw Flynn's preface it came as 'a nasty shock'[219]), felt that, as Flynn had taken the trouble to compile and edit the book, the preface should remain. As a result, Faber and Faber never did publish Bunting's poetry, an omission that should finally be rectified in 2014. Pound certainly felt that Eliot was at least partially responsible for Bunting's neglect. In 'Canto CX' he explicitly linked it with *The Waste Land*:

> Bunting and Upward neglected,
>   all the registers blacked out,
> From time's wreckage shored,
>   these fragments shored against ruin ...[220]

Hugh Kenner wrote a substantial review of *Poems 1950* for *Poetry*, considering that 'of these 54 pages some five may or should enter the corpus poeticum; a way of saying that Bunting's subjects and treatment have an interest outlasting the age in which they were conceived'.[221] Bunting was quietly pleased with Kenner's review. He had seen the proofs and wrote to Dorothy Pound in August 1951: 'not unintelligent reviews, though like most reviews of anybody, apt to chase irrelevancies ("influences", "content") and look only obliquely at the shape and texture of poems which are, after all, as much manufactured objects as a teapot or a dance tune'.[222] Bunting was rightly sensitive about the apparently unavoidable mention of Pound's influence on his work. As he frequently complained, if you grew up with Eliot, Yeats and Pound how could you not be influenced? It didn't mean that you couldn't have an individual voice.

Louis Dudek described Bunting as 'a gifted poet … who has been writing for twenty years without due recognition … The poems have real impact. Rarely, one reads a book which makes one, in desperation, almost give up writing. This is the effect of Basil Bunting … The whole poetry breathes a liberated personality that could not be smothered by any influence.'[223] Vivienne Koch thought the collection moderately impressive although 'one would be happier … had Mr. Bunting excused his prefacer, Mr. Dallam Flynn, from writing one of those Poundian and crack-pot essays which only the Master – who really had the wit – could bring off.'[224] Thomas Cole celebrated Bunting's 'easy, fluent line' and 'bare beauty … It is difficult to believe that the poetry of Basil Bunting has gone uncollected until this excellent edition appeared … Bunting's poetry can hold its own against any England has produced these past fifty years.'[225]

We tend to see *Poems 1950* as a failure (the literary world hardly noticed it) but it was an important milestone for Bunting, and he wasn't entirely ignored in the 1950s. Selections of his poems were read on the BBC's Third Programme in November 1954 and in July 1957.

ITALY, 1950

Bunting returned with his family to Throckley in May 1950 and stayed with his mother. He was offered a job by an Italian newspaper syndicate as foreign correspondent but lack of newsprint soon closed this opportunity and the following month they were back in the north east of England. Peter Quartermain suggests that when Bunting lost his job on *The Times* in 1950 he was immediately sent to Italy by the British Foreign Office 'to stop a Russian takeover but some fool from the embassy met him at the plane and blew his cover'.[226] He would have got this from Bunting and there is no way of verifying it.

Bunting told Zukofsky in November that he had with some difficulty persuaded the Westminster Press, which owned fifteen regional newspapers, to employ him as its first foreign correspondent in Italy,[227] but that before he left he was required to spend 'a bloody six weeks of senseless, pointless, useless drudgery' in London learning the newspaper business he already knew.[228] At first he felt that *The Times* had been generous: 'The Times was awfully nice about it and paid my wages after I came home until I found another job. Since I hadn't given them above a week's warning of the move, I think that was bloody generous.'[229] He had brought with him some fresh caviar for Astor but didn't think that was a factor. His attitude to *The Times* was to change sharply in the coming months.

The Buntings drove from Newcastle to Rome, a long and tedious journey with a new baby, and rented a 'villattino' 'some way from the sea and out of sight of it, but with a view of the Alpi Apuana when it isn't raining';[230] 'rather a nice house', he told Zukofsky, 'belonging to a marchesa who unfortunately wants it back again as soon as the weather improves in May'.[231] It was the start of a hectic period for Bunting. 'I have just got back from Milan,' he told Dorothy at the end of November, 'driving far too fast over the Cisa pass in a fog, and leave tomorrow for Siena, and thereafter Garda. That will be followed by Rome again, and I may also have to make a trip to Sicily before I get time, sometime in January, to look in at Rapallo ... I see little except the surface of the road and the cyclists who get in my way: and even in an inn I just gobble my spaghetti, swig my wine, and away again at 60 mph, no time to talk or taste.'[232]

He was busy in Italy but at least beginning to re-engage intellectually. He corresponded with Pound about a proposed series of translations from Oriental classics mainly, he told Zukofsky, to 'give EP something to think about. Nothing can come of it. At present he's rushing after it most magnificently. Especially since I revealed that Arabic historians aren't totally blind to economic and currency problems.'[233] Bunting put a fair amount of effort into something that was conceived only to give Pound something to think about. In December 1950 he sent Pound, Bertrand Russell, Ahmad Suratgar, Arthur Waley (a celebrated Sinologist but also a member of the Bloomsbury Group, so despised by Pound and Bunting) and the Arabist, G. M. Wickens, the draft of a prospectus for the proposed Oriental 'Loeb' and asked for their permission to use their names as a 'provisional and (I hope) temporary committee'. He was aware that this was not a committee that would have fallen together naturally: 'If any of you does not entirely like the company you are asked to keep, please reflect that the ends for which you keep it are limited and common to all. If we get the thing going we can, I hope, part and let others carry on with it.'[234] The response was discouraging.[235]

He also started work on a new sonata and began to read some contemporary poetry. 'I looked at the fellers I'd more or less missed out,' he told Pound in March 1951, 'the Audens and Day Lewises and the Welsh blighter [Dylan Thomas], and found I'd done damn right to miss them out.'[236] He expressed this rather more forcibly to the less strait-laced Zukofsky: 'Feeling I'd maybe been over severe on too little acquaintance I recently bought a collection of Auden & his friends. I was wrong. I was far too indulgent. They are a useless set of cunts.'[237] Hundreds of Bunting's letters survive in various libraries in the US and the UK, as well as in private hands, and in not one of them is there vocabulary like this. 'Auden & his friends' enjoyed a fruitier send off from Bunting than his real hate figures Margaret Thatcher, Ayatollah Khomeini, Mosaddeq, Hugh Astor, Hitler.

The notorious Fascist Bandit

He had clearly learned a thing or two about propaganda. In contrast with the 'Audens and Day Lewises' Zukofsky was the real article and Bunting deeply (and generously in the circumstances) lamented the fact that Zukofsky's genius was going unnoticed. Perhaps if Pound were to raise his voice in support? 'If you,' he wrote, 'the notorious Fascist Bandit and arch-anti-semite were to recommend him as he ought to be recommended, people might be non-plussed, but they'd take notice.'[238]

Privately Bunting had conceded that Pound might have been losing his mind. He told Peter Russell in May 1950 that he wanted to help get Pound released but that 'it would be difficult to maintain that Pound is NOT mad. He always had some eccentricities, and they have grown steadily queerer during the thirty years I have known him.'[239] Reading Pound's correspondence it is impossible to disagree with Bunting's diagnosis, but his circumstances were not being helped by his friends. Olga Rudge, Bunting told Zukofsky,

> seems to me to have become embittered by jealousy of Dorothy, who, of course, has all the honour and glory, besides being infernally unjealous, which must be maddening … I think she now disapproves of me because I don't take sides in family squabbles which she magnifies until everybody who isn't a partisan of her or at least her point of view is an enemy to be maligned and combated. It is all damn silly. She goes so far as to assert that Dorothy prevents Ezra from being released for fear he should run away to her, Olga … Old Pea says she is much madder than Ezra, and he ought to know: mad as a hatter himself.[240]

A month later he told Zukofsky that the point about Pound was that 'he is mad, a prisoner, and getting I think, very near the end of the nervous strength which has enabled him to put up an undaunted and unrepentant show so far ...'[241]

Bunting knew that Olga Rudge's demands for more direct action could only be counterproductive, given the mood of the American public, although he did recommend a change of lawyer. The husband of his old friend Margaret de Silver had a partner, George Richards, a Wall Street lawyer who looked after accounts such as General Motors. Bunting was friendly with Richards and considered him a man of 'great kindliness and immense worldly wisdom'.[242] Dorothy responded positively to Bunting's suggestion that she get Richards to take on Pound's case and Bunting enquired but Richards told him that he was too old and ill, and anyway busy 'prosecuting gangsters in New York'.[243]

Bunting was frustrated by Rudge's unsubtle maneouvring. He wrote to Eliot in May 1952:

> It seems that some of Ezra's friends here and in England have got impatient at his long incarceration and are planning in a vague and restless way some move which, I fear, might only make things worse by setting up the backs of the Great American People and perhaps also of their rulers. To keep these folk quiet ... I've undertaken to recommend EP and DP to consult another lawyer, namely George Richards of Wall Street, if he will be consulted ... Meanwhile I am told (for I haven't seen her) that Gabriela Mistral wants to make a letter, manifesto, petition or something of that nature to be signed by all the literary Nobel Prize winners and a few others of similar standing. If it were tactfully drafted such a performance might do no harm, even conceivably a very little good: and it seems to me that you, American by birth and much experience, would be the obvious bloke to do the drafting.[244]

Part of Pound's problem was his inability to compromise his lunatic beliefs even to those people with whom he had fallen out, such as Bunting. 'An unexpected note from EP,' Bunting wrote to Zukofsky in July 1953, 'after silence. He thinks the Kikes are terrifying the Americans and seems to want me to go there and reveal this horrible business to the world. They have made schoolteachers afraid of expressing anti-Semitism ... I am discouraged from argument. It is beyond argument.'[245]

Bunting recognised that Pound's anti-Semitic ravings were, if obnoxious, unlikely to cause any real damage. By now Pound's credibility as a social scientist, if he ever had any, had evaporated. There was even less chance of him affecting the political classes in the 1950s than there had been in the 1930s. Bunting pointed out to Zukofsky that Pound's 'hebraiophobia' was 'as mad as Yeats's Rosicrucianism and perhaps hardly more mischievous. See WBY's diary: he was thrust into awful doubt when the devil whispered to him that that fellow Bunting didn't believe in anything: and that fellow Bunting had written some quite decent poetry.'[246]

Pound wrote to Bunting in 1955 to criticise him directly for not doing anything to 'contradict lies' told about him. Bunting replied that he 'would make considerable efforts for any plan that seemed to me likely to help, or even not to harm, your prospects or your reputation'.[247] But there never was a coherent plan to liberate Pound, and Bunting's suspicion from the outset that Pound's case would have to wait until the American public had forgotten him, and that Olga Rudge's manoeuvring was only likely to keep him in the spotlight, to his detriment, was correct.

For someone so uncompromising and absolutist, Bunting had an extraordinary ability, sometimes, to bury the hatchet. In 1964 he wrote to Pound just to remind him that 'silence doesn't mean lack of love'.[248] He didn't expect a reply, having been told that Pound neither talked nor wrote by then. He merely wanted to reassure Pound that he had 'forgotten neither what I owe you nor the deep affection I now and always feel for you. And so it will be, whether I write or not, and whether you reply or not.' Even in the mid-1960s he thought that it was Rudge rather than Pound who was still fomenting discord. He told Goacher, as he was finishing *Briggflatts*, that Pound wouldn't be pleased with *Briggflatts*, 'partly for sound reasons, I expect, but partly because Olga has him persuaded that I (and probably TSE) wouldnt cooperate in getting him out of the madhouse, whereas we merely wouldnt cooperate with her in publicity which seemed likely to make it harder than ever to get him set loose.'[249] Bunting continued to write sporadically until Pound died in 1972.

TEHERAN 1951–1952

The Italian job didn't work out. He had, as usual, been complaining about lack of money and the cost of living since the day he arrived, and by the end of January 1951 he reported to Dorothy that his job was 'extremely shaky'. By the middle of May he knew he was 'definitely finished here at last' though a desk job in London was a possibility.[250] Before he left he wrote to Margaret de Silver in April 1951 with family news. Sima Maria was now fourteen months old and he longed to see his three children from his first marriage but was certain that 'Marian would find some way of preventing it and turning it to my harm'.[251]

In June 1951 the Buntings returned to Northumberland by car, an 'overstrenuous' journey that included one stretch of uninterrupted driving for twenty-four hours because the hotels in England were full with visitors to the 1951 Festival of Britain.[252] At that stage he was hoping to return to Iran for *The Times*, the Italian job having rendered him even poorer than he had been when he began it.[253] He was beginning to despair of Britain where 'everything involves papers and permits, the limits that are set to you in every direction, the assumption that if you aren't a civil servant you must be predatory or in some way dishonest'.[254]

But matters were worse elsewhere. On 20 July 1951 Abdullah bin al-Hussein, King of Jordan, was assassinated while attending Friday prayers in Jerusalem. Abdullah, friend of T. E. Lawrence and one of the moderate nationalists in the region, was one of the giants of Middle Eastern politics in the twentieth century and Bunting was deeply shocked by his death. 'Today they've murdered Abdulla,' he wrote to Dorothy Pound. 'In two years, three men I knew and admired, one my friend: Hazhir, Razmara, Abdulla.' Abdolhosein Hazhir, who had been Prime Minister of Iran in 1948, was assassinated on 5 November 1949. Sepahbod Haj Ali Razmara, Prime Minister of Iran in 1950 and 1951, was assassinated on 7 March 1951. 'They kill the patient men,' Bunting explained to Dorothy, 'who do the best the conditions allow: never the fools whose brains can't contain more than one political idea, & who are therefore loudmouthed, the extremists. They get killed only after they've brought a generation to ruin.'[255] 'Razmara was a good guy and my friend,' he wrote to Zukofsky,

> ready to tackle the extraordinarily difficult job of reforming Persia without defying facts or initiating a new dictatorship. He released the jailed communists, including the several-times-over murderer Boghrati, and imagined that would ease tension. An error. And I was stopped from advising him, even when he asked it, for fear of 'British interference'. He took on the PM job just after I left Iran, and he was the man for it, but I'd have liked him to let the Nationalists make a mess of it first and discredit themselves. Now there's no one left with both sense and authority. Even uprightness is none too common among politicians in Persia as elsewhere.[256]

Bunting's assessment of the post-assassination political situation in Iran was astute. He wrote to Dorothy Pound on 20 July 1951:

Hazhir could do very little: only whisper to the Shah the names of those who were shamelessly dishonest. His funeral was hissed by a hired mob. Razmara, whom I regarded as a friend, saw that he could best serve the West by composing the disputes with Russia: so those who benefited by his sense were calling him a traitor before he was shot. Abdulla has been the most patient statesman of this age: counter-mining for a whole generation: not personally ambitious (his kingship was a move in the long attempt to unite the Arabs). He has never risked the peace: nobody has ever been killed to serve his purposes. And he has found no ally – his own people full of jealousy, the British backward, [Sir John Bagot] Glubb an impetuous intriguer ... And now he's dead, the poor muddled Regent of Irak will muff the business: the little king is too young, & his British tutors too determined to minify him & kill the military spirit he was born with (something of Feisal in him) ... This assassination has filled me with horror.

It's hard to fault the diagnosis. Bunting understood the region better than any of his Western contemporaries. He overheard a colleague at *The Times* on the phone to someone at the *News Chronicle* saying, 'he told us two years ago exactly what was going to happen in Persia, & the Foreign Office said Pooh! & so did the oil people.'

On the positive side *The Times* had 're-doubled [his] salary & brought the News-Chronicle into the partnership, so between the two of them I can afford to go back to Persia'. In June he was in London 'buttering' Ali Soheili (a former Prime Minister of Iran) who was the Iranian Ambassador to Britain, to secure a visa. He was aware of the stakes in this dangerous game: 'Soheili knows I know more of his past than he likes anyone to know, but I couldn't judge by his face what he intends to do. I hope the visa isn't delayed. Maybe the Fedayan will murder me too (or Hosein Makki [a key figure in the nationalisation of Iran's oil industry] might like to), but I've been threatened before & by more formidable folk, & it's a reasonable risk.'[257] Bunting was acutely aware of the issue that was driving the politics of the region, then as now. 'Oil, oil, oil,' is the first sentence of a letter to Dorothy in August 1951.[258]

Although he still hadn't acquired a visa in August 1951 his work for *The Times* continued and it is clear that there was a strong overlap between his journalism and diplomacy. 'I've managed to keep the Times more reasonable than other English papers,' he wrote to Dorothy, and even conspired with them to influence the govt. Difficult article to write – mustn't be detected attacking the foreign office that is, not by the general reader: but must be perfectly plain to the cabinet etc that we know all about their neglect and disapprove of their policy. Since we disapprove even more strongly of what the Tories would have liked to do and are in fact pretty completely isolated in England, the caution is justified. The Times wants its say on other matters attended to, as well as Persia.[259]

Meanwhile the BBC had turned down his application for a job in Northern news, even though, he believed, he was the only northerner who had applied and the only 'seriously experienced journalist … Not even an interview.'[260] Fortunately his visa came through and he returned to Teheran in the autumn of 1951. The city was uncontrollable and foreign correspondents were abandoning it as quickly as they could:

They were terrified, by mobs and by other threats. I have never seen people like them. Very few of them showed the slightest spunk of any sort. There was just one from the *Daily Express* who was not afraid to go with me into the middle of a big riot. But, after the Greek journalist got hit on the head and was killed during a riot, the rest departed. It was shocking. I think all the cheap English papers and the American papers, without exception, disappeared within the next two or three days. In fact, all these kinds of things are much less dangerous than people imagine. You can go about with threats against your life for a long time and nothing happens at all – there's no use taking the slightest notice of them. I've been shot at once or twice, and often had people looking for me supposed to be going to kill me if they could, but they never got around to it. If somebody hires a man to kill you, that man doesn't want to earn the money. He wants to get the money, but once he kills you he's taking a risk for it and he's not likely to kill you at all. One time there was a mob. I don't know quite who had hired them but I've no doubt they were hired all right. They came around and began shouting outside the door of the Ritz in Teheran for my life. They *wanted* to kill me. And I sat in the flat of the Reuter's correspondent and watched for some time and then said I want to go hear what they're saying. And Reuter's man was a bit afraid to go out. I said what the hell, no one knows what I look like or anything. I went out. I walked into the crowd and stood amongst them and shouted DEATH TO MR. BUNTING! with the best of them, and nobody took the slightest notice of me. Another time, two men with pistols arrived at our door while I was taking an afternoon nap. My wife told them I wasn't in. That was all;

they accepted that and went away again. There's no great determination on the part of hired assassins.[261]

He held American foreign correspondents in especially low regard. He told Dorothy in June 1949 that he couldn't understand how a word of truth ever made its way into even the best US newspapers. 'The chaps who write for the [New York] "Times" and the "Herald-Tribune" not only wouldn't be tolerated by the London Times, I believe the Daily Mail itself would sack them for irresponsible inaccuracy. One who was here for a few weeks practically advertised for anybody to sell him false news so long as it was sensational. I have begun to look at any telegram marked UP or APA as untrue until I see evidence to the contrary.'[262]

According to Peter Stothard his filed copy didn't seem the work of a literary genius, although 'like all correspondents in those days, the reports which he sent back to senior editors were better than the articles those editors chose to publish. There is a fine dry sketch of the Persian Queen Mother who "has always had an itch to interfere in politics".'[263] I'm not sure how an article on the intricate politics of the Majlis could ever 'seem the work of literary genius'? I doubt that T. S. Eliot's daily summaries of the financial pages did either. Bunting didn't get a byline and we can be sure of his authorship of only one article because he copied it in a letter to Dorothy Pound.[264] 'Persia's Present Leaders: The Maturing of National Policy, from a Special Correspondent' appeared in *The Times* of 22 August 1951. It may not show signs of 'literary genius' but it is a compelling piece of writing, very much Bunting's authentic voice. He wasn't deliberately endearing himself to Mosaddeq: 'Dr. Moussadek might seem, in normal times, merely the ordinary Persian politician and not a very distinguished one ... He is not, in the ordinary sense, a brave man: perhaps, rather, a timid one. But he can be brave when his emotions are sufficiently aroused, and when he can speak for Persia he has a martyr's temerity, marred by nervous instability and the tears he sheds as a result of it.'[265] This survey of the Persian political classes is uncompromising and deeply informed.

He told Dorothy in November that the 'only kind of intelligence I am able to have any contact with is that of the British chargé d'affaires who argues the state of Persian politics with me twice a week or so'.[266] The British chargé d'affaires, George Middleton, was the most able diplomat Bunting had ever come across. He told Ezra Pound that he was 'intelligent, quick, knows his own mind, doesn't have to surround himself with pomposities'.

Bunting's impression of Middleton's diplomatic abilities may have been affected by the fact that he had Pound's works on his shelves, was familiar with them, and even knew Bunting's work from Pound's *Active Anthology*.[267]

He described a typical day working for *The Times* to Zukofsky. It was

> an all-day and nearly all-night job. I used to begin reading the local press as soon as I was shaved, by say 6.30, and I'd never have a pause in the work until it was too late to telegraph for the next day's paper, about nine at night. I hardly saw Sima or Maria unless it was Friday, and even the Friday picnics were few. In a way exciting, in a way dull: Mosaddeq kept doing sensational silly things that had to be reported more shrewdly than the agencies and other papers could do it, and I was under threat of expulsion from the beginning of December.

Most other foreign journalists fled, and by February he was practically alone,

> and having to intrigue to prevent the police serving an expulsion order on me … For nearly twelve weeks I had no papers at all – passport and identity card impounded by the cops … I found myself notorious for a few weeks. Some politician had told the police to make trouble about Sima's exit visa, and there was a beastly period of continual cross-examinations and efforts to persuade her to leave me and remain in Persia. They even announced that Maria was to be regarded as a Persian subject and kept there by force.[268]

By March 1952 his position was distinctly precarious; 'Mossy Dick can't make up his mind to expel me and can't bring himself to let the cops give me a permis de séjour,' he told Ezra Pound in March. The restrictions Mosaddeq placed on his life and movements were irritating. Apart from not being able to secure legal papers, he couldn't retrieve his luggage and books from the customs authorities where they had been 'rotting for ten weeks', couldn't get a sugar ration card, couldn't move more than fifty miles from Teheran or spend a night away from his own house.[269]

The most dramatic cable in Bunting's employment file describes his expulsion from Iran by Mosaddeq in May 1952: 'Bunting arrived Baghdad postexpulsion expersia accompanied wife ettwo yearold daughter. Made difficult journey parcar viaheaviest rainstorm … wife grilled, repeat grilled parpolice attempt force her upgive british nationality but she refused despite threat treat infant daughter as persian national prevent child leaving country cumparent.'[270]

The Times reacted unsympathetically to this tale of woe and three days later the news editor cabled a return: 'we sympathise and regret no other vacancy abroad stop.' Although the newspaper's accounts department allowed him to keep his company car, a Ford Mercury, Bunting maintained a healthy disrespect for the newspaper for the rest of his life. On the one occasion *The Times* stuck up for Bunting it did so from a safe distance. A leader on 14 April 1952 explained why Mosaddeq had expelled its correspondent:

> the real reason for excluding all these correspondents is the Persian Government's dislike of criticism and its desire to hold the truth from both other countries and its own people. Our Correspondent's dispatches in *The Times* were frequently quoted in the Persian Press. Inside Persia elections can be rigged and the Opposition bought or suppressed in various ways; foreign correspondents cannot be silenced unless they are expelled. It is the remedy of all weak and dictatorial Governments and it always wrong.[271]

In the light of ensuing events it isn't altogether surprising that Bunting came to regard this as hypocritical cant. A similar leader three years later provoked a letter from Bunting that put his case in characteristically forthright style: 'Sir, you expressed as much indignation three and a half years ago, when your own correspondent was expelled from Tehran, but showed the depths of your concern for the freedom of the press by leaving him to starve.'[272]

I kept on telling the truth

His account of his expulsion to Margaret de Silver contains elements of the Leighton Park School incident nearly thirty-five years previously – refusal to compromise, commitment to tell the truth as he saw it, contempt for those who didn't:

> The grounds [Mosaddeq] gave were absurd, namely, that I had once been a consul, that I had a Persian wife, and that Persian newspapers continually quoted my despatches. These things supposedly made me dangerous. I had been under threat of expulsion for several months, but didn't allow that to affect my despatches. I sent facts – things actually seen – that other correspondents were afraid to send, and made comments which were afterwards proved accurate by events – was, in short, always ahead of what was happening: and that no doubt seemed a danger to a man whose game is as intricate and unavowable as Mosaddeq's.[273]

He told Ezra Pound a few months later that he had been 'under threat' for several months before his expulsion. During that period he had had 'several messages from Mossy and his pals, hinting strongly that if I would modify the news (I was the only foreigner reporting it) he'd see what could be done for me. Instead I kept on telling the truth, which is reputed to be a virtue, and imagined that the Times (which had previously promised to back me up if I got expelled) would impute it to me for merit.'[274]

'This is pretty bad,' he wrote to his boss at *The Times*.

> Mossy has no common sense, and the idea of expelling a man because he likes Persia and has a real interest in Persians doesn't seem to him grotesque. But in addition; (a) Ansari [head of the Iranian Foreign Office] lied to me when he said he hadn't got my passport – it was visible on his tray (b) another time Ansari kept me waiting nearly an hour in the corridor when not only was he disengaged, as I could see once or twice when his room door was opened by servants, but the comfortable waiting room was quite empty. This kind of discourtesy is rare in Persia and always deliberate. It means he thinks I've got to be treated as an enemy to secure his own position in the eyes of the ultimate authorities.

According to Tom Pickard,

> after many days of bureaucratic shove-halfpenny, he unhappily accepted his fate. *The Times* suggested that he could cover Persia from Basra. Bunting thought not, although 'one could greatly annoy the Persians with the sort of stuff one could send from there.' Instead he suggested Kuwait might be better: 'since large numbers of unemployed from Khuzistan are believed to be smuggling themselves in there.' Musaddiq was determined he should leave, and the Persian evening press reported the story in detail. Bunting was unable to file anything to *The Times* because he had 'spent two whole days in government offices, collecting the papers necessary to collect other papers necessary to show at the frontier, and I'm far from done.' The authorities proved particularly obstructive in supplying an exit visa for 'my poor wife [who] is stricken at leaving her country, family and friends.'[275]

For all his complaints Bunting must have known that his expulsion was inevitable. In 1951 Mosaddeq nationalised the Iranian oil industry and began negotiations with the Anglo-Iranian Oil Company for a smooth transfer to the newly created National Iranian Oil Company. The British responded by evacuating all AIOC personnel, blocking the export of oil from Iran and lodging a formal complaint at the United Nations. When Mosaddeq broke diplomatic relations and closed the British Embassy and consulates Britain retaliated by freezing Iranian assets and sending more warships to the Persian Gulf. As Ervand Abrahamian says, 'by the end of 1951 Mosaddeq was embroiled in a full-blown crisis with Britain'.[276] In August 1951 Christopher Montague (Monty) Woodhouse, British hero of Greek resistance to the Nazis, was sent to Teheran as head of British Intelligence and found a country 'already on the brink of catastrophe'.

Bunting can hardly have been surprised by his enforced departure. All British officials were expelled from Iran early in 1952 and, from Mosaddeq's perspective, with good reason. Bunting had no reason to feel singled out for special attention by Mosaddeq. On the other hand he may well have *deserved* special attention and a footnote buried in Darioush Bayandor's *Iran and the CIA* may explain why.[277] We know that Bunting was active among the Bakhtiari tribesmen in the Zagros mountains throughout his time in the region. Bayandor claims that low-level plots and subversion were a continuous threat to Mosaddeq, and not long after Bunting's expulsion the Bakhtiari started an insurgency against Mosaddeq's government. It is unlikely that Bunting had not been involved, especially as the British government, according to Woodhouse, had been secretly arming tribesmen to resist a Russian insurgency if Iran descended further into chaos.[278] Perhaps unsurprisingly Britain's repeated covert attempts to subvert the Mosaddeq regime were all about oil.[279]

By October the last remaining officials of the Anglo-Iranian Oil Company withdrew from Iran and Richard Stokes, a minister in the Labour government, was sent to try to restart negotiations with Mosaddeq, who was immensely popular at the time 'although with little sense of direction', according to Woodhouse, and with a track record of principled opposition to the autocracy of Reza Shah as well as strong and consistent advocacy of Iranian national integrity and constitutional government.[280] Mosaddeq closed all the British consulates early in 1952 and a Soviet sponsored coup in Iran seemed inevitable. The British Foreign Office, under Herbert Morrison, mounted a covert campaign to remove Mosaddeq but the British cabinet forced him to cancel the operation. Attlee's Labour government lost the October 1951 election and Anthony Eden returned to the Foreign Office for the third time. Eden withdrew government support from the destabilisation plot and Iranian politics were left to run their course, Mosaddeq continuing to believe until his overthrow in 1953 that the British were actively working to overthrow his regime, which they were.[281]

In the summer of 1952 Mosaddeq resigned because of differences with the Shah, although he was quickly reinstated, and he broke all diplomatic links with Britain in October, by which time he had almost certainly got wind of the fact that the British were conspiring with the US to foment a coup to remove him. The coup d'état, Operation Ajax, finally went ahead in August 1953 and Mosaddeq was arrested and tried for treason. The coup could not have happened, as Nikki R. Keddie shows, without the intervention of the CIA and the British SIS.[282] Britain's pivotal role in the coup was spearheaded in Teheran by Nancy Lambton, who had run British propaganda in Iran during the war, and Robin Zaehner. It was Lambton who made the decisive recommendation that Mosaddeq should be overthrown by a deliberately fomented coup.[283]

In the context of massive social unrest, loss of oil revenue following Mosaddeq's nationalisation of the country's oil industry, the British imposition of major trade sanctions, hostility at home from the Shah and his foreign advisers, the US support for a worldwide boycott of Iranian oil and an impending US/UK sponsored coup, it isn't really surprising that Mosaddeq expelled Bunting, who reflected on all this ruefully in a letter to Zukofsky in October 1953: 'A letter a few days ago, that the Govt now realises that my work in Persia in 1947 could have prevented the whole oil trouble if it had been attended to … but the man who refused to attend [Sir John Le Rougetel] is a knight and a High Commissioner; and I'm on the dole.'[284] At this distance it is hard to be certain but Bunting's complaints have the genuine indignation of honesty underneath them. He could embellish stories innocently as well as Ford could, but on matters about which he cared, as we saw at Leighton Park School, he told the story exactly as he saw it: 'Attlee, told of the Persian nationalisation demand, wrung his hands, wept and cried: "Why wasn't I told?" He wasn't told because Sir John le Rougetel wouldn't forward my reports, and when they were sent another way, Sir William Strang sat on them. Then he let them send Stokes – thus making certain that no agreement wd be reached – out of pure ignorance, deliberately unenlightened by the blokes who are paid to enlighten him.'[285]

Bunting did however have some reason to feel singled out for special *inattention* from the British establishment, and in particular *The Times*, which, along with the British Embassy in Teheran, he claimed, had always encouraged him 'to take the boldest course', implying that if his 'indifference to Persian threats brought me into trouble in the end, my family and my income shouldn't suffer for it'.[286] *The Times*, as we have seen, published a 'violent leader' in protest at Bunting's expulsion but refused him alternative employment and though contractually obliged to continue to pay him until October halved his pay from the moment of his expulsion in April.[287] Bunting complained that the Foreign Office didn't even issue a protest about the expulsion and refused to intervene in the Persian customs' confiscation of the Buntings' property, including all their household linen, baby clothes, toys and the priceless collection of Persian books and manuscripts that Bunting had been collecting for the previous twenty years. The Foreign Office, he felt, could easily have found him a place in its Information Service, in the British Council or in the BBC's foreign department, but were not prepared to 'make a precedent'. It is a minor but nevertheless shameful example of tight-lipped British establishment callousness, but it is not helped by the fact that its victim was always hovering on paranoia about 'them'. He held the British Council in special contempt:

> I never could [secure work with the British Council], even in their earliest days, and with a recommendation from T. S. Eliot O.M. They wiped their noses and said I had no qualifications, which is Greek for teacher training college. I was delighted when a repulsive darvish took a bath stark naked in the pool of their building in Isfahan, thus shocking them all, for a moment, to silence. The ladies pretended they hadn't noticed, though he practically shook his stick at them.[288]

If Bunting was contemptuous of the British Council he came to positively detest *The Times*. The feeling seems to have been mutual. He complained in September 1953 that the newspaper had refused to publish his short letter to the editor about Persian affairs, 'and that is a grave discourtesy to a former staff-correspondent'.[289] He told Denis Goacher that 'somebody in the *Times* set-up was against him. He said he was never offered another job with the newspaper except one in Chile and, for whatever reason, he didn't want to go out to Chile.'[290]

Bunting for his part, however, just as he had been in Charles Evans' office nearly forty years' previously, was determined to be fair. A letter to Margaret de Silver in May 1953 contains a passage that rang warning bells that are still pealing:

I think diplomacy (and American diplomacy even more than British) is making such a series of huge blunders out there [the Middle East] that they will ultimately make a present of it all to [Georgy] Malenkov [Russian Prime Minister after Stalin's death in 1953], but not before they have produced chaos and massacre on a considerable scale. The Times did its best for a while with me in Persia and an excellent man in Cairo: but now they have only halftime men from the Egyptian frontier to Pakistan. They are trying to prevent the British Government making an equally unnecessary mess in Africa, and all their spare energy seems to have gone to Rhodesia and Kenya ... the moral atmosphere of Islam is NOT the moral atmosphere of Xtianity (nor is the Shiah atmosphere the same as the Sunni) and the persistent Western attempt to impose Christian morals on Moslems is FATAL. Especially when you remember that the morals Xtians take for granted and expect people to conform to have hardly any relation to the ones advocated in the New Testament. Money doesn't mean the same between Stambul and Karachi as it does in the West, success in our sense is unimportant, our notions of honesty aren't theirs. In short, anyone who brings economics to the East is wasting his time.

Secondly, they lump it all together: 'The Middle East': they read Persian (Shiah, Aryan, squirearchical) problems in terms of Egyptian (Sunni, Hamitic, plantation) or Arabian (Wahabi, Semitic, demi-autocratic). Idiots! And so they are always surprised and baffled.

Thirdly they are plain ignorant ... one meets perpetual confusions: between tribes and dervish orders; between nomad tribes and nomad herds, whose tribes, except the shepherds, stay put; between systems of landholding and water-owning; between religions and races.[291]

Bunting told a story from his time in Baghdad which illustrates his first point beautifully:

I do know a man in Baghdad; he was a ferryman working a very tough job, for the Tigris is an extremely fast river; the labour of getting across it is considerable. I felt sorry for the old man and was very much astonished when one day he invited me to come to the wedding of his daughter. I went along and it was the most magnificent affair. There inside the mud compound that he lived in were all manner of magnificent carpets and there were no less than three bands of musicians, everything on the most tremendous scale; all the dishes were silver and so forth – it was admirable. I was in a position then when I could get things found out for me and I got some people on to finding out all about this old boy and it turned out that he owned ... the only efficient dairy farm in Iraq – he was a very wealthy man – but because he was a good religious man he also had to earn his living by the labour of his hand and went on being a ferryman.[292]

Is it an exaggeration to suggest that Mosaddeq's expulsion of Bunting and the refusal of *The Times* to support him set back diplomacy for sixty years in what I'm afraid we still call the Middle East? Possibly, but at any rate the loss of someone as knowledgeable and politically sensitive as Bunting was clearly a blow to stability in the region.

THROCKLEY AND WYLAM, 1952–1964

The Buntings' journey back to Britain was eventful. He told Denis Goacher that he was 'fired at twice, out of the blue; one bullet hit the windscreen, just above his head, and the other one dented a back mudguard but by a miracle didn't penetrate the tyre'.[293]

Bunting wrote to Ezra Pound in May about his journey home, unaccountably forgetting the bullets. The family had reached Sirmione in the Italian lakes after only a

> very moderate crop of disasters – half drowned by torrents of rain in Persia, washed out the electric system, hid the quarry like holes in the asphalt under two inches of muddy water, hence a broken back spring & 4 days delay in Baghdad: our good battery stolen in Baghdad & a dud put in its place: 5 days delay in Istanbul (3 too many) in a cursed German garage: an unfindable short circuit between Belgrade & Zagreb: but our first puncture happened in Italy.[294]

Once again, Bunting's en route letter to Pound gives us a glimpse of the travel writer that could have been in a filmic description of his experiences:

> The Iraqi customs officer who gave us a feast in his poverty-stricken lodging: the petrol pump attendant at Mafraq (Jordan) who sent out for tea & gave Maria a live starling (which we afterwards set free): the innkeeper at Gerede (Turkey) who'd never had foreign guests before & overcame the language difficulty by drawing pictures while his mother took Sima into the larder to choose our food; and was with difficulty persuaded to present a bill for his hospitality: the Greek soldiers who built a fire at our bivouac in Macedonia & made coffee & gave us cheese & wine: even the Servian [Greece] communist officer who, after examining our luggage & passports pretty strictly with a

grim face, finally borrowed Sima's accordion & gave us a tune to which the frontier sentry danced; duty sat heavily on him, but he had enough spirit left to be a man again once it was over.[295]

They arrived back in Britain in June and shared his mother's 'very small house in Throckley'.[296] Bunting tried to find work as a journalist but found that other newspapers were put off by the fact that *The Times* had let him go. Working for *The Times* had cost him whatever savings he had accumulated, Sima was heavily pregnant with their second child, and because he had worked overseas for so long he had 'no rights in the vaunted Welfare State. We can draw no insurance nor help of any kind. In short, I don't think I've been in a worse situation in the whole of my life, hard as it mostly was.'[297] Bunting closed his letter with an entreaty to Margaret to help him find work in the US, summarised his by now considerable skills and experience, enclosed copies of his curriculum vitae and signed off with an admission that he had not even tried to be 'social and interesting' in his letter, such an activity being unthinkable 'while my anxiety lasts'. He also asked Zukofsky to spread the word that he was willing to move to the United States if he could find a job. Zukofsky forwarded Bunting's letter to William Carlos Williams who returned it on 17 October: 'I return Bunting's letter as you asked me t. The CURRICULUM VITAE I have sent on to Norman Pearson at Yale who as far as I know is more likely than any one else to be of assistance. I sent him also Bunting's address on the chance that he want to communicate direct with him.'[298]

Nothing came of this. Williams wrote to Pound on 17 April 1954 telling him that, 'when I last heard from him [Bunting] via Louis Zukofsky he included in his letter a summary under a Latin title giving a summary of Buntings scholastic accomplishments. It was impressive so I sent it off as it was to Norman Pearson of Yale asking him if he could find a place for him as a teacher of Persian there. He said in reply that no one there was interested in learning the language.'[299]

Bunting had written, as Williams had suggested, to Professor Norman Holmes Pearson who had returned to Yale, after intelligence work in London during the war, to set up a new American Studies department. He believed that he 'could be of real use in a University, either to bring a rather wider range of reading in foreign languages than is usual to the exposition of English poetry or, more directly, to teach Persian as a literature from which we can learn much that has never been absorbed into European literatures and at least something that used to be got from Latin and Greek before the syllabus was choked with philology,'[300] but a few weeks later he told Zukofsky, 'Pearson. Never a word.'[301] Academic orientalists were something of a bugbear for Bunting but he got his own back on one of them. In his quest for employment he had written to America's most distinguished orientalist, Arthur Upham Pope, recently retired Chancellor of the Asia Institute in New York. Pope had replied to Bunting that, '(1) there aren't any jobs, (2) I am retired and can't be asked to know of jobs (3) if there were any jobs there are lots of people much better qualified than you, Sir.' Bunting told Zukofsky a story about 'the high priest of USA Orientalism' that I am sure he hoped would one day become public: 'Well, Louis, last time I saw [Pope] he stopped his car to beg me to translate to his chauffeur the difficult piece: "I want to go to the railway station." I suppose I could manage that in at least a round dozen of languages, let alone those I profess to know something about or would presume to teach.'[302]

The Spoils

Bunting wasn't entirely unpublished in the post-war years. 'The Complaint of the Morpethshire Farmer' was published in *Four Pages*, a periodical edited by Dallam Flynn mainly to promulgate Pound's social theories. In May 1948 Bunting told Zukofsky that Flynn hadn't asked for permission to publish but 'they were most flattering. I like butter (in moderation)'.[303] 'All the teeth I ever had...', 'Night is hard by' and 'Last night without sight of you' were published in Peter Russell's *Nine*; Rainer Gerhardt's German translation of 'Empty vast days...' appeared in *Fragmente*, and 'Now that sea's over that island' was published in *Imagi*.[304] *Nine* published 'You there', 'This I write' and 'The Thundercloud' in its April 1956 issue and Hugh Kenner included 'Let them remember Samangan' and 'Vestiges' in *The Art of Poetry* in 1959, each poem followed by a series of critical questions. In 1960 'Darling of Gods and men' was included in *Poetry for Pleasure: The Hallmark Book of Poetry*. 'You leave' (from 'Aus dem Zweiten Reich') was reproduced in Kenneth Patchen's privately published *Journal of Albion Moonlight* in 1961, but without attribution to Bunting. Bunting couldn't complain, he had grandly announced to Zukofsky in 1948 that 'I hereby inform my literary executor that I disapprove of copyright, and anybody can print whatever they like of mine anywhere and over any name, so long as they don't alter it.'[305] So as far as Patchen was concerned he had little to complain about, although he didn't like his longer works being dismembered.

Much more importantly, however, 'The Spoils', Bunting's poem of the Second World War was published in *Poetry* in November 1951. 'The Spoils' is one of the more 'difficult' poems Bunting wrote, something the poet himself acknowledged at a reading in 1977.[306] It is condensed almost to the point of paralysis and the oriental references sometimes seem alien to a Western ear so that getting to the memorable episodes can feel like hard work. Even Bunting's explanation of some of the terms of the poem can feel like heavy going:

> Bashshar bin Burd was an Arabic poet of Persian race who was put to death for heresy in the eighth or ninth century. It's not clear exactly what his heresy was, but it seems that he 'glanced back' at the achievements of the Sassanian kings and the Zoroastrian religion, and in particular at the communist rebellion of Mazdak which was put down after a temporary triumph in about 570 a.d. He was probably some kind of pantheist, though he didn't get as far as Hallaj, who said 'Ana'l-haqq', or some kind of Manichean, but most likely a bit of both. He 'speculated whither' by forseeing [*sic*] only evil from the caliphate and rousing a rather vague spirit of rebellion. The first great Persian poets who wrote in Persian, a century or more later, thought well of Bashshar, at least as a poet.[307]

He told an audience in London that 'The Spoils',

> begins with the four sons of Shem ... They are here to show four different aspects of the Semitic peoples. Arabs and Jews are very much alike. Perhaps they wouldn't like to hear that in New York but it's true. And not only in their language but in much of their habits and way of looking at things. So I have a rather militant Jew and an Arab merchant and a Badu and a Zionist ... and then go on in the 2nd part to another fine thing, finer than I think the Semitic thing too, the civilization of Persia, for one part. But the poem became lopsided. It was intended to have four parts as a sonata ought to have of course, and I sent it all to Louis Zukofsky who wrote back and complained that the last two parts were pretty thin. And I read them through again and he was quite right. They were pretty thin. And the only thing I could think to do about it was to shrink them both into one. So the sonata is a lopsided affair ... One of the suras of the Koran deals with what is to be done with the spoils of war, and it begins with the words 'The spoils are for God, the spoils are God's'... and it struck me during the last war that that was precisely the

state of affairs. What you got out of it was nothing you could enrich yourself with much, but in a way it was something you could dedicate to God, or to whatever in the modern mind takes the place that God would have taken in the medieval mind.[308]

Bunting worked hard on 'The Spoils'. He told Peter Quartermain that he had taken six months or more to find the last half of one line and when he did it contained just three words, 'Halt, both, lament'. These were a translation from the *Mu'allaqát* of 'Amr al Qais, two Arabic words represented by the three English words, though 'four syllables in somewhat the same rhythm'.[309]

'The Spoils' is obscure but some passages shimmer with conviction and beauty, the lines that describe the North Sea convoys for instance (p. 274). Bunting describes a real scene from the Malta campaign in part 3 of the poem:

> Tinker tapping perched on a slagheap
> and the man who can mend a magneto.
> Flight-Lieutenant Idema, half course run
> that started from Grand Rapids, Michigan,
> wouldn't fight for Roosevelt,
> 'that bastard Roosevelt', pale
> at Malta's ruins, enduring
> a jeep guarded like a tyrant.
> In British uniform and pay
> for fun of fighting and pride,
> for Churchill on foot alone,
> clowning with a cigar, was lost
> in best blues and his third plane that day.[310]

This stanza tilts, I think playfully, at Yeats' 'An Irish Airman Foresees his Death' and does so with complete integrity. Yeats had no direct experience of participation in war. The answer to his question in 'The Man and the Echo', 'Did that play of mine send out/Certain men the English shot?', is probably 'no', and even if it did the question is more about Yeats than about the men. But Bunting counted his pilots home after every flight and felt the direct pain of each loss. The day Flight Lieutenant Idema didn't reach his home airfield Bunting was searching the skies for him. A few years later, desperate for work, he wrote to Idema's father, Walter Idema, to ask if he knew of a job. 'Lord knows I did it reluctantly,' he told Zukofsky. 'He is the father of one of my pilots when I looked after Spitfires in 43 and 44. His son was one of the bravest men I ever met and a particularly individual and picturesque one. You'll maybe remember the lines in *The Spoils*. Father Idema saw them and wrote to me when I was in Persia, and I was able to give him some particulars of his son's last hours which must have wrung his heart with pride.'[311]

Keith Alldritt described 'The Spoils' as a work of 'ironic undeludedness and quiet stoicism. It is more sensuous than *Little Gidding*; it is more restrained than *The Pisan Cantos*. But it has the same kind of literary stature as theirs and its essential purposes as a work of art are the same.'[312] *Little Gidding* and *The Pisan Cantos* are good enough company for any poem to keep but 'The Spoils' didn't dazzle the literary world (although it was read on the BBC's Third programme in July 1957).[313]

Bunting was armed with 'The Spoils' when he visited T. S. Eliot in 1952 to, as Denis Goacher puts it, 'beg for a favour'. Bunting wanted Faber & Faber to publish *Poems 1950* in the United Kingdom but, according to Goacher, Eliot turned him down because, 'he considered that Basil's style was too notably influenced by Pound – that there wasn't sufficient divergence to really justify his being published by them. Now, timing is everything, Eliot died in January 1965, so he didn't live to see *Briggflatts*. If he had, I am perfectly certain that Fabers would have published Basil.'[314] If 'Villon', 'Chomei at Toyama' and 'The Spoils' weren't enough to convince Eliot that Bunting had a powerful, distinctive voice of his own I doubt that even *Briggflatts* would have done the job. In fact Eliot had told Bunting that he thought 'the poetry is good, some of it very good indeed, and writing is clean and workmanlike, with no fluff, but … they are still too much under the influence of Pound, for the stage which you have reached'.[315] Bunting certainly felt that Eliot was deaf to his music. He told Pound that 'TSE must always have been a bit muddled and he gave up the chance of unmuddling himself when he took to smokescreens such as religion to hide his poetry behind. The screen distracted his own attention from the poetry, I imagine, as well as that of the public, and his perception of poetical technique diminished.'[316] It's unlikely that Eliot was as deaf to Bunting's music as Goacher claims, and it is hard not to conclude that his rejection of Bunting was inspired by some personal animus. Eliot wouldn't have forgotten Bunting's heavy handed criticism of his influence in the 1930s and Goacher tacitly admits as much when he refers to Bunting's attitude to Eliot: 'He was always trying to cut Eliot down to size … He would say, "Oh, history will show that Eliot is a minor poet, like

Coleridge.'"[317] Goacher had a point here. Bunting seems to have enjoyed comparing Eliot unfavourably with, particularly, Rudyard Kipling. Bunting held Kipling in high regard but to a wider audience a comparison of Eliot with Kipling, even a favourable one, would have seemed like damning with faint damnation. As early as 1935 he was delighted with his discovery of the 'astonishing correspondence' between Kipling's story, 'How the Kangeroo got his Legs' and Eliot's 'Sweeney Agonistes', noting that 'The rhythm exactly corresponds, the diction is very similar. Some phrases seem to be perfectly parallel with phrases in the Eliot.'[318] And thirty years later he told Gael Turnbull that he thought *Four Quartets* was 'badly flawed' and that Eliot had a dead ear. 'He beats a drum. His beat is too obvious and boring. It goes thump thump thump. It isn't even as subtle as Kipling can be.'[319]

Bunting was too astute to believe that Eliot was really a minor poet. There was a lurking mutual mistrust between Bunting and Eliot that doesn't do great credit to either of them. Bunting even managed to be condescending about Eliot's Nobel Prize in 1948: 'I hope he enjoys it, but fear he will try to do good instead.'[320]

In the mid 1960s Bunting showed Tom Pickard a letter from Eliot that Pickard described as 'mean spirited'. Eliot once again refused to publish Bunting at Faber, which was no great surprise, but the 'bitterness' puzzled Pickard and he asked the poet Ed Dorn about it. Dorn's reply sheds some light on the way Eliot used his position of power:

> Eliot occupied the position of power and one of his strategies was to write essays and redefine what literature could be and was according to his own lights. Basil wouldn't have been a threat exactly. I mean what could threaten T.S. Eliot? But he certainly wouldn't have conformed to what Eliot wanted, as a buttressing element in his own position in the canon … T.S. Eliot was the midwife who was constantly trying to kill the baby. He was the abortionist of the post modern movement; he controlled who was going to be born and who wasn't insofar as he could.[321]

But Bunting knew Eliot's worth. In later life he reflected on Eliot's achievement. He told Dennis Goacher, 'I said a few hard words about TSE from time to time. I thought he surrendered too easily to the damned orthodoxies he had no real need of. But he was a kindly man, affectations and all; and people of my age remember how much Prufrock and the Waste Land did for English taste and understanding. Even persistence in what everyone said was a foolish marriage was a fault of kindness, though it was there he first put his foot in the grave, I think.'[322]

For all the mutual mistrust Bunting's relationship with Eliot is best expressed by Bunting himself in a letter he sent to Zukofsky before the meeting about 'The Spoils', which reprimanded Zukofsky for his stand-offishness:

> I like the gin-sodden holy reprobate, long may he flourish and exhort us to repentance. No malice more certain, no kindness more ready. A good bloke, Zuk, not to be shied off from on skimpy excuses. Don't be so goddamned proud. He's busy, he's plagued by idiots, he doesn't answer letters if they're difficult to answer nicely, BUT he leaves word with his sec. Don't let BB get through London without seeing me, if you have to cut an engagement with Almighty God out of my diary. Considering he don't really like anything I've ever written, and knows I got a lot of reservations about his work, and considering he's now an OM and Nobel Prize and high archangel of English lit., I think it's a sign of something somewhere. In the Café Royal the waiter remembered him after a while. Then he stood in thought and finally remembered me too, 'Weren't you the man who was always being turned out drunk?'[323]

Grimmer and grimmer

But rock bottom had still not been reached. The joy at the birth of the Bunting's second child, Thomas Faramarz Bunting, on 29 November 1952 came on the back of disaster. In October Roudaba called Bunting to tell him that Rustam had died at the age of sixteen at a boarding school in New Hampshire, apparently after an eighteen-hour polio attack. His sense of estrangement is painful. 'My son Rustam died last autumn,' he wrote to Dorothy Pound in March 1953, 'far from his home, and so far as I can learn, amongst strangers.'[324] Father and son had never met.

'Grimmer and grimmer', begins a letter to Margaret de Silver in April 1953. He had reached the final stages of a selection board for a government 'information service' job, which sounded as though it could have been glamorous but which was in reality routine journalism with a salary that was 20 per cent higher than that of a dustman. He would have jumped at it even so but was rejected because he had not been a journalist in the 1930s, 'only in the 20s and 40s and 50s'.[325] The fact that he had reached the rank of General Staff Officer Grade 2 during the war also told against him. How could someone of that calibre not 'be safely fixed in a very highly paid job'?

The Buntings were now so poor that he was facing the possibility of having to send Sima and their children back to Persia to live with her relatives, and a hint of suicidal thinking crept into his letter to Margaret. How much of this was emotional blackmail it is impossible to say. Margaret certainly had the resources to help his family out of starvation, but his letters to other, less financially secure friends, also reveal a level of despair that was clearly becoming unbearable. There's no doubt that the Buntings and their young family were wretchedly poor. He wrote to Margaret de Silver in desperation:

> Things here – I mean our personal affairs – seem to be very close to a climax. We spent the last few days entirely without money and with very little to eat, though we managed to feed the babies. Mother has run her overdraft to the limit the bank will allow: it is secured on her house, and she is being pressed to sell the house to pay the bank its five hundred pounds. Meanwhile I've been applying for 'National Assistance' – the new name for outdoor relief. They are not polite, and I doubt whether we will get it. We have not sold Sima's engagement ring nor my irreplaceable Persian and Arabic books, and I am still nominally owner of a car, or the rusty remains of one, which the customs will not let me sell; and they cannot even make up their minds how much duty they mean to charge on it. It is clear that the car will not fetch even the minimum they can charge – they have caused it to lie rusting for over a year. Unfortunately our National Assistance area is the Marxist stronghold hereabouts – Blaydon – and we are bourgeois parasites, or so I gather.
>
> I had been led to believe several times during the past ten years that I had deserved well of my country in a small way, and eighteen months ago half the papers in the country were praising me for my work in Persia – just after Mosaddeq chucked me out. But in that time I have earned only about ten pounds.

He owed £150 on his own account and, as he told Margaret, he was also really responsible for half of his mother's considerable overdraft. This is an abject letter:

> What is to happen now I don't know. Perhaps the bank will insist on Mother selling her house: if so, she will have to go and live with my sister who does not want her and with whom she quarrels terribly, frequently and bitterly. My sister is generous in an overcalculated way, without any apparent kindness, and it would be a wretched life for the old lady, who is happy with Sima. Mother would have only just enough to keep herself (and she has nothing to leave). I suppose I would have to beg whatever balance remained from the sale of the house to send Sima and my children to their relatives in Persia

– if the Persians would allow it. They could manage there for some years, declining little by little into the helpless starvation of the Armenian poor in Teheran. Then I would be left alone, with no place even for my few books, no money, no prospect of reuniting the family.[326]

It is surprising that Margaret did not offer him funds, if only to stop the tidal wave of relentless misery that accumulated in letter after long letter from her former protégé.

He was becoming bitter. He wrote to Zukofsky in March 1953 that 'my very considerable services to the state haven't entitled me to anything whatever. They are even, by the workings of the Official Secrets Act, sometimes a handicap – I mustn't satisfy the perfectly legitimate curiosity of prospective employers about what I did in such and such a post. Penalty, fourteen years in jug.'[327] A few months later, on 18 June 1953 Bunting wrote again to Zukofsky, noting the painful irony of his position:

'"Dispatches ... always been scrupulously fair and objective," said the Times leader writer "a sound judge of Persian affairs ... deep sympathy with the Persian people ... devoted his life to the country". Another time, "Persia's best friend in the West." For which my children must starve and I be denied any chance to show sagacity elsewhere. This week we cannot pay the butcher.' Also in the same letter we learn that:

The government is applying a last turn of the screw, demanding duty and purchase tax on the car the Times abandoned to me. I can't pay, I'm not even allowed to sell the car which is running up debts in a garage. But if now they fix a government debt on me I'll end in gaol for having refused to falsify news to the disadvantage of our government. Such is democratic gratitude ... And little worms who hardly know enough Persian to construe a few pages of the Chahar Maqaleh have lectureships, because they listened to professors nearly as ignorant as themselves, but I who know their literature – and their newspapers – and their conversation – and the ways of their tribesmen – I cannot be the slightest use, or at any rate, cannot be paid for it.[328]

In July 1953 he wrote to Pound: 'I can't get a job at seven quid a week (no experience) let alone get listened to. What they mean by experience Lord knows. Last board that interviewed me simply refused to believe my record. Wouldn't even take the trouble to check up and find it true. "You mean to say a former GSO2 and Counsellor is applying for a piddling little job like this? Make your claims more modest next time.'"[329] And in September he complained to Zukofsky that,

> Mother's bank won't let her overdraw any more – she owes them £500 – and I owe £150 that I'm sure of and an unspecified amount to the Customs and something like another sixty to the garage … the Bank might want to sell Mother's house to repay itself – I don't think so, but it's possible. And we may get from the State, if we're lucky … enough to pay the grocer and the butcher, but not the baker, not the gas, water, electricity, nor any share of the rent, nor clothes, postage, travel, tobacco … So I reread the Times' leader after my expulsion from Persia – what a fine fellow I am, what high qualifications; how unrighteous to kick me out, and I wonder a bit where the hell I am. And the Manchester Guardian asks my advice, but expects it for nothing (though it did pay £8 when I wrote its first leader for it – well over twice my train fare).

> And the Air Force expects me to keep my uniform handy for the next war 'to serve in the same position you occupied before demobilisation,' ie, chief of intelligence for a very big region. I wonder, by the way, how many General Staff Officers, Grade Two, are now drawing public assistance?

Not many, probably. He asked Zukofsky to help him find work: 'What! Do you think you'll ever have the chance of such a bargain again? GSO2, Times staff-correspondent, diplobloodydoormat, Middle East expert, poet, unofficial scholar, all under one shirt and for the price of one. Oh yes, and listed by the Communists as a dangerous adversary: that should go down with the Re Publicans and Sinners.'[330]

Bunting was once again at odds with the establishment in his usual self-destructive way. He had a point though and his friend Peter Quartermain made it forcefully:

> His own damn pride no doubt got in the way, that Victorian or is it Edwardian rectitude, that code of gentlemanly conduct, of not making a fuss, of not airing your linen (clean or dirty) in public. But if he was at all bitter in his later years he had every right to be. Because he had lived so much abroad, he did not qualify for a full old-age pension, which at 65 was pitifully small. So at the Queen's pleasure he was awarded a Civil List pension to make up the difference – but, indexed at a lower rate and taxed at a higher one, it barely paid for his cigarettes. In the middle 1950s Basil Bunting and his family, valued servants of the state, were supported with food parcels sent by Ezra Pound, inmate of St. Elizabeths Hospital for the Criminally Insane. The British treatment of Basil Bunting is a national disgrace.[331]

It was.

He had sent Pound a copy of 'The Spoils' and asked for his help finding work. Pound had clearly replied in ferociously negative terms on both counts, prompting an extraordinary riposte from Bunting that is eloquent in its self-justification while defending his position in a much more mature way than would have been the case before the war:

> Well, well! Ole Ez does shy a profuse shower of stones when I ask him the way to the baker's. It is almost exhilarating. One of the craters on Etna does the same if you provoke it. (I used a snowball; but its aim was no better than Ez's – that is, if he really intends to break any heads or windows.)

> Or else he doesn't know the knob from the ferrule. But I haven't time to put him right, and maybe its twenty years too late anyway. I mean, he did so much for me in so many ways that I never had the heart to argue with him, and I suppose he often thought I agreed – or acquiesced – when I didn't: for I dare say I began by having to see the rough of the world at closer quarters than he, and never valued men and their works at his estimate: but I've come in the end to think of Man (capital M) a detestable nuisance invented to decoy Ez and other remarkable energies away from their game.

> I had a hand in saving Azerbaijan from Uncle Joe Stalin, and I spent a long time trying to save Britain and Persia from mutual follies which only profit the lovers of uniformity (in this case especially Russian and American). After I'd been choked in the Foreign Office (by le Rougetel and Strang) I tried through the Times, and eventually persuaded the leader-writers to come half way: difficult, because by then the Persians had Mosaddeq on their back, and to put it shortly he was indifferent to the fate of the Persians if only he could destroy the Shah. And through the Times I got a little, too little, sense into the Brit govt, and might have kept it there if the Astors hadn't saddled themselves with an editor after doing without one very nicely for several years. (Barrington-Ward was dead before I joined, and Sir William Haley came in just in time to decide to drop me after I'd returned to England.) To weigh, I had to have the news, all of it and all correct. And to get that I took risks. My wife, the Embassy and the Persian correspondents thought I'd be murdered: I think they exaggerated. However, I was stoned, I was continually threatened, I stood on the pavement and watched a crowd of thugs howling for my life at the door of the Ritz Hotel (after which the remaining foreign US correspondents packed and ran away): and because I wasn't 'their man' my own Embassy made only a very halfhearted, very formal attempt to protect me – nothing like what they did for the tame Reuters' man. I went into the riots – after that Greek got thwacked

and bayoneted during the November one I never succeeded in getting another journalist to go near one, except Bill Hamsher of the Daily Express, though my wife once went into the thick of it without my knowledge and got me some useful facts. Apart from that, I worked more than twice as long every day as anybody else on the job. Well, even worse errors might have been made if I hadn't – Loy Henderson seemed likely to give bad advice to your govt at one time, but after a whole afternoon with me he didn't send the despatch. Well, is that 'ganging up with criminals'? It is trying to prevent follies which, even in the world ruled by its rulers, are preventable, instead of wasting my time howling at the moon … The same invincible repugnance to whole-hog lying which prevented me complying with the wishes of either Mossy Dick or Sir John le Rougetel prevents me from pretending to believe the things you'd like me to believe (or at any rate Ez would), and I on my part see no reason why I should deplore Ez merely because he isn't another me.

On 'The Spoils' he notes that, 'If Ole Ez had had time or inclination to read "The Spoils" attentively instead of being put off by the pair of Jews in part one of it, he might have noticed plumb in the middle of it a remark that God is the dividing sword. It isn't there just for the noise. That's what I'm writing about, and that's why the spoils are for God in the epigraph from the Qor'an. It is shorthand for quite a lot, or if you like for something I think fundamental.'[332]

Wretched newspaper job

In September 1953 Bunting was given some low paid, part-time work by the *Manchester Guardian*, which promised much but paid next to nothing. According to Denis Goacher he briefly found work as a ticket collector at the local railway station,[333] but this may be a confusion because he worked for Thomas Reid & Son, a publishing business, proofreading bus and train timetables.[334] This wasn't very fulfilling. He wrote in an exasperated tone to Zukofsky in October 1953:

> You are not likely to get many more letters, old friend, because at the end of this week, if the trade-union concerned gives its exalter permission, I shall start a 9½ hour day plus 1½ hours travelling, correcting the proofs of railway time-tables: and for that I shall get, after off-takes, (tax, insurance, fares, union subscription) less than 25% above what I get on the dole: or, to put it in Sir W. Beveridge's terms, still a good deal less than a minimum subsistence wage. Maybe that's all the stupid work is worth, but the poisonous task and the

starvation pay, looked at as the reward for all the years of strenuous, intelligent and uncorrupted service at, however modestly I try to look at it, a highish, a certainly influential level … I shall end by hating the Western world. Even for this I must express loud gratitude: it is a most generous gesture (if they make it) for a trade-union to allow someone who has 'written for Conservative papers' to correct time-table proofs.[335]

Within weeks he had moved on from timetables to 'seedsmen's catalogues and from those to electoral lists, which now occupy about six of my daily nine hours. The rest is bill-heads, receipt-forms and technical journals of such unbelievable illiteracy that it is often not possible to guess what the authors imagine themselves to be saying.'[336] He spent an enormous amount of time doing this exasperating proofreading for the National Coal Board's magazine. He complained bitterly about it to Dorothy Pound:

The National Coalboard runs a magazine called 'Mining' for the technical information of mining engineers, and the firm I work for prints it. Considering the illiteracy of most mining engineers they might have been expected to appoint an industrious and skilful editor, but though I hear he's very highly paid, you cannot imagine anyone more slovenly. I have to correct about half the proofs for his paper: but I may not make a verb agree in number with its subject, or supply a verb that's been omitted, or put in or take out a comma that's making nonsense or even see that a word is spelt the same way twice if it occurs twice. It might hurt the customer's feelings. As the proofs leave me they often contain whole paragraphs of which nobody could possibly make head and tail without protracted study. The authors get their friends to put in corrections, which adds handsomely to the bill the Coal Board pays my boss and still leaves the magazine, when it goes to press, short of verbs and entangled to such a degree that I wonder how many engineers ever read each others articles.[337]

He was hankering after Persia and took a week off work to go to London in the early summer. He had been invited to the Persian Embassy for an interview, but when he got there

Hamzavi only wanted to give me the gist of a letter from Foreign Minister Entezam without committing anything to paper or showing me the script. Entezam wanted him to convey to me discreetly and noncommittally the idea that Zahedi's govt was perfectly aware that my expulsion was not only indefensible but a bad mistake which had left Persia without its only friend in the English press, but that they were afraid to cancel it just yet because Baqai and his thugs were still capable of rioting about it and even more capable of putting an end to me, which would embarrass Zahedi: so would I please wait a few months and then apply ... No doubt they have some colour for this. I think they exaggerate. After all, Baqai has had at least two shots at murdering me before, but between inefficiency and irresolution he couldn't get his thugs to do the job properly, and that was when he was really powerful: now he's not. Hamzavi added some interesting stuff about his and Makki's efforts to prevent Mosaddeq turning me out, and Mosaddeq's consternation when he saw what the press in general had to say about it. But since I'm not altogether convinced that Zahedi's government will survive very long unless the oil consortium offers him better terms than I think they are doing, I don't feel much nearer Teheran.[338]

He also had interviews at *The Times* and the BBC, where Bridson, who by now held a senior position at the BBC, tried to help and told him he would do a Bunting programme on the Third Programme in the autumn. This was, it seems, the only promise that Bunting collected during his week in London that was ever fulfilled. Denis Goacher had approached Bridson on Bunting's behalf and recordings of his poems (not read by Bunting himself, but by a Scottish actor) were broadcast by the BBC in 1954 and 1957.[339] The cheque for the broadcast 'provided Sima with a superfine sewing-machine, which will of course contribute to the family budget as long as she and the children need clothes'.[340]

He landed what seemed to be a better job as a sub-editor on the Newcastle *Daily Journal* on 26 July 1954.[341] He loathed it. His 'wretched newspaper job' was 'a tiresome drudgery and there is nothing good to be said about it. It brings in very little money but, at least, it keeps the children fed.'[342] He described his Sisyphean life on the *Journal* to Pound in a letter of 28 November 1954: '5 p.m. to 2 a.m, or later ... usually in bed by 3.30, but sometimes not till 4 or later, and I have to read several papers in the time between getting up and getting on the bicycle again'.[343]

He tried to find other work. In 1955 he wrote to Bridson to tell him that he had applied for a job as a BBC reporter and given Bridson's name as a referee: 'I'm above the age they mention, but please endeavour to earthquake them into taking me nevertheless, for I am perishing in the swamp still where Mosaddeq threw me and the Times left me ... We have kept alive, but it has taken all our leisure and all our energy to accomplish it.'[344] He didn't get the job and in June 1957 he asked if Bridson could find him work at the BBC's Newcastle office as the family was now committed to the area because of accommodation and schools.[345]

He said a few years later that he had lasted at the *Journal* a year beyond the normal retirement age of 65, 'because I don't think they could get anybody else to do such dreary work or such heavy work for anything like the money they pay me. They would have to get two men, or they would have to pay one man a lot more than they pay me.'[346] He was as contemptuous of local journalists as he was of the national and international press who had fled Teheran. In one of those flashes of prescience of which Bunting was so capable he excoriated the local media in a way that suggests he could see fifty years ahead:

> Provincial journalists are not capable of any thought of any sort at all ... By now I've had a long life. I've seen very many odd situations and I have never at any time seen people so wholly without experience of life as journalists. They go to newspaper offices from the most ignorant parts of secondary-modern schools. That's where they're recruited. And they are never outside the newspaper office again for the rest of their days, except to do a little shorthand writing in the police court or something like that. They see nothing and their notions of life are probably adopted from out-of-date novels. The stupid things you see in newspapers are going to be there as long as newspapers are run the way they are. Like anything else that lives upon advertising – they'll be run the same way. That is the horror of all these attempts to extend the sphere of advertising to television and so on.[347]

His job on the *Journal* was a far cry from the high political intrigue of his years in Teheran but it had its compensations. He worked a late shift, and after work he rode his moped home through the Northumbrian countryside to Throckley. He told Jonathan Williams, 'that was worth doing. In the middle of the night you saw all sorts of creatures on that road that you never see in the daytime. Every kind of owl I got familiar with, and foxes carrying chickens in their mouths, and things of that sort. It was very nice in some ways, of course you were terribly tired, a tiring business being up all night working on a newspaper and then trying to sleep when everyone else is up and about in the day.'[348]

These are generally regarded as Bunting's empty years. He was bringing up a young family in poverty, was writing no poetry and was working at a job he detested. In 1957 he moved from the night job on the Newcastle *Daily Journal* to a day job on its sister paper, the *Evening Chronicle*. Even the move from daily to evening backfired. 'That was a great mistake I made,' he told Victoria Forde. 'I wanted to see more of my children and I could by working on the Chronicle that had reasonable working hours. But they put me on to doing the damned stock exchange report and that sort of thing.'[349] 'It gave me some grim satisfaction,' he told Gael Turnbull, 'to print as prominently as I could in the Evening Chronicle the Board of Trade's estimate of average incomes for 1963. It seems that, pensioners included, the average income then was £22 per week ... at that time what the Chronicle paid "Our Financial Expert" to advise its readers what to do with their money and to perform the longest, drudgingest task in its daily round, was £17.'[350]

He didn't entirely lose his spirit. Caddell and Flowers describe the way he was perceived by colleagues:

> Bunting is remembered by a colleague on the 'subs' bench as an unassuming man, with a good financial brain. He was responsible for, among other things, the financial page with its listing of the movement of stocks and shares: 'he could always tell you where to put your money!' A popular man, he told stories of his times in Persia and how he had had to leave while correspondent for *The Times.* He was always writing, and fellow journalists were aware of his poetry, although he was also known for his humour – the story is told of a local councillor who had risen to the rank of Major during the war – a fact that he regularly reminded the local press of, when they reported on him. On one occasion he rang the *Evening Chronicle* and was put through to Bunting: 'WING COMMANDER BUNTING here,' said Basil, with impressive solemnity.[351]

He had little contact with the literary world. Zukofsky wrote to Pound from Brooklyn on 1 October 1956: 'P. sent an announcement to Basil – but the perennial question? Where is he? Do you know? Has not answered to several letters since I saw you last.'[352] The poet Gael Turnbull, however, did visit Bunting in Throckley in 1956:

> It was his mother's home, a fairly substantial terraced [actually semi-detached] house. Sima and the two children were in Persia ... up some high steps, to an ordinary door, any door. With a man to open the door, to say, 'Yes, I am ...' and to greet me. A little amused perhaps at my obvious surprise that he existed. How could it be? And how could it be otherwise? My first bizarre reaction: how much he was the story-book image of a scout-master. Then, another image of dignity and humour.[353]

According to Caddell and Flowers Bunting, when he read this account later, said 'that would be Wing Commander Bunting'. But another poet, the American Robert Creeley, turned up in Newcastle in 1964 and was surprised to hear that Bunting was still alive. The journalist and poet Barry MacSweeney was a trainee reporter with Bunting at the *Chronicle*. He would have been in his late teens at the time. He showed a poem, 'Walk', to Bunting and 'it came back sliced down to about four lines and a note: start again from there'.[354] The older poet also taught MacSweeney how to calculate correct tide times for the crossing to Lindisfarne after MacSweeney had published potentially disastrous incorrect information. 'You have always to be accurate,' Bunting admonished the teenager.

An aged aunt died in 1956 leaving 'a few thousand pounds' to Bunting, and the family moved, with his mother, from Throckley a few miles further up the Tyne valley to Shadingfield, a good-sized semi-detached house in the village of Wylam, 'a pleasant house,' he told Gael Turnbull, 'with some space in it … There's a big garden over the river, pleasant walks all round a pleasant village …'[355] He spent the next twenty years trying to pay off the mortgage, he reflected ruefully in a television interview in 1984.[356] At the time though the legacy was a lifesaver. He wrote to Zukofsky in April 1957:

> I had an astonishing legacy from an aunt – not enough to change the wretched way I have to live, but enough to do two mitigations. Sima took the children off to Persia for a long holiday. When they get back at the beginning of June they will have been eight months gone. And, by selling the house we live in, which has been engulfed in the suburbs of Newcastle and poisoned by a power station, with the balance of the legacy, I've bought a great hideous house with lots of space, a splendid garden and a beautiful view … It is nearly twice as far from town as this house, and I shall probably kill myself riding home at night on the scooter, at least when things ice up next winter. But it's a genuine warranted village, complete with eccentric squire and six pubs to serve its minute population.[357]

The inheritance was indeed 'astonishing', as far as Bunting was concerned. He told Pound that his aunt had led 'such a starveling existence I supposed her to be penniless, but she left several thousand pounds'.[358] With this legacy he bought Wylam 'at the very bottom of the market … Edwardian, not a modern dog-kennel and about half an acre of garden where the children get strong playing and I cultivate cabbages. The view is very pleasant, down the garden to the river, across the cricket field to the village jammed around its church, and up the hill to the Roman Wall.'[359]

Bunting summarised his situation in the early 1960s in a rather depressing letter written in February 1963 that began his long friendship with Jonathan Williams. Williams had written to the older poet to enquire about publishing a selection of his work. Bunting's reply offered Williams accommodation at Shadingfield on the nights of 17 and 18 March, and longer if Williams cared to stay on: 'a friend of Zuk's is bound to be welcome in my house'. Hospitality offered, the rest of the letter is a series of dispirited grumbles:

> But you must be warned that the drudgery by which I feed my family will probably make it impossible for me to be at home on a Monday before 5:30 p.m. I shall try to get off for the day, but haven't much hope of it. That doesn't mean that you must waste your time at Wylam. Sima, my Persian wife, is not a reader even in her own language, but she is lively and entertaining: and if you prefer to write, there's a room for it. Also, Wylam is a pleasant place. The children don't get home from school until late afternoon, so their inquisitiveness and noise need not interrupt you much … No, it wasn't that I wouldn't have liked you to do an edition of my poems: but (a) I had little to offer you beyond what Flynn printed – only, in effect, *The Spoils.* (b) I didn't, and don't, know what became of Flynn and his edition: there must have been complications (c) I thought you were better occupied in printing Zuk, who is still a poet, than in reviving an extinct man. You will see for yourself how my circumstances prevent correspondence: what I would write would be too depressing.[360]

After a long silence Bunting was back in touch with Zukofksy, prompted by 'old affection'. In November 1962 Zukofsky urged him to raise some cash by selling his papers to the Humanities Research Center at the University of Texas. Letters from Pound, Eliot and Williams were particularly prized and Zukofsky thought Bunting would 'fetch at least a thousand bucks'.[361] Zukofsky had been planning such a sale for many years. Bunting wrote disapprovingly about his scheme in 1953: 'Letters are meant to be written to affect one bloke, not a public. What is true in the context of sender and recipient may be a bloody lie in the context of author and public … secondly: the bane of the age is running after remnants and rubbish heaps to avoid having to face what a man has made with deliberation and all his skill for the public.'[362]

Bunting wrote to Denis Goacher in 1964 that he felt as though he 'had been dead for ten years now, and my ghost doesn't walk. Dante has nothing to tell me about Hell that I don't know for myself.'[363] By November that year his despair was deepening. He told Goacher that 'they've cut off our gas, and the water is threatened, there's no coal, the mortgage and the rates are due, and the prospect is so bleak that with a wife less courageous than Sima I'd despair'.[364]

Bunting captured the spirit of this period of his life in a section of *Briggflatts* that strikes a jarring note for many readers:

Tides of day strew the shingle
tides of night sweep, snoring;
and some turned back, taught
by dreams the year would capsize
where the bank quivers, paved
with gulls stunned on a cliff
not hard to climb, muffled
in flutter, scored by beaks,
pestered by scavengers
whose palms scoop droppings to mould
cakes for hungry towns. One
plucked fruit warm from the arse
of his companion, who
making to beat him, he screamed:
Hastor! Hastor! but Hastor
raised dung thickened lashes to stare
disdaining those who cry:
Sweet shit! Buy!
for he swears in the market:
By God with whom I lunched!
there is no trash in the wheat
my loaf is kneaded from [365]

This is grim portrait of the journalist's trade, and especially of Hugh Astor of *The Times*.

A BOY OF EIGHTEEN, LONG-HAIRED AND FAIRLY RAGGED, 1964–1965

In the midst of this financial despair in the summer of 1964 Bunting's life took an enormous change for the better. He recalled the turning point in a letter to Dorothy Pound written a year later: 'First, about a year ago, somebody rang me up on the phone and asked if I would like to read some poetry. It turned out that the voice thought it belonged to a poet of sorts, so I said: Come out. He took the next train and turned up inside an hour, a boy of 18, long-haired and fairly ragged, with a fist full of manuscript. He said: I heard you were the greatest living poet.'[366]

Jonathan Williams had advised the young Newcastle poet Tom Pickard to contact Bunting for some poems for a new magazine he was starting. As Caddell and Flowers observe[367] that the two Newcastle poets should be

355

introduced via Black Mountain College (although by then the college had been closed for several years) in North Carolina is a measure of Bunting's obscurity at the time. Pickard remembers their meeting:

> One Sunday night shortly after receiving Jonathan's letter I decided to look up Mr. Bunting in the telephone directory, and I gave him a ring from a public box. His Persian wife Sema [*sic*] answered the call, then sent Basil to the phone. Nervously I explained that I was putting together a magazine and wanted some contributions from him. He invited me over, and I caught the next train out ... The door was opened by a man of sixty-three with a bushy moustache and thick glasses. He took me into the kitchen where I met his Persian wife Sema and her mother, who spoke no English. The kitchen overlooked the Tyne and their garden, well kept, ran down to the railway line. They had a small dog and a cat, which was famous in the village for accompanying the Buntings on walks. Their two children, Maria and Thomas, lived with them as did Basil's mother. She was a proud old woman with all her own teeth and a piano in her room. Until her death at ninety-odd she would take unaccompanied trips to Newcastle and back.
>
> I was given a whiskey and sat at the table while Basil kindly asked me what I was up to. Sema's mother had brought a lot of caviar from Persia, and since neither she nor Sema enjoyed it, Basil and I were given heaps of it on bits of toast. I got the impression there was very little else in the pantry. Sema was a happy, strong, wild-eyed Armenian, who looked a little pale in those northern days. We always got on well. I remember a number of visits in which I was pinned to the wall in an Armenian arm-lock and rib tickled, while Basil laughed coughing into his Senior Service, pleading for my release. Over the caviar sandwich he read me the 'Spoils', which I took away to publish.[368]

Which he did. 'The Spoils' was published by The Morden Tower Book Room in 1965 with a photograph of a Persian mosque on the cover and at a price of 5/-, beginning an extraordinary period in an already extraordinary life. Bunting started to write in earnest once more and the result was the biggest event in the world of poetry (in English at least) since the publication of *The Waste Land* in 1922, *Briggflatts*. Tom Pickard, and his wife Connie, were responsible for more than Bunting's reawakening. They fostered a local cultural revolution more generally. The *Evening Chronicle* of 12 June 1964 noted that: 'Newcastle's ancient city wall will become the centre of modern poetry for the area if an 18-year-old youth's scheme proves successful. Thomas Pickard of Buston Terrace, Jesmond has rented the famous Morden Tower from Newcastle Corporation for 10 shillings a week and is busily turning it into a bookroom where he plans to stage exhibitions and poetry readings.'[369]

Pickard's visit and the constant encouragement of friends such as Zukofsky, Jonathan Williams and Gael Turnbull released the genie and Bunting re-engaged with his art. By November 1964 well-known poets such as Robert Creeley were beating a path to Wylam, and he was thrilled by the response to his readings at Morden Tower. Tom Pickard described the reaction to Bunting's first reading there:

> … we had a packed house, maybe seventy people. The audience was mainly young. There were students, grammar school kids, apprentices and the unemployed. We charged less money, nothing, to those like myself 'on the dole'. The young people loved him and were attentive. We listened carefully, not always understanding, but hearing. We recognized and respected this sailor come home. He sat by gas-light (we had no electricity then), his safe-door glasses gleaming, and he read (for the first time in how many years?) to a young audience, who literally sat at his feet (we couldn't afford chairs and besides they took up precious space).[370]

Bunting wrote to Zukofsky in July 1964:

> it was a curious experience, reading to these youngsters. They were not hindered by the difficulties that annoy their elders. They took poetry as poetry – a nice noise – without questions about its 'meaning'. They laughed at the comic bits, they were rapt at the passages of intricate metric that nobody ever took any notice of before – not that they understood what was attracting them, but it certainly did attract – and the piece about the sick child made at least one girl cry. I found it all very encouraging.[371]

On 7 September he acknowledged the role that Zukofsky and Pickard had played in his sudden revival. He wrote again to Zukofsky: 'Perhaps it is enough to say that between you and Tom Pickard and Denis Goacher, somehow the old machine has been set to work again, and I have actually been writing. Therefore I send you the first fruits.' The poem Bunting enclosed with this letter was his heartbreaking 'A song for Rustam', 'facing at last the death of my elder son, I have courted the risk of platitude and even cliché by trying to banish "literature" as far as I can from the statement of what I feel, or felt'.[372]

In September 1964 he wrote to Zukofsky:

> I owe poems to Rustam – part paid; to Cooper Stephenson, who was killed in the great battle of March 1918, the closest of all friends I've had; and to

Peggy Greenbank and her whole ambience, the Rawthey valley, the fells of Lunedale, the Viking inheritance all spent save the faint smell of it, the ancient Quaker life accepted without thought and without suspicion that it might seem eccentric: and what happens when one deliberately thrusts love aside, as I then did – it has its revenge. That must be a longish poem. Presumably the effort will breed little poems too. And then I'll be ready to write a great hymn to death that cleanses the world and puts an end to its stench. Well, that looks like the programme of an old man revisiting the scenes of his youth, casting up his accounts, as my father did in the few months before he died. I have no means to carry it out, but I must try.[373]

Within the next two years of this creative resurgence he wrote eight odes and one of the century's poetic masterpieces.

'A thrush in the syringa sings' was written in 1964 and published in *Paris Review* in 1965.[374] It became the first poem in the *Second Book of Odes* and announces a theme that runs consistently through the twelve poems in that sequence, mortality:

> A thrush in the syringa sings.
>
> 'Hunger ruffles my wings, fear,
> lust, familiar things.
>
> Death thrusts hard. My sons
> by hawk's beak, by stones,
> trusting weak wings
> by cat and weasel, die.
>
> Thunder smothers the sky.
> From a shaken bush I
> list familiar things,
> fear, hunger, lust.'
>
> O gay thrush![375]

'Birthday greetings', also written in 1964, briefly celebrates life at the other end of the continuum:

> Gone to hunt; and my brothers,
> but the hut is clean, said the girl.
> I have curds, besides whey.

> Pomegranates, traveller;
> butter, if you need it,
> in a bundle of cress.
>
> Soft, so soft, my bed.
> Few come this road.
> I am not married: – yet
>
> today I am fourteen years old.[376]

The 'yet' at the end of the penultimate line shifts the girl's yearning subtly. 'I am not married:– yet' sounds like a confident assertion that she soon will be, but in fact the final line shows clearly that she is, if anything, bewildered by the fact that she is not married *even though* she has turned fourteen.

If nothing else a new Ezra Pound was teaching condensation to younger poets. Tom Pickard recalls,

> on many lunch hours I would meet Basil at the Rose and Crown, which was close to the news-factory, and over a pint of bass he'd go over some recent effort of mine, saying 'Well, you've almost got it there, Tom … ' All that was left of two pages was a line.
>
> 'What shall I do with it?'
>
> 'Oh keep it hanging around … until just the right place for it turns up … '
>
> Only one line out of two pages. I was horrified, and it happened often. Over a period I got small complete poems chiselled out of the slag. He would patiently look at a typed page for a while, a cigarette in his mouth … blow the smoke with great force out of his nostrils, and take a pencil faintly round a few chosen lines.
>
> 'Try that. It's not what you wanted to say, but it makes a poem,' or 'Take this line from here and try it at the end … '
>
> 'But what I wanted to say was …'
>
> And he kindly: 'Oh well, what the hell. It's not important to the poem.'[377]

It was around this time that Tom Pickard introduced Bunting to Hugh MacDiarmid. 'I'd gone to North Yorkshire to give my first public poetry reading and MacDiarmid was there,' Pickard told me.

We got on very well, spending the night drinking in the local bars where he introduced me to Glenfiddich. It was a weekend festival and on the Monday morning we travelled north together on the train – he on his way to Scotland and I to Newcastle. I persuaded him to stop off in Newcastle for a few hours so he could meet Basil on his lunch break from Thompson House. It was my habit in those days to meet BB for a lunch time drink in a bar close to his work in the centre of town. BB was delighted to find MacDiarmid waiting there and they got on well immediately.[378]

After a reading at Morden Tower a few months later the poets went back to the Pickards' flat:

The old men were bubbling with the Glenfiddick Fire Water and the youngsters blissful on beer and marijuana.

BB: 'MacDiarmid, this working class lad here spells cunt with a K, but writes marvellous poetry … '

HMcD: 'I hate the fucking working class … '

Mischief sparkled in their eyes all night long, and Bunting sang from his seemingly endless repertoire of bawdy songs.[379]

FOUR

AN ACKNOWLEDGED LAND

It is time to consider how Domenico Scarlatti
condensed so much music into so few bars
with never a crabbed turn or congested cadence,
never a boast or a see-here; and stars and lakes
echo him and the copse drums out his measure,
snow peaks are lifted up in moonlight and twilight
and the sun rises on an acknowledged land.

Briggflatts IV

THE PULSE OF GOD'S BLOOD

It is time to consider *Briggflatts*.

Bunting eventually felt compelled to write an explanatory note about *Briggflatts*, although he suppressed it during his lifetime. As it is the poet's only complete statement about one of the twentieth century's most important poems it is worth considering in full:

> *Briggflatts* is a poem: it needs no explanation. The sound of the words spoken aloud is itself the meaning, just as the sound of the notes played on the proper instruments is the meaning of any piece of music. Yet I have been teased so much by people who cannot be content to listen without reasoning, and by people who think they detect in the poem notions alien to it and sometimes repulsive to me that I will set down, if I can, some hint of the state of its maker's mind.

> Commonplaces provide the poem's structure: spring, summer, autumn, winter of the year and of man's life, interrupted in the middle and balanced

around Alexander's trip to the limits of the world and its futility, and sealed and signed at the end by a confession of our ignorance. Love and betrayal are spring's adventures, the wisdom of elders and the remoteness of death, hardly more than a gravestone. In summer there is no rest from ambition and lust of experience, never final. Those fail who try to force their destiny, like Eric; but those who are resolute to submit, like my vision of Pasiphae, may bring something new to birth, be it only a monster.

What Alexander learns when he has thrust his way through the degraded world is that man is contemptibly nothing and yet may live content in humility. Autumn is for reflexion, to set Aneurin's grim elegy against the legend of Cuthbert who saw God in everything, to love without expectation, wander without an inn, persist without hope. Old age can see at last the loveliness of things overlooked or despised, frost, the dancing maggots, sheepdogs, and particularly the stars which make time a paradox and a joke till we can give up our own time, even though we wasted it. And still we know neither where we are nor why.

All old wives' chatter, cottage wisdom. No poem is profound.

The name 'Briggflatts', that of a remote hamlet and a Quaker meeting house, ought to warn people not to look for philosophy. Unfortunately T. S. Eliot's *Four Quartets* are also named after little hidden places, and they do expound the mystical Christianity that nineteenth century theologians brewed from a mash squeezed ultimately, I think, from Plotinus. No scheme of things could be further from my own.

Yeats too professed Plotinus, though his spirit seems nearer to that of Iamblichus. Pound took his gods from Ovid, close cousins to the gods of *The Golden Bough*, never truly pagan but spangles on a neo-Platonic chiffon. Both Pound and Yeats fancied the dreary notion of a history that repeats itself, not as the Buddhists see it, nor as Toynbee, but the cruder Spengler, and that too is part of the neo-Platonic outlook. Pound had too much sense to be consistent. A kind of pragmatism often hidden under the robes of his own private Confucius represents him best. He was not averse to reason, much more a moralist than a metaphysician; yet the scheme of *The Cantos* rests in the mood of Spengler, even, but not consciously, in the mood of Hegel.

Hierarchy and order, the virtues of the neo-Platonic quasi-religion, were prime virtues also to Yeats, Pound and Eliot. They are not virtues to me, only expedients that chafe almost as vilely as the crimes they try to restrain. Amongst philosophers I have most sympathy with Lucretius and his masters, content to explain the world an atom at a time; with Spinoza who saw all things as God, though not with his wish to demonstrate that logically; and with David Hume, the doubter. The men I learned poetry from did not much value these. Perhaps that is why it took me so long to make a poem that reflects, fragmentarily, my whole mind.

Call it God, call it the universe, all we know of it, extended far beyond our telescopes or even inferences, detailed more minutely than our physicists can grope, is less than the histology of a single cell might be to a man's body, or to his conduct. The day's incidents hide our ignorance from us; yet we know it, beneath our routine. In silence, having swept dust and litter from our minds, we can detect the pulse of God's blood in our veins, more persuasive than words, more demonstrative than a diagram. That is what a Quaker meeting tries to be, and that is why my poem is called *Briggflatts*. Let the incidents and images take care of themselves.[1]

Shining slowworm part of the marvel

The poem opens in Brigflatts itself:

> Brag, sweet tenor bull,
> descant on Rawthey's madrigal,
> each pebble its part
> for the fells' late spring.
> Dance tiptoe, bull,
> black against may.
> Ridiculous and lovely
> chase hurdling shadows
> morning into noon.
> May on the bull's hide
> and through the dale
> furrows fill with may,
> paving the slowworm's way.[2]

Hugh Kenner asked in a review of *Briggflatts* if the first four words of this poem had ever been together in a line of poetry before. It seems unlikely. The opening image is one of the most arresting in twentieth-century verse. The soundscape conjured in these lines is enchanting, exactly capturing the essence of May in the fells of the north Pennines. The madrigal sung by the swollen River Rawthey, which runs just behind the hamlet, is the authentic voice of the fells; each pebble on its bed applying tiny modulations to create a song sung in thousands of counterpoint parts. It is an effect Bunting caught beautifully in a later lyric:

> Stones trip Coquet burn;
> grass trails, tickles
> till her glass thrills.[3]

Above the Rawthey's main melody and harmonising with it is the bull's tenor descant. The contrasts suggested by the descant on Rawthey's madrigal are paralleled by the figure of the black bull set against the brilliant white may blossom hedge, and the harmony is supplied by the reflected contrast of the pale blossom on the bull's black hide as it drops and fills the furrows to pave the slowworm's way.

The behaviour of the bull had been in Bunting's notebooks for at least a dozen years before he worked it into the opening of *Briggflatts*. 'The bull had been in my mind for ages,' he told an interviewer in 1970,

> but he hadn't been put down as having anything to do with [*Briggflatts*] until quite late in the process … the bull I noticed one day in a farm near Throckley … it struck me, at once, nobody had noticed the bull has a *tenor* voice. You hear of the bull bellowing and this, that, and the other. But in fact he bellows in the most melodious tenor, a beautiful tenor voice. In spring, the bull does in fact, if he's with the cows, dance, on the tips of his toes, part of the business of showing off, showing that he is protecting them, you see. He's not really doing anything, but he sees somebody walking by the hedge and he begins to dance at once, just to demonstrate to the cows what an indispensable creature he is. It is delightful, and it bears such a, a strong resemblance to the behaviour of young men in general …[4]

It struck him as, 'comically like a young man … his voice was a tenor voice, more like a young man's still, his attitude to the field of heifers, he's showing off all the time …'[5] The temptation to read the bull as the thirteen-year-old Bunting displaying for his best friend's young sister is one to be resisted. We should take the poem as it comes and not be derailed by the (natural enough) desire to read in autobiographical meanings.

The second stanza sharpens the focus to the sounds of the hamlet itself:

> A mason times his mallet
> to a lark's twitter,
> listening while the marble rests,
> lays his rule

at a letter's edge,
fingertips checking,
till the stone spells a name
naming none,
a man abolished.
Painful lark, labouring to rise!
The solemn mallet says:
In the grave's slot
he lies. We rot.

John Greenbank's father, the stonemason, is at one with his environment, the tempo of his work set by the rhythm of the lark's song, more contrasts and harmony. The mason chisels the name of the dead man into the marble and we can feel Bunting reaching back forty years to the poet 'broody all night over the bones of a deadman' in 'Villon', the 'deadman' who is something other than a 'dead man'. Here he is 'a man abolished'. Bunting also takes the opportunity to repeat a sly dig at Vaughan Williams, whose lark he accused of ascending apparently interminably in *The Outlook* in 1928.

Part one of *Briggflatts* consists of twelve thirteen-line stanzas which describe a day and night of tender intimacy between two very young lovers on the fells around Sedbergh;

Stocking to stocking, jersey to jersey,
head to a hard arm,
they kiss under the rain,
bruised by their marble bed.

The young lovers walk in the fells and, after a brief meditation on the death of Eric Bloodaxe,

they trudge and sing,
laying the tune frankly on the air.
All sounds fall still,
fellside bleat,
hide-and-seek peewit.

Their song reflects Rawthey's madrigal from the first stanza, and the bull's descant is replaced by the sounds of the sheep and lapwings.

Their caresses continue at night when her parents are asleep:

Gentle generous voices weave
over bare night
words to confirm and delight
till bird dawn.
Rainwater from the butt
she fetches and flannel
to wash him inch by inch,
kissing the pebbles.
Shining slowworm part of the marvel.
The mason stirs:
Words!
Pens are too light.
Take a chisel to write.

By this, the ninth stanza, the pebbles and slow-worm have returned in different guises in true sonata style. 'I have a very slight knowledge of some of the most elementary tasks of masonry,' Bunting told an interviewer.

> I've rubbed down a gravestone in the days when it was a matter of doing it by hand ... 'Pens are too light. Take a chisel to write'... is very good advice if you translate it from the figure into the way one actually does write with a typewriter. Namely don't be in any hurry about it and think it bloody thoroughly out before you put down a word! ... If you're writing with a chisel you have to be certain of every word, and they have to be the fewest you can possibly use, and the shortest you can possibly find.[6]

The chisel is an important point of inflection in the first part of *Briggflatts*. The tender lyricism of the first nine stanzas has celebrated a love that is both innocent and sexual, full of childlike wonder at the part love plays in a world which is not separate from nature. The chisel ends that brutally. We move from a prelapsarian world of endless innocent delight to bitter reflection on one that is forever lost. The chisel and marble, hard and inflexible, mark a transition to a world of words:

Every birth a crime,
every sentence life.
Wiped of mould and mites
would the ball run true?
No hope of going back.
Hounds falter and stray,
shame deflects the pen.

Love murdered neither bleeds nor stifles
but jogs the drauftsman's elbow.
What can he, changed, tell
her, changed, perhaps dead?
Delight dwindles. Blame
stays the same.

The poet has betrayed love and his words coalesce as 'sentences', lifelong imprisonment for the guilty man. The final stanza of part one returns to its beginning, but it is no longer spring and the world has changed irrevocably:

Dung will not soil the slowworm's
mosaic. Breathless lark
drops to nest in sodden trash;
Rawthey truculent, dingy.
Drudge at the mallet, the may is down,
fog on fells. Guilty of spring
and spring's ending
amputated years ache after
the bull is beef, love a convenience.
It is easier to die than to remember.
Name and date
split in soft slate
a few months obliterate.

This is, for me, one of the most moving stanzas in English poetry.

Love is a vapour, we're soon through it

The second part of *Briggflatts* continues the theme of guilt but individualises it, 'sick, self-maimed, self-hating'. It begins in London but quickly shifts to the far north. In between the London and polar scenes is a short, discrete lyric that Bunting sent to Zukofsky in a letter written in November 1964:

You who can calculate the course
of a biased bowl,
shall I come near the jack?
What twist can counter the force
that holds back
woods I roll?

You who elucidate the disk
hubbed by the sun,
shall I see autumn out
or the fifty years at risk
be lost, doubt
end what's begun?

These lines were enclosed as a handwritten postscript: 'This occurred to me after I had sealed the envelope, but what the hell. Perhaps by tomorrow I shall think it's shit, but tonight it seems to be words for music. If you don't play bowls (not ten-pins, but on the grass with biased balls) in America you may not quite get it. On the other hand, it may amuse you.'[7] These lines make one wonder if the whole *Briggflatts* enterprise was planned to effect a reconciliation with Peggy. The image elaborates on the question asked in part one of the poem: 'Wiped of mould and mites/would the ball run true?' In the first stanza if Peggy is the jack then Bunting is both bowler and bowled. He is rolling the woods as well as *being rolled* towards the jack. The poet is writing the future just as Villon did in his cell.

After London the hardship of life at sea in the northern ocean numbs memory:

No tilled acre, gold scarce,
walrus tusk, whalebone, white bear's liver.
Scurvy gnaws, steading smell, hearth's crackle.
Crabs, shingle, seracs on the icefall.
Summer is bergs and fogs, lichen on rocks.
Who cares to remember a name cut in ice
or be remembered?

A name carved in ice is no more durable than those that are 'split in soft slate' in Brigflatts' graveyard.

The chisel in part one signals an abrupt shift in tone and in part two there is a similarly sudden move from cold to warm, hardship to ease:

About ship! Sweat in the south. Go bare
because the soil is adorned,
sunset the colour of a boiled louse.
Steep sluice or level,
parts of the sewer ferment faster.

Days jerk, dawdle, fidget
towards the cesspit.
Love is a vapour, we're soon through it.

Life is still without hope, and our fate sealed whichever part of the sewer we
inhabit, but there may be incidental pleasures to be found along the way:

Flying fish follow the boat,
delicate wings blue, grace
on flick of a tissue tail,
the water's surface between
appetite and attainment.
Flexible, unrepetitive line
to sing, not paint; sing, sing,
laying the tune on the air,
nimble and easy as a lizard,
still and sudden as a gecko,
to humiliate love, remember
nothing.

In lines 6–8 Bunting is, according to Donald Davie, 'honouring the *cantabile*
art practised by Lawes and Jenkyns, by Waller and Dowland and Lovelace,
in the seventeenth century, as by Arnold Dolmetsch and Pound … in the
twentieth'.[8] Davie may be correct in this but it is a reductive interpretation
that robs the lines of some of their magic. Song is certainly the hero but
it is song found in the behaviour of lizards and geckoes. The 'flexible,
unrepetitive line' is the surface of the sea, about which the flying fish dart
to satisfy appetite below and aspiration above. It is a purely natural rhythm,
irreducible to art. But Bunting does not deny appetite and the relaxed
Italian idyll of 'submarine Amalfitan kisses' that follows is a celebration of
the senses although, as we have seen, still loaded with guilt.

Part two stays in Italy for a little longer:

White marble stained like a urinal
cleft in Apuan Alps,
always trickling, apt to the saw. Ice and wedge
split it or well-measured cordite shots,
while paraffin pistons rap, saws rip
and clamour is clad in stillness:
clouds echo marble middens, sugar-white,

that cumber the road stones travel
to list the names of the dead.

In the heat of Italy the cold of the north is recalled by locating to a marble quarry in the Alps, the mason's yard at Brigflatts recalled by the industrial carving of headstones. 'There is a lot of Italy in churchyards,' the poem continues, wittily pointing to the Italian appetite for marble monuments as well, perhaps, as a sense of a culture that has been suffocated by the Church. Another 'self-contained fragment' that Bunting sent to Zukofsky, acknowledging his debt to Kipling along the way,[9] follows the quarry section and, as with the bowling lyric, reintroduces the direct voice of the poet:

> Win from rock
>   flame and ore.
> Crucibles pour
>   sanded ingots.
>
> Heat and hammer
>   draw out a bar.
> Wheel and water
>   grind an edge.
>
> No worn tool
>   whittles stone;
> but a reproached
>   uneasy mason
>
> shaping evasive
>   ornament
> litters his yard
>   with flawed fragments.

The 'reproached uneasy mason' of part two is a travesty of the atoned mason of part one, the distance between them measured by the Brigflatts mason's understanding that 'rocks happen by chance' and the poet-mason's attempt to shape 'evasive ornament'. It returns the scene to the fells, and to Eric Bloodaxe:

> Loaded with mail of linked lies,
> what weapon can the king lift to fight
> when chance-met enemies employ sly

sword and shoulder-piercing pike,
pressed into the mire,
trampled and hewn till a knife
– in whose hand? – severs tight
neck cords? Axe rusts. Spine
picked bare by ravens, agile
maggots devour the slack side
and inert brain, never wise.
What witnesses he had life,
ravelled and worn past splice,
yarns falling to staple? Rime
on the bent, the beck ice,
there will be nothing on Stainmore to hide
void, no sable to disguise
what he wore under the lies,
king of Orkney, king of Dublin, twice
king of York, where the tide
stopped till long flight
from who knows what smile,
scowl, disgust or delight
ended in bale on the fellside.

Bloodaxe's stuttering achievements are reduced and restricted by his infidelity, 'no sable to disguise what he wore under the lies'. At this stage part two of *Briggflatts* swings back into lyric:

Starfish, poinsettia on a half-tide crag,
a galliard by Byrd.
Anemones spite cullers of ornament
but design the pool
to their grouping. The hermit crab
is no grotesque in such company.

Asian vultures riding on a spiral
column of dust
or swift desert ass startled by the
camels' dogged saunter
figures sudden flight of the descant
on a madrigal by Monteverdi.

But the music's power is limited. It cannot penetrate places nature has fled:

But who will entune a bogged orchard,
its blossom gone,
fruit unformed, where hunger and
damp hush the hive?
A disappointed July full of codling
moth and ragged lettuces?

Once again the music is driven by nature:

Yet roe are there, rise to the fence, insolent;
a scared vixen cringes
red against privet stems as a mazurka;
and rat, grey, rummaging
behind the compost heap has daring
to thread, lithe and alert, Schoenberg's maze.

In the previous stanza the attempts to turn nature into ornament fail; there
is no fruit, no honey, no produce. But nature will not be shut out. The deer
have no fear, the fox performs her folk dance undeterred, and the rat, which
will reappear dramatically in part four, reproduces Schoenberg's sinewy
rhythms.

But we desired Macedonia

The third part of *Briggflatts* has consistently caused readers more difficulties
than the rest of the poem, partly because it departs from the autobiography,
albeit a minimalist one, that we have come to expect from the first two
parts, partly because it presents an almost Blakean vision that is not very
transparent, and partly because it depicts a world that many readers do not
recognise.

Bunting told Donald Davie that the theme of part three, Alexander's
meeting with the angel on the mountain top, 'is the rejection of what is
usually reckoned as success and as consistency. But it's not a piece of theology
or philosophy. Its reason for existence is only to be a poem.'[10] Elsewhere
he described Alexander's encounter with Israfel as 'the confrontation of
ambition with something more full-fated that's in store for all of us ... the
futility of mankind' though he was quick to point out that this was just
one of many possible 'meanings'.[11] It is uncompromising, a pitiless view of
human ambition:

Tides of day strew the shingle
tides of night sweep, snoring;
and some turned back, taught
by dreams the year would capsize
where the bank quivers, paved
with gulls stunned on a cliff
not hard to climb, muffled
in flutter, scored by beaks,
pestered by scavengers
whose palms scoop droppings to mould
cakes for hungry towns. One
plucked fruit warm from the arse
of his companion, who
making to beat him, he screamed:
Hastor! Hastor! But Hastor
raised dung thickened lashes to stare
disdaining those who cry:
Sweet shit! Buy!
for he swears in the market:
By God with whom I lunched!
there is no trash in the wheat
my loaf is kneaded from.
Nor will unprofitable motion
stir the stink that settles round him.
Leave given
we would have slaughtered the turd-bakers
but neither whip nor knife
can welt their hides

As we have seen, this passage is a barely concealed sneer at journalism in general and *The Times* and Hugh Astor in particular (Bunting explains dismissively in a note that Hastor is 'a Cockney hero'), but it may also describe a world in which turd bakers could flourish. If we regard the word 'rubbish' in Sir Reader Bullard's description of Teheran during the war as the euphemism of a career diplomat we can envisage the scene Bunting describes: 'The task of supplying the bakers of Tehran with enough flour was stupendous. At times the American Food Adviser, in spite of occasional loans of flour from the British Army, had only a three days supply in hand, and had to use barley or some other foodstuff to eke out the wheat flour. Some bakers increased the difficulties by selling in the black market part of their quota of flour and replacing it by rubbish.'[12] We know from Bullard's letters from Teheran that bran, straw, charcoal dust and 'all kinds of chaff and muck' were mixed into Persian bread at the time.[13]

The poem then drops many circles in this *Inferno* before Alexander climbs the mountain to meet Israfel:

> Guides at the top claim fees
> though the way is random
> past hovels hags lean from
> rolling lizard eyes
> at boys gnawed by the wolf,
> past bevelled downs, grey marshes
> where some souse in brine
> long rotted corpses, others,
> needier, sneak through saltings
> to snatch toe, forearm, ear,
> and on gladly to hills
> briar and bramble vest
> where beggars advertise
> rash, chancre, fistula,
> to hug glib shoulders, mingle herpetic
> limbs with stumps and cosset the mad.

The *Shahnameh* was the source for this story:

> But we desired Macedonia,
> the rocky meadows, horses, barley pancakes,
> incest and familiar games,
> to end in our place by our own wars,
> and deemed the peak unscaleable; but he
> reached to a crack in the rock
> with some scorn, resolute though in doubt,
> traversed limestone to gabbro,
> file sharp, skinning his fingers,
> and granite numb with ice, in air
> too thin to bear up a gnat,
> scrutinising holds while day lasted,
> groping for holds in the dark
> till the morning star reflected
> in the glazed crag
> and other light not of the sun

dawning from above
lit feathers sweeping snow
and the limbs of Israfel,
trumpet in hand, intent on the east,
cheeks swollen to blow,
whose sigh is cirrus: Yet delay!
When will the signal come
to summon man to his clay?

We really need Ferdowsi's original, in which Alexander is Sekandar, to supply some context here:

Sekandar made his way to the mountain summit alone. There he saw Esrafil, the angel of death, with a trumpet in his hand, his head raised at the ready, his cheeks filled with breath, his eyes brimming with tears, as he waited for God to order him to blow. Seeing Sekandar on the mountain Esrafil roared with a voice like thunder,

'Stop struggling, slave of greed! One day, at last,
Your ears will hear the mighty trumpet's blast –
Don't worry about crowns and thrones! Prepare
To pack your bags and journey on elsewhere!'
Sekandar said, 'I see that I'm to be
Hurried about the world perpetually,
And that I'll never know another fate
Than this incessant, wandering, restless state!'

He descended the mountain, weeping and praising God, then set out on the dark road again, following his guides.[14]

For Bunting this was one of the greatest moments of poetry: 'The one in Firdosi which I made use of in 'Briggflatts' of Alexander climbing the mountain and seeing on top the Angel of the Resurrection ready to blow the trumpet and put an end to the world. And it's not merely because the incident itself is striking but because the words make it so much more striking.'[15] Only with Ferdowsi can we see 'the confrontation of ambition with ... the futility of mankind' that is Bunting's thrust. For once the condensation is too intense (Bunting claimed to have cut the poem down from twenty thousand lines to around seven hundred).[16] He insisted that *Briggflatts* needed no notes although 'a few may spare diligent readers the pains of research'.[17] Even a diligent reader is likely to miss the point here without a note of explanation.

Bunting, of course, wouldn't have had much sympathy with this, but his stated 'meaning' is all but invisible.

Bunting's own gloss is also necessary if we are properly to follow the transition from Alexander's encounter with the Angel of Death to the passage which follows it:

> Alexander wanders through country after country where the most horrible things are going on, and ultimately comes to the mountains of Gog and Magog on the edge of the world. And his troops refuse to follow him, but all alone he climbs up to the top of the mountain, and there he sees the Angel sitting exactly as in my poem, with the trumpet ready to his lips to blow, and looking anxiously to the east for the signal to blow the trumpet and put an end to the world. And that of course does Alexander's business *for* him: he falls off the mountain, comes to, and leads everybody home in peace to Macedonia.[18]

In *Briggflatts* Alexander's fall from the top of the mountain is condensed out of existence. After Israfel's delayed sigh we return from the 'edge of the world' to a world that is very similar to that around the River Rawthey, but it is Alexander who wakes:

> Heart slow, nerves numb and memory, he lay
> on glistening moss by a spring;
> as a woodman dazed by an adder's sting
> barely within recall
> tests the rebate tossed to him, so he
> ascertained moss and bracken,
> a cold squirm snaking his flank
> and breath leaked to his ear:
> I am neither snake nor lizard,
> I am the slowworm.

The bowls and slow-worm themes re-emerge and interweave as in a sonata.

In his brilliant comparison of *Briggflatts*, *The Waste Land* and Pound's 'Canto 47' (which, incidentally, shows how much more Bunting had been influenced by Eliot than by Pound), Thom Gunn, one of Bunting's most sensitive critics, observed that,

> when Alexander falls stunned from the mountain, Bunting has him fall to a ground very like that of Northumberland. As he lies there, Alexander, the Achiever, hears the song of the slowworm at his ear – and the slowworm

sings, among other things, 'I prosper/lying low.' The song gives Alexander pause:

So he rose and led home silently through clean woodland

where every bough repeated the slowworm's song.

It is the song of the natural world, which is clean of the achiever and his ambition, and which is also helpless before him.[19]

I hear Aneurin number the dead

Part four of *Briggflatts* takes us back to the north of England, many miles north of Brigflatts, where the poem started, to the banks of the River Till.[20] It is autumn:

Grass caught in willow tells the flood's height that has subsided;
overfalls sketch a ledge to be bared tomorrow.
No angler homes with empty creel though mist dims day.
I hear Aneurin number the dead, his nipped voice.
Slight moon limps after the sun. A closing door
stirs smoke's flow above the grate. Jangle
to skald, battle, journey; to priest Latin is bland.
Rats have left no potatoes fit to roast, the gamey tang
recalls ibex guts steaming under a cold ridge,
tomcat stink of a leopard dying while I stood
easing the bolt to dwell on a round's shining rim.
I hear Aneurin number the dead and rejoice,
being adult male of a merciless species.

Aneirin, as his name is now usually spelt, a seventh-century court poet, described in his bloody poem, *Y Gododdin*, the fate of the warriors of Gododdin, a small Brythonic kingdom located between the Firth of Forth and Hadrian's Wall, at the Battle of Catraeth (now Catterick in north Yorkshire). In the post-Roman sixth century the land between the Antonine Wall and Hadrian's Wall, the 'Intervallum', was a battleground for the native Britons and Picts, and the incursive Germanic Angles and Gaelic Scots from Dalriada in Ulster. The Battle of Catraeth was fought in about 600 by Britons and Angles and Aneirin recorded it in a celebration of the warrior class and its glorification of slaughter, feasting and death. As Norman Davies has shown, the slaughter at Catterick was 'shocking even for a society that lived from warfare'.[21] The native tribes were wiped out and just one of the three hundred chieftains who had taken part survived. The heavy loss opened the door to the Angles who proceeded to occupy the entire region in the following decades. In Bunting's poem Aneirin numbers the Catraeth dead, as he does in *Y Gododdin*, as a prime specimen of his 'merciless species'. The proximity of this to the cold-eyed Bunting gazing on the dying leopard he has just shot clearly suggests that we should amalgamate the poets as we amalgamated Bunting and Villon. Aneirin–Bunting's job is to record death without pity or shame.

> I see Aneurin's pectoral muscle swell under his shirt,
> pacing between the game Ida left to rat and raven,
> young men, tall yesterday, with cabled thighs.
> Red deer move less warily since their bows dropped.
> Girls in Teesdale and Wensleydale wake discontent.
> Clear Cymric voices carry well this autumn night,
> Aneurin and Taliesin, cruel owls
> for whom it is never altogether dark, crying
> before the rules made poetry a pedant's game.[22]

After Aneirin and Taliesin the story of north Britain is taken on by the great Christian missionaries:

> Columba, Columbanus, as the soil shifts its vest,
> Aidan and Cuthbert put on daylight,
> wires of sharp western metal entangled in its soft
> web, many shuttles as midges darting;
> not for bodily welfare nor pauper theorums
> but splendour to splendour, excepting nothing that is.

Four generations of inspiring, mainly Celtic, Christian evangelists were responsible for the greatest achievements of the early Church in the British Isles. Columba, who was born in 521, founded the monastic community at Iona; a generation later Columbanus (born in 540) took his mission to the Franks; Aidan (who died in 651) founded the great monastery and the See of Lindisfarne in about 635; and Cuthbert (who died in 687) founded the city of Durham. It was these saints who introduced the distinctly Celtic architecture and design that is so prevalent in the north of Britain, and that Bunting valued so highly – the 'wires of sharp western metal entangled in its soft web'.

He had been enchanted by the Lindisfarne Codex since he was a small child, when the illustrated edition of J. R. Green's *A Short History of the English*

People 'was in our house always',[23] and the design of the Lindisfarne Codex was in Bunting's mind while he worked on the interrelationships between parts of the poem: 'The image of history is that of continually changing racial identity but continually recurring and lasting cultural identities, and the flowering of art and literature and history in ancient Northumbria has been a lasting thing.'[24]

After the Celtic saints Bunting moves on to the beautiful lyric about Scarlatti that opens this chapter. As the sun 'rises on an acknowledged land' an extraordinary and tender celebration of love unfolds. Bunting tended to slow his pace markedly when he reached this point in his reading:

> My love is young but wise. Oak, applewood,
> her fire is banked with ashes till day.
> The fells reek of her hearth's scent,
> her girdle is greased with lard;
> hunger is stayed on her settle, lust in her bed.
> Light as spider floss her hair on my cheek which a puff scatters,
> light as a moth her fingers on my thigh.
> We have eaten and loved and the sun is up,
> we have only to sing before parting:
> Goodbye, dear love.
>
> Her scones are greased with fat of fried bacon,
> her blanket comforts my belly like the south.
> We have eaten and loved and the sun is up.
> Goodbye.

With that 'goodbye' the brief idyll ends. The images of applewood and ashes, cobwebs, hair and puffs that do so much to sustain the almost weightless happiness of the lovers return in a different guise in a mirror image of innocence; grief, loss, betrayal:

> Applewood, hard to rive,
> its knots smoulder all day.
> Cobweb hair on the morning,
> a puff would blow it away.
> Rime is crisp on the bent,
> ruts stone-hard, frost spangles fleece.
> What breeze will fill that sleeve limp on the line?
> A boy's jet steams from the wall, time from the year,
> care from deed and undoing.

> Shamble, cold, content with beer and pickles,
> towards a taciturn lodging among strangers.

Her scones and her blanket are replaced by beer, pickles and cold.

At this point, perhaps the lowest of the entire poem, the tone changes once again. Up to now the poet has been a 'rat' in the colloquial sense, the 'love rat' who betrays and deceives a young love. At the end of part four of *Briggflatts* the poet becomes a rat proper, and embraces his new state:

> Where rats go go I,
> accustomed to penury,
> filth, disgust and fury;
> evasive to persist,
> reject the bait
> yet gnaw the best.
> My bony feet
> sully shelf and dresser,
> keeping a beat in the dark,
> rap on lath
> till dogs bark
> and sleep, shed,
> slides from the bed.
> O valiant when hunters
> with stick and terrier bar escape
> or wavy ferret leaps,
> encroach and cede again,
> rat, roommate, unreconciled.

The unreconciled rat shares some characteristics with the poet; both are intelligent, both are adult males of a merciless species. In her study, *The Nets of Modernism*, Maud Ellmann doesn't mention the poet-rat in *Briggflatts* specifically but she notes the importance of rats in modernist literature generally: 'popping up irrepressibly in modernist texts, the rat signals the breakdown of boundaries, at once calamitous and liberating'.[25] Ellmann's fascinating analysis of 'the Modernist rat' in Freud's transformation of Dr Ernst Lanzer into the Rat Man and in key modernist texts such as *Ulysses*, *The Waste Land* and Beckett's *Watt*, describes early twentieth-century laboratory experiments using rats in mazes. 'The influential behaviorist John Broadus Watson argued that ... stripped of baggage such as language, intellection, will, and feeling, rats performed their tasks with greater alacrity than human beings. In Watson's experiments, rats had to find their way to rewards placed in the center of the maze. Their success was measured by speed, which reduced behaviour to a matter of mechanical efficiency.' Watson's discoveries were published in *Psychological Review* in 1907.[26] Bunting's rat 'threaded Schoenberg's maze' in part two of *Briggflatts*. By the end of part 4 the poet has transformed himself into a modernist trope. He has embraced the rat world.

Starlight quivers

The fifth part of *Briggflatts* immediately announces the arrival of a new season:

> Drip – icicle's gone.
> Slur, ratio, tone,
> chime dilute what's done
> as a flute clarifies song,
> trembling phrase fading to pause
> then glow. Solstice past,
> years end crescendo.

The rest of part five is a long meditation on natural beauty not as it is found in the great Romantic tradition, in the sublime and the magnificent, but in its everyday manifestations:

> Conger skimped at the ebb, lobster,
> neither will I take, nor troll
> roe of its like for salmon.
> Let bass sleep, gentles
> brisk, skim-grey,
> group a nosegay
> jostling on cast flesh,
> frisk and compose decay
> to side shot with flame,
> unresting bluebottle wing.

Not many poets have discovered the divine in maggots (gentles) on rotting flesh. Bunting moves on to celebrate man's relationship with nature, at its simplest, in an enigmatic stanza that for me carries the full weight of the poem. It is perhaps its central statement, clean, deliberate and full of wonder:

> Shepherds follow the links,
> sweet turf studded with thrift;
> fell-born men of precise instep
> leading demure dogs
> from Tweed and Till and Teviotdale,
> with hair combed back from the muzzle,
> dogs from Redesdale and Coquetdale
> taught by Wilson or Telfer.
> Their teeth are white as birch,
> slow under black fringe
> of silent, accurate lips.
> The ewes are heavy with lamb.
> Snow lies bright on Hedgehope
> and tacky mud about Till
> where the fells have stepped aside
> and the river praises itself,
> silence by silence sits
> and Then is diffused in Now.

I use the word 'deliberate' to describe this passage so as not to repeat Bunting's 'precise' or 'accurate', but precision is the guiding principle. Peter Makin had some shrewd things to say about this stanza. Makin asks how exactly an instep can be 'precise', how lips (not teeth) can be 'accurate' and records his answer in the context of Bunting's many statements about the poet's responsibility to record the world as accurately as a scientist would. Makin's comments on the opening couplet of this stanza are rewarding:

> Bunting has put, not fells, or rough bent, or hillsides, but 'links': firm, smooth, grassy mounds. On them, move shepherds. But it is said here, 'Shepherds follow the links.' That is another denotative (semantic) choice. They don't walk, they don't stride: they are not Wordsworth being sublime on a felltop, or Kaspar David Friedrich being dramatic: they 'follow' the links. It seems that the path is quietly evident. Then again, these links have flowers. How? D. H. Lawrence's bundles of flame? Enthusiastic little Wordsworthian armies? Medieval patches of enamelling? Seas of thrashing Van Gogh irises? No; no; no; no.
>
> Sweet turf studded with thrift.

That is (the metaphor also tells us), small flowers, decisively, firmly, neatly inserted at intervals in the links: they are studded with them.[27]

Bunting's observations of nature were consciously scientific. Lucretius, the only poet who turned the 'vocabulary of science into magnificent poetry', was an important early influence on Bunting, as was Darwin.

> I think that a man who wants to write in the 20th century makes a great mistake if he doesn't begin by reading *The Origin of Species*, where he will find the most magnificent example of the building up and testing of hypothesis … Darwin was a very good prose writer. He does not of course go in for purple patches, but for what he wants to do, his prose is not only adequate, it's very hard indeed to think of any way of improving it.[28]

In the twentieth century only Hugh MacDiarmid had come close. Reviewing MacDiarmid's *More Collected Poems* in 1970 Bunting asked if any other poet since Lucretius had:

> used the vocabulary of science with such skill as Hugh MacDiarmid? It hardly hampers him, but moves evenly at a clear, demonstrative pace through the long syntax … There is sharp focus. The matter is new to nearly all of us, facts worth learning, a brilliant show we could enjoy without caring whether it were a simile or not … Pound and Zukofsky have sought a poetry of facts too, but neither, I think, has ever quite separated facts from metaphysics. MacDiarmid has his mysticism; and no doubt science itself is founded on undefined faith: but MacDiarmid sees things washed clean of irrelevancies as Darwin did. Suckling poets should be fed on Darwin till they are filled with the elegance of things seen or heard or touched.[29]

The precise observation of the maggots and the bluebottles' wing in the previous stanza might have alerted us to this unexpected debt. As Thom Gunn says, this passage is, 'like an old dream of order … in this specific and fecund scene, seeming spontaneity is a re-enactment of tradition; each detail recognizes its relation to each other detail, and is at ease in that established relation. Bunting's comparison of the dogs' teeth to the color of birchbark is as much a matter of course as the dogs' relation to their masters and to the sheep.'[30]

From gentles, to sheepdogs to the skies, *Briggflatts* reaches its magnificent conclusion by contemplating the stars, Aldebaran, Capella, Betelgeuse, Rigel, Orion, Procyon:

Furthest, fairest things, stars, free of our humbug,
each his own, the longer known the more alone,
wrapt in emphatic fire roaring out to a black flue.
Each spark trills on a tone beyond chronological compass,
yet in a sextant's bubble present and firm
places a surveyor's stone or steadies a tiller.
Then is Now. The star you steer by is gone,
its tremulous thread spun in the hurricane
spider floss on my cheek; light from the zenith
spun when the slowworm lay in her lap
fifty years ago.

The sheets are gathered and bound,
the volume indexed and shelved,
dust on its marbled leaves.
Lofty, an empty combe,
silent but for bees.
Finger tips touched and were still
fifty years ago.
Sirius is too young to remember.

Sirius glows in the wind. Sparks on ripples
mark his line, lures for spent fish.

Fifty years a letter unanswered;
fifty years a visit postponed.

She has been with me fifty years.

Starlight quivers. I had day enough.
For love uninterrupted night.

The selection of the stars is as precise as the shepherds' insteps. 'They came in first as a means of fixing the time and date,' he told an interviewer. 'If you notice where the stars are at the beginning of the star passages and where they are at the end of them, and go to a nautical almanack and work things out backwards, you'll find that you must be in approximately the latitude of the Farne Islands at approximately New Year's Eve.'[31]

Night, float us

Bunting was by no means ashamed that the Coda to *Briggflatts* was not written with its eventual purpose in mind: 'I'd written three-quarters of *Briggflatts*, was busy in fact on the last part, when I had to turn over papers on my desk to get something for the bloody income tax commissioners, and on the back of an old bill I found a poem that I'd written long before and forgotten when I wrote it, which required three or four lines cut out, and with those three or four lines cut out it was the Coda, and was obviously a part of *Briggflatts*.'[32]

As Thom Gunn says, although the poet has arrived at 'the essential beginnings by returning to his own beginnings' that arrival is not permanent. 'The Coda, if nothing else, would take care of such a cheerful notion.'[33] It does indeed, and the poem is a kind of celebration of ignorance:

> A strong song tows
> us, long earsick.
> Blind, we follow
> rain slant, spray flick
> to fields we do not know.
>
> Night, float us.
> Offshore wind, shout,
> ask the sea
> what's lost, what's left,
> what horn sunk,
> what crown adrift.
>
> Where we are who knows
> of kings who sup
> while day fails? Who,
> swinging his axe
> to fell kings, guesses
> where we go?

If the Coda celebrates ignorance, or at least accepts it as an essential part of the human condition, Bunting decisively rejected pessimism:

As for pessimism, no, though I'm a lot more at home with Timon or Schopenhauer than with Leibniz or the passing Pippa, but nihilist if you like. Yeats was perturbed by that in my very earliest published poems. But the last lines of The Well of Lycopolis and the Spoils are hopeful; even if Briggflatts closes in darkness. Those are the 'thoughtful' poems. It's only humanists who must find the world hopeless. It's a good enough world for stars or mushrooms, and why assume that it was meant for us.[34]

BRIGGFLATTS, AN AUTOBIOGRAPHY, FOR PEGGY

Briggflatts contains no detachable meaning but that is not to say that it is not 'about' something. Bunting considered it 'a description of my life, what I have made of it and what it has made of me'.[35] He told Bridson that *Briggflatts* was about love, 'in all senses, beginning with a kind of Daphnis and Chloe and ending with St Cuthbert in love with all creation'.[36] If nothing else *Briggflatts* is an enormous feat of memory, something he distrusted: 'I distrust memory extremely, but the effort to remember the various episodes in *Briggflatts*, for they are all however altered based upon my own past, the effort to remember it was a severe one which went on for many months. So that to make then into now is not something you can just say … it takes some doing!'[37]

Briggflatts was published in 1966 in *Poetry*, which celebrated its one hundredth anniversary in 2012. As part of that celebration its current editors, Don Share and Christian Wiman, published a selection of one hundred poems, including the first part of *Briggflatts*, which exemplify the magazine at its best over its distinguished history. Wiman's introduction reflects on the fact that much of the poetry of the last hundred years is extremely demanding of its readers, and that Bunting is sometimes taken as an example of that difficulty, even though *Briggflatts* 'now seems obviously one of the greatest poems of the twentieth century'. Wiman's observations on the 'difficulty' of *Briggflatts* are apt:

> If you are not very familiar with poetry, you will likely have some trouble figuring out exactly what is being described, which is fine, which is, in fact, exactly what the poet intended. Besides being 'about' a man who realizes, way too late, that the most intense and defining experience of his life occurred during an adolescent love affair, *Briggflatts* is a palimpsest of history, nature, learning, loss. It is the testament and artefact of a man who has lived so thoroughly into the language, so thoroughly *through* the language, that it has become a purely expressive medium. Because of cadence and pacing, and the way sounds echo and intensify sense, the word is restored to a kind of primal relation with the world; language itself takes on the textures and heft of things … As a general rule, it's safe to say that if you can paraphrase a poem, it's not a poem. There's

no other way of saying what Bunting is saying in *Briggflatts*. The language is *action*. Great poetry is usually difficult in some way, and then clear in ways we would never expect. ('It is easier to die than to remember' – Bunting) Its difficulty, you might say, makes new clarities possible in and for us.[38]

This seems to me one of the best summaries of 'meaning' in *Briggflatts* and in Bunting's poetry generally. Thom Gunn's comparison of the poem with *The Waste Land* and 'Canto 47' concludes with a remarkable disclaimer: 'I am not trying to say that Bunting's poem is better than Eliot's or Pound's. Certainly *The Waste Land* has meant too much to several generations of readers, and Canto 47 means too much to me, that I should want to supplant them.' Bunting's masterpiece is so towering an achievement that such a thought – that it *might* be the greatest poem in the English language in the twentieth century – is permissible. For Gunn *Briggflatts* sits alongside its peers and somehow illuminates them:

> *Briggflatts* addresses itself to certain of the same barely formulable needs of ours as they do. We seek some kind of reconciliation with our beginnings, or at least an understanding of how such a reconciliation might be brought about ... In *Briggflatts* Bunting – among his many other achievements there – shows us a full reconciliation, though brief, tentative, and qualified by its own transience. Ceremony has matured to tradition; the representative man has become the specific man of autobiography; a montage of places has become one place. He does indeed show us.[39]

As for the poem being an 'autobiography', Bunting said that *Briggflatts* follows the, 'phases of a lifetime in line with the phases of a year without any attempt to bring in historical facts'.[40] As Gunn says: '"Then is diffused in Now." He has recovered those [memories of natural] rhythms in the present, and more than Pound has recovered them in terms not only of the imagination but of literal fact. This is the sense in which *Briggflatts* is autobiography: he has arrived at the essential beginnings by returning to his own beginnings.'[41]

SCARLATTI AND LINDISFARNE

If *Briggflatts* is a feat of memory it is an even more impressive triumph of technique. The sonata patterns were thoroughly structured: 'there are symmetries – matching one another here and there. They are not followed out pedantically in full detail and so forth, but they are there. There's the contrast between Bloodaxe here and Saint Cuthbert here, the extreme opposite of each other in things.'[42] Bunting drew a map of *Briggflatts* during an interview in 1970.

He explained that

> you're going to have five parts because it's got to be an uneven number. So that the central one should be the one apex, there. But what is new, the only new thing ... was that instead of having one climax in the other parts you have two. In the first two the first climax is the less and another immediately comes out of it when you're not expecting it. So you have it for those two. In the others the first climax is the greater and it trails off ... the second part rises up slowly to a very nice climax with the murder of Eric Bloodaxe ... but then it rises up to a still higher climax which has to fade almost immediately afterwards.[43]

Later in the interview he annotated the first drawing:

'The middle one is a nightmare or a dream or whatever you fancy ... Spring is around Briggflatts, Summer is all over the place – London, the Arctic, the Mediterranean. Autumn is mostly in the Dales, and the last part is mostly on the Northumberland coast.'[44]

The two structural models for *Briggflatts* were Scarlatti's sonatas, particularly the B minor Fugato which was to accompany Bunting's readings of the fourth section of the poem,[45] and the Lindisfarne Codex. In an interview in 1981 he explained of the latter that, it's all interlacings of one sort or another. Nothing follows through without being crossed by something else, which is a good analogy to some kinds of poetry. On the best of these pages the theme is always the cross, but on the best of those pages you've got to look twice and three times before you can spot the cross. It's not in any way underlined. It emerges slowly out of this extremely complex design around it. There's no mistaking it. It is there, it does emerge, but it's not thrust at you. That again is a parable for poetry.[46]

In 'The Codex', a lecture at Newcastle University in 1969, Bunting displayed a surprisingly intimate knowledge of the *Codex Lindisfarnensis*. It was to him one of the triumphs of Northumbrian art, but by no means the only one: 'There are perhaps half-a-dozen books in the world comparable with the *Codex Lindisfarnensis*,' he told his audience, and they were all of them produced by Northumbrians or people who were working under the immediate influence of Northumbrians. He described one particular page in a way that helps us to understand the patterning of *Briggflatts*:

The abbreviation for Christ's name, 'chi rho iota', occupies the whole top of the page, more than half the page, and the three letters are woven together into a single monogram, very irregular in its shape, and yet perfectly balanced ... Every millimetre of the letters in the monogram is occupied by an enormously complex system of ribbons and spirals, and knots, and circles, and they spill over at the corners and in the loops of the letters and at the cross of the 'chi', yet without disturbing either the clarity of the writing or the proportions of the design ... There must be hundreds of elements in this one monogram. They repeat, and they echo and they balance one another, and yet I think none is ever repeated without some variation.

This could be a description of *Briggflatts*. 'That is the way you've got to write poetry,' he said later in the lecture, 'every word has got to be thought of with all that care.'[47] The Lindisfarne Gospels were, for Bunting, the ultimate manifestation of a uniquely Northumbrian art that had at one time been the wonder of the world.

Bunting didn't regard *Briggflatts* as a 'long' poem, as Pound's *Cantos*, Zukofsky's *"A"* or William Carlos Williams' *Paterson* are long. Indeed he felt that such poems, written over a working life, were impossible for modern writers because the world changed so quickly in a way that it hadn't for, say, Dante. 'I think it's important there shouldn't be great lengths to a poem in times like these,' he said in an interview in 1984, 'because otherwise you dislocate your structure because the world will have changed and you won't be able to fit it together without the signs of this dislocation showing ... that's true of both the *Cantos* and of *A*'.[48] He included Wordsworth's *The Prelude* in this list of failed poems; failed not because they did not contain great poetry and great poems, but because they cannot in themselves constitute a single coherent poem.[49]

A QUAKER POEM?

Bunting inscribed a copy of the Fulcrum edition of *Briggflatts* that is on display at Brigflatts Meeting House with the words 'I hope this book may have leave to lie quietly in the meeting house where I worshipped as a boy and again when I grew old.' Unease among some Quakers about the seemliness of a poem that celebrated carnality so lustily caused him to add a postscript in 1977: 'Some Friends think words I have used to picture Hell unseemly, yet it is as much of God's making as heaven. Good poetry praises all his work. This is my small contribution to his glory.'

During his first visit to Brigflatts and on subsequent visits, Bunting attended meetings in the seventeenth-century Meeting House there. Though Bunting was profoundly affected by his Quaker education he stopped short of becoming a member of the Society of Friends, never describing himself as more than an 'attender'; there are no records of his attending meetings in Newcastle. Despite this Bunting didn't discourage his Quaker image. Even a close friend such as Jonathan Williams thought that Quakerism was deep-rooted in Bunting's family. It wasn't at all, but in his reply to Williams' query regarding his supposed Quaker roots Bunting emphasised the small part that was: 'I don't know much of the history of my family, but, certainly, between my uncle, who was a member of the Society of Friends, and others, there was a great deal of Quakerism about and I was brought up entirely in a Quaker atmosphere.'[50] This is disingenuous. It is difficult to detect any specifically Quaker influence on him before the age of twelve. There was a similar interchange in 1975 when Eric Mottram interviewed Bunting for a BBC radio broadcast. Mottram recalled that Bunting had told him 'quite recently' that he considered himself a Quaker poet. 'Yes,' Bunting had replied, 'I'm a Quaker by upbringing', which isn't strictly true, although clearly he was a Quaker by (secondary) schooling.[51] In his lecture to the Yeats Society in Sligo in 1973 he claimed he was 'a Quaker if not in intellectual persuasion, at least by temperament and education',[52] so if you take away belief and six years' education at Quaker schools you are left only with 'temperament'. This suggests to me that the extent of Bunting's Quakerism was a meditative and relatively non-judgemental nature. The most significant Quaker influence on Bunting was Ellen Mary Fry at Ackworth School, who Bunting described as an old lady well past retirement age and the sister of a celebrated Quaker: 'She was a very penetrating woman with children. She found out a great deal more about me in the course of a very few conversations than I think anybody else has done in the whole of my life. And she certainly encouraged me to take Quaker doctrine seriously.'[53] Ellen Fry was forty-nine when Bunting joined Ackworth, so not exactly ready to be put out to pasture, but Bunting's recollection of her ability to understand children was certainly shared by many, as her obituary in *Ackworth Old Scholars' Association Report* in 1941 generously demonstrated.[54]

Bunting made an important statement about the limits of his Quakerism in an interview published in 1977:

> Quakerism is a form of mysticism no doubt, in that it doesn't put forward any logical justification whatever, only the justification of experience. It is comparable pretty easily with a pantheistic notion of the universe. It would be very difficult to avoid picking logical holes in it if you approached it from any other aspect. It is an extremely liberal organisation, that is to say it will tolerate almost anything so long as you behave yourself reasonably … what you believe in is your own affair, so long as you follow out the process of simply waiting quietly and emptying your mind of everything else to hear what they would call in their language the voice of God in your inside … I should say that mainly my view of things is an extremely pantheistic one which finds no expression in any organised society except, perhaps to a limited extent but still a very useful extent, in the Society of Friends.[55]

There are so many implied caveats in this passage that one can only assume that he was firmly trying to distance himself from the reductive 'Quaker poet' tag.

In another interview Bunting clarified his position on God and religion generally. He shared Swift's disgust with the human species and conceded that it's 'true that by considering oneself as just a product of the various chemicals that one is made up of, it is easy not to bother'; but that shouldn't necessarily open a door for God:

So long as you stay clear of humanism there is nothing to complain of. But if one is obliged to judge things from a humanistic point of view, there is no escape from pessimism. The Middle Ages distorted God, making a God who cared only for humans. Then the Renaissance came along and substituted man for God at the centre of things. If you do that, Swift's pessimism is inevitable. The universe is very large and in it man is no more important than animals or trees ... I have no use for religion conceived as church forms or as believing as historical fact what are ancient parables, but I do believe that there is a possibility of a kind of reverence for the whole creation which I feel we all ought to have in our bones if we don't, a kind of pantheism, I suppose. If the word 'God' is to have any use it must include everything. The only way to know anything is to consider yourself a student of histology, finding out as much as carefully controlled commonsense can find out about the world. In so doing, you will be contributing to the histology of God.[56]

In 1981 Bunting was asked how important 'being a Quaker' had been to him. There is a long pause while he considered his answer. Although it is a question he had faced on many occasions I suspect that it had rarely been formulated in quite this way before. Interviewers tended to ask about the influence of Quakerism on the poet, rather than describing him as a Quaker:

I think it has affected me one way or another all my life. At first I paid more attention to their literal doctrine and so on than I would now, but I believe my outlook and their outlook are fundamentally the same, though they might differ in almost every detail ... Putting together the kind of things believed by the very earliest Quakers and those which are now regular, things which rather faded from sight during the 19th and 20th centuries, you have something amounting to pantheism. The God worshipped by Quakers is just as manifest in all the little beasts and the trees and the grass and so on as it is in anything else, and in the rocks. Man does not have the central place which he has in most modern thought ... I think that old fashioned Quakers, 19th century Quakers, certainly would regard me as an atheist and I'm perfectly certain that Roman Catholics, Anglicans, probably Wesleyans and so forth would regard me as an atheist too.[57]

Those (such as Sister Victoria Forde and Donald Davie)[58] who want to find Quakerism, mysticism or any form of religion or belief in Bunting's life and work have some hard evidence to the contrary to sidestep. He described himself as one 'who believes nothing because he can't, not because there are no pleasing or even useful beliefs to choose from'.[59] In 'Pages from a Diary Written in Nineteen Hundred and Thirty' Yeats wrote respectfully of Bunting's pantheism:

> A poet whose free verse I have admired rejects God and every kind of unity, calls the ultimate reality anarchy, means by that word something which for lack of metaphysical knowledge he cannot define. He thinks, however, that a baptismal and marriage service and some sort of ceremonial preparation for death are necessary, and that the Churches should stick to these and be content. He now writes in the traditional forms because they satisfy a similar need ... I find among some of the newer school of poets hatred of every monotheistic system.[60]

Nevertheless we can certainly acknowledge something deeply meditative in the life and work of this atheist and no doubt that can be attributed to his lifelong attachment to the Society of Friends. Peter Lewis remembered Bunting wishing to see Durham Cathedral one night after a reading. The snow was falling and the floodlights lit up the great space.

> He was in one of his celebrated meditative moods and for a while he contemplated the Cathedral, outlined by snow, without saying much. What he did say indicated that for him the Cathedral embodied in its very fabric the turbulent history of Northumbria, not only the nine centuries since the Normans had begun work on the present building, but the Anglo-Saxon and Christian centuries before that, encompassing the world of Aidan, Bede and Cuthbert ... When Basil, gazing at the Cathedral, said that no-one could ignore this, he wasn't referring to the vast stone structure in front of him but to the long history it represented, a history which also contained him, he made clear, however much he wanted to distance himself from religious authoritarianism and dogmatism. He did admit that there were ways in which he could be considered a 'religious' poet. Yet it was surely the bare meeting house at Brigflatts that spoke to him more clearly about *lux eterna* than the great Cathedral in Durham.[61]

It wasn't just the history of the Church he was referring to, however. 'Religion is not a matter of intellect or desire or anything,' he wrote in 1976. 'It's just that you cannot avoid it. It's so bred into you when you are young that it becomes part of your general system.'[62]

In his interview with Eric Mottram Bunting went on to explain the appeal of Quakerism to him:

fortunately it is a religion with no dogma at all – and consequently there's very little you can quarrel with, and I don't have to believe this or that or the other. I think what the real essence of the Quaker business is exactly what it was at the beginning: if you sit in silence, if you empty your head of all the things you usually waste your brain thinking about, there is some faint hope that something, no doubt out of the unconscious or where you will, will appear – just as George Fox would have called it, the voice of God; and that will bring you, if not nearer God, at any rate nearer your own built-in certainties.[63]

Among the 'this or that or the other' that Quakerism didn't force Bunting to believe in was God.

Quakerism gave Bunting what he needed spiritually, but not religiously. In a letter to Louis Zukofsky in 1939 he insisted that he was, 'fundamentally averse to acts of faith. Faith being belief contrary to the available evidence.'[64] He forcefully rejected the idea that religion had any influence on his poetry: 'You know quite well that no muse, no Apollo, no Holy Ghost whispers in my ear. Nothing outside a man's mind suggests what he should write.'[65] Mysticism was worse than religion. In his lecture on Wordsworth at Newcastle University in the 1969–70 series he ridiculed the concept: 'As for mysticism, whenever that word turns up those who use it can find support in anything or nothing. It is by definition an unreasonable belief. There is no arguing about it. You like what Plotinus tells you, or you don't: there is no room for evidence, and hardly any for discussion.'[66]

'The meeting [at Brigflatts] has formally accepted me as an "attender",' he told Gael Turnbull. 'They called that ass Whittier "The Quaker poet". Absit omen.'[67] That 'absit omen' clinches it. The last thing Basil Bunting wanted to be known as was a 'Quaker poet'.

FIVE

THEN IS NOW

Then is Now. The star you steer by is gone,
its tremulous thread spun in the hurricane
spider floss on my cheek; light from the zenith
spun when the slowworm lay in her lap
fifty years ago.

Briggflatts V

ALL MY LUCK HAS TURNED

Bunting's letters are generally gloomy. Partly this was the deliberately curmudgeonly persona he adopted, but much of it was his customary desire to look life in the face and tell his story as it was. A life of sapping poverty and disappointment had taken its toll on the poet, but in June 1965 a glimmer of hope appeared. 'My own news,' he told Dorothy Pound, 'for now nearly a year, is a series of small miracles, or things as unexpected and welcome. I am still tied to my deadly drudgery, make no mistake, with hardly any leisure and a mere pittance to feed the family on, but everything else seems changed.'[1] He told Dorothy about Tom Pickard's first visit and his decision to start writing again, his recent completion of *Briggflatts*, the start of the Morden Tower readings which had become 'famous with extraordinary speed', the gathering media attention (all this before publication of *Briggflatts*), the Northern Council for the Arts' decision to subsidise publication of 'The Spoils', a proposal from 'a guy I'd never heard of in London' to reprint *Poems 1950* and an Arts Council grant of £300. He suddenly found himself at the heart of the swinging sixties: 'The Beats, apparently are among my admirers: and though they seem to me mere improvisers, they are amusing company. I am also informed … that the Beatles, no less, spent a lot of

money getting secondhand copies of Poems 1950 and carry them around.'
Even family life was looking up:

> My children are pleasant to have about. Maria is a painter ... I've the
> impression that she really is an artist of sorts ... Lately she has begun to take
> an interest in poetry and a pride in her dad ... The boy, Tom Bunting, after
> lethargic beginnings, has astonished his prep school, is a year ahead of others
> of his age, and, after failing his exam at 11, passed into the Royal Grammar
> School here at 12 as one of two admissions out of more than 300 trying for it
> ... Sima is still all I ever hoped, dear lass ...

This is the first inkling of Basil Bunting the proud father and contented
family man, and it comes as a bit of a shock. No wonder his letter to Dorothy
was excited. 'I find it very hard to believe myself,' he confessed. 'I keep
waiting for the bubble to burst. But even if it does, I will have had a lively
year after all the deadliness.'

He was interviewed on Tyne Tees Television in August 1965 and read a
selection of his poems. In October the BBC's Third Programme celebrated
Pound's eightieth birthday and Bunting read parts of Cantos 2, 4 and 81;
and in November 1965 a rather bizarre collection of twelve of Bunting's
poems, and notes and images relating to him were published in a loose-leaf
collection, *King Ida's Watch Chain*,[2] but it doesn't seem to have greatly engaged
the wider world, even when it turned itself into a band.[3] *Briggflatts*, even
before it was published, continued to turn Bunting's fortunes. 'Its magic still
goes on,' he wrote to Dorothy in September 1965. 'All my luck has turned
good since I began to write it more than a year ago. More to your point, it's
the best thing I've done by miles.'[4]

Bunting's first reading of *Briggflatts* was at Morden Tower on 22
December 1965, the month before its first publication in the January 1966
edition of *Poetry*, and the poem turned Bunting into a celebrity, or as much
of a celebrity as a poet ever makes. His poetry suddenly started to become
available in a way that it had never been before. Pickard had published
'The Spoils' earlier in the year to mixed reviews. Richard Howard described
it in *Poetry* as being: 'like the best of the *Cantos*, or anyway the prettiest:
Turkish delight, and indigestible without something more fibrous along the
way'. Charles Tomlinson, however, wrote of it in *Agenda* that 'experience
prepares the ground and music plays over against that ground', and praised
its 'intricate rhyme and line'.

Other reviewers predictably drew attention to Bunting's apparent debt to Pound: '*The Spoils* is a difficult, pamphlet-sized poem which sometimes reads as if the Master of the Cantos had got to work refurbishing not the classical-Mediterranean brand of English nostalgia but the gorgeous-East tradition that erupts in Flecker or in *Sohrab and Rustum*.' This review from the *New Statesman* by Francis Hope goes on to identify 'Poundian jokes' and 'Poundian rhetorical simplicities' that are no more Poundian than Shakespearean, but this reviewer had a 'savage disciple' point to hammer home.

Al Alvarez was supportive in the *Observer*: 'Bunting deserves all the recognition he can get. He has kept unflaggingly out of the limelight and never relaxed the standards of his verse,' without ever getting out 'from the aegis of ol' Ez's style.' Cyril Connolly reviewed 'The Spoils' in the *Sunday Times* noting that it was 'undoubtedly a good poem, repaying several readings', but was baffled by obscurity that he too attributed to the Pound effect.[5]

Stuart Montgomery's Fulcrum Press published Bunting's *First Book of Odes* in November 1965. Montgomery was the 'guy I'd never heard of in London' but he became a good friend of Bunting and was one of the catalysts of the poet's resurgence. The selection is the same as that of *Poems 1950* although the order of appearance was rearranged so that Bunting's poems were published for the first time in chronological order with the dates of their composition. Bunting also took the opportunity to add two poems, 'On highest summits dawn comes soonest' and 'On the Fly-Leaf of Pound's Cantos'.

The following month Fulcrum published *Loquitur* as a limited edition of a thousand copies. It was effectively a new edition of *Poems 1950*, minus 'They say Etna' and with the addition of 'On highest summits dawn comes soonest' and 'Verse and version' as well as four or five poems that had been written in 1949, too late for Simpson's edition. This was a rather baffling piece of publishing. *Loquitur* must have been in production at the same time as *First Book of Odes* and it contains all the poems included in the earlier book, even using the same typesetting. *First Book of Odes* was given just one month to earn its keep before it became redundant.

Martin Seymour-Smith, in a hugely positive review in the *Scotsman*, described *Loquitur* as, 'certainly one of the most important poetry-publishing events for many years.' Bunting, he thought, was the only English poet to solve the problem of how to assimilate the lively spirit of American poetry without losing his own sense of identity.

The Newcastle *Evening Chronicle* was confident that *Loquitur* would find a place in any collection of the work of major twentieth-century English poets: 'It is highly wrought, chiselled with the care and love of a true craftsman … a book that everyone who cares for modern literature needs to have.'

John Raymond, in a *Sunday Times* review, after the inevitable introduction of Bunting as 'friend and disciple of Ezra Pound', said that Bunting, 'has played many parts, fulfilled many roles in a life seemingly crowded with interest and excitement. Always he has possessed the password.'

Thomas Clark gave *Loquitur* a positive review in *Poetry*. His response to the poetry was sensitive and arresting:

> A great and (at its best – as in *Villon*) simple dignity in the placement of words provides an equal light and clarity in Bunting's poems – the consummation and creation of experience as language is so complete that the central personality is reduced to a transparency through which the action of the words can be seen … The similarity to Pound in Bunting's works is less a matter of technique than of attitude, a toughness of regard that makes possible the expression of bitterness as a description of realities and not simply as a complaint.

This was a considerably more nuanced assessment of Pound's influence on Bunting than most. Clark captured the experience of many readers who come to Bunting for the first time: 'The first time I read this book I was shaken, without knowing anything more about Bunting than a few biographical facts concerning his relation with Pound. Today, copying out some words to include them in this review I was struck by their integrity as I was on first reading. The poetry here is permanent – it's a really important publication.'

Charles Tomlinson reviewed *Loquitur* in *Agenda* ('a lucid music') and in the same issue Robert Creeley praised the 'lovely dense sensuousness' of Bunting's work. Richard Kell, however, damned it with faint praise in the *Guardian*: 'stylish in a Poundian or Black Mountain Way … there are things worth discovering but the search can be tedious.' An anonymous review in the *Observer*, was much more encouraging, noting that: 'One poem, 'Villon', hovers on the edge of being a masterpiece.'[6] 'Villon' is a masterpiece.

The *Times Literary Supplement* wrote off both *Loquitur* and 'The Spoils' as Poundian pastiche. You can track Bunting 'everywhere in Pound's snow', the anonymous reviewer sneers in a tone that is reminiscent of Bunting of *The Outlook* nearly forty years previously. He makes fun of Bunting's name ('put out more Bunting') as Bunting had of Norman Haire's. Michael

Hamburger sprang to Bunting's defence (and that of Christopher Middleton, who had also been scornfully dismissed in the same review), prompting another supercilious response from the reviewer, which Hamburger deflated effectively.[7]

Zukofsky wrote in February to thank Bunting for a copy of *Loquitur*, and particularly for its preface which had identified Zukofsky as one of 'the two greatest poets of our age'.[8] He wrote again in March to commiserate with him about some poor reviews: 'The hell with 'em – there'll be "good" ones come fawning etc ... So don't feel low.'[9]

Montgomery followed *Loquitur* two months later with *Briggflatts*, issuing a second edition in December 1966. *Briggflatts* opened the floodgates. Herbert Read rather threw up his hands at it in *Agenda*, recognising it as a work of art that had to be heard to be properly appreciated: 'I can only say that here is the score of a great oral symphony, one that awaits a worthy performance.' In *Encounter* Charles Tomlinson celebrated its combination of 'strength and delicacy in patternings that to the reader are a constant delight and that to the young poet should prove of intense and liberating technical interest'. Read's position was ridiculed by Patric Dickinson in the same issue of *Encounter*. 'It might seem from such different viewpoints as Nicolson and Bunting that poetry was a noise. The words don't matter. Bunting goes further in his horrible analogy: "Music in the stave is no more than instruction to the player. Poetry must be read aloud." This is muddled thinking indeed but it implies an interpreter – what sort?' But Alasdair Clayre was positive, praising Bunting's 'firm, individual voice' and hoping that the poem would be a springboard for new poetic.

Jim Burns drew attention to Bunting's music in *Tribune*: '*Briggflatts* is as finely constructed as a well-wrought symphony, the different movements having common themes, and the skilful instrumentations forming dense, but perfect, textures of sound and meaning ... I admire it immensely, and that a man can speak with such nobility in our mealymouthed age astounds me.' Edward Lucie-Smith interviewed Bunting for the *Sunday Times* and praised his 'meticulous craftsmanship' and, refreshingly, while acknowledging Pound's influence on Bunting's early work, was careful to point out that they are, 'by no means imitations. They have, for one thing, a certain obstinate Englishness, a close-knit organization which is alien to Pound.'[10] Bunting wrote to Gael Turnbull entertainingly about the Lucie-Smith interview: 'Mr Lucie Smith has got the editor of the Sunday Times to send him to Wylam to interview me at length ... He met me at the Arts Council and fed me expensively. Golly, what a BOUNDER. The old word fits perfectly. His remarks revealed that he hasn't read (though he may have glanced through) any of my work, but he is clearly convinced that I am the coming thing and he means to be in on it.'[11]

Cyril Connolly in the *Sunday Times* was, 'quite unprepared for *Briggflatts*, which seems to me one of the best poems I have read and re-read for a long time'.[12] Denis Goacher thought the Connolly review was 'great good luck', but didn't think Bunting cared to acknowledge it as such.[13] Donald Davie put *Briggflatts* in its historical context in the *New Statesman*. Bunting was 'very important in the literary history of the present century as just about the only accredited British member of the Anglo-American poetic avant-garde of the Twenties and Thirties'.

Tom Pickard reviewed *Briggflatts* in the Newcastle *Evening Chronicle*, and perhaps made rather too grand a claim for it in his enthusiasm. Picking up on Sir Herbert Read's comparison Pickard claimed that, 'since "The Seafarer" it [*Briggflatts*] is the only poem in this language to deal adequately with man exiled from that which he loves.' That seems to sideline a great deal of sixteenth-century verse, if nothing else, but Pickard was quick to pick up the theme of exile in *Briggflatts*.

In the *Scotsman* Martin Seymour-Smith rejected the Poundian label that had dogged Bunting for forty years, and described him as, 'one of the most consciously English of English poets', concluding that *Briggflatts* is a 'notable English poem, and there can no longer be any excuse for the neglect of its author'.

The Nottingham poetry magazine *Tarasque* praised *Briggflatts* as 'an important poem that demands attention. Important because it is one of the few poems of real maturity since "Four Quartets".' This thoughtful essay was accurate in predicting Bunting's impact on a wider readership:

> I suppose there is not much chance of his being read generally, largely because 'Loquitur' and 'Briggflatts' are cumbersomely printed and prohibitively priced, and 'The Spoils' is perhaps too wilfully Middle Eastern to be read with much sympathy. Moreover Larkin and Hughes are too much in the ascendance. I believe he is known and read by practising poets. Graves once wrote: 'To write poems for other than poets is wasteful.' That, of course, is pernicious: it is also full of point.

Robert Woof was positive in *Stand*: 'surely a properly large and appreciative audience will read this poem', as was, once again, Charles

Tomlinson: 'Bunting has come, in his late poetry, to a music that combines strength and delicacy in patternings that to the reader are a constant delight and that to the young poet should prove of intense and liberating technical interest.' Robert Creeley praised the, 'lovely dense sensuousness to Bunting's poetry and it is as much the nature of the words as the nature of the man who makes use of them'. Kenneth Cox contributed a thoughtful essay on 'The Aesthetic of Basil Bunting' in the same issue. Hugh Kenner inevitably pointed to *Briggflatts* as a beacon of hope: 'If there's a hope just now for English poetry ... it's here, in this return to actual plain speech (not "simplicity": Bunting isn't an easy poet).'

These were heavyweight reviewers but there were plenty of complaints. Bernard Bergonzi in the *Guardian* thought *Briggflatts* a 'rambling, bitty, and extremely obscure autobiographical poem ... [which] suggests that [Bunting] has a very limited talent, and that he has inherited more of Pound's vices than his virtues.' The *Observer* agreed: Bunting 'has only recently been rediscovered and – like most literary exhumees – overpraised ... line by line its blunt alliterating progress offers faint basis for the current fuss.' The *Times Literary Supplement*, never a Bunting cheerleader, thought *Briggflatts* 'a failure; lacking any theme other than the poet's sense of home after much travel, it has no forward driving movement. Its exoticism is attractive but finally unsatisfying.' And a young D. M. Thomas, many years before *The White Hotel* brought him fame, really disliked it: 'absence of strict metrical pattern, added to telegrammatic clumsiness and his expressed contempt for the printed poem, leads to many an irritating confusion of meaning.'[14] Clumsiness doesn't get much clumsier than the telegrammatic kind.

'Briggflatts is selling well, in spite of the T.L.S.', Bunting wrote to Pound from California in March 1967. 'Herbert Read and Hugh MacDiarmid have been boosting it, and Connolly did a silly but very "pro" review, which helped the publisher. Here Ginsberg and Creeley are the missionaries.'[15] Allen Ginsberg was certainly doing his best. He wrote in the *International Times* that Bunting was the most alert prosodist in England and that poetry had become a ghost there because Bunting's work had been ignored.[16]

His new fame brought him an Arts Council Bursary for 1966 although it is a measure of how little known he was that the *Guardian* reported that 'for the first time the [Arts] council is making four awards of £300 each – with no strings. One recipient is Basil Bunting, who does the stocks and shares list for the 'Newcastle Journal', and who says he has been writing poetry for 65 years.'[17] That 'says' speaks volumes.

Agenda released a Basil Bunting Special Issue with two new odes ('Birthday greeting' and 'Carmencita's tawny paps') in Autumn 1966, coinciding with the publication of George Steiner's *Penguin Book of Modern Verse Translation*, which included parts of 'Villon', in November 1966.[18] Bunting read *Briggflatts* on the BBC's Third Programme in February 1967 and at Harvard and the Guggenheim Museum in New York in March. There were television and radio interviews and unprecedented press attention. He was back on the BBC reading *Briggflatts* in November 1968 and in February 1969 he read at the first Albert Hall Poetry Festival (a reading that was later broadcast by the BBC). Suddenly poetry magazine publishers were hungry for new work. He wrote to Anthony Rudolf, founder of Menard Press, in January 1969: 'I've written nothing for a long time, and have no poems, no translations at all on hand or in hand ... What's wanted? Current poetry – most of it, I imagine, Spanish. Competent version of Gongora, swift version of the Cantar del Cid, an attempt on Metastasio, almost anything Arabic or Persian. You know, I expect, Omar Pound's bits of Arabic. I am sorry I've nothing.'[19]

Philip Norman wrote in the *Sunday Times* that 'almost everyone is at his feet or studying hard to be ... At the age of 66, Bunting was revealed and applauded as among the most important poets of the century ... the work is as hard as tombstones'[20] After decades of being ignored, by the public, if not by poets, he took to celebrity gladly. William Corbett recalled hearing Bunting read *Briggflatts* at Harvard in the spring of 1966 (actually 27 March 1967) and feeling that the poet was enjoying being at the centre of a Bacchanalia:

> seated in a chair, to his left seated on pillows a teenage girl acted as his cup bearer. Between sections of *Briggflatts* a tape recorder played Scarlatti and Bunting drank with obvious savor – his pleasure made you thirsty – from a glass of red wine offered by the blonde girl at his feet. His reading was vigorous, precise ("Each pebble its part") and masterful. The words and lines shaped and fitted each to each with an emphatic tang. When he finished, the audience sat stunned as if waiting out the poem's resonance. The trembling I experienced was a sensation so powerful that to remember it now is to feel it again.

Corbett's experience was similar to Thomas Clark's, that sense that, even though you don't entirely understand it, you know that you have encountered extraordinary art.

At a party after the reading, Corbett recalls, 'Bunting sat in a baronial armchair, his cup bearer on his lap, talking with a semi-circle of people. A friend came up to me chuckling and, pointing towards Bunting, said, "Jesus! Look at that old man will you." Bunting's arm was around his cup bearer's waist and his hand delicately stroked her ribs and breast as he nodded his head and his eyebrows – large flecks of gray ash – moved up and down.'[21]

He was back on Tyne Tees Television in June 1969, reading from *Briggflatts*, of course, but also visiting Brigflatts itself. The following August he read at the Harrogate Arts Festival and the following year he did no fewer than three BBC broadcasts.[22]

His friend Denis Goacher noticed a gradual change in Bunting's approach to celebrity. After the publication of *Briggflatts* his characteristic modesty prevailed, but was 'slightly modified' as time passed. 'If you have got a lot of young men and people like Allen Ginsberg coming round and soaping you up like mad, then you are bound to be ever so slightly corrupted … He began, ever so gradually, to start playing the Grand Old Man.'[23]

CHANGED, ALL CHANGED

But all this glamour and attention seems to have been nothing compared to his rekindled relationship with the girl he had famously failed to reply to for fifty years, Peggy Greenbank. In July 1965 he wrote to Denis Goacher about the momentous fallout from *Briggflatts*:

> The extraordinary effects that have flowed from Briggflatts are still in full spate. Peggy has her copy of the poem, and has written to her sister, obviously proud and excited, but worried to death about the jealous husband. I am full of hope and delight. Clearly, she will see me, as soon as she can contrive to. Clearly, she will leave her name on the poem and risk scandalising her neighbours if she has the least reason to hope her husband will not see it. She is minimising the past suddenly served up to her, perhaps only because she is writing to her sister; but she certainly does not reject it. Can I make it become the present? Her letter was so alive and vivid, it was like having her with me.[24]

A few days earlier he had written somewhat cryptically to Dorothy Pound about this latest transformation in his fortunes:

> I told you I find myself in the last chapters of a Hardy novel? Approaching the denouement, with no idea what it is to be, but a strong premonition of something tragic. [Gael] Turnbull could tell you the story. He knows most of it. The rest is between myself and her. I never told you about her in the

old days. I was too ashamed to speak. But the poem Briggflatts has exploded the past into the present, and I am largely living in 1915 in the remotest dale country, whatever seems to be going on around me. No, a happy ending is not out of the question, only very unlikely.[25]

Gael Turnbull could indeed have told the story but he didn't for nearly fifty years. Turnbull died in 2004 and in 2012 his second wife, the glass historian Jill Turnbull, published his memoirs, essays and journal pieces about twentieth-century poets and poetry. Bunting was still working on *Briggflatts* in May 1965 when Turnbull visited him at Shadingfield with his first wife, Jonnie, and their children. Bunting persuaded them to return to their home near Worcester via Brigflatts. When he got there Turnbull sat alone for a while in the meeting house but eventually fell into conversation with an older man and told him that he had a friend who had known the hamlet as a boy and had visited the family of a local stonemason. Turbull's new companion told him that the stonemason's daughter still lived in the house across the lane and suggested that Turnbull went to see her. He didn't: 'As I walked back up the lane, I was full of troubled thoughts. Had I any business blundering into someone else's past? We drove home.'[26] Turnbull wrote up his account of his visit to Brigflatts in a letter to Bunting and received a reply by return:

> You knew of course that your report on Briggflatts [his spelling] would strike very deep. Yet what you tell me is no more than I foresaw and expected before I began to write the poem ... But first I must be sure ... her elder sister had no health. Still, unexpected things happen, the weakling often survives ... It would be cruel to leave her to hear of the poem from anyone else. And if she is quite indifferent, it would even be discourteous ... She has been with me all this half century often when nobody else was.

There is a moving postscript to this letter that was not published in Turnbull's article: 'Peculiar recesses there are in man that he knows very little about. I went into a pub at lunch time, thinking about your letter. While I was drinking my beer a middle-aged man came up and said: Why, Grandad, whatever is the matter? And only then I became aware that the tears were running down my face as they haven't done since I was a little boy.'[27]

Bunting finished *Briggflatts* three days later, at midnight on 16 May 1965. The prospect of some sort of rapprochement with Peggy threw Bunting into a state of enormous confusion. He wrote a series of excited letters to Gael Turnbull on 13, 16, 18 and 26 May 1965. He was convinced that Peggy, rather than her sister, was still living in the stonemason's house and at the weekend of 18 to 20 June he visited Brigflatts himself. He wrote an emotional letter to Turnbull the following Monday:

> Such a weekend. My mind and emotions in a turmoil. No, it was not Peggy, but her sister [Cissie]. Peggy is alive and married, elsewhere ... Changed, all changed. A different world ... I told her [Cissie] I had come to seek Peggy, to beg her forgiveness and tell her how ashamed and unhappy I had been for so long, and that I would never have had the courage to face a meeting but for the absolute need of getting her permission before I let them print her name on the poem ... Little by little I learned: After my last, terrible refusal to see my dear love, she, Peggy, despaired altogether, and her face turned sad, the smile that I knew gone, almost forever.

His excitement was causing him to project a little incoherently. He reported Edward, Peggy's husband, as being 'jealous almost to a madness' before Edward could have known anything about an affair that hadn't yet started. By now his sense of being at the heart of one of Hardy's novels was picking up: 'Cissie's history of the family was like a series of stories by Hardy, all sad, some tragic. And what am I doing in the most melodramatic novel of all? I love Sima and my children. I cannot wrong them to right the wrong I did to Peggy: yet I told Cissie I would carry Peggy off if she loved me and wanted to escape from her present life.'[28]

Peggy, he discovered, was living at Hope in Shropshire, coincidentally not far from the Turnbulls, with her husband, Edward Edwards, and teaching in a village school. They had had three children of whom only one, Gillian, survived. In July Peggy and Edward visited Cissie in Brigflatts and Cissie showed Peggy the poem while Edward was occupied elsewhere. Edward worked away from home during the week and by 22 July Peggy and Bunting were corresponding, carefully at first, but soon Bunting was able to time his letters to arrive while Edward was away. In August he was still hoping for an imminent meeting with Peggy. He told Goacher that he was unlikely to find time to do a reading of *The Cantos* for the BBC during his next visit to London. 'Does the august BBC work on Sundays?' he asked. 'But even if it does, if Peggy Greenbank comes to London for the reading, as she may, I wont do anything on Sunday except sit and look at her. There is half a century of looking to be caught up with somehow ... If Peggy makes up her mind to what seems the inevitable break with her husband, how shall I feed her?'[29]

Bunting made covert arrangements to meet Peggy in October while he was staying with the Turnbulls, and towards the end of the month Turnbull drove Bunting to Hope to meet, at last, the woman who had been with him for fifty years. 'The intensity of their emotion and happiness,' according to Turnbull, 'was not uncomfortable, if amazing.'

'At Hope', Bunting reported to Goacher, 'Peggy was all any man could wish. I shant leave her at Hope for ever, insha'allah. But complications are more complicated for the impecunious and there are awful complications.'[30] So began an affair that was conducted surreptitiously at first. Bunting wrote letters to Peggy 'with a variety of orthography' so as not to arouse Edward's suspicions if he chanced to be at home when the letters arrived. During holiday periods, when he certainly would have been, Turnbull became the couple's postman. Bunting wrote a long account of his life for Peggy so that she would know the real person and not an idealised one.[31] He was anxious about her health and confided to Turnbull in January 1966 that he didn't know how he could go on if 'she were taken away from me.' There were practical as well as emotional difficulties in conducting a secret, long range affair after a gap of fifty years. He pined constantly for Peggy; 'Peggy has been ill,' he told Goacher in February. 'I shall see her in May, but its an awful long time to wait. I want a private helicopter to annihilate those 200 and odd miles.'[32]

He told Turnbull in September 1966 that he was,

suffering from Peggy's determination to have a good conscience ... Let people love and unlove without having to go after divorces ... I never felt like claiming exclusive rights in any of my women, after I was about 22 or 3, and I don't see why they should require exclusive rights in me. Contracting to keep a household together is a different matter ... I was 'faithful' to Marian, unfaithful to Sima and to Peggy ... but it certainly isn't Marian who loves me in consequence.

Peggy's 'conscience' was something Bunting didn't really understand. He reflected 'with some astonishment at where she draws the line between a good and a bad one'.[33] Conscience notwithstanding he was prepared to undergo a fair amount of discomfort to spend time with Peggy. 'She lives on the Welsh border, nearly two hundred miles away, hard to get at by train and bus,' he told Roudaba, 'but nothing soothes me more than a few days with her, even if I must hang about dismal railway stations in Leeds and Manchester, waiting for trains. She seems busy with many little things, helping all the various village institutions; and when she needs distraction, she makes pottery in a kiln in her cellar.'[34]

Sima was not overly impressed by this turn of events, but she seems to have found distraction in the presence of her cousin Edmond. According to Turnbull she was, 'mostly scornful, at least affecting not to stoop to jealousy, just remarking, "Silly old man!" … There was also Edmond, who squired Sima about, was involved with her buying and renovating and selling cottages, although also refurbishing Shadingfield. They were sometimes away on holiday together.'[35] Perhaps Bunting genuinely didn't understand how his relationship with Peggy might have affected Sima. He complained from California to Gael Turnbull, with a straight face, that, 'as for wives, one's own or others, nobody at Wylam has written to me since the beginning of March. Has the Tyne washed the village away? Am I toiling for a set of ghosts?'[36]

It may seem strange to characterise Bunting's relationship with Peggy as one of the great love stories of the twentieth century – after all they spent nearly fifty years apart and with no communication at all – but a passage from a letter to his daughter, Roudaba, in 1966 shows that it was nothing less:

> When I was very young I met, at the hamlet of Briggflatts in the mountains of Westmorland, a girl four years younger than myself, and loved her. The story of that love is the skeleton of the poem. As the poem grew, I understood that I had never stopped loving the girl, and that our parting (my fault) was foolish as well as wrong. I felt certain that she and I were so much one that she must feel the same, still be in love with me, after forty-five years of separation. So I took my courage in both hands and went in search of her with the finished poem in my hand. It was a slow search; but I found her, found her exactly as I had felt she must be. So I have a love again, one that has survived a lifetime's separation and will surely last till Peggy and I die. There are great difficulties: we are both married, both have children, are both poor. But there is also, now and then, when we can meet, great happiness, such as I have not known since I was a boy.[37]

Reunion with Peggy seems to have stimulated the poet; 1965 was a productive year. Denis Goacher thought that Bunting had, a sexual crisis at the age of sixty-five or so. He wasn't so unfortunate as Pound was, who had a prostatectomy around seventy-five; he was not afflicted with impotence, as far as I know, as Graves was around sixty, and Yeats also around sixty-five. But he knew, because he was perfectly ready to speak about himself, that he was no longer attractive to women and he couldn't bear it … It was at this time that he wrote the ODE that starts, 'You idiot! What makes you think decay will/never stink from your skin?' Now, the bitterness in that poem is entirely – and consciously – applicable to the position and stage of his life that he had got to.[38]

This is a peculiar observation given the enormous changes in Bunting's personal life, and there is no hint of a 'sexual crisis' in any of his surviving letters. 'You idiot! What makes you think decay will', written when Bunting was sixty-five, does not seem to me at all bitter. It is a caricature of the ageing lover, almost a reply to Wyatt's 'They flee from me that some time did me seek':

> A lame stag, limping after the hinds, with tines
> shivered by impact and scarred neck – but
> look! Spittle fills his mouth, overflows,
> snuffing their sweet scent …[39]

'Under sand clay', also written in 1965, was, as we have seen, consciously evoking the desert but also dealing with historical events in which Bunting played a part:

> Under sand clay. Dig, wait.
> Billy half full, none for the car.
> Quartz, salt in well wall,
> ice refract first ray.
> Canvas udders sag, drip,
> swell without splash the mirage
> between islands. Knee-deep
> camels, lean men, flap-dugged
> matrons and surly children.
>
> Aneiza, kin to the
> unawed dynast haggling with God.
> This brine slaked him as
> this sun shrinks.[40]

Bunting wrote to Dorothy Pound from Goleta in May 1967 with a version of 'Under sand clay' that is slightly different from the published version. 'Arabic poetry,' he explained,

> is extremely hard and even rocky. That's the desert. When they went to live in cities the poets usually became ornamental and tiresome. I was trying to evoke the desert just before I began to teach, and the results were rather contorted and tough; dry, forbidding … You dig in the wadi for a slow drip of brackish water, which freezes at night. The canvas water cooling bags drip above what looks to the eye like a shallow sea with islands, but is the heat refraction of morning. There I met the tribe Aneiza.[41]

Bunting's well-known satire on philistinism, particularly northern philistinism, 'What the Chairman Told Tom', was also written in 1965. The poet's point is made in the first three stanzas, but it winds on for another eight:

> Poetry? It's a hobby.
> I run model trains.
> Mr Shaw there breeds pigeons.
>
> It's not work. You dont sweat.
> Nobody pays for it.
> You *could* advertise soap.
>
> Art, that's opera; or repertory –
> The Desert Song.
> Nancy was in the chorus.[42]

It isn't inspired, but it is short and unusually accessible, so therefore found its way into anthologies.

More interesting is 'O, it is godlike' which was, as he told an audience, stolen almost entirely from Catullus. 'People have tried again and again to do the poem as Catullus from which I take the first four or five lines there, and they've all failed, every one of them, failed in various ignominious degrees, and where Ben Jonson and Campion failed I'm not ashamed to fail too.'[43]

> O, it is godlike to sit selfpossessed
> when her chin rises and she turns to smile;
> but my tongue thickens, my ears ring,
> what I see is hazy.

I tremble. Walls sink in night, voices
as unmeaning as wind. She only
a clear note, dazzle of light, fills
furlongs and hours

so that my limbs stir without will, lame,
I a ghost, powerless,
treading air, drowning, sucked
back into dark

unless, rafted on light or music,
drawn into her radiance, I dissolve
when her chin rises and she turns to smile.
O, it is godlike![44]

Although the source for this powerful lyric is Catullus 51 (itself a translation from Sappho) it is very difficult to keep Peggy out of these lines.

'Carmencita's tawny paps', about 'a young lady I met in the Canary Islands',[45] and 'Three Michaelmas daisies' were the other poems from Bunting's *annus mirabilis* that survived into *Collected Poems*, and both tend to undermine Goacher's claim that Bunting was suffering some kind of sexual crisis:

Three Michaelmas daisies
on an ashtray;
one abets love;
one droops and woos;

one stiffens her petals
remembering
the root, the sap
and the bees' play.[46]

There's no doubt about the context – Michaelmas represents the fading of the year and a gift of a Michaelmas daisy has traditionally been a way of saying goodbye. But Michaelmas daisies are one of nature's final acts of defiance of winter, providing colour and life deep into the autumn months, and the second stanza is a rousing affirmation of life even as death beckons.

In 1966 he told Robert Creeley that he had 'half a notion in my head to do a Salome, as different as possible from Wilde, Flaubert, Laforgue and so on. She jigs and wiggles and makes no fuss about stripping off. No wiles, no purpose, no afterthoughts. She probably dances to the sound of the

21. (*top left*) Sima Alladadian in Ronald Oakshott's garden, Isfahan, c.1947.

22. (*top right*) and 23. (*below left*) Bunting, Qolhak, Teheran, c.1948.

24. (*below right*) Bunting, 1958.

25. (*above*) Bunting and Allen Ginsberg in Tom and Connie Pickard's apartment, Jesmond, 22 May 1965.

26. (*below*) Bunting and Peggy Edwards (Greenbank), Brigflatts, 1960s.

27. (*above*) Bunting with Gael
Turnbull, Wylam, winter 1965.

28. (*below*) Bunting and Cissie
Greenbank (Jean Armstrong),
Brigflatts, c.1965.

29. (*above*) Bunting
with Tom Pickard (*left*),
Gael Turnbull (*rear*) and
Stuart Montgomery
(*front*), Wylam, 1966.

30. (*below*) Bunting in
Aspen, Colorado, 1967.

1. (*above*) Bunting at
Clifford's Bridge during a
visit to the Turnbulls, 1970.

2. (*below*) Bunting and
Allen Ginsberg, Durham
Cathedral, 1973. Ginsberg
wrote on the bottom of this
photograph: "'Haic sunt
in fossa/Bedae venerabilis
ossa." At Bede's tomb,
Durham Cathedral 1973,
Basil Bunting, & Allen
Ginsberg sightseeing.
Camera in Connie or Tom
Pickard's hands.'

"Haic sunt in fossa / Bedae venerabilis ossa." At Bede's tomb, Durham
Cathedral 1973, Basil Bunting & Allen Ginsberg sightseeing. Camera
in Connie or Tom Pickard's hands.
                                                    Allen Ginsberg

33. (*above*) Bronze portrait of Bunting by Alan Thornhill, spring 1973.

34. (*opposite, above*) Bunting in his 80s.

35. (*opposite, below*) Bunting, 1983.

36. Bunting looks down at Sima and Diana Collecott from the wall of the Reading Room, Palace Green, Durham, March 2004.

Beatles.'[47] It was still cooking a couple of weeks later when he told Gael Turnbull that it was beginning 'to show some very faint, misty outlines of a shape',[48] but by his sixty-eighth birthday in March 1968 it 'had refused to take shape'[49] and he appears to have entirely dropped the idea.

It was around this time that another ghost from Bunting's distant past appeared, this one rather less welcome than Peggy. Stuart Montgomery's wife Deidre told Tom Pickard this strange story:

Shortly after they had set up as publishers in the mid sixties the Montgomerys were living in a couple of attics in Lawn Road, Hampstead, with their new baby. Despite the cramped accommodation Basil, who had become good friends with them, used to stay there on his rare visits to London. They looked forward to his coming because he was an excellent storyteller especially when his vocal chords were oiled with good drink, and he was happy amongst children. In other words he was an amiable, amusing and illuminating guest. In the basement of the house in Lawn Road a handsome but elderly woman lived. Stuart and Deidre knew her as a neighbour with a beautiful bone structure and thought it a mere coincidence that one of Basil's early poems had been dedicated to a woman of the same name, Helen Egli. One day the Montgomerys were walking around the Tate Gallery and discovered a portrait by Augustus John of a beautiful young woman whose features reminded them immediately of their elderly neighbour living in the basement. They were curious to know; was she the Helen Egli of the John portrait and the Bunting poem? They weren't on sufficiently intimate terms to ask her, but on his next visit to London they would ask Basil.

So, after the baby was put to bed, a meal and a good wine, and as the single malt whisky bottle was opened, they told him about the handsome old woman who lived in the basement and could she be the same Helen Egli? The cheery flush of alcohol drained from his face and the hand holding the glass discernibly trembled. Stuart said, 'he turned white as a sheet and stood up saying, "I'll never come and visit you again, never come back to this house again."'

According to Montgomery, 'the affair was quite tempestuous and he couldn't get on with her at all and the child that she had by somebody else Basil's parents helped to bring up at the time. But Basil actually left England and went to France, originally, to get away from her effectively. And for years he would avoid all comment on her.'

Some three or four weeks later she died, so they never met and he returned as a visitor to their house. But the coincidence didn't end there; Helen had a son who was also the local postman and he would see letters addressed to Basil Bunting c/o Montgomery, his publisher. Even though he was aware of their past relationship he had never mentioned Bunting's current connection with the house on Lawn Road to his mother. After her death the son carried out the requirements of her will, to burn the letters that Basil had written to her three or four decade earlier.[50]

BUFFALOONATICS AND SANTA BARBARIANS, 1966–1967

Bunting was invited in 1966 to the State University of New York at Buffalo where he first met the poet and academic Eric Mottram, who spent every day with him from 27 June until 5 August.[51] It was the start of a long friendship. Shortly after Bunting's death nineteen years later Mottram published extracts from the diary he kept at the time. On 29 June Bunting gave his first reading in the US, followed by a reception at the Main Book Centre, which 'went off very well'. Mottram recalls Bunting being in a sociable mood, enjoying the company of other writers 'very freely'. Bunting and Mottram went to a concert in Blair Hall on 11 July and drank whisky in Mottram's room afterwards, talking and listening to Schumann's *Fantasia*. On 16 July the pair went with a party of six others (including the poet Tony Connor, who recorded his impressions of Bunting in verse, Ed Davidson, Aaron Poulker and 'three girls') to Niagara Falls, 'marvellous weather, completely ideal. Evening: Basil, Aaron, and I dined well and amusingly at the Chinese'. On 19 July Mottram had 'dinner with Basil, who was celebrating some letters and contacts which made him happy – his sister [daughter] in Wisconsin, and Peggy, his girl-friend, among others.' Four days later there was a party 'at Professor Thomas Connolly's place ... everyone there. Lots of beer. John Barth on drums, with Jack Clarke on piano, and two others on saxes. In fact, Basil and I had drinks with Barth beforehand at his place.'

Mottram's diary records five or six weeks of endless drinks, parties, dinners, readings, singing and lectures but Mottram was open to Bunting's darker side. On 13 July he went with 'Bunting to Eduoardo's on Bailey Street, for a huge Italian meal and excellent Valpolicella and Bardolino. Bunting spouted and said some shrewd, and some very silly, things – about Lawrence and Ginsberg especially. He *is* sometimes garrulous and pig-headed.' Two weeks later (on 28 July) they spent a 'sad evening somehow' at Stephen Rodefer's house: 'Idle talk never got far beyond the relaxed stage.

Basil asserted and laid down the law … (Everyone behaved aggressively that evening. Perhaps the endless hot rain did it?).' Three days later they went to Alan DeLoach's house for dinner and Mottram recorded an 'excellent conversation about poetry, Basil's saying how his sense of poetic vocation came on his grandfather's knee when he was five – and that this is what carried him through all the difficult years. But, also some strangely reactionary views of art.' Bunting had a tendency to 'mythicize these weeks together and tell a number of highly amusing stories about it, but always with a sense of a happy time he could draw on'.[52]

Tony Connor captured moments with Bunting at SUNY in his poem 'Reminiscences Remembered'. Bunting is seen throwing off anecdotes to faculty and students in Tiny's Modern Café:

'It must have been the summer/of '28. Fordie had/taken me to visit/one of Proust's minor duchesses …'/'Yes, Eliot/didn't hit it off at all/with Isadora. He threw,/or tried to throw, Ezra's coat/from the window of her flat,/as a gesture of protest/at Isadora's neatness./I should say 'her studio' –/which was bare, completely bare;/as – so it must be confessed –/was 'Dora, who greeted us/in the hall stark naked!…'/ … 'Cat's-piss! – which reminds/me of that cat Willie was/always fondling: Minnaloushe./Used to pedicure its paws,/claimed it had psychic powers –/especially after it peed/all over George Moore's valise/stuffed full with reams of his prose./I got the tale from Arthur –/Symons: he witnessed the deed!'

This is the professional raconteur in action but Connor's poem goes on to give a snapshot of a more private Bunting at SUNY:

His private being, shrunken/and myopic, occupied/the apartment next to mine –/where, sometimes, I'd visit him./With memory fixed upon/himself among the great dead,/the rest of his mind would strain/nobly to deal with the dim/fellow-countryman he saw/in the room … /He endeared himself to me/by late summer: he refused/to allow the library,/or anybody, to tape/his reminiscences./'No,/my boy: I won't have them *used*./Damn these university/confidence-tricksters, in lip-/service to literature!/They want articles, footnotes,/anything in black and white/that'll help 'em get tenure…'/The old poet shook his head,/as though to be rid of flies./He popped a couple of pills/into his mouth, muttered 'Turds!'/saw me beside him, and said:/'There are lies, and there are lies./What you'll remember of me –/years from now, in some pub, say,/or perhaps in a poem,/speaking from the pure pleasure/of telling a good story –/will be warped, changed, pulled awry/into your own idiom./You'll soon make *my* stories *your*/stories – that's how it should be./

Murrain take accuracy!/Speak with a rich man's freedom,/leave facts to the sober poor!'[53]

One can't help but feel that Connor has caught Bunting's authentic voice in this caricature.

Denis Goacher considered Bunting 'a tremendous pedagogue, a really born teacher, which is one of the reasons why young people were so impressed by him. He had a way of stating things so *ex cathedra* that you felt that he *must be* right. He told me, *à propos*, that when he was living in Italy Ezra Pound once said to him that he ought to go back to London and set himself up as a new Dr. Johnson.'[54] Bunting certainly tried to bring some by then already old-fashioned concepts to the classroom. Peter Lewis recalls Bunting's stories about his teaching in America, 'including the women students who "were prepared to do anything for an A" – to which his reply was: "Are you prepared to work?"'[55]

Robert Creeley also considered Bunting a gifted teacher[56] but his style would certainly fall foul of current educational requirements. On 2 August Mottram took Bunting's class on Yeats: 'He had been teaching Eliot, Pound, and Yeats to the SUNY students by getting them to read the poems aloud in class. But he was aware that they had to gain other information about poetry – this is where I was supposed to be the channel.'[57]

We don't really associate Bunting with action for a common good. Although he hated oppression of any kind we rarely see him doing anything other than inveighing against it. He left SUNY, however, with an unusual gesture of militancy on behalf of his visiting colleagues. Never good with figures of authority Bunting was clearly stung into action by the conditions under which visiting lecturers were hired: 'For some reason I did not record Basil's fight to get visiting professors paid at the end of the session, rather than have to wait months and have nothing to spend in America. He won for us all by storming the President of the University's office, and by writing a sharp letter to him. Nor did I record his final gesture to the office he had been assigned to and to its regular occupant: he cellophane-taped the tables, desks and drawers together – and called for me to approve.'[58] Buffalo wasn't 'stupider than other universities,' he wrote to Pound in July 1966, 'just dead'.[59]

His visit to the US was, culturally, a disappointment. He wrote to Cid Corman in April 1967 that it had given him none of the lift he had come to expect in America: 'Too many shams, too little disposition to distinguish between the sham and the real article. Brains absent or in cold storage, often. I'm not sure that I don't prefer the bitter philistinism of England to this sludge of culture.'[60] He was also considerably preoccupied while he was in Buffalo with events at home, and the burden of managing his domestic finances by remote control. Sima infuriated him by borrowing £50 from Turnbull to pay bills:

> (a) I left Sima more money than I ever have to meet the bills, and all bills but one small one paid. I also sent her an extra £30. (b) she has gone, or is going, to France for a holiday with the children, which horrifies me, for wherever the money came from (Edmond, I expect), it could have been used for the bills or to repay you. This kind of thing makes me ashamed and angry. She had already committed quite a large slice of the Arts Council £1,000 before I left England, though she knew I needed it to pay off our mortgage and so improve our weekly budget.[61]

(He repaid the debt two days later.) The domestic situation hadn't improved much by the time he returned. For one thing he found 'Sima deeply disturbed by bad (and I believe false) news of her mother. Ma-in-law is a cunning and very selfish old woman who is constantly dying, and has been for the last 28 years at least. She does not worry about the possible effect of these demonstrations on a distant daughter, and of course she really will die someday, so Sima gets upset.'[62]

This was compounded by new financial problems. Bunting was planning to take his daughter, Maria, to California but 'Edmond (nothing new in this) has waited to the last moment and then tried to throw a spanner in the works, demanding instant repayment of a debt. What the real state of the account is I cannot tell, for I do not believe that he has ever paid a regular board-and-rent (certainly I've never seen a penny of it); but if I pay him, Maria cannot go to California, and I doubt whether I can, so I wont.'[63]

A few days later he told Pound he had returned from 'six weeks among the Buffaloons' and was off 'to pass a year among the Santa Barbarians on the Specific Coast', a prospect he didn't relish: 'I'd rather not go to California; rather stay in my own place, Northumberland, go to meeting once in a couple of months at Brigflatts, keep away from the horrors of the literary life. Avoid pontificating.'[64] But the children had to be fed, and he found himself in Goleta, California, just two months later.

Bunting left his detested job at the *Evening Chronicle* on 30 August 1966. He was replaced by the journalist, Peter Stansill, who recalled his awe at being led to Bunting's chair:

> The deputy editor steered me to the huge subs' table, around which clustered a dozen journalists, and pointed to the vacant seat that I was to occupy for the next seven months. 'You're filling the chair of an officer and a gentleman,' a neighbouring colleague announced, 'a poet and a scholar who translates from the ancient Persian.' I had inherited not only the chair but also the workplace effects (though not the job) of Basil Bunting, who had retired only a few days before. These included a foot rule, a copy of the house style book and thick wads of copy paper, all kept in a locker in the hallway to the printing plant.

> It was a terrifying honour … Even more worrying was my recent pathetic attempt to write something intelligent about *Briggflatts* for *International Times*, London's first countercultural publication. The review was cryptic and hurried, silly but enthusiastic. I can just imagine his 'violently alarming' laugh as he read it (if he did) … Seeking some trace of this glory, I searched for Bunting the poet in his workaday world, for some clue to the 'remote blood and ancestry' that preoccupied him. Nothing but a few squiggles on scraps of paper which I took for shorthand notes and discarded, though they may indeed have been immortal lines from some Persian epic he was translating between copy-editing and headline-writing for the evening financial page.[65]

Safe from drowning

In 1966 Bunting accepted a Visiting Lectureship at the University of California, Santa Barbara, where Alan Brilliant and Jack Shoemaker had just founded the Unicorn Press and Bookshop. He was distressed at leaving Peggy[66] but was straightaway in their midst, contributing poems for a Unicorn chapbook and giving readings at the book store. Alan Brilliant recalls that he 'wasn't a garrulous person while among us … he seemed to be gently tolerating all of us while his mind was elsewhere'.[67] Unicorn Press published Bunting's *Two Poems* ('Birthday Greeting' and 'All You Spanish Ladies') in May 1967 with a cover price of $1 in a short run of 250 copies, of which 30 were numbered and signed by the poet at the reading on 27 May 1967 at the Unicorn Bookshop.[68] (Both poems had been published in *Agenda* the previous year.)[69] In the same month Pym-Randall Press in Cambridge, MA, published 'What the Chairman Told Tom' in a limited signed edition of two hundred copies. 'Pym, by the way, was a cat,' he revealed to Dorothy Pound. 'Randall took him into partnership to satisfy the law about how many shareholders a limited company has to have. The firm is now in mourning for its senior partner, dead of old age at sixteen or so.'[70]

He was enjoying himself, although he expressed it cautiously, and he must have had some money for once. If his claim, in a letter to SUNY in January 1970, is to be believed the University of California paid him $16,500 per annum, worth well over $100,000 today.[71] He wrote to Jonathan Williams in December 1966:

> The Pacific – what there is of it under the oil – cuts back our cliffs, but I believe it will be several years before it reaches this house, so I'm safe from drowning. The sun does shine, mostly: but I understand it does that in North Carolina too. (Maria has discovered a headline: "Southern Black farmers fading..." Perhaps you've observed this peculiar physiological phenomenon? It should solve the colour problem in the end.) ... Here I talk to silent rows of milk-shakes, with never a dash of salt in a classroomful. I am endeavouring to make David Jones known to their elders, and annoying people by saying obvious things that they didn't expect about Carlos Williams or The Cantos. Kenner, however, is a pleasure, and one or two others are kind and friendly to the poor prisoner on the campus who has still no car to go to town with or explore the country. Any chance of seeing you here? A nice hike across the desert? We have cheap wine and can cook cakes and bacon.[72]

His apartment was seven minutes from the beach, fifteen from his office at the university.[73] It could have been worse. On the whole though he preferred the Buffaloonatics to the Santa Barbarians. They might drive one crazy but at least they were 'more aware of the world around them than the Santa Barbarians, who look like the milkshakes they live on and seem as tasty'.[74]

The following February, he told Dorothy Pound, he was unwell – 'dragged myself to class then subsided in or on my bed, for several weeks'.[75] He may have been depressed by news from home. On 10 January he had discovered that his mother had cancer and couldn't 'hope to add much to her 92 years', as he told Robert Creeley.[76] In fact his mother held out for another eighteen months; she died in July 1968: 'She was about the house until a few hours before she died, but she had a bad night and the next day she seemed to be failing rapidly – fainted a couple of times. Then she rallied, talked a lot about a new frock and joked with Sima and ate her dinner. A little later I saw her lying half asleep, complaining quietly to herself, and an hour after that we found her dead. She would have been 93 in a few more days. Nothing there to grieve about. She is buried with my father.'[77]

417

March saw a tour of Texas, for a Pound symposium, where the 'locals tried to drown me in Bourbon',[78] New York and Harvard. He complained to Pound that 'it rained whiskey' at the conference: 'They bath the babies in whiskey in Texas. They drink it out of their ten-gallon hats. They wash their clothes in it. I asked for beer, but that consternated everybody. I asked for water and they looked puzzled.'[79] Bunting met Pound's daughter (with Olga Rudge), Mary, for the first time at the symposium and warmed to her. He thought she was moved by meeting her father's old friend. Mary aside, his view of such conferences was caught in a poem written in 1969, 'All the cants they peddle':

> All the cants they peddle
> bellow entangled,
> teeth for knots and
> each other's ankles,
> to become stipendiary
> in any wallow;
> crow or weasel
> each to his fellow.
>
> Yet even these,
> even these might
> listen as crags
> listen to light
> and pause, uncertain
> of the next beat,
> each dancer alone
> with his foolhardy feet.[80]

'Whoever has been conned,' he noted in *Collected Poems*, 'however briefly, into visiting a "poets' conference" will need no explanation of this ode.'[81] Although 'All the cants they peddle' was written in 1969 it wasn't finished to Bunting's satisfaction until 1974, when it was published in *Agenda*. 'Finished at last, after five years,' he wrote to Jonathan Williams in April 1974, 'the 16 lines about current literary amenities which has been on my desk all that time, waiting for one word in the last line, now supplied. At least the delay removes the lines from suspicion of personal animosity.'[82]

In New York he read at the Guggenheim to 'a considerable audience who took their cue from Ginsberg and stamped, jumped, clapped and yelled when it was over'.[83] The Harvard reading was a more sedate affair but he enjoyed a 'charming, quiet time', and his hosts drove him out to Gloucester and Concorde.

The New York leg of the tour provided some painful encounters. He met the poet Denise Levertov and 'disliked her heartily'. More importantly he called on Zukofsky but found him 'very bitter and, strangely, very jealous. A painful hour. He did not go to the reading because of "drafts".'[84] He wrote to Pound that Zukofsky was 'sunk in bitterness, in spite of all the American poets calling him father (you're grandfather now).'[85]

Bunting's time in California coincided with a period of immense student unrest and riots on campus were frequent. 'Mr Ronald Reagan, Governor of Californa, has dismissed the head of the university,' he told Gael Turnbull. 'He will charge students about £150 a year on top of the £100 they already pay ... Protests are going on.'[86] In spite of the chaos in the California university system J. M. Edelstein remembered that Bunting was comfortable there and that he was liked by his students:

> He would walk, sandaled, with a tweed jacket on, through that Goleta campus which looks like a stage set, sand blowing through the streets, weeds growing in the gutters in front of new glass and stone buildings, and he was always followed by a retinue of kids.
>
> One day we went to hear Robert Duncan lecture on poetics; I remember many allusions to Dante. It was a Saturday afternoon and there were twenty, or maybe thirty, people in the dimly lit, abandoned movie house where the lecture was being given. Duncan spoke brilliantly, but dryly – and for hours. Bunting slept soundly and snored loudly. When it was over, he said: 'I like talks like that.' Personally and poetically, that is what we expect from Basil Bunting: the heart of the matter. And that is what we get.[87]

Bunting frequently dined with Hugh Kenner's family during his year at Santa Barbara 'to the repeated delight of one of [Kenner's] daughters, who thought that for once a poet looked like a poet. He looked trim and twinkly-eyed, with a white moustache, and I suspect she was projecting on his features the undoubted fact that he *sounded* like a poet.'[88]

He was an inexperienced but memorable teacher. At one of his Santa Barbara classes he asked his students to read aloud Wordsworth's 'Idiot Boy': 'as first one, and then another, took up the reading, they gradually began to find that tall tale – funny. (It has *never* been officially acknowledged that Wordsworth might anywhere be funny.) And the laughter grew contagious, and the roomful of California adolescents were helpless with hysterics, and from the next classroom there came bangs on the wall to get them to shut up.'[89] Bunting wrote to Jonathan Williams about this event in April 1967: 'The class are astonished to find that Wordsworth was not a humourless old woman. They even laughed often and long at the Idiot Boy. I've hopes of them. We'll see what they make of The Old Cumberland Beggar.'[90] Bunting didn't always reciprocate this enthusiasm. One of his Santa Barbara students 'had eaten rattlesnake in all but one of the 50 states, but my interest was not excited'.[91] He was, he wrote to Ezra Pound, 'pretending to teach, a kind of unteacher, trying to prevent the kids getting the sort of education they do get in such places'.[92]

He tried to supplement his income with readings in California, but it was slow work. He wrote to the poet Cid Corman in April 1967 that in the previous eight months he had given only two readings, one free at the university and another for $100 in San Francisco, but he had been required to pay his own expenses.[93]

Much is forgotten and all forgiven

The year 1966 was important for the man as well as the poet. Victoria Forde, until very recently the source of nearly all the information we have about Bunting's American family, reports that he met his daughters Bourtai and Roudaba for the first time in thirty years.

> Although they had corresponded sporadically throughout this time, they had never been reunited. The summer he arrived in the States he first travelled to Wisconsin where Bourtai and her family lived near their mother. His grandchildren immediately loved their newly found grandfather and his fabulous stories. Bourtai more slowly renewed her acquaintance with a pleasant stranger, a father she had idealised and fantasised about all through her youth. Earlier he had tried to convince Rou to go to nursing school in England, but Rou had decided on the University of Honolulu. That Christmas Bunting sent Rou a ticket to California for their first reunion. Though Bourtai had been invited also, she was unable to accept. In her last year at the University of Wisconsin, she was trying to balance her family responsibilities and studying by getting up at four in the morning and staying up late at night. When Rou travelled from Hawaii to see Bunting in Santa Barbara, she expected a flamboyant 'Poet' – something like the barefoot Poet with swirling cape who had been described to her. To her amazement she met an ordinary looking, quiet, cultured, gentle man with whom, from that time

on, she and her family never lost close contact. Later when her father had a cataract removed from one eye, Rou, a nurse, was able to be with him in California for the operation.[94]

Forde describes what seems to have been an idyllic summer for the reunited family:

> From Wisconsin Bourtai and her son Ahab, Bunting and Maria drove on to Montreal's Expo 67 before Maria and Ahab set sail for Wylam where Ahab lived for a year. Returning to Madison, Bourtai packed up her four youngest sons and their belongings to travel to California with Bunting. Leaving with her mother one son who wished to finish high school in Madison and dropping off another and his pet monkey in Chicago with his father, Bourtai with her three youngest sons and Bunting drove across the country in a holiday spirit. Crossing the Nevada desert, Bunting pretended with the children that they were in the Sahara with water and dates rationed. At Isla Vista in Bunting's home close to the Pacific, they all lived together companionably for several months until Bourtai found a job in Los Angeles.
>
> To make up for all the lost years, Bourtai with her family travelled from Los Angeles to see her father on weekends. One time he had made kidney stew for them, but he was not sure what was in it since his cataracts hindered his sight. But to be sure it would be ready, he had had it cooking on the stove for three days.[95]

In 2006 Roudaba Bunting Davido deposited letters to her from her father at the Basil Bunting Poetry Archive in Durham and this rich resource allows us to fill out the picture sketched by Victoria Forde. In the summer of 1966 he met Marian for the first time since Christmas 1936 when she left London with their two children, while pregnant with their third. 'I saw your mother,' he told Roudaba, 'and made friends with her again – she told me all her woes, without much pause for me to get a word in, but I tried to make the few things I could say helpful to you and Bou. Poor woman. I think she brought most of her troubles on herself needlessly, and I don't think they have taught her much.'[96]

According to Marian, Bunting congratulated her on her parenting of his two daughters. 'They were just what he would have liked them to be – free, unconcerned about public opinion, independent, living the lives of their choice. So he said.'[97] She was quite right about this. Bunting never seems to have lost his intense dislike of Marian's family and considered that in the circumstances she had done a good job. Bourtai and Roudaba were 'like the rest of the people I love best – free of humbug, free of greed, very open ... to love'.[98] He told Roudaba that peace had been established between himself and Marian:

> Much is forgotten and all forgiven. I know the difficulties she found, better than she knew them when she chose to face her awful family rather than poverty. Eau Claire has left a powerful mark on her, and it would be false to pretend that I am not glad she divorced me, for I could not long endure contact with her as she now is. But there would have been no divorce, no separation, if I could have prevented it, for I loved my two daughters beyond anything else in the world. I would have put up with anything to have kept you with me. Dear girl, you tell me that when you were a little girl you wrote to ask me to take you; believe me, I never received any such letters.[99]

We saw how profoundly Bunting's experiences in the Second World War affected him. By 1950 he was a man of action, a diplomat, spy, a mover and shaker in one of the world's most sensitive, dangerous and politically vital theatres. He honed his Wing-Commander Bunting act and cut a commanding figure throughout the Middle East. *Briggflatts* and the reunion with Peggy, Roudaba and Bourtai seems to have had an equally profound effect. There is something of the spirit of the final scene of *King Lear* in Bunting's letters to Roudaba; the anger and paranoia have abated and he appears reconciled, gentle, atoned:

> What else can I say to you dear daughter now? Only, I think, that I hope very earnestly that you can come to Santa Barabara: that I love you: that writing poetry is a skill like weaving carpets or shaping bowls on a potter's wheel and is not an intellectual exercise to make people afraid of the poet. Bourtai feels that she needed a father, and I that I needed a daughter even more. I think it will be the same with you and me.
>
> Sun is shining here. All omens good! (except the rheumatism!) Goodbye for now, dear Roudaba, and let us meet and kiss soon, soon.
>
> Love from your stranger father.[100]

When he got back to California Bunting wrote to Jonathan Williams in August 1967:

I'm back here again at last; now accompanied by my eldest daughter and three of my grandsons, but for how long I don't know. Bourtai is looking for a job in California ... I had to give up the idea of revisiting Harvard, and came home instead by way of the forests in northern Ontario, very dense and tangled. We saw Sullivan's bank in Iowa (Maria disdainful) and Lloyd Wright's monastic school at Taliessin (a bit too pious-memory for me), and visited Lorine Niedecker (very nice).[101]

He was amused to find Niedecker living in dread that her neighbours would discover that she was a poet. 'It's almost a crime in rural Wisconsin,' he told Tom Pickard.[102] He described Niedecker to Gael Turnbull as a 'shy, nervous old lady (though some years younger than me) terrified lest the neighbours should find out that she is anything as eccentric as a poetess. She is, I think, poor; but not so poor as to be uncomfortable in her pretty village.'[103]

Niedecker certainly enjoyed the visit. She wrote excitedly to Cid Corman:

Basil came! With two daughters. I was staying out home on the river and they came down from Madison where the older girl, Bourtai, lives. Not having planned for company so far as groceries were concerned, I took them to a tea room in Fort for lunch. Basil, 'I don't suppose it would be possible to get a glass of beer here?' Have you ever met him? His manner is timid and tender. Withal so kindly. O lovely day for me. He had seen the LN *Origin* – 'so much more there than is implied'. Asked if I'd ever written a long poem. And of course the question came up of reading poems aloud ... Would somebody would start Meditation Rooms, places of silence, so silent you couldn't help but hear the sound of your page without opening your mouth, and reading books would come back. Glad, tho, that Basil is earning a living thru reading poetry. (He teaches but does it he says mainly by reading good poetry aloud to his classes.)[104]

She clearly loved his gravelly Northumbrian voice: 'It was so pretty as we drove into our yard the evening we came home,' she wrote to Cid Corman in October 1968. 'So pr-r-r-it-ty as Basil said.'[105] Niedecker confided to Jonathan Williams that Bunting's visit was a high point in her later life[106] and by the end of 1967 she had completed 'Wintergreen Ridge':

Nobody, nothing
    ever gave me

          greater thing
  than time
          unless light
              and silence
  which if intense
          makes sound
                  Unaffected
  by man
          thin to nothing lichens
              grind with their acid
  granite to sand
          These may survive
              the grand blow-up
  the bomb
          When visited
              by the poet
  From Newcastle on Tyne
          I neglected to ask
              what wild plants
  have you there
          how dark
              how inconsiderate
  of me[107]

Niedecker and Bunting had the highest regard for each other. Her 'The Ballad of Basil', in mentioning Bunting's influences, quickly identifies him as completely his own poet:

  They sank the sea
      All land
          Enemy

  He saw his boats stand
      and he
              off the floor

  of that cold jail
      (would not fight
          their war)

```
        sailed anyway
                Villon went along
                        Chomei

Dante
        and the Persian
                Firdusi –

rigging
        for his own
                singing[108]
```

Bunting said of Niedecker that 'No one is so subtle with so few words',[109] and when she died in 1970 Roudaba remembered her father's anger that the event didn't get the media attention he felt it deserved.[110] A few years later he paid her a significant posthumous compliment: "There are some very fine female poets. One of the finest American poets at all, besides being easily the finest female American poet … – Lorine Niedecker never fails; whatever she writes is excellent.'[111] When Jonathan Williams was considering an edition of Niedecker's poems in the 1960s Bunting was delighted. 'Nobody else', he complained, 'has been buried quite so deep.'[112] He considered her a 'much better' poet than Emily Dickinson for instance.[113]

In early 1967 Bunting went to New York. The Academy of American Poets paid him $500 to read there but, he complained to Cid Corman, 'left me to pay my own fare there and back. (If I'd realised that before I'd have refused to go.)'[114] His profit, he told Denis Goacher, was $150.[115] If the pay was insulting the accommodation was worse. He wrote to Gael Turnbull from 'The Filthy Hotel, New York': 'They've lodged me where Dylan Thomas died.'[116]

Jane Kramer recalls Allen Ginsberg teasing Bunting about his reading of *Briggflatts* at the Guggenheim Museum and confessing that he had 'tried to write a poem like you once … The one about Piccadilly. I set it up for myself like kind of an exercise. I said, like, "How would Basil write this poem?" and then I went ahead. Like I revised and revised. It ended up pretty rigid and condensed.' Ginsberg laughed, 'That kind of writing's not my scene – I haven't got the strength,' he said. 'I know that poem,' Bunting said. 'I thought it was rather good myself.'[117]

Bunting was being kind. Ginsberg's poem, 'Studying the Signs', had been written eighteen months previously and published in the Oxford magazine *Isis* in November 1965, and although it is much more terse than most of his work one wouldn't know that Bunting's *Briggflatts* was an influence if the fact had not been announced in an introductory note.[118] Bunting liked Ginsberg, but not his poetry. 'I like the notion of Ginsberg singing to the sheep,' he wrote to Jonathan Williams in September 1973, 'but I myself find his music so dismally platitudinous that I don't think even my friendly feelings towards him will ever get me to sit out another hour of it.'[119] A few years later even Ginsberg's kindness was becoming a nuisance. He told Williams that he had been

> put to great confusion and embarrassment by Allen Ginsberg. He wrote, offering me an obviously manufactured place in his Boulder Buddhist tushery, full of kindness and concern; and then offering me his farm up New York State; and then telling Cape to send me a cheque – his royalties, I suppose. His motives are as kind as they well can be, and that hinders me from explaining how ill all these plans strike me. I detest Gurus, Tibetan or any other breed. I am utterly sick of students, couldn't face them now. A rather rickety farm scares me. And I can't accept his royalties. If Cape actually sends the cheque, I'll put it in the bank to be held for Allen. But how do you tell a kind, friendly man that you prefer any misery that comes along to the kind of help he can give you? I must invent some excuse, and I not only lack invention but am quite clumsy enough to give offence. I'm postponing my answer as long as I can in the hopes of some inspiration. Do you think I am being perverse? I fear a lot of people would think so.[120]

A lovely gaudy world

Bunting struggled with his eyesight all his life. The earliest recording of it appears to be the doctor's certificate he presented to the London School of Economics in June 1922 and, as we have seen, he was only able to join the Royal Air Force during the Second World War because a doctor who had known his father allowed him to cheat in the eye test. Tom Pickard recalled that by the time he met Bunting in the early 1960s the lenses of the poet's glasses were 'as thick as a safe-door'.[121]

Eric Mottram recalled that he and colleagues went regularly to the cinema, 'Basil never. His eyesight at this time was extremely poor. He needed guiding over curbstones and across the busy main road between Clement Hall and the shopping and restaurant district.'[122]

By the end of May 1967 he had a serious disability. He complained to Dorothy Pound that he was becoming 'blinder and blinder'. Although he could still read books in large font and good light 'the stars disappeared three years ago, but I can make out the moon. I fall over invisible steps and kerbs, but see enough of the traffic to get across the road. And I can see the girls' legs if not their faces. Not too bad.'[123]

Bunting responded to Jonathan Williams in April 1967 that 'on present schedules I'll have full use of my one working eye just in time to catch the plane home. And I want a job for 1969–70, but it can't be in the US because of your laws. I wonder what they pay in Trinidad, Ubangi-Shari, Seychelles, Upper Amazon etc etc.'[124] Suddenly in the middle of December 1967 his right eye 'retired from business'. He wrote to Tom Pickard that it was now very difficult to read and write and that he could lose his job as a consequence: 'I'd expected to go more or less blind, James Joyce fashion, bit by bit; but this was sudden (a few hours) and I can just distinguish light from darkness with that eye.'[125]

He wrote to Turnbull at the same time about the cataract in his left eye. His doctor had told him that he required an immediate operation but Bunting's insurance didn't cover his eyes and he needed to find $1,000 to pay for it.[126] He went ahead with the operation and on 7 January dictated a fairly cheerful letter to Turnbull: 'They dug a bit out of my left eye in the Cottage Hospital in Santa Barbara where they also overfed me for a week until I insisted on going home for fear of getting too fat for my clothes.'[127] The first letter he typed himself after his operation was also written to Turnbull, reporting success: 'If you start from a state of complete blindness every little step in recovery is a delight. The first time the surgeon took the bandages off and I saw a shapeless red thing that must have been his hand – like the Ancient Mariner enjoying the sunrise. Then as the eye cleared the colours, untampered even by the normal lens which filches some of their exuberance – a lovely, gaudy world.'[128]

On 30 January 1968 Lorine Niedecker wrote to Cid Corman about 'Basil's eyes. Has had cataract removed from the one and will have to have the other eye done. Students come in and cook and write letters for him. He seems to have a great companionship with his students.'[129] He had to wait until the summer to have his other eye operated on, 'not quite such a long job as the left', he told Jack Shoemaker in November, 'and it did not disable me so much or for so many weeks. Now I see well with glasses, and by March I'll be able to return to contact lenses. Only at arm's length I cant see well, so I still drop cups and spill my food.'[130]

FEAR ADJECTIVES, THEY BLEED NOUNS

In 1968 Fulcrum Press published one thousand hardcover copies of *Collected Poems* at 35/- and Stream Records recorded *Briggflatts*. The Fulcrum *Collected Poems* brought together for the first time everything Bunting felt was worth keeping. His preface is a rueful retrospective:

> A man who collects his poems screws together the boards of his coffin. Those outside will have all the fun, but he is entitled to his last confession. These verses were written here and there now and then over forty years and four continents. Heaped together they make a book.

> If ever I learned the trick of it, it was mostly from poets long dead whose names are obvious: Wordsworth and Dante, Horace, Wyat and Malherbe, Manuchehri and Ferdosi, Villon, Whitman, Edmund Spenser; but two living men also taught me much: Ezra Pound and in his sterner, stonier way, Louis Zukofsky. It would not be fitting to collect my poems without mentioning them.

> With sleights learned from others and an ear open to melodic analogies I have set down my words as a musician pricks his score, not to be read in silence, but to trace in the air a pattern of sound that may sometimes, I hope, be pleasing. Unabashed boys and girls may enjoy them. This book is theirs.[131]

Collected Poems was well received. Andrew Wylie praised it in *Agenda*: 'permanent ... must be heard'. Martin Dodsworth, however, in the *Listener* was unimpressed. Bunting aimed for 'crisp, curt perfection' but it 'left a rather gritty taste in the mouth ... The diction, careful, heavily monosyllabic and particular, certainly commands respect, but rhythmically he is very monotonous, the omission of definite and indefinite articles is an irritating mannerism, and there is an overall want of originality.' Richard Holmes was much nearer the mark in *The Times*. He noted the link between *Briggflatts* and *The Waste Land* in terms of impact: 'In 1922 a generation recovering from war opened a slim volume and read. "April is the cruellest month, breeding/ Lilacs out of the dead land", finding its own voice in the painful, regretful cadences. Now our own Spring comes round. In 1966 we opened *Briggflatts* to find a tough, intricate music, full of hope.' Holmes went on to praise the translations from Villon, Dante, Horace, Rudaki and Chomei, poets who were 'crushed to a dense mineral glitter in the substrata of his work'. For once there was no use of the words 'Poundian' or 'disciple'. Peter Stansill, who, as we have seen, replaced Bunting at the Newcastle *Evening Chronicle*, celebrated *Collected Poems* in the *International Times* with a bewildering mixture of metaphors as 'a concentrate of bristling, clanking words formed into a sculpture of timeless myth and continuous motion'. At the time most readers would have agreed with Stansill that Bunting's was 'English Poetry – the Eng. Lit. that our kids will ponder over in the decades to come in their spacious comprehensive schools', but that is a prediction that is yet to be fulfilled. Patrick Kavanagh in the *Guardian* singled out 'Chomei at Toyama' for special praise and noted Bunting's 'splendid ear, not for tinkles but for strong, rhythmic speech, the words hard, clear-edged'. Cyril Connolly gave *Collected Poems* an enthusiastic review in the *Sunday Times*.

Roy Fuller, the newly appointed Professor of Poetry at the University of Oxford, praised the 'fresh energy and simplicity' of the later poems, their 'narrative subtlety' and 'integrity', in the Newcastle *Evening Chronicle*, but a by now predictably negative review of *Collected Poems* appeared in the *Times Literary Supplement*, though this time sweetened by an acknowledgement that Bunting had talent: 'Phrase after phrase demonstrates his command of resources that better-known poets have not acquired.' On the whole though it suggested that Bunting's entire career had been a waste of energy.

Alan Brownjohn in the *New Statesman* praised Bunting's 'stark, powerful and chastening poetry ... a poetry of barren magnificence and no ease', while noting that he could be 'coldly impenetrable'.

Reviews in America (where *Collected Poems* was published by Horizon) were positive. Thomas Lask in the *New York Times* praised the later poems in particular: 'Now the lines are hard, spare and weighted. The beat is almost reminiscent of Anglo-Saxon verse ... His is not the kind of poetry that wears away with a single reading.' In *Library Journal* Robert Regan described the collection's 'superbly wrought poems'. *Atlantic Monthly* averred that 'this remarkable poet has dragged the whole history of English verse into the twentieth century and proved it relevant'.

Roger Guedalla, who compiled the first Bunting bibliography, accepted Pound's influence but put it in perspective. His use of 'alliteration and hard, compressed consonants derives as much from his independent reading of Anglo-Saxon as it does from his reading of Pound ... He defies classification, and his contribution to English poetry is unique. But this very independence [from universities and schools of poetry] seems to limit his reputation, much to the frustration of his admirers.' *Queen* lamented the public's neglect of Bunting but decided that 'time is on his side'.[132]

Perhaps the most illuminating review of *Collected Poems*, however, appeared in the Quaker magazine, *The Friend*. It illustrates why many Quakers were suspicious about acknowledging Bunting as a Quaker poet, even if non-Quakers were sleepwalking into it: 'Skimming through the volume one might at first be inclined to lay it down in disgust,' wrote Wyatt Rawson, 'nauseated by the outspoken portrayal of the flesh and its desires. But a second and slower reading could give quite a different impression. For beneath the repellent surface there will begin to glow an ever-present love and compassionate understanding in which men's scars and failings, pains and tragedies, are seen in a diviner light.'[133] This is a more profound insight into Bunting's poetry than anything to be found in the broadsheets or the *Times Literary Supplement*.

Douglas Jones reviewed *Collected Poems* in *Odysseus* and added a note from Denis Goacher which claimed that Bunting was the only one of Pound's close associates to have managed a long poem ... which will 'hold a permanent place in our literature',[134] which might have disappointed Zukofsky and which certainly would have puzzled Eliot had he been alive.

On 16 August 1968 Jonathan Williams' Gnomon Press published *Descant on Rawthey's Madrigal: Conversations with Basil Bunting*, which included 'A Statement', an uncompromising document which deals with the relationship between poetry and the arts establishment that he soon had even greater reason to condemn: 'All the arts are plagued by charlatans seeking money, or fame, or just an excuse to idle. The less the public understands the art, the easier it is for the charlatans to flourish. Since poetry reading became popular, they have found a new field, and it is not easy for the outsider to distinguish the fraud from the poet. But it is a little less difficult when poetry is read aloud. Claptrap soon bores. Threadbare work sounds thin and broken backed.'[135]

Bunting's influence was beginning to be acknowledged and for the first time he was able to make such comments from a position of strength. The editor of *New Measure*, Peter Jay, noted that with the publication of 'The Spoils', *Loquitur* and *Briggflatts* Bunting now occupied a position similar to that of William Carlos Williams.[136] The poet Roy Fisher recalls sitting 'at a table in Stuart and Deirdre Montgomery's flat overlooking Southampton Row, correcting the galleys for *City* for the Fulcrum Press *Collected Poems 1968*, with Basil sitting quietly in the corner peering at *The Times* with the pages held close to his face. Every time I looked in his direction I felt for an adjective to cut or a construction to contract. It was the nearest I could get to asking for a blessing on my prose.'[137]

Publication had also brought Bunting the recognition in Great Britain that he deserved. The North East Arts Association's proposal to create a two-year Poetry Fellowship depended on the financial support of the Universities of Durham and Newcastle upon Tyne and after protracted negotiations that subsidy was secured, although the NEAA still supplied most of the funding. By the time the negotiations had been successfully concluded in 1967 Bunting had accepted an offer from the US and his Fellowship was delayed until 1968.

Bunting was a controversial choice for academic institutions. When he was awarded the NEAA Fellowship one senior academic at Durham is reported to have asked 'Who's Basil Bunting?'[138] He had never courted academic favour. He described his experience of proofreading an academic journal to Zukofsky in the 1950s: 'I am also responsible for one University journal: in two numbers of it I haven't found one sentence which wasn't humbug – conscious and deliberate humbug in my opinion – which has enormously increased my regard for soldiers and politicians, not usually thought of as very intelligent or scrupulous classes, but less dishonest and less fatuous than the academics.'[139]

He was consistently hostile towards any academic influence on poetry and particularly towards academics' drive to uncover 'meaning'. But, according to Peter Lewis, 'once in post ... Bunting made it clear that his quarrel was not with academe as such but with certain prevalent modes of literary study.'[140] Indeed Bunting broke with tradition to give a series of lectures, which Fellows were not expected to give, at Newcastle University. Bunting saw his students regularly, and directed them – sometimes forcefully – on their apprentice writing. He printed a postcard for young poets embodying the wisdom of half a century of experience, and advised them on how best to develop their poetic voice:

I SUGGEST

1. Compose aloud; poetry is a sound.

2. Vary rhythm enough to stir the emotion you want but not so as to lose impetus.

3. Use spoken words and syntax.

4. Fear adjectives; they bleed nouns. Hate the passive.

5. Jettison ornament gaily but keep shape

Put your poem away till you forget it, then:

6. Cut out every word you dare.

7. Do it again a week later, and again.

Never explain – your reader is as smart as you.[141]

An interview with the Durham University student newspaper, *Palatinate*, in October 1968 reveals him in characteristically uncompromising form. He was 'highly critical of the charlatans who get away with imitation and he thinks that many of the young see the Arts as an excuse for being lazy'.[142] That criticism, as we shall see, was to deepen sharply in the coming decade.

One student from the south of England (Wilko Johnson, later of Doctor Feelgood) asked which 'southrons' wrote well. 'Keats,' said Bunting after some thought. 'Keats is for Cockneys.'[143] (In fact Bunting thought the only way Keats' poetry becomes even tolerable is when it is read in the poet's own 'old cockney' accent.) Bunting thought that one half-line from the ode 'To Autumn', 'Hedge-crickets sing', was the only impressive phrase in the whole of Keats' work.[144] Another of Bunting's Newcastle students astutely noted that 'obscurity seems to have given him a freedom that few major poets have had and a means for personal expression without the inhibitions of public taste and morality'.[145]

He could be as curmudgeonly with students as he was with bureaucrats. Roy Fisher recalls turning up at a 'new and fashionable university' to give a reading:

My student host was a bright, optimistic young woman, running a well-organized reading series. I asked who the other poets were and she named the names of the day. Then:
– We *did* invite Basil Bunting.
– And he sent you a dreadful letter that made you cry.
– Well yes!
– I hope you sold it for a lot of money?
– *I tore it up and flushed it down the loo!*

… his standard refusal-note, in some such terms as that poets should not have to peddle their wares for mean fees in the public markets … seemed to [be delivered] with renewed vehemence each time. When he chose, he could be generous. At about the same time, Eric Mottram and I tutored a course at Lumb Bank and invited Basil to be guest reader, a two-hour engagement, modestly paid. He arrived early, and left only on the third day, having given two long evening readings … and conversed amiably and usefully with anybody who wanted to talk to him.'[146]

Bunting was neither proud nor ashamed of his grumpy approach to readings and their organisers. He was pragmatic, although with an element of barely disguised class contempt. He wrote to Jonathan Williams:

> Your adventures in Cambridge don't surprise me. Never a year goes by but I am invited to Cambridge in terms which, at their extreme, reached: 'Of course we cannot afford to pay any fee, but we will make sure you get a good meal.' I answer roughly. Oxford doesn't quite treat me as a beggarman, still, it's much the same. Poorer universities have more sense, but yet one's usually out of pocket by going to them. London institutions are worse, if you allow for the extra expense. So far as my experience goes only Cardiff and Newcastle try to make a reading worthwhile.[147]

Tom Pickard remembered Bunting's disgust at the expectation that poets would perform without being paid:

> One day I showed Bunting a letter from the Oxford Poetry Society responding to my refusal to read without payment and it outraged him. The society secretary told me that most people consider it an honour to read for them, and money was never mentioned. It was bad form. Basil was getting similar letters, and a few days later someone gave him a John Bull hand printing set with which he produced this:

> 'Thank you for your invitation; but I am not keen to read. Reading poetry is much like playing music. I find it hard to understand people who read who are too haphazard, with no matched or contrasted programme and no rehearsal. I think that people who pay to see films or hear concerts should pay no less for poetry, if they want it; but some are willing to sponge on poets who never think of treating a fiddler so. I believe readings will go on being sloppy till poets insist on proper pay and conditions.
> So I have fixed these fees for readings:
> In the North Country (Humber & Ribble to Solway Firth and Tweed)
>   forty guineas
> Elsewhere in Britain eighty guineas
> Overseas 500 US dollars
> _____ all plus fare, bed and board.
> Most school societies have no money. I will oblige them if I can conveniently. Many student societies could squeeze rich colleges but don't. If you think your case is special by all means state it. (Letters addressed to Shylock may not always reach their destination.)'

He was always sympathetic and knocked the self pity from my helpless rage at the dole authorities with a "What the hell! You keep at those poems and you'll have a good book in no time." Then he might break into a music hall song because we were next to the Empire Theatre, or a bawdy one from the First World War, assuming for the latter frowning eyebrows, a chin firmly set on chest and ponderous bishop-like scowl from which he uttered the brilliant trench profanities that inspired him to a howl of appreciative laughter.[148]

Curmudgeonly or not, his readings were attracting audiences that poets today can only dream about. The poet and academic Charles (Mike) Doyle wrote to Sylvia Bowman at Twayne Publishers on 19 January 1971 with a proposal for a book he was proposing to write on Bunting: 'Some months ago he gave a reading at U.B.C., Vancouver, and the noted American poets Robert Creeley and Robert Duncan flew from San Francisco specifically to attend the reading. An audience of about 500 gave Bunting a standing ovation at the end.'[149]

A SHREWD AND MISCHIEVOUS KIPLING

By now Bunting was beginning to be anthologised. He had already, as we have seen, been included in anthologies collected by Zukofsky, Hugh Kenner and Pound, but in the early 1970s he attracted the attention of editors with whom he was not closely associated. In 1970 Anthony Howell's collection of *Erotic Lyrics* included 'Yes, it's slow, docked of amours', Geoffrey Summerfield included twenty-five lines from *Briggflatts* in the third volume of his *Junior Voices: An anthology of poetry and pictures,* a book designed for classroom teaching, and Edward Lucie-Smith included 'The Spoils' in Penguin's prestigious *British Poetry since 1945.* John Matthias included 'Vestiges', 'What the Chairman told Tom', 'Chomei at Toyama' and parts of *Briggflatts* (stanzas printed in the wrong order) in his *23 Modern British Poets* and 'A thrush in the syringa sings' appeared in William Cole's anthology of 'short, short poems', *Poetry Brief.* In 1973 Jon Stallwothy included Bunting's translation from Rudaki , 'Came to me', in *The Penguin Book of Love Poetry.*

Anthologies presented a real problem to Bunting. As he explained in an increasingly acrimonious exchange of letters towards the end of 1970 about 'An Active Anthology', which the 'axial' artist and poet, George Quasha, was preparing: 'I am not inclined to figure in Mr. Quasha's anthology, for several reasons. If you have examined 'Briggflatts' Part 3 you must have seen that it needs what goes before and what follows. By itself it would have no excuse, either as sense or as music.'

There were other reasons for Bunting to spurn Quasha's exercise. The financial offer was 'funny'; he required at least $1,000 for a contribution of the length suggested. In any event, 'Mr. Quasha must have noticed, and very many people could have told you, that my work is at the furthest possible distance from 'Found Poetry', 'Concrete Poetry', 'Mixed Media Poetry', 'Protest Poetry', etc. I prefer to work at the job and make as good a poem as I can without looking for short cuts to notoriety.'[150] Quasha's response to this rejection hasn't survived but however it was couched it prompted a long Christmas lecture from Bunting: 'I don't give a damn whether anybody reads the poems I make or listens to them: never did. I am not on show, and if ever I want to "communicate" anything I'll do it in prose. I never dreamt of making a living out of poetry. If what I make seems to me well-made, that's an end of my interest in it; and if it doesn't, I suppress it so far as I can. If what I write is really good it is likely that people will find it out sooner or later, but that is their affair, not mine.'[151]

The increased attention should have secured Bunting's enduring reputation but, if anything, it harmed it. Bunting's great work is painted on large canvases. It is possible to select parts of the longer poems that seem to stand alone but the effect of those poems is cumulative and gradual, and dismembering them for anthologies diminishes both the whole and the part. Bunting wrote many short poems, of course, but even the best of those considered in isolation give the impression that he was a meticulous and skilled but essentially minor poet. The great poems, 'Villon', 'Chomei at Toyama', 'The Spoils' and *Briggflatts* are essentially irreducible to the anthology format.

In August 1968 *The Times'* Pooter column carried a feature on Pickard and Bunting, 'looking with his high forehead, minatory eyebrows and total moustache, like a shrewd and mischievous Kipling',[152] and wider public recognition of Bunting's achievements allowed him to pass the acid test of celebrity; he became the subject of satire. Edward Pygge ribbed Bunting in *The Review* in June 1970:

After years of cringing and soul-destroying notoriety, Basil ("Crushed Grit") Bunting has at long last been granted the obscurity he deserves. Born in Hailey, Idaho in 1785, this dour and remorseless skald has of recent years been tempted into a cryptic silence. We visited him in his eleventh century granite nightsoil pit in Newcastle last week. Pulling a plaid scarf round his inert and aristocratic neck, he listened attentively when we asked him to describe how he first met young Tom Pickard. After a moment's ruminative silence, he began to move his grizzled lips, and spoke: 'Pickard, ay, the fluffy bum, the shite hawk. Telt meyis name wus Stoppard. On to a gid thing, I telt mesel. Wait till I seeyim. Kick ees pills, ah will, boorim in the nackers, wipe ees face wiya rasa, suck ees plums …' We could bear it no longer and as he ranted on, we slipped quietly out into the damp Tyneside air, his rich verbs ringing unforgettably in our offended ears.[153]

Pygge's satire provoked a rather po-faced response from Jonathan Williams:

> Sir, I don't know who Edward Pygge is (Bill Hook? Or, perhaps, Aeon-Ton-Ill-Ham?), but I don't think he's very funny when he subjects Basil Bunting to the sort of undergraduate calumny received in No. 22 of your magazine. Bunting's major crime has been to devote a life quietly to making decent durable poems and staying out of Soho pubs and editorial offices. His Northumbrian burr, even to my foreign ears, connects him to Morpethshire and the Cheviot hills, not to the Geordie sound of the streets of Tyneside.[154]

Williams was right with his 'Aeon-Ton-Ill-Ham' suggestion. Ian Hamilton, editor of *The Review*, invented the pseudonym Edward Pygge to write a page at the back of the magazine 'where somebody would get it in the neck'.[155] I think Bunting would have enjoyed the joke. Only a few letters separate Tom Pickard from Tom Stoppard but they constitute an unlikely couple.

Bunting caught the eye of reference book editors as well as that of anthologists, feature writers and satirists. He told Jonathan Williams in 1970 that *World Who's Who* was proposing to list him as the author of *Briggflatts*, *Loquitur*, 'The Spoils' and *The Rise of the South African Reich*. 'I am thinking of adding *Papist Malignancy in Northern Ireland* and *A Child's Guide to the Cello*.'[156]

Bunting hadn't been entirely happy with his selection for Fulcrum Press' 1968 *Collected Poems* and he took the opportunity of a second edition in 1970 to exclude nine previously published poems and introduce a couple of new ones, including the beautiful, reflective 'Stones trip Coquet burn':

> Stones trip Coquet burn;
> grass trails, tickles
> till her glass thrills.

The breeze she wears
lifts and falls back.
Where beast cool

in midgy shimmer
she dares me chase
under a bridge,

giggles, ceramic
huddle of notes,
darts from gorse

and I follow, fooled.
She must rest, surely;
some steep pool

to plodge or dip
and silent taste
with all my skin.[157]

He sent this poem to Jonathan Williams in March 1970 and told him that Mottram thought it 'sexy',[158] and that was clearly an intentional effect. He told an audience that 'Coquet is a little river in Northumberland. It struck me a long time ago that the Greeks thought all rivers had nymphs, and so if you go near the fountains of a river, where it is very little, it must have nymphettes, and I decided to write a poem which, without going into great detail, would suggest that.'[159]

Bunting also read Wordsworth's 'The Brothers' and 'Michael' for BBC Radio 3 in October 1970. He told his audience that all he could claim for his reading, 'is that my vowels are nearer to those Wordsworth uttered than a Londoner's might be, and my intonation perhaps less foreign to his ... His music is lost if his poems are read in Southern English, and no doubt that is why so many of his critics imagine he had none.'[160]

Kenneth Cox helped Bunting with the Wordsworth recording:

Bunting's attitude to the job throughout was in the highest degree 'professional'. At his home I heard him practising passages behind closed doors. When the day came to record he kept silence while we journeyed to the studio. It was as though he were carrying something in his head too precious to be disturbed or distracted from, or something too fragile to be exposed to the air. In studio he referred to me questions about pronunciation of certain words which might, he thought, affect comprehensibility in other countries. When something he had recorded seemed to him to fall below the result he had rehearsed, or aside from the one he had intended, he corrected himself on the instant without reference to me. When I returned to London I was told a bill for the bottle of whiskey we had shared had already been received from the regional office.[161]

According to Hugh Kenner he read 'Michael' with the vowels and burr he shared with Wordsworth as well as with Spenser and Swinburne 'to reclaim the regionality of these poets … from the awful subsuming dominance of London received pronunciation. It was part of his lifelong protest against the BBC.'[162]

Bunting thought that the broadcasts had been a great success, and a thoughtful review in the *Guardian* by Keith Dewhurst suggests that he was right to. Dewhurst thought that Bunting had touched on 'one of the central and most important mysteries of the English literary tradition'.[163] In July 1971 he expressed some surprise to Dorothy Pound that 'how much of what I said about Willy Wordsworth two years ago has been taken up and is now being said by all sorts of people who dont very well understand what they are repeating; and lots of people seem to have found the two broadcasts … quite exciting'.[164]

Wordsworth came back into Bunting's life significantly in his later years. He read from 'The Excursion' for the BBC in August 1972[165] and in February 1978 he told Jonathan Williams that he had been to London to read Wordsworth for the fund to repair the roof of Dove Cottage, Wordsworth's Lakeland home, but that the reading had been poorly attended because it was at 6 o'clock when most people were struggling to get home from work.[166] According to Gael Turnbull he was pleased that scholars had begun to notice what he had been saying about Wordsworth, that he didn't speak 'Standard' English but Westmorland and that Wordsworth alone constituted one of the four great pivotal movements in English poetry in English.[167]

Goacher never understood what he called Bunting's 'over-estimation' of Wordsworth:

> I think this, perhaps, indicates the weakness of too strong an identity with one's roots. He liked to marshal himself up alongside Wordsworth, because Wordsworth was a great North Country poet. This is why he loved Dunbar so much. It's why he vaunted MacDiarmid so much and why he championed the young Tom Pickard – because he wanted to feel there was a continuity of great Northern poets who were distinct from us softies down South. I'm not exaggerating on this point.[168]

He wasn't. You could add Joseph Skipsey and Swinburne to the list of poets Bunting admired because they were northerners not because they were great poets; but it is still a depressing observation. How can you 'over-estimate' Wordsworth? Wordsworth was what he was to Bunting. The fact that Goacher rated Wordsworth less highly than Bunting did is trivial.

CANADA, 1970–1971

'No, life is not comfortable often or for long, but fortunately life isn't long either.'[169]

Poverty pushed Bunting back to North America. As his Fellowship at Newcastle and Durham Universities was drawing to a close he wrote to dozens of universities in North America to try to secure a position for the following academic year. He told Rodger Kingston in May 1970 that it was possible that he would be in Canada by autumn:

> 45 Canadian and US universities have no use for me. My appointment here ends in June and when it ends I must endeavour to live on my old age pension – about £6 a week – and a Civil List pension which has just been awarded me of £5 a week less income tax! Not much for a man and wife and two university age children in a country where £25 a week is considered too little for a bricklayer's hodman ... As you'll gather, I'm depressed. Perhaps it's only due to the long winter, longest for many years; but I do see a general resurgence of everything unscrupulous, illiberal and brutal in Great Britain. Lord Chief Justice Parker, the worst LC in fifty years, is in favour of abolishing the rules of evidence because they hamper the police. Lesser lights advocate police perjury – the police are so honest they would never perjure themselves except to convict someone whom they know to be guilty. Besides, even when the prisoner isn't guilty, his conviction is a warning to those who are. We had better send all the Pakistanis in England home for fear the sight of them annoys the South African cricket team.[170]

He taught briefly at the University of British Columbia in Vancouver in 1970, describing his flight there to Pound with a poet's eye:

> the plane showed me northern Greenland. Like Dante's worst circle: and the needle sharp rocks and razor ridges sticking out of the ice for Judas's nose and Satan's fangs. Near the west coast an ice-fall, perpendicular for maybe 2,000 feet, ending in a huge conical moraine, started in Noah's time or before. I scarcely believed what I saw. If Harald Fairhair could scare people so badly

that they preferred Greenland to Norway I think he must have been an ugly bugger.[171]

He wrote fairly cheerfully to Tom Pickard at the beginning of term, seemingly comfortable in his 'little flat, four miles from my work',[172] but within a month had come to dislike Vancouver. 'The students are like oxen,' he told Pickard, 'but they don't moo.' And the charms of the city itself were illusory: 'it's incredible how a place so beautifully sited can be so damned uninteresting'. To Bunting Vancouver was obsessed by size, nowhere better exemplified than by Simon Fraser University at the other end of the city, which he hated: 'a monstrous building … stairs and stairs, wider than the M1, and a central room you could drill a couple of regiments in … The very essence of a bully's architecture.'[173] 'You can't teach British Columbians,' he wrote to Ezra Pound. 'They are made of the timber they trade in. And if there is anything more disheartening than the class it is the faculty.'[174] This letter to Pound had been prompted by a welcome, if typically terse, letter from Pound. Peter Quartermain recorded that in October 1970 'a depressed Ezra Pound wrote to Bunting in Vancouver: "If I had paid your attention to detail, I might have done something decent." (Bunting showed me this letter the day he received it, when I immediately copied it from memory in my notebook. So far as I know Bunting destroyed the original.)'[175] He did destroy Pound's letter but not before writing in some excitement to Tom Pickard: 'a surprise letter from Ezra Pound. First time I've seen his fist for years. Concise – he wasted no energy on superfluities. "Dear Basil, Thanks for your note from Vancouver. If I had your eye for detail I might have done something decent. Yours E.P." What it means I'm not sure. I thought he had demonstrated fairly often that he had at least as good an eye for detail as anyone whatever. However, it's a fine compliment and I'm not disposed to quarrel with it.'[176] He wrote a generous reply to Pound: 'I don't know anyone with a keener eye for detail than the chap who wrote the Cantos: not in every line, but whenever he wants it. If you had had my taste for looking at things when I can and books only when I have to, you would have been as ignorant as I am, and there would not have been any Cantos.'[177]

On 2 November Lorine Niedecker wrote to Cid Corman: 'Yes, Basil is in Vancouver according to Deirdre Montgomery … at least she said he would be there for one term, however long that is up there.'[178] Niedecker had seen Bunting for the last time. She died on 31 December 1970 at the age of sixty-seven. Bunting's contribution to Jonathan Williams' *Epitaphs for Lorine* expresses his sense of loss as it celebrates the precision of her art:

> To abate what swells
> use ice for scalpel.
> It melts in its wound
> and no one can tell
> what the surgeon used.
> Clear lymph, no scar,
> no swathe from a cheek's bloom.[179]

He spent the second half of the 1970–71 winter at the State University of New York at Binghamton, and didn't much enjoy it. 'The snow melted last night,' he wrote to Jonathan Williams in April 1971, 'nearly all of it, ending, I hope, a winter which has kept me more or less in solitary confinement since early December … (I'm sick of universities – students and faculty).'[180]

Once he had escaped he wrote to Eric Mottram from Wylam in June 1971 to complain: 'Binghamton was a dreadful climate and in every way a most discouraging place. Dull, dull students; boring faculty; continual snow – the last fall about May 9; air line on strike, so that I was a prisoner in my apartment, except for three days in Ottawa to read there. I didn't love British Columbia … Victoria BC, where I'm due in September, wants to work me far too hard.'[181]

The following month he wrote to Peter Quartermain about his ordeal:

> Can you imagine me teaching poor devils to read Bellow, Styron (who's he?), Cary, to say nothing of Lawrence, Brecht, Beckett, Fitzgerald; or in another course Stevens, Hart Crane, Berryman, Lowell, somebody called O'Hara, Cummings, Duncan? The prospect appals me. If I hadn't dependants I'd never pretend to do it. It makes me quite sick to anticipate it, and the only comfort is that … I should save enough to live a year or more without working, if the work doesn't kill me first. This syllabus will prevent me being the only real use I can be to the university, which would be to let them know of the existence of David Jones, Zukofsky, MacDiarmid and so on. Even by A-level standards their syllabus is fifteen years or more out of date. By what I'd reckon of university standards, thirty years.[182]

During this bleak and unhappy winter Bunting had been negotiating new contracts for the following academic year with the Universities of Victoria and Glasgow. He could, of course, take only one of them and he made the wrong decision.

The only poem Bunting preserved from 1971, 'You cant grip years, Postume', a translation from Horace, is a reflective meditation on death that perhaps draws on his recent experience of life. A single, thoughtful sentence winds through the first three quatrains giving an easy rhythm that suggests that the poet has learned from experience that resistance is useless:

> You can't grip years, Postume,
> that ripple away nor hold back
> wrinkles and, soon now, age,
> nor can you tame death
>
> not if you paid three hundred
> bulls every day that goes by
> to Pluto, who has no tears,
> who has dyked up
>
> giants where we'll go aboard,
> we who fed on the soil,
> to cross, kings some, some
> penniless plowmen.

The following two quatrains explain the consequences of resistance:

> For nothing we keep out of war
> or from screaming spindrift
> or wrap ourselves against autumn,
> for nothing, seeing
>
> we must stare at that dark, slow
> drift and watch the damned
> toil, while all they build
> tumbles back on them.

The poem ends with a mature acceptance that the future is for others:

> We must let earth go and home,
> wives too, and your trim trees,
> yours for a moment, save one
> sprig of black cypress.

Better men will empty
bottles we locked away,
wine puddle our table,
fit wine for a pope.[183]

An old, old, probably too old guy from England

Bunting, said the poet and academic Charles 'Mike' Doyle, 'stirred things up in Victoria over forty years ago'.[184] Doyle had been trying to secure a position for Bunting at the University of Victoria for months. At that time the English department was dominated by the flamboyant and charismatic poet Robin Skelton who was pioneering the new field of Creative Writing. Although Skelton had a devoted following he also aroused deep scepticism in the department and in the university as a whole. He cheerfully admitted to having an enormous ego and he enjoyed his considerable influence on the English department. Skelton, while a tactician, was not very tactful and Bunting was a not entirely innocent victim of Skelton's domineering style.

Doyle proposed to the head of department that Bunting teach Doyle's own course on modern American poetry but warned that even if accepted Bunting would be required to teach another course in return for a full professor's salary. He presented Bunting's curriculum vitae to the departmental appointments committee in the hope that if it wasn't going to be possible to offer a position in the visiting poet category, then 'any appropriate position' would be better than not having the poet on campus at all.

An undated (but December 1970) memo from Skelton to the head of department contains in its opening line the seeds of the problem that was about to unfold, although Bunting himself was to play his full part in it: 'I am a little surprised that Dr. Doyle should profess not to understand why I was not eager to support Bunting as a full-time member of the Creative Writing Division.' Skelton goes on to cite Bunting's lack of experience of Creative Writing, which rather points up the difference between Creative Writing and creative writing, a difference that Bunting was cruelly to expose later on. Skelton then makes the point that he wouldn't support a similar application from his friend, Robert Graves, whom he considered a more significant poet than Bunting.

On 4 January 1971 Bunting copied to Doyle a letter he had sent to the head of department. It is a quiet model of Bunting's style, a curious mixture of intense honesty, self-parody, modesty and occasional mocking self-regard:

A telegram from Mike Doyle which has been relayed to me here [Madison] and reached me yesterday says that there may be a position vacant at Victoria University next year and that I should write to you about it. I need a post.

I shall be at the above printed address [Binghampton] after about January 20 till the end of May, when I must return to England to undergo an honorary degree from the University of Newcastle. My address there is Shadingfield, Wylam, Northumberland.

I do not know what I can say about myself. I think my work is now fairly well known: and I have taught at Buffalo, Santa Barbara, Newcastle, Durham, and British Columbia without any manifest disaster, though I daresay my amateur methods are not in accordance with academic precedent …

… I am fairly honest and often sober, vigorous for my age.

This application assumes that its recipient has a developed sense of irony. Claiming that he has taught without manifest disaster, is often sober and that he is looking forward to 'undergoing' a degree, even an honorary one, as though it were a haemorrhoid operation is a high-wire strategy for securing an academic position that he clearly needed. He finished his letter to Doyle with a personal note that may have had some bearing on events: 'Thankyou very much for taking so much trouble. Here snow and lumbago limit me, and will, no doubt, at Binghampton too. If I survive such horrors, it seems I may see you again next year. Excellent.'[185]

Bunting arrived in Victoria in September 1971 and rented a cottage on the southern shore, with a view of the Olympic Mountains across the US border, getting around in an old car that he bought. It seems as though someone was gunning for him from the outset. Brent Mackay recalls that the 'academic advisor from the creative writing department informed me that that section of creative writing was Bunting's, "an old, old, probably too old guy from England".'[186]

On 14 October 1971 he gave a reading at the university. According to Quartermain, 'Robin Skelton introduced Mike Doyle who introduced BB. The reading was packed (people sitting in the aisles, standing at the back, in a room whose official capacity was about 200). That day, or the one before, BB was interviewed in two local papers.'[187] Doyle had set up the interviews with the *Victoria Daily Times* and *Daily Colonist* and at some point in the course of each of them Bunting told the reporters that 'the only thing worse than a creative writing student is a creative writing professor'.[188] Perhaps unsurprisingly Skelton accepted this as the personal insult that was probably intended.

On 16 October 1971 Bunting wrote about the interviews to Quartermain:

I'm writing because the reading had a curious sequel. After you'd gone I called at the University for mail; and amongst it was a letter from Skelton, the most astonishing I have ever received (not excepting the book-long essays in abuse of Hamilton Finlay). He took exception to things the newspaper reporter said I said: to the effect (near enough, as reporters go) that classes didn't help to make poets, and that academicism is not being good for north American poetry. He does not understand how I 'find it possible to accept a salary for teaching students the writing of poetry' (which, of course, I never pretend to teach). This is 'the most despicable cynicism', leads to the 'demoralization' of my students, undermines my colleagues authority, prevents students registering for writing classes, and so on. I owe an apology to my colleagues, particularly the 'poet-professors'. He does not understand how I can face my students, or the faculty, without shame. I ought not to be teaching a subject where honesty is a necessary qualification.

This bundle of stupid pomposities was addressed, not to me only (when I could have despised it completely) but to five others in the department. It is obviously intended to make my position here impossible. If there were any doubt about that, he demands that I shall write to the newspaper and contradict myself under penalty of some imperfectly expressed threat.

Two of the other addressees ... came round to see me at once: not, however, to disown Skelton but to beg me to forgive him, because, poor fellow, he is under such provocation. (From me? Who have spoken to him perhaps three times in all, to pass the time of day!) I do not think Skelton knew they were coming, and they did not even pretend that he could be brought to apologise.

Now, of course, it will spread. Five people do not remain discreet. I do not know how far the wording of Skelton's letter will bear the interpretation of libel, though the intention is obviously libellous. However, I pretended to have no doubts about it and told his pals to tell Skelton that if the letter were not retracted instantly and completely I would take it to a lawyer, and had no doubt of what the ultimate result would be. I know they were convinced I was determined, and I hope they may affect him.

If not, I certainly will have to see a lawyer and whether there is a court case, with all that bother, or whether he advises me that it's too uncertain to go to law on, it is obvious that the peace and quiet I'd expected here, as some mitigation of the exile, is gone, and forever, in Victoria. Somebody or other in England told me that Skelton would try to get me out (can't abide a better poet), but I never imagined such a gratuitous assault. Russell implied that it is, in some obscure fashion, a part of the war Skelton and Doyle wage endlessly, and even that it was a result of the misunderstanding about who was to introduce me at the reading, which I would have put down to sheer inefficiency, which this place abounds in.

Anyway, here's pore ole granpa up to his neck in shit. And even the best in prospect will leave me regarding about half my colleagues with contempt, not a nice feeling.

I dunno why I bother you with it: but I have no other friend nearer than London. I'd quit here on the spot, but for the money. I need that.

May no such nastiness engulf you![189]

Two weeks later he started to escalate the circulation of Skelton's letter: 'I have stumbled into what must be the most unpleasant society I have ever had to frequent,' he told Gael Turnbull. 'Skelton (with whom I have only spoken once, on introduction) saw fit to address a letter to eight or nine people in which he called me a cheat and several other kinds of thief, who ought to be ashamed to meet his classes. The object, I'm told, is to discredit the man who got me invited here.'[190]

Bunting refused to teach again until Skelton withdrew what Bunting saw as his libel, proposing a deadline in early December. Skelton offered some form of apology on that very day, which happened to be the last day of term. The apology seems to have broken some kind of departmental dam: 'Skelton signed a letter of retraction and apology – approximately one hour before the writ was to be issued,' he told Turnbull. 'The sequel is almost past my own belief: several people who hadn't spoken to me for three months rang up and asked me to meals. I had to leave the phone off the hook so as to economise the number of lies I had to tell to avoid their unwelcome attentions. Can you imagine such worms?'[191]

He told Jonathan Williams in November 1971 that: 'this university is full of the most repugnant people you can imagine. Those who are not blackguards are bores ... None of them seem to mean any good and my situation is very precarious ... I've had to bring a libel action against Skelton, an outrageous attack, without provocation, calling me all sorts of cheat ... there's a smell of blackmail pervading the campus like a whole tribe of skunks, and public scandals in every department.' [192] He summed up his relationship with

Victoria in a single sentence in a letter to Dorothy Pound on 1 December 1971: 'This is a foul place I don't want to mention.'[193]

Bunting taught only two courses in the second term, one of which he took over from Doyle. (One student characterised Bunting's courses as 'Pound and Zukofsky' and 'Zukofsky and Pound'.[194]) He might have been unhappy (it seems that he was ostracised by virtually the entire faculty) but he left his mark on at least one young poet. August Kleinzahler was at the University of Victoria in 1971, having just discovered *Briggflatts*:

> When I got to Victoria, I had one of the real shockers of my life, and I used to not tell people about it because they wouldn't believe it. It was a startling coincidence. Six months earlier I was living with my brother in Greenwich Village, and I went to the Eighth Street Bookshop where I discovered the Fulcrum edition of Basil Bunting's Briggflatts. I went hog wild over that. As soon as I got to Victoria, I went to see whether I could get into the contemporary poetry course. I was told that the professor couldn't see me right away, so I went to the library, where I looked up Loquitur — Bunting's poems other than Briggflatts — and I sucked it up like a beer on a warm day. After that, I went racing back to register for the course, and the person there said, It'll be taught by an elderly British poet you won't have heard of. His name is Basil Bunting. And I said, You're not going to believe this. Oh, he said, 'you've heard of him?[195]

Kleinzahler got into Bunting's class and recalled him as a controversial teacher:

> I took two classes with him. One was called Problems in Contemporary Poetry, which ... well, there weren't any problems at all. He began with some poems by Hardy and Hopkins, The Wreck of the Deutschland, and went up to Yeats and Pound, then David Jones, Williams, the poets who were important to Bunting, Hugh MacDiarmid, Lorine Niedecker, and H.D. All he did was smoke unfiltered Player's and read to us – the entirety of the Cantos, Jones's Anathemata, including the introduction – and when he got tired, or out of breath, he'd say, 'Do you have anything to say?' Someone would start talking gibberish, and he'd start reading again. There was a revolt: he's not interested in what we have to say! I remember telling one of the girls, 'Why should he be interested in what you have to say? He's the world's greatest living poet.' 'Well', she wanted to know, 'why aren't we reading E. E. Cummings or Richard Brautigan? Why doesn't he care what we want?' You could see the seeds of what poetry in creative writing programs was to become thirty

years down the road. A lot of people were very unhappy and the class got rather small, and he just read to us, beautifully. There were only three of us in his creative writing class by the end. Everyone was very upset with him, the department was upset, and we began to meet in his bungalow. There he'd read to us, give us beer – Charrington Toby – and play music. He liked the seventeenth-century English musicians, Dowland and Purcell, and Bach's Goldberg Variations. He'd tell us stories. He was very much disapproved of.[196]

Kleinzahler also enjoyed the mentoring style that Tom Pickard had learned to endure a few years earlier:

I recall two poems I gave to Mr. Bunting, one close to the beginning of our year together, and one toward the end. The first poem was an ornate jam of tropes and queer rhythms which had taken me weeks to confect. Mr. Bunting looked at it for a long time, then put his face in his hands for a considerable length of time. Perhaps he was dozing. But no; he finally took his hands away from his face, looked again at the poem and then at me.

'Mr. Kleinzahler, I am suddenly very tired and dizzy; I'm not certain if I've taken ill or if it's your poem.'

The final poem I gave to Mr. Bunting ... was much shorter, plainer, had come rather swiftly, and I was concerned that it was too thin. The old man considered the poem for a long time and then looked up.

'Mr. Kleinzahler, the difference is so slight as to be indistinguishable, but there may be some very minor improvements here. Throw it out and try again.'[197]

In fact he was mildly impressed. He wrote to Tom Pickard in June 1976 that Kleinzahler seems 'to have some glimmer of how to set about it ... economical and fairly objective'.[198]

Brent Mackay, having overcome the 'dubious bit of p.r.' that announced Bunting's arrival, also remembered Bunting's classes as rigorous and inspiring. Bunting clearly expected a lot from his students, and those who remained loyal to his class seem to have delivered it: 'The tapestry unfolded firsthand to an eager handful.'[199]

It was a lonely time for Bunting. In February 1972 he complained to Mottram that: 'you must know something about the kind of muck I am compelled to read and comment on, not too harshly, in this job. The staffs of this and other universities are much worse than the students, and their pet outside poets hardly better.'[200] He was longing for home and looking forward to spending some time with Mottram in the North East: 'It'd be fine to run you round the moors and fells, and through the forest to Liddesdale (Hermitage about the grimmest castle in the island) or over the enchanting run to Briggflatts – 100 miles with never a factory or a town above 3000 population in sight, unlike anybody's idea of England. And if we see any bloody Jutes or Saxons we can chuck dirt at them. Or Bewcastle. Or even just Hexham and Bywell, next door to us, splendid places.'[201]

Doyle remained close to Bunting during his remaining weeks at Victoria: 'The distance between my house and Bunting's cottage was about twelve miles, but every now and again I brought him to my house for a Sunday dinner or some such and he formed an attachment to my youngest child, my daughter then a two-year-old … Other than that I would visit him at his cottage and drink Bols gin … with him. There were always just the two of us.'[202] Even with Doyle's occasional visits he was very lonely: 'I sit here, looking at the sea,' he wrote to Roudaba,

> and sometimes the mountains across the sea, but I have no visitors. Often the only voices I hear for two or three weeks together are the shopkeepers or students in class. It has been a vile four months … If anything could drive me mad this place would have done it by now. A harmless, quiet old man, knowing not a soul in the place; but libelled and shunned because a sinister sort of fool imagines that by discrediting me he can discredit the rival who got the job for me … They snake around, the whole faculty, looking for chances to bite one another. I haven't found a trace of learning or even of commonsense among the lot of them … One woman came up to me in the faculty club and screamed a lot of abuse about conspiracies at me. I'm not sure whether she thought I was a conspirator or was warning me against others.[203]

Mike Doyle's is not the only surviving account of Bunting's miserable winter in Victoria. Kleinzahler's review of Keith Alldritt's biography of Bunting in 1999 in the *London Review of Books* sparked a lively correspondence. Another former student, the Canadian writer Marilyn Bowering, claimed that it was Skelton who, knowing that Bunting was short of money, had invited Bunting to apply to Victoria:

> The story went that the committee (all non-writers) reviewing applications had turfed out Bunting's at once on the grounds that they had never heard of him. It may have been Bunting himself who later told the story that he had been turned down, similarly, for a Guggenheim many years before when the committee refused to recognise the validity of references from Yeats, Eliot and

Pound. In any case, once that embarrassment was out of the way, Bunting
arrived to lead what was by all accounts an inspired class, although he was
quoted in the local press, to Robin's great chagrin, as saying that creative
writing could not be taught.

Bunting was always courteous, if not courtly, and often wore a blue tweed
jacket that brought out the blaze of his eyes. I am surprised that Kleinzahler
didn't comment on his eyebrows, unlike any I have seen before or since. It
wasn't just their size – each the wing of a small bird – but that they were
groomed and waxed, predatory and, well, sexy. They gave me shivers: odd, I
thought then, when he was such an old man, although it doesn't seem so odd
now.[204]

While Marilyn Bowering's recollection of Skelton's role (and the date of
Bunting's visit) may be faulty her remarks about the poet's eyebrows rather
undermine Denis Goacher's 'sexual crisis' theory. A chivalrous Kleinzahler
replied in the issue of 29 April:

> Marilyn Bowering was apparently so smitten by Basil Bunting's eyebrows that
> she has forgotten what year he was at the University of Victoria. It was 1971–72.
> Rod Stewart's 'Maggie May' was on the jukebox and my distinguished fellow
> alum was, if I recall, in charge of the mimeograph machine at the English
> Department, which always made visits there worth looking forward to.

> Bunting that year got himself into a nasty scrape with Robin Skelton, one that
> eventually involved lawyers; but of course you can't teach someone to write
> poetry, just as you can't teach someone to be kind or a wizard with languages.
> Bunting's method of teaching was simply to read good poetry aloud and,
> when possible, to have us listen to music. In this he favoured Dowland,
> Byrd and Purcell. I remember him playing a recording of Bach's *Goldberg
> Variations* as well, the first time I'd heard it. I believe he thought we might
> absorb some of the possibilities for rhythm in poetry by keeping our mouths
> shut and listening. Can you imagine trying to get away with teaching a writing
> course in this manner now?[205]

The last word was left to the Scottish poet and translator Alexander
Hutchinson who had been part of the attempt to mediate between Bunting
and Skelton:

> Marilyn Bowering and August Kleinzahler, in conjuring up Basil Bunting's
> eyebrows, and memories of a dispute during his visit to Victoria in the early

Seventies provide details which could still be improved on. I'm pretty sure wax didn't come into the picture, for instance – though it could have stiffened Bunting's beard and moustaches in the very early days. There were at least two factions involved in inviting the poet to the University of Victoria – Robin Skelton being party to one of these – and there were tensions throughout the visit. Once there, Bunting did, as Bowering relates, say to a local paper that poetry couldn't really be taught – inflaming Skelton, who had fought to get creative writing on the university curriculum. He fired off a reproachful and intemperate letter to Bunting, and made the mistake of putting copies in various faculty pigeon-holes. Bunting, discovering this, threatened suit. When my colleague Lawrence Russell was sent as an intermediary, I went along as someone friendly to both parties. Basil met us at the door of the house provided for him on the Victoria waterfront and said: 'This is a bad business!' He then said something along the lines of 'Skelton retracts, or I blow him out of the water.' Lawrence and I said nothing to this, though it was clear the message would be relayed. We moved inside to be regaled with drams and stories. Skelton in due course had a change of heart, and any lawyers on the scene would have twitched their tails in disappointment.[206]

A few weeks into the winter term of 1972 Bunting succumbed to lumbago. If he hadn't already referred to it in his letter from Binghampton one might assume that it was psychosomatic. He claimed to be unable to drive and therefore unable to get to the university, which was about six miles away. He stayed at home, Doyle apparently his only regular visitor, until he decided to return prematurely to the UK, on the way pocketing a full year's professorial salary for about one third of a year's teaching.[207]

A GABERLUNZIE MAN

Despite increasing celebrity Bunting was beginning to feel under intense financial pressure, real or imagined. He did have assets. As Jonathan Williams said a few years later: 'There's still a copy of Mina Loy's *Lunar Baedecker* [*sic*], 1923, on the shelf, which he would never consider selling for the thousand dollars it's worth in 1983.'[208]

By August 1971 he had bought 150 shares in ICI and a few debentures, and was beginning to feel like a man of property for the first time since 1919 when he sold some Armstrong shares to pay his fare to Russia. It added about ten shillings a week to the family's income.[209]

This brief glimpse of prosperity apart, however, his complaints about poverty became relentless. Liquidity was a problem and his supporters and friends rallied to secure him an Arts Council grant. In a superb example of Bunting churlishness he made a lot of trouble for himself and others. He wanted no charity from 'desk and pen vermin'.[210]

Arts Council Confidential Council Paper number 446 reported that:

> At their last meeting on 24th June [1970], the Council discussed the letter from Mr. Basil Bunting, the poet, that The Times had printed the same day and the Secretary-General's reply which was subsequently published ... As a consequence of the Council's withdrawal of the requirement that Mr. Bunting's next volume should contain the acknowledgment 'The author of this book received financial assistance from the Arts Council in 1970–71', Mr. Bunting then accepted the grant. In the light of this exchange of correspondence, which resulted in considerable publicity for the offer of £750 to Mr. Bunting, the Council will wish to decide upon the type of acknowledgment (if any) to be required of recipients of grants of this nature in the future.[211]

The writer of this paper, Mr K. H. Jeffery, goes on to condemn, politely, Bunting's ingratitude and points out that other recipients of grants had not reacted as Bunting had, drawing particular attention to a letter received by The Times, but not published, by Mr R. Breckman, dated 26 June 1970. Bunting's letter to The Times appeared on 24 June. It is not exactly a model of fawning gratitude:

> The Arts Council of Great Britain has made me an offer of £750, which I have not solicited, on condition that my next published book should contain the sentence: 'The author of this book received financial assistance from the Arts Council of Great Britain in 1970–71.'
>
> I do not know whether the Council requires a similar sentence to be carved on the pedestals of statues, painted on the frames of pictures or sung before the opening bars of symphonies; but I do know that nobody in this generation who is not an artist of some sort is expected to wear the badge of a gaberlunzie man in public. Even those who administer what used to be called the Poor Law are careful not to demand such a humiliation.

Bunting quickly gets into his stride with a series of accusations that seem designed specifically to get under the skin of London mandarins:

The condition is arrogant, for I am sure neither Parliament, which votes most of the funds, nor any other subscriber has authorised it. It is impudent, since it claims for a set of clerks and bookkeepers a share of the credit for work made possible only by a life-time of concentrated effort such as they, perhaps, cannot imagine. It is dangerous because men who find they can impose one condition are quick to impose others. If the Arts Council can enforce such a public obeisance I do not think it will be long before it undertakes to censor literature and art.

It is also needless, since the Arts Council can claim all the credit it is entitled to by publishing and publicizing its accounts; but I do not think it will call any more attention to its accounts than it must, for fear Parliament and the public should notice the disproportion between the salaries it pays to administrators with neither artistic competence nor conspicuously good taste and the income it considers appropriate to the men and women who are engaged in making art.

In sum, it seems to me that to accept the condition attached to this grant would be to betray artists into the hands of their parasites. I prefer anxiety, labour, exile and perhaps, later, starvation to such a slavish means of survival.[212]

He was hard to help. In this particular case he clearly used the opportunity to attack the arts establishment, not to justify his own highly principled position. We know this because the Secretary-General of the Arts Council, Hugh Willatt, wrote to *The Times* to explain that he had telephoned Bunting as soon as he received his letter to tell him precisely that they would *not* require their usual acknowledgement. He fairly hoped that Bunting 'will feel that his attribution of motives is unjust, and that he may be now willing to accept a grant for which, as a poet, he was so strongly supported'.[213]

Those supporters must have been deeply frustrated by Bunting's very public intransigence, by his 'which I have not solicited' and by his continuous complaints about lack of money. There's no doubt that the Arts Council won the public relations battle on this occasion although in later confrontations with the Arts Council the establishment lost the PR battle badly. Bunting's letter drew hostile (and well-reasoned) responses from other beneficiaries of Arts Council largesse, J. C. Hall, Phoebe Hesketh and the unpublished letter from Breckman. Over fifty years later we could be once again back in Charles Evans' office at Leighton Park School looking at a bewildering series of unfounded attacks presented with barely concealed hysteria and paranoia. He certainly put the Arts Council on the alert as far as the issue of acknowledgement of grants was concerned and the minutes indicate that a lot of hard work went into generating suitable formulae for various forms of artistic output.

The Arts Council file contains clippings from the Newcastle *Evening Chronicle* which, predictably enough, supported its own with headlines like 'Basil Bunting faces the dole' and 'Bunting takes on the Arts Council and wins'. Even the *Yorkshire Post* got in on the act. One of the clippings has a note in the hand of one of the 'parasites'. 'I see he doesn't mention his Arts Council grant!' In another article in the *Evening Chronicle* Peter Anthony claimed that Bunting had won a famous David and Goliath victory having 'emerged with a significant victory for himself and other writers'. Bunting apparently told Anthony that the Council had 'given in completely. "They have withdrawn this demand both from me and all other artists in the future."' In the margin of the copy in the Arts Council archive the parasite muses, 'Have we indeed?'

As Roy Fisher observed:

> He had a variable attitude to his paymasters and benefactors, quite often prickly, particularly when the assistance came from official quarters or from those who would sentimentalize him, for he was a very tough man. He kept ready to hand a shifting *persona*, made up from a cast of archaic roles – the medieval mendicant poet, the cultured Imperial slave, the dispossessed exile – and employed it from time to time in whatever way suited him ... Along with the affable, anecdotal man one met there was something that remains to me inscrutable. On the one hand there was the high and genuine sense of artistic standard, respect and ethics. But there was also the inaccessible sense of a demon of delinquency and improvidence – the absences, the goings-to-ground, the impulsive initiatives, the periods of yielding to circumstance in a curiously – I'm tempted to say suspiciously – passive manner. A sort of anti-matter countering the will to achieve good things, and in some way ministering to it.[214]

Nevertheless, and perhaps not surprisingly, towards the end of 1971 Bunting's financial problems were deepening and he complained to Mottram: 'I have had a lot of troubles ... which have kept me away from the typewriter except to deal with tax collectors and equally unwelcome business.'[215]

In July 1973 Bunting wrote to Mike Doyle in Victoria: 'The University of Newcastle takes up very little of my time, but contributes, accordingly, very little to my income, so that I expect to be finally broke, for ever and ever, in about four months. No means of livelihood offers and at my age even American State Universities in their prosperous days (now past) would hesitate to take me on.'[216] This could have been lifted verbatim from one of his letters to Margaret de Silver in the 1950s.

After the predicted four months of financial survival he sounded defeated in a letter to Mottram: 'By this time you must have forgotten that you ever knew anybody of the above name. However, local irritations, progressive bankruptcy, and chores, chores, chores, haven't yet completely banished you from my mind ... That's all the news, except the cheerless item that I set out tomorrow to sell my tiny investments, which may just carry us through the winter. If you know any university anxious to pay a good salary to an antediluvian zombie for doing nothing in particular, let me hear of it.'[217] It seems that Mottram responded positively as by January 1974 Bunting was rising to the bait: 'Sure, if you can raise the wind for me in USA, I'm not above earning something. In fact, I've just told a correspondent that I can see the workhouse door agape for me, even if they've changed the place's name.'[218] He was aware enough of the financial problems of his friends, particularly those of Tom and Connie Pickard,[219] but his grumbling about his own plight was relentless. In June 1974 he told Mottram, 'the last items of my income have ended, except the old age pension and the civil list pension. The Lord Chamberlain has ordered me and Sima to show ourselves (morning dress or lounge suit) at Buckingham Palace for the garden party on July 23, but thinking of the train fare, taxi fare and clothes – I suppose Sima would have to have a new frock – I fancy we'll find ourselves unfortunately too ill to attend. What a pity if her majesty should miss the chance of gazing on me! In my 1947 suit.'[220] As it turned out it seems that Sima was the star of the show. Bunting wrote to Jonathan Williams in August that 'Sima, looking very elegant for the first time in her life, had a conversation with the queen, which made her next neighbour in the crowd faint with envy. She tackled the Chinese embassy contingent too. Enough to exalt her at Wylam Tennis Club for a long time to come.'[221]

A DROP OF MOLTEN SILVER

Little of Bunting's verse written after 1965 survives although he was busy repaying a fair number of poetic debts. In 1971 Bunting edited the *Selected Poems* of his second boss, Ford Madox Ford, and in 1976 those of Joseph Skipsey, the miner poet who had held him on his knee ('one small lifelong commitment discharged at last' as he told Jonathan Williams).[222] He prefaced his edition, unusually, with a brief biography. Needless to say it starts from his familiar anti-biographical position: 'A man's circumstances seldom matter to those who enjoy what he makes. We buy our shirts without asking who the seamstress was, and should read our poems without paying too much attention to the names they are printed over. Things once made stand free of their makers, the more anonymous the better. However, there are exceptions.'[223]

Bunting made this exception out of a sense of regional solidarity. His interest in Skipsey was two fold: 'First of all he was a very local man who has been neglected. He was not a great man but he was one who ought not to be completely neglected, and secondly, Skipsey lived just long enough to come as a visitor to my father's house and hold the baby on his knee, which was me, so I suppose the whole poetic afflatus must have been passed on to me and there's a pious duty towards Skipsey.'[224]

Skipsey really was a local poet, an autodidact who went to the Percy Main pit near North Shields at the age of seven and, apart from a brief and unhappy period when he was, improbably, custodian of Shakespeare's Birthplace in Stratford-upon-Avon, barely emerged from coal mines for the rest of his life.

A report in the *Newcastle Journal* of 1975 announced a reading of Skipsey's poems by Bunting, and once again regional pride seems to cast a glow on 'one of the North East's remarkable literacy [*sic*] sons'. The report announces with some justifiable pride that 'There's never been a reading of Skipsey's work, but tomorrow, in the Northern Arts Gallery, New Bridge Street, Newcastle, another famous Geordie Bard, Basil Bunting, makes a rare appearance to read Skipsey's poems. For Basil, there's more than a literary interest. As a young child Skipsey would visit the Bunting household and bounce the youngster on his knee.' Bunting wouldn't have liked the 'Geordie' bit. He spoke Northumbrian, the voice of the region before 'Irish navvy immigrants had made "geordie" of it'.[225] 'Geordie is a bastard language,' he told Tom Pickard. 'It's a mixture mainly of south Northumbrian with the Irish that was brought in by the labourers who came first to dig canals, then to build railways, and finally settled down largely in the coal mines ... Where I was born, Scotswood wasn't Geordie. Geordie stopped at Newcastle, and we were in those days separated from Newcastle by two miles of fields.'[226]

Sister Victoria Forde was completing her PhD thesis on Bunting in 1972 and he wrote to her frequently. On his return voyage to the UK from Canada in May he had time to write as the quantity of books he was bringing back with him had forced him to return by boat through the Panama Canal. Back in England Bunting wrote to Forde about an epiphanic moment that had occurred on this voyage:

> I'd had a number of themes in my head for at least three years, some longer, but could do nothing with them because they didn't seem to join together or oppose each other in any way that suggested their proper shape. Then one night I saw the new moon, the very first new moon, emerging from the old moon as Helen, Selanna, the new moon, must have emerged from Leda's egg; and the next night I watched Jupiter occulted by the then invisible old moon reappear as a drop of molten silver sliding down the flank of the new moon. And as I turned away from this marvellous sight I caught a glimpse of a very young girl who seemed obviously the new moon in flesh, slim, graceful, blond; and instantly many old themes began to assemble themselves as though this were the keystone enabling them to form an arch, themes of renewal, mainly, closely bound, though I had never perceived it. And this was wonderfully reinforced when I spoke to the girl and found her name was Linnaea and she a descendant of Linnaeus who named all the flowers, as though she were Persephone as well as Selanna. There was even the germ of an antitheme ready to fit in, though that needs more perception before I can use it. I cannot say more yet: but it seems to me that I shall soon be able to begin work on a sonata, or what is more likely to prove a sonata than not, with the transformations of the first theme all worked out though those of the second may delay me.[227]

He enclosed thirty lines of a sonata that, had it been completed, would perhaps have been even more powerful than *Briggflatts*, such was its promise:

> Such syllables flicker out of grass:
> 'What beckons goes'; and no glide lasts
> nor wings are ever in even beat long.
> A male season with paeonies, birds bright under thorn.
> Light pelts hard now my sun's low,
> it carves my stone as hail mud
> till day's net drapes the haugh,
> glaze crackled by flung drops.
> What use? Elegant hope, fever of tune,
> new now, next, in the fall, to be dust.
>
> Wind shakes a blotch of sun,
> flatter and tattle willow and oak alike
> sly as a trout's shadow on gravel.
> Light stots from stone, sets ridge and kerf quick

as shot skims rust from steel. Men of the north
'subject to being beheaded and cannot avoid it
of a race that is naturally given that way'.
'Uber sophiae sugens' in hourless dark,
their midnight shimmers like noon.
They clasp that axle fast.

Those who lie with Loki's daughter,
jawbones laid to her stiff cheek,
hear rocks stir above the goaf;
but a land swaddled in light? Listen, make out
lightfall singing on a wall mottled grey
and the wall growls, tossing light,
prow in tide, boulder in a foss.
A man shrivels in many days, eyes thirst for night
to scour and shammy the sky
thick with dust and breath.[228]

The image of light that 'stots from stone' is precise. Bunting almost certainly has the Scots word for 'bounce' in mind but not far beneath the surface is the stotting gait of gazelles, which flash their brilliant white rumps as they flee.

By October, however, he was losing heart: 'A whole host of interruptions, trivial at first, but now becoming really serious, have prevented me doing real work for months; and it looks as though I will have to try to find a job again, if anybody will employ me at my age, thus making poetry not far from impossible for a long time to come; and I haven't got a long time to come (though I'm healthy for my age).'[229] Little of his work from the 1970s survives.

THE BATTLE OF EARLS COURT

In 1972 Bunting became President of the Poetry Society, founded in 1909 and by 1969 boasting '1,500 members, many Affiliated Societies and Centres, Examinations for adults and in the schools in Spoken Poetry and Drama, and a journal of world authority, *The Poetry Review* [sic]'.[230] *Poetry Review* had a distinguished record, having 'sponsored the emerging Ezra Pound and also T. S. Eliot, Walter de la Mare, W. H. Davies and Rupert Brooke' from the outset. In the same pamphlet in 1969 Poetry Society Council member G.

B. H. Wightman declared that the mission of the society was to 'bridge the gap between the traditional and the "avant garde": to remind people of the value of the poetry of the past (including that of the recent past which tends to be obscured in the dust of fashion) and to introduce the work of new poets beginning to raise the dust'. And then in a passage of astonishing prescience and lyricism Wightman turns his eye to the future and the society's role in it:

> It will be a frighteningly overpopulated world dominated by a technological culture in which analytic thinking is supreme. Moreover, not only the media of information but also the media of education will be increasingly centralised and vested in fewer hands. The Early Bird satellite is a beginning of the universal direct broadcast system we can expect in the future. There will therefore be a growing need to know the minds of men who consider the effects of the age upon the individual, who recall the values we require to employ our technical resources sensibly, who speak with a private voice, who state their impressions in an original way and who thereby communicate to the human pulse rather than to the system analyst's computer. Such men we term poets.[231]

In spite of this apparent commitment to eclecticism Wightman was to pay an important part in the events which tore the Poetry Society apart in the 1970s.

Bunting privately despaired of *Poetry Review*, writing to Mottram in June 1971 that he had never heard of the people who ran it having done anything sensible before they appointed Mottram as editor, but lamenting the fact that he couldn't contribute any new work: 'you catch me unprovided. I've not a line unpublished except one tiny poem which I cant get right. It's been hanging around for a year and a half because of one word in the last line, and I dunno whether I can get it fixed in time for you.'[232]

By the beginning of 1972, however, he was becoming very aware of the people who ran the Poetry Society because he had been invited to become its President. His acceptance is characteristically larded with cavils:

> I was much astonished by your letter of January 20th, which reached me two days ago, saying that the Council of the Poetry Society wanted me to be president. I feel the honour; yet I must also consider that I am an old man, not fit for many duties, and not able, perhaps, to attend many of your meetings, and that I am not a member of your society and know very little about its activities.

However, I think I remember that you are partly concerned with encouraging people to read poetry aloud, which is something I thoroughly approve of; so, if you can put up with the disabilities I have mentioned, I am content to accept the society's offer.[233]

Classic Bunting: I'm too old, I can't do anything, I won't attend your meetings, I'm not a member and I don't know anything about you, but, if you want …

Mottram's first edition of *Poetry Review* was the Autumn 1971 issue, which introduced a radical cover redesign. Bunting was impressed by Mottram's improvements. He singled out Tom Pickard's contribution for particular praise and, while recognising that any editor of a poetry magazine needed 'secondary stuff to fill it out' he inveighed against contributing poets he considered sub-standard: 'All the same, say it aloud, listen to the wild shamble of Gary Snyder, the dislocated echo of [Robert] Nichols, the record player running down of Miss [Elaine] Feinstein: and then turn to our Tom, hard and sharp (though he still stumbles here and there). Jonathan [Williams], of course, is himself, out of their class, not too familiar, and yet, essentially small stuff. Tom's voice seems to me like that of a great poet – if they'll let him get on with it long enough and not starve him into compromises.'[234] He received an immediate and doubtless huffy riposte from Mottram and a few days later sent a hurried corrective: 'Don't get the idea that I am running down your other poets: it's only by contrast with Tom Pickard that they look so woolly. There aren't many of us who could come out of that confrontation at all well.'[235]

Looking at Mottram's second edition of *Poetry Review* one can sympathise with Bunting's frustration. The concrete and sound poetry that was so prevalent at the time seems as fatuous now as it did to many then, but Mottram's task was to 'bridge the gap between the traditional and the avant garde', as Wightman had said, and he needed to include progressive, experimental verse even if the quality was questionable; and in any event Mottram was undoubtedly aligned with the radical wing of contemporary British poetry. Bunting wasn't happy with the balance of Mottram's selection and told him about a Poetry Society member who had written to him 'in violent expostulation' against the concrete and sound poetry in the most recent issue, demanding that Bunting, as President, denounce it publicly as 'the nonsense which I do, in fact, think it is'. He refused to comply however because: 'I think such a society can only function by complete inclusiveness

– everyone who says he's a poet is, so far as such a society is concerned; concretists to one side, the muttering zombies to the other; and the genuine poets, whoever they may be, must stand their chance amongst the crowd of frauds.'[236]

He continued to praise Mottram's editions, in public and privately. He opened the Poetry Society's Annual General Meeting on 16 June 1973 with an expression of his appreciation of Mottram's work; there were poems in recent editions, he thought, which the Society would be 'proud in the future to have published'.[237] But privately he urged Mottram to pay more attention to work the majority of members would consider 'respectable', to promote inclusiveness while 'keeping a certain technical standard'. He acknowledged that Mottram was under conflicting pressures from different factions but encouraged him to resist any influence that would make the Poetry Society even smaller than it already was.

In fact at the age of seventy-two Bunting found himself caught up in another war, the British Poetry Wars and, particularly, the Battle of Earls Court. The idea of a poetry war is so impeccably ludicrous that, forty years later, it seems astonishing that its combatants didn't laugh themselves into a ceasefire. But in 1970s Britain it was possible to apply the word 'militant' to the most inoffensive occupation and immediately find oneself confronted by the bitterest of enemies. This was a decade when, whatever your interest, if you didn't take an extreme position in it you didn't count, a point wistfully made by Roger Guedalla in a letter to Eric Mottram after the war, from his point of view, had been lost: 'I have taken it all very seriously but have been constantly reduced to being forced to make puerile gestures to prove that I am more radical than somebody else.'[238] This was the year, after all, when the British Royal Navy dispatched warships to Iceland in an argument about fish. In the Poetry Wars it was the very soul of the Poetry Society, and the expression of that soul, *Poetry Review*, that was at stake. This bizarre episode in twentieth-century British cultural history is recorded in Peter Barry's even-handed *Poetry Wars: British poetry of the 1970s and the Battle of Earls Court*. A brief sketch of the war and Bunting's small role in it will suffice here.

The Poetry Society was one of Britain's most conservative cultural institutions and by 1970 a radical counterculture had developed around a small group of poet activists that included Bob Cobbing, Anthony Rudolf, Mottram, and Bunting's publisher, Stuart Montgomery. All, as members of the General Council, were Poetry Society insiders who were determined to challenge the status quo. In Mottram's words the Poetry Society before the revolution was 'then exemplary in being a non-entity. It was dead. It had been dead for centuries. It was establishment dead – as it is now.'[239] In 1971 this small group of radicals seized control of the Poetry Society, installed Bunting as President and Mottram as editor of what became the most exciting, innovative and controversial poetry magazine in Britain, and started six years of rancorous and aggressive internal politics that tore the British poetry establishment apart and severely tested the patience of many genuine poetry lovers.

Mottram, a combative type, took an antagonistic stance towards the Poetry Society as soon as he was appointed as editor of *Poetry Review*.[240] But it was his editorial strategy, rather than his hostility to the poetry establishment, that turned the conservative element of the Poetry Society against him. George Wightman who, as we saw, had proposed a balanced presentation of traditional poetry and the radical poetry of Mottram's British Poetry Revival, quickly turned against the new editor. As early as the General Council meeting in April 1973 Wightman proposed an alternative editor, Gavin Ewart. Although Mottram won the ensuing vote comfortably Wightman was to remain his most vocal opponent throughout the 1970s.

Mottram was confrontational but he had more than enough reason to be so. An embarrassed Chair of the General Council, Laurence Cotterell, wrote to him in November 1975: 'An apology is due and overdue for the offensiveness to which you were subjected when taking the chair at a recent meeting here. This sort of thing on our premises shames us all ... I am told that you soldiered on and rode it all out admirably.'[241] The 'offensiveness' got much worse despite Cotterell's apology.

Other members of the General Council resented the coup, as did the Arts Council, which emerges as one of the real villains of the saga. (Iain Sinclair's comment on Barry's book would have had Bunting cheering: 'a warning to future poets. Never mix with bureaucrats. Destroy your correspondence. And count your fingers after shaking hands with the Arts Council.') In 1973 the Arts Council, in the person of Charles Osborne, was preparing to declare war on the Poetry Society. (Mottram claimed that Osborne had 'declared himself at one point to be the "undertaker" of British poetry.'[242]) When Osborne announced a full internal enquiry into the workings of the Poetry Society headed by Sir John Witt, Vice-Chair of the Arts Council, the radicals refused to co-operate. Witt found that the Poetry Society was underfunded but entirely dysfunctional and that any improvements in the former should be dependent on improvements in the management and organisation of the society and an ending of the factionalism that had split it asunder. The General Council meeting of 13 November 1976 was a disaster for the radicals who themselves split into two factions in yet another suicidal act of tribalism. Three officers in the radical faction resigned, setting the stage for meltdown of the radical cause at the General Council meeting of March 1977 when fourteen radical officers resigned in protest at Arts Council interference and walked out of the society to begin a series of ineffective boycotts against it and publicly flay those who stayed. This effectively ended the revolution. Osborne, who manages to seem obnoxious even in his own account of the meeting that ended the revolution, boasted that:

> One Saturday afternoon, I found myself yet again at a meeting, waiting for it to begin ... They were nearly half an hour late in starting, because they were too busy shouting accusations at one another about the Chairman's desk being removed without permission, or something equally ridiculous. Finally, having had enough of this, I took a deep breath, projected my voice as though I were declaiming at the Theatre Royal, Drury Lane, and managed to make myself heard above the clamour. 'For Christ's sake pull yourselves together and start the bloody meeting,' I yelled. 'I have better things to do than waste my weekends here.'
>
> What the Arts Council's investigating team had failed to achieve in months I accomplished in seconds. One of the poets, Jeff Nuttall, stood up. 'I am not going to bow down to this kind of official censorship,' he exclaimed. 'I resign in protest.' 'So do I,' said another, Bob Cobbing. And one by one, their followers did the same. They marched out of the room, and I asked the Secretary to be certain to record their resignations in the minutes, for fear they should come to what senses they possessed and march back in again. But they didn't return.[243]

Anyone who remembers Britain in the 1970s may have some doubt as to whether any of this actually had much to do with *poetry*. A letter to Mottram from Bunting's bibliographer, Roger Guedalla, written on 20 April 1977 reveals a context that permeated every aspect of British society at the time:

> I am also very depressed at what has happened at the Society ... We have handed the Society back to the most reactionary elements and it seems that all the efforts of the past five or eight years have come to nothing and Osborne and his friends have achieved exactly what they wanted. I did think, and I continue to think that we had a great chance to break their stranglehold but I never thought it would be easily or quickly achieved. I thought it was

a serious and continuing struggle and I never thought we would give in so easily ... I have read a great deal and thought a great deal about the role of the radical artist in a capitalist society struggling in just the ways we have been doing. I have discussed the problems at length, in particular with friends at the I.M.G., the I.S. and the W.R.P. as well as with Tribunite members of the Labour Party and associates of the Militant Faction. I have always seen it as a political struggle, and thus as a question of tactics and organisation.[244]

Not a mention of poetry. The I.M.G. is the International Marxist Group; the I.S. are the International Socialists; the W.R.P. is the Workers' Revolutionary Party. The Poetry Wars and the Battle of Earls Court were never about poetry; it was about who controlled the soul of the Left. No wonder Bunting despaired. He had no time for propaganda, let alone poetry as propaganda. He wrote to Jonathan Williams in December 1979:

> I am infuriated by the unshakeable naivety of people (Tom Pickard is one) who will believe any propaganda which looks as though it came from the left, and would sign their own death warrants if asked in the name of Humanity or the Proletariat. The success of the Persian priests and landlords with their anti-Shah stuff is a case in point. Whatever the Shah is, he is far further to the left than the present regime or its supporters; but who is to persuade students and such?[245]

He had made the same point, more publicly and more personally, earlier in the year at a reading in London:

> Poetry hampers itself when it undertakes advocacy, however indirectly. I would have maintained that even against my much-loved Hugh MacDiarmid, whose advocacy was mostly *against* unreason, *for* thought and tolerance and renewal. But poetry that advocates obscurantism, or on the other hand advocates naïve slogans of liberalism is a nuisance to everybody who can read. What I have tried to do is to make something that can stand by itself and last a little while without having to be propped by metaphysics or ideology or anything from outside itself. Something that might give people pleasure without nagging them to pay their dues to the party or say their prayers, without implying the stifling deference so many people in this country still show to a Cambridge degree or a Kensington accent. It's brought me just what I expected from the first ... nothing.[246]

One might sympathise with those who were hostile to Osborne. It is difficult not to be, even after an interval of forty years. There's no doubt, however, that the Poetry Society in the 1970s was unfit for public subsidy. Some cameos from the period paint an unlovely scene. This is the Cardiff-based poet and performer Peter Finch:

> We're sitting in the White House, the hotel bar next to the Poetry Society in Earls Court Square. Criton Tomazos is standing on the mantle piece ripping bits out of a book and chanting. Bob [Cobbing] has drunk almost half a bottle of whiskey and is still standing, or leaning. Jennifer [Jennifer Pike, Cobbing's wife] arrives in her small car to take us home. The vehicle is full of boxes, papers and bits of equipment. We push Bob into the front seat but there's no room for me in the back. I climb onto the roof rack. We drive. Somehow we get back.[247]

For ordinary poetry lovers who were not part of what the poet Ira Lightman called the 'beer-sipping, anarcho-syndicalist tendency with scattered residual Marxist undertones' an evening at the Poetry Society could be an intimidating experience. One member complained about a reading by David Jaffin that it had been a 'distressing and disgusting experience' for all present, '13, including the poet': 'The smell of beer pervaded everything, the hallway was dirty and the noise from the bar made one think of a back alley public house. After ten minutes of struggling to hear David Jaffin, the door flew open and a long-haired lout screamed "Bomb" – it was dirty paper which fell all over the disillusioned audience. We cleared up the mess, only shortly after to have the same fool plus half a dozen more come shoving into the room shouting "Litter Bomb".'

One staff member's statement to the Witt Panel paints an unforgettable picture: 'She said she did not know Jeff Nuttall [poet, painter, jazz musician, anarchist] very well, but when he had given a reading at the Society she had found broken eggs on the rostrum next morning, a tin of golden syrup underneath the piano, with a doll stuck in the syrup and there was talcum powder everywhere. Mr Nuttall had also run around in his underwear. There were only twelve people at the reading.'

Bunting had a view on all this and was always willing to express it. The *Guardian* reported that he sent 'a fierce little message to the [Poetry Society's extraordinary general] meeting: "If the reformers succeed in their ludicrous aims, the society will be cutting its own throat and bankrupt in six months."'[248] His real, and unlikely, role in the Poetry Wars, however, was as a behind-the-scenes peacemaker, a job for which the previous seventy years had hardly prepared him. By the end of 1972 he was already finding the politics of the Poetry Society distinctly tedious, and his attempt to reconcile two friends was conducted with resigned grumpiness. A distance had grown between Mottram and Stuart Montgomery:

> In London I found that Montgomery had tried to phone you several times, but couldn't get through, no doubt because you were moving house; and you hadn't phoned him, as I asked you to, perhaps for the same reason – he was moving house simultaneously. Then, so I'm told, you rejected his attempt to get in touch with you at the reading, and that, I'm afraid, has huffed him. So there's a pair of you.

> It is bloody silly, since I think, so far as I'm kept in touch at all (not very much I'm afraid) that Montgomery has done more than anybody else to keep you editor against the impatience of a lot of old dumbbells. You resent the financial calculations which he made in answer to specific questions by the committee because the committee decided, against his advice, to cut down the size of the paper. Unfortunately he is badly overworked at present, which prevents him doing much beyond his medical stint and isn't good for his temper either. He thinks mal-distribution is the magazine's trouble, and since it seems I can't get it anywhere, I'm inclined to suppose him right.

You can almost hear Bunting's energy for this kind of mollifying politics draining away in the course of this letter: 'You cant suppose it gives me any pleasure to hobnob with the crowd I've now met three times. It is very difficult not to show my impatience with them. I do it because I want a platform on which whatever good poets turn up (and I'm not the judge of that) can prove themselves by showing brightly amongst the mass of dullness.'[249]

A week later Bunting urged Mottram to recognise that he and Montgomery were essentially on the same side in seeing the main problem of *Poetry Review* as distribution. He went on to explain that if Mottram was himself 'busy and harassed' Montgomery's day job ('enduring the conversation of lunatics, largely incurable') meant that his publishing, literary and family interests needed to be squeezed into the limited time that remained. He clearly sympathised with Montgomery in this disagreement: 'I have watched Stuart trying to get you on the phone fruitlessly. Now I will send him your address and number, but I think the response you gave him at the reading may have put his back up.' It is clear, though, that he considered this trivial stand-off between two friends as symptomatic of a much deeper problem within the British arts establishment:

I am president of the damned outfit (and now of the Northern Arts too) not because I like either the aims or the set-up of either institution, but in the hope that the people who are really concerned will pay a little attention to my advice, and that so I may steer each of the outfits a trifle nearer usefulness. It is not a very hopeful enterprise, but a weary one. And in each case the direction must be inclusiveness – unless both Cobbing and the post- Georgian zombies can be heard, there'd be nothing left shortly but a ring of mutual backscratchers of the usual pattern. [You and Montgomery] both want the Poetry Society to represent Good Poetry. But unless it also represents bad poetry (within very wide limits) its chances of advancing good poetry will diminish.

As well as distribution and finances there was also a row about the cover price of *Poetry Review* in which Bunting felt obliged to play the peacemaker. It is uncomfortable to see such an uncompromising character actively seeking compromise in order to make bureaucratic progress. This was a job he was simply unfitted for, and you can feel the strain in this letter: 'Probably some rise in price is inevitable ... But what is all this about 'elitists'? What a word! The Poetry Society can't give a free service. Even Adrian Henri charges people to hear him read. The review costs a good deal less than a cinema ticket. There's a point in between charging yourself out of the market and charging so little that you can't carry on ... An accountant's opinion is likely to be nearer than the rest of us get, but wont necessarily be right either.'

In no other aspect of his life would Bunting have countenanced such a compromise or been interested in any point between two extremes if he believed in one of them. As a senior officer of a society he was obliged to do exactly that. Later in this letter he comes close to expressing that explicitly in his denunciation of the Arts Council, particularly with its preoccupation with a plan for a Poetry Centre ('whatever the meaning of that notion may be. It is the kind of irrelevance they seek by nature. Anything, so long as it can be of no direct use to the chap who actually writes the poetry.') The Arts Council is managed by 'zombies' so: 'Codding them along towards tolerable decisions must be a ticklish job at best. Nothing to be got by intransigence, beyond a momentary publicity.'[250]

It is unimaginable that Basil Bunting could say 'nothing to be got by intransigence' in any environment other than one that was grinding him down so relentlessly. Poetry Society politicking would have broken his heart if his heart had ever been in it. He wrote to Mike Doyle as early as July 1973:

No, the Poetry Society is no pleasure, but another chore I undertook to help other people rescue it from the fools who have run it for so long: but with very limited results so far. The president has no duties and hardly any privileges, nine tenths of the members are dullards; but I've tried to prevent some of the more sordid wrangles and, vainly, to persuade them to adjust their subscriptions to inflation before bankruptcy puts an end to their society. I am also president of Northern Arts, with even less influence.[251]

Predictably enough, the problems at the Poetry Society rumbled on beyond Bunting's presidency. By the middle of 1974 it had started to act in a way that Mottram approved of. Bunting avoided the AGM on grounds of age and infirmity but the real reason was the issue he thought he had left behind, the society's continuing financial crisis and its executive's continuing refusal to face it: 'Refusing the Arts Council's dictatorship (as they should) makes it more necessary than ever to multiply the subscription by a pretty large factor. They can't count on W H Smith every year. And if they don't pay poets better, they'll end up with only the duds to read to them.' He concluded, somewhat against the grain of his letter, with the hope that a 'more intelligent contingent in council' would address the issue properly.[252]

Bunting continued to support Mottram's editorial position (though he regarded editing as an 'insidious vice') but warned that he shouldn't carry on for too long even though he predicted that a 'booby' would be selected to replace him: 'No man, said Thomas Eliot, can edit a magazine WELL for more than two years. As he demonstrated later.'[253]

THE GREATEST POET OF THE TWENTIETH CENTURY

By now though another challenge was appearing, this time on his own doorstep. In December 1972 Columbia Broadcasting made a film about him: 'I rashly took them to Blanchland for lunch, and they'd never seen anything like that before, so I was kept reading poetry and walking about in icy winds on the fells near the top of Bolt Law for three days ... There was some fun. When I was feeling fed up I warned them that the place swarmed with vipers, and enjoyed watching them step delicately around, examining every tuft of heather before gingerly putting their feet down.'[254]

The ensuing film, rather bizarrely narrated by the actor Patrick Macnee at his most urbane and Steed-like, has no interview with Bunting. Instead it links readings by the poet mixed with moody footage of a bleak Northumbrian landscape. The winds do indeed look as though they were icy, and Bunting looks stoic rather than enthusiastic. The film's writer, Stephan Chodorov, wrote in April 2011 that Bunting was 'affable, cooperative, in no way a primadonna. I was particularly interested in anything he might have to say about Ezra Pound but he didn't offer much. We had a small BBC crew and shot it in a couple of days. Stayed in a local inn, drank various great whiskeys, walked on the heath.'[255] He doesn't mention the vipers.

Bunting had a sharp eye for situation comedy. He wrote to Quartermain in September 1972:

> One day I stopped at the Farmer's Arms in Muker, in Swaledale, for a sandwich. I ordered two, one beef, one cheese. I'd forgotten I was in Yorkshire, where people really eat, and the sandwiches were enormous by English standards (you wouldn't gasp at them in North America). The girl brought them in and set them down and went off to the kitchen again. Within a minute a man came in, went to the bar and ordered two sandwiches, one beef, one cheese. The barman hollered out to the kitchen: "Another beef and another cheese, quick", and there came back the most astonished voice I have ever heard saying: "What! Has he eaten them *already!*"[256]

But the mood was soon to become heavier. On 1 November 1972 Bunting's old friend Ezra Pound died in Italy at the age of eighty-six and the *Sunday Times* published an obituary by Bunting. As he had in the 1930s he put Pound ahead of every other twentieth-century literary figure: 'There are not many people left, perhaps, who remember the rice-pudding poetry on sale before Ezra Pound restored crispness and density to English verse ... When Mauberley and Homage to Propertius and the earliest cantos were published, before The Waste Land and before Ulysses, Pound had set a standard capable of lasting.'

He paid tribute to his kindness. Pound had little enough money himself but he was unusually generous with what he did have. He remembered his conversation: 'Unexpected ideas, surprising phrases, leapt out continually. I have listened to other good talkers, but to none whose wit was so sudden, so unfailing and, when you recalled it, so illuminating. He did not talk to himself aloud in company, he conversed, he kept his mind on what the other man said, answering and inciting.'[257]

This doesn't square with Humphrey Carpenter's analysis of the older poet's conversational skills. Carpenter's judgement is that Pound was a 'bad conversationalist':

'If there IZ anything qui ne m'interesse pas,' he wrote in 1935, 'c'est de la CONversation. especially yawpin' 'bout licherchoor.' He could be a consummate verbal performer if he had the chance to construct his aphorisms in advance, or was allowed to pursue paths he knew well already, but throughout his life he was unable to respond quick-wittedly to unexpected verbal challenges ... When in the company of others, he had to have free rein to say everything he wanted, in his own time, or he could contribute next to nothing to the proceedings.[258]

I think we have to give this one to Bunting. He had spent a huge amount of time in Pound's company and was well placed to judge his conversational skills. He didn't hesitate to criticise Pound when necessary so the fact that he singled out Pound's conversation skill in his obituary suggests that it was striking. As Bunting said in an interview in 1984, 'before I got things clear about poetry I was over 30 ... it was arguing with Ezra that helped to get it clear in my head. Where I differed from Ezra, the more violently I differed the more likely I was to get things clear. I spent three years arguing with Ezra four or five times a week.'[259]

Bunting went on to celebrate Pound's physicality, his sporting prowess and swaggering walk, and his moral rectitude. (Pound despised drunkenness for instance. Bunting told Zukofsky that Pound 'stiffens and is unable to disguise his disgust at even mild parlour drunkenness'.)[260] Most of all though Bunting celebrated Pound's elusiveness:

It took the critics a long time to forgive Ezra for puzzling them with new, misleading, complex, endless poetry. He said in the Thirties that Eliot had got stuck because he could not understand Propertius, and all the rest had got stuck a few books earlier still ... If you will read the Cantos aloud and listen without troubling your head about their meaning, you will find, especially in the later Cantos, a surge of music that is its own meaning. Every year more people seem to hear it. By now there must be considerable backing for my opinion that Ezra Pound has been the greatest poet of the twentieth century.[261]

In spite of all their differences Bunting bitterly resented anything that he felt trivialised Pound's memory. The *Guardian* reported in February 1973 that Bunting:

upset the Mermaid Theatre by withdrawing yesterday from a poetic tribute to Ezra Pound, planned for tomorrow night. Sir Bernard Miles arranged the evening ... and invited Bunting to read: Frank Kermode divised [*sic*] a programme of readings and recollections, which he describes as a fairly light-hearted portrait of Pound as a person and as a poet. A summary was sent to Bunting in Newcastle a fortnight ago. Bunting arrived in London yesterday, saw the full script for the first time, and pulled out – on the grounds, apparently, that it was not the straightforward poetry reading he expected. What has upset the organisers is that Bunting must have known well enough from the summary two weeks ago that it was planned to include discussion.[262]

This prompted an immediate response from Omar Pound: 'Sir, – For the record: Basil Bunting withdrew from the Programme at the Mermaid Theatre, intended to honour my father, Ezra Pound, because he considered the script denigrated E.P. Had I seen the script beforehand, I, too, would not have attended. Bunting's integrity is completely vindicated.'[263]

Bunting sent his own version of events to Denis Goacher: 'Maybe you have already seen in the papers that I shall not be reading at the Mermaid on Sunday. Kermode's "script", which only reached me this morning, was more than I could stomach, with its constant belittling of Ezra ... I don't want to influence you: but if you too feel like walking out on this ugly minstrel show, I'd surely welcome your company.'[264]

Any interference with Pound's literary legacy angered him. In 1977 Faber's Editorial Director, R.B. Woodings, asked Bunting for an endorsement for the cover of Pound's *Collected Early Poems*, prompting a stinging response:

Dear Mr Wooding – Thank you for sending me the book. It makes me shudder. No doubt it is fitting that maggots consume us in the end, or at least the rubbish we scatter as we go; but I'd rather leave the lid on my dustbin and the earth on my friends' graves. Piety takes curious forms: the toenail clippings of Saint What's His Name are revered. I don't think religion is much advanced by that. It would be more profitable, more to his glory, to throw away some of the poems Pound printed than to print those he threw away himself. I apologise for my lack of sympathy for the industrious compilers.[265]

He was pragmatic about Pound's influence on his own work and generous about his influence on that of everyone else. An interviewer asked him about Pound's influence, noting that some reviewers regarded Bunting as no more than a follower of Pound:

I don't think it's surprising. They knew of me, in so far as they knew of me at all, only as somebody who was mentioned by Pound from time to time. And

it must be obvious to anybody that I, like all the poets worth mentioning, all
the poets worth bothering with, have learned a great deal from Pound. Pound
tried out very many styles and ways of doing things which it would be folly
to ignore. You can save yourself a lot of work by just going over what he did.
It is an extraordinary parallel between the career of Ezra Pound and that of
Edmund Spenser. In the beginning trying every conceivable form of verse;
the amount of concentrated experiment there is in *The Shepherd's Calendar* for
instance is something very similar to those multitudinous attempts to revive
this or alter that of Pound's youth. And the fact that Spenser undertook
an enormously long poem, which he had indeed planned but not in that
complete detail with which Dante planned the *Divina Commedia,* and that this
was undertaken in an age when it's impossible to write an enormously long
poem because things were changing too fast. They were changing far too fast
in the sixteenth century and they were changing far too fast in the twentieth
to allow the long poem to have the kind of coherence that Dante gives to the
Divina Commedia or even the kind of coherence, at a much lower level I think,
that Virgil gives to the *Aeniad.* The similarity in the characters of Pound and
Spenser is very great and I have the feeling that the influence of Pound is
likely to be as lasting as that of Spenser. Which means that three centuries
hence, though they may have forgotten to be aware of it by then, anybody
who knows the history will still be able to trace it all over the place.[266]

While generous in his acknowledgement of Pound's influence on him
Bunting was always firm about the fact that he (and Zukofsky) would have
got to where they did get to, or somewhere very close to it, without Pound:

> It wasn't a question of absorbing a man and then reproducing. It was a
> question of finding a man whose thoughts were working on parallel lines who
> happened to be senior. But I think both Zukofsky and myself would have got
> exactly where we are, not exactly but in the main, without Pound and Eliot.
> So that I reckon we both belong to the rather small group of innovators as
> Pound does. I should say that the most important is certainly Ezra Pound;
> Eliot was the one who first and most decisively got to the public; Zukofsky is
> the one who has taken things furthest.[267]

Bureaucrats and tinkers

As we have seen, Bunting saw incompetent, overpaid bureaucrats as the
cause of much of the woe of contemporary British culture, and he seems
to have had a point. On 4 July 1973 Bunting wrote to Jonathan Williams to

report that a Pound reading had gone well, but that the infrastructure was dreadful:

> The stink of condescension and patronage at the ICA and at the Arts Council is overpowering. The other reading was buggered up by [Charles] Osborne, who informed me and MacDiarmid two minutes before it started that we must cut down our prearranged time by about a third to make room for an appalling bore who speechified in a somewhat Will Rogerish way, but much duller, in between our dos (and took a good deal more than HIS allotted time)...They will have to pay a lot to get me back to London.[268]

Bunting is referring here to the annual Poetry International summer festival of spoken poetry which the Arts Council had been presenting each year in London since 1967. Charles Osborne became the festival's sole director in 1973, and his own belligerent account of his years at the Arts Council form a large part of his 1986 memoir, *Giving it Away: Memoirs of an Uncivil Servant*. He takes centre stage in his own first festival and certainly doesn't stoop to mention Bunting or MacDiarmid:

> As usual, Wystan Auden was the star attraction, and at Wystan's request I also invited his friend Chester Kallman to read. For my sideshows I engaged John Betjeman (who was then the Poet Laureate) and Roy Fuller to present 'Homage to C. Day Lewis: poetry and prose by the late Poet Laureate', a programme in which Cecil Day Lewis's widow, Jill Balcon, also participated. I encouraged Ian Hamilton and Clive James to devise and present 'The Poetry International Revue' (out of which grew those long narrative poems of Clive's).

> I also presented a programme, 'The Poet as Lyricist', in which the lyrics of Noël Coward, Cole Porter, Lorenz Hart, Ogden Nash and others were introduced by Benny Green and read by Constance Cummings, John Gielgud, Vincent Price and me. I asked Jack Lambert to chair a discussion on 'The Poet as a Librettist', but on the night he was indisposed and I had to step in and do it myself. The other participants included Auden, Kallman, Ronald Duncan, Elizabeth Lutyens, Nicholas Maw, Myfanwy Piper and Malcolm Williamson. The most enjoyable of the sideshows, however, so people told me, was 'An Evening of Innocent Austral Verse', in which Mrs (as she then was) Edna Everage was assisted by Mr Barry Humphries and myself.

> It was a highly successful week. *The Times* wrote: 'This has been the most various and ambitious season of Poetry International, which can now be regarded as a miniature poetic equivalent of the Proms. Nursed through

infancy by Patrick Garland, helped by Ted Hughes, and now in the capable and imaginative hands of Charles Osborne, it was a triumphant week, Ginsberg or no Ginsberg.[269]

Even in his own account the 1973 festival was more about Charles Osborne than it was about poetry. Along the way he seems to have turned the entire festival into an antipodean pantomime. I have little doubt that celebrating contemporary poetry with a combination of the saxophonist Benny Green, the horror movie actor Vincent Price and Edna Everage irritated more than just purists.

A few months after the festival MacDiarmid spent a week with the Buntings at Shadingfield: 'I ferried him from and to Biggar, and drove him a bit about the Northumberland countryside. He is a reformed character. In seven days (apart from what he got in the pubs) he only drank four bottles of Glen Fiddich, and even diluted it with water to a slight extent. Seven or eight years ago he managed three bottles (and at least another in the pubs) in 36 hours. I like talking with him. He is a thoroughly good chap as well as our best island poet.'[270]

Further confirmation of Bunting's increased acceptance in the poetry establishment came with Philip Larkin's *The Oxford Book of Twentieth-Century Verse* in 1973, in which Larkin included 'On the Fly-Leaf of Pound's Cantos', 'Chomei at Toyama' and 'What the Chairman Told Tom'. Furthermore an invitation to address the Yeats Summer School in Sligo that year confirmed him as one of the grand old men of modernism. He was there to talk about the Yeats he knew in Rappalo rather than Yeats the poet. He told Peter Quartermain a classic story of Bunting cussedness from that visit:

> I had a conversation with three donkeys. They were wandering along a road, where I was taking a morning stroll. I patted the first that reached me, whereupon it instantly laid its head in my bosom, while its mates joined it. One donkey isn't too hard to manage, but three, all trying to eat your jacket at the same time, are a handful. A tourist car arrived and couldn't get past. The man honked awhile, then stuck his head out of the window and bawled: "Take your bloody asses out of my way!"; so I let on to be a bit stupider than I am, and held him up quite a while.[271]

Bunting enjoyed his visit to Ireland. It satisfied his taste for the absurdity of the human condition. He wrote to Jonathan Williams in September 1973:

I worked hard at Sligo amongst dull people – a lecture, two readings, and five seminars (where the students were all university lecturers) in a week – to earn a total of fees and alleged expenses which together came to just a pound or two short of real expenses; but I got a glimpse of preposterous Ulster and two days wandering about Connemara, a place worth seeing. Witnessed a fight of tinkers, thirty of them, men and women, fighting each against all; and saw the same thirty an hour later sitting in a line by the church wall looking crestfallen and silent. I suppose all defeated each, a fairly satisfactory result. As picturesque as Spaniards were 40 years ago. All Irish cars have bent front fenders, and are driven at night without lights on the wrong side of the road. Bulls, rams, donkeys etc obstruct all roads, dead dogs and cats litter them anywhere near a town. Perhaps you know the place.[272]

The poet Mike Shayer accompanied Bunting in Sligo:

We had agreed to meet at Cleggan quay, where the boat went to Inishbofin. He had driven down from Northern Ireland. I had some kind of re-meeting with people on the island in mind (where I had written Poems from an Island) … We arranged that I would spend a night on Inishbofin, while he stayed at the bar in Cleggan. It was there that he had his adventure with the donkeys. The next day we set off toward Sligo – where on the way I regret not having followed my own intuition that we explore the local life around Lough Mask. We stayed overnight on the coast somewhere, and the next day on the way in to Sligo we encountered the tinkers well-sloshed and fighting alongside a church. In a pub around lunch we met the red-haired tinker lass and had a little conversation … later, or the next day, in the pub the girl (who I think had met with some hostility from the locals) went straight up to Basil and kissed him on the lips. [273]

More evidence that Goacher's 'sexual crisis' theory has feet of clay.

DELIGHT IN TRANSIENCE, 1975

'I did what I could to prevent 75th birthday celebrations,' he told Victoria Forde after the event, 'but I couldn't dodge the Poetry Society of which I am still president for a final year, so I had to turn up in London for two days of what seemed to me suspiciously like a rehearsal for my funeral.'[274] In March 1975 the Poetry Society (or, rather, Eric Mottram) organised a two-day event in Bunting's honour.

A few days before his birthday Bunting contemplated the prospect of the celebrations: 'I lack experience of being 75 and am not sure what I should or what I want to say.' A reading had been planned but Bunting was doubtful that *Briggflatts* was the right poem on account of its length (it takes an hour to read, and an hour and a quarter if accompanied by the Scarlatti sonatas). He suggested Tom Pickard reading his own *Dancing under Fire* as an alternative, and Colin Simms or 'my fellow-struldbrug [*sic*] Hugh MacDiarmid … always a pleasure, whether he reads his very excellent best or his incomprehensible worst … My close or closish personal friends, Gael Turnbull, Stuart M.[ontgomery], (Gael has a new poem, unfinished, which sounds interesting) – Roy Fisher, Mike Shayer I'd like to see. D.G.Bridson remains an asset to all occasions.'[275]

In fact Bunting read the beautiful meditation, 'At Briggflatts Meeting House', and according to Peter Barry the event was 'a great success, a defining moment of the radicalised Poetry Society, and by paying homage to Bunting the radicals celebrated their own lineage, linking themselves, through Bunting, to the pioneer modernists like Yeats and Pound'.[276] Bunting sent the poem to Mottram on 16 June 1975 with a short note, 'I sit anxiously, waiting for the editor-regrets note', but Mottram published it in *Poetry Review* that year, the only poem by Bunting that *Poetry Review* did publish.[277]

Written to mark the tercentenary of Briggflatts Meeting House it is the only poem, he told an audience in 1982, that he was ever able to write for a particular occasion. 'I can't do that kind of thing. But, I did it that time – it took me about six months of doing.'[278]

> Boasts time mocks cumber Rome. Wren
> set up his own monument.
> Others watch fells dwindle, think
> the sun's fires sink.
>
> Stones indeed sift to sand, oak
> blends with saints' bones.
> Yet for a little longer here
> stone and oak shelter
>
> silence while we ask nothing
> but silence. Look how clouds dance
> under the wind's wing, and leaves
> delight in transience.[279]

Peter Barry compares 'At Briggflatts Meeting House' with Wordsworth's Lucy poems, and, rather less plausibly in my view, with Gerard Manley Hopkins: 'The poem is like the last echo of that intensely stark Poundian lyricism which Bunting was heir to, a lyricism which had its roots deep in the nineteenth century. Certainly this is one of the poems which (in Bunting's own words, though he did not say it of his own work) *Poetry Review* should be proud to have published.'[280] It actually took Bunting four months to write this short lyric. He told Jonathan Williams that 'The rhymes (as they might call them) dissembled in the Welsh manner hold it up, more or less, I fancy.'[281]

Bunting's own account of the Poetry Society celebration was unusually generous. He told Jonathan Williams that 'the intentions were good. One night they read poems at me, the other they listened to Briggflatts and got very enthusiastic. I got a double sized bottle of very good wine, everybody else had to drink plonk of the plonkiest.'[282]

Was Peggy at Bunting's seventy-fifth birthday celebrations? It is difficult to know for certain, but probably not. She has disappeared from the record rather since the end of the 1960s. The person who was closest to the couple, Gael Turnbull, didn't have the heart to track down the date of the second, final, parting:

> How much was it a mutual decision, how much hers, how much Basil's? I don't know. [Aldritt quotes from a letter to Denis Goacher, that it was Peggy who insisted on the break.] Certainly, as late as 1974, he was still corresponding with her, but unable to go to visit her. Some of the initial emotional intensity undoubtedly faded. Basil was aware that he had, perhaps once again, upset her life. Peggy was uneasy about it almost from the start. Whatever the details, a decision was made. Certainly, Peggy could not face abandoning Edward, who had been very upset at the possibility, of which he was aware, even if the practicalities of money would have allowed it.[283]

After Peggy's husband's death there was apparently no attempt to re-establish contact. As Turnbull says, Bunting was not someone to compromise a decision he had already made, and Turnbull himself lost contact with Peggy towards the end of 1974.

JUST THE MISCHIEF OF IT

In October 1975 Jonathan Williams and Larry Fagin, Director of the Poetry Project in St Marks Church in the Bowery in New York City's East Village, cooked up the idea of a US reading tour for Bunting. They told him that if he had the strength and time at seventy-six to visit in April they would be sure to get him $5,000 net from ten readings.[284] The idea of the tour was that Bunting would read in America's major poetry centres and universities where there was established interest in Pound and his circle. Each of the readings would net Bunting $500 plus travel expenses. Bunting arrived in Boston from the UK on 2 April 1976. Over the next ten days he gave readings at Harvard, the University of Maine at Orono, Yale and the Poetry Center, New York, before flying to Charlotte, North Carolina, on 13 April, where Jonathan Williams and Tom Meyer met him and drove him to Davidson College.

As far as Bunting was concerned the entire tour was a disaster. He wrote to Jonathan Williams on 4 May 1976:

> I think I'd better rehearse the tour now, to avoid errors. Corbett and wife were kind and their children dears, but Harvard paid only 200 dollars for what I think was a reading much more valuable than that ... But Yale's cheque for 150 dollars seemed to me a deliberate insult. Even English provincial universities pay as much or more, sometimes twice as much. This angered me ... For some reason, maybe only forgetfulness, I was left to pay my own trainfare to New York – no great sum.
>
> In New York Monahan had appointed himself my mentor. I don't know what to make of him. He talks too much, flatters too blatantly, and I suspect him over overreaching me, or trying to, in his bargain for a copy of 'Redimiculum Matellarum'; but he took a lot of trouble and seems as angry as I was with the doings of Fagin. But the hotel, Pickwick Arms, is a dirty place, unswept, undusted, and with linen that may have been washed or not. The photographic lady bored me extremely, but was better than the hotel room or than Monahan's incessant chatter ... The reading was possibly the best I ever gave, judging as well as I can, and the audience enthusiastic, with a crammed hall, people standing wherever there was space to stand on. It was also exhausting, so that though I was glad to see Ginsberg, I had no spirit left to talk with him. Naturally, when I found they had given me a cheque for 300 dollars, in spite of having insisted I cable an acceptance of an offer of 900

plus all expenses; and in spite of the fact that the full hall and the sale of some sort of program which I never saw must have brought them in well over 4000 dollars, I was exceedingly angry.[285]

David Gordon recalled collecting Bunting from a motel in Orono during the tour to return him to the English department. He was 'genially nonchalant in manner and gesture … He was wearing brown tweed jacket and pants, and carrying a walking stick in his right hand, and in his left, a satchel of dark, tooled leather with a rain-proof slung over it. His patent leather shoes fastened with black buckles. His bearing, his being at ease, self-confident and compact, the natural-born traveller.'[286] At their conversation over a lobster lunch Bunting seems to have led Gordon a bit of a dance, with stories that become more improbable (to me at least) with each arriving Manhattan:

> He described his Northumbria as very hilly and filled with bracken (a kind of fern). It was being reforested and a lot of new wildcats and ptarmigans were re-appearing; many of the new species that were showing up were those that had been thought extinct …
>
> Bunting said that he would drive the 25 miles over to the coast of Northumbria (cruising at 80 mph) and catch lobsters. One day his child, knowing that he liked them, caught a bucket of them, carried them in a sack to his room, and emptied the sack on the floor … he liked horses; had raised Clydesdales …
>
> … once in Provence he has asked a waitress which was the best wine and the young girl had blushed to the roots of her hair as she moved her thumb down the menu, 'La pisse de vieille' [The old woman's piss] …[287]

I'm sure Bunting expected these innocent tall tales to appear in a biography some time in the future, and now they have. But there haven't been ptarmigans in Northumbria for a very long time, if ever, certainly not in the twentieth century. The wine exists though, and Bunting was careful to mix his stories, so who is to say that the family home in Wylam wasn't occasionally awash with disoriented lobsters? It doesn't solve the mystery of where the poet kept his Clydesdales. His own version of the lunch was recorded in a letter to Jonathan Williams: 'At Orono the man in charge had vanished. His substitute did all he could; nevertheless the time was harassing and money only turned up two minutes after the bank closed and four minutes before I had to leave for the plane. The hotel was comfortable, and a man, name forgotten, who took me to lunch, though unpunctual even beyond American wont, was agreeable and fed me an admirable lobster.'[288]

Bunting was fond of teasing Americans. A note in Gael Turnbull's unpublished journal of a visit to Bunting in Washington New Town recalls:

> laughing at the pub, the Honest Boy, and the mural of the chopped cherry tree. 'Cashing in on the Americans. When Washington never had any connection with this place. His family went to America from somewhere down south, in Northampton I think. Though they came from here before that. Someone once bought up a field next to the hall and subdivided it into 1 ft. square sections. Went to America and sold them as parts of the Washington Estate. Made a fortune out of it. But the Americans will believe anything.' He seemed pleased, however. Just the mischief of it.[289]

Carroll F. Terrell recalled an eventful drive across northern England in Bunting's DAF car during his first visit to Britain. On the way he learned that DAF is short for 'daffodil – a Swedish [?] invention'; and discovered that part of their journey was on the top of Hadrian's Wall; he was forced to brave a terrifying but in the event inoffensive bull on a detour that Bunting himself avoided; he learned that the entire curriculum of Sedbergh School, one of England's most celebrated private schools, consisted of rugby and cricket. Eventually he realised that the purpose of the narrowly missed traffic accidents was that Bunting was 'having tons of fun trying to scare the pants off me and succeeding very well'.[290] He told Victoria Forde an implausible story about his dog, Fortnum, having nearly killed the Ambassador's pet European brown bear in Persia, the bear later recognising Bunting in London Zoo.[291]

He arrived with Williams and Meyer at St Andrews College on 15 April. Whitney Jones, who was teaching at the small, liberal arts college in Laurinburg, North Carolina, had invited Bunting to read to what he expected to be a receptive audience and then spend a few days with a chance to rest and catch his breath in the middle of a hectic tour. According to Whitney Jones:

> Spring had hit Laurinburg in full force that week and temperatures were in the high 70s. Basil arrived wearing a heavy, dark wool suit. The features of his face, looking both chiselled and weathered, and the posture of his walk, in which he used a cane, not so much for support as for touching out the pattern of his footprints in advance, both reminded me strangely of the films of Ezra

Pound I had seen. He seemed at once very frail and yet very resilient, a reed who had survived a lifetime of buffeting about by winds stronger than most of us even dream of.[292]

Later that day he found the poet reading an essay on Pound and wondered what he thought of it:

> He seemed to grope for the exact way of replying to my question and for a moment the silence made me feel that I had asked the wrong question. At last he broke the silence by saying that people who wrote about Pound all meant well, and he liked many of them very much, but quite frankly literary criticism was of little interest to him. Poetry, he said, is above all else sound. What a poem says might be interesting, but the way a poem sounds is what gives it true meaning. He then began talking of Spenser's poetry and the importance of sound to Spenser. He recited several verses out loud as an example and I was struck by the beauty of his voice. I had read Spenser in numerous undergraduate and graduate courses, had written a dissertation on Spenser, and had been teaching Spenser for six years, but I had never *heard* Spenser before. For the next several days I was to hear Basil read or recite from memory lines from Spenser, and I never failed to be enthralled by the experience.[293]

The following day, 16 April, Bunting gave an influential talk to a creative writing class about the poets of the sixteenth century and that evening 'was in rare form' for a public interview with Williams, Whitney Jones and Meyer. Meyer asked Bunting if 'there's another poem coming'; Bunting's reply was self-deprecating:

> I have no idea. I wish there were. I would like to write another thing before I get too old to be credible. Old men become silly, so I've begun distrusting myself. In another 4 years I shall be 80, and God knows men of 80 are not fit to listen to. I have doubts, but I hope something else may yet be written … I think that all men ought to be put an end to at the age of 70. The humane killer ought to be applied to them. I think a great mistake was made by the British government in the early 1930s when in the Southern Sudan they prevented one of the tribes, I think it was the Dinka, from eating every woman who became a grandmother. Obviously that's the time to eat her, isn't it? She's no more use to anybody after that.[294]

He answered questions about his poetry, read 'Chomei at Toyama' in its entirety and explained his selections for his anthology of English poetry.

According to Whitney Jones: 'The conversation was frequently punctuated by sounds from a rock band warming up outside for a student beer party, but the audience was with Basil all the way. Knowing that Basil really frowns upon interviews and literary discussions, Jonathan brought along a bottle of Basil's favorite scotch.'[295]

The following morning Williams and Whitney Jones took Bunting and a small group on a tour of the birthplace of the local dialect poet, John Charles McNeill, in Wagram, about nine miles north of Laurinburg. Bunting was delighted to find that a Temperance Hall shared McNeill's property and that it sported an upside down wine glass on its roof. The following day was Easter Sunday and Bunting joined faculty and students for a picnic by the lake in the middle of the St Andrews campus:

> Basil chatted with a few students and faculty, but he seemed to enjoy being by himself, enjoying the sun of a beautiful Sunday. At one point I noticed him standing in front of a large magnolia by the lake. He told me of a mockingbird in the tree which reminded him of home. In all our later correspondence he referred to that mockingbird. He seemed especially relaxed on Sunday, and my image of his frailty had long since faded. He had abandoned his cane and was in a lively mood.

> That evening we had dinner with a suite of girls who shared an interest in feminism. They served homemade bread and various kinds of health foods, and we sat on the floor in their suite, enjoying the food and the wine. Outside, on the lake, the coots were chattering, and the evening had a kind of homemade exotic feeling about it. Basil suddenly began regaling everyone with a story of dining in the palace of the Shah of Iran. The girls, who really had little interest in poetry, had invited us over because they know that I was desperate for hospitality since none of the faculty had invited Basil to dinner. Nonetheless, they all warmed up to Basil, and by the end of the evening he seemed to feel very much at home with them.[296]

The following day Bunting began yet another reading with a lengthy introduction to *Briggflatts*. He seems to have felt the need to explain the obscurer references in the poem. Whitney Jones noticed at this reading that Bunting's voice was 'strong and his energy level was running high' and concluded that Bunting's reluctance to talk about specific poets was largely due to the fact that he was pacing himself, saving his strength for the public readings: 'The reading was indeed a great success, and it was a success on Basil's own terms. It was an evening of pure sound. Most of the audience left without a single line to quote the next day, without a single image to remember. Instead, they remembered *the voice*. In fact, the audience responded so well to the voice that Basil read for over two hours, covering all of *Briggflatts* and much of his other work, and ending with a very recent poem.'[297]

Carroll F. Terrell had helped to organise the tour but was unable to be there during Bunting's visit. His students, however, were extremely positive about the elderly poet:

> ...they liked him because for his age he had a remarkable eye for any female who wasn't too old or too skinny, and he enjoyed the local pub more than other more scenic places and would talk freely about anything anyone brought up while the beer was flowing. They also admired the fine figure he cut with his beard, his loose-flowing garments, his walking stick, his tall and straight posture, and a clear-cut no-nonsense attitude. And they liked his dislikes: his hatred of shame and hypocrisy, of the fake and the meretricious. In a word, for the young 'a wonderful old coot' was someone they would like to become at the age of seventy-five, but knew in their secret hearts they couldn't or wouldn't.[298]

Bunting, however, was not positive about any part of the tour:

> In North Carolina all went well and as agreeably as my still indignant mind would let it. I liked the campus, though I don't think I'd like to be a student at St. Andrews – rather like a jail, so far from the things students value. I liked the mocking-birds that are ready to converse, and to learn a tune, and the countryside ... Buffalo is still itself, dignified, etc; but I couldn't escape two hours in the Poetry Room at the library, looking at mss of James Joyce which don't interest me in the slightest ... Alas for Madison! That agreeable-looking city hasn't changed. It consists of academics and politicians exclusively. The academics are quite indifferent to me, the politicians are all over me. Barbara Lesch is unfortunately one of those New Yorkers who believe that the smallest gap in the chatter is a disaster to be averted at all costs. In her laudable desire to protect me from the other academics she more or less confined me to a narrow circle of exactly similar people. She cannot have any idea how tiring she and they are. They took a lot of trouble and were kind, and that was at least a refuge from the famous Student Union, where I was put up in a pleasant enough room, but where the food is possibly the worst in America, or even in the world ... I was taken to a horrible party where six professors and their wives, besides a number of less exalted persons, asked silly questions on

the assumption that I must be an admirer of Lowell and Larkin, and pressed whisky on me, without any food (I'd been told it was a dinner party but it wasn't) till I fell decorously asleep ... The reading the next day was a disaster. Few people came, and those few almost unanimously disapproved of me. I didn't even read really well.[299]

His complaint to Williams doesn't stop in New York – he found little to like in any of the locations he visited.

A STENCH OF REPRESSION

In 1966 Jonathan Williams had half jokingly asked if Bunting was ever likely to become head of the Northeastern Council of the Arts, an idea that Bunting met with characteristic scorn: 'Oh, *most* improbable. Most improbable. No seat on the Committee should ever go near an artist. They're unreliable people. They actually like art.'[300]

The Arts Council files in the archive of London's Victoria and Albert Museum reveal the period of Bunting's presidency of Northern Arts to have been an intensely political one, with Northern Arts actively pursuing a devolution agenda. Bunting's name appears little in the correspondence but he can't possibly have been too distant from the high-energy wrangling between 105 Piccadilly in London and New Bridge Street in Newcastle, where Director David Dougan was 'clearly determined to establish Northern Arts as the Arts Council of the North, and is pushing devolution to the limit in his region'.[301] Bunting wanted independence for Northern Arts, not just devolution. His experience with the Poetry Society had shown him that subsidies came with intolerable interference. 'The men who run the Arts Council,' he said in his final Presidential Address to Northern Arts in 1977, 'are quite aware of the power that [money] gives them to impose their own views. They will not, they say, interfere in detail; yet the recent history of the Poetry Society shows them interfering in considerable detail with the society's internal affairs, exerting their power, as it seems to me, almost always to stifle and to thwart.'[302]

Minutes of the Literature panel on 4 November 1974 reported on Bunting's proposed fellowship that 'the University has now agred [*sic*] to continue the visiting Fellowship for Basil Bunting for the next two years when it would terminate finally. The officer was congratulated on achieving this as a result of delicate negotiations.' I'm sure they were. The minutes of the previous meeting on 9 September record that the English Department of the University of Newcastle had agreed to contribute £300 towards Bunting's fellowship for the coming academic year, with the hope that the Senate, when the proposal was put to them, would increase it to £400, the amount Bunting had received for the previous two years. The committee recommended that £500 would be contributed by Northern Arts with the hope that the university would match that amount.

In any event Northern Arts wasn't much better than the Poetry Society or Arts Council: 'There's a Pound Memorial concert here on Sunday Nov. 26 … But I've got to cope with idiocy here: one of the readers wants to make a speech denouncing EP's fascism before he reads! I got the guarantee out of Northern Arts, and now I must find a way round this folly.'[303]

His Presidential Address to Northern Arts in 1974 makes a point of celebrating the fragile distinctiveness of northern culture:

> The beautiful work of northern Britain was coarsened and almost disappeared during the years of Roman domination, but it was capable of blazing again with extraordinary splendour as soon as the Romans were gone … The great power of design that produced the Codex Lindisfarnensis, the astonishing originality of the sculpture on the Bewcastle Cross, the two Acca crosses, and the stone at Hexham called the tomb of King Aelfwald, survived war and havoc, conquest by Wessex and by the Danes, for at least four and a half centuries, as you can see by visiting the gravestones of the Bolbec family now built into the church wall at Bywell, still fertile in distinctly Northumbrian designs.[304]

All this was to be encouraged and yet the Arts Council continued to fail British artists, in Bunting's view, by spreading what few subsidies it did grant too thinly. He wanted arts administrators to place their bets on fewer artists and accept that they would back many losers. He developed this theme the following year, urging administrators to take 'startling chances' and pointing to the most 'triumphant patrons' who 'never backed anything unless the odds were at least ten-to-one against it'.[305] By 1976 he was criticizing Arts bodies for evading responsibility, encouraging censorship and spending too much money on 'rich men's recreations'.[306] He told Jonathan Williams that he thought this particular speech might have had some effect: 'I believe I stirred up Northern Arts a bit more deeply than usual this year by opening their annual general meeting with an attack on Lord Redcliffe-Maud's long dull report on the arts. Some of them looked seriously uneasy, and I hope they may, for once, reflect. Doing such things and still keeping one's phrases "diplomatic" is at least good exercise.'[307] Some members of Bunting's audience may have been looking 'seriously uneasy' because the tone of his address was not in the least diplomatic, and its target was plain for all to see.

By the time of his resignation speech in 1977 he had run out of hope. If the Northern Arts administrators had been wondering why their own President despised them so much, they were about to be enlightened:

> When you made me your president I still hoped [that Northern Arts would be useful to artists], though I was beginning to feel impatient. I believe now that we are further from what was our aim than we were several years ago. The mistakes have been made and the false steps taken mainly in London, not here; but we have acquiesced. A system that leaves many artists, men of some achievement, as poor as some of them are after a life of putting up with poverty has something seriously wrong with it ... I now ask you please to relieve me of the task of being your president.[308]

If Bunting was contemptuous of the cultural micro-politics of the Poetry Society and Northern Arts and, at a higher level, the Arts Council, he positively despised the prevailing national political culture. 'It seems to me that every kind of reactionary is flourishing just now,' he wrote to MacDiarmid in November 1973. 'The infection spreads quickly from politics to morals to literature. I've been patient all my life, but it's got progressively harder to resist the conviction that nothing short of the guillotine will ever make this island tolerable.'[309] He told Jonathan Williams about a visit to Cardiff:

> a very attractive city, new to me, and looks alive too ... But they told me the speculators have persuaded it to get rebuilt in huge flatsided towers of offices. To no useful end whatever, merely to fill the pockets of fools who are too rich already. However the bulldozers haven't got there yet, and I hope some general bankruptcy of all the greedy idiots may yet save Cardiff and what's left of Newcastle. There's a smell of bankruptcy in the air, something like, say, 1928; and a stench of repression such as I don't remember even in 1926. It's hard to compare depths of stupidity and baseness, yet I've a suspicion that I'm watching the worst bout of misgovernment there's been in my lifetime, and not only in England. I'm not usually a revolutionary, too aware of what's rightly permanent, but I'd welcome a 1789 or a 1917 rather than another decade of this. Also I think that unless financial incompetence destroys the system first, as it almost did in 1930, some revolution, whether from the people

or from a lot of would-be Diocletians and Mussolinis, is sure in much less than a generation. I don't often bother you with politics. Overlook it.[310]

We saw how prescient Bunting could be as early as 1928 during his stint at *The Outlook* and this survey of the gathering political crisis in Britain in the early 1970s is remarkable. Edward Heath's Conservative administration was an economic and social disaster. In January 1972 the number of unemployed people in the UK rose to one million for the first time since the 1930s, having doubled in the eighteen months of Heath's government. A miners' strike had resulted in a national state of emergency being declared in February, followed by a second state of emergency in August after a prolonged strike by dock workers, and what are always euphemistically referred to as 'the Troubles' began in Northern Ireland. The day after Bunting wrote this letter to Williams rail workers and civil servants went on strike, and in May 1973 1.6 million workers withdrew their labour to protest at the Heath government's pay policies, and the Lonrho scandal became the very first 'unacceptable face of capitalism'. Apart from IRA bombing campaigns in Northern Ireland and on the mainland and the continuing Cod War with Iceland, there were serious disasters at Lofthouse and Markham collieries and troops were drafted in to cover striking firefighters in Glasgow. All this was before the real chaos and misgovernment of 1974 with the three-day week, the oil crisis, the arrival of Harold Wilson's toothless minority Labour government in March, IRA bombs on the M62 motorway and in London, the Birmingham and Guildford pub bombings, the lethal explosions at the Flixborough chemical plant and Golborne colliery near Wigan, the emergence of the far-right National Front as a politically significant force and the street rioting it caused. And it was well before the 'winter of discontent' in 1979 under James Callaghan's government, when lorry drivers went on strike in January causing serious fuel and food shortages, gravediggers went on strike leaving thousands of corpses unburied, tens of thousands of public sector workers went on strike to protest against the pay freeze, refuse collectors went on strike leaving millions of tons of rubbish rotting in Britain's streets, National Health Service ancillary staff went on strike, blocking access to hospitals to all those who were not emergency cases. And there was yet another explosion at Golborne colliery in March.

Bunting wasn't just another old codger complaining that the country was going to the dogs. It really was. If his diagnosis of the situation was spot on, his prediction of the likely outcome was even better. The Secretary of State for Education and Science in Heath's appalling administration became the leader of the Conservative opposition in February 1975, and when she won the general election in 1979 Margaret Thatcher began a neo-Diocletian revolution that transformed British society for ever. Given the woeful catalogue of disasters in 1970s' Britain the fact that the Thatcher revolution was and is regarded in many quarters as an even greater national disaster is some measure of how deep that revolution was. Bunting stuck to the basic premise of his prediction that the emergence of 'a lot of would-be Diocletians and Mussolinis' would be the consequence of the political chaos of the 1970s. He wrote to Jonathan Williams in December 1983:

> I'm afraid I have left Christmas greetings too late to reach you; but after all I don't feel much devoted to such ecclesiastical holidays, especially since the BBC now expends so much time on reminding us of our proper station – low, low – before God and Die Fuehrer, whose latest feats of near-abolishing the trade unions and local government might easily bring us to civil war or something like it before the time comes for new elections. More Tories are complaining, but there are so many that she still has a majority of 100 in parliament. She is about where Hitler was in 1933. And accelerating.[311]

He retained his liberal outlook to the end, albeit grudgingly: 'I'm disgusted by the general reactionariness of everything and everybody lately. It laps over from politics into morals and literature, as though there were a universal hate of anything honest. I've just told McDiarmid [sic] I'll back him when his party reintroduces the guillotine. I don't like Communism, but at least it might butcher off a decent proportion of even worse folk.'[312] Jonathan Williams asked him in 1980 what he thought of the Thatcher government, provoking an unambiguous response: 'It shows an intention of being the worst government since 1906. And the people in it seem as bad as those in Lloyd George's 1919 cabinet.'[313]

He was contemptuous of the Thatcher administration but he also derided Labour's retreat from socialism, and the claims to it of some of the left's more iconic figures of the period. He wrote to Jonathan Williams on Guy Fawkes Night (5 November) 1984:

> The bonfire waiting to be lit tonight in the pub's paddock is ample to celebrate a man who made as good a near miss as the IRA scored at Brighton. James I was a pretty target too; but poor Guy actually precipitated the long eclipse of his church in Britain, Holland and Denmark, just as the IRA puts an

end to all wishes to rearrange Northern Ireland in a workable, tolerant way. Assassination always risks its intentions against an incalculable reaction, and Lord knows we have reaction enough in this country, where men who would have been called *mild* socialists by Webb or Shaw, such as Arthur Scargill and Tony Benn, are half-repudiated by a Labour party that has quite forgotten its origins and most of its history. Scargill hasn't even got a jail record like some of his predecessors, or 'Lord' Manny Shinwell who has just been much praised by the Tories for living long enough for them to forget how frightened of him they used to be. I don't often get political with you. But I *was* active once upon a time.[314]

He reserved his supreme contempt, however, for Ayatollah Khomeini, the despotic leader of the revolution in Iran in 1979: 'An exemplar of the very worst breed of political reactionary, from which one can expect nothing whatsoever. He's a bloody priest ... The man is as bad as St. Bernard.'[315] A year later he was hoping that Khomeini would soon 'die at last by the assassination he has done so much to make customary'.[316]

NO HOME ... NO GRUB

Bunting was capable of putting a brave face on his poverty. He wrote to Jonathan Williams in May 1976: 'The tax people look menacing, and prices are about to increase again, with no corresponding increase in pensions; but the May seems sunny, and I consumed a pint of beer yesterday that tasted pretty.'[317] But by 1977 poverty was really depressing him: 'Midst of crisis – the last, I hope, till a final crisis which I'd welcome. It seems I'll have no home these coming months; soon, perhaps, no grub.'[318]

Shortly after he wrote this letter to Eric Mottram Bunting and Sima separated and he was effectively ejected from the family home in Wylam. Bunting's own account of the break up of his second marriage carries more than a whiff of the paranoia that coloured the first. At no point does he seem able to have acknowledged that he may have played a part himself. He wrote to Jonathan Williams in January 1977 that

Sima has been behaving as though she were actually mad, though I fancy it is only an exaggerated form of the 'change of life' trouble women undergo. She finally drove me out (after miscellaneous violence and what seemed to be a try at strangling me) into a snowstorm. I had nowhere whatever to go. At Hexham the snow was thick: up the Hexham Rothbury road it became very dangerous driving with lots of skids, next to no visibility and some drifts. When I stopped in a lay-by to smoke a cigarette and rest, a lorry driver told me the road was impassible [*sic*] on the high ground beyond Wallington. I had to turn back a long way before I could find a side road to Morpeth.'[319]

After an exhausting journey the 77-year-old poet eventually made it to Belford, where he stayed the night at the Blue Bell. That night the locals told him of a furnished cottage nearby that was rented cheaply during the winter and the following morning a gang of men dug his car out of the snow and Bunting moved into 4 Fenwick Village in Beal. 'It's a cold place,' he told Williams,

fixed for summer visitors only, I suppose, and in this weather thoroughly forbidding. I am sitting almost on top of an electric fire, with a car blanket round my head and shoulders, and still shivering. For the first time in my life I've had to thaw out my fountain pen – not very completely, it seems – by toasting it in front of the fire. But the type-writer has not enjoyed its journey and is not co-operating. Besides, I'd have to go to the table and freeze myself to use it … Next door – old Scotsman – has just been in with the cheerful news that two old people, one in this village, one in the next, died of cold last night.

His friends were deeply concerned about his accommodation. Tom Pickard recalls:

It took me a couple of weeks to locate his refuge, along rain soaked roads lined with bushes dripping sea fret. With a miserable fire burning and not much in the pantry I found him, cigarette in his mouth, reading Dante, a historical biography and a couple of detective novels. He was wrapped in a short woollen scarf and a woollen jacket that his wife had purchased from a church jumble sale.[320]

Michael Shayer and his wife, Denise, visited with Tom Pickard and were convinced that he would die if he remained there for long.

Although there is some of the old paranoia in his account of his eviction another 'new' Bunting emerges from this period of temporary homelessness: 'I worked very hard at very disagreeable tasks for nearly 20 years to buy Shadingfield,' he told Roudaba, 'and when at last it was paid for I made it over to Sima, to give her some feeling of security that she seemed to lack. There was nothing else to give. But little by little, over a good number of years, Sima has grown more and more implacable; and lately, with the approach of the change of life, I think she has become, in some respects, mad.' But Bunting clearly felt responsible: 'She is so obviously and extremely unhappy – and I feel so responsible for her, having brought her so far from her family and her country – and there's long companionship as well as love to reckon in – that I am afraid of some irrational act.'[321] Given the circumstances of his departure from the family home, as he told it himself at least, this is a remarkably generous view of events. There is no rancour, just compassion.

Sima sold Shadingfield, and Bunting had no desire to make any trouble for her. 'I am sorry for her. She has sold it and bought a bungalow in the next village, where I hope she will be able to be content and get back her balance. And also, she has divorced me – after 29 years of marriage.'[322] A few months later Bunting and Sima were on cordial terms. 'I see Sima once in every ten days or so,' he told Roudaba, 'drive over to her bungalow at Ovingham, near Wylam, and drink a cup of tea or eat a curry. I think whatever was wrong with her a year ago has pretty well cleared up, and I even get the impression that she would like to remarry me, but it would be very hard to arrange now everything is dispersed and no real room for me in her bungalow.'[323] By the summer he reported that he was on 'excellent terms' with Sima.[324]

Jonathan Williams offered him Corn Close until he and Tom Meyer returned in June,[325] but Bunting hesitated as matters with Sima seemed to be on the mend and she asked him to return to Wylam. 'Everything was tranquil and fine,' he told Williams, 'for exactly one week. Then as soon as she got a bit of life in her again she started the old ploy – not with violence indeed; but I am not able to cope with what I think is some kind of madness.'[326] So, with some reluctance ('I don't like to make free with things or places other people set a high value on'), he accepted Williams' offer and moved into Corn Close on 16 February. It must have been a relief. Fenwick was four and a half miles away from the nearest shop, an impossible journey when Bunting's car failed to start, as it frequently did. He sent regular 'Corn Close Bulletins' to Williams in the following months. He had a few visitors; the poet Gael Turnbull spent some time with him before Easter,[327] and Kelsey Thornton and his wife and Robert Creeley also visited in April.

Bunting loved Corn Close and his letters became gradually more relaxed, but the problems with Sima ('domestic atom bombs' as he described them to Cid Corman[328]) were getting worse. He had found her, he told Williams, 'without a penny in her pocket and no food in the house but a couple of eggs. She has always been foolish about money, but mustn't be left to starve as a result, so I parted with a bit of my fast dwindling bank balance which, it's fair to say, she was reluctant to accept. She is getting public assistance, but not enough, and can't budget for what she does get.'[329] He was also convinced that Sima had been swindled by an unscrupulous relative.

He wrote to Williams and Tom Meyer from Corn Close in May 1977 with the catalogue of an accomplished natural historian. He was sensitive to all the activity in his environment:

> The last ten days have been brilliant. A few of the sheep have reappeared, but find the bull and his eleven concubines in possession of the field. A second [pine] marten got indoors and shit here and there before I persuaded it to use an open window as an exit. The heron which fishes the Corn Close reach of the beck every afternoon has been missing for a couple of days – I hope no jealous angler has shot it. Where is the heronry? One of the cuckoos behind the house stammers and cries 'Cu' cuckoo'. It needs psychoanalysis, no doubt. Cuckoos must have frightful complexes, with infantile murders and what not on their consciences. A very cocky cock-mizzle-thrush bosses the back garden. One large bird of prey noted, spreading its wing feathers to prevent stalling, but against the sun I couldn't guess what it was – buzzard, maybe. Or perhaps just a raven. No recent sight of the weasel. If the family has grown up she probably finds foraging less pressing and waits for concealment. The inexhaustible succession of large spiders who get into the bath and can't get out again has culminated in a monster. Let him stay there for a few days – I prefer the shower. Or should I exhibit him as the Dentdale Tarantula?[330]

Bunting seems to have had a problem with the local wildlife soiling his accommodation. He wrote to Jonathan Williams on 4 December 1982: 'The blue tits are beginning to remind me that winter is here and they would like to find breadcrumbs on my window sill. The nearest robin has taken to coming into the lobby where he makes my telephone his shit house. He takes no notice of the cards that say "WASHROOM FURTHER IN".[331]

SIX

CODA

A strong song tows
us, long earsick.
Blind, we follow
rain slant, spray flick
to fields we do not know.

Briggflatts, Coda

AN INTENTIONAL SLUM

'Do you think if I made my tea with whisky instead of water', Bunting asked
Tom Pickard in June 1978, 'I would find Washington more endurable? ...
The New Slum Development Corporation has made a splendid job of it.
All we need is a large Borstal and a big annex to Durham gaol.'[1] Bunting
left Corn Close on 29 June 1977 (according to the 'welcome home' letter
he left for Williams and Meyer) and moved to 107 Stridingedge, Blackfell,
Washington New Town, at the beginning of July 1977. He hadn't been
looking forward to the move to a 'huge slave barracks designed by a team of
lunatics', as he put it in a letter to Roudaba.[2]

'I must change the country and the fells for a loathsome industrial town
on the latest improved principles,' he lamented to Eric Mottram. The
town had offered a house to Northern Arts and Northern Arts offered it to
Bunting. He conceded that his new home was better designed than standard
council accommodation, indeed that it was a lot bigger than it seemed,
but he wasn't terribly happy: 'Outside, you might hold a competition for
hideousness without finding anything so ugly; and the view is of its twins, or
of the unrelieved brick walls of garages. There is a minute burn running by
the door, spared as a sop to nature; but already a dump, with wrecked prams
and skinned umbrellas in it. And the distance to <u>fields</u> is in all directions

15–20 miles of frantic traffic and squalid houses.'[3] To some extent, as Gael Turnbull noticed, his new environment was no more than a symbol of a world that had self-destructed:

'Those buildings are a disgrace. Only put up 10 years ago. From prefabricated sections. Falling to bits already.' But he couldn't specify exactly where and how they were defective. It was all just part of the general slovenliness of a world that admired the poetry of Geoffrey Hill. 'He's got all the technique. He knows just how to do nothing wrong. Except that there's nothing right. Just nothing there. And they once had the cheek to ask me to write something praising it. Even the Tower isn't what it was. But then, nothing is. Everything changes. It's a natural process.'[4]

He quickly developed a jaundiced view of his new home. He told Carroll F. Terrell that he 'lived in a nest of criminals; that most of the people in Black Fells village had been in jail one time or another; and that hardly a family in his row of houses didn't have one member, male or female, in jail right now.'[5] With at least four spells in jail himself in four different countries perhaps he felt that he had a right to such a view. Tom Pickard thinks that Northern Arts was using Bunting as a guinea pig in a social experiment to see what happens when a poet is embedded in one of the most deprived estates in the region.[6]

One compensation was the presence of the local children. According to Peter Quartermain 'his great tolerance of and patience with children extended to, embraced, and delighted in children of three shouting "fuck off!" or "kick the dog in the balls!"'[7] Bunting wrote to Jonathan Williams in August 1977 that

children alone make the place endurable. Four or five boys last night who had made their bicycles horses to drag home-made chariots racing round our nearest spot of green at a great pace, in defiance, apparently, of the police, who do not notice that if they prohibit such an entirely harmless infringement of the laws there'd be nothing left for the boys to do but break street lamps, telephone kiosks and people's cars. They got on fine with me, made me Emperor to start the races. Or two little boys and a little girl so loquacious that she kept me sitting ¾ of an hour on my doorstep without ever closing her lips for ten consecutive seconds, telling me about a deceased goldfish.[8]

The admiration was mutual. Carroll Terrell described his arrival in Blackfell: 'A few hundred yards into a dell from the bus stop, two little girls around nine or ten ran down to greet Basil and give me a careful scrutiny. He called them by name, answered their questions, paused to be pleasant, and after a bit waved them back to their play. His smile said he liked them. They certainly liked him.'[9] Tom Pickard also noted the permanent presence of the children: 'the children are always knocking on his door. And he answers it. Children love him. Sometime I hear Washington intonations dancing in his speech.'[10]

Bunting had a real affinity with young children. During his disastrous visit to the University of Victoria in 1971–72 he made friends with Mike Doyle's youngest daughter, Meki, then two years old. He wrote to Doyle from Wylam in July 1973: 'I'm glad to have news of my friend Meki. I was reminded of her strongly the other day when, in Newcastle Central Station, a little girl of two or two and a half ran up to me and embraced my legs, then held up her hand for mine – a child who had never seen me before but knew a grandfather when one hove in sight.'[11] William Corbett recalled Bunting's two-week visit to his family home in 1975: 'Our daughter Arden, then six, took a shine to him as he did to her. Opening our front door late one afternoon Beverley saw and heard Basil charging up our very steep stairs with Arden on his back. Both of them flushed and yelling for joy. Unabashed boys and girls indeed, and he meant to keep them that way.'[12]

Terrell described his first impressions of Bunting's home in Washington New Town and doesn't seem to have been shocked by the deprivation:

> The hall was about eight feet long with a small but complete kitchen to the left. It opened onto a large L-shaped room with an alcove under a staircase to the right, which had a telephone stand and chair and bookcases against the wall. To the left was a large oblong dining table of old gleaming wood, which could seat ten people with no trouble. A bookcase against the wall held a small radio. The dining area opened without walls to a long rectangular room about ten by twenty feet, which formed the base of the L. On the left, some wide windows and a glass door opened onto a garden area outside. To the right another large glassed-in bookcase was against the wall. In the center of the back wall was a working desk jutting at right angles into the room. One sitting at the desk and typewriter would look down the base of the L. The desk was covered with papers and correspondence. In the area before the windows, which reached from ceiling to floor, there were three overstuffed easy chairs, where one could sit and talk. Altogether the setting seemed bright and cheerful.[13]

To Quartermain, however, the environment was bleak: 'he lived in a bare and ugly row house in a cramped jungle of concrete-block and brick houses in dead-end curving streets where by car it is a mile or even two to a neighbour's house less than fifty yards along the footpath; impossible to police; crammed with unemployed (like many another 'new town'); hundreds of snotty-nosed kids running round with nothing to do and nowhere to play except scruffy minute patches of grass, or the dead-end street.'[14]

Apart from the children the only other compensation in Washington New Town was the supermarket which, perhaps surprisingly, had a 'truly excellent range of cheeses. Their wine too is not bad. And the fish. Not up to Lisbon, of course, but quite impressive. Not that I buy any. It stinks up the house. I prefer my fish from the fish and chip shop.'[15] Turnbull painted a deft portrait of the ageing poet in Washington New Town:

> Coming away, up the path, past the roses gone wild and all to hips, reminding [me] of MacDiarmid 'umber burnt madder and straw', and the fire-weed, and two white butterflies on the thistles, very attentive to the purple heads, and to each other. 'They'll be off to lay their eggs on Mr. Rutherford's cabbages.' Having showed me a typescript of his introduction to his last reading in London. 'It was my last. I'll never go there again. It's a dreadful place.' Very much the 'poor old man'. After 'sixty years of work without pay.' While the children shouted at him 'Hello, Mr. Bunting!' and he'd reply 'Hello, hinny.' Muttering 'On two tiny pensions, together not as much as the standard Old Age Pension.'[16]

Another visitor to Washington New Town was the poet August Kleinzahler who has left a touching anecdote about Bunting and Sima, now semi-reconciled. Even after their divorce, Kleinzahler noticed that

> there remained great affection between them and Sima liked nothing better than taking the piss out of him, especially in front of an adoring, young American admirer. She made us a beautiful Persian dinner of lamb in pomegranate sauce and said: 'Do you know why I divorced him? Because he promised me he would die twenty years ago and he never did. The old bastard will never die. He's preserved in whisky and cigarette smoke!' Basil laughed his always alarmingly violent, sixty years of unfiltered Players, chain-smoker's laugh. Sima was very much a Near Eastern woman: warm, voluble, emotionally intense, sharp as a tack. And at 44, still extremely handsome and a strong sexual presence. Basil was very proud of her.[17]

During this visit, in spring 1978, Bunting told Kleinzahler how Robert Lowell had written to him to tell him how much he admired Bunting's work and that he wished to pay Basil a visit. As Bunting put it to Kleinzahler, 'as is my custom with visiting writers I went to the library to find a book of his so I could quote to him a poem, or passage from a poem, that I especially admired. I wound up wasting an entire fooking afternoon going through his entire output and not finding a single poem worth a damn. Fortunately, he changed his mind at the last minute about coming up for a visit.'[18]

Bunting was convinced that his health suffered as a consequence of his accommodation. In the summer of 1977 he had what his doctor described as: 'the ghost of a stroke. It hasn't disabled me, only all my right side is numb. My hand does what it's told, but it doesn't feel things – light things not at all – so that I cannot pick up a needle anyhow and my handwriting has become very laborious and more illegible than ever. Also it affects the corner of my mouth so that once in a while a word is slurred, which rather hampers my public reading though I can control it with an effort.'[19] He told MacDiarmid he was in 'the nastiest place I've ever had to inhabit … a stroke has made my right side numb – cant hold a needle, cant help dropping my cigarette, which complicates life for an old man all alone'.[20] Turnbull noticed that he turned his right hand over on the table and moved his fingers, 'like a sheep dog, once entirely faithful, now a bit suspect.'[21]

He had had in 1970 a 'rodent ulcer, which they've burned, and forbidden me to wash the north-west corner of my face for the next three months',[22] and since then he had undergone an annual check-up on his 'cancerous tendencies'.[23] Constant poverty can't have helped his health, but his friends continued to be generous. He told Jonathan Williams in May 1978 that:

Ping Ferry and his wife Carol came and were very pleasant … They left, secretly, an envelope on my desk with a cheque for 500 pounds … And still I'll be broke. Sima is in great difficulties and though she hasn't asked me for anything I'll have to come to her rescue. How she gets into these messes is partly mysterious, but just as I couldn't leave her with empty cupboards a few months back or with no heating during the cold spell, I can't leave her to be sold up for rates and taxes. Being divorced is proving almost as expensive as being married, though there's no alimony.[24]

Bunting was generous himself when he could be. He sent Tom Pickard a cheque for £50 in July 1978 to help with the cost of his wedding, but the overall picture is consistently bleak.[25]

He delivered an extraordinary peroration the following year at a reading at Keats House in London, during which he told his audience that it was almost certainly the last time he would speak in London given his age (it wasn't):

> I've noticed in the past few years a darker reaction than any I remember except at the beginning of the 1930s, in all things, in politics, in social morals, in literature. To be sure there are always of course wild men to be laughed at – not pelted – by people who refrain from making rash experiments in order to follow recipes that have been tried before and didn't work ... I do find a ridiculous number of young men who are, as Pound said of Dante ... 'ideas of long ago, unburied though rotten'. Of course I'm thinking chiefly of poetic techniques, but there's also a great rush to throw reason overboard and trust in one magic or another, to achieve wisdom without toil by practising the rights of some church or other, or stilling the argumentative parts of your brain with drugs. Those who have neither gone Buddhist nor psychedelic are apt still to desert God for the church which exists by concealing God, and which is partly responsible for the revival of censorship by irresponsible police or customs men, and for blasphemy prosecutions and laws against undefined obscenity, for all that Mrs Whitehouse symbolises. ... If I set aside the handful of people who over-praise my verses and the few who take the trouble to run them down, I think nobody takes any notice of them ... I live on two small pensions, which together amount to somewhat less than the usual old age pension, in a house which is not mine, where Northern Arts allows me to stay, in part of a new town, planned for the greatest possible density of population; in short, an intentional slum. I'm not complaining, but describing conditions an honest poet must expect, and they will get worse not better. Yet I think something is wrong where arts administrators draw salaries immeasurably more generous than any income that they find appropriate for an originating artist, though they can be quite generous to performers. And I think it's unfortunate for England, as well as for myself, that after 60 years of fairly good work without pay I haven't even a house of my own to die in.[26]

This is classic Bunting rhetoric, rolling up a number of sincerely held criticisms of the modern world – 'in all things, in politics, in social morals, in literature' – in an overarching metanarrative of disgust at the way society treats some of its most talented individuals, with himself as the prime example.

He wasn't enjoying his old age, he told Denis Goacher: 'I cannot really blame anybody for even a part of it, since I chose the path I have followed with my eyes open. If I am very poor and very uncomfortable and decidedly lonely, I foresaw it all when I took to poetry. And yet I don't kick myself. I know I was right to do so.'[27]

ACKNOWLEDGEMENT OF HIS GREATNESS

In 1976 Stuart and Deirdre Montgomery decided to fold Fulcrum Press and so *Collected Poems* went out of print. Bunting offered a third (revised) edition to Oxford University Press although James Laughlin had been trying to obtain the rights for New Directions in the US.[28] He told Jonathan Williams in February 1977 that the syndics had accepted a third edition of his *Collected Poems*, although he was predictably scathing about the proposed royalty.[29]

Oxford's new edition of *Collected Poems* was released in 1978. Philip Toynbee reviewed it in the *Observer* and agreed with Cyril Connolly's judgement that *Briggflatts* was 'the finest long poem to be published in English since "Four Quartets"'. *Collected Poems* was one of Toynbee's three books of the year in the *Observer*. Martin Booth celebrated the poetry's 'truth, its integrity and its intense, soft power' in *Tribune*. The *Guardian* described the appearance of *First Book of Odes* and *Loquitur* in 1965 as 'one of the most electrifying literary moments of the sixties resurgence' and thought that *Collected Poems* put 'a major literary collection ... back into circulation'. Jeff Nuttall, in the *Guardian*, dismissed some new collections, despairing of public taste as much as Bunting did: 'It is obviously not widely understood among both the amateurs and the conservative literati that form and tradition are not the same thing, that there is more painstaking craftsmanship and metrical skill in one line of Basil Bunting than there is in the entire work of John Betjeman.'

Nigel Wheale gave *Collected Poems* a baffling review in *Poetry Review* in which he considered Bunting's poetry as falling back 'to Tennysonian orderings of the poetic surface'. It is difficult to understand how anyone might reach this conclusion. In fact Craig Raine, in the *New Statesman*, had already specifically excluded any 'Tennysonian' effect where he hailed *Briggflatts* as Bunting's 'great, tragic masterpiece ... the voice is totally achieved, consonantal, shy of Tennysonian *bel canto*, chary of the definite article, mutedly alliterative. The overdraft is paid off.'

Donald Hall put Pound's influence in context in the *New York Times Book Review* and pointed out that Wordsworth and Browning are just as important. G. S. Fraser noted in the *Times Literary Supplement* that the publication of a poet's 'Collected Poems' by Oxford University Press was 'an acknowledgment of his greatness, a recognition that he belongs to the canon'. Roger Guedalla was quick to point out in *Time Out* that, OUP notwithstanding, there wasn't much reward in 'a life devoted to exploring all the possible resources of language. Little fame and no reward to speak of, but the sense of a very difficult job very well done.'[30]

In 1978 Bunting was also fretting about publishing *The Pious Cat*, a loose translation of a fouteenth-century Persian children's story by Obaid-e Zakani: 'You must call him "Obeyed", like the English word "obeyed a command", "obeyed a zaw-kaw-nee"; and save most of the breath for the "nee",' Bunting wrote in a note to the poem. 'He wrote this story about six hundred years ago, and Persian children still read it at school, or they used to, twenty years since. Any story that lasts as long as that is worth listening to, I think. Perhaps not everything in it is true, but bits of it are very true indeed.'[31]

He wrote to Mottram on 7 February 1978 to apologise for the delay in sending the manuscript, 'Put it down to irresolution', and the sources of that irresolution were numerous: 'I doubt whether it is worth preserving, whether the time when it was apposite (1939) will ever have a parallel; and I feel that publishing it might look like a severe criticism of Omar Pound's version (Gorby and the Rats) which I don't intend in the least. All the same, having gone so far, read it to an audience, interested Susan Bland, it might be difficult and might look pusillanimous to draw back now.' As though an unintentional slight of Dorothy Pound's son Omar were not enough, there were other sensitivities: '"Matamora"[*sic*], Guedalla's concern, wants to print it, but cant take pictures, or only line drawings, which Mrs Bland hasnt been asked for. I'm in two minds about that too. On the one hand it might increase the chance of snaring a commercial publisher, on the other it might look like an attempt to jettison Mrs Bland.' Even if this dilemma could be reconciled, 'in such a high-flown, ambitious publication as Matamora it would look out of place and cause some eyebrow raising, I suppose that might have worried Guedalla.'[32] It's something of a shock to find the resolute Basil Bunting in such a dither. Bunting didn't admire Omar Pound's 'Gorby and the Rats'. It was as though, he told William Cookson, Omar had 'written in gloves and with an eye on the orientalists. Mine cant be called a translation, beyond a line here or there, but an adaptation, which seems to me funny, and the only audience I've read it to laughed a good deal.'[33] He was still worrying it to death in March, though with an element of hand-washing: 'I dunno about the Pious Cat. I'm not so fearfully keen

on printing it. I'm chiefly concerned about Mrs Bland and her drawings.
Still, if you want it for your new paper I'll try to square it with her provided
you let me know in time to write a little fore-note, bowing to Omar Pound
etc etc.'[34] I'm sure he wouldn't have struggled like this when he wrote the
poem forty years previously, but forty years previously Omar Pound, Roger
Guedalla and Susan Bland weren't around to be consulted and Bunting
wasn't a lonely old man of seventy-eight living on an unlovely council estate
in Washington New Town.

The reissue of Bunting's *Collected Poems* by Oxford University Press in
March 1978 should have been cause for celebration but he had little time for
OUP. He complained to an audience at a reading at Keats House in London
in 1979 that 'even my publisher hasn't bothered to let me know for all but a
year whether any copies of my *Collected Poems* have been sold or not; and I've
never seen the book on sale in a bookshop.'[35]

It seems that the contempt was mutual. Even the launch of the OUP
edition was a disaster. Eric Mottram recalled it bitterly, although the occasion
gave him the opportunity to rehearse his hatred of the Poetry Society:

> Of course when Oxford University Press published Basil Bunting finally,
> was there any acknowledgement at all, as to who had published Basil over
> the years, and looked after him? Not in the least. Oxford University Press
> just crowed. There was no acknowledgement and thanks anywhere to Stuart
> Montgomery, or Tom Pickard, or Migrant Press, at all. Just to support Basil,
> I went to the launching of Oxford University Press's edition of his *Collected
> Poems*. When I got there, Basil was seated on his own, in a pretty ragged jersey
> and jacket and trousers, and nobody was talking to him at all. He didn't even
> have a glass in his hand. But the dreaded Abcess was there, yacketing on.
> A ghastly person called Josephine Fox, who was Charles Osborne's assistant
> at the trial that interrogated me [the Witt enquiry], was there. She comes
> marching across and says: "I wonder if you remember me?", I said "Yes I do.
> Fuck off, you bitch!". "Oh" she says. I said "Yes, oh". They think it's all some
> sort of game. It was dreadful, in fact; humiliating for Basil and everything he
> stood for.[36]

In a review of *Collected Poems* Peter Mortimer described Bunting's life and
noted that living in Washington New Town 'must simply seem gruesomely
unimaginative to one who has led such a life'.[37] *Collected Poems* was not a
major success. In 1984 he complained to Tom Pickard that his publisher
had taken 'no pains to sell anything – I had last year's statement from O.U.P.

Royalties £4. Back where E.P. was in 1930, or worse, since £4 then was worth about £100 now.'[38]

WE HAVE NO COURSE TO SET

Grudgingly accepting an invitation from Mottram for an event in August 1977 Bunting complained about the accommodation to be provided ('hugger-mugger bunk beds'), the fee ('nowt'), the young ('let them find out by failing, as I had to') and, most of all, the trappings of age: 'It's bad enough to be old without advertising one's disabilities – obscene teeth, fuzzy lenses, worn out clothes and skin. What I didn't mind when I was vigorous and curious, among soldiers and barbarian huns, has become hard to endure.'[39]

Bunting's health was now starting to fail. He suffered a slight stroke in 1979 and he was deeply lonely. Colin Simms wrote to Victoria Forde on 27 November 1979 that 'his loneliness, since the departure of most local poets to the South, is more acute. A great tragedy.'[40] Old friends were beginning to fade. He visited Hugh MacDiarmid on 25 April 1978:

> ... Valda had warned me I might only be allowed to talk to Chris for a few minutes – she would give the signal when he might be getting too tired. But the signal never came, and when I myself insisted on going after four and a half hours they both lamented. Valda said he had been better than she had seen him for a long time, she wished there were other old friends to come and put life into him.
>
> I'd taken a bottle of Glenfiddich. With a little help from Valda we finished it in the afternoon.
>
> In sum, rather better than I feared; but no doubt I saw him at what is now his best, and I rather gathered that the day to day scene is pretty depressing. I don't suppose I am likely to see him again, which will be goodbye to quite a lot that I can share with nobody else ...
>
> His huge Collected Poems is due out next month. "They'll take no notice," he said. "They'll boycott you and me till the end." I think he suggested that that was because we were not gentlemen, but maybe that was something I thought later at the inn.[41]

The following month he wrote wistfully to Jonathan Williams about the death on 12 May of his old friend Louis Zukofsky:

I had heard nothing about Zukofsky's dying until your letter arrived, nor had I any idea that he was ill, except in so far as he had always been ill since the 1920s. None of my friends told me, and I imagine it is quite possible that no English newspaper took any notice of it. Now, if it had been Mr. Larkin there'd have been acres of obituaries.

For a long time I've had to think sadly of Louis as a man who had no further use for my friendship – no quarrel, just apparent indifference: nevertheless I'm saddened further to think that there's no chance now of any renewal of our long correspondence; and that there'll be no more gritty poems to puzzle us. A step further towards isolation. Another affection banished to memory … I'm glad he finished 'A'. I daresay that he felt his business was completed.[42]

MacDiarmid's death on 9 September 1978 was no shock but Tibor Serly's on 8 October hit him hard. He wrote to Diana Collecott on 20 November 1978:

McDiarmid's [sic] death I expected and was prepared for. But Tibor Serly was killed by the London traffic actually on his way to meet me. The ghosts of his friends, Bartok and Kodaly are wailing regularly over the radio, and his death seems to me to snap the very last link with music, painting and poetry of the 1920s apart from my shaky recollections. Oh, maybe there are hangers-on still hanging on, but no originator left. And this town is like a tomb in a very bad part of the Inferno.[43]

Perhaps the loss of Zukofsky and MacDiarmid in 1978 prompted Bunting to put his own affairs in order. His last will and testament was drawn up in 1979. It left everything, such as it was, to Sima but expressed 'the clear wish and desire that she shall take account of the advice left in a letter which is to be found with this will and that she should deal with the items mentioned in the letter accordingly'. Though he and Sima had separated nearly three years before the will was lodged he clearly felt a keen responsibility towards her. His final ode is dated 1980 and deals unflinchingly with his marriages. It is addressed to his imaginary boat, and the first two stanzas show the ageing sailor reflecting on life:

Now we've no hope of going back,
cutter, to that grey quay
where we moored twice and twice unwillingly
cast off our cables to put out at the slack

when the sea's laugh was choked to a mutter
and the leach lifted hesitantly with a stutter
and sulky clack,

how desolate the swatchways look,
cutter, and the chart's stained,
stiff, old, wrinkled and uncertain,
seeming to contradict the pilot book.
On naked banks a few birds strut
to watch the ebb sluice through a narrowing gut
loud as a brook.

The poem was originally titled 'Perche no spero' (perhaps to recall Cavalcanti's 'Perch'i' no spero di tornar giammai') when published in *Agenda* in 1978. Bunting improved the poem in 1980 and it was published in its final version in the US edition of *Collected Poems* in 1985. The final stanza turns to face a certain future:

Soon, while that northwest squall wrings out its cloud,
cutter, we'll heave to
free of the sands and let the half moon do
as it pleases, hanging there in the port shrouds
like a riding light. We have no course to set,
only to drift too long, watch too glumly, and wait,
wait.[44]

There is no sentimentality in this poem, no self-pity and, for once, no self-recrimination. Somehow the way that the poem is spoken to the cutter removes the element of loneliness and allows the poet to speak as a kind of Everyman rather than as a disillusioned old man facing death.

I HAVE LIVED FOR TEN YEARS TOO LONG

'The eightieth birthday is past. I managed to ward off all proposals for celebrations, at least for a time, and just had my immediate family to lunch with me at a Greek place in Newcastle where we drank plenty of retsina and ouzo.'[45] Literary celebrations of Bunting's eightieth birthday were, however, unavoidable. At Warwick University, where Tom Pickard was Writer-in-Residence, Roy Fisher, Eric Mottram, Charles Tomlinson, Gael Turnbull and others read alongside Bunting but the event seems to have been something of a shambles, at least in Bunting's view. He wrote to Denis Goacher in April 1980 that the entire congress was organised by the students' union while Pickard was in Poland and that some of the invited poets had been selected by the students against Pickard's advice: 'The only invitees present whom I had suggested were Turnbull and Roy Fisher; and one or two had been brought against my express wishes. I think perhaps a lot of the students would have been quite happy to have me omitted if I hadnt been the excuse for the jamboree.'[46] If it was a shambles it was, at least, a shambles that Bunting fully expected:

> They crowded into Tom's little rooms and ate and drank everything they found there without consulting him or Joanna [Pickard's partner]. They talked alternatively bawdy with little point to it and the politics of their calling. One section seceded to some other room to devise means of ridding the Arts Council of Mr Osborne, pointless because his successor, whoever he might be would soon be up to the same tricks and manipulations. Others spoke ill of those who were absent from the room. All of them insisted on disorganising the programme that had been fixed by exceeding their alloted time, usually by about 60%. Many read so badly they couldn't be heard – a dreary drone: yet perhaps it was as well they werent heard, for there was no sense or point in their stuff ... an alleged 'folk' singer from the group called Lindisfarne, hitting a guitar the way these people do, as though it were a banjo or a ukelele. No 'folk' I can imagine had ever had anything to do with his words, which he'd doubtless concocted himself ... The universities own music man played the harpsichord, but did not understand how to phrase the Scarlatti sonatas he had practised for the occasion.[47]

The boorish behaviour that enlivened the Poetry Wars appears to have outlived the Battle of Earl's Court.

Birthday celebrations aside, Bunting's melancholy was growing. He wrote to Forde in May 1980:

> I am to go to a sort of miscellaneous jamboree at Orono, Maine, in August. It is partly concerned with Pound, partly with me, and partly just a general (pointless) gathering ... After that, I'll be finished with public reading, except for the two local universities and the Morden Tower, to which I feel some obligations; but first I may possibly read in Paris where my French translator Jacques Darras seems to be arranging something ...

> I have lived ten years too long. It is cheating the Bible to keep on after three score and ten; and so all my surviving friends of the past have died and I

sometimes feel very much alone. MacDiarmid died, Zukofsky died; Tibor Serly gave me the hardest blow, because he was on his way to see me. He telephoned about his journey from London, stepped out of the telephone kiosk and was knocked over by a bus and killed – within a minute of talking to me about our old, dead friends.

Old men talk nonsense and write silly stuff, so I don't write any more.[48]

Orono and Europe, 1980

Bunting went to Orono in Maine in August 1980 and stayed with the Kenners. Bourtai joined her father for the final time. Kenner's daughter, Lisa, published her own version of Bunting's visit after Bunting died in 1985. Lisa told how she flew up with her parents to Orono, where she was told that the family would be hosting

> an illustrious, and probably crabby, old poet in our summer house. Upon first seeing Basil Bunting I was taken by his ferocious grey eyebrows. His face, too, was intriguing – constantly seeming ruffled, annoyed, yet in control. At dinner that night, as Dad taught him how to crack lobster claws and suck out the meat and juices, I watched his eyes closely. They were hypnotically bright and expressive for such an old man. I thought this was perhaps the sign of a great poet … Before long Basil had taken an interest in this chubby ten-year-old who laughed and gibbered continuously, but who became remarkably quiet whenever he spoke. Maybe it was my giggles, or my love of producing all sorts of sounds, my youth, or perhaps even *my* brown expressive eyes; in any event, Basil informed me that I was to be his *saqhi*. It was at lunch that Basil clarified the duties of a *saqhi*. Ideally, the following sequence of events would take place in Persia. I, being the saqhi, would sit bowed on an embroidered pillow and pour wine for the hallowed poet. It would be a potent, exotic wine which I would pour into a thick goblet … The plans for the reading began with a banquet given in his honor. Then we would all go to hear him in the auditorium. I was to sit on a little wooden step-stool while he sat in an armchair and read *Briggflatts*. The wine was to act as a 'poetic aphrodisiac,' and I was to keep his glass filled.

Lisa was terrified at the prospect of being a saqi, but performed her duties well. Her account of the reading and of the rest of the week in Bunting's company is a moving account of friendship across generations:

I was inexplicably moved. All thoughts of the hard bench and the itches on my nose and my aching back left me. I was no longer mesmerized by his eyes; actually, I felt that I could not truly see them, because they were not registering on this plane. It was his voice – raspy, deep, purring, falling like water – that carried me away to a level of thinking which I can barely describe, truly remember or convincingly relate. All I know is that we were alone (he and I) in poetry. We were a self-sufficient unit which read poetry and poured wine … What else could I feel but love for this old man who linked arms with me at cocktail parties … After going upstairs and pulling out the book of poetry he autographed for me, I flip through the pages trying to impress on myself the genius of this man. All the same, it is not a celebrated English poet whom I miss; rather an old man who shared a week of his life with a lonely ten-year-old.[49]

Bunting accepted an invitation to Seattle from Roudaba after the Orono convention. 'I have to talk or read or lecture or something for three days at Orono, and then sit through four or five days of other people's literary guff.' After Seattle he was expecting to go 'to read and talk' in Paris and he was also planning a visit to Venice 'to see some pictures'.[50]

Paris turned out to be 'rather a queer trip':

They never left me alone for a second … I was driven about in Embassy cars and Ministry cars. When I wanted to see the only Balthus picture the French government owns, it turned out that the Museum of Modern Art was having its weekly day off, so I was quite reconciled to being disappointed: but someone telephoned to the Ministry, a number of the staff were recalled from their holiday, including the Director of the Museum, who showed me round, and I had the whole place to myself. Much the same happened at Amiens, where they closed the cathedral (on a Sunday afternoon!) so that the alleged chief expert could show me all its beauties in private.[51]

Venice was even better: 'Mr Ferry took it into his head to pay my expenses to go to Venice to see the show of Balthus's paintings. They were marvellous, better even than I'd expected.'[52] During this trip to Venice, he told Diana Collecott, he sat near Olga Rudge's apartment but couldn't knock on her door because he was so ashamed that he hadn't the wherewithal to buy her lunch.[53]

GREYSTEAD, 1981–1984

Bunting was never happy in Blackfell and was looking for an alternative home as soon as he moved in. He told Jonathan Williams in December 1979 that there were few options:

> Disappointments succeed one another, even when the cottage is suitable – I'm too old, or the landlord wants it back in six months to put his mother in, or I must have a wife who will help in the farmhouse etc etc. Mostly they are too small to get the books in, or too tumbledown. But we keep looking, while Blackfell grows more and more loathsome. There's a colony of 'skinheads' now amongst the boys of early teenage. One tried to hold me up with a knife the other day, demanding ten pounds. I told him he was going the right way towards the gaol and walked on, whereupon he stood and shouted abuse at me as long as I was within sight, but he hadn't the courage to knife me. Another pair tried to hold me up at my own door. I shut it, whereupon they crapped on the doorstep. An old man elsewhere in Washington was beaten up by such boys. There are still pleasant boys too, mostly very young. I chased most of the girls away who used to visit me. Too many of them stole in a small way.
>
> Altogether the place has grown more solitary than any rural cottage is likely to be.[54]

Bunting moved to The Cottage at Greystead in Tarset in May 1981 just as construction of the nearby Kielder Water, the largest artificial lake in the United Kingdom, was being completed. He was happy enough with the reservoir but unimpressed by the fact that the Queen was travelling north to officially open it: 'royalty's a big expense, no use'.[55] He was happier for the move, writing in an upbeat mood to Victoria Forde:

> But first let me call attention to my new address. It signifies that I have at last escaped from Washington, a place I detested, and am just settling in to a little house, pretty nearly where I've wanted to be for many years. I look out over a big garden (not mine but I can use it) to the hills of the dale of the North Tyne, covered with sheep, and lambs too at this season, with a glimpse of the river and quiet all around. Very big trees shelter me from most winds – an enormous ash grows right up against my chimney, and an owl lives in it which never fails to say goodnight to me. I'll miss the children who were the only good things about Washington, since the population of Tarset is only about 30, and no doubt I'll find shopping awkward, for the nearest shop is six miles

away and for anything more than basic needs I'll have to drive 25 miles into Hexham, down an exceedingly twisty road, which makes it nearly an hour's drive. But the place is so lovely nothing of that sort matters.[56]

Forde described Bunting's new home as a 'comfortably renovated stable, two stories. A small entryway led into a living room with a fireplace, the only heat source, with postcards on the mantel and books on each side, and wood and materials for a fire which he went down on his knees with difficulty each time to light, morning and evening. Stairs led to the second floor, icy cold, his small spare bedroom, the bathroom, and the small guest room with bed, chair, and dresser under a slanted roof with a skylight.'[57] He was clearly happy to be in the heart of his favourite landscape, watching the wildlife, even if it did lead to complications. He wrote to Peter Quartermain in September 1972:

Did I tell you about the cats? The snake-and-lizard man [poet and naturalist Colin Simms] came to see me, hunting a lizard said to have been seen in Northumberland, where it had no business to be. I mentioned casually the wild cats (Felix Sylvestris) now plentiful in the border forests. He got enormously excited, got on his motor-bicycle and rushed off to the forest, where he found three wild cats in a single evening. Apparently none of the farmers or forestry people had ever thought of mentioning wild cats to the naturalists, so it was news to *Nature*, which ran an article, and to the BBC's natural history section. They asked Simms *who* was an expert on wild cats and the damn man said I was; so for a week the BBC was ringing me everyday, trying to get me to admit that I knew all about wild cats. Now I had never even seen one loose, only heard about them in the pubs near the forests. They wouldn't believe me. At last I choked them off (their photographers got a good picture of one eating a pheasant), and went out for a ride, which took me into the forest. Coming down a very narrow remote lane I stopped to examine a hedgehog, deciding not to take it home to our garden because the dog and two cats would have gone mad trying to bite it, and just as I was about to get into the car again I saw a wild cat, stalking a couple of young rabbits. It was unmistakeably the wild creature, heavier on the haunch than the domestic cat, and with a head smaller in proportion to the body.[58]

The move was good for his health. He reported to Roudaba that he was in 'excellent health … far better than I ever was at Washington. I even walked nearly a mile the other day without my stick. It can only be (a) the good air here (what we had to breathe in Washington I don't know); (b) that

I am content, and happy every time I look out of the window and see the hills and the sheep.'[59]

Greystead is as remote a location as any to be found in England, and much more remote than most. Five miles of upland moor separates it from the nearest tiny village. The minor road on which the two Greystead properties are situated winds up for another ten miles or so past the source of the North Tyne river and over the Cheviot Hills and the border with Scotland. It is classic Reiver country. Throughout the Middle Ages and well into the early modern period the area around Tarset suffered from cross-border raids most winters, and the bastles (squat stone-built, earth-covered homes) the local communities built provided little protection. 'I'm not sure that you realise how remote my cottage is,' he wrote to Diana Collecott in November 1981. 'When you get to Hexham there are still 25 twisty miles to drive'.[60]

There was even a possibility of starting to write again in this isolated spot on the edge of the Kielder Forest: 'I don't expect to write any more. What a man of my age writes can seldom be any good. Nevertheless in such a splendid place, if there are no nagging worries, something might happen to get down on paper at last – even perhaps "The New Moon".'[61]

His confidence in May 1980 that his reading days were over, except locally, was wide of the mark. In the winter of 1982 he travelled to London for a series of readings, accompanied by Victoria Forde:

> people stood outside in the cold evening drizzle, uselessly hoping to squeeze into an already overcrowded room. At Riverside Studios where crowds were able to be accommodated, Bunting's unassuming son Tom could not get in because he did not have a ticket. When I discovered this and because I knew Tom from his welcome visits to our Notre Dame classes in London, I explained at the door and of course they let him in to hear his father. The Michael Henshaws were his attentive and gracious hosts who had small and large gatherings for him and his friends. Once after a three-hour dinner at a fine French restaurant with two publishers, we walked in and out of bookshops on our way to Foyles. At some places he asked quietly about the sales of his poems. A shop manager who recognised him treated him with deference, getting him a chair so he could browse at a table in a small room. With evident pleasure Bunting looked carefully through books about friends he had known in Paris and Italy and also earlier ones. But the walk to Foyles became too long and taxing, and he had to return to the Henshaws' home by taxi.[62]

Back in Greystead he wrote to Forde in February 1982, still enthusing about the local wildlife:

Since two days after I got home we have been having beautiful weather, bright sunshine and warm enough to do without a fire until the evening. There are hundreds and hundreds of snowdrops and crocuses out in the garden besides other flowers ...

I was very tired after London. It took almost a week to wear off, but I'm much as usual now. The Henshaws must be tired too. [The Henshaws had taken Bunting back to Greystead from London.] It was very cold the two days they stopped here.

The wild pheasant is back on the garden wall crowing, and the other birds were making quite a noise this morning, though the winter must have killed some of them. I don't see the finches around. I did see two of the peacocks from the farm, a bit bedraggled, but very selfpossessed strutting down the middle of the road, holding up the traffic.[63]

Barry Miles described Henshaw in his obituary in the *Guardian*:

Michael waged a one-man crusade against what he saw as the unfair treatment of artists and writers by tax inspectors. He insisted that the arts made a substantial contribution to the economy and, as far he was concerned, for a poet to go on a walking tour of the Lake District was just as valid a business expense as a visit to a factory by a businessman – a concept the Inland Revenue had trouble understanding. But many artists and writers were delighted to discover someone who appreciated what they were doing and was prepared to take on their financial problems, and his reputation quickly spread ... Michael's other media clients [other than the BBC's then director-general, John Birt] included television and film producers Ken Loach, Ken Trodd and Tony Garnett, theatre director Michael Bogdanov, broadcaster Humphrey Burton and actor Anthony Hopkins. Among his writers were David Mercer, David Hare, Fay Weldon, Alexander Trocchi, Simon Gray, Monty Python collectively, then Terry Jones and Michael Palin, as well as poets Ted Hughes, Basil Bunting, and even Allen Ginsberg when he was in Britain.[64]

No wonder Bunting liked him. Henshaw's creative energy made a real difference to his life. 'Maria has got a very good grant from the Northumberland County Council for her university,' he told Roudaba, 'the result of the rascality of an accountant whom I have employed to deal with my income tax. He's a nice chap, who does it for next to nothing "for the love of art" and who used to be an income tax collector himself. Somehow he conjures up allowable expenses which eat up almost all the income, thus reducing the tax and making a deplorable show of poverty which the County Council has to count in when it assesses Maria's grant.'[65]

Forde visited Bunting in March. Sima had prepared a room for her but, to Forde's regret, the two didn't meet: 'ever since I had read Basil's letter to Louis Zukofsky about Sima's surreptitiously putting a piece of the Communion Bread in her husband's meal so that he made his Easter Communion in Persia, I had wanted to meet her.'[66] It isn't clear whether Sister Victoria Forde, Sister of Charity, admired Sima's piety or her mischief.

They must have made an odd couple. Bunting, the octogenarian 'atheist Quaker' and the young, devout, Catholic, American research student, but he made her welcome, ensuring that the windscreen wipers worked on his car so that he could drive her around the country he loved so much:

> Basil drove me all over the countyside proudly pointing out so much that would help me to absorb the atmosphere of Northumberland. Its distant past was like recent history to him, and in the evenings he could enthrall a listener by telling stories of past and present before the fire which warmed his small cottage.
>
> His deep love of the north was evident as he showed me such places as Hadrian's Wall, nearby Hermitage Castle and Newcastleton, and the little pub in Liddisdale, Scotland. At Hexham Abbey he persuaded someone to open the crypt so we could see the ancient fragments. Each place he knew so well, not only geographically but historically, with all the famous people of each age discussed as if they were intimate friends. He was not strong enough to share everything he spoke of – a walk along the Roman Wall, Lindisfarne when the tide was out, and Briggflatts. But with the help of his daughter Maria when his car broke down, we covered even more of the area around Hexham.[67]

The fabled anthology

Jonathan Williams described discussions about Bunting's 'fabled *Anthology*' in 1983:

> Along with 1983's longest day and the mysterious advent of actual sunshine on the center court at Wimbledon, Mr. Bunting has arrived in his venerable, rusty Daf motor car at Corn Close for his annual siesta-cum-fiesta. This

features Tom Meyer as *chef de cuisine* and conversationist, serving up opinion, linguistics, joints of beef, pesto, Blue Wensleydale, curries, apple tarts, etc., for washing down with Theakston's bitter beer, the Wine Society's aged Rioja, and Hugel's Gewürztraminer. Tennis and the deracination of dandelions from the garden occupy my mind this week until evenings. And then it's time to open the Caledonian fire-water and discuss the vagaries of poetry and the miseries of the times. Last night we did considerable damage to a bottle of Lagavulin malt whiskey from the Island of Islay ... Basil got to grumbling about the infirmities of the aged. But, he's still driving a car at 83 (often at 83 mph); he's quicker in the head than most men in Northumberland or anywhere else.[68]

I wish Bunting's anthology had appeared. It would have been a wonderful book, with few of the obvious candidates and many surprises. Williams tried. While Bunting was asleep he 'got to thinking that we should devote some time this week to putting down on paper the poems and poets he would put into the fabled *Anthology* that he has spoken of compiling for many years now. Lest he never get around to the job, the basic information ought to be made available.'[69] Bunting had described his proposed anthology to Williams six years previously:

> The plan was not to put in the best poets necessarily, or the best poems, but to try and demonstrate, from the English everybody knows – without going to Old English, and even excluding Middle English – to try and show the principles on which poetry works ... Right up to 1640 you can say that a poet wasn't a poet unless he was capable of playing a musical instrument and composing his poems to that ... If you will read Wyatt and Sidney and Campion you'll get a good idea of poetry as song. But Sidney's slightly older contemporary, Spenser, invented a new thing which has given a complexion to English verse ever since, so one must have Spenser there also. Spenser made the words produce their own music, instead of depending on the musician to do it.[70]

Williams wanted Bunting to list 'the Great Instructors, the ones you read to learn how to construct your poems'. For some reason he started this riveting series of conversations with a bizarre suggestion that Bunting's friendship with Pound had been sexual. Once Bunting had parked that ('Ezra would have been absolutely horrified. He was a bit of a prude in some ways.') he was free to describe his project. The anthology would begin with the Greeks, Sappho and the 'firm architecture' of Homer's *Iliad*, before moving on to the Welsh poets, Aneirin and Heledd, and the medieval Persian poets Ferdosi, Manuchehri and Hafez. Then:

Dante: 'The combination of extremely terse and vivid language with a sonority which is always adapted to what is going on makes practically the whole of the *Commedia* (for people who bother to read it in Italian) absolutely unforgettable. You'll remember more lines and passages of Dante than any other poet.'

Wyatt: 'Wyatt learned to write lyric poetry in Italy to his own accompaniment on the lute, which is what the Italian poets were used to doing. Naturally, he made use of the devices of song-writers and composers of his day ... All Wyatt's editors until well into this century thought they could write better poetry than Wyatt and altered him accordingly. Notably, Sir Arthur Quiller-Couch in the *Oxford Book of English Verse*. Wyatt's poetry is practically all for singing.'

Malherbe: 'still writing to be sung. He complained to his friend Racan that he had been handicapped all his life because he had never been taught to finger the lute. He paid immense attention to the texture of his verse, so that he could make a perfectly smooth stanza out of the ordinary spoken syntax of French.'

Spenser and Sidney: 'They were particularly interested in the sound of English words. Sidney spent a great deal of time investigating quantity in verse instead of stress. Spenser tried his hand at it, but he was interested in so many aspects of versification that he let it drop. He wrote "The Shepherd's Calendar" to show the great variety of English versification, so that poets, for several generations after, could dip into Spenser and find what they wanted to imitate.'

Wordsworth: 'very musical. He wrote in very plain language, usually with very plain syntax, and made it musical and forceful all at once ... What's never mentioned is his extreme narrative skill, greater than any other English poet save Chaucer, perhaps. Secondly, they overlook entirely his humour. Very comic stuff, an early kind of humour that again reminds one of Chaucer.'

And ... Darwin: 'I sometimes recommend a non-poet to aspiring writers as someone who can teach them about putting things together: and that is Charles Darwin ... Any competent writer must know the importance of *things*. The moment you leave off into abstract words you lose touch, with the reader and the music and the world. So stay away from Plato.'

So there was to be no Chaucer, Shakespeare or Keats, but he included two poems by Tom Pickard, rather implausibly, between Zukofsky and Cranmer. Yeats had only three poems included and Eliot just the first part of *The Waste Land*. The eccentricity of this splendid enterprise is nowhere better celebrated than by the inclusion of 'John Lennon's "Yellow Submarine"' (actually Paul McCartney's) between Ben Jonson and Edward Lear.

The interview must have got lost in the Lagavulin. We know from an earlier interview that Bunting planned to include Samuel Butler, Lewis Carroll and Swinburne and it's inconceivable that he would have omitted Pound.[71]

What innocence!

In March 1983 Bunting celebrated his eighty-third birthday in London with Stuart and Deirdre Montgomery, who 'had a little party ... much wine, much laughter, going home at 2.30 a.m. I stayed at Henshaw's house by Regent's Park, but I have aged enough to prevent me going out onto the streets of London even once.'[72] But not so much to prevent him from travelling the length of the country to Devon later that month to help judge the Arvon International Poetry Competition. Anyone who submits poems to national competitions will be interested in Bunting's description of the selection process:

> In the South I spent several days with six other poets in Devonshire, as guests of Ted Hughes, finishing the judging of 33,000 poems! Three of them had first of all reduced the number to 1,800 or so by throwing out those they thought the very worst. Adrian Mitchell lightened his share (11,000) by making a private collection of the most preposterous entries. He read us a few of them for fun. A poem about the soldiers who were killed by a bomb while parading through Hyde Park began 'Klip-klop, klip, klop, kilp-klop, BANG!' but then, I'm afraid, fell off into maudling. I read all my 1,800 poems without finding a good one, or more than three or four that were excusable. That was exhausting, if you like! One of the judges was a tiresome fool, who spent half a day reading entries aloud in order to tell us why he didn't recommend that one. That might have gone on for ever, if I hadn't made an alliance with Stephen Spender to reverse the procedure and get them to exhibit only the poems they did recommend for the main prizes, and in that way we polished the poems off at a good pace and finished with half a day to spare. They were all so bad that I didn't care what the result was, yet three of the first five prizes

were poems I had chosen. After the choice, we were told the names of the authors, and not one of the 35 prizewinners was anybody we had ever heard of. Earlier, I had recognised, from the style, one poetess, but her poem was bad and I chucked it out, and nobody else mentioned it.[73]

This process was written up by Michael Davie in the *Guardian*. Bunting

> sits attentively, beard jutting forward: a spry presence, not saying a great deal, but when he does speak, being very much to the point, like Attlee in Cabinet … his sharpest expression of disapproval is to say that a poem is 'an English Department poem' … Over the pheasant Mr Bunting reminisced. He went to Paris in 1922 with 10s. 6d., and left for Italy a year later with £25. He met everyone. What was Ford Madox Ford like? 'Fat. Enormously fat.' Eliot? 'You could joke with him, and you could laugh at him. You can't be friends with someone you can't laugh at.' George Barker, sitting next to him, whispered to me behind his hand: 'What a man! What innocence!' Back in the hotel where the poets were staying, the conviviality continued. Mr Bunting sat beside a huge log fire, upright, hands resting on his stick in front of him. At two o'clock in the morning, glass at his side, aged 83, he seemed immortal. He said he had put Eliot on to Kipling, but didn't think Eliot had done him justice.[74]

Bunting made a tremendous impression on Spender, who recorded his memories in the *London Review of Books*. He recalled that Bunting told the other judges, Gwendoline Brooks, Adrian Mitchell, George Barker and Spender himself, 'stories that held us spellbound. With his domed head, beard, glittering eyes under Mephistophelean eyebrows, Basil Bunting has the buccaneering look of one who has sailed a *bâteau ivre* through oceans of poetry and arrived in port. I envy him. Of the 33,000 poems submitted there were only about five lines that Basil Bunting – harking back to the crystalline standards of Pound and Eliot's generation – approved.'[75]

Bunting was clearly on form but it was a huge effort. He returned to Tarset exhausted 'having been nearly three weeks in the South judging that silly poetry competition'.[76] One wonders which element of this he found more painful, the competition or the 'South'.

He may have been tired of London but he loved the environment around Greystead, and there is a poignant identification with the self-possessed dog fox in his description of the local wildlife to Forde in March 1983:

Your flowers are further on than ours. Our daffodils are only promising to blossom, though we have our usual early profusion of snowdrops, thousands of them, amongst the trees and by the path.

We've a very fine fox about, astonishingly big and astonishingly bold. He often comes to raid our rubbish bins. Sometimes he brings his lady friend with him, so that we could reconstruct what they were up to from their tracks in the snow while there was snow. The fox goes and peeps through the pub window to see who is there, and the vixen goes every night to a house at the Eals where they put out food for her. She is partial to bread and marmalade. No one will help the Tynedale hunt to get either of those two. We are really proud of the dog-fox, who walks amongst the flocks of an afternoon, scared of no one and nothing.[77]

He was thrilled by the visit of a rare goshawk. 'I'd no idea it was such a lovely bird till it trapped itself in my lobby,' he told Tom Pickard. 'In fact I'd been told that it did not live in this island but that seems to have been a mistake. Its red-brown zigzag bars and rounded wings, its tail and its claws were all shown to me in detail before I could manoeuvre it safely out to the air again.'[78]

Bunting loved the quiet environment of Greystead but he hadn't forgotten how to enjoy himself in company. Derek Smith remembered the 83-year-old poet after a reading he filmed before Newcastle's literati:

The magnificent job done, our 83-year-old poet revelled until late, oblivious of the party going on in full swing around him. Basil was busy entertaining two attractive young women, one on his knee, while the other seemed to be enjoying the grip of his right arm and frequent kisses. The last drops of wine and whisky consumed, Basil and Colin Simms staggered to a taxi and headed towards the Keelman's Hospital on Sandgate for Hexhamshire and home, singing bawdy songs in thick Northumbrian to the tune of 'Cushy Butterfield.'[79]

An inoffensive old piece of rubbish

In the autumn of 1983 a film crew led by Richard Else spent a week making a documentary about Bunting at Corn Close. Jonathan Williams facilitated it and, according to Else, Bunting too 'got fired up – the notion of a plan devised around good beer and food guides; the run of Corn Close and a whole week talking about anything BUT his work was novel.'[80] Else brought a case of Glenfiddich to lubricate the process. Bunting talked more freely than usual about his life and told stories about climbing in the Lake District with the Abraham brothers of Keswick, imprisonment as a conscientious objector at the end of the First World War and exotic opium-laced tales from Persia:

> So our days continued: B.B. walking amongst the ruins of Pendragon Castle. Sixty-five and more years ago he cycled here as a kid up from Sedbergh and Garsdale ... Looking at those images the day after his death it became more clear. Another friend of Basil's rang and confirmed what I sensed: that in allowing us into the lives, Basil had a clear sense of a few glimpses that would do to remain after he'd gone. "I think I'll fade away quite soon ... probably this winter," he said on film. J.W., visibly alarmed, reached for the Bells, determined to put it off a little longer. Basil thought our film "wouldn't do any harm." Praise indeed.[81]

In fact Bunting was impressed by the result. He wrote approvingly to Williams in March 1984: 'Else's film proved to be good – I even think, very good. Not that there was any fearfully good photography, but he not only avoided the usual T.V. claptrap and impertinence, he put his bits together without explaining to viewers who need no explanation, just leaving them to add up to their own total, Ezra-fashion. Colin Simms said it was "moving" – not an adjective I would have picked – and at least it seemed to show me as an inoffensive old piece of rubbish, which is reasonable.'[82]

Bunting seems to have been plagued by film-makers in his eighties. He told Roudaba in June 1981 that he was 'worn out by a damned film that is being made of me'.[83] Another 'infernal camera crew are coming here again on the 10th to tire me out,' he complained to Victoria Forde in March 1982.[84] Just a few months later another crew arrived from the US 'making yet more film, an exhausting business'.[85] In December he reported that: 'Philip Trevelyan has at last finished that film, eighteen months in the making, and I am told that the Arts Council is showing it in London on the fourteenth. Philip suggests showing it here first, in Mrs Grierson's [Bunting's landlady] big sitting room, to a very small invited audience.'[86]

WHITLEY CHAPEL, 1984–1985

Later in 1983 Mrs Grierson's lack of funds forced a move from the home he loved so much. He wrote to Jonathan Williams in April: 'Mrs Grierson's debts have multiplied till she feels obliged to sell the house, cottage and all, so I'm under sentence of moving again but at a date yet to be fixed. The best hope is that she will be too greedy to attract any buyer. Otherwise I must look about for a new home, and I'm not likely to find one as good as this – if any at all.'[87]

That year was spent in an increasingly dispirited search for suitable new accommodation. By the end of the year he was hoping to secure a National Trust property at Cambo but, as ever, the establishment had parked its tanks between the poet and his goal. He wrote to Williams again on 19 November 1983:

> The prospects of the house at Cambo seem dim, though not quite vanished, chiefly because of the red-tape in the National Trust. God knows how many people have to agree before they can let it to me, and I think a lot of that many must have their own candidates. Officials of the Trust seem to have first call, and then perhaps relatives of the Trustees. Poets come low in the scale, after ruined county gentlemen. They asked me whether I hunt! (I should have responded "Only Tories – out of season.")'[88]

He was in good shape in spite of his accommodation worries. He wrote to Tom Pickard in fine spirits in November 1983: 'I stay healthy. It is wonderful how my rheumatisms have disappeared since I came to live here, and I am afraid of them coming back when I move away, but though I can't walk more than ¼ mile or so I am fairly spry, eat fearfully, drink a lot and sleep perfectly. Not bad, for nearly 84.'[89]

He stayed with friends and family and then spent the winter in rented accommodation in Bellingham. This wasn't ideal. He wrote to Williams in March 1984:

> No home has been traced yet, though there is one which will not be finally struck off the list of possibilities till Monday, so I am likely to take advantage of Corn Close in the first week of April, in spite of the extreme unreliability of my car. (I have to be out of here on March 31, but can probably stretch it a few days.) This address will do a bit longer because my landlord here is the postmaster and will take care of forwarding mail – he's an obliging ex-policeman. His is, however, the coldest house I have ever inhabited. The only fire in it has been ingeniously designed to send all the heat up the chimney. You can hang a damp handkerchief on the fireguard and after an hour it will be just as damp as ever. I am only warm in bed, this cold March.[90]

He was still at Corn Close on 15 May when he wrote to Williams to give news of the spring – plenty of cuckoos but no ospreys – and appended a limerick:

> An overfat guest at the Ritz
> Tried a diet of casseroled tits.
> But it can't be denied
> It did no good. He died
> Of a series of fits of the squits.[91]

He continued to write in his eighties but circulated little and published nothing. He worked on poems on Linnaeus, the new moon and on his old school friend, Ernest Cooper Apperley Stephenson. Only one complete work, 'Such syllables flicker out of grass', was circulated to friends. Jonathan Williams asked him in 1980 how his new long poem was going and received the reply, 'Stuck. S-T-U-C-K.'[92]

But he continued to play a bit part in the war the Arts Council was waging against British literature. The egregious Charles Osborne contributed a typically belligerent 'Diary' entry to the *London Review of Books* in June 1984:

> A few weeks ago, in New York, I accompanied a friend on a shopping expedition. While we were in a novelty gift shop on Columbus Avenue, she bought me a rubber stamp which she said I'd find useful when I got back to my Arts Council office in London. I know what she means, though, in fact, I've found myself using it, not on office memos (strong at times though the temptation has been), but on press clippings relating to the Arts Council. The stamp reads 'BULLSHIT' and it has recently been slapped on articles in the *Sunday Times*, *Publishing News* and the *Times Educational Supplement*. As the 1940 Deanna Durbin song says, 'it's foolish but it's fun'.[93]

This provoked a lengthy, stinging reply from Michael Horowitz, editor of *New Departures*, part of which put some distance between poets like Bunting and the mediocrity that Osborne promoted:

> It's typically irrational and prejudiced of Osborne to have stayed away from the Albert Hall reading at Easter, yet smugly to cast his judgment on what was done by whom: 'Ginsburg, Corso, Ferlinghetti and our own ... survivors of the Sixties' Beat generation, all read ... sloppy, mindless ersatz poetry.' For your readers' information Ferlinghetti wasn't there, and none of the British poets who were are definable as survivors of the Beat generation, which was the Fifties. Liz Lochhead, Tom Pickard and the Liverpool poets were going

strong in their respective styles and dialects before they'd heard of the Beats, whilst Basil Bunting, Bob Cobbing, Roy Fisher and Adrian Mitchell (though invariably open and internationalist) are unimpeachably their own men as poets.

It's hypocritical, self-persuasive and patronising of the Director to boast his abhorrence 'of deciding which of my fellow poets should be supported', and then to insult makers of the above-mentioned's calibre as 'poets' in quote-marks only – 'amiable enough non-talents who have never even understood that poetry is made of words'. Anyone who knows contemporary oral verse in English knows that Bunting, Corso, Fisher, Ginsberg, Patten and Pickard are among the most fastidious word-musicians alive. One deduces from his 'less-means-better' touchstone that it's Osborne's fearless conviction that he is 'a real poet' which has made him publish an output of verse incomparably more banal in quality, as well as laughably more sparse in volume, than any of these.[94]

On 13 June Bunting wrote to Jonathan Williams. He was looking forward to moving into Fox Cottage in Whitley Chapel:

I hope to be there by the end of June. If I am not in the workhouse – for the balance sinks fast and steadily. It's not Greystead and no Corn Close, but a presentable spot for all that, with air I can breathe without disgust and fields not yet strewn with bubblegum wrappers, old condoms and plastic wrappers of all kinds. The move will be vexation and chaos, I've no doubt, but that done, I can reach my books, my files, my spoons and corkscrews without a week's work and maddening frustrations. If the car is ready at the same time I can begin to live at something better than half-throttle again (I hope).

They've been putting in a damp-course, or what passes for one and murdering woodworm larvae, and I, with what hands I can press-gang, will have to do some painting, in and out, and twisting screw hooks here and fixing glue hooks there and no doubt fifty jobs I have never dreamt of. You must come, with whisky, to placate the spirits of past owners, as soon as you have been welcomed back to Dentdale. I *hope* there will be enough money to put in a decent stove for Tom to play with instead of the squalid wreck now in situ. A disagreeable large Alsatian may have been placated by that time (I'm told I'm good with dogs, which perhaps is merely a way of saying I'm not too good with girls), and I ought by then to know what beer is best in the pub next door.[95]

On 20 June Bunting wrote to Tanya Cossey to tell her that he had not yet taken possession of his new home but that it was his from that day and that he will visit it every day to air it to dry out the new plaster. Meanwhile he stayed with his daughter in Corbridge.[96] Bunting moved into Fox Cottage in July 1984. Whitley Chapel is another remote village, though not as remote as Tarset. At least his new home had a pub next door (sadly no longer), and Fox Cottage enjoys stunning views north over the Tyne valley. Once the move was over he wrote to Forde about his despair during the ordeal: 'I've been so hassled and worried and confused by being turned out of my pretty cottage at Tarset that I've not had either a calm mind or a trace of energy … For a very long time we searched for a new home, I, helped by my daughter and son-in-law, my ex-wife and Colin Simms, but there was nothing even tolerable.'[97]

His son-in-law, John Halliday, helped him to secure a mortgage on the property in spite of his age, but the repairs necessary to secure it put him in debt that he found stressful. He made the best of it, while acknowledging that it wasn't 'a patch on Tarset':

> The cottage stands next door to a well-kept pleasant old pub. It has no immediate outlook, but as soon as I go out of my door I have pretty wide views, still with forest on the horizon – Slaley forest, oak and other deciduous trees, but open and very windy and comparatively high up. It may be cold in winter. I wish it were on the North Tyne, of course, but these parts (Hexhamshire) are also thought beautiful, and the lanes are narrow and twisting. I shall be a little more cramped than I was, but not badly, and when we can finish furnishing it there will be a bed for visitors. The pub's drinkers park their cars all around me, which is noisy at night, but I'll get used to that in the end.[98]

It took some time to settle in. On 17 July he invited Jonathan Williams to visit him, complaining that:

> I'm surrounded by grotesque details. At this moment none of the doors in the house will shut, or if they shut, nothing will open them again. That may be only a matter of a few days, but while it lasts the weekend evening crowds leaving the pub are perfectly capable of engendering some surprise. All my tools except a screwdriver and saw have strayed during their migration, having fled with a number of the more valued books, a rolling pin, and other things mysteriously dissatisfied with a career in my society. In spite of these disconcerting, anti-hospitable circumstances, I think a short sojourn here would not cripple you permanently.[99]

The Niedecker scholar Jenny Penberthy recalls meeting Bunting in his new home:

> We arrived, Peter and Meredith Quartermain and I, at his bare home in Whitley Chapel, Tyne Valley, Northumbria, to be met at the door by a delighted, even festive host. Companionship came too seldom, it seemed. Over strong tea and Bellingham bramble tart he told stories that would, I feel sure, have enchanted Lorine – the small creatures and birds that entered through the never-closed doors of his succession of Northumbrian homes; the fox that tapped for its evening meal at a local pub window. When I ventured to say that I was writing about Lorine Niedecker and Louis Zukofsky he was, for a while, no longer the indulgent raconteur. He fixed on me a sad, heavy stare and after many seconds, he growled: "Be sure to do her justice."[100]

As well as a new home he acquired a new car in July. 'It is very little, and has a very little engine,' he wrote to Tanya Cossey.[101] He remained physically strong, enjoying walks and whisky right up to his death, although in 1984 he complained to Victoria Forde that his latest visit to London had tired him 'beyond reason ... I keep well, free of rheumatism, but in some ways feeble. My utmost walk must be about a mile, and I wont willingly venture on foot more than half a mile.'[102]

His eye for the written word was as sharp as ever. In Hexham with Peter Quartermain and others in November 1984 he waited in a shop while his watch was being mended: '"There's a watch that has an eye in it where it shouldn't have." Facing us, a placard promoting ACCURIST. Our slow wits took some time to read "accurst."'[103] He had an eye for ambiguous signs. He saw one in Prescott, Ontario: '"ST PAUL ST BILLIARDS. Popular saint, that last."'[104]

He never lost his strange blend of political radicalism and cultural conservatism. In November 1984 he wrote to Jonathan Williams: 'I *hate* our bosses. Only old age, and the uselessness of resisting them keeps me quiet. If England goes to hell via Thatcherian economics, as it may, we might eventually escape, and Hugh MacDiarmid and I will share a bottle of celestial malt to celebrate the break-up of Great Britain into a new heptarchy.'[105] Earlier in the year he had written 'in jest' to Victoria Forde: 'And let us have a new Pope please, this one is too conservative.' I doubt he was jesting.[106]

Bunting began to weaken physically early in 1985. He wrote to his young friend, Tanya Cossey, in January to complain that he had been 'struggling with a kind of gastric flu, very unpleasant ... I have hardly even cooked, but lived on whisky and a little bread and butter bit by bit ... Sima got here once only. Apart from that and a crack with the landlord of the Fox and Hounds, I've not heard a human voice for 12 days. (I don't really miss it, but it is odd.)'[107] 'I am only wreckage,' he told Gael Turnbull in February 1985. 'It is weeks since I ventured as far as Hexham. Eating is a chore – cooking an imposition – making my bed is labour. I can't even read for more than about an hour, and only old stuff that spares me the effort of understanding. I sleep.'[108]

On 3 February 1985 Bunting wrote to Jonathan Williams in a reflective but touchingly anticipatory way:

> I'll be blest if I can imagine why I have begun a letter to you today, seeing that I have no news whatever to give you and no business to transact. Between Tanya's long visit over Christmas and New Year and the snow that's been falling ever since, I've been imprisoned in my cottage, except that the pub opens at midday to sell me a pint on Saturdays and Sundays, but none of my acquaintances turns up ...

> Makin has been comparing my verse with Dante's: amusing, but not very convincing. I put right one or two wild mis-conceptions for him. Two young men from Hull did a taped-interview, and I have cut a good deal of it out. I am too old to be trusted near a tape, and they are too young to dare blue-pencil me as they should.

> I daresay there is now some ground for expecting that I might reach the age of 85 in less than four weeks, bar accidents; but why? I've been good for nothing for fifteen years and most people have very properly forgotten me. No doubt the *Times* has an acid obituary ready in its morgue, but three days after the funeral I'll be in Limbo for a long stay. I've filled out a coupon for Littlewood's Pools. If I win a million, there might be some fun yet![109]

The recording of the interview with the 'two young men from Hull' survives, and he was right to suspect the outcome. If he did cut a good deal of it out he didn't go far enough. At times, especially on the relationship between meaning and sound, he becomes uncharacteristically incoherent. He acknowledges that it is difficult for him to 'talk about it clearly, especially since I no longer read anything. I'm not familiar even with my own works any more.' The interviewers were not particularly generous to the old man.[110]

He was starting to say his goodbyes. On 19 March 1985 he wrote to Forde, still worried about debts but in good humour: 'My central heating is effective but costs an awful lot to run. Fortunately people sent me so many bottles of whisky for my birthday that I am thinking of bathing in it. That should warm me up … Last week there were crocuses and such blossoming and we all thought spring had come; but they were just codding us. Inches of snow lying again today. The rooks, which had all come home, escorted by flocks of starlings and a few jackdaws, seem to have gone away again.' He then began the closing paragraph unusually, with the prophetic, 'Goodbye now …'[111]

In an undated (but February 1985) letter Bunting wrote to invite Tanya Cossey to visit him at Easter: 'Tanya dear … Did I tell you that my daughter Roudaba has decided to come and see me? She is due about the 8th of April. She is quite able to share your room. She's a very energetic, lively, amusing person, though of course about 49 or 50 now.'[112] According to Forde it proved to be:

> a very enjoyable time although the little cottage was quite crowded with visitors and Rou had to share a room with Tanya Cossey, a young art student who had been almost a daughter to Bunting for years (and his saki on television). Another good friend, Michael Shayer, arrived on April 15 and slept on the small couch in the living-room with his feet hanging over one end. Maria, his youngest daughter, was in and out during the visit, often taking Rou sightseeing since Bunting had given his car to the Cosseys, afraid that he would injure someone if he kept on driving.

> The cottage itself was small and poor with grey cement walls unpainted except for the bedroom Rou and Tanya shared which Tanya had painted white. Shelves of books which covered the living-room walls softened its starkness, but the kitchen/dining room were not so camouflaged. Maria and others who wished to make his life more comfortable were continuously and adamantly refused by this proud man who wished to remain independent to the end. Though Bunting had trouble walking, the group occasionally went to the next door pub for a meal. The week passed pleasantly, and the night before Shayer was to go back south, they all stayed up till the early hours, reminiscing, talking about poets and poetry, drinking and singing ballads, including the bawdy Northumbrian ones Bunting knew so well. These Rou had learned in childhood from her mother who used to sing them while they washed up the dishes together.[113]

Tanya wrote to thank 'Uncle Basil' on 15 April. She told him how much she had enjoyed her visit and particularly the company of Roudaba and

Mike Shayer: 'Tell Roudaba I miss her company very much. I never met anyone so happy and fun to be with as her.'[114]

Bunting felt unwell the following day but put it down to a hangover, although Roudaba, who had trained as a nurse, had misgivings. Bunting refused to see a doctor but his daughter prevailed in this rather sad but familiar battle of wills, and he reluctantly agreed to call one. Bunting was shocked when the doctor immediately summoned an ambulance to get him into intensive care at Hexham General Hospital as quickly as possible. He was ill but in good spirits:

> As soon as he was settled in the cot too short for him to stretch out in, he began half-seriously complaining, "What's the use of having daughters? One comes all the way from America to put me into hospital!" ... As [Roudaba and Maria] were about to leave, with a loud crash the man next to her father fell out of bed with his bedpan, and Bunting exclaimed, "See what happens in hospital?" But everyone in good spirits teasingly consoled him with the thought of all the pretty nurses about.[115]

The following morning Maria and Roudaba called the hospital early and were told that their father was well. They were just leaving Maria's home 'when another call came, about 10 a.m., to tell them that their father was dead. For exercise he had walked down the hall with a nurse and returned to bed, but something had made the nurse, who was leaving, turn back – to find he had just died.'[116]

Shortly after Bunting's death Jonathan Williams reflected that it was 'curious to think that his contemporaries – dead 50 years ago – were Hart Crane, George Gershwin, and Thomas Wolfe. Basil was precisely one day older than Kurt Weill, dead since 1950. Bunting was the last of the Victorians.'[117]

His ashes were scattered in the Quaker graveyard at Brigflatts, and a suitably understated stone was placed among the other memorials. A more elaborate memorial in the Botanic Gardens at Durham University quotes from *Briggflatts*:

> Words!
> Pens are too light.
> Take a chisel to write.

Peggy attended Bunting's funeral, which Gael Turnbull thought was 'much dominated by one of the American daughters from his first marriage'.

Peggy wasn't mentioned at the funeral, an omission which upset Turnbull who wrote to her afterwards to assure that she had not been forgotten, by him at least. His letter was returned with a note, 'No Longer at this Address'. Michael Shayer tracked her down and called on her in the social services home in Bishop's Castle where she died in February 1988. Turnbull recalled that one of the poets at Bunting's funeral 'did publish a little account of that event, which, among other stupidities, does contain a reference to her, but derisory in context … She was a warm and gallant lady, much torn and jolted by the hazards of life and passion.'[118]

* * *

'Three days ago,' Bunting wrote to Tom Pickard in 1978,

> I learned, from Jonathan W. by letter, that Louis Zukofsky had died. That thins the population of good poets rather drastically. I hope MacDiarmid can make a fool of the doctors, but I fear that, bar road accidents and strokes of lightning, I'll soon be the only survivor of what was rightly a famous generation. Louis had finished 'A', and maybe it seemed to him that his business in this world had been completed.

W. B. YEATS

EZRA POUND	W. C. WILLIAMS
T. S. ELIOT	LOUIS ZUKOFSKY
DAVID JONES	HUGH MACDIARMID

> And a lot of pretty good secondaries, such as Marianne Moore, Mina Loy, Hilda Doolittle and what not, besides, rather isolated, yet part of it, Lorine Niedecker. All these, except H.D., were among my friends; and I think there have been a great many generations that could not match them. Perhaps I could claim, like WBY, that my best epitaph would be 'He had such friends'.[119]

The fact that he set them up as if on a tombstone suggests that he meant it.

NOTES

ABBREVIATIONS

The following abbreviations have been adopted for frequently recurring publications, names and places. Otherwise, for printed sources the usual convention has been adopted of a full citation in the first instance, followed by a recognizable shortened form.

AG   *Agenda*, 16, 1978

BB   Basil Bunting

BBNL   R. Caddel and A. Flowers, *Basil Bunting a Northern life* (Newcastle upon Tyne, 1997)

BRBML   Beinecke Rare Book and Manuscript Library, Yale University

CHIC   Ronald Lane Latimer Papers, University of Chicago Library

CONJ   *Conjunctions* 8, 1985

CP   B. Bunting, *Complete Poems*, edited by R.Caddel (Newcastle upon Tyne, 2000)

DESC   J. Williams (ed.), *Descant on Rawthey's Madrigal: Conversations with Basil Bunting* (Lexington, 1968), unpaginated

DG   Denis Goacher

DISJ   P. Quartermain, *Disjunctive Poetics: From Gertrude Stein and Louis Zukofsky to Susan Howe* (Cambridge, 1992)

DP   Dorothy Pound

DUR   Basil Bunting Poetry Archive, Durham University Library

EM   Eric Mottram

EP   Ezra Pound

FORDE   V. Forde, *The Poetry of Basil Bunting* (Newcastle upon Tyne, 1991)

GT   Gael Turnbull. Bunting's letters to Gael Turnbull are currently in the private collection of Jill Turnbull.

HM	Harriet Monroe
HR	Harry Ransom Center, the University of Texas at Austin
JW	Jonathan Williams
KCL	Eric Mottram collection, King's College, London
KD	Karl Drerup
KEW	The National Archives, Kew
LILLY	The Lilly Library, Indiana University, Bloomington, Indiana
LR	Lionel Robbins
LSE	Lionel Robbins Papers, London School of Economics and Political Science
LZ	Louis Zukofsky
MAK	P. Makin (ed.), *Basil Bunting on Poetry* (Baltimore, 1999)
MONT	*Montemora* 3, Spring 1977
MS	Margaret de Silver
MT	*Meantime*, 1, April 1977
MTBB	J. Williams (ed.), *Madeira & Toasts for Basil Bunting's 75th Birthday* (Highlands, 1977), unpaginated
PAID	*Paideuma* (9, 1), Spring 1980
PI	*Poetry Information* (19), Autumn 1978
RBD	Roudaba Bunting Davido
SSLT	R. Caddel (ed.) *Sharp Study and Long Toil: Basil Bunting special issue* (Durham, 1995)
SUNY	The Poetry Collection, State University of New York at Buffalo
SYSB	J. McGonigal and R. Price (eds), *The Star You Steer By: Basil Bunting and British Modernism* (Amsterdam, 2000)
TERR	C. F. Terrell (ed.), *Basil Bunting: Man and Poet* (Orono, 1981)
TP	Tom Pickard
VF	Victoria Forde
WCW	William Carlos Williams

INTRODUCTION

1. This is how Bunting thought poetry should be written. Bunting offered an anecdote about his contemporary, the poet David Jones: 'A year or two ago I had tea with David Jones while he was engaged on a piece of lettering in the Roman manner ... He'd got the letter T at the beginning of one line. As we talked, he suddenly fell silent. A look of abstraction came into his face. And he set down his teacup and his piece of cake, fiddled about till he got a pencil, and stood up to his easel, and slowly, slowly, very carefully, drew in the letter H. Then he sat down again; with a sigh, he said, "I'll have the E by Friday!" ... That is the way you've got to write poetry, you know: every word has got to be thought of with all that care' (MAK, 8–10).
2. DESC. Williams decided not to reproduce Bunting's final sentence, 'Damned if it isn't bugging ____' (undated note from Bunting to Jonathan Williams, SUNY).
3. I felt the heat of Bunting's posthumous scorn less intensely when I discovered that he used this medieval manuscript-like sign-off for all documents he regarded as 'official'. Diana Collecott interprets the flourish of Bunting's formal signature as signifying 'Artist/Poet' and believes the Arts and Crafts Movement may have been an influence. (Conversation with author, May 2012.)
4. J. Skipsey, *Selected Poems*, ed. B. Bunting (Sunderland, 1976). His careful research didn't prevent several important factual errors from marring his account. See http://gerald-massey.org.uk/skipsey/index.htm
5. MAK, 151–70.
6. PAID, 132. Bunting's 'autobiography' appeared in the Who's Who of modern poetry, J. Vinson (ed.), *Contemporary Poets* (London, 1975), 213–14.
7. Bunting might have argued that he was merely restoring a 'g' that had been stolen from the hamlet by the Ordnance Survey after the 1950s series of maps. Until then it had been 'Briggflatts' since the beginning of organised government mapping of the country.
8. Almost every verifiable assertion in Alldritt's book, from Thomas' entry on Bunting's birth certificate to the cause of death cited in his death certificate, is wrong.
9. BB to TP, 18 January 1979, SUNY.
10. MTBB.
11. H. Kenner, *A Sinking Island: The Modern English Writers* (London, 1988), 7.
12. Dilworth's account of this interchange was published in *Poetry Review*, Summer 2010, 122–3.
13. MAK, 151.
14. CP, 80.
15. BBNL, 9. Folk culture had an enduring appeal for Bunting. He told Tom Pickard that he had made a small selection of skipping songs in the 1920s. (Interview recorded at Bunting's home in Whitley Chapel on 17 and 18 June 1981, published by Keele University, 1995.)

16. BBNL, 9.

17. P. Quartermain, *Basil Bunting: Poet of the North* (Durham, 1990).

18. *Basil Bunting 1900–1985: A life in images*, catalogue for an exhibition in Durham University Library, January–February 1987.

19. 'A statement' in DESC. Poets are 'mostly dismal' readers of their own work, he said in an interview in 1981, and 'actors will bugger up any poetry they're allowed to speak unless they're drilled hard' (interview with Peter Bell, 3 September 1981, recorded at Bunting's home in Greysteads, published by Keele University, 1995).

20. BBNL, 33–5.

21. Quartermain, 5.

22. Quartermain, 10.

23. C. Johnson, *The Disappearance of Literature* (Amsterdam, 1980), 51.

24. T. Pickard, *High on the Walls*, preface Basil Bunting (London, 1967), 7.

25. 'A statement' in DESC.

26. Johnson, 57.

27. 'A statement' in DESC. Bunting thought that *The Waste Land*, for instance, should be read without the notes. The poem 'needs no explaining that is not contained in its own lines. Every reference is a red-herring to drag the reader away to hunt the "meaning" of the poem anywhere but in the poem itself' (*New English Weekly*, 8 September 1932, 500).

28. A. Clarke, *Collected Poems* (Manchester, 2008), 314.

29. Hazlitt remarked on the 'great depth and manliness and a rugged harmony in the tones of his voice … His language may not be intelligible; but his manner is not to be mistaken.' This could be a description of Bunting's reading voice. J. Cook (ed.), *William Hazlitt: Selected Writings* (Oxford, 1991), 224–5, 353.)

30. MAK, 103.

31. MAK, 103.

32. See Stephen Logan's fascinating analysis of Wordsworth's voice at www.english.cam.ac.uk/cambridgeauthors/conversation-with-stephen-logan

33. He got it from Yeats. Pound was introduced to Yeats in London in 1909 by Yeats' lover Olivia Shakespear, whose daughter, Dorothy, thought Pound's accent 'odd … half American, half Irish'. When Pound first heard a recording of himself reading he was surprised by his own 'Irish brogue'. Whether conscious or not Pound's imitation of Yeats' unique chanting sounded ridiculous to Bunting and sounds ridiculous now (H. Carpenter, *A Serious Character: The Life of Ezra Pound* (Boston, 1988), 133, 138).

34. PI, 4. Bunting and Zukofsky may well have had a profound effect on the development of literary modernism with this intervention. Carroll F. Terrell has pointed to the striking prosodic differences between Canto XXX, written after Bunting and Zukofsky made their recommendation, and those beginning *Eleven New Cantos* (PAID, 35.) In any event anyone who has heard Yeats reading 'The Lake Isle of Inisfree' is unlikely to disagree with Bunting's broader point about Yeats.

35. Gael Turnbull, 'An Arlespenny: Some notes on the poetry of Basil Bunting', *King*

Ida's Watch Chain (Newcastle upon Tyne, 1965), unpaginated.

36. Diary, 11 May 1925, DUR.
37. SSLT, 204.
38. PI, 40.
39. '83 Answers ... and Some Questions'. Basil Bunting and Jonathan Williams, introduced by Eric Robson, BBC North East, 17 August 1984 and 19 April 1985.
40. DISJ, 144.
41. E. Pound, *Polite Essays* (London, 1937), 153–4.
42. SSLT, 110.
43. C. D. Heymann, *Ezra Pound: The Last Rower* (London, 1976), 222–3.
44. Quartermain, 15.
45. M. Hart, *Nations of Nothing but Poetry: Modernism, Transnationalism, and Synthetic Vernacular Writing* (Oxford, 2010), 85–6.
46. SSLT, 93.

CHAPTER 1:
GUILTY OF SPRING

1. DESC.
2. In theory anyway. Much of the action shown had been staged.
3. G. R. Searle, *A New England? Peace and War 1886–1918* (Oxford, 2004), 285–6.
4. *Manchester Guardian*, 2 March 1900.
5. *Evening Chronicle*, 1 March 1900, 3.
6. Weather reports for 1 March 1900 from *Evening Chronicle*, 28 February 1900, 4, and *Newcastle Courant*, 10 March 1900, 7. Ferocious storms during the week had seen two ships from the north east sunk without survivors.
7. Cheap wheat from Canada and frozen meat from New Zealand, brought over in the newly developed refrigerated ships on the one hand, and chemicals and electrical goods from Germany, for instance, on the other.
8. Searle, 177–8.
9. Freud's *The Interpretation of Dreams* was published in 1899. Daimler's first production motor cars had been seen on British roads since 1896 and aircraft were exploring a new spatial dimension by 1900 (the first Zeppelin).
10. G. R. Searle, *The Quest for National Efficiency: A Study in British Politics and British Political Thought, 1899–1914* (Oxford, 1971), 51–2.
11. BBNL, 8, 11, 57.
12. Lawrence's birthplace, Eastwood, is just two miles from Heanor. Bunting came to regard Lawrence as a 'terrible jerk' according to the poet, August Kleinzahler (PAID, 28). He 'detested Lawrence, first for locking him out on a window-ledge at a party (in Paris, I think) and then for slipping him some hashish baked into a pastry of some sort and not telling him. Bunting did, however, greatly admire *Sons and Lovers*' (A. Kleinzahler, 'Blackfell's Scarlatti', *London Review of Books*, 21 January 1999).

13. B. Bunting, 'The Village Fiesta', *Paideuma*, Winter 1981, 621.
14. DESC.
15. 'Blaydon Races', *Allan's Illustrated Edition of Tyneside Songs and Readings* (Newcastle upon Tyne, 1891), 451.
16. The salmon story crops up in every account of Bunting's childhood but I have been unable to find it in any of Bunting's own recollections. Certainly there is photographic evidence of salmon fishing on the Tyne in the 1890s but the industrialisation of the river would have made it a pretty miserable way of earning a living by 1900. See FORDE 17; BBNL, 11; K. Alldritt, *The Poet as Spy* (London, 1998), 3; *Basil Bunting: 1900–1985: A life in images*, 3.
17. The patient, Dorothy Ellison, remembered that Thomas wore rabbitskin gloves which led her to adjust the 'Bye Baby Bunting' nursery rhyme to include a reference to Dr Bunting going a-hunting. See BBNL, 62.
18. J. M. Taylor, *England's Border Country: A History of Northumberland County Council 1889–1989* (Morpeth, 1989), 3–5.
19. BB to EP, 21 March 1934, BRBML.
20. Taylor, 19–33. For Messer see, for example, N. G. Rippeth, *Newburn in Old Pictures* (Eindhoven, 1993).
21. J. Forsyth, *Scotswood Road* (Newcastle, 1986), 17.
22. DESC.
23. PAID, 127. Bunting recorded his debt to Edith Nesbit a few years later in a note to *Villon*: 'catalytic making whisper and whisper/run together like two drops of quicksilver', of which he wrote: 'The image of two drops of quicksilver running together is from the late E. Nesbit's *Story of the Amulet*. To her I am also indebted for much of the pleasantest reading of my childhood' (CP, 225).
24. DESC.
25. DESC.
26. In a curriculum vitae produced in 1952 (BBNL, 14) and repeated in 1963 (DESC). Newcastle Grammar does not feature in a curriculum vitae Bunting sent to the State University of New York in 1966 (BB to Mrs B. White, 24 April 1966, SUNY). Bunting claimed to have spent 'about a year and a half' at Newcastle Grammar (DESC) and it is unlikely that such a prolonged period of education would have gone unrecorded.
27. DESC.
28. E. B. Collinson (ed.), *List of the Boys and Girls admitted into Ackworth School from the year of the Centenary of the School, 1879, to the end of 1930* (Scarborough, 1932), 67–9.
29. Ackworth School Committee meeting minutes, 25 March 1912.
30. FORDE, 24. After graduating from Edinburgh University Joyce completed a postgraduate course in Dublin before becoming a locum GP in London, after which she returned to the north east to become a Schools Doctor for Northumberland. Looking back in her mid-eighties she described her career to Victoria Forde as 'partly assistant to doctors in general and partly in the School Medical Service'. Joyce and her brother were not close as adults but according to her son, Alexander Christie, there was no antagonism between them and he

remembers normal family visits during holiday periods. Joyce died in March 1992.

31. Ackworth School, *Ackworth School 1779 to 1929* (York, 1929), 17–18.

32. DESC. In later life he came to prefer 'the Great Bible of 1539, which is Coverdale; or, Coverdale revising Tyndale' (PAID, 128).

33. E. Vipont, *Ackworth School* (London, 1959), 145–6.

34. Vipont, *Ackworth School*, 158–9. These peace celebrations were scuppered in 1914 by the outbreak of one of the bloodiest wars in history.

35. Leighton Park School, *Leighton Park 1890–1940* (Reading, 1940), 1.

36. M. Dawson, 'Memories of Briggflatts', MTBB.

37. E. Vipont Foulds, *The Birthplace of Quakerism: A handbook for the 1652 country* (London, 1952), 18.

38. Vipont, 13–15.

39. E. Vipont, *George Fox and the Valiant Sixty* (London, 1975), xiii. Unless the ghost is that of John Handley, the cabinet maker who married Miss Elizabeth Rushford at the Meeting House in Brigflatts in 1810. See *Monthly Magazine and British Register*, Volume 30, Part 2, 278.

40. The first Meeting House was built at Hertford in 1670. Brigflatts was the first to be built in the north of England.

41. PAID, 168.

42. Interview with Peter Bell 3 September 1981, published by Keele University, 1995.

43. Interview with Peter Bell.

44. CP, 61. Bunting clearly involved himself in the mason's work. 'I've rubbed down gravestones,' he told an interviewer in later life, 'and that's how I know how it feels to rub down a gravestone. And how your fingers ache on the damn job ... and so on. I take care not to write anything that I don't bloody well know' (AG, 12).

45. Ackworth School archive. The dream device seems to have been Stephenson's default position. 'A Winter Dream', an essay submitted to the Essay Society in autumn 1915, applied the same conceit to an Elizabethan ball. Yet it is deeply moving to read these dreamy romantic fantasies in the knowledge that a few months later Stephenson's body was lying in pieces in a field in northern France. The AOSA Report of 1914 reported 'a falling-off in the quality of the work of the Essay Society' but praised Stephenson for being 'gifted with the skill of the pen'.

46. Bunting himself was elected as a member of the Lit & Phil on 10 July 1968 and was then made an honorary member on 11 July 1978 until his death.

47. C. Parish, *The History of the Literary and Philosophical Society of Newcastle upon Tyne*, Volume II, 1896–1989 (Newcastle upon Tyne, 1990), 28.

48. Parish, 30.

49. BBNL, 29. According to Caddel and Flowers Whittaker's influence on Bunting extended to 'musical performance: Bunting owned a copy of Whittaker's *North Countrie Ballads, Songs and Pipe-tunes*, from which he played (on recorders) and sang throughout his life'. He told an interviewer in later life that as a young man he had been 'a good amateur singer and of course got some control over my voice that way' (interview with Peter Bell, 3 September 1981).

50. DESC.

51. S. Sadie (ed.), *The New Grove Dictionary of Music and Musicians* (London, 2001), iv, 723 and viii, 660–1.

52. Parish, 75.

53. CP, 236.

54. CP, 235–6.

55. W. Blake, *The Poems, with Specimens of the Prose Writings, of William Blake, with a Prefatory Notice, Topographical and Critical by Joseph Skipsey*, ed. J. Skipsey (London and Newcastle upon Tyne, 1885), 32–3. Bunting observed in his introduction to Skipsey's poems that Skipsey's prefaces 'like those of his contemporaries, are too long and too verbose, but sometimes unexpected or acute'. This is one such example.

56. E. R. Pease, *The History of the Fabian Society* (London, 1925), 33–5. The Fabians were named after the Roman soldier and politician Quintus Fabius Maximus Verrucosus, nicknamed 'Cunctator' for his patient war of attrition that defeated Hannibal.

57. Pease, 40.

58. The Fabian Society's membership records are kept in the London School of Economics archive.

59. Hyndman had a habit of larding his speeches with generous layers of Latin, not a failsafe demonstration of class solidarity.

60. Searle, 231.

61. Fabian Tract No. 3 *To Provident Landlords and Capitalists*, 1885, and Fabian Tract No. 45, 277–8.

62. DESC.

63. L. Robbins, *Autobiography of an Economist* (London, 1971), 87.

64. N. and J. MacKenzie, *The Diaries of Beatrice Webb* (London, 2000), 175.

65. MacKenzie, 176.

66. K. Martin, *Father Figures* (London, 1966), 93. According to his membership record Wallas resigned in January 1904.

67. MacKenzie and MacKenzie, 370.

68. CONJ, 212.

69. PI, 6. Perhaps this was the prize Bunting was referring to when he told Gael Turnbull that he had 'won prize of £50 when aged 16 to be spent on books. Bought (and read) Abraham Cowley' (Gael Turnbull, 'A visit to Basil when he was at Washington New Town', unpublished journal). It's a little unlikely; £50 in 1916 would be worth over £4,000 today.

70. MAK, 92.

71. *Ackworth Old Scholars' Association Report*, 1915, 73.

72. *Ackworth Report*, 1915, 81–2. The other end of the spectrum was occupied by a boy who, when upbraided for poor results, assured his teacher that he was doing his best 'but you see I am naturally rather thick'.

73. *Ackworth Report*, 1915, 105.

74. *Ackworth Report* 1916, 43.

75. *Ackworth Report*, 1916, 52.

76. 'Roncevaux', Ackworth School archive.
77. 'Into the vale they rode …' Perhaps Bunting had been reading Hazlitt's *The Life of Napoleon* which draws an explicit parallel between the Emperor and Child Roland, the legendary French courtly hero who defended Christian Europe. See W. Hazlitt, *Selected Writings* ed. J. Cook (Oxford, 1991), 240.
78. Letter to Anthony Flowers in Ackworth School archive dated 21 September 1997. This visit took place in November 1968 (BB to GT, 29 November 1968).
79. Letter from Frederick Andrews, Pontefract, to Charles Evans, 30 May 1916, Leighton Park School.
80. T. Newell Price, manuscript at Leighton Park School.
81. The form gives the Buntings' address as 38 Moorside, Newcastle-on-Tyne.
82. C. Townshend, *Easter 1916: The Irish Rebellion* (London, 2005), 279.
83. Newell Price.
84. DESC.
85. Newell Price.
86. *Leightonian*, December 1916, 95.
87. Newell Price.
88. Although he is mentioned as a member of the Grove tennis team in *The Leightonian* of July 1917, so perhaps Bunting wasn't as determinedly unsporting as he seemed. *The Leightonian* of December 1917 recorded that he had also been awarded a Bronze Medallion in the examinations of the Royal Life Saving Society.
89. Memorandum from Bunting to Charles Evans, Leighton Park School archive. The file note Evans made to himself and the correspondence between T. L. Bunting and Evans are all to be found in the Leighton Park archive.
90. Leighton Park School, *Leighton Park The first 100 years* (Reading, 1989), 34.
91. *Leightonian*, April 1917, 126. The writer quotes directly from the minutes of the meeting of 19 February 1917. It is likely that the earlier date, that in the minutes, is correct.
92. W. Blake, *The Poems, with Specimens*, 27.
93. BB to TP, 1 October 1974, SUNY.
94. Minutes of Meeting 141 of the Debating Society, Leighton Park School.
95. Charles Evans file note, 17 April 1917, Leighton Park School.
96. 'The Present Social Condition of Shinfield', July 1917, Leighton Park School.
97. Charles Evans, file note, July 1917, Leighton Park School.
98. Or 'present Russian Dictator' as the minutes record, although someone has later added 'Prime Minister?'
99. Not quite idle speculation this. In his introduction to his selection of Blake's poems Skipsey draws a direct parallel between the young Blake and the young Poe. Bunting would have been familiar with Skipsey's edition of Poe. See E. A. Poe, *The Works of Edgar Allan Poe with a Prefatory Notice, Biographical and Critical*, ed. J. Skipsey (London and Newcastle upon Tyne, 1885).
100. *The Leightonian* of December 1917 recorded the 'unusual merit' of the paper, 178. Diana Collecott has pointed out to me that this story might tell us more about Bunting's alienation from Leighton Park than the medical account of his state of

mind favoured by his father and headmaster. It might also tell us something about the way he viewed his relationship with Peggy.

101. Judges' report on senior essay prize, 1917, Leighton Park School.
102. *First Hundred Years*, 14–15.
103. *First Hundred Years*, 153.
104. Leighton Park School, *Leighton Park 1890–1940*, 6.
105. *First Hundred Years*, 43.
106. *First Hundred Years*, 13.
107. S. Brown, *Leighton Park: A History of the School* (Reading, 1952), 100.
108. Brown, 102.
109. *First Hundred Years*, 52.
110. *First Hundred Years*, 144. It seems that Evans himself may have taken on that role. See Brown, 104.
111. Brown, 115.
112. *First Hundred Years*, 14. This general attitude softened in the twenty years following Bunting's departure. By 1940 thirty-six of the sixty Old Boys who were at university were at Oxbridge, a remarkable 60 per cent, albeit in a system with far fewer universities than today. See *Leighton Park 1890–1940*, 4–5.
113. CP, 236. Perhaps Bunting had heard Newbolt's lecture, *Poetry and Patriotism*, at the Lit & Phil in 1914.
114. H. D., *Selected Poems*, ed. Louis L. Martz (Manchester, 1997), 25.
115. See C. Reilly, *English Poetry of the First World War* (London, 1978), xix.
116. *Leightonian*, December 1916, 96.
117. The AOSA Report of 1918 is sobering. On page 26 John Allen Greenbank is mentioned as having 'received grants for training expenses, uniforms, renewal of outfit, insurance premiums or maintenance'. Six pages later Stephenson appears in a lengthy list of old boys who had lost their lives since the previous report: 'Ernest Cooper Apperley Stephenson (Scholar 1912–1916). 2nd Lt. R. F. C. Killed in action, March 21st, 1918'.
118. Searle, 510.
119. Brown, 119.
120. Vipont, *Ackworth School*, 159–60.
121. *Ackworth Report*, 1915, 81–2.
122. *Ackworth Report*, 1915, 82. It is only fair to point out that the crack had existed since the birth of Quakerism in the middle of the seventeenth century. In the 1650s many Quaker leaders were ex-soldiers and Fox and other Quaker leaders broadly supported the activities of the British army and navy. See A. Bradstock, *Radical Religion in Cromwell's England* (London, 2011), 107.
123. *Ackworth Report*, 1919, 15.
124. I. H. Wallis, *Life of Frederick Andrews of Ackworth* (London, 1924), 281.
125. K. Robbins, *The Abolition of War: The 'Peace Movement' in Britain 1914–1919* (Cardiff, 1976) 32–3.
126. A. Hochschild, *To End all Wars: How the First World War Divided Britain* (Basingstoke, 2011), 353.

127. Newell Price.
128. D. Stevenson, *With our backs to the wall: Victory and defeat in 1918* (London, 2011), 53. Stevenson's account of the spring offensives shows just how far the Allies were from scenting victory as Bunting faced a hostile tribunal.
129. Searle, 723–8.
130. Searle, 742.
131. Searle, 743.
132. Hochschild, 188–9.
133. Hochschild, 323.
134. We might recall the effeminate peacemonger Ganelon in Bunting's 'Roncevaux'.
135. Quoted in letter from George Simmers, *Times Literary Supplement*, 23 November 2011.
136. BBNL, 23.
137. Searle, 766. Not all COs justified their stance on religious grounds. Many socialists felt that the working class had no business fighting to maintain a ruling class status quo.
138. A. Brown, *English Society and the Prison: Time, culture and politics in the development of the modern prison, 1850–1920* (Woodbridge, 2003), 145–7.
139. S. Hobhouse, *An English Prison from Within* (London, 1919), 5.
140. Searle, 766. The other was the United States.
141. *Leightonian*, December 1918, 254. Wormwood Scrubs was commonly spelt with two Bs at the time. It is referred to as such throughout *English Prisons Today: Being the Report of the Prison System Enquiry Committee* (London, 1922).
142. Bunting told Philip Norman in a feature in the *Sunday Times* in 1969 that at the Newcastle barracks six men at once were taken out dead. 'There would have been an even greater scandal, but it happened to coincide with the last big battles of the war' (P. Norman, *Sunday Times Supplement*, 19 January 1969, 34–8).
143. Quoted in K. Alldritt, *The Poet as Spy: The Life and Wild Times of Basil Bunting* (London, 1998), 21.
144. Hochschild, 190–1, 301.
145. *Leightonian*, July 1919, 42–3. The 'Cat and Mouse Act', actually the 'Prisoners' Temporary Discharge for Ill-health Bill', had been brought in by Herbert Asquith's Liberal government in 1913 to curb the effect of hunger-striking suffragettes.
146. SSLT, 197.
147. S. Hobhouse: *Forty Years and an Epilogue: An Autobiography, 1881–1951* (London, 1951), 162–4.
148. BB to TP, 15 November 1982, SUNY.
149. *transatlantic review*, Volume 2, No. 1, 132.
150. DESC.
151. Hochschild, 366.
152. R. Dahrendorf, *LSE: A History of the London School of Economics and Political Science 1895–1995* (Oxford, 1995), 9, 41–3, 104–6.
153. G. Rose, *The Struggle for Penal Reform* (London and Chicago, 1961), 108.

154. W. D. Wills, *Stephen H. Hobhouse: a Twentieth Century Quaker Saint* (London, 1972), 58.
155. S. Hobhouse and A. F. Brockway (eds), *English Prisons Today: Being the Report of the Prison System Enquiry Committee* (London, 1922), 488–500, 636–50.
156. Hochschild, 325.
157. PAID, 76.
158. E. Pound, *The Cantos of Ezra Pound* (London, 1987), 431. It should, of course, be 'Redimiculum Matellarum'.
159. DESC.
160. Interview with Lawrence Pitkethly and James Laughlin, October 1982, in R. Swigg, 'Basil Bunting on Ezra Pound', *Paideuma*, 38, 2011, 9.
161. Interview with Peter Bell, 3 September 1981.
162. FORDE, 17. Bunting claimed in 1966 that his poetic vocation came to him on his grandfather's knee at the age of five (CONJ, 154–7).
163. The *Leeds Mercury* did occasionally publish short (and usually intensely patriotic) poems, including one by Thomas Hardy that I have not seen collected elsewhere ('Up and be doing, all you who have a hand' on 13 March 1917) as column fillers. No issue of the *Leeds Mercury* of 1916 and 1917 carries a poem attributed to Bunting. The only unattributed poem, a dialect poem entitled 'T'War Loan', is so terrible that one hesitates to suggest that Bunting had anything to do with it.
164. DESC.
165. DESC.
166. MT.
167. CP, 226.

CHAPTER 2:
FELLS FORGET HIM

1. *Leightonian*, July 1920, 157.
2. DESC.
3. CONJ, 157.
4. PAID, 40.
5. See G. Wallas, 'An Historical Note', London School of Economics Archive, Wallas 2/6 91701, 67.
6. L. Robbins, *Autobiography of an Economist* (London, 1971), 75.
7. Although Bunting joined the Royal Air Force at the beginning of the Second World War he spent the first part of it flying balloons in the North Sea.
8. Robbins, 76.
9. J-P. Potier, *Piero Sraffa: Unorthodox Economist* (London, 1991), 1–4.
10. R. Murray Schafer, *Ezra Pound and Music: The complete criticism* (London, 1978), 336. Susan Howson has, however, made the very valid point to me that it is likely that Bunting knew Piero Sraffa because of the Rapallo connection but that it is less likely that they knew each other earlier at the London School of Economics, where there would not have been much contact between a research student and

an undergraduate, especially one who attended as infrequently as Bunting did.

11. S. Howson, *Lionel Robbins* (Cambridge, 2011), 65.
12. BB to EP, undated but August or September 1934, BRBML. Nearly sixty years after Robbins introduced him to *Ulysses* Bunting still thought it the funniest book he knew in English (PAID, 128).
13. MONT, 68.
14. Interview with Lawrence Pitkethly and James Laughlin, October 1982, in R. Swigg, 'Basil Bunting on Ezra Pound', *Paideuma*, 38, 2011, 12.
15. In a letter written over sixty years later he explained that Orage's writers 'were few, and mostly turned out to be Ezra Pound in disguise, yet I never met EP till later' (BB to 'Mr Bradshaw', 25 September 1982, SUNY).
16. H. Carpenter, *A Serious Character: The Life of Ezra Pound* (Boston, 1988), 356.
17. Although even an issue as apparently straightforward as Pound's anti-Semitism is not clear cut; see Carpenter, 359–62.
18. J. L. Finlay, *Social Credit: The English origins* (Montreal, 1972), 103–4.
19. As did the British Communist Party, and particularly a poet who later became a close friend of Bunting's, Hugh MacDiarmid; see Finlay, 176, 193–4, 196.
20. Interview with Pitkethly and Laughlin, 1982. When Orage died in November 1934 Bunting told Pound that Orage 'was the first chap ever gave me any serious encouragement' (BB to EP, 22 November 1934, BRBML).
21. PAID, 42–4.
22. Carpenter, 315.
23. Carpenter, 314.
24. Carpenter, 235.
25. Carpenter, 346.
26. Howson (66) quotes Lionel Robbins: 'In the diggings which I then inhabited at St John's Wood, there was also residing a student from the London School of Economics', who introduced him to other students. Through Basil Bunting he met Jacques Kahane. See Howson, 66. Bunting's Fabian Society membership card shows that he also lived at 63 Brocash Road, near Clapham Common in south London.
27. 'Passed Internal Intermediate B.Sc. (Econ.) Examn. 1921' added as a handwritten note. Michaelmas was the first term of the 1920–21 session.
28. BB to LR, undated but 1920, LSE. I am grateful to Dr Susan Howson for alerting me to the existence of these ten letters from Bunting to Robbins.
29. BB to LR, 12 October 1920, LSE. Bunting told Dorothy Pound in August 1971 that he had 'sold my few Armstrong shares' to pay his fare to Russia (BB to DP, 6 August 1971, LILLY).
30. This experience gathered patina over the years. In 1965 he told Edward Lucie-Smith that he had embarked on this journey to Russia 'to convert Lenin and Trotsky to more peaceable means of creating heaven on earth. But they wouldn't let me in', the consequence being a 'wild tour of Scandinavia' (E. Lucie-Smith, 'A man for the music of words', *Sunday Times*, 25 July 1965, 33).
31. Howson, 75.

NOTES

32. Bunting's 'Attendance Record Sheet' for 1922–23, the third year of his course, has figures for the Michaelmas term only, so he had left by December 1922. He attended only twenty-six of his seventy-seven lectures that term.

33. Not unreasonably since Thomas was covering his son's costs. His annual applications show the cost of Bunting's fees for the third year of his course as £22 1s 0d, which he paid on 4 October 1922. He applied to do his final exam in 1923 with Honours in Currency and Banking.

34. Howson, 107. BB to LR, 22 April 1923, 1 May 1923 and 6 October 1926, LSE. The first of these letters reveals that Bunting was still being subsidised by his long-suffering father.

35. So-called because Bonar Law and Lloyd George, leaders of the Conservative and Coalition Liberal parties in the coalition government, had sent letters (which the Independent Liberal leader H. H. Asquith derided as 'coupons' to link them to wartime rationing) to 159 prospective Liberal MPs endorsing their candidacy.

36. Bell died in 1922 and Barnes contested the seat again in the 1923 by-election but the Labour candidate, Arthur Henderson, increased Bell's majority from 13 per cent to 18 per cent. Barnes stood in Tynemouth at the 1923 and 1924 general elections, losing the first narrowly and the second emphatically to the Conservative Sir Alexander Russell. His final attempt to return to parliament was in the July 1928 by-election in Halifax, in which he lost heavily to Labour's Arthur Longbottom.

37. Hansard, 13 February 1919, vol. 112, cc325–407.

38. Hansard, 13 February 1919, vol. 112, cc384–5.

39. Hansard, 13 February 1919, vol. 112, cc387.

40. Hansard, 18 February 1919, vol. 112, cc795–6.

41. H. Barnes, *Valuation & Revaluation for Poor Rate and Income Tax (Post War)* (London, 1923). *Housing: The Facts & The Future* (London, 1923) is slightly less testing and its dedication would have mollified the young socialist:

    To the Homeless

    One dwelling, one family

    Every family, a dwelling

    We have seen that Bunting misremembered his deathless footnote in a book supposedly written by Graham Wallas on prison reform. He almost certainly worked on one of Harry Barnes' books on tax and possibly confused the Royal Commission he referred to with the Royal Commission on Income Tax of 1920. Not so romantic perhaps but Bunting was prone, as we shall see, to talking up his part in events that are historically obscure.

42. BBNL, 30.

43. DESC.

44. BB to LR, 1 May 1923, LSE.

45. BB to LR, undated but spring 1923, LSE.

46. BB to J. J. Adams, undated but 1923, DUR.

47. BB to J. J. Adams, undated but 1923, DUR.

48. F. M. Ford, *It was the Nightingale* (London, 1934), 255. The artist, sculptor and

architect, Fernand Léger, was that time in the middle of his 'mechanical period'.

49. W. Lewis, *Rude Assignment* (Santa Barbara, 1984), 131.

50. R. Aldington, *Life for Life's Sake* (London, 1941), 150–1.

51. J.J. Wilhelm, *Ezra Pound in London and Paris, 1908–1925* (Pennsylvania, 1990), 332.

52. *Nightingale*, 259.

53. *Nightingale*, 259–60.

54. See M. Sanouillet, *Dada in Paris*, revised by A. Sanouillet, transl. S. Ganguly, (Cambridge, 2012).

55. Interview with McAllister and Figgis, 10 November 1984.

56. CP, 29.

57. BB to HM, 30 Nov 1930, CHIC.

58. DESC.

59. J. Turnbull and H. White (eds), *More Words: Gael Turnbull on Poets and Poetry* (Bristol, 2012), 45.

60. S. Bowen, *Drawn from Life* (London, 1941), 116.

61. Bowen, 120.

62. R. M. Ludwig (ed.) *Letters of Ford Madox Ford* (Princeton, 1965), 160–1.

63. *Nightingale*, 273.

64. *Nightingale*, 272.

65. *Nightingale*, 258.

66. *Nightingale*, 301–4.

67. H. Kenner, *The Pound Era* (London, 1991), 527.

68. TERR, 41–2.

69. Reading in spring 1977 at the Air Gallery, London, published by Keele University, 1995.

70. *Nightingale*, 311. For date see M. Saunders, *Ford Madox Ford: A Dual Life*, vol. 2 (Oxford, 1996), 156. Ford spells it 'Bede'.

71. *Nightingale*, 310.

72. B.J. Poli, *Ford Madox Ford and the Transatlantic Review* (Syracuse, 1967), 28.

73. *Times Literary Supplement*, 20 May 2011.

74. BB to WCW, 7 October 1930, BRBML.

75. Poli, 144.

76. DESC.

77. F. Madox Ford, *Selected Poems*, ed. Basil Bunting (Cambridge, Mass., 1971), vii.

78. Ford, *Selected Poems*, viii.

79. Ford, *Selected Poems*, ix. Hemingway's malicious caricature of Ford is made the more incomprehensible by his observation in 1925 of 'Pound the major poet devoting, say, one fifth of his time to poetry. With the rest of his time he tries to advance the fortunes, both material and artistic, of his friends ... And in the end few of them refrain from knifing him at the first opportunity' (Carpenter, 200). Bunting doesn't always seem to have loathed Hemingway so. He told Philip Norman of the *Sunday Times* a story in 1969 of going to meet Hemingway after Hemingway had reported discovering a 'deposit of pre-war Guinness. That was in 1922, so the Guinness would have been almost 10 years old. Ford was removed

after eight hours or so, by business; and Hemingway and I remained two days and three nights, playing billiards until we had drunk *all* the Guinness.' (P. Norman, *Sunday Times* supplement, 19 January 1969, 34–8).

80. A. Judd, *Ford Madox Ford* (London, 1990), 350–1.

81. C. Burke, *Becoming Modern: The Life of Mina Loy* (Berkeley, 1996), 344–5.

82. Burke, 345.

83. BB to EM, 27 March 1978, KCL. Was Bunting in La Conciergerie or La Santé as Ford believed? La Santé was a relatively new prison (built in 1867) and had none of the bloody history or terrifying Gothic echoes that reverberate around La Conciergerie, a Valois palace that had been converted into a prison in 1391. La Conciergerie had effectively been the office accommodation of the Terror in the aftermath of the French Revolution and its prisoners included the most romantic and bloodstained characters in modern and early modern French history. The fact that Bunting believed the subject of his first great poem, François Villon, to have been one of them doesn't add much to his claim, but Villon was arrested so frequently that it is far from impossible.

84. Interview with Pitkethly and Laughlin, October 1982, *Paideuma*, 38, 2011, 3–28. Another version, intended primarily to illustrate Pound's prudish nature, substitutes the sculptor Brancusi for Boris de Kruschev. See PAID, 65.

85. BB to James Leippert, 30 October 1932, CHIC.

86. BB to EM, 27 March 1978, KCL. Pound did despise Wordsworth, 'a silly old sheep with a genius ... for imagisme, for a presentation of natural detail, wild-fowl bathing in a hole in the ice, etc., and this talent ... he buried in a desert of bleatings' (Carpenter, 222). Pound's ability to dragoon long dead poets into his Imagiste movement stretched as far as the third century BCE Chinese poet 'Chu Yüan, Imagiste' (Carpenter, 220).

87. BB to J. J. Adams, 14 January 1924, DUR.

88. BB to J. J. Adams, 19 February 1926, DUR.

89. Hemingway wrote to Pound on 17 March 1924: 'Bunting, they say, is in jail in Genoa.' C. Baker (ed.), *Ernest Hemingway Selected Letters 1917–1962* (New York, 1981), 112.

90. DESC.

91. E. Pound, *The Cantos of Ezra Pound* (London, 1987), 108.

92. DESC.

93. Interview with Peter Bell, 3 September 1981.

94. Wilhelm, 335.

95. BB to James Leippert, 30 October 1932, CHIC.

96. DESC.

97. PI, 43.

98. FORDE, 16–17.

99. FORDE, 17.

100. Letter from Matthew Kahane to the author, 19 April 2011. According to Kahane his father had been:

   born Jacques Cahane (the spelling of the surname was changed to Kahane when he was travelling from the UK to Romania via Berlin in 1916) in Galati in Romania on 25 September 1900. After the collapse of the Austro-Hungarian Empire in 1918 Kahane was able to obtain Polish citizenship on the basis of his father's birth in Czernowitz, which the resuscitated Polish state claimed. He came to the UK on a Polish passport and enrolled at the London School of Economics where he met Bunting, and on graduating joined the London office of the prominent grain merchants Louis Dreyfus, for which he worked until the autumn of 1950. He took a number of walking tours in the UK, mainly in England, and became a British subject by naturalisation on 20 September 1932, being described as 'of uncertain nationality'. (Letter to author, 7 May 2011.)

101. Robbins, 264.
102. BB to James Leippert, 30 October 1932, CHIC.
103. According to James Laughlin (a disciple of Pound's from the age of eighteen, and later his somewhat undiscriminating publisher) who 'studied' at the Ezuversity, 'EP disapproved of the funivia. He preferred to walk.' Quoted in M. Bacigalupo 'Tigullio itineraries: Ezra Pound and friends' in M. Bacigalupo and W. Pratt (eds), *Ezra Pound, language and persona* (Genova, 2008), 413.
104. CP, 97.
105. FORDE, 102
106. Reading in 1980 in London, published by Keele University, 1995.
107. BB to EP, 29 April 1926, BRBML.
108. *British Medical Journal*, 28 February 1925.
109. *The Lancet*, 14 March 1925.
110. Supplement to the *British Medical Journal*, 11 April 1925.
111. FORDE, 26.
112. Excerpt from Christabel Dennison's Diary, 11 May 1925, DUR. See also V. Nicholson, *Among the Bohemians: Experiments in living 1900–1939* (London, 2002), 192–3.
113. BB to J. J. Adams, 19 February 1926, DUR.
114. BB to LR, 6 October 1926, LSE.
115. BB to J. J. Adams, 19 February 1926, DUR. According to Richard Caddel and Anthony Flowers Bunting also wrote speeches and lectures for the shipping magnate William Noble, First Baron Kirkley (BBNL, 32). This is likely to be the 'rich man' he referred to in a letter to J. J. Adams who promised him a job, promises on which he lived 'for months' (BB to J. J. Adams, 19 February 1926, DUR).
116. BB to LR, 6 October 1926, LSE.
117. BB to EP, 2 December 1926, BRBML.
118. FORDE, 26.
119. MONT, 75. Bunting regarded Keynes as a consummate crook (BB to EP, undated but 1931 or 1932, BRBML).
120. DESC.
121. BB to EP, 10 April 1927, BRBML.

122. V. Eliot and J. Haffenden (eds), *The Letters of T. S. Eliot*, Volume 3 (London, 2012), 467.

123. DESC.

124. By 1968 Bunting had inflated Eliot's observation a little: 'Oh, you know what Eliot says about that restaurant – it is one of the three most expensive restaurants in the world now' (SSLT, 203).

125. See A. Conover, *Olga Rudge and Ezra Pound* (New Haven, 2001), 5–6. Pound had written two 'Villonauds' in 1907, when he was 21 (Carpenter, 72–3).

126. Conover, 66.

127. P. Norman, *Sunday Times* supplement, 19 January 1969, 34–8.

128. PI, 38.

129. MAK, 19.

130. By 'cadence' Bunting means those recurrent phrases at the end of clauses that are so familiar in sixteenth-century religious writing, such as Cranmer's liturgy of 1544: ' ... from everlasting damnation, Good Lord, deliver us ... from envy, hatred, and malice, and all uncharitableness, Good Lord, deliver us ...'

131. MAK, 85.

132. MAK, 106.

133. MAK, 93.

134. Interview with Tom Pickard on 17 and 18 June 1981, recorded at Bunting's home near Hexham, published by Keele University, 1995. Bunting had no intention of giving ground to Eliot on this issue. 'I do claim copyright, and bugger TSE', he wrote to Zukofsky. 'He was before me with Preludes, but I'd a bunch of Sonatas before he thought up his Quartets' (BB to LZ, 22 March 1951, HR).

135. Interview with Andrew McAllister and Sean Figgis, recorded at Bunting's home near Hexham on 10 November 1984, published by Keele University, 1995.

136. MAK, 154–5.

137. MAK, 160.

138. MAK, 170.

139. BB to VF, 23 May 1972, DUR.

140. Interview with Peter Bell, 3 September 1981.

141. TERR, 107. Pound referred to Lavignac in *Guide to Kulchur* (London, 1952), 136.

142. A. Lavignac, *Music and Musicians*, transl. W. Marchant (London, 1904), 346.

143. TERR, 110.

144. CP, 26. Steven Matthews plausibly cites these lines as a crucial influence on Yeats' 'Crazy Jane Talks with the Bishop', which was written shortly after the publication of 'Villon' in *Poetry*. K. Williams and S. Matthews (eds), *Rewriting the Thirties: Modernism and after* (Harlow, 1997), 100.

145. AG, 22. Quizzed a few months before he died about the introduction of Marot into the poem Bunting said, 'I like Marot. I have respect for him. The fact that he was wrong about Villon doesn't destroy that.' (Interview with McAllister and Figgis, 10 November 1984).

146. FORDE, 151.

147. BB to Donald Davie, 25 September 1975, BRBML.

148. 'Yes or be it the Emperor of Constantinople of the golden fist' in Galway Kinnell's translation. G. Kinnell (transl.), *The Poems of François Villon* (London, 1982), 51.

149. See I. Kalavrezou, 'Helping hands for the empire: Imperial ceremonies and the cult of relics at the Byzantine Court' in H. Maguire (ed.), *Byzantine Court Culture from 829 to 1204* (Washington DC, 1997), 53–79. Peter Makin thinks it 'fairly clear from his poem that Bunting thinks Villon's lines refer to manuscript illuminations. Villon students have generally taken them to refer to the gilded tomb of Alphonse, court of Eu, at saint-Denis, whose inscription stated that he was the son of the emperor of Constantinople. However, it has been pointed out that Villon is more likely to be speaking of the gilded orb in such a figure's hands, as commonly depicted in the *danse macabre*' (P. Makin, *Bunting: the Shaping of His Verse* (Oxford, 1992), 28). There are, of course, many ways of interpreting 'Villon'. Brian Conniff, for instance, sees it as Bunting's first strike in a class war that he single-handedly conducted for forty years. See B. Conniff, *The Lyric and Modern Poetry: Olson, Creeley, Bunting* (New York, 1988), 137–61.

150. Pound 'chopped out at least one fifth, perhaps one quarter of the first two parts [of 'Villon'], maybe more than that. He didn't touch the third part because, he said, "I don't know what you young fellows are up to nowadays!"' (MONT, 72). According to Barbara Lesch, Bunting claimed that Pound reduced 'Villon' to half its original length. See FORDE, 151.

151. BB to EP, 'Last of 1928', BRBML.

152. BB to LZ, 9 September 1953, HR.

153. CP, 99.

154. BB to Roger Guedalla, 6 May 1969, DUR. There is also a clear echo of Matthew Arnold's 'Dover Beach'.

155. Carpenter, 339.

156. T. S. Eliot (ed.), *Literary Essays of Ezra Pound* (London, 1953), 7.

157. Eliot, 232.

158. *Criterion*, 15, 41, July 1936, 714–16. Bunting told Pound that this was 'a bad review of a bad book', BB to EP, 28 March 1936, BRBML.

159. CP, 228.

160. CP, 149.

161. BB to HM, 19 October 1926, CHIC.

162. *Leightonian*, October 1927, 280. *The Leightonian* seems to have found Bunting difficult to let go. The July 1928 issue noted that Bunting was 'supposed to be in Fleet Street, but little is seen or heard of him. This can only be because our "outlook" is in the wrong quarter' (*Leightonian*, July 1928, 67).

163. Howson, 145.

164. DESC. It was Nina Hamnett who introduced Bunting to the poetry of Ezra Pound in 1919. She lent him 'Homage to Sextus Propertius' and 'Quia Pauper Amavi'. (Interview with Pitkethly and Laughlin, October 1982.)

165. S. Fiber, *The Fitzroy: The Autobiography of a London Tavern* (Lewes, 1995), xi.

166. Fiber, 2–3.

167. Fiber, 11. She didn't have far to go. At that time she was living above the Etoile

restaurant in Charlotte Street. See D. Hooker, *Nina Hamnett: Queen of Bohemia* (London, 1986), 173.

168. Fiber, 18.

169. BB to Roger Guedalla, 25 November 1974, DUR.

170. BB to EP, 2 December 1926, BRBML. See also Howson, 77.

171. BB to LR, 22 April 1923, LSE.

172. Excerpt from Christabel Dennison's diary, 18 May 1925, DUR.

173. CP, 101.

174. Polyhymnia, the Muse of lyric poetry, was often associated with sacred songs.

175. CP, 102.

176. 'Throb: An Inquiry', *Outlook* 59, 1516, 188–9.

177. 'Observations on Left-Wing Papers', SSLT, 44–7.

178. 'Alas! The Coster's End', *Outlook* 59, 1521, 328–9.

179. 'Squares and Gardens', *Outlook* 59, 1527, 542.

180. 'Small Holdings', *Outlook* 59, 1530, 674.

181. 'Crime and Punishment', *Outlook* 59, 1531, 718.

182. For instance 'Capital punishment: a century of discontinuous debate' by Carol S. Steiker and Jordan M. Steiker, *The Journal of Criminal Law and Criminology*, Vol. 101, No. 3, Northwestern University School of Law, 654.

183. 'Readers and Librarians', *Outlook* 60, 1537, 87.

184. 'Some of Our Conquerors', *Outlook* 60, 1538, 126–7 and 1547, 407.

185. 'Conducted Tour to Parnassus', *Outlook* 60, 1538, 132–3.

186. 'Philosophic Criticism', *Outlook* 60, 1540, 188.

187. 'Marvellous Moscow!', *Outlook* 60, 1543, 283–4.

188. 'Mr. Lindsay and Mr. Blake', *Outlook* 60, 1548, 453–4.

189. 'What are we coming to?', *Outlook* 60, 1550, 520. Bunting's joke about Haire's name is made even lamer by the fact that Norman Haire's father was Henry Zajac, a Polish Jew. 'Zajac' is Polish for 'hare' so Haire had already made Bunting's jibe for him when he changed his name in 1919.

190. BBNL, 45.

191. '83 Answers … and Some Questions', Basil Bunting and Jonathan Williams, introduced by Eric Robson, BBC North East, 17 August 1984 and 19 April 1985.

192. BB to VF, 28 February 1972, DUR.

193. DESC.

194. DESC.

195. DESC.

196. MAK, 120.

197. MAK, 120–1.

198. DESC. The reference to 'writing music' is doubtless a transcription error.

199. BB to LR, 24 September 1927, LSE.

200. 'Pianists', *Outlook*, 60, 578–9. Bunting missed just three issues, 24 March, 7 April and 5 May 1928.

201. 'Medium Calibre', *Outlook*, 60, 620.

202. L. Foreman, *Bax: A composer and his times* (Woodbridge, 2007), 254. See also Hubert

Foss' glowing review in *The Dominant* of December 1927, 257–8. Bunting also described Sibelius' wonderful seventh symphony, premiered in London in 1927, as dull, 'unwieldy and disappointing' with no more life than 'a jelly-fish or slug' (17 December 1927).

203. 'String-players', *Outlook*, 60, 648.

204. 'Chamber Orchestras', *Outlook*, 60, 676. For Bunting's relationship with Warlock see p. 148–9. 'Liszt', *Outlook*, 26 November 1927; 'The Third Philharmonic Concert', *Outlook*, 17 December 1927; 'César Franck', *Outlook*, 25 February 1928; 'The London Programme', *Outlook*, 7 January 1928. 'The Opera Question', 3 December 1927 and passim; 'Gurrelieder', 4 February 1928; 'Too many concerts', *Outlook*, 24 December 1927, 845; 'The influence of the ballet', *Outlook*, 14 January 1928, 56. Walton was just twenty-five at the time of this review and attracted Bunting's 'serious, if guarded, praise'; 'Recent fiddlers', *Outlook*, 18 February 1928, 209.

205. 'Threes and fours', *Outlook*, 3 March 1928, 265; 'Sackbuts and harpsichords', *Outlook*, 10 March 1928, 307; 'Song and folk music', *Outlook*, 17 March 1928, 344; 'Handel mishandled', *Outlook*, 31 March 1928, 404.

206. 'Symphonies for children', *Outlook*, 14 April 1928, 472; 'Musical stimulants', *Outlook*, 21 April 1928, 508–9; 'Criticism and music', *Outlook*, 28 April 1928, 526–7; 'Committing musical archeology, *Outlook*, 12 May 1928, 594–5; 'The whole man', *Outlook*, 19 May 1928, 636–6.

207. B. Smith (ed.), *The Collected Letters of Peter Warlock*, Volume iv 1922–30 (Woodbridge, 2005), 113.

208. Smith, 196.

209. Percy Scholes, the music critic of the *Observer*, had referred to Fellowes' 'discovery' in the *Radio Times*, prompting Warlock to write an (unpublished) letter to the magazine. In a letter to Scholes of 14 June 1925 Warlock repeated his claim that it was Richard Terry rather than Fellowes who had discovered Byrd's masterpiece. Something of the flavour of Warlock's relationship with Scholes is captured by the closing paragraph of this letter: 'Permit me to suggest that, abandoning the pretence that you are in any way qualified to pass judgment on music, you would be much better employed in playing tennis than reporting concerts at any time, and that you would be still better employed in buggering yourself with a pair of exceptionally well-greased bellows' (Smith, 130–1).

210. PAID, 130.

211. DESC.

212. DESC.

213. N. Pernicone, *Carlo Tresca: Portrait of a Rebel* (Oakland, 2010), 246–7. Margaret de Silver was also friendly with Trotsky.

214. T. Page (ed.), *The Diaries of Dawn Powell 1931–1965* (South Royalton, 1995), 75. Unkind given that she owed de Silver $800 at the time, more than she owed any other individual (82).

215. DESC.

216. PAID, 46–7. If Bunting was suggesting Margaret de Silver he was also confusing J.

J. Adams with Tresca, and London with New York.

217. DESC.
218. DESC.
219. BBNL, 35.
220. PAID.
221. DESC.
222. CP, 103.
223. P. Quartermain, 'Take Oil/and Hum: Niedecker/Bunting' in E. Willis (ed.), *Radical Vernacular: Lorine Niedecker and the poetics of place* (Iowa City, 2008), 282.
224. Judges 15:15–16, King James Bible (Cambridge).
225. CP, 103.
226. CP, 104.
227. SSLT, 6.
228. BB to James Leippert, 30 October 1932, CHIC. In 1965 he told the Newcastle *Evening Chronicle* that he didn't like the 'spurious liveliness' of Berlin ('Eldon', *Evening Chronicle*, 9 June 1965, 6).
229. DESC. One of Bunting's least attractive characteristics is this ability to generalise unfavourably. He didn't get over his prejudice towards Germany; he wrote to Peter Russell, editor of *Nine*, in May 1950 that 'I've loathed the Germans for so many years that I approach anything of theirs with hostility … ' (BB to Peter Russell, 18 May 1950, SUNY). He didn't like Spaniards much either: 'I like them better than Germans, but they are a cruel people, the Spaniards. One gets tired of their cruelty, one gets tired of the neglect of comfort, of the horrible food the Spaniards find good enough for themselves even when they're rich enough to afford very decent food'(DESC). He 'detested' Arabs (BB to DP, 14 April 1949, LILLY) and he had a problem with America's Midwest, nowhere more explicit than in a letter to Karl Drerup in 1938: 'disgusting Middle West – America in excelsis – all the worst traits at their worst … The middle class [of Los Angeles] comes from the Middle West, and is as beastly as the Middle Westerner can be … [their] truculent hatred of all foreigners, self-complacency, and bad manners, and contempt of anything that isn't a money-success, is very hard to put up with. They are a disgusting lot' (BB to KD, 27 August 1938, DUR). We might recall his rant about 'southerners' at Leighton Park School.
230. M. de Rachewiltz, A. D. Moody and J. Moody (eds) *Ezra Pound to his Parents: Letters 1895–1929* (Oxford, 2010), 671.
231. BB to EP, 'Last of 1928', BRBML. The tragedy has never been explained.
232. de Rachewiltz, Moody and Moody, 683.
233. Marian Bunting to Roger Guedalla, 25 September 1968, DUR. Marian recalled in 1970 that Bunting was still being financed by Margaret de Silver when they met in Venice (Marian Bunting to Roger Guedalla, 20 November 1970, DUR). Otto Theis told Pound in January 1930 that Margaret de Silver was 'thumbs down on any further aid' to Bunting. He wrote that he would try to help Bunting to find work if he returned to London but added that his 'work is rather too highly individualised for ordinary journalism. If the *Outlook* hadn't died he would by now

have established himself as a provocative and original writer on music. Damned good stuff he used to do' (Otto Theis to EP, 7 January 1930, BRBML). Bunting repaid the compliment by telling Pound that Theis appeared to be 'completely booze-sodden and useless now' (BB to EP, 22 May 1930, BRBML).

234. Marian Bunting to Roger Guedalla, 7 March 1969, DUR.
235. BB to C. H. Rickword, 26 April 1929, BRBML. C. H. Rickword was not the brother of the pioneering communist and poet, Edgell Rickword, but his cousin. Edgell Rickword's *Rimbaud: the boy and the poet* had been published in 1924. A hasty postscript to this letter asks 'How's London? In particular, you, Edgell & Bertram?' Bertram Higgins, the Australian Modernist poet who spent much of the 1920s in London working as a book reviewer, was to feature entertainingly in the correspondence a couple of years later between Bunting and Harriet Monroe regarding Bunting's 'British' edition of *Poetry*.
236. C. H. Rickword to BB, 30 April 1929, BRBML.
237. BB to C. H. Rickword, 3 May 1929, BRBML.
238. Rickword to BB, 6 May 1929, BRBML.
239. BB to Louise Morgan (Theis), 11 April 1929, SUNY.
240. Reading, February 1982, Riverside Studios, London.
241. CP, 105.
242. FORDE, 87.
243. CP, 107.
244. CP, 108.
245. FORDE, 92.
246. B. Mackay, 'Basil Bunting, Mentor', DUR.
247. BB to Louise Morgan, 11 April 1929, SUNY.
248. Lot 77 of Poetical Manuscripts and Portriats of Poets, the Roy Davids Collection, auctioned by Bonhams in London in April 2013.
249. BB to Louise Morgan, 18 October 1929, SUNY.
250. BB to Louise Morgan, 4 January 1930, SUNY.
251. BB to Louise Morgan, 6 May 1930, SUNY.
252. BB to EP, 17 June 1930, BRBML.
253. Marian Bunting to Roger Guedalla, 18 December 1968, DUR.
254. Marian Bunting to Roger Guedalla, 25 September 1968, DUR.
255. BB to LZ, 11 July 1930, HR.
256. C. Bernstein (ed.), *Louis Zukofsky Selected Poems* (New York, 2006), 154.
257. Bernstein, xiii.
258. Bernstein, 102.
259. Bernstein, xvii.
260. Bernstein, 41–2.
261. Eliot, 273.
262. Bernstein, 75.
263. Bernstein, 104.
264. Bernstein, xviii. This seems to have been a notion that was in the zeitgeist. Count Dionys in D. H. Lawrence's novella, *The Ladybird*, delivers a lengthy lecture on the

darkness of the sun.

265. MAK, 152. Bunting also noted (153) that Zukofsky was 'more completely a city poet' than any other poet he could think of.

266. Bernstein, 121.

267. Bernstein, 50.

268. Bernstein, xix.

269. BB to EP, 28 July 1935, BRBML.

270. MT.

271. Interview with McAllister and Figgis, 10 November 1984, published by Keele University, 1995. For an excellent comparison of Bunting and Zukofsky's poetry see P. Quartermain, 'Parataxis in Basil Bunting and Louis Zukofsky', SSLT, 54–70.

272. DESC.

273. J. Parisi and S. Young (eds), *Dear Editor: A History of Poetry in Letters* (New York, 2002), 289–90.

274. BB to EP, undated but 1930, BRBML.

275. Marian Bunting to Roger Guedalla, 25 September 1968, DUR.

276. BB to WCW, 7 October 1930, BRBML.

277. BB to EP, 27 October 1930, BRBML.

278. B. Ahearn (ed.), *The Correspondence of William Carlos Williams and Louis Zukofsky* (Middletown, 2003), 77.

279. FORDE, 28. He also told Forde that 'the New Jersey State Police guarded the tunnel into New York so that the Feds could not get the bootleg liquor for themselves!' (V. Forde, 'Background for Letters of Basil Bunting and a Remembrance of My Visits with him, March 1982', DUR).

280. *Contempo*, 5 February 1932.

281. Marian Bunting to Roger Guedalla, 18 December 1968, DUR.

282. This quotation from the seventeenth-century French philosopher Jean de La Bruyère can be translated as: 'The same justice of spirit that makes us write good things makes us stop and suspect that they are not good enough to merit praise.'

283. These are the titles Bunting gave the poems in *Complete Poems*. These odes had different titles in *Redimiculum Matellarum*.

284. 'Here check we our career/Long works I greatly fear.'

285. *Poetry* 38, no. 3, June 1931, 160–2.

286. Pound, *Cantos*, 431–2.

287. BB to Louise Morgan, 6 May 1930, SUNY.

288. DESC.

289. FORDE, 32.

290. EP to HM, 11 November 1931, CHIC.

291. Marian Bunting to Helen Groves, 11 September 1968, DUR.

292. BB to DP, 14 September 1932, LILLY. The 'Balilla' was the Opera Nazionale Balilla, an Italian Fascist youth organization.

293. Marian Bunting to Roger Guedalla, 25 September 1968, DUR.

294. CP, 67. The reference to Antonietta indicates that Bunting was recalling an earlier visit to Italy. Nearly 50 years later Bunting still remembered Antonietta. William

Corbett recalled that during a visit in 1975, 'late on the night after his reading of *Briggflatts* at Harvard, Basil told us of swimming to a grotto with a young girl he once loved in Italy. Perhaps forty years ago. He paused to ask, "I hope I'm not speaking too roughly." He wasn't, and the gentle regard in which he held us, his listeners, and the girl in his memory has remained with me' (CONJ, 186).

295. Pound, *Cantos*, 473.

296. W. B. Yeats, *A Vision* (London, 1937), 3.

297. CP, 37–8. Bunting added a note: 'The great man need not be identified but will, I believe, be recognized by those who knew him' (CP, 225).

298. Yeats, *Vision*, 3–4.

299. BB to James Leippert, 30 October 1932, CHIC.

300. BB to James Leippert, 30 October 1932, CHIC.

301. Interview with Pitkethly and Laughlin, October 1982.

302. A. Wade, *The Letters of W. B. Yeats* (London, 1954), 759.

303. 'Yeats Recollected', *Agenda*, 12 (Summer 1974), 37.

304. *Agenda*, 12, 41.

305. *Agenda*, 12, 37.

306. Reading in 1980 in London.

307. *Agenda*, 12, 37.

308. R. Foster, *W. B. Yeats: A Life*, Volume 2, *The Arch-Poet* (Oxford, 2003), 400.

309. DESC.

310. *Agenda*, 12, 42. The goat story is best told by Nathalie Blondel in her biography of Butts:

> The final straw came at the end of the summer [1921] when Mary Butts and Cecil Maitland witnessed an attempt at copulation set up by Crowley between the 'Body of Babylon [Leah Hirsig] and the Virgin He-goat.' In the event the goat refused to co-operate. However, according to Crowley's biographer, 'immediately afterwards, the Beast had cut the goat's throat and the blood spurted over Leah's bare back. In an aside, she asked Mary, "what shall I do now?" And Mary replied, "I'd have a bath if I were you"' (N. Blondel, *Mary Butts: Scenes from the life* (New York, 1998), 105–6).

311. *Agenda*, 12, 41.

312. FORDE, 31.

313. The names Jack and John are, of course, interchangeable in many households but in the Yeats family they are essential in distinguishing between different artists a generation apart.

314. *Agenda*, 12, 42.

315. *Agenda*, 12, 38.

316. BB to William Cookson, 18 April 1974, BRBML.

317. *Agenda*, 12, 41–2.

318. *Agenda*, 12, 43–4.

319. See, for instance, R. Burton, *The Spiring Treadmill and the Preposterous Pig: The Accommodation of Science in the Occult, Political and Poetic Development of W. B. Yeats, 1888–1904* (University of London, PhD thesis, 1984).

320. *Agenda*, 12, 44–5.

321. See for instance A. J. Gregor, *The Ideology of Fascism* (London, 1969), 23.

322. S. U. Larsen et al., *Who were the Fascists?: Social roots of European Fascism* (Bergen, 1980), 52–5.

323. Quoted in T. G. Otte, *The Foreign Office Mind: The Making of British Foreign Policy 1865–1914* (Cambridge, 2011), 328.

324. Carpenter, 552–3.

325. Marian Bunting to Roger Guedalla, 18 December 1968, DUR. 'Do you still swear as much?', Bunting asked Karl Drerup in January 1938. 'People don't in America. But here [in Devon] no one opens his mouth without swearing' (BB to KD, 25 January 1938, DUR).

326. Carpenter, 458.

327. Carpenter, 492.

328. BB to EP, 3 September 1936, BRBML. He wrote to Eric Mottram thirty-six years later about the poet and artist J. P. Angold, who was killed in action with the RAF in 1943: 'I met him only a couple of times, when I was in great trouble with my first wife and couldn't pay much attention. He seemed intelligent, but I cant say I found much in his poetry, though I'm not clear enough to speak with certainty. I think he was one of the set EP was in with then, Green Shirts, or something, half Fascist half Douglasite' (BB to EM, 13 November 1973, KCL).

329. *Agenda*, 12, 45–6.

330. FORDE, 34–5. Forde quotes from an article of 5 January 1932 that Bourtai kept from her mother's collection.

331. Bacigalupo, 382–3. Bacigalupo's chapter is essential reading for any visitor to Rapallo.

332. Bacigalupo, 384.

333. Bacigalupo, 398–9.

334. R. Murray Schafer, *Ezra Pound and Music: The complete criticism* (London, 1978), 332.

335. N. Stock, *The Life of Ezra Pound* (Harmondsworth, 1970), 316.

336. FORDE, 35.

337. Schafer, 332.

338. Interview with Pitkethly and Laughlin, October 1982.

339. *Musical Times* (August 1934), 750.

340. Carpenter, 521.

341. Zukofsky arrived in August 1933; the Buntings left in September. Bunting sent a postcard to Zukofsky in Budapest in June asking him to stay with them in Rapallo and another on 8 August arranging to meet him off his train at Genoa (BB to LZ, June 1933 and 8 August 1933, HR).

342. C. Norman, *Ezra Pound* (London, 1969), 317.

343. FORDE, 35–6. Margaret de Silver had withdrawn her regular financial support, according to Marian, when Bunting married but she continued to supply them generously with cash (Marian Bunting to Roger Guedalla, 18 December 1968, DUR).

344. Norman, 318.

345. DESC. Bunting's generation was perhaps more familiar with Ferdowsi's epic than we are today. Matthew Arnold's beautiful 'Sohrab and Rustum' was adapted from an episode in the *Shahnameh*.

346. FORDE, 46.

347. BB to DP, 14 September 1932, LILLY.

348. *Morning Post*, 1 October 1934, 14.

349. Pound, *Cantos*, 474. Bunting had written 'Firdowsi' in Persian script on his door in Rapallo. When Pound wished to reproduce it in 'Canto 77' Bunting sent the script to Dorothy Pound, explaining that 'it is as near as I can make it from memory to the lettering used on the oldest tiles in buildings of the Seljuk dynasty, which began about 1050 – half a century after Firdausi died' (BB to DP, 27 November 1946, LILLY).

350. H. Witemeyer (ed.), *The Selected Letters of Ezra Pound and William Carlos Williams* (New York, 1996), 163.

351. D. D. Paige (ed.), *The Letters of Ezra Pound 1907–1941* (New York, 1950), 305.

352. BB to EP, 'Twentyumpth' January 1934, BRBML.

353. EP to BB, 17 January 1935, BRBML. Reading Pound's correspondence for longer than thirty seconds is not for the faint-hearted. His execrable spelling and grammar, absurd contractions, swaggering jargon and, worst of all, his man-to-man, backslapping alternation between chumminess and abuse are hard to take for extended periods. Zukofsky's is nearly as bad. This is not a twenty-first-century prejudice. Ford Madox Ford complained in 1938 about Pound's 'incomprehensible scrawls' and suggested that he ask the waiter at his hotel to write his letters for him. Yeats told him that he read his letters without much understanding them and asked him to write in future in 'old-fashioned English' (Carpenter, 557).

354. O. Pound, *Arabic & Persian Poems* (London, 1970), 5.

355. BB to Peter Russell, 8 Sept 1949, SUNY.

356. BB to HM, 20 November 1932, CHIC.

357. Document in BRBML.

358. D. Share (ed.) *Bunting's Persia: Translations by Basil Bunting* (Chicago, 2012).

359. P. Loloi, *Hâfiz, Master of Persian Poetry: A critical bibliography* (London, 2004), 18, 328.

360. Share, back panel.

361. Marian Bunting to Roger Guedalla, 7 March 1969, DUR.

362. *St Andrews Review*, Spring–Summer 1977, 38.

363. Interview with Tom Pickard, 17 and 18 June 1981.

364. CP, 110.

365. CP, 114.

366. Reading in 1980 in London. Bunting was well aware of the danger of being inextricably associated with a single, often not particularly distinguished work. The poet Gael Turnbull visited Bunting in 1964: 'While there, an anthology arrived from Philadelphia. Co-edited by Ezra Pound. And we both laughed in glee, that he has two poems in it, and only one each for Eliot, William Carlos Williams, Marianne Moore etc. I remark, "But you must be getting a little tired of the 'Morpethshire farmer'. You'll notice that we didn't ask you to read *that* last

night." He laughs. "Yes, I can see it's going to be to me what 'The Lake Isle' was to Yeats!'" (Turnbull and Whyte, 48).

367. CP, 113.

368. C. Burke, *Becoming Modern: The Life of Mina Loy* (Berkeley, 1996), 345.

369. D. Annwn, 'Her pulse their pace: Women poets and Basil Bunting', SYSB, 126–7.

370. CP, 227.

371. CP, 150.

372. H. Gilonis, 'Soiled Mosaic: Bunting's Horace Translations', SYSB, 209.

373. SYSB, 214.

374. CP, 225.

375. P. Hobsbaum, 'Beyond the Iambic Norm', SYSB, 48.

376. CP, 30–1.

377. BB to HM, 13 July 1931, CHIC.

378. Reading in spring 1977, London.

379. Interview with Peter Bell, 3 September 1981.

380. P. Quartermain, 'Take Oil/and Hum: Niedecker/Bunting' in E. Willis (ed.), *Radical Vernacular: Lorine Niedecker and the Poetics of Place* (Iowa City, 2008), 276. In later life he regretted that his early poems were not as skilful as they might have been (A. Hall, 'The Irony of Bunting's Climb to Fame', *Newcastle Journal*, 6 December 1968, 8).

381. CP, 118.

382. First published in *Poetry*, October 1934, 13, as 'Fishermen'.

383. 'Verse and version', also written in 1932, is unusual in that it is a translation into Latin. Louis Zukofsky had sent Bunting a poem, 'In that this happening', and asked him to translate it into Italian. Bunting's Italian, however, was not yet up to the job so he translated it into Latin instead which seemed to him more suited to the poem's 'monumental terseness' (BB to LZ, 'September ?th [*sic*] 1932', HR).

384. Reading in February 1982, London.

385. BB to HM, 20 November 1932, CHIC.

386. BB to James Leippert, 30 October 1932, CHIC.

387. Turnbull and Whyte, 46.

388. FORDE, 146. Letter from Niedecker to Cid Corman, 7 March 1969, L. P. Faranda (ed.) *'Between Your House and Mine': The Letters of Lorine Niedecker to Cid Corman, 1960 to 1970* (Durham, 1986), 186, and letter from Niedecker to LZ, 30 December 1950, in J. Penberthy (ed.), *Niedecker and the Correspondence with Zukofsky 1931–1970* (Cambridge, 1993), 172.

389. BB to William Cookson, undated but before his Round House reading of Wordsworth on 14 February 1978, BRBML.

390. V. Slade, *Tarasque*, 3.

391. A. Hall, 'Basil Bunting Explains How a Poet Works', *Newcastle Journal*, 17 July 1965, 7.

392. PI, 37.

393. CP, 85–6.

394. BB to WCW, 'August the umpth' 1932, BRBML.

395. BB to EP, undated but 1935, BRBMB.

396. B. Ahearn (ed.), *Selected Letters of Ezra Pound and Louis Zukofsky* (London, 1987), 37.

397. Pound wrote to Zukofsky from Rapallo on 22 November 1931 that 'Intellectual life costs about ten dollars a week in europe. Basil must do it on less, but he is a bit torpid and can't be said to be plumb in the centre etc. etc.' (Ahearn, 105).

398. Ahearn, 39.

399. Carpenter, 184–8.

400. Carpenter, 189. The development of Imagist theory, such as it was, is well charted in S. K. Coffman, *Imagism: A chapter for the history of modern poetry* (New York, 1972), 120–62.

401. W. C. Williams, *The Autobiography of William Carlos Williams* (London, 1968), 264–5.

402. H. Kenner, *The Pound Era* (London, 1972), 404.

403. BB to LZ, 2 October 1932, HR. Bunting wrote in 1976 that 'a work of art is something constructed, something made in the same way that a potter makes a bowl. A bowl may be useful but it may be there only because the potter liked that shape ...' (*Multi: Basil Bunting from the British Press* (1976), unpaginated).

404. BB to EP, 18 November 1933, BRBML.

405. MONT, 72.

406. Interview with McAllister and Figgis, 10 November 1984.

407. Ahearn, 47. Pound refers to Bunting's 'Scrittori Inglesi Contemporanei' which appeared in *L'Indice* of 20 May 1930 and which was reprinted in English as 'Directory of Current English Authors' in *Front*, 3, April 1931. Pound considered this article a 'very good summary of state of things in Briton' (EP to HM, 28 January 1931, CHIC).

408. Ahearn, 49.

409. Ahearn, 58

410. Ahearn, 52.

411. Ahearn, 64.

412. Ahearn, 71. By 'prized' Zukofsky meant he would lobby Monroe to award Bunting the Lyric Prize for poetry. Zukofsky's reference to La Bonne Lorraine relates to lines from Villon's *Ballade des dames du temps jadis*:

> Et Jehanne, la bonne Lorraine,
> Qu'Anglois bruslèrent à Rouen;
> Ou sont-ils, Vierge souveraine? ...
> Mais où sont les neiges d'antan!

which Bunting rendered as:

> In those days rode the good Lorraine
> whom English burned at Rouen,
> the day's bones whitening in centuries' dust (CP, 26).

413. Ahearn, 89.

414. Ahearn, 92.

415. BB to HM, 15 December 1930, CHIC.

416. EP to HM, 16 February 1931, CHIC.

417. B. Ahearn (ed.), *The Correspondence of William Carlos Williams and Louis Zukofsky*

(Middletown, 2003), 409.

418. BB to HM, 5 March 1931, CHIC.

419. HM to BB, 19 March 1931, CHIC.

420. BB to HM, 13 July 1931, CHIC.

421. BB to HM, 1 May 1931, CHIC.

422. BB to HM, 13 July 1931, CHIC.

423. BB to HM, 28 October 1931, CHIC. For a while Bunting was under the illusion that Samuel Beckett was English. 'Found I like Mr Becket,' he told Pound in 1931, 'glad he's English, as a matter of national pride. Sorry he's English, since he's thereby liable to succumb to the triplecursed gentleman-idea, destruction of all things' (BB to EP, undated but January 1931, BRBML).

424. *Poetry*, February 1932, 264.

425. F. R. Leavis, *New Bearings in English Poetry* (London, 1932), 58.

426. BB to HM, undated but 21 January 1932, CHIC.

427. M. Schmidt, *An Introduction to 50 Modern British Poets* (London, 1979), 196: 'T. S. Eliot … appears as a eunuch (Attis's self-emasculation in service of Cybele is the legend at the back of the poem). Bunting claims his target was Lucretius and Cino de Pistoia – in fact, it is an ageing Prufrock.' Schmidt's ridiculous misreading of the opening lines of *Briggflatts* (197) renders this interpretation rather suspect. Schmidt seems to have taken this theory somewhat uncritically from Anthony Suter's commentary on the poem in *Durham University Journal*, March 1973, 189–200.

428. Parisi and Young, 303.

429. *The New English Weekly*, 8 September 1932, 499. Incidentally Bunting had a letter published in the same edition in which he sought to distance himself forcefully from the work of another contributor: 'Sir, Kindly make it known to your readers that the B. C. B. who contributes occasionally to your paper is NOT me. Those are indeed my initials, well enough known to a certain number of people, but I have never signed them to any printed work, and the only work I know of the other "B. C. B." I don't like' (508). It is interesting that the two reviews 'the other "B. C. B."' contributed in 1932 were written very much in the sarcastic and superior tone of some of Bunting's pieces for *The Outlook*. See *New English Weekly*, 19 May 1932, 119–20 and *New English Weekly*, 7 July 1932, 287. Perhaps Bunting was looking to distance himself from *New English Weekly* generally. Its pro-Douglas economic position was attracting anti-Semitic contributors including, needless to say, Pound.

430. MT, 77–8.

431. Kenner, 444.

432. BB to Morton Dauwen Zabel, 4 January 1933, CHIC.

433. *Poetry*, February 1932, 264.

434. *Poetry*, February 1932, 265.

435. BB to EP, 2 December 1926, BRBML.

436. *Agenda*, spring 1969, 42.

437. *Agenda*, Spring 1969, 42.

438. MONT, 74. Bunting told Denis Goacher that he had met Auden and was 'baffled

by a sort of heaviness and dullness of mind' (BB to DG, 4 July 1973, DUR).

439. Ahearn, 96.

440. The short-lived *Pagany: a native quarterly* published 'Please stop gushing about his pink' in the Summer 1931 issue and this translation from Horace reappeared in the Winter 1931 edition of *New Review.*

441. EP to HM, 30 November 1929, CHIC.

442. EP to HM, 2 March 1930, CHIC. Bunting was sincere in his desire for anonymity. He wrote to Pound:

> Hope you wont think me ungrateful or something – I have replied to Poetry that I don't like blurbs, prefer to be as near anonymous as practically possible … I do intensely detest personal publicity and wish I could put out my productions in papers or elsewhere as Op 23 by Writer 347 … I was always like that. It has nothing to do with 'being a gentleman' to which animal I have small resemblance, but simply with my idea of what poetry is or ought to be – the opposite of gossip (BB to EP, undated but February 1930 , BRBML).

443. BB to HM, 21 January 1932, CHIC.

444. Ahearn, 100.

445. E. Pound (ed.), *Profile* (Milan, 1932), half title verso.

446. S. Vines (ed.), *Whips & Scorpions* (Glasgow, 1932), 40–3. These were 'To a POET who advised me to PRESERVE my Fragments and False Starts', 'Crackt Records: Number One' ('Please stop gushing about his pink') and 'Number Two' ('Yes it's slow, dockt of amours') and 'Reading X's Collected Works'. *The Leightonian*, ever keen to get in on Bunting's act, noted that 'two of the famous 'Crackt Records' were composed in part at least while he was at Leighton Park, and the opening lines of the second have all the world-weary disillusion of the Upper VIth' (*Leightonian*, December 1932, 251).

447. *Hound and Horn*, 6, 1, Oct–Dec 1932, 158–60.

448. BB to James Leippert, 30 October 1932, CHIC.

449. *Hound and Horn*, 6, 2, Jan–Mar 1933, 322–3.

450. Marian Bunting to Roger Guedalla, 7 March 1969, DUR.

451. Turnbull and Whyte, 49.

452. A copy of this letter, dated 22 January 1933, was sent to EP, BRBML.

453. E. Pound (ed.), *Active Anthology* (London, 1933), prelims.

454. *Active Anthology*, 9. In the case of Hemingway's single poem, 'They all made peace – What is peace?', I'm on the side of the British literary bureaucracy. It is dreadful. But so is the Eliot poem included, 'Fragments of a Prologue', representing the greatest poet of his generation at his embarrassing pseudo-demotic worst. To be momentarily fair to Pound he did concede that '20 or 30 poets between the ages of 20 and 40 have written better poems than some of those here included' (253). Nowhere can the unevenness of the anthology be better appreciated than by reading Bunting's cool sonata against Hemingway's tuneless whistling.

455. *Active Anthology*, 23–4.

456. The complete list is: 'Villon', 'Attis – Or, Something Missing', 'How Duke Valentine Contrived', 'They Say Etna', 'Yes, it's slow, docked of amours'

(previously published as 'Crackt Records: Number Two'), 'Weeping oaks grieve, chestnuts raise', 'Molten pool ... ', 'The Passport Officer', 'Chomei at Toyama', 'The Complaint of the Morpethshire Farmer' and 'Gin the Goodwife Stint'. He told Gael Turnbull that he wanted to suppress 'They say Etna' but 'Pound wouldn't have that ... I think it sounds horrible ...' (BB to GT, undated but January 1965). It is as bad a poem as he wrote, but he recognised the futility of suppression. He told an interviewer late in life that 'it's very difficult to suppress something once you have printed it, and I think it is usually best not to try to suppress it. So there are several poems in the *Collected Poems* which I feel ought not to be there, but it would be no use leaving them out because as soon as I'm dead somebody will print another collection that will include them. Better to chop them a little myself' (PI, 39). Which is exactly what happened. In any event, according to Pound Bunting was 'NOT satisfied with HIS stuff. Finds Marianne better on rereading (enforced in Canary Isles, as he has no other books) thinks W. C. W. the best (apart from me and Possum [Eliot], who are merely umbrellas to the vol), but uneven' (D. M. Gordon (ed.), *Ezra Pound and James Laughlin: Selected Letters* (New York, 1994), 8–9).

457. Interview with McAllister and Figgis, 10 November 1984.
458. Bridson commissioned two broadcasts from Bunting for the BBC's Third Programme in 1963 and 1964.
459. Paige, 250.
460. Paige, 272. Letter dated 28 March 1935.
461. E. Pundit, *Superman: being the complete poetical works of Robert Baby Buntin-Dicebat* (London, 1934), xiii.
462. BB to HM, 26 February 1932, CHIC.
463. BB to James Leippert, 17 July 1932, CHIC.
464. Interview with McAllister and Figgis, 10 November 1984.
465. BB to James Leippert, 'September nth 1932', CHIC.
466. BB to James Leippert, 26 September 1932, CHIC.
467. BB to James Leippert, 26 September 1932, CHIC.
468. BB to HM, 27 September 1932, CHIC.
469. BB to HM, 20 November 1932, CHIC.
470. BB to HM, 20 November 1932, CHIC.
471. BB to Morton Dauwen Zabel, 4 January 1933, CHIC.
472. BB to Morton Dauwen Zabel, 24 March 1933, CHIC.
473. EP to HM, undated but 1933, CHIC.
474. BB to HM, 2 August 1933, CHIC.
475. BB to HM, 30 August 1933, CHIC.
476. R Caddel (ed.), *Basil Bunting: Three Essays* (Durham, 1994). There is some doubt about the authorship of 'The Written Record', Andrew Crozier having suggested it is the work of Zukofsky's friend Irving Kaplan.
477. T. S. Eliot, *Selected Essays* (London, 1951), 13.
478. For instance this: 'The poet's mind is in fact a receptacle for seizing and storing up numberless feelings, phrases, images, which remain there until all the particles

which can unite to form a new compound are present together'; and: 'The business of the poet is not to find new emotions, but to use the ordinary ones and, in working them up into poetry, to express feelings which are not in actual emotions at all'; and 'to divert interest from the poet to the poetry is a laudable aim', (Eliot, *Selected*, 19, 21, 22). I think Bunting may have been alienated by Eliot's implausible accommodation of chemistry into the creative process in this essay. What is certain is that Bunting was deliberately picking a fight that couldn't possibly advance his career.

479. *The Lion and Crown*, 1.1, October 1932, 26–33. It is mentioned in a letter from Bunting to Pound written on 21 November 1930.

480. Caddel, 30–31.

481. Caddel, 4.

482. SSLT, 212.

483. BB to LZ, 27 April 1934, HR.

484. BB to EP, undated but January 1931, BRBML.

485. R. Murray Schafer, *Ezra Pound and Music: The complete criticism* (London, 1978), 333. According to Omar Pound, Bunting and Pound were 'on the "foreign affairs" staff of the literary supplement of *Il Mare*'. O. Pound and R. Spoo, *Ezra and Dorothy Pound: Letters in Captivity, 1945–1946* (Oxford, 1999), 162.

486. BB to James Leippert, 26 September 1932, CHIC.

487. An exclusion made the more unforgivable for being justified by Eliot at his condescending worst: 'I have omitted one long poem, which Mr. Pound might himself have included: the *Homage to Sextus Propertius*. I was doubtful of its effect upon the uninstructed reader, even with my instructions. If the uninstructed reader is not a classical scholar, he will make nothing of it; if he be a classical scholar, he will wonder why this does not conform to his notions of what translations should be.' E. Pound, *Selected Poems*, ed. T. S. Eliot (London, 1948), xxiii.

488. *New English Weekly*, 1, no. 6, 26 May 1932, 137–8.

489. Carpenter, 510.

490. E. Pound, *ABC of Reading* (London, 1961), 92.

491. BB to EP, 18 July [1934], BRBML.

492. BB to William Cookson, 21 December 1979, BRBML.

493. Interview with Pitkethly and Laughlin, October 1982.

494. BB to James Leippert, 4 January 1933, CHIC.

495. BB to Morton Dauwen Zabel, 4 January 1933, CHIC.

496. BB to Morton Dauwen Zabel, 24 March 1933, CHIC.

497. Marian Bunting to Helen Groves, 11 September 1968, DUR.

498. Ahearn, 145 and 149. See also DESC.

499. BB to Peter Russell, 18 May 1950, SUNY.

500. Marian Bunting to Helen Groves, 11 September 1968, DUR.

501. SSLT, 193.

502. FORDE, 36. This account is a little incoherent.

503. BB to EP, 18 November 1933, BRBML.

504. BB to EP, 18 November 1933, BRBML.
505. BB to EP, 'Twentyumpth' January 1934, BRBML.
506. BB to EP, 8 April 1934, BRBML.
507. BB to EP, 8 April 1934, BRBML.
508. BB to EP, 21 March 1934, BRBML.
509. BB to EP, 18 November 1933, BRBML.
510. DESC.
511. FORDE, 36.
512. BB to EP, 21 March 1934, BRBM.
513. BB to EP, 21 March 1934, BRBML.
514. FORDE, 36.
515. Postmarked (Tenerife) 16 April 1935, DUR.
516. BB to EP, 5 March 1935, BRBML.
517. Marian Bunting to Roger Guedalla, 25 September 1968, DUR.
518. DESC.
519. BB to EP, undated but 1934, BRBML.
520. Ahearn, 158.
521. BB to EP, 'Twentyumpth' January 1934, BRBML.
522. BB to EP, 21 March 1934, BRBML.
523. BB to EP, 21 October 1934, BRBML.
524. CP, 153.
525. CP, 168.
526. Reading in February 1982, London.
527. *The Lion and the Throne: Stories from the Shahnameh of Ferdowsi*, transl. D. Davis (Washington DC, 1998), 117–8.
528. FORDE, 39.
529. BB to LZ, 28 October 1932, HR.
530. Plymouth State University, *Karl Drerup: A Modernist drawn to life* (Plymouth, 2010), 22–3.
531. CP, 124–5. Bunting told Gael Turnbull that 'The Orotava Road' is 'a tribute to Dr Williams. Just a deliberate exercise in his style. Trying to use what he discovered. That's all it is' (Turnbull and Whyte, 49). Fittingly *Cambridge Opinion* published 'The Orotava Road' in a special William Carlos Williams issue in 1965 (*Cambridge Opinion*, 41, 1965, 21).
532. Reading in 1980 in London. This was the first of Bunting's poems to be translated into Spanish by Andres Sanchez Robayna of La Laguna University, Tenerife.
533. Quoted in Stock, 283.
534. B. Ahearn (ed.), *The Correspondence of William Carlos Williams and Louis Zukofsky* (Middletown, 2003), 176.
535. Marian Bunting to Roger Guedalla, 18 December 1968, DUR.
536. FORDE, 39–40.
537. BB to EP, 23 June 1934, BRBML.
538. BB to EP, 18 July 1934, BRBML. 'I lived,' he wrote in 1976, 'for some weeks in a hotel where they gave me a bedroom and a sitting room and all my meals, very

good meals, and did all my washing for the equivalent of about 11d a day.' (*Multi: Basil Bunting from the British Press* (1976), unpaginated).

539. BB to EP, 18 July 1934, BRBML.

540. BB to EP, 5 March 1935, BRBML.

541. BB to EP, 11 December 1935, BRBML.

542. BB to EP, 8 April 1934, BRBM.

543. BB to EP, 21 October 1934, BRBML.

544. BB to EP, 22 November 1934, BRBML.

545. In a letter to Louis Zukofsky, 29 September 1935, FORDE, 129.

546. FORDE, 131.

547. SYSB, 202–3.

548. Reading in 1976 at the University of Essex, published by Keele University in 1995.

549. CP, 126.

550. BB to DG, 13 December 1964, DUR.

551. Reading, February 1982, London. Bunting described 'The Well of Lycopolis' as 'a very bitter poem' at an earlier reading in London in spring 1977.

552. E. Gibbon, *The Decline and Fall of the Roman Empire* (London, 1994), Volume II, 64.

553. CP, 39–40. Pound urged Bunting to cut the opening of 'The Well of Lycopolis'. 'Much thanks suggestion re first lines of Lycopolis, wh. seems likely to be very useful. Don't know how you do it (find the key to weaknesses). Said excision suggests many emendments' (BB to EP, 28 March 1936, BRBML). He accepted much of Pound's advice but was conscious that Pound would not have accepted some of the fundamental conceits: 'I have parodied part of the Belle Heaulmiere for a poem now in the making. But I don't think you'd approve' (BB to EP, 'Day after saint bloody John' [so 25 June], 1935, BRBML).

554. CP, 40–1.

555. CP, 41.

556. CP, 43.

557. BB to LZ, 28 October 1935, HR.

558. Dante, *The Divine Comedy: Hell*, transl. Dorothy L. Sayers (London, 1949), 113.

559. CP, 44–5.

560. BB to LZ, 28 October 1935, HR.

561. B. Ahearn (ed.), *The Correspondence of William Carlos Williams and Louis Zukofsky* (Middletown, 2003), 199.

562. 'Carlos Williams' Recent Poetry', *Westminster Magazine*, 23, 2, Summer 1934, 149–54.

563. 'The Roots of the Spanish Revolt', *Spectator*, 24 July 1936, 138.

564. *Criterion*, 15, 41, July 1936, 714–16.

565. *Criterion*, 15, 41, July 1936, 762–3.

566. B. Bunting, 'Mirage and Men', *Spectator*, 5648, 25 September 1936, 510–12.

567. SSLT, 36. Anyone who has doubts about the interconnectedness of the British literary establishment should consult V. Cunningham, *British Writers of the Thirties*, (Oxford, 1988), 134–5, for an almost comical, certainly biblical, account of the English public school and Oxbridge connections of virtually every literary name

one can think of.

568. *New English Weekly* 9, no. 25, 1 October 1936, 411–2.
569. Marian Bunting to Roger Guedalla, 7 March 1969, DUR.
570. I. Hunter, *Malcom Muggeridge: A Life* (London, 1980), 97.
571. Hunter, 106.
572. G. Wolfe, *Malcolm Muggeridge: A Biography* (London, 1995), 148.
573. Hunter, 106.
574. For instance by Peter Quartermain and Roger Guedalla, SSLT, 36.
575. M. Muggeridge, *Chronicles of Wasted Time*, Volume 2 (London, 1973), 32–3.
576. J. Bright-Holmes (ed.), *Like it Was: The Diaries of Malcolm Muggeridge* (London, 1981), 152.
577. 'Mr Wordsworth', *The Spirit of the Age* (1825) in J. Cook (ed.), *William Hazlitt: Selected Writings* (Oxford, 1991), 357.
578. Ahearn, 194–5.
579. L. Zukofsky, *Ferdinand* (London, 1968), 38.
580. 'Observations on Left-Wing Papers', SSLT, 46–7.
581. Marian Bunting to Roger Guedalla, 25 September 1968, DUR.
582. DESC.
583. BB to EP, 22 January 1936, BRBML.
584. Ahearn, 187.
585. BB to EP, 22 January 1936, BRBML.
586. BB to EP, 13 July 1936, BRBML.
587. BB to EP, 3 September 1936, BRBML.
588. FORDE, 40–3.
589. Marian was eventually granted a decree absolute in 1940. Martin Duberman describes how, in 1949, Bourtai made a rather bizarre announcement to members of the Black Mountain community: 'The Buntings and Ezra Pounds had shared a house in Rapallo for a time, and Bortai [*sic*] let the community know that her younger brother was a Pound and that she suspected the youngest Pound might be a Bunting' (M. Duberman, *Black Mountain: An exploration in community* (New York, 1972), 317). Ezra was almost certainly not Omar Pound's father, but neither was Bunting. Dorothy Pound became pregnant with Omar during a visit to Egypt. (Bunting referred to Omar cheekily as 'Omar-i-bin-Ezra' (Carpenter, 453–6). Rustam was conceived in September 1936 when the Buntings were living in London. In any event, there is no evidence that the Buntings shared a house in Rapallo with the Pounds. Pound already had a virtual *ménage à trois* at the time with Dorothy and Olga Rudge in Rapallo.
590. *Criterion*, April 1936, 421–3.
591. CP, 209.
592. BB to DP and EP, 9 January 1937, BRBML.
593. Ahearn, 191.
594. BB to LZ, 31 August 1939, HR.
595. Ahearn, 191.
596. Paige, 277.

597. Ahearn, WCW–LZ, 323.

598. BB to DP, 22 November 1946, LILLY. *Poems 1950* was published in the US by Dallam Flynn.

599. Marian Bunting to Roger Guedalla, 7 March 1969, DUR.

600. Pound, *Cantos*, 518.

601. B. Bunting, 'The Village Fiesta', *Paideuma*, Winter 1981, 619–20.

602. *Paideuma*, Winter 1981, 620–21.

603. BB to KD, 19 January 1940, DUR.

604. BB to DP and EP, 9 January 1937, BRBML. The reference to 'unco guids' is taken from Robert Burns' 'Address to the Unco Guid, or the rigidly Righteous.'

605. DESC.

606. DESC.

607. BB to KD, 25 January 1938, DUR.

608. BB to KD, 25 January 1938, DUR.

609. BB to KD, 25 January 1938, DUR.

610. BB to KD, 25 January 1938, DUR.

611. SSLT, 50.

612. SSLT, 206.

613. Interview with Andrew McAllister and Sean Figgis, recorded at Bunting's home near Hexham on 10 November 1984, published by Keele University, 1995.

614. BB to EP, 11 November 1938, BRBML.

615. CP, 127, 227.

616. *Criterion*, April 1938, 557–9.

617. DESC. According to Garth Clucas, 'Basil Bunting: A Chronology' in PI, 71. The chronology of this period of Bunting's life is difficult to establish exactly. Caddel and Flowers, for instance, claim that he spent 1938 sailing in the Mediterranean and joined Nellist's in 1938 (BBNL, 39–40). He couldn't have done this as he sailed to Montreal in April 1938. In any event Bunting claimed that 'the chap [Clucas] who compiled an alleged chronology, one page in Poetry Information, got almost every item wrong' (BB to TP, 18 January 1979, SUNY).

618. *Edinburgh Gazette*, 19 June 1923, 899.

619. DESC.

620. BB to LZ, 12 April 1938, HR.

621. DESC.

622. DESC.

623. BB to C. D. Abbott, 2 June 1938, SUNY.

624. Faranda, 88.

625. Ahearn, 196. In fact Bunting did have work. He wrote to Drerup in May 1938: 'I got a job and have to leave for Annapolis at once … I come north again, with the yacht, in June. Then I'll be at Oyster Bay …' (BB to KD, 11 May 1938, DUR.)

626. BB to KD, 27 August 1938, DUR.

627. BB to WCW, 14 October 1938, BRBML.

628. EP to BB, 24 November 1938, BRBML.

629. Carpenter, 481.

630. R. Preda (ed.), *Ezra Pound's Economic Correspondence, 1933–1940* (Gainesville, 2007), 115–16. See also Howson, 268–9.
631. BB to EP, 5 March 1935, BRBML.
632. EP to BB, undated but December 1935, BRBML.
633. BB to EP, 31 December 1935, BRBML.
634. BB to EP, 22 January 1936, BRBML.
635. BB to EP, 16 December 1938, BRBML.
636. Ahearn, 198.
637. BB to KD, 25 January 1938, DUR.
638. Paige, 324–5.
639. Ahearn, 203. The 'kumrad' was e. e. cummings.
640. Witemeyer, 294. Bunting did not appear in the series.
641. CP, 65.
642. B. Ahearn (ed.), *The Correspondence of William Carlos Williams and Louis Zukofsky* (Middletown, 2003), 262–3.
643. Ahearn, *Williams and Zukofsky* (Middletown, 2003), 265–6.
644. BB to EP, 11 November 1938, BRBML.
645. W. C. Williams, *The Autobiography of William Carlos Williams* (London, 1968), 264.
646. BBNL, 41.

CHAPTER 3:
SWEET SHIT! BUY!

1. BB to LZ, 3 November 1939, HR.
2. BB to DP, 28 August 1948, LILLY.
3. BB to LZ, 3 November 1939, HR.
4. BB to KD, 2 May 1939, DUR.
5. BB to LZ, 3 October 1939, HR. Bunting was certainly caught up in it. He wrote to Zukofsky about 'the tremendous display of energy on the part of the English people – "One thinks of … Rome in Hannibal's time; military genius, superior wealth & the command of the seas were all helpless against it. And yet nearly all the Roman leaders were mediocrities or worse" (BB to LZ, 18 December 1939, HR).
6. Annie Bunting to KD, undated but 1939, DUR.
7. *Manchester Guardian*, 10 June 1939.
8. BB to LZ, 3 October 1939, HR.
9. BB to LZ, 18 December 1939, HR.
10. BB to LZ, 3 November 1939, HR.
11. BB to LZ, 18 December 1939, HR.
12. BB to KD, 19 January 1940, DUR.
13. BB to LZ, 27 April 1940, HR.
14. BB to LZ, 11 July 1940, HR.
15. BB to LZ, 9 August 1940, HR.

16. BB to LZ, 9 August 1940, HR. This complaint about Marian resurfaced frequently until the couple were partially reconciled in the 1960s. In 1951, for instance, he complained to Zukofsky that he wouldn't 'list the series of dirty tricks she has played using the children as a kind of bait. Bourtai, since her marriage or a bit before it, seems to be completely estranged' (BB to LZ, 19 April 1951, HR).
17. DESC.
18. DESC.
19. I am indebted to *Hull's Own Air Force Station* by Leonard C. Bacon (Hull, 2002) for information about 17 Balloon Centre.
20. There are ten Luftwaffe folders in the Imperial War Museum, London, dated March 1939, which contain details of eleven specific targets in Hull, with accurate descriptions, locations and accounts of the strategic importance of each, as well as guidance on how to find them, and their likely defence capacity. See Revd P. Graystone, *The Blitz on Hull (1940–1945)*, (Hull, 1991).
21. Bacon, chapter 3.
22. The effects of the attacks on Hull are vividly described by Esther Baker in *A City in Flames: A Firewoman's Recollections of the Hull Blitz* (Beverley, 1992).
23. AIR 27/2287, 5 November 1940, KEW.
24. J. Penberthy, *Niedecker and the Correspondence with Zukofsky 1931–1970* (Cambridge, 1993), 128.
25. AIR 27/2294, KEW.
26. DESC.
27. DISJ, 141. Quartermain is probably correct. Bunting wrote to Dorothy Pound that the *Golden Hind's* job was protecting convoys, (BB to DP, Throckley, 22 November 1946, LILLY). On the other hand, 'I got a beautiful job,' Bunting told the Newcastle *Evening Chronicle* in 1965, 'taking balloons up and down the coast from Flamborough Head to Aberdeen' ('Eldon', *Evening Chronicle*, 9 June 1965, 6).
28. DISJ, 134. In fact Bunting wasn't promoted to leading Aircraftman until May 1942.
29. AIR 27/2294, KEW.
30. AIR 27/2294, KEW.
31. BB to GT, 20 January 1965.
32. BB to LZ, 9 September 1941, HR.
33. BB to LZ, 12 September 1941, HR.
34. CP, 129.
35. BB to LZ, 9 September 1941, HR.
36. BB to LZ, 22 September 1941, HR.
37. BB to LZ, 15 December 1941, HR.
38. BB to LZ, 18 February 1942, HR.
39. BB to KD, 1 April 1942, DUR. Bunting enjoyed the company of adolescent girls. Apart from Peggy and Violet there was his second wife, Sima, and in later life Tanya and a string of 'saqis'. I have come across no evidence (with the possible exception of *Briggflatts* itself, although that is a *poem*) that these girls ever became more than companions. He was intensely attached to some of them but there is no

evidence that any of them became either muses or lovers.

40. CP, 57–8.
41. BB to VF, 23 October 1972, DUR.
42. BB to KD, 1 April 1942, DUR.
43. Gael Turnbull, 'A visit to Basil when he was at Washington New Town', unpublished journal.
44. BB to LZ, 4 October 1942, HR.
45. DESC. 'When that finished, I wrote the Air Force authorities in medieval, classical Persian – I only knew it as a literary language' ('Eldon', *Evening Chronicle*, 9 June 1965, 6).
46. AIR 27/2266, KEW.
47. AIR 27/2266, KEW.
48. AIR 27/2329, 14 May 1942, KEW. The chain of command in the Middle East was, as we shall see, Byzantine, and Iraq was HQ for many who were actually operating in Iran and elsewhere.
49. BB to LZ, 4 October 1942, HR.
50. BB to DP, 29 June 1947, LILLY.
51. BB to LZ, 4 October 1942, HR.
52. BB to LZ, 4 October 1942, HR.
53. AIR 27/2329, KEW.
54. BB to LZ, 4 October 1942, HR.
55. AIR 27/2329, KEW.
56. DESC.
57. DESC.
58. A. H. Layard, *Early Adventures in Persia, Susiana, and Babylonia* (London, 1894), 162).
59. Layard, 162.
60. BB to LZ, 9 May 1943, HR.
61. PAID, 126.
62. BB to LZ, 4 October 1942, HR.
63. DESC. Bunting was already in Cairo, according to his service record, when he became an officer.
64. PAID, 63. Tom Pickard, for one, thinks this story a fabrication designed to tease Bunting's young American friend (conversation with author, May 2013).
65. S. Johnstone *Where No Angels Dwell* (London, 1969), 121.
66. Johnstone, 121.
67. AIR 27/1419, KEW.
68. BB to DP, 22 November 1946, LILLY.
69. AIR 27/1419, KEW.
70. AIR 27/1420, KEW.
71. BB to DP, 10 December 1946, LILLY. Bunting was much taken by this token of religious gratitude. He told Victoria Forde in 1972 that, 'there is a convent in Sicily where I'm told they still pray for me because of some trifling politeness I was able to show them during the war. It is something to value' (BB to VF, 11 January 1972, DUR).

72. Turnbull and Whyte, 48.
73. BB to DP, 8 January 1947, LILLY.
74. BB to DP, 22 November 1946, LILLY.
75. CONJ, 157.
76. BB to DP, undated but November 1949, LILLY.
77. BB to LZ, 25 July 1944, HR.
78. Turnbull, 48.
79. BB to DP, Throckley, 22 November 1946, LILLY.
80. Turnbull and Whyte, 50–1.
81. DESC.
82. BB to EP, 21 January 1947, LILLY.
83. K. Jeffery, *MI6: The History of the Secret Intelligence Service, 1909–1949* (London, 2010), 421–2.
84. Jeffery, 436.
85. R. Bullard, *The Camels Must Go: An Autobiography* (London, 1961) 221–2.
86. A. Milani, *The Shah* (London, 2011), 67.
87. Milani, 69.
88. Milani, 69.
89. PI, 44–5.
90. JIC Report quoted in F. H. Hinsley, *British Intelligence in the Second World War*, Volume 2 (London, 1981), 81.
91. Hinsley, 83.
92. *The Security Service 1908–1945: The Official History* (Kew, 1999), 271.
93. Jeffery, 688.
94. BB to LZ, 21 April 1945, HR.
95. BB to KD, 18 July 1945, DUR.
96. BB to KD, 18 July 1945, DUR.
97. BB to LZ, 6 August 1945, HR.
98. BB to DP, 27 November 1946, LILLY.
99. BB to LZ, 21 April 1945, HR.
100. BB to DP, 1 May 1947, LILLY.
101. BB to LZ, 17 October 1947, HR.
102. Turnbull and Whyte, 50.
103. Turnbull and Whyte, 48.
104. BB to LZ, 6 August 1953, HR.
105. BB to LZ, 3 November 1948, HR.
106. BB to LZ, 10 June 1946, HR.
107. FORDE, 49.
108. DISJ, 141.
109. BB to LZ, 13 March 1951, HR.
110. BB to LZ, 19 April 1951, HR.
111. B. Butters, 'Don't keep poetry to yourself – read it aloud', *Victoria Daily Times*, 13 October 1971, 3.
112. BBNL, 49.

113. Paige, 346.
114. O. Pound and R. Spoo (eds), *Ezra and Dorothy Pound: Letters in Captivity 1945–1946* (New York, 1999), 249.
115. Witemeyer, 224.
116. Pound and Spoo, 281.
117. Pound and Spoo, 303.
118. Pound and Spoo, 327.
119. Pound and Spoo, 349.
120. BB to MS, 2 September 1949, DUR.
121. BB to KD, 24 January 1947, DUR.
122. BB to Robert Creeley, 12 July 1951, DUR.
123. B. Ahearn, *The Correspondence of William Carlos Williams and Louis Zukofsky* (Middletown, 2003), 385.
124. BB to DP, 22 November 1946, LILLY.
125. BB to LZ, 21 January 1947, HR.
126. BB to Mary Baratti (later de Rachewiltz), 21 March 1947, DUR.
127. BB to LZ, 5 May 1947, HR.
128. BB to DP, 10 December 1946, LILLY.
129. BB to LZ, 10 June 1946, HR.
130. For example in BB to DP, 10 December 1946, LILLY, and BB to LZ, 10 June 1946, HR.
131. BB to EP, 7 December 1946, LILLY.
132. BB to EP, 7 December 1946, LILLY.
133. BB to EP, 25 March 1947, LILLY.
134. BB to LZ, 4 November 1946, HR.
135. BB to DP, 10 December 1946, LILLY.
136. BB to DP, 10 December 1946, LILLY.
137. DESC.
138. BB to DP, 8 January 1947, LILLY.
139. BB to DP, 24 January 1947, LILLY.
140. BB to DP, 11 February 1947, LILLY.
141. BB to DP, 20 April 1948, LILLY.
142. BB to DP, 20 February 1947, LILLY.
143. BB to DP, 29 June 1947, LILLY.
144. BB to DP, 22 November 1946, LILLY.
145. BB to LZ, 5 May 1947, HR.
146. BB to DP, 17 May 1948, LILLY.
147. BB to DP, 29 June 1947, LILLY.
148. BB to DP, 17 December 1947, LILLY.
149. BB to DP, 17 May 1948, LILLY.
150. BB to LZ, 20 August 1947, HR.
151. BB to DP, 17 December 1947, LILLY.
152. BB to LZ, 'June the New Moonth' 1953, HR.
153. BB to DP, 11 April 1948, LILLY.

154. BB to DP, 17 May 1948, LILLY.
155. BB to DP, 17 December 1947, LILLY.
156. CP, 130.
157. BB to LZ, 28 July 1949, HR.
158. CP, 131.
159. BB to LZ, 28 July 1949, HR.
160. CP, 228.
161. T. Cole, 'Bunting: Formal Aspects', *Poetry* (78, 6) September 1951, 366–9.
162. 'Just about a thousand years ago Rudaki wrote a dialogue which I find fresh to this moment' (Reading in 1978 in Leeds, published by Keele University in 1995).
163. Bunting noted that this poem was probably wrongly attributed to Sa'di. (CP, 159.)
164. Reading, 9 December 1970, the University of British Columbia, published by Keele University, 1995.
165. CP, 160.
166. L. Zukofsky, *A Test of Poetry* (New York, 1948), 107–8.
167. CP, 132.
168. Reading in February 1982 in London.
169. SSLT, 207.
170. BB to MS, 28 August 1948, DUR.
171. BB to MS, 28 August 1948, DUR.
172. BB to DP, 28 August 1948, LILLY.
173. BB to DP, 17 May 1948, LILLY.
174. BB to MS, 2 September 1949, DUR.
175. BB to MS, 2 September 1949, DUR.
176. BB to LZ, 5 March 1949, HR.
177. BB to DP, 14 April 1949, LILLY. *The Times* was his new employer.
178. BB to DP, 11 April 1948, LILLY. The ageing officer referred to is Oakshott rather than himself.
179. BB to LZ, 3 November 1948, HR.
180. BB to DP, 30 May 1967, LILLY.
181. BB to DP, 30 May 1967, LILLY. Bunting certainly prized Islamic culture. 'Reverting to the West,' he wrote to Zukofsky, 'has made me more convinced than before that we've got to learn almost everything from the East (which, to the measure of my limited experience is the lands of Islam) before there's a chance of any peace of mind or dignity for most of us' (BB to LZ, 10 May 1953, HR). *The Spoils* 'said more to the point about Islam, Israel, Persia, and what they should show us than ten dozen special reports', he wrote in a splenetic letter to Margaret de Silver in 1953 (BB to MS, 9 April 1953, DUR).
182. See C. Tripp, *A History of Iraq* (Cambridge, 2007), 105–34.
183. BB to DP, 26 September 1948, LILLY.
184. *Multi: Basil Bunting from the British Press* (Berkeley, 1976), unpaginated.
185. BB to Charles Deakin, 2 November 1948, *Times* archive, quoted by Tom Pickard.
186. BB to Charles Deakin, 10 January 1949, *Times* archive, quoted by Tom Pickard.
187. BB to MS, 2 September 1949, DUR.

188. BB to MS, 28 August 1948, DUR.

189. BB to MS, 2 September 1949, DUR.

190. BB to MS, 2 September 1949, DUR.

191. R. Payne, *Journey to Persia* (London, 1951), x.

192. Payne, 194–6.

193. BB to DP, 15 May 1949, LILLY.

194. BB to LZ, 29 March 1953, HR.

195. BB to MS, 28 May 1953, DUR.

196. BB to TP, 18 January 1979, SUNY.

197. BB to DP, 9 June 1949, LILLY.

198. B. Ahearn (ed.), *The Correspondence of William Carlos Williams and Louis Zukofsky* (Middletown, 2003), 414.

199. BB to LZ, 17 June 1949, HR.

200. BB to LZ, 17 June 1949, HR. Nasser Khan Qashqai was the tribal chief of the politically important Qashqai people.

201. BB to LZ, 6 August 1949, HR.

202. BB to LZ, 5 September 1949, HR.

203. BB to MS, 3 January 1950, DUR.

204. BB to MS, 3 January 1950, DUR.

205. BB to MS, 27 April 1951, DUR.

206. BB to DP, 13 April 1950, LILLY.

207. BB to DP, 25 July 1950, LILLY.

208. BB to DP, 14 May 1950, LILLY.

209. BB to DP, 20 July 1951, LILLY.

210. BB to DP, 14 May 1950, LILLY.

211. BB to LZ, 20 July 1950, HR.

212. BB to LZ, 12 November 1950, HR.

213. BB to DP, 14 April 1949, LILLY.

214. BB to LZ, 12 November 1950, HR.

215. MONT, 71.

216. B. Bunting, *Poems 1950*, ed. D. Flynn (Galveston, 1950), ii.

217. Mary de Rachewiltz, 'For B. B.', SSLT, 193.

218. BB to DP, 3 September 1950, LILLY.

219. BB to GT, undated but January 1965.

220. Pound, *Cantos*, 781. Eliot wrote, in *The Waste Land*, 'these fragments I have shored against my ruins'. The other neglected poet is Allen Upward.

221. H. Kenner, 'A resurrected poet: The Chisel', *Poetry*, September 1951, 361–5.

222. BB to DP, 24 August 1951, LILLY.

223. *Northern Review of Writing and the Arts in Canada*, IV, 5 (1951), 45–7.

224. V. Koch, 'The Necessary Angels of Earth', *Sewanee Review*, LIX, 1951, 670–1.

225. T. Cole, 'Bunting: Formal Aspects', *Poetry* (78, 6) September 1951, 366–9.

226. DISJ, 141. According to Tom Pickard, who would also have had this from Bunting, there is some evidence to suggest that the journalistic trip to Italy was a cover. Bunting was known to be an expert on Italy, and 'there is a strong possibility

that he may have been acting as a stringer for them. The communists formed the largest political party in Italy, and there was a fear that they would take the country into the Soviet sphere of influence. Bunting was being sent there to assess the likelihood of that happening. Unfortunately his cover was blown at the airport "by some fool from the embassy" who recognized him.'

227. BB to LZ, 12 November 1950, HR.
228. BB to DP, 12 November 1950, LILLY.
229. BB to LZ, 12 November 1950, HR.
230. BB to DP, 12 November 1950, LILLY.
231. BB to LZ, 12 November 1950, HR.
232. BB to DP, 29 November 1950, LILLY.
233. BB to LZ, 14 March 1951, HR.
234. BB to EP, Bertrand Russell, Ahmad Suratgar, Arthur Waley, G. M. Wickens, 30 December 1950, BRBML.
235. BB to EP, 14 February 1951, BRBML.
236. BB to EP, 14 March 1951, LILLY.
237. BB to LZ, 14 March 1951, HR.
238. BB to EP, 14 March 1951, LILLY.
239. BB to Peter Russell, 14 May 1950, SUNY.
240. BB to LZ, 14 March 1951, HR. 'Pea: Italian novelist, pretty good. Peasant origin' (BB to LZ, 19 April 1951, HR).
241. BB to LZ, 19 April 1951, HR.
242. BB to DP, 16 April 1951, LILLY.
243. BB to DP, 14 May 1951, LILLY.
244. BB to T. S. Eliot, 2 May 1951, HR.
245. BB to LZ, 9 July 1953, HR.
246. BB to LZ, 28 September 1953, HR.
247. BB to EP, 14 November 1955, BRBML.
248. BB to EP, 11 November 1964, BRBML.
249. BB to DG, 26 May 1965, DUR.
250. BB to DP, 12 November 1950, 31 January 1951, 14 May 1951, LILLY.
251. BB to MS, 27 April 1951, DUR. He had told Margaret the previous year that the only news that year from his 'ex-family … is a card which reached me a few days ago, printed, indicating that my daughter Bourtai married a man called Scudder two or three months ago' (BB to MS, 3 January 1950, DUR).
252. BB to DP, 24 June 1951, LILLY.
253. BB to MS, 30 June 1951, DUR.
254. BB to MS, 30 June 1951, DUR. ·
255. BB to DP, 20 July 1951, LILLY.
256. BB to LZ, 14 March 1951, HR.
257. BB to DP, 20 July 1951, LILLY.
258. BB to DP, 24 August 1951, LILLY. It was 'oil troubles' that delayed his visa (BB to Karl Shapiro, 22 August 1951, DUR).
259. BB to DP, 24 August 1951, LILLY.

260. BB to DP, 24 August 1951, LILLY.

261. DESC.

262. BB to DP, 9 June 1949, LILLY.

263. P. Stothard, 'Put out the birthday Bunting', *Times*, 29 January 1999. To be fair Stothard does acknowledge that Bunting was a 'great' poet.

264. BB to DP, 24 August 1951, LILLY.

265. *Times*, 22 August 1951.

266. BB to DP, 30 November 1951, LILLY.

267. BB to EP, 24 March 1952, LILLY.

268. BB to LZ, 17 June 1952, HR.

269. BB to EP, 24 March 1952, LILLY.

270. P. Stothard, 'Journalist spies', *Times Literary Supplement*, 27 September 2009.

271. *Times*, 14 April 1952.

272. Stothard, *TLS*.

273. BB to MS, 1 October 1952, DUR.

274. BB to EP, 17 March 1953, LILLY.

275. BB to *The Times* quoted by Tom Pickard in George Oppen Memorial Lecture, 2004.

276. E. Abrahamian, *A History of Modern Iran* (Cambridge, 2008), 117.

277. D. Bayandor, *Iran and the CIA: The Fall of Mosaddeq Revisited* (Basingstoke, 2010), 203–4.

278. C. M. Woodhouse, *Something Ventured: An Autobiography* (London, 1982), 115.

279. Bayandor, 64–8.

280. See M. Axworthy, *Empire of the Mind: A History of Iran* (London, 2007), 239–44.

281. Woodhouse, 108–19.

282. N. R. Keddie, *Modern Iran: Roots and Results of Revolution* (New Haven, 2003), 130.

283. C. de Bellaigue, *Patriot of Persia: Muhammed Mossadegh and a Very British Coup* (London, 2012), 194–7.

284. BB to LZ, 27 October 1953, HR.

285. BB to EP, 9 July 1953, BRBML.

286. BB to MS, Throckley, 1 October 1952, DUR.

287. 'I'm on half pay until October, and would be sent back to Persia by the Times if Mosaddeq should fall' but 'we'll cease to have an income just about the time we are due to have another baby' (BB to LZ, 17 June 1952, HR).

288. BB to TP, 13 June 1976, SUNY.

289. BB to MS, 27 September 1953, DUR.

290. SSLT, 197.

291. BB to MS, 28 May 1953, DUR.

292. *Multi: Basil Bunting from the British Press* (1976).

293. SSLT, 196.

294. BB to EP, 18 May 1952, LILLY.

295. BB to EP, 18 May 1952, LILLY.

296. '83 Answers … and Some Questions', Basil Bunting and Jonathan Williams, introduced by Eric Robson, BBC North East, 17 August 1984 and 19 April 1985.

242 Newburn Road was certainly not 'very small'. It is a large, semi-detached, family house.

297. BB to MS, 1 October 1952, DUR.
298. B. Ahearn (ed.), *The Correspondence of William Carlos Williams and Louis Zukofsky* (Middletown, 2003), 455.
299. Witemeyer, 292.
300. BB to LZ, 29 October 1953, HR.
301. BB to LZ, 5 December 1953, HR.
302. BB to LZ, 5 December 1953, HR.
303. BB to LZ, 28 August 1948, HR.
304. *Nine*, 4, August 1950, 217–19; *Fragmente* 1, 1, 1951, 7; *Imagi*, 5, 3, 1951.
305. BB to LZ, 28 August 1948, HRC.
306. 'The Spoils' 'is said to be the most difficult poem I have written' (Reading in spring 1977, London). He told Victoria Forde in 1972 that he had cut out more of the poem than Zukofsky had wanted him to, and condensed two movements into one, 'thus keeping a dense tissue, but losing the symmetry I had planned. That makes it lopsided. And too obscure' (BB to VF, 23 October 1972, DUR).
307. BB to VF, 23 October 1972, DUR.
308. Reading in February 1982, London.
309. P. Quartermain, 'Take Oil/and Hum: Niedecker/Bunting' in E. Willis (ed.), *Radical Vernacular: Lorine Niedecker and the Poetics of Place* (Iowa City, 2008), 276.
310. CP, 56.
311. BB to LZ, 18 June 1953, HR.
312. K. Alldritt, *Modernism in the Second World War: The Later Poetry of Ezra Pound, T. S. Eliot, Basil Bunting and Hugh MacDiarmid* (Berne, 1989), 96.
313. *Guardian*, 15 July 1957.
314. SSLT, 201.
315. BB to LZ, 22 June 1951, HR.
316. BB to EP, undated but April 1954, BRBML.
317. SSLT, 201.
318. BB to EP, 5 March 1935, BRBML.
319. Turnbull and Whyte, 52.
320. BB to LZ, 2 December 1948, HR.
321. T. Pickard, George Oppen Memorial Lecture, 2004.
322. BB to DG, 20 January 1965, DUR.
323. BB to LZ, 31 December 1950, HR.
324. BB to DP, 17 March 1953, LILLY.
325. BB to MS, 9 April 1953, DUR.
326. BB to MS, 27 September 1953, DUR.
327. BB to LZ, 29 March 1953, HR.
328. BB to LZ, 18 June 1953, HR. The Customs authorities eventually valued Bunting's car 'at exactly six times the highest price I have been offered for it' (BB to LZ, 27 October 1953, HR).
329. BB to EP, 9 July 1953, BRBML.

330. BB to LZ, 28 September 1953, HR. He also revealed in this letter that the Colonial Office had turned him down for an 'excellent job in Trinidad'.
331. DISJ, 142–3.
332. BB to DP, 11 December 1953, LILLY.
333. SSLT, 197.
334. PAID, 156.
335. BB to LZ, 27 October 1953, HR.
336. BB to LZ, 5 December 1953, HR.
337. BB to DP, 14 December 1953, LILLY.
338. BB to EP, 1 July 1954, BRBML.
339. SSLT, 198.
340. BB to EP, 28 November 1954, BRBML.
341. D. Foreman, Senior Librarian at the *Evening Chronicle*, to Roger Guedalla, 9 March 1970 DUR.
342. DESC.
343. BB to EP, 9 July 1953, BRBML.
344. BB to D. G. Bridson, 23 August 1955, LILLY. He was still railing against Mosaddeq and *The Times* ten years later. Poverty 'brings so many unforseen [*sic*] humiliations besides the daily ignoble drudgery among foul people. I curse Mosaddeq and the Astor family every day.' (BB to GT, 4 January 1965).
345. BB to D. G. Bridson, 26 June 1957, LILLY.
346. DESC.
347. DESC.
348. '83 Answers … and Some Questions'.
349. FORDE, 55–6.
350. BB to GT, 27 March 1965.
351. BBNL, 44–5. Bunting's RAF file records that his commission was relinquished on 10 February 1954 and that he retained his rank of Squadron Leader under the Navy, Army and Air Force Act 1954. It isn't clear when he promoted himself by a rank to Wing Commamer.
352. Ahearn, 214. 'P' is Zukofsky's son Paul who was thirteen at the time and a talented violinist. The 'announcement' probably relates to Paul's debut recital at Carnegie Hall that year.
353. BBNL, 46.
354. BBNL, 45.
355. BB to GT, 9 August 1957.
356. '83 Answers … and Some Questions'.
357. BB to LZ, 11 April 1957, HR.
358. BB to EP, 11 December 1957, BRBML. Hettie had enjoyed a successful career at the Post Office and died a wealthy woman.
359. BB to EP, 11 December 1957, BRBML.
360. BB to Jonathan Williams, 22 February 1963, SUNY.
361. LZ to BB, 21 November 1962, DUR.
362. BB to LZ, June the New Moonth 1953, HR.

363. BB to DG, 13 June 1964, SUNY.
364. BB to DG, 23 November 1964, SUNY.
365. CP, 71.
366. BB to DP, 11 June 1965, LILLY.
367. BBNL, 47.
368. PAID, 158–9.
369. *Evening Chronicle*, 12 June 1964.
370. PAID, 160–1.
371. BB to LZ, 28 July 1964, HR.
372. BB to LZ, 7 September 1964, HR.
373. BB to LZ, 16 September 1964, HR.
374. *Paris Review*, 34, Summer 1965, 92–3.
375. CP, 135.
376. CP, 137.
377. PAID, 162.
378. TP to author, 15 March 2013.
379. PAID, 163. That seems to have struck a chord. Jill Turnbull found a limerick from Bunting in her husband's papers after Gael Turnbull died:

    There was a young lady called May
    who was got in the family way
    by the mate of a bugger,
    an ignorant bugger
    who always spelled c___ with a 'k'.

CHAPTER 4:
AN ACKNOWLEDGED LAND

1. B. Bunting, *A Note on Briggflatts* (Durham, 1989).
2. CP, 61.
3. CP, 144.
4. AG, 11.
5. Interview with Tom Pickard, 17 and 18 June 1981.
6. Interview with Peter Bell, 3 September 1981.
7. BB to LZ, 10 November 1964, HR. The one change from the original wording in the published version was the replacement of the word 'spheres' with 'woods'.
8. D. Davie, *Pound* (London, 1975), 83.
9. BB to LZ, 6 December 1964, HR.
10. BB to Donald Davie, 9 October 1975, Essex University Library.
11. Interview with McAllister and Figgis, 10 November 1984.
12. R. Bullard, *The Camels Must Go: An Autobiography* (London, 1961), 245.
13. R. Bullard, *Letters from Tehran: A British Ambassador in World War II Persia* (London, 1991), 138, 145, 166.
14. A. Ferdowsi, *Shahnameh: The Persian Book of Kings* (transl. Dick Davis), (London,

2007), 513–4.

15. MONT, 79.

16. AG, 17. Don Share suggests it was more like fiteen thousand lines (donshare. blogspot.com).

17. CP, 226.

18. AG, 9–10.

19. T. Gunn, *Shelf Life* (London, 1993), 61.

20. BB to Roger Guedalla, 28 May 1970.

21. N. Davies, *Vanished Kingdoms: The History of Half-Forgotten Europe* (London, 2011), 59.

22. Ida was the king of Bernicia. Taliesin was a sixth-century court bard.

23. Interview with Peter Bell, 3 September 1981.

24. PI, 5.

25. M. Ellmann, *The Nets of Modernism: Henry James, Virginia Woolf, James Joyce, and Sigmund Freud* (Cambridge, 2010), 22.

26. Ellmann, 14–34.

27. P. Makin, *'Silent, accurate lips': Precision in Bunting's poetry* (Durham, 2000), unpaginated. Bunting regarded Makin as a sensitive reader of his poetry but ridiculed his readings in of meaning: 'Makin amuses me that way. As I say, I think he's one of the good critics. He takes great pains, but he is apt to read meanings in that you never put there!' He was generally scathing of any analysis of his work, even that of his friends. He said of Eric Mottram's readings that 'where he got his guesswork from I didn't know. Some of it was a load of rubbish' (interview with McAllister and Figgis, 10 November 1984).

28. PI, 9.

29. *Agenda*, 8, 3–4, Autumn–Winter 1970, 118–19.

30. Gunn, 63.

31. Interview with Peter Bell, 3 September 1981.

32. AG, 14. In another interview he said that the poem had been written on an old income tax return (MT, 79).

33. Gunn, 64.

34. BB to DG, 4 September 1965, DUR.

35. Interview with Philip Trevelyan, 3 September 1981, published by Keele University, 1995.

36. BB to D. G. Bridson, 20 April 1965, LILLY.

37. nterview with Peter Bell, 3 September 1981.

38. D. Share and C. Wiman (eds), *The Open Door: One Hundred Poems, One Hundred Years of Poetry Magazine* (Chicago, 2012), 6–7.

39. Gunn, 64.

40. Reading on 20 April 1976 at Allentown Community Center, Buffalo, NY, donshare.blogspot.com

41. Gunn, 64.

42. AG, 9–17.

43. AG, 14.

44. AG, 15. The slightly mistranscribed quotation is from Catullus 5, his celebrated

'Vivamus mea Lesbia', in Thomas Campion's translation, 'then must we sleep one ever-during night'. Bunting explained that *'nox est perpetua una dormienda ... is a much more complex line than any of the translators has ever got across. The una is never given its full value ... Nox est perpetua: there is an everlasting night. Una dormienda doesn't mean one night, it means a night that is all one, that never varies ... I think that it's probably from that line that the whole train of thought started, that brought back the various things that become matter in the poem.'* The line clearly inspired the close of *Briggflatts* (AG, 12–13).

45. The full references for the Scarlatti sonatas to be used in readings of *Briggflatts* are L204 G major, L25 E major, L10 C minor, L275 E minor, L33 B minor, L58 D minor, L33 repeated (BB to VF, 6 June 1971, DUR).

46. Interview with Peter Bell, 3 September 1981.

47. P. Makin, *Basil Bunting on Poetry* (Baltimore, 1999), 10.

48. Interview with McAllister and Figgis, 10 November 1984.

49. Stephen Gill makes this point expertly. S. Gill, *Wordsworth's Revisitings* (Oxford, 2011), 83–154.

50. DESC. Williams clearly noticed something fishy about Bunting's Quaker credentials:

> BB: The First World War was on and I had decided to refuse service, and I just had to wait until the police arrested me, almost on my 18th birthday.
> JW: Did your family support that position?
> BB: No.
> JW: They didn't, with all that Quakerism?
> BB: No...

51. PI, 9.

52. Agenda, 12, 2 (Summer 1974, 37).

53. DESC.

54. Frederick Andrews celebrated Ellen Fry's 'natural gift for teaching, her buoyant temperament, [and] her prowess at cricket' (Headmaster's Address, 1920, 43). She seems to have been the real thing. There is not an inauthentic syllable in the encomium to friendship in her Presidential Address to Ackworth Old Scholars of Easter 1921.

55. MT, 72.

56. MONT, 68–9.

57. Interview with Peter Bell on 3 September 1981.

58. SYSB, 246–50. Davie's claims that Bunting's writing forms part of a long line of Protestant dissent were made in *The Times Literary Supplement* of 23 May 1986. They were partially, and unsatisfactorily, refuted by Richard Caddell in the issue of 20 June 1986, before being thoroughly demolished by Peter Makin in the 1 August 1986 issue.

59. BB to LZ, 3 February 1951, HR.

60. W. B. Yeats, *Explorations* (London, 1962), 295–6.

61. SSLT, 9.

62. *Multi: Basil Bunting from the British Press* (1976).

63. BBC Radio 3 broadcast 7 March 1975 (KCL).
64. BB to LZ, 18 December 1939, HR.
65. SSLT, 66–7.
66. MAK, 102.
67. BB to GT, 12 August 1965. ('Absit omen' means 'may no such misfortune befall us'.)

CHAPTER 5:
THEN IS NOW

1. BB to DP, 11 June 1965, LILLY.
2. *King Ida's Watch Chain* (Newcastle upon Tyne, 1965).
3. M. Horowitz (ed.), *Children of Albion: Poetry of the 'Underground' in Britain* (Harmondsworth, 1969), 326. *King Ida's Watch Chain* received very little attention but John Clare reviewed it and pointed approvingly to Bunting's craftsmanship. Bunting was a poet's poet: 'If Mr Bunting achieves a permanent resurrection … it will be because poets at least will always remember a man who has done a few things exceedingly well' (J. Clare, 'A Critical Look at Bunting's Poems', *Newcastle Journal*, 1 September 1965, 6). King Ida's Watch Chain is the huge anchor chain that hangs in Bamburgh Castle. The band of the same name was fronted by Tom Pickard.
4. BB to DP, 29 September 1965, LILLY.
5. *Poetry*, June 1967, 195–7; *Agenda*, Autumn 1966, 11–17; *New Statesman*, 17 December 1965, 976; *Observer*, 24 October 1965, 27; *Sunday Times*, 26 September 1965, 47.
6. *Scotsman Week-end Magazine*, 19 March 1966, 5; *Evening Chronicle*, 29 January 1966, 4; *Sunday Times*, 19 June 1966, 29; *Poetry*, November 1966, 110–2; *Agenda*, Autumn 1966, 12; *Guardian*, 18 February 1966, 8; *Observer*, 2 January 1966.
7. *Times Literary Supplement*, 17 February, 3 March and 10 March 1966.
8. LZ to BB, 28 February 1966, DUR.
9. LZ to BB, 19 March 1966, DUR.
10. *Agenda*, Autumn 1966, 10, 17; *Encounter*, January 1970, 54–62; *Encounter*, 29, November 1967, 74–5; *Tribune*, 3 March 1967, 14; E. Lucie-Smith, 'A man for the music of words', *Sunday Times*, 25 July 1965, 33.
11. BB to GT, 17 June 1965.
12. *Sunday Times*, 7498, 12 February 1967, 53.
13. SSLT, 199.
14. D. Davie, 'Privately Published', *New Statesman*, 4 November 1966, 672; *Evening Chronicle*, 26 February 1966, 4; *Scotsman Week-end Magazine*, 8 October 1966, 3; *Tarasque*, 3; *Stand*, 8, 2, 1966, 34; *Agenda*, Autumn 1966, 17, 18, 20–8; *National Review* (19, 43), 31 October 1967, 1217–8; *Guardian*, 3 March 1967; *Observer*, 26 March 1967; *Times Literary Supplement*, 16 February 1967; *London Magazine*, May 1967, 70–3.
15. BB to EP, 29 March 1967, BRBML.
16. A. Ginsberg, 'On Basil Bunting', *International Times*, 16–19 January 1967, 14.
17. *Guardian*, 15 June 1965.

18. G. Steiner (ed.), *The Penguin Book of Modern Verse Translation* (Harmondsworth, 1966), 154–6.
19. *Menard Press 1969–2009* (London, 2010), 18.
20. *Sunday Times* supplement, 19 January 1969, 34–8.
21. W. Corbett, 'Remembering Basil Bunting', MTBB.
22. A reading to celebrate his seventieth birthday on BBC 2 on 2 March, a reading of Wordsworth's 'The Brothers' on the Third Programme on 7 April and repeated on 9 September, and a reading of Wordsworth's 'Michael' on 19 April.
23. SSLT, 200.
24. BB to DG, 17 July 1965, SUNY.
25. BB to DP, 11 July 1965, LILLY.
26. Turnbull and Whyte, 67.
27. BB to GT, 13 May 1965. The fact that Bunting 'foresaw and expected' Turnbull's finding lends weight to the possibility that Briggflatts was conceived specifically to encourage a reconciliation with Peggy. This suggestion is only strengthened by Tom Pickard's comment that 'it was as though his creation had stepped out of the canvas.' When the relationship started to falter, 'like a dream … he couldn't seem to write himself into his own creation.' (George Oppen Memorial Lecture, 2004).
28. BB to GT, 21 June 1965. Cissie's memories of Bunting stretched back to when she was 'only 4 or 5 years old – my lasting impression was of Edinburgh rock. He always brought me a box' (Jean Armstrong (née Greenbank) to W. S. Milne, 8 July 1978, DUR).
29. BB to DG, 11 August 1965, DUR.
30. BB to DG, 8 November 1965, SUNY.
31. The irony is that Bunting could not see beyond the Peggy he knew as a child. She took Stuart Montgomery to one side shortly after the reunion and said, "I don't understand what he sees in me … he sees me as a small child, he looks at me and sees me as I was. He doesn't see me as I now am." (quoted in T. Pickard, George Oppen Memorial Lecture, 2004).
32. BB to DG, 25 February 1966, DUR.
33. BB to GT, 3 September 1966.
34. BB to RBD, 4 August 1969, DUR.
35. Turnbull and Whyte, 72.
36. BB to GT, 16 April 1968.
37. BB to RBD, 14 April 1966, DUR. Ed Dorn considers *Briggflatts* 'the greatest love poem of the twentieth century, ' (T. Pickard, George Oppen Memorial Lecture, 2004).
38. SSLT, 206.
39. CP, 138.
40. CP, 139.
41. BB to DP, 30 May 1967, LILLY.
42. CP, 140. Tom Pickard revealed the identity of the model for the Chairman of what he called 'Bunting's satirical poke at municipal morons' in 2000. She was 'the Lord Mayor [of Newcastle City Council] and the chairman of the Cultural

Activities Committee, Mrs. Gladys Robson, magistrate, leader of the council' (T. Pickard, 'Rough Music (Ruff Muzhik)', *Chicago Review*, Spring 2000).

43. Reading, February 1982, London.
44. CP, 141.
45. Reading, February 1982, London.
46. CP, 136.
47. BB to Robert Creeley, 20 November 1966, DUR.
48. BB to GT, 3 December 1966.
49. BB to GT, 1 March 1968.
50. T. Pickard, George Oppen Memorial Lecture, 2004.
51. CONJ, 154.
52. CONJ, 154–7.
53. T. Connor, *Things Unsaid: New and Selected Poems 1960–2005* (London, 2006), 124–8.
54. SSLT, 205.
55. SSLT, 5.
56. PAID, 13.
57. CONJ, 157.
58. CONJ, 157.
59. BB to EP, 8 July 1966, BRBML.
60. BB to Cid Corman, 29 April 1967, SUNY.
61. BB to GT, 24 July 1966.
62. BB to JW, 4 May 1976, SUNY.
63. BB to GT, 9 September 1966.
64. BB to EP, 13 September 1966, BRBML.
65. *London Review of Books*, 18 February 1999.
66. Turnbull and Whyte, 71–2. Peggy was equally distressed. She sent Bunting a 'heart-broken letter' in September when she discovered that he was going to be away for so long (BB to RBD, 7 September 1966, DUR).
67. Letter from Alan Brilliant to author, 28 March 2011.
68. B. Bunting, *Two Poems* (Santa Barbara, 1967).
69. *Agenda*, Autumn 1966, 3.
70. BB to DP, 28 March 1971, LILLY.
71. BB to Department of English, 21 January 1970, SUNY.
72. BB to JW, 11 December 1966, SUNY.
73. BB to GT, 5 October 1966.
74. BB to Robert Creeley, 20 November 1966, DUR.
75. BB to DP, 21 May 1967, LILLY.
76. BB to Robert Creeley, 10 January 1967, DUR.
77. BB to GT, 16 July 1968.
78. BB to DP, 21 May 1967, LILLY.
79. BB to EP, 29 March 1967, BRBML.
80. CP, 143.
81. CP, 228.
82. BB to JW, 23 April 1974, SUNY.

83. BB to DP, 21 May 1967, LILLY.
84. BB to TP, 30 March 1967, SUNY.
85. BB to EP, 29 March 1967, BRBML.
86. BB to GT, 22 January 1967.
87. MTBB.
88. TERR, 64.
89. TERR, 64.
90. BB to JW, 21 April 1968, SUNY.
91. PAID, 129.
92. BB to EP, 29 March 1967, BRBML.
93. BB to Cid Corman, 29 April 1967, SUNY.
94. FORDE, 59.
95. FORDE, 60.
96. BB to RBD, 30 August 1966, DUR.
97. Marian Bunting to Helen Groves, 11 September 1968, DUR.
98. BB to RBD, 7 September 1966, DUR.
99. BB to RBD, 7 September 1966, DUR.
100. BB to RBD, 7 September 1966, DUR.
101. BB to JW, 27 August 1967, SUNY. By 1968, when Marian updated Roger Guedalla on the Bunting family history, their two daughters were married, one living in Inglewood, California, and the other in Madison, Wisconsin. There were by now ten grandchildren (Marian Bunting to Roger Guedalla, 25 September 1968, DUR).
102. BB to TP, 28 August 1967, SUNY.
103. BB to GT, 26 August 1967.
104. L. P. Faranda (ed.) *Between Your House and Mine: The Letters of Lorine Niedecker to Cid Corman, 1960 to 1970* (Durham, 1986), 127.
105. Faranda, 172.
106. *Truck*, 16, 1975, 52.
107. J. Penberthy (ed.), *Lorine Niedecker Collected Works* (Berkeley, 2002), 253–4. 'I don't know why it was that I couldn't have done a better poem,' she wrote to Cid Corman in March 1970. *Conjunctions*, 5, 1983, 167.
108. 'The Ballad of Basil' appeared in *Stony Brook*, 3–4 (1969), 31. Cid Corman collected it in *Blue Chicory* (New Rochelle, 1976).
109. Gail Roub, 'Getting to know Lorine Niedecker' in J. Penberthy (ed.), *Lorine Niedecker: Woman and Poet* (Orono, 1996), 81.
110. FORDE, 60.
111. PI, 44.
112. SYSB, 256.
113. Interview with McAllister and Figgis, 10 November 1984.
114. BB to Cid Corman, 29 April 1967, SUNY.
115. BB to GT, 21 March 1967.
116. BB to GT, 21 March 1967.
117. J. Kramer, *Allen Ginsberg in America* (New York, 1968), 142.

118. *Isis*, 1502, 26 November 1965, 12.

119. BB to JW, 1 September 1973, SUNY.

120. SYSB, 267.

121. PAID, 160–1.

122. CONJ, 156.

123. BB to DP, Goleta, 30 May 1967, LILLY.

124. BB to JW, 21 April 1968, SUNY.

125. BB to TP, 17 December 1967, SUNY.

126. BB to GT, 19 December 1967.

127. BB to GT, 7 January 1968.

128. BB to GT, 10 February 1968. This letter contains many typing errors which I have silently corrected as it was the first he wrote after his operation.

129. Faranda, 150.

130. BB to Jack Shoemaker, 5 November 1968, SUNY.

131. CP, 21.

132. *Agenda*, Spring 1969, 46–8; M. Dodsworth, 'Sea-Town Records', *Listener*, 27 March 1969; R. Holmes, 'Poets: Bunting to Ginsberg', *Times Saturday Review*, 25 January 1969 (Holmes chose Bunting's *Collected Poems* as his book of the year for *The Times* on 27 December 1969); *International Times*, 1–16 January 1969, 5; *Guardian*, 27 December 1968; C. Connolly, 'Profession: Poet', *Sunday Times*, 26 January 1969, 60; *Evening Chronicle*, 4 December 1968, 8; *Times Literary Supplement*, 27 February 1969; A. Brownjohn, 'Craft and Art', *New Statesman*, 13 December 1968, 843–4; T. Lask, 'Each in His Own Voice', *New York Times*, 8 March 1969; *Library Journal*, 15 June 1969, 2473; *Atlantic Monthly*, May 1969, 114. Horizon published *Collected Poems* in the US; R. Guedalla, 'Struggler in the Wilderness', *Nation*, 15 February 1971, 216–8; *Queen*, June 1970, 71.

133. W. Rawson, 'Poems of Basil Bunting', *Friend*, 18 September 1970, 1123.

134. D. Jones, 'Basil Bunting: The Line of Succession', *Odysseus* (Portland, Oregon) Oct–Nov 1971, 1–2.

135. DESC.

136. *New Measure* 4 (Winter 1966–7), 60.

137. SYSB, 13–14.

138. BBNL, 48.

139. BB to LZ, 5 December 1953, HR.

140. SSLT, 6.

141. Postacrd, DUR.

142. *Palatinate*, 24 October 1968, 14.

143. Interview with Tom Pickard on 17 and 18 June 1981.

144. Peter Quartermain, 'Thinking with the poem (Zukofsky)', *Golden Handcuffs Review* 1, 5, Summer–Fall, 2005.

145. T. B. Webster, 'Basil Bunting – A Poet in Our Time', *Courier* (Newcastle University) 5 February 1969, 6.

146. SYSB, 14.

147. BB to JW, 1 September 1973, SUNY.

148. T. Pickard, 'Rough Music (Ruff Muzhik)', *Chicago Review*, Spring 2000.

149. Mike Doyle to Professor Sylvia E. Bowman, 19 January 1971, privately held.

150. BB to Alexander Nelson, 25 November 1970, copy DUR.

151. BB to George Quasha, 26 December 1970, copy DUR. The whereabouts of the original is unknown.

152. *Times*, 3 August 1968, 19.

153. *Review* 22, June 1970, 63.

154. *Review* 23, September–November 1970, 68.

155. 'Ian Hamilton in Conversation', *The Dark Horse*, 3, 1996, 34–3.

156. BB to JW, 18 March 1970, SUNY.

157. CP, 144.

158. BB to JW, 12 March 1970, SUNY.

159. Reading in February 1982, London.

160. *Listener*, 8 October 1970, 484.

161. K. Cox, 'Basil Bunting reading Wordsworth', *Jacket*, 28, October 2005.

162. Hugh Kenner, quoted in 'A Conversation with Stephen Logan', Cambridge Authors, http://www.english.cam.ac.uk/cambridgeauthors/conversation-with-stephen-logan

163. *Guardian*, 14 October 1970.

164. BB to DP, 14 July 1971, LILLY.

165. BB to DG, 19 September 1972, DUR.

166. SYSB, 267.

167. The others being Wyatt, Sidney, Spencer 1500/1600, Denham, Waller (especially 'Cooper's Hill') and Campion 1600/1700 and Pound, Eliot, Yeats and William Carlos Williams. He expected the next great change to occur at the end of the 1900s or early 2000s (Gael Turnbull, 'A visit to Basil when he was at Washington New Town', unpublished manuscript in private hands).

168. SSLT, 201–2.

169. BB to Rodger Kingston, 25 May 1970, DUR.

170. BB to Rodger Kingston, 1 May 1970, DUR. Lord Justice Parker was regarded as a relatively moderate Lord Chief Justice but was criticised for politicising the criminal justice system. Although Bunting does not mention it specifically he is referring here to the 'D'Oliveira scandal'. Basil D'Oliveira was a popular member of the England cricket team. South African by birth and designated 'coloured' by the South African apartheid regime, 'Dolly' became a catalyst of the international boycott of all South African sport in 1968 when the South African cricket authorities refused to allow the England team to tour in South Africa if he was selected.

171. BB to EP, 12 September 1970, BRBML.

172. BB to TP, 7 September 1970, SUNY.

173. BB to TP, 4 October 1970, SUNY.

174. BB to EP, 14 October 1970, BRBML.

175. DISJ, 222.

176. BB to TP, 4 October 1970, SUNY.

177. BB to EP, 14 October 1970, BRBML.
178. Faranda, 236–7.
179. CP, 198.
180. BB to JW, 3 April 1971, SUNY.
181. BB to EM, 1 June 1971, KCL. To be fair Bunting does praise the University of British Columbia's beautiful campus and admirable faculty club, as well as one or two attractive people on and off site. The Ottawa reading Bunting refers to earned him $500 for three days' readings and supplied a 'good change of scene and voices' (BB to JW, 19 April 1971, SUNY).
182. DISJ, 143.
183. CP, 161.
184. Mike Doyle to author, 26 March 2012.
185. BB to Mike Doyle, 4 January 1971. He wrote to Dorothy Pound about his honorary degree: 'When I was getting that degree I told the Public Orator it was a shame not to do it in Latin, because it was embarrassing to listen to one's own praises in one's native tongue. I then learned that Wordsworth, the first doctor made by the university, said word for word the same thing to the Public Orator in 1838. A characteristic of Northern poets?' (BB to DP, 14 July 1971, LILLY).
186. B. Mackay, 'Basil Bunting, Mentor', DUR.
187. Letter from Peter Quartermain to author, 21 April 2011.
188. Letter from Doyle to author, 26 March 2012. The interviews were by Brian Butters (*Victoria Daily Times*, 13 October 1971, and Bill Thomas (*Daily Colonist*, 14 October 1972).
189. 'Pore ole granpa' refers to Bunting's status as an honorary grandfather to the Quartermains' two children who were seven years old at the time (letter from Peter Quartermain to author, 21 April 2011). Doyle regards Bunting's reference to his 'war' with Skelton as an exaggeration and says that although the two were at loggerheads for about five years, it was hardly a war.
190. BB to GT, 31 October 1971.
191. BB to GT, 8 January 1972.
192. BB to JW, 14 November 1971, SUNY. He repeated his claim that the attack on him was 'really aimed to discredit the man who got me invited here', that is Mike Doyle.
193. BB to DP, 1 December 1971, LILLY.
194. Letter from Doyle to author, 26 March 2012.
195. 'August Kleinzahler, The Art of Poetry No. 93', interview with William Corbett, *Paris Review*, Fall 2007.
196. *Paris Review*, Fall 2007.
197. PAID, 28–9.
198. BB to TP, 13 June 1976, SUNY. It seems that Bunting was at his most acerbic when confronting poems that he felt had something good buried in them. Where he saw nothing he was merely polite. He wrote to one poet to thank him for 'the pleasant poem. I'm too impressed to say more' (BB to Rodger Kingston, 9 August 1969, DUR). Kleinzahler's later success as a poet rather justifies Bunting's assessment.

199. B. Mackay, 'Basil Bunting, Mentor', DUR.

200. BB to EM, 22 February 1972, KCL.

201. BB to EM, 22 February 1972, KCL.

202. Letter from Mike Doyle to author, 26 March 2012.

203. BB to RBD, 10 December 1971, DUR.

204. *London Review of Books*, 1 April 1999.

205. *London Review of Books*, 29 April 1999.

206. *London Review of Books*, 10 June 1999.

207. Mike Doyle to author, 26 March 2012. According to August Kleinzahler another reason for leaving Victoria was Bunting's discovery that he was being taxed by both the Canadian and British governments, which rather defeated his reason for being there in the first place (Kleinzahler to author, 4 February 2013).

208. *Conjunctions*, 5, 1983, 75.

209. BB to DP, 6 August 1971, LILLY.

210. As he described administrators in a letter of 25 July 1944 to Louis Zukofsky, HR.

211. The papers relating to this episode are to be found in the Victoria & Albert archive ACGB/119/27.

212. *Times*, 24 June 1970, 11.

213. *Times*, 25 June 1970, 9.

214. SYSB, 14–15.

215. BB to EM, 28 October 1972, KCL.

216. LBB to Mike Doyle, 14 July 1973, privately held. He clearly excluded Doyle from his blanket condemnation of the Victoria faculty.

217. BB to EM, 13 November 1973, KCL.

218. BB to EM, 28 January 1974, KCL.

219. BB to EM, 29 June 1974, KCL. In January 1977 he blamed the Arts Council for leaving Pickard 'so close to starvation that it's plausible for the police to clap him in gaol if he's found anywhere near an offence' (BB to EM, 8 January 1977, KCL).

220. BB to EM, 29 June 1974, KCL. The last sentence is not typed but added in Bunting's hand.

221. BB to JW, 7 August 1974, SUNY.

222. BB to JW, 27 January 1976, SUNY. He told Roudaba that he was never paid for the Skipsey book and so didn't complete a selection from Swinburne that was planned (BB to RBD, 9 February 1973, DUR).

223. J. Skipsey, *Selected Poems*, ed. B. Bunting (Sunderland, 1976), 7.

224. MONT, 70.

225. Skipsey, *Selected Poems*, 13. Bunting describes Skipsey's pronunciation as 'Tyneside' here. Bunting didn't exaggerate his relationship with Skipsey. In his preface to his selection of Skipsey's poems he noted that: 'His son William was inspector of schools at Durham, his eldest son, James, master shifter at the Montague colliery at Scotswood, where Joseph Skipsey sometimes visited my father, the colliery doctor there; but I was too young to have any memory of him. He died at Harraton in September 1903.' (11)

226. Interview with Tom Pickard on 17 and 18 June 1981, recorded at Bunting's home

near Hexham, published by Keele University, 1995.

227. BB to VF, 23 May 1972, DUR. The image of a drop of molten silver reaches back to 'Villon' and, further back, to Bunting's childhood reading of Edith Nesbit's stories. See Chapter 1: Guilty of Spring, note 23.

228. CP, 199.

229. BB to VF, 23 October 1972, DUR.

230. The Poetry Society, *Poetry Gala*, (London, 1969), 35.

231. *Poetry Gala*, 39.

232. BB to EM, 1 June 1971, KCL. The unfinished poem was 'All the cants they peddle'.

233. BB to Denys Thompson, 29 January 1972, Poetry Society.

234. BB to EM, 13 February 1972, KCL.

235. BB to EM, 22 February 1972, KCL.

236. BB to EM, 28 October 1972, KCL.

237. P. Barry, *Poetry Wars: British Poetry of the 1970s and the Battle of Earls Court* (Cambridge, 2006), 38.

238. Barry, 109–10.

239. P. Skelt (ed.), *Prospect into breath: Interviews with north and south writers* (Twickenham, 1991), 17.

240. Barry, 21.

241. Barry, 56.

242. Skelt, 37.

243. C. Osborne, *Giving it Away: Memoirs of an Uncivil Servant* (London, 1986), 204–5.

244. Barry, 109.

245. SYSB, 270.

246. Reading, London, 1979.

247. Barry, 162–4.

248. *Guardian*, 12 January 1976.

249. BB to EM, 28 October 1972, KCL.

250. BB to EM, 8 November 1972, KCL.

251. BB to Mike Doyle, 14 July 1973, privately held.

252. BB to EM, 29 June 1974, KCL.

253. BB to EM, 26 March 1975, KCL. Mottram's last issue was Volume 67, Nos. 1 and 2, 1977. The next two issues were edited by Edwin Brock, not really a booby.

254. DISJ, 136.

255. Stephan Chodorov to the author, 30 April 2011. The shooting of the film created quite a stir locally. Mary Dawson recalls the day the crew arrived affectionately in 'Memories of Brigflatts', MTBB.

256. DISJ, 136.

257. B. Bunting, 'Prince of Poets', *Sunday Times*, 12 November 1972, 38.

258. H. Carpenter, *A Serious Character: The Life of Ezra Pound* (Boston, 1988), 117.

259. Interview with McAllister and Figgis, 10 November 1984.

260. BB to LZ, 17 June 1949, HR.

261. *Sunday Times*, 12 November 1972.

262. *Guardian*, 3 February 1973.

263. *Guardian*, 6 February 1973.
264. BB to DG, 2 February 1972, SUNY.
265. Letter at SUNY, quoted by Tom Pickard.
266. MT, 67–8.
267. MT, 69.
268. BB to JW, 4 July 1973, SUNY.
269. Osborne, 201.
270. BB to EM, 8 November 1972, KCL.
271. DISJ, 135–6.
272. BB to JW, 1 September 1973, SUNY.
273. Mike Shayer to author, 6 February 2013.
274. BB to VF, 11 May 1975, DUR.
275. BB to EM, 19 February 1975, KCL. Bunting took a wry view of his predicament. Struldbruggs were denizens of the kingdom of Luggnagg in Swift's *Gulliver's Travels*. Struldbruggs 'commonly acted like mortals, until about thirty years old, after which by degrees they grew melancholy and dejected, increasing in both until they came to fourscore … When they came to fourscore years … they had not only the follies and infirmities of other old men, but many more which arose from the dreadful prospect of never dying. They were not only opinionative, peevish, covetous, morose, vain, talkative; but uncapable of friendship, and dead to all natural affection' (J. Swift, *Gulliver's Travels* (London, 1975) 225–6).
276. Barry, 48–9.
277. Barry, 53.
278. Reading, London, February 1982.
279. CP, 145.
280. Barry, 53–4. Indeed Bunting's remarks about poems that the Poetry Society should be proud of were made two years before this.
281. BB to JW, 16 March 1975, SUNY.
282. BB to JW, 30 June 1975, SUNY.
283. Turnbull, 73
284. PAID, 141.
285. BB to JW, 4 May 1976, SUNY.
286. PAID, 149.
287. PAID, 150–1.
288. BB to JW, 4 May 1976, SUNY.
289. G. Turnbull, 'A visit to Basil when he was at Washington New Town'.
290. PAID, 55. DAF has nothing to do with daffodils; it is short for Van Doorne's Automobiel Fabriek after its Dutch, not Swedish, founder.
291. V. Forde, 'Background for Letters of Basil Bunting and a Remembrance of My Visits with him, March 1982', DUR.
292. PAID, 142.
293. PAID, 143.
294. PI, 46.
295. PAID, 144.

296. PAID, 145.
297. PAID, 146.
298. PAID, 33.
299. SYSB, 262–4.
300. DESC.
301. Arts Council minute to Secretary-General, 26 May 1976, Victoria and Albert Museum.
302. *Presidential Address by Basil Bunting: An Artist's view on Regional Arts patronage*, 1977.
303. BB to EM, 8 November 1972, KCL.
304. *Presidential Address by Basil Bunting: An Artist's view on Regional Arts patronage*, 1974. He didn't have much hope that his voice would be heard. He complained to Tom Pickard that he was required to 'spout to the Annual General Meeting of Northern Arts, pretending to be the Great Poet, pretending to think they might listen to anything I say' (BB to TP, 1 October 1974, SUNY).
305. *Presidential Address by Basil Bunting: An Artist's view on Regional Arts patronage*, 1975.
306. *Presidential Address by Basil Bunting: An Artist's view on Regional Arts patronage*, 1976.
307. BB to JW, 27 September 1976, SUNY.
308. *Presidential Address by Basil Bunting: An Artist's view on Regional Arts patronage*, 1977.
309. BB to Hugh MacDiarmid, 13 November 1973, Edinburgh University Library.
310. BB to JW, 26 February 1973, SUNY.
311. SYSB, 276.
312. BB to EM, 13 November 1973, KCL.
313. PAID, 125.
314. SYSB, 281.
315. PAID, 127–9.
316. BB to Roger Guedalla, 1 April 1980, DUR.
317. BB to JW, 4 May 1976, SUNY.
318. BB to EM, 8 January 1977, KCL.
319. BB to JW, 12 January 1977, SUNY.
320. T. Pickard, George Oppen Memorial Lecture, 2004.
321. BB to RBD, 15 March 1977, DUR.
322. BB to RBD, 5 July 1977, DUR.
323. BB to RBD, 27 February 1978, DUR.
324. BB to RBD, 23 June 1978, DUR.
325. BB to TP, 21 March 1977, SUNY.
326. BB to JW, 11 February 1977, SUNY. 'Sima knew she was a bit off her head,' he told Roudaba, 'and I stayed with her a few days again before going to occupy Jonathan Williams' cottage in Dentdale' (BB to RBD, 5 July 1977, DUR).
327. BB to JW, 8 April 1977, SUNY.
328. BB to Cid Corman, 26 April 1977, SUNY.
329. BB to JW, 8 April 1977, SUNY.
330. SYSB, 265.
331. SYSB, 274.

CHAPTER 6:
CODA

1. BB to TP, 3 June 1978, SUNY.
2. BB to RBD, 5 July 1977, DUR.
3. BB to EM, 19 June 1977, KCL.
4. G. Turnbull, 'A visit to Basil when he was at Washington New Town'.
5. PAID, 37.
6. Conversation with author, 31 May 2013.
7. DISJ, 137.
8. BB to JW, 22 August 1977, SUNY.
9. PAID, 38.
10. PAID, 161.
11. M. Doyle, *Paper Trombones: Notes on poetics* (Victoria, 2007), 20.
12. CONJ, 186.
13. PAID, 38.
14. DISJ, 137.
15. G. Turnbull, 'A visit to Basil when he was at Washington New Town'.
16. Turnbull, 'A visit'.
17. A. Kleinzahler, 'Blackfell's Scarlatti', *London Review of Books*, 21 January 1999.
18. August Kleinzahler to author, 4 February 2013.
19. BB to RBD, 27 February 1978, DUR.
20. BB to Hugh MacDiarmid, 15 January 1978, Edinburgh University Library.
21. Turnbull, 'A visit to Basil'.
22. BB to Michael Shayer, 2 April 1970, DUR.
23. BB to JW, 1 September 1973, SUNY.
24. SYSB, 269. Mike Shayer thought Sima was 'a good deal more canny with money than Basil realised. My memory was of her driving around in a big red Landrover at the same time as Basil was very hard up. She got money from Iran – and was leading quite a social life' (Mike Shayer to author, 6 February 2013).
25. BB to TP, 10 July 1978 and 13 November 1978, SUNY.
26. Reading in 1979 at Keats' House, London.
27. BB to DG, 29 April 1980, DUR.
28. BB to TP, August 1976, SUNY.
29. BB to JW, 11 February 1977, SUNY.
30. *Observer*, 26 March 1978, 17 December 1978; M. Booth, 'Poetry for our humanity', *Tribune*, 19 May 1978; 'Put out more Bunting', *Guardian*, 10 March 1978; J. Nuttall, 'The odious creed of self-expression', *Guardian*, 23 August 1980; *Poetry Review*, June 1978, 52–3; C. Raine, 'Amputated Years', *New Statesman*, 21 April 1978; D. Hall, 'A Gorgeous Sound', *New York Times Book Review*, 2 July 1978; G. S. Fraser, 'Sound before Sense', *Times Literary Supplement*, 5 May 1978; R. Guedalla, 'Put out the Bunting', *Time Out*, 9 June 1978.
31. CP, 228.

32. BB to EM, 7 February 1978, KCL.
33. BB to William Cookson, 5 September 1977, BRBML.
34. BB to EM, 27 March 1978, KCL.
35. Reading, London, 1979.
36. Skelt, 39–40. It is not clear if the obfuscation of identities is deliberate here. 'Abcess' is a fairly easily identifiable British poet and Josephine 'Fox' has appeared earlier in these pages.
37. Newcastle *Journal*, 16 March 1978.
38. BB to TP, 29 February 1984, SUNY.
39. BB to EM, 21 July 1977, KCL.
40. FORDE, 62.
41. SYSB, 268.
42. SYSB, 269.
43. BB to Diana Surman (later Collecott), 20 November 1978, DUR.
44. CP, 146.
45. BB to RBD, 13 March 1980, DUR.
46. BB to DG, 29 April 1980, DUR.
47. BB to DG, 29 April 1980, DUR. See also *Basil Bunting at 80: A celebration*, Warwick, 1980. The singer was Lindisfarne's singer/songwriter, Alan Hull. Bunting's attitude was a little churlish, considering that Tom Pickard had persuaded the students to pay Bunting a fee of £500 plus expenses, a considerable sum in 1980 (TP to author, 11 March 2013). Pickard was also responsible for some of his London readings: 'Even though I knew they were a chore for him I made sure he was well paid.'
48. BB to VF, 7 May 1980, DUR.
49. CONJ, 204–6.
50. BB to RBD, 17 July 1980, DUR.
51. BB to RBD, 2 December 1980, DUR.
52. BB to RBD, 13 March 1980, DUR.
53. Author interview with Diana Collecott, 2012.
54. SYSB, 270–1.
55. V. Forde, 'Background for Letters of Basil Bunting and a Remembrance of My Visits with him, March 1982', DUR.
56. BB to VF, 2 June 1981, DUR.
57. V. Forde, 'Background for Letters', DUR. There was also 'a tennis court where I am not likely to prance' (BB to RBD, 1 June 1981, DUR).
58. DISJ, 134–5.
59. BB to RBD, 9 December 1981, DUR.
60. BB to Diana Collecott, 7 November 1981, DUR.
61. BB to VF, 2 June 1981, DUR.
62. FORDE, 63. The restaurant was Mon Plaisir in Monmouth Street and the publishers were Jackie Simms of Oxford University Press and Peter Jay of Anvil Press (Forde, 'Background for Letters', DUR).
63. BB to VF, 28 February 1982, DUR.

64. *Guardian*, 4 October 2007.
65. BB to RBD, 4 August 1969, DUR.
66. FORDE, 64.
67. FORDE, 64–5.
68. *Conjunctions*, 5, 1983, 76–7.
69. *Conjunctions*, 1983, 77.
70. PI, 41.
71. *Conjunctions*, 1983, 75–86. James McGonigal was surprised by the extent to which Darwin featured in the conversation during his first meeting with Bunting in 1973 (James McGonigal, 'An XYZ of Reading: Basil Bunting in the British Tradition', M. Alexander and J. McGonigal (eds) *Sons of Ezra: British poets and Ezra Pound* (Amsterdam, 1995, 119).
72. BB to VF, 16 March 1983, DUR.
73. BB to VF, 16 March 1983, DUR.
74. M. Davie, 'How the poets pick a winner', *Guardian*, 6 March 1983.
75. S. Spender, 'Diary', *London Review of Books*, 21 April 1983.
76. BB to VF, 16 March 1983, DUR.
77. BB to VF, 16 March 1983, DUR.
78. BB to TP, 20 November 1983, SUNY.
79. CONJ, 210–11.
80. CONJ, 219.
81. CONJ, 220.
82. SYSB, 277.
83. BB to RBD, 29 June 1981, DUR.
84. BB to VF, 7 March 1982, DUR.
85. BB to Sandra Cossey, 23 Sept 1982, DUR.
86. SYSB, 274.
87. SYSB, 275.
88. SYSB, 275.
89. BB to TP, 20 November 1983, SUNY.
90. SYSB, 276–7.
91. SYSB, 278–9.
92. PAID, 135.
93. *London Review of Books*, 7 June 1984, 21.
94. *London Review of Books*, 19 July 1984.
95. SYSB, 279.
96. BB to Tanya Cossey, 20 June 1984, DUR.
97. BB to VF, 14 July 1984, DUR.
98. BB to VF, 14 July 1984, DUR.
99. SYSB, 281.
100. CONJ, 163.
101. BB to Tanya Cossey 28 July 1984, DUR.
102. BB to VF, 14 July 1984, DUR.
103. DISJ, 134.

104. DISJ, 134.
105. SYSB, 282.
106. FORDE, 67.
107. BB to Tanya Cossey, 14 January 1985, DUR.
108. BB to GT, 8 February 1985.
109. CONJ, 150.
110. Interview with McAllister and Figgis, 10 November 1984. A letter (DUR) to Bunting of 19 December 1984 from Figgis and McAllister makes it clear that Bunting had complete control over how this interview, which was published in *Bête Noire* in 1987, appeared to the public. I suspect that a couple of years previously he would have cut a great deal more of it.
111. BB to VF, 19 March 1985, DUR.
112. BB to Tanya Cossey, February 1985, DUR.
113. FORDE, 67–8.
114. Tanya Cossey to BB, undated but 15 April 1985, DUR.
115. FORDE, 68.
116. FORDE, 68. The official cause of death was mesenteric thrombosis.
117. CONJ, 149.
118. Turnbull, 73–4
119. BB to TP, 3 June 1978, SUNY.

ACKNOWLEDGEMENTS

Basil Bunting moved into our home in 2010 and as I write this he is still to move out. Elizabeth, Jamie and Jo have been remarkably tolerant of his extended visit and have raised their voices at him only rarely.

Many people have gone a long way out of their way to help me as this book has developed. Comments on an early draft from Andrew McNeillie, Stuart Crainer, Mark Allin, Neil Astley, Diana Collecott and Steve White helped me in their various ways to find a direction.

I owe a great debt to Jamie Burton for nuanced and insightful readings of some of Bunting's early odes. I have reproduced almost verbatim his surefooted account of 'Loud intolerant bells'.

The archivists at Ackworth School, Celia Wolfe, and at Leighton Park School, Tim Newell Price, were enormously kind and helpful, and I am grateful to the schools for permission to use material from their archives. I am also grateful to the librarians and staff at the Beinecke Library at Yale University, the University of Chicago Library, The Lilly Library at Indiana University, the Poetry Collection at the State University of New York at Buffalo, the Harry Ransom Center at the University of Texas at Austin, the Division of Rare and Manuscript Collections at Cornell University, the London School of Economics, Kings, the University of London, The National Archive at Kew, Edinburgh University, the Bodleian Library, Oxford, and the British Library. I would particularly like to thank Sally Harrower at the National Library of Scotland and Mike Harkness and Richard Higgins at Durham University Library.

Tess Satchell in Briggflatts, Lucy and David Sutcliffe of Coldside Farm, Rebecka Mustajarvi of the Poetry Society were all welcoming and helpful during the early stages of my research. August Kleinzahler, Peter

Quartermain and Charles (Mike) Doyle helped clarify the events surrounding Bunting's disastrous season at the University of Victoria in the early 1970s. Helen Keane at the Air Historical Branch (RAF), Ministry of Defence, very helpfully deciphered the notes on Bunting's war records. Many of Bunting's friends have been extremely helpful. Tom Pickard, Michael Shayer, Jill Turnbull and Colin Simms, in particular, have clarified issues that would have remained a mystery without their contribution.

I have had very useful correspondence with academics around the world and I am grateful for contributions from Stephen Regan at the University of Durham, Massimo Bacigalupo at the University of Genoa, Thomas Dilworth at the University of Windsor, Dick Davis at Ohio State University, Edward Burns at The William Paterson University of New Jersey, Susan Howson at the University of Cambridge, Claire Sawyer at the Henry Moore Institute, and Richard Swigg. I am also grateful to the following for various kindnesses and contributions: Enid Thompson, Tom Meyer, Anthony Rudolf, Matthew Kahane, Stephan Chodorov, Alan Brilliant, Jack Shoemaker, David Wilk, Britt Bell, Tony Connor, Don Share, Alan Thornhill, Alexander Christie, Jonathan Greene and Lindsay Gordon. I am grateful to Bloodaxe books, and by extension New Directions in the US, for permission to quote from Bunting's poetry and to John Halliday for permission to quote from Bunting's unpublished work.

This book is infinitely better for the intervention of my editor, Rebecca Clare, a publishing professional without peer, and I am grateful to Simon Witter for an elegant design. I must also record my thanks to the publishing professionals at Infinite Ideas: Laura Sandford, David Grant, Elaine Collins, Arthur Diggle and Tim Moore, in no particular order.

It goes without saying, so I'll say it, that none of those cited are responsible for any lapses of scholarship or taste in *A Strong Song Tows Us*.

* * *

Every effort has been made to trace the copyright owners of the images reproduced in the plate section, but not always with success. Unacknowledged copyright owners should contact the publisher, and reprints will contain full acknowledgements.

I am grateful to the following for permission to reproduce images:
Front cover and 1, 2, 3, 4, 7, 8, 9, 10, 11, 12, 13, 14, 15, 18, 20, 21, 22, 23, 24, 25, 32, 34, 35 courtesy of Special Collections, Durham University.

5 courtesy of Newcastle City Library.

6 courtesy of Ackworth School.

16, 17, 19 courtesy of Lindsay Gordon.

26, 30 © Jonathan Williams, reproduced with permission of Tom Meyer and Jonathan Greene.

27, 28, 29, 31 courtesy of Jill Turnbull.

33 courtesy of Alan Thornhill.

36 courtesy of Diana Collecott.

front flap image © Karl Drerup, courtesy of Oliver Drerup.

INDEX

Note: Numbers in brackets after a page number refer to the note on that page.

B

Bacigalupo, Massimo 180
Bacon, Friar Roger 235
Bacon, Leonard 270
Bainbridge, Isabella 23
Bakhtiari tribes 277–8, 332
Barnes, Major Harry MP 91–2, 542(36)
　Housing: The Facts & The Future 542(41)
Barrati, Mary, née Pound 294
Barry, Peter 461, 476–7
Basil Bunting Poetry Archive 421
Basra, Iraq 276
Bates, E. Stuart 133
　Modern Translation 239–40
Battle of Mount Sorrel 43
Bax, Arnold 147
Bayandor, Darioush 332
BBC
　application to 327
　programme on Bunting 350
Be patient (Horace) 237
Beatles, The 395–6
Beckett, Samuel 558(423)
Beede, Ivan 103
Belgion, Montgomery 142
Bell, Miss A. M. 26–7
Bell, Clive 118, 141
Bell, Joseph 91, 542(36)
Bergonzi, Bernard 401
Berlin, Germany 157
Bernstein, Charles 163
Berrichon, Paterne 157–8
Berryman, John 319
Beveridge, Sir William 88
Bird, Otto 184
Bjerre, Andreas 139
Black Mountain College 356
Blake, William 37
　BB's essay on 52
　Book of Thel, The 37, 52
Bland, Susan 500–501
Blondel, Nathalie 553(310)
Bloodaxe, Eric 365, 370–71, 388
Bloomsbury Group 118, 141, 237
Blunt, Alfred, Bishop of Bradford 251
Boer War (1899–1902) 19–21
Bomberg, David 141

Booth, Martin 499
Bowen, Stella 99
Bowering, Marilyn 449–51
Brace, William MP 91
Breckman, R. 452
Bridson, Douglas Geoffrey 211, 350, 386
Brigflatts 363–4
　birthplace of Quaker movement 30–31
　burial ground 1
　BB's visit to Greenbank family 31–3
Briggflatts 2–5, 7, 77, 341, 354–5, 428, 434
　Briggflatts I 19, 363–7
　　first stanza 363–4
　　first three stanzas 32–3
　　second stanza 364–5
　Briggflatts II 79, 367–72
　Briggflatts III 265, 372–7
　Briggflatts IV 361, 377–81
　Briggflatts V 381–4, 395
　Briggflatts: Coda 165–6, 385–6, 493
　account of London 262–3
　autobiographical elements of 386–7
　bull, in opening 364
　change in BB's fortunes 396
　chisel in 366
　introductory note 361–3
　Kleinzahler's admiration of 447
　love, theme 365–7
　meaning 386–7
　musicality 120–21
　praise for Italy 171
　Quakerism 390–94
　rat theme 380–81
　read aloud by BB 10, 13, 15–16, 396
　references to Peggy Greenbank 403–4,
　　581(27)
　reviews 399–401
　spelling 531(7)
　stars theme 383–4
　stonemason character in 165
　structure 387–90
　talk on 482–3
Brilliant, Alan 416
British Columbia, University of 439–40,
　586(181)
British Council 334
British Embassy in Teheran, Iran 300–312
British Medical Journal 114–15